THE LEGAL RESEARCH AND WRITING HANDBOOK

ASPEN PUBLISHERS

FIFTH EDITION

THE LEGAL RESEARCH AND WRITING HANDBOOK

A BASIC APPROACH FOR PARALEGALS

ANDREA B. YELIN
Loyola University, Chicago

HOPE VINER SAMBORN

Wolters Kluwer
Law & Business

AUSTIN   BOSTON   CHICAGO   NEW YORK   THE NETHERLANDS

Aspen Publishers
Attn: Permissions Department
76 Ninth Avenue, 7th Floor
New York, NY 10011-5201

To contact Customer Care, e-mail customer.care@aspenpublishers.com, call 1-800-234-1660, fax 1-800-901-9075, or mail correspondence to:

Aspen Publishers
Attn: Order Department
PO Box 990
Frederick, MD 21705

Printed in the United States of America.

1 2 3 4 5 6 7 8 9 0

ISBN 978-0-7355-6738-2

Library of Congress Cataloging-in-Publication Data

Yelin, Andrea B.
    The legal research and writing handbook: a basic approach for paralegals / Andrea B. Yelin, Hope Viner Samborn. — 5th ed.
        p. cm.
    Includes index.
    ISBN 978-0-7355-6738-2
    1. Legal research—United States. 2. Legal composition. I. Samborn, Hope Viner. II. Title.

KF240.Y45 2009
340.072'073—dc22

2008045719

About Wolters Kluwer Law & Business

Wolters Kluwer Law & Business is a leading provider of research information and workflow solutions in key specialty areas. The strengths of the individual brands of Aspen Publishers, CCH, Kluwer Law International and Loislaw are aligned within Wolters Kluwer Law & Business to provide comprehensive, in-depth solutions and expert-authored content for the legal, professional and education markets.

CCH was founded in 1913 and has served more than four generations of business professionals and their clients. The CCH products in the Wolters Kluwer Law & Business group are highly regarded electronic and print resources for legal, securities, antitrust and trade regulation, government contracting, banking, pension, payroll, employment and labor, and healthcare reimbursement and compliance professionals.

Aspen Publishers is a leading information provider for attorneys, business professionals and law students. Written by preeminent authorities, Aspen products offer analytical and practical information in a range of specialty practice areas from securities law and intellectual property to mergers and acquisitions and pension/benefits. Aspen's trusted legal education resources provide professors and students with high-quality, up-to-date and effective resources for successful instruction and study in all areas of the law.

Kluwer Law International supplies the global business community with comprehensive English-language international legal information. Legal practitioners, corporate counsel and business executives around the world rely on the Kluwer Law International journals, loose-leafs, books and electronic products for authoritative information in many areas of international legal practice.

Loislaw is a premier provider of digitized legal content to small law firm practitioners of various specializations. Loislaw provides attorneys with the ability to quickly and efficiently find the necessary legal information they need, when and where they need it, by facilitating access to primary law as well as state-specific law, records, forms and treatises.

Wolters Kluwer Law & Business, a unit of Wolters Kluwer, is headquartered in New York and Riverwoods, Illinois. Wolters Kluwer is a leading multinational publisher and information services company.

To David, Rachel, and Henry with all my love.
—ABY

To my youngest students and teachers, Eve, Sarah, and Benjamin, and to my favorite teacher and friend, Randy. You have all of my love and thanks.
—HVS

SUMMARY OF CONTENTS

CONTENTS

CHAPTER 2   WHAT LAW GOVERNS   19

CHAPTER OVERVIEW   19

CHAPTER 3 COURT DECISIONS 35

PART 2   LEGAL WRITING   337

CHAPTER 15   GETTING READY TO WRITE   339

LIST OF
ILLUSTRATIONS

PREFACE

As paralegals, you can be invaluable to attorneys and clients when you have adequately mastered legal research and writing skills. This book is a step-by-step guide that explores the twists and turns of legal research and writing, teaching you how to avoid the dead ends and conquer obstacles along the way. Examples, exercises, and checklists help make it a smooth and enjoyable road.

Part 1 features an introduction to the legal system and legal authorities: the state and federal legislatures, the courts, and administrative agencies. It explains the relationship between state and federal governments and between other governing bodies.

The research component of Part 1 begins with hard-copy resources. Proficiency in hard-copy research will bring you greater success when performing research using a computer. You will also learn how to use online resources. All significant resources will be explored, and you will learn how they are interrelated and how to find the best sources for your particular project. Legal writing pointers are integrated throughout the research chapters where relevant.

Part 2 focuses on basic legal writing, with an emphasis on legal memoranda and letters—the most common documents that paralegals draft. Objective memos inform the attorney of all of the relevant law, both for and against the client's position. Having paralegals brief cases expedites the research process. Delegating research and writing tasks to the paralegal is cost-effective for the client and saves the client money.

Part 2 also guides you step-by-step through the legal writing process. You will be introduced to the case brief, the legal memorandum, the questions presented statement, the brief answer, and the facts statement. You will learn how to identify the legal issues and relevant facts of a case and how to organize

and present them in a written brief or memorandum. As the culmination of your legal writing skills, you will learn to synthesize—to distill a general legal concept that applies to a case and then state it in writing (citing more than one case or statute). Synthesis is essential to writing most case-related documents. A clear methodology—IRAC—will introduce you to the important components of synthesis: Issue, Rule, Application, and Conclusion. Using IRAC, you will learn to synthesize effectively and consistently.

A valuable reference tool, *The Legal Research and Writing Handbook* reviews letter writing, grammar, and editing—all essential skills you will use every day as a paralegal. Also, the examples and citation appendix will help you draft documents.

The Legal Research and Writing Workbook gives you hands-on exercises that reinforce the concepts in this textbook and provide you with practical applications for future work experiences. Practice pointers and ethics alerts included in this text are designed to guide you in your day-to-day work as a paralegal. This edition provides Net Notes to help you navigate the Internet to review points raised in the text. Computer resources, both paid and free, and integrated throughout the book.

You should view *The Legal Research and Writing Handbook* as a launching point from which to begin developing your research and writing skills. You will want to refer to the guidelines and concepts in this book throughout your career as you continue to expand in knowledge and experience.

November 2008   *Andrea B. Yelin*
                                                Hope Viner Samborn

ACKNOWLEDGMENTS

We would like to acknowledge all of the people who have helped us create this text and who have shaped its contents.

Thank you to Betsy Kenny for helping us to hone our continuing revisions of the text, the workbook, and the teacher's manual and for countless hours spent guiding us. Thanks to Lisa Wehrle for her great job copyediting the first and second editions of this text.

Thanks to Julie Grady and Rebecca Logan for their work copyediting the fifth edition, to Candice Adams for her assistance with the fourth edition, and to Peggy Rehberger, Melody Davies, Ellen Greenblatt, Curt Berkowitz, Suzanne Rapcavage, and Barbara Roth for their editing and additional help with the text. Thank you to Dave Herzig, Charles Gass, and Lou McGuire for their terrific marketing of the text.

Thanks to the U.S. Attorney's office library in Chicago, Loyola University Law School Library in Chicago, West Group, Lexis Law Publishing, Bureau of National Affairs, Martindale-Hubbell, Shepard's, the U.S. District Court in Toledo, Premark Corporation, and the Arlington Heights Memorial Public Library for assistance in obtaining illustrations for this book.

Thanks also to Julia Wentz, Patricia Scott, and Fred LeBaron of Loyola University Law School for all of your assistance past and present. A special debt of gratitude goes to Fred LeBaron for his wise counsel and professional guidance. Thank you to Lauren Grodsky and Eve Samborn for your research assistance.

Thanks to our families and friends, whose continued support has helped us to revise this text.

We continue to be indebted to the people whose assistance, direction, and support led to the first edition of this text and ultimately this revised text as well as individuals who helped with our text *Basic Legal Writing for Paralegals,* a project that led to some of the revisions in this text.

To that end, we thank Jean Hellman, Director of the Loyola University of Chicago, Institute for Paralegal Studies, who encouraged us to write our first book and who introduced us to Carolyn O'Sullivan of

Little, Brown and Company, the predecessor of Aspen. We cannot thank Carolyn O'Sullivan, Betsy Kenny, Lisa Wehrle, Joan Horan, John Lyman, and Katie Byrne Butcher enough for their assistance with our books.

We also thank our students who have helped us to hone the text and the exercises. Their writing and use of the exercises helped form the skeleton for the book and then mold its contents. Their continued use of the book assisted us in revising the text. Our students have taught us more than we ever could teach them, and we appreciate all that they have done. Some of our students who deserve special thanks for their critiques, suggestions, and encouragement include Kelly Barry, Amy Berezinski, Nanette Boryc, Mara Castello, Patricia Cochran, Jessie Cohen, Nan Crotty, Beverly Dombroski, Susanne Grant, Stephen Gromala, Chris Harrigan, Marion Kahle, Michael Luckey, Mitchell McClure, Brenda Mondul, Cheryl Morgan, Patricia Naqvi, Melissa Pederson, Shay Robertson, Louise Tessitore, and Amy Widmer.

Thanks to Terri Rudd, David Harris, Marc Steer, the late Debbie Freudenheim, and Linda Kahn for your insightful ideas and assistance.

We would also like to thank the reviewers listed below. Their careful review of the first manuscript and the *Basic Legal Writing for Paralegals* manuscript produced many valuable comments and suggestions. We greatly appreciate their efforts.

Jonathan H. Barker
George Washington University

Laura Barnard
Lakeland Community College

Suzanne Cascio
Manhattanville College

Charles E. Coleman
New York City Technical College

Holly L. Enterline
State Technical Institute at Memphis

Andrew T. Fede
Montclair State College

William J. Heimbuch
Montclair State College

Patricia Hohl
Boston University

Mary Holland
Manchester Community College

Paul Klein
Duquesne University

Gina-Marie Reitano
St. John's University

Brenda L. Rice, J.D.
Johnson County Community College

Kay Y. Rute
Washburn University

Helene Kulczycki
Briarcliffe, The College for Business and Technology

Adelaide Iagnese
University of Maryland

Cynthia B. Lauber
Denver Paralegal Institute

Sy Littman
Platt College

Judith M. McAuliffe
Quincy College

Robin O. McNeely
McNeese State University

Joy O'Donnell
Pima Community College

Eric Olson
Barry University

Elaine Puri
Univeristy of North Florida

Julia O. Tryk
Cuyahoga Community College

Sue K. Varon
National Center for Paralegal
Training

Lastly, we would like to thank the following publishers for allowing us to reprint the illustrations listed below.

Illustrations 3-3, 3-4, 3-6A. Reprinted with permission of Thomson Reuters/ West.

Illustration 3-6B. Reproduced by permission of LexisNexis. Further reproduction of any kind is strictly prohibited.

Illustration 3-6C. Reprinted with the permission of Loislaw, www.loislaw.com.

Illustrations 3-6D, 3-8, 3-9, 4-1, 4-3, 4-4, 4-6, 4-7, 4-8, 4-9, 4-10, 4-11, 4-12, 4-13, and 4-14. Reprinted with permission of Thomson Reuters/West.

Illustrations 4-15, 4-16, 4-17, 4-18, 5-1, 5-2, 5-3, 5-4, 5-5, 5-6, 5-7, 5-9, 5-10, 5-11, 5-12, 5-13, 5-14, and 5-16. Reproduced by permission of LexisNexis. Further reproduction of any kind is strictly prohibited.

Illustrations 5-17, 5-18, 6-1, 6-2, 6-3, 6-4, 6-5, 6-6, 6-7, 6-8, 6-9 and 6-10. Reprinted with permission of Thomson Reuters/West.

Illustrations 6-11 and 6-12. Copyright ©1981 by the American Law Institute. Reprinted with permission. All rights reserved.

Illustration 7-1. Reproduced by permission of LexisNexis. Further reproduction of any kind is strictly prohibited.

Illustration 7-6. Reprinted with permission of Thomson Reuters/West.

Illustration 7-7. Reprinted with permission of LexisNexis. Further reproduction of any kind is strictly prohibited.

Illustration 7-8. Reprinted with permission of Thomson Reuters/West.

Illustration 7-9. Reprinted with permission of LexisNexis. Further reproduction of any kind is strictly prohibited.

Illustration 7-10. Reprinted with permission of Thomson Reuters/West.

Illustrations 7-11 and 7-12. Reprinted with permission of LexisNexis. Further reproduction of any kind is strictly prohibited.

Illustration 7-13. Reprinted with permission of Thomson Reuters/West.

Illustrations 7-14, 7-15, and 7-16. Reprinted by permission of LexisNexis. Further reproduction of any kind is strictly prohibited.

Illustrations 8-1, 8-2, and 18-1. Reprinted with permission of Thomson Reuters/West.

PART 1

LEGAL RESEARCH

CHAPTER 1

INTRODUCTION TO LEGAL RESEARCH

CHAPTER OVERVIEW

Before you begin to research and to write about a legal problem, you must understand your role as a paralegal. You are an important member of a team. To function effectively, you must know which legal system governs and how that system operates. This chapter first considers your role in researching a legal problem. Next, it discusses the legal system. It focuses on the organization of the U.S. federal government, which is divided into three separate branches: the legislative, the executive, and the judicial. It also provides a general explanation of how state governments are structured. Finally, the role of major governmental bodies is explored.

A. INTRODUCTION TO LEGAL RESEARCH AND WRITING

1. The Role of the Paralegal in Legal Research and Writing

Legal research and legal writing are among the tasks paralegals can perform efficiently and cost-effectively for law firms and their clients. But to do so effectively, paralegals must understand the legal system and a variety of legal concepts. They must be able to use all the research tools available to lawyers and their staffs, including the computer. Paralegals retrieve information regarding the law as well as nonlegal information, such as financial information and test results.

▼ Why Do Paralegals Perform Research?

Often research is done to determine whether a client has a case. Other times, you must research a particular issue raised after a case has been filed. Some research is done to support motions to be filed with courts. Research also may be done when a client is involved in a transaction and the attorney needs to determine the law and the steps to take in the transaction.

▼ What Tasks Do Paralegals Handle in the Research and Writing Process?

In practice, paralegals act as an arm of an attorney. The amount of research and the type of assignments paralegals perform vary throughout the country.

In some law offices, paralegals undertake all the research in preparation for the filing of motions but attorneys draft the motions. In others, paralegals research and prepare rough drafts of motions. Once a research project is completed, you must communicate your research results effectively. To do this, you must understand the fundamentals of legal writing and be able to write detailed, clear, and thoughtful memoranda. Paralegals often are asked to prepare memoranda that summarize their research results. Some paralegals who work with judges prepare rough drafts of court decisions. This book is designed to help you complete each of these tasks.

When you are assigned a research problem, you are expected to work as a professional. You should complete the assignment in a timely fashion. More important, however, the research results must be accurate, complete, and current. This book teaches you how to approach a research problem, about the resources available to uncover the legal standards, and about the various methods for ensuring that those standards are current, complete, and valid.

▼ What Are You Trying to Accomplish with Your Research?

In completing your tasks, you are looking for legal standards that will apply to the legal problem you must research. The ideal standards of authorities would be ones that are based on facts and circumstances identical to those posed in your legal problem. This quest is difficult. Do not be discouraged if you do no find such standards easily or at all. If you do find legal authorities that apply to the facts of a case, then you try to analyze the problem using the legal authorities you have found. Finally, discuss the issue and the research results with the assigning attorney. For a full discussion of research strategy, see Chapter 14.

ETHICS ALERT

Paralegals work under the supervision of attorneys, except in very limited, statutorily sanctioned situations. As a result, all research results should be submitted to an attorney before they are provided to a client.

ETHICS ALERT

All legal documents filed with a court should be reviewed and signed by an attorney, if required.

B. INTRODUCTION TO THE U.S. LEGAL SYSTEM

1. The Organization of the Legal System

The United States consists of a multi-tiered system of government. The **federal government** and the **state governments** are the top two tiers. See Illustration 1-1.

Several lower-tier governmental bodies, including **city, village, township**, and **county governments**, exercise authority over the citizens of the United States. For the most part, your research will concern either federal or state law. Therefore, this book focuses its discussion on the federal and state systems and how to find the law they generate. The knowledge of these systems, the types of laws they adopt, and how to find legal standards for these systems later can be applied to any research you undertake concerning other government bodies and their laws.

ILLUSTRATION 1-1.   U.S. and State Government Systems

*Most, but not all, state courts consist of three tiers.

▼ How Did the Federal and State Systems Originate?

Representatives of the states adopted a **constitution** for the United States that is the framework for the operation of this federal/state system of government. To that end, the U.S. Constitution creates three branches of government and defines their powers. You can think of the Constitution as an umbrella over all of the United States' governing bodies as it covers questions of not only federal government powers, but some state powers as well. The Constitution reserves for the states all the remaining powers not specifically designated to the federal government bodies. In addition, the Constitution establishes the rules for the relationship between the federal and state governments. The U.S. Constitution is the supreme law of the United States. For example, Congress, the legislative body of the federal government, cannot enact a law that is contrary to the U.S. Constitution. The state legislatures similarly are prevented from adopting laws that violate provisions of the U.S. Constitution.

2. Components of the Federal System and Governing Law

The federal government consists of three branches of government: the legislative, the executive, and the judicial. The U.S. Constitution created each branch and defines the relationship between them. The Constitution establishes a system in which each branch of government can monitor the activities of the other branches to prevent abuses. Each branch has the ability to alter actions of another branch. In this way, the Constitution provides **checks** and **balances** concerning the actions of each branch of government.

a. The Legislative Branch

The **legislative branch** of the federal government is called the **Congress.** It is comprised of two houses or chambers called the **Senate** and the **House of Representatives.** Both houses are comprised of individuals

who are elected. The Congress creates laws called **statutes.** Some statutes are new rules of law. Other statutes supersede or adopt court-made law. Court-made law is commonly referred to as **case law** or the **common law.** When Congress adopts common law as its own, the process is called **codification.** One pervasive example of this is patent law. Many laws were adopted based on court decisions concerning this area of the law. The statutes and the U.S. Constitution comprise one body of law called **enacted law.** The laws enacted by the federal government apply to all U.S. citizens and residents.

▼ How Is a Law Created?

Anyone can propose that Congress adopt a new law, and either chamber can introduce a law for consideration. When a proposed law is introduced, it is called a **bill.** Before the bill can become a law, both chambers must approve it. If both houses approve the same version of the bill, it is sent to the chief of the executive branch, our President. The President can sign or veto the bill or withhold action on it. If the President signs the bill, it becomes law. If the President does not act within ten days and the legislative session is still in progress, the bill becomes law. If the President vetoes the bill, Congress may override the veto by a two-thirds majority vote of each house.

If the President fails to act on the bill within the ten days and the legislature is out of session, the bill does not become law. This action is called a **pocket veto.**

b. The Executive Branch

The **executive branch** of the government, headed by the President, is the primary enforcer of the law. The President appoints the cabinet and oversees many federal agencies. The executive branch is responsible for the day-to-day management of the federal government. With the assistance of the Vice President, the cabinet members, and the heads of federal agencies, the President helps to guide the day-to-day operations of the government. The President can issue executive orders to direct the operations of various agencies and the actions of the citizens of the United States. In addition, the President is the commander in chief of the armed forces and with the advice and consent of the Senate, he can enter into treaties. Most federal administrative agencies are part of the executive branch. See Illustration 1-2.

NET NOTE

Illustration 1-2 can be found at http://bensguide.gpo.gov/files/gov_chart.pdf.

ILLUSTRATION 1-2. The Government of the United States

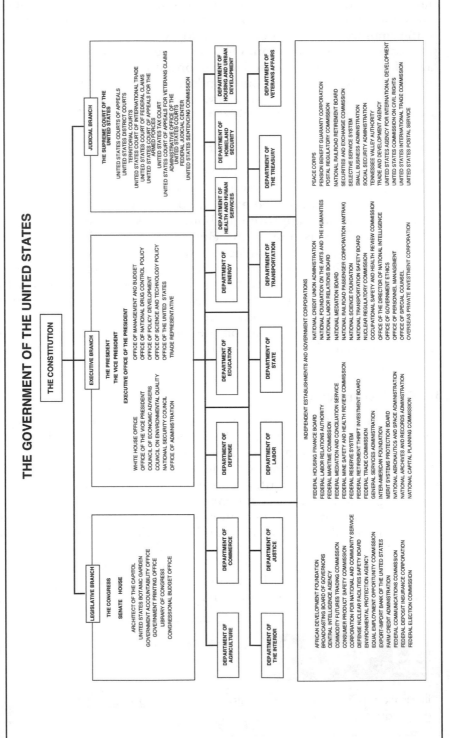

As the country's top executive, the **President** has the authority to control many administrative agencies. However, some administrative agencies are independent rather than part of the executive branch. For example, the Department of Justice that includes the Office of the Attorney General is part of the executive branch. However, the Federal Trade Commission is an independent agency.

Administrative agencies enforce many of the laws of the United States. These agencies are responsible for the daily regulation of activities controlled by federal law. For a listing of some of the many administrative agencies, see Illustration 1-2.

Congress creates the agencies and delegates some of its own power to them because it alone is unable to handle the day-to-day enforcement of the overwhelming number of federal laws. Agencies, however, have the staff and often the technical expertise to deal with the daily enforcement of Congress's enacted laws. To do this, agencies often make rules that explain in detail how individuals should act to comply with congressional mandates. In some cases, agencies hold hearings to enforce the law. These agencies, therefore, function in quasi-judicial and quasi-legislative roles.

For example, Congress enacted the Consumer Product Safety Act and delegated its enforcement power to the U.S. Consumer Product Safety Commission. Congress charged the commission with the responsibility for the daily enforcement of that act. As part of the commission's duties, it adopts rules or regulations. It also has administrative hearings, which often result in decisions.

In some cases, agencies use their **police powers** to enforce the law. For example, the U.S. Environmental Protection Agency will assist in prosecuting individuals or corporations that violate the Clean Air Act or other laws designed to protect the environment.

Search for federal agencies and information at <u>usasearch.gov</u>. Details about cabinet members, proclamations, executive orders, and issues facing the executive branch can be found at <u>whitehouse.gov/index.html</u>. Another government source of information is usa.gov. Information on federal government agencies can be found at <u>usa.gov/Agencies/federal.shtml</u>.

c. The Judicial Branch

The third branch of government is the **judicial branch.** The federal judicial system includes three levels of courts that resolve disputes. See Illustration 1-3.

ILLUSTRATION 1-3.   Federal Judicial System

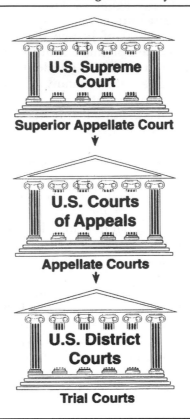

The entry-level court is the **trial court.** In that court, disputes are heard and decided by either a judge or a jury. The second level or intermediate level of courts is called **appellate courts.** These courts consider appeals of decisions of the trial court. The final level is the **U.S. Supreme Court.** Its decisions cannot be appealed to any court.

The Web site www.uscourts.gov provides links to all the U.S. appellate and district courts and U.S. bankruptcy courts, as well as the U.S. Supreme Court. Information is provided about judges, court personnel, locations, and court rules.

▼ Who Can Bring an Action in Federal Court?

A court can only consider a case if it has **jurisdiction** to hear it, that is, if the court is authorized to consider such cases. The federal court can

consider all cases involving issues of federal law. In addition, it may hear cases involving disputes between parties of different states. Such cases are called **diversity cases.** Cases in which both the plaintiff, who is the party bringing the lawsuit, and the defendant are citizens of different states are examples of diversity cases. Diversity cases often involve issues of state law.

PRACTICE POINTER AND ETHICS ALERT

If you are assisting an attorney in preparing a claim, be certain that the claim is made in the court that has jurisdiction over such a claim.

PRACTICE POINTER

State and federal courts can decide issues of state or federal law.

---

i. The Trial Courts

The **trial court** is the court that hears the facts concerning a dispute. It is generally the first place in which a party can seek a remedy in federal court. In that way, it is considered a court of **original jurisdiction.** However, this court also hears appeals from some administrative agencies and the federal bankruptcy courts. Some administrative agency decisions, however, are appealed directly to the appellate courts.

In the federal system, the trial courts are known as the **district courts.** These courts decide disputes when a party (which can be a person, corporation, or other entity) brings an action against another party. In such cases, the trial courts often are asked to interpret congressional enactments such as statutes, ordinances, charters, or executive branch-created laws, including agency rules or decisions. When a court interprets a statute or regulation, it is overseeing the actions of other government branches. Courts often consult a body of law called the common law before rendering any decisions. Common law is court-created law found in the judicial opinions or cases; it is not found in the statutes.

ii. The Appellate Courts

The federal trial courts' decisions can be appealed to one of the 13 **federal appellate courts** known as the **U.S. Courts of Appeals.** See Illustration 1-3. This second tier of federal courts is broken into

numbered and named **circuits.** Eleven circuits are known as the First through Eleventh. The remaining circuits are the Federal Circuit and the District of Columbia Circuit. The circuits are geographic, except for the Federal Circuit. See Illustration 1-4. An online map is available at www.uscourts.gov/images/CircuitMap.pdf. These courts decide issues of law posed in appeals of trial court decisions. These courts do not consider new factual evidence. Witnesses are not brought before these courts. Instead, judges review transcripts of trial court proceedings to make decisions concerning appeals. Decisions of the federal appellate courts can be appealed to the U.S. Supreme Court.

iii. *The Supreme Court*

The U.S. Supreme Court is the highest court in the United States. See Illustration 1-3. The U.S. Constitution establishes this court. Today nine justices, appointed by the President and confirmed by the U.S. Senate, sit on this tribunal. The U.S. Supreme Court has discretion to consider many issues. This discretion is called **certiorari.** If the court decides not to hear an issue, it denies certiorari. The effect is that the decision of the appellate court is final. If the U.S. Supreme Court decides to hear an issue, it grants certiorari. It then will consider whether the appellate court's decision should stand. By law, the U.S. Supreme Court alone has the authority to hear appeals of a state court of last resort decision when a substantial federal constitutional issue is presented. The U.S. Supreme Court also may hear a dispute between two states.

The Federal Judicial Center provides information about the federal judiciary and its history. See www.fjc.gov.

3. Relationship Between Federal and State Governments

▼ Can a Federal Court Decide an Issue of State Law?

Yes. A federal court can decide an issue of state law if the state issue is presented with a related federal issue or if the state question is raised in a dispute between parties of different states in a case called a diversity action.

ILLUSTRATION 1-4. Circuit Map of the U.S. Courts of Appeals

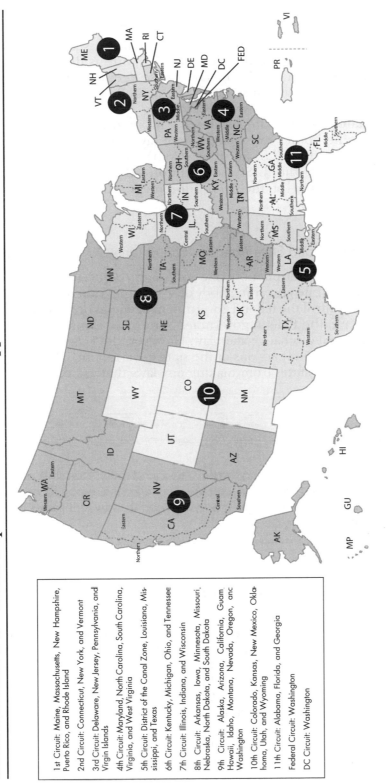

1st Circuit: Maine, Massachusetts, New Hampshire, Puerto Rico, and Rhode Island

2nd Circuit: Connecticut, New York, and Vermont

3rd Circuit: Delaware, New Jersey, Pennsylvania, and Virgin Islands

4th Circuit: Maryland, North Carolina, South Carolina, Virginia, and West Virginia

5th Circuit: District of the Canal Zone, Louisiana, Mississippi, and Texas

6th Circuit: Kentucky, Michigan, Ohio, and Tennessee

7th Circuit: Illinois, Indiana, and Wisconsin

8th Circuit: Arkansas, Iowa, Minnesota, Missouri, Nebraska, North Dakota, and South Dakota

9th Circuit: Alaska, Arizona, California, Guam, Hawaii, Idaho, Montana, Nevada, Oregon, and Washington

10th Circuit: Colorado, Kansas, New Mexico, Oklahoma, Utah, and Wyoming

11th Circuit: Alabama, Florida, and Georgia

Federal Circuit: Washington

DC Circuit: Washington

▼ What Effect Does a Federal Decision Have on State Law?

A federal court decision generally cannot change state law. It may persuade the state courts to review state law, but its decision usually does not force any change in the law. These decisions, therefore, are advisory for future litigants, but must be followed by the parties directly involved in the case in which the decision was rendered. Because states are separate sovereigns, in almost all cases only the state governing bodies can change state law. One exception to this rule does exist. The U.S. Supreme Court can determine whether state law violates the U.S. Constitution. If such a violation is found, the decision of the U.S. Supreme Court could invalidate state law.

▼ Are Federal and State Agencies Part of One Governing Body?

No. The federal government is one sovereign or governing body and the state is a separate governing body or sovereign. That means that the state cannot control the federal government agencies or change federal law. In general, the federal government branches cannot control the state government or change state law. However, the U.S. Constitution, the umbrella, can limit actions of the state government. The Constitution prohibits the states from making any laws that are contrary to its provisions.

PRACTICE POINTER

Often attorneys choose to bring a case in a federal rather than state court or the other way around for tactical reasons. More often the reason for bringing an action in a particular court is based solely on the law that serves as the basis for the claim.

---

4. Organization of State Governments

Most state governments are organized in a manner similar to that of the federal government. State governments are governed by constitutions. That constitution defines the organization of the state's government and the relationship between the branches of government. The states have legislative, executive, and judicial branches.

The legislative branches operate in a manner similar to that of Congress and often feature two chambers. Some legislatures enact enabling laws that create administrative agencies and provide such agencies with the responsibility for the daily enforcement of state laws. The chief executive in each state is a governor.

Each state has a judicial system. However, not all state systems mirror the federal government's three-tier court system. Each state establishes which courts can hear different disputes. Some states have a three-tier system similar to that of the federal judicial branch. In some states, the intermediate appellate court is eliminated. The following systems do not include an intermediate appellate court: Delaware, District of Columbia, Maine, Montana, Nevada, New Hampshire, North Dakota, Rhode Island, South Dakota, Vermont, West Virginia, and Wyoming.

NET NOTE

For more information about the state trial courts, see the National Center for State Courts Web site, ncsconline.org. A diagram and summary of courts' structures within the states is found from the links at the NCSC Web site.

PRACTICE POINTER

The Supreme Court may not be the highest court in a state. This is the case in New York.

▼ What Are the Duties of the State Courts?

In most state court systems, a trial court determines the facts and legal issues of a case. A trial court might include a family, a municipal, or a small claims court. The jurisdiction of these courts is generally limited, sometimes according to the amount of money in dispute.

The next level generally is an appellate level court. However, as noted above, some states do not have this level. As in the federal court system, this court usually does not hear new facts or evidence. Instead, it decides whether the lower court erred in deciding substantive law or procedural issues. Finally, most states have another appellate level court, similar to the U.S. Supreme Court, which is the final arbiter of disputes. In some states, there are two such courts—one for criminal cases and the other for civil cases. Texas and Oklahoma are two states that have such courts.

PRACTICE POINTER

An appellate court may hear facts and evidence if it is the court of original jurisdiction. That is the court charged with first hearing the case.

▼ Can State Courts Decide Issues of Federal Law?

Yes, state courts can decide issues of federal law. Although a state court decision concerning federal law does not change the federal law, it may persuade federal governing bodies to change federal law. The state court decision's impact is limited to the case in which the federal issue was presented, and therefore only parties involved in that case are bound or required to follow that ruling.

The federal government controls all issues of federal law. The state governments exercise authority over all issues of state law. These areas are not always well defined. In some areas, both the state and federal governments exercise authority. For example, both the state and federal governments control how industries dispose of their wastes. Do not be discouraged if you have difficulty separating state and federal issues in some cases. Many times courts struggle with these issues.

CHAPTER SUMMARY

In this chapter, you learned about the branches of the U.S. government and their functions, as well as the general structure of the state governments. The United States has three branches of government: the legislative, the executive, and the judicial. All of these branches were created by the U.S. Constitution, which guides their activities. In addition, administrative agencies enforce the laws created by the legislature.

The legislature, which consists of the House of Representatives and the Senate, creates laws called statutes.

The executive branch enforces the laws of the United States, and the judicial branch resolves disputes and interprets the laws.

The judicial branch is comprised of a three-tier court system. The highest court is the U.S. Supreme Court; the middle courts are the U.S. Courts of Appeals; the trial or lowest courts are the U.S. District Courts. All three branches of government create law.

KEY TERMS

administrative agencies
appellate courts
balance

bill
case law
certiorari

checks
circuits
city government
codification
common law
Congress
constitution
county government
district courts
diversity cases
enacted law
cxccutive branch
federal appellate court
federal government
House of Representatives
judicial branch
jurisdiction
legislative branch
original jurisdiction
pocket veto
police powers
President
Senate
state governments
statutes
township government
trial court
U.S. Courts of Appeals
U.S. Supreme Court
village government

EXERCISES

HOMEWORK

1. Draw a diagram of your state government.
2. How many houses does your legislature have? What are the names of each chamber?
3. Diagram your state court system. Is there an intermediate court?
4. Draw a flow chart of the federal bill process.
5. Draw a flow chart of the state bill process for your state.
6. Who is the chief executive?
7. Go to the National Center for State Courts Web site and review the structure of your state court.
8. What are the monetary requirements for filing an action in the trial court in your state?
9. Go to usa.gov and click around the site to find links to the Congressional Budget Office and the Domestic Policy Council.
10. What are the branches of the U.S. government and what are the responsibilities of each branch?
11. What are Congress-created laws called?
12. What is the body of law created by the courts called?
13. Name the judges on your high court. Where did you find this information?
14. Find your state's Web site. Note it.
15. Find a Web site for your courts. Note it.
16. Find a Web site for your legislature. Note it.

CHAPTER 2

WHAT LAW GOVERNS

CHAPTER OVERVIEW

In researching legal issues, you must have goals and understand the value of the legal authorities you find. This chapter explains the concept of legal authority and the determination of governing law. It discusses the value of various authorities and how authorities interrelate with each other. You will learn which authorities should determine the outcome of a case and which authorities merely provide persuasive support for a case.

A. DETERMINATION OF GOVERNING LAW

To determine what law controls your case, you must first determine the jurisdiction. Next, you must identify the current law that applies to your case by examining the hierarchy of authorities. Looking at relevant precedent and dicta completes your strategy for determining the governing law.

1. Jurisdiction

Jurisdiction is a complex concept that has several different definitions. It is the authority of a government body to exercise control over a conflict. In the broadest sense, jurisdiction is the right of a state or of the federal government to apply its laws to a dispute. It also is the right of a court to interpret and apply the law to a particular case. When a court or a governing body has jurisdiction over a case or situation, it has the authority to control the case or outcome of the situation.

▼ What Factors Determine Which Jurisdiction Governs Your Case?

A variety of factors affect which jurisdiction governs a claim in a particular case, including where the dispute arose, the parties involved in the case, and the nature of the dispute. Sometimes making this determination is a complex task. Ask the assigning attorney to assist you in making this determination. Various statutes, procedural rules, and cases also can assist you in understanding which court has jurisdiction. For example, federal court jurisdiction is specified by federal law.

2. Precedent

You already have learned that the courts generate decisions of cases that become law. The basic rule of law decided by the court is the **holding.** If the court is presented with more than one issue, the decision includes more than one holding. The holding also is called the **precedent.**

Theoretically, the lower courts must follow decisions or precedents of the higher courts in their jurisdiction. This theory is called **stare decisis.** The idea behind it is that parties should be able to rely on what the courts have done in the past. Doing so allows parties to predict how a court is likely to rule in their cases.

The doctrine of stare decisis makes your job as a researcher important. You must determine what the courts have decided in the past to assist the attorneys in predicting what the court is likely to do, or likely to be persuaded to do, in your case. Sometimes a court will not follow precedent. Even though stare decisis and precedent are the controlling doctrines, courts decide cases based on the facts before them and the changes in society. This allows the law, through the holdings, to evolve

and to meet contemporary needs. It is these holdings that you must consider after reviewing the theories of hierarchy of authorities.

3. Hierarchy of Authorities

Once you have determined the jurisdiction, you then must identify the current law that applies to the case. To determine what law applies to your case, you must determine the **hierarchy of authorities.** This is a system in which legal authorities such as court decisions, statutes, administrative rules and decisions, and constitutions are ranked according to the effect they have in controlling the law of a governing body. You can think of this in part as a chain of command. For example, U.S. Supreme Court cases outrank federal appeals and trial courts concerning issues of federal law. Determining the hierarchy of authorities can be simple or complex depending in large part on the system of government and structure of the courts, the law applicable to the dispute, and the underlying claim. Other factors that play a role in determining whether one authority outranks another is the currency of an authority and competing laws within a jurisdiction.

a. Currency

You must first determine which authority is most current. Suppose you find that the law governing your case is a federal law and the case involves a question of federal constitutional law. At first glance the highest legal authority would appear to be the U.S. Constitution because it is the supreme law of the United States and because the legal issue in question is constitutional in nature. However, if the U.S. Supreme Court has interpreted the Constitution on the issue presented in your case, its decision is more current and would therefore be the highest legal authority.

In another case that does not involve a constitutional issue, a federal statute might be the highest authority. This would depend on whether a court had interpreted the statute. If a federal court had interpreted the statute's language and that language affected the issue involved in your case, you would need to determine whether the court decision or the statute is more recent. The most current authority is the highest authority.

EXAMPLE OF THE HIERARCHY QUESTION BETWEEN A STATUTE AND A CASE

Your case involves a statute that was enacted on December 1, 2007. All the court cases you have found that may have a bearing on the issue involved in this case were decided before December 1, 2007. Therefore, the statute—the most current authority—is the highest authority concerning this issue. For another example, see Illustration 2-1.

ILLUSTRATION 2-1.   Example of Ranking Authorities

Consider a question concerning the constitutional provision that requires due process. Does it apply to aliens held under the USA Patriot Act?

> Applicable law:
>
> U.S. Constitution
>
> The USA Patriot Act (2001)
>
> Supreme Court case 2005 determining that the Due Process Clause of the U.S. Constitution is not applicable to persons held under the USA Patriot Act

Rank of authorities and reason for the ranking:

1. Supreme Court case 2005 interpreting the Constitution and the USA Patriot Act would be first. It is the most current authority.
2. The next authority is likely to be the USA Patriot Act if it directly addresses this point. It is the second most current authority.

b. Levels of Court

Next, you must consider the level of each authority, that is, where the court or government body ranks in order of its authority. The trial courts, appellate courts, and U.S. Supreme Court do not carry the same weight. For example, a decision of the highest court, the U.S. Supreme Court, would be at the top of the hierarchy of authorities of federal court decisions. Its decisions would trump those of other federal courts.

Except for the U.S. Supreme Court, all the federal courts are within defined groups called **circuits.** Within each circuit are a group of district courts and one circuit court of appeals. The key to the relationship between the federal courts is that the district courts, which are the entry-level courts, must follow decisions of the U.S. Circuit Court of Appeals within its circuit. A district court does not have to follow decisions of appellate courts that are outside of its circuit. However, these decisions often are used to persuade a court to make a certain decision if it has not addressed that issue earlier. Such a decision is **persuasive authority** discussed later in this chapter.

PRACTICE POINTER

Make a chart of authorities for the jurisdictions in which you regularly handle cases. If you have multiple authorities to consider, this chart will be helpful.

Two examples of how such a hierarchical ranking would work in practice follow.

EXAMPLES OF HIERARCHY BETWEEN COURTS

The U.S. District Court for the Northern District of Illinois, which is in Chicago, falls in the Seventh Circuit. See Illustration 1-4. If the federal district court in Illinois was asked to determine whether federal law permitted a union to charge a fee to nonmembers for activities that benefit nonmembers, it would be bound to follow any U.S. Seventh Circuit Court of Appeals decision concerning this issue. This is because this appellate court is a higher court than the district court within the Seventh Circuit. If the U.S. Sixth Circuit Court of Appeals in Cincinnati handed down a decision on this issue that conflicted with the Seventh Circuit Court of Appeals, the District Court for the Northern District of Illinois, a trial court, would be bound to follow the decision of the Seventh Circuit Court of Appeals, a court that is above it in rank and status, not the Sixth Circuit Court of Appeals, as the Illinois court is within the Seventh Circuit. The Seventh Circuit decision would be considered **mandatory binding authority** for the Illinois court. But the Illinois district court would not have to follow decisions of the U.S. Sixth Circuit Court of Appeals in Cincinnati concerning the above issue because it is not part of the Sixth Circuit. The Sixth Circuit opinion would be primary persuasive authority.

Similarly, the U.S. District Court for the Northern District of Ohio, based in Cleveland, falls within the Sixth Circuit. See Illustration 1-4. That district court must follow decisions of the Sixth Circuit appellate court, not those of the Seventh Circuit Court of Appeals in Chicago, because decisions of the Sixth Circuit Court would be mandatory binding authority for the Ohio court. Decisions of the Seventh Circuit would be primary persuasive authorities for the Ohio court.

c. Conflicting Decisions Between Circuits

Each circuit is independent of the other circuits. Therefore, their decisions may conflict. Each appellate court can make its decision independent of any decisions concerning the same issue rendered by other appellate courts. If two appellate courts have conflicting decisions concerning the same issue, how can you, as a researcher, decide what law governs? You must determine what circuit court authority is **mandatory authority** for your case. If the question is a particularly significant federal issue, check if the U.S. Supreme Court has decided the issue or is about to render a decision concerning such an issue. If so, a decision of the Supreme Court—the highest level of court—will be at the top of the hierarchy of authority.

Often, however, one appellate court may be guided in its decision by the decision of another appellate court. For example, if the Seventh Circuit had not rendered an opinion in the union fee case, but the

Sixth Circuit had issued a decision concerning that matter, the Illinois district court facing a decision in a union fee case or even the Seventh Circuit Court of Appeals may be guided by the Sixth Circuit opinion. That decision rendered by a court outside of the Seventh Circuit would be persuasive authority rather than mandatory or binding authority. That is because the two courts would not be bound to follow the Sixth Circuit's decision.

d. State and Federal Decisions Concerning an Issue

What happens if the issue in your case involves both state and federal decisions? How do you make sense of the hierarchy of authorities in such cases? The key is to determine which court has jurisdiction or the right to hear the case. The court systems of the state and federal governments operate in tandem. As explained above, the federal courts may decide issues of both federal or state law. For example, a federal diversity case may involve a negligence issue—a state law issue.

Next, you must determine whether federal or state law applies. If you find this difficult, ask the assigning attorney. The federal courts must look to decisions of the highest court of the state to make a determination of state law. The federal court decision, however, does not bind later state court decisions.

State courts also may decide issues of either federal or state law. The state court decisions concerning federal law are merely persuasive authority, however, because federal courts are not required to follow these decisions. For instance, a plaintiff may bring an age discrimination case based on both the state and federal age discrimination in employment statutes. State courts will look to federal courts for guidance in deciding issues of federal law. However, they are not bound to follow those decisions. Similarly, a state court may decide a federal age discrimination issue, but the federal courts can disregard that decision when facing the same question.

e. Conflicts in Federal and State Authority

Although the federal and state governments are independent governments, they sometimes regulate some of the same areas, such as environmental pollution and securities. In some cases, the federal government by congressional action will control an area extensively, and a state will attempt to monitor the same area. Who controls varies. Often, a determination of which of the **conflicting authorities** governs is decided by reviewing the Constitution. Other times, federal or state law might specify which law governs.

The federal courts sometimes are asked to decide who controls. The courts may look to the Constitution for guidance or may consider who has pervasively regulated an area. For example, if a case involves a section of the U.S. Constitution, the U.S. Supreme Court is the final authority. In other cases, it depends on the area being regulated.

f. State Court Decisions

Each group of state courts is a separate court system. State courts of one state are not required to follow decisions made by courts of other states. Often, however, state courts consider other states' court decisions for guidance in how to decide a case. Decisions of one state's courts are merely advisory or persuasive decisions for another state's courts, not decisions that control the law of the first state.

4. Dicta

Often a court addresses an issue that is not directly presented by the parties. In such cases, a court states what it would do if it was presented directly with the issue. When the court makes such statements, they are called **dicta.** Dicta do not have the same force and effect as holdings. They are not authoritative, and lower courts are not bound to follow such statements.

You might use dicta when no court has ever been asked directly to decide the issue addressed. The dicta explain how the court would decide the issue if it was directly presented to the court. Because of this, the dicta might help you to predict how a court might decide an issue. Dicta also can be used to persuade a court to decide an issue in a certain manner. Although dicta may be helpful, finding dicta is not the goal of your research.

B. GOAL OF YOUR RESEARCH

Your task is to find primary authority "on point" or "on all fours" with your case, in other words, cases that are similar in fact and in legal issue to your case and whose holdings address an issue presented in your case.

1. Primary Authority

Primary authority is law generated by a government body. Cases decided by any court are primary authority. Legislative enactments such as constitutions, statutes, ordinances, or charters are primary authorities. See Illustration 2-2. Administrative agency rules and decisions are primary authorities.

These authorities often are published chronologically. However, statutes are arranged by subject. Some sources of primary authorities will be more appropriate for your research than others. In some cases, primary authority is mandatory or binding authority because a government body must follow that authority when it makes future decisions. The words *mandatory* and *binding* are interchangeable.

ILLUSTRATION 2-2. Authorities and Finding Tools

Primary Authorities	Secondary Authorities	Finding Tools
Court decisions	Encyclopedias	Digests
Statutes	*American Law Reports*	Citators
Agency rules and regulations	Periodicals and law reviews	Updaters
Constitutions	Dictionaries	Annotated statutes
Charters	Thesauri	
Ordinances	Model codes	
Adopted pattern jury instructions	Unadopted uniform laws	
Court rules	Treatises	
State-adopted model code provisions	Restatement of the Law	
State-adopted uniform laws		

▼ How Do You Determine Whether a Case Is Mandatory or Binding?

To determine whether a case is mandatory or binding, you must consider the rank of the authorities. Follow the steps below.

1. Determine the jurisdiction that applies to your case. Then, look to the hierarchy of the courts within that jurisdiction.
2. Note what court decided the case you are reviewing.
3. Determine whether this is a court within the jurisdiction that applies to your case.
4. If the court is within the appropriate jurisdiction, you must determine the level of that court within the court system. Is it a trial court or an appellate court? Is it the highest court of the system? States often have rules that specify the effect of a court decision on other courts within the same system. In general, the lower courts in a system must follow the decisions of the highest court in the system. The rules concerning which courts must follow the decisions of the intermediate-tier courts vary by jurisdiction. Consult the rules for that jurisdiction.

An authority is only mandatory if it controls or shapes the law of a particular jurisdiction, for example, an opinion from a state appellate court or an applicable state statute.

An authority is persuasive when it is made by a court outside of a particular jurisdiction. For example, decisions of one state court are not binding on courts of other states. Decisions of the Arizona Supreme Court are mandatory or binding on the lower courts in Arizona, but these decisions are merely persuasive primary authority in Michigan.

A decision is also persuasive rather than mandatory if it is made by a court whose decisions according to the law do not bind other courts. For example, decisions of the federal trial courts do not have to be followed by other federal courts.

Persuasive authority can be invaluable in persuading a court. This is especially true in decisions concerning statutory interpretation that involve statutes that are identical. For example, Kansas and Ohio adopted the same comparative negligence statute at different times. Kansas courts faced challenges concerning the statutory language. The decisions were highly persuasive authority when Ohio courts faced similar challenges years later, particularly since it was likely that the Ohio legislators were aware of the Kansas interpretations when they adopted the Ohio statute.

PRACTICE POINTER

Use persuasive authority if you do not have primary authority on point. For statutory disputes, determine whether legislators would have been aware of the persuasive authority when the statute was adopted.

---

2. Secondary Authority

Another type of authority is **secondary authority.** Such authority is not generated by government bodies. Instead, secondary authority includes commentary of attorneys or other experts. Secondary authority is persuasive only, and it is never binding or mandatory. In general, an attorney would not base an argument to a court on a secondary authority.

Secondary sources are helpful in understanding an issue of law, in determining other issues, and in finding primary authorities. Sometimes secondary authorities help to interpret primary authority for you and the court. Secondary sources include treatises, Restatements of the Law, dictionaries, encyclopedias, legal periodicals, *American Law Reports,* books, and thesauri. See Illustration 2-2. Often these sources direct you to cases, statutes, and other primary authorities.

Some secondary authorities are more persuasive than others. Many Restatements and treatises are authoritative and can be noted in court documents and legal reports called memoranda addressed to attorneys. However, most secondary authorities should not be noted in these reports.

One type of secondary authority that is often confused with primary authorities is uniform codes. Many uniform codes exist throughout the country. These are suggested laws, often devised by experts. If a state adopts the uniform code in total or in part, its adopted statute is

primary authority, but the recommended or uniform code remains as secondary authority. This, however, is often very persuasive secondary authority.

PRACTICE POINTER

If you have a primary authority on point, do not cite a secondary authority to make the same point.

PRACTICE POINTER

Secondary authorities are rarely cited. However, some secondary authorities carry significant persuasive weight, for example, commentaries to uniform laws.

---

3. Finding Tools

To find primary and secondary resources, often you need to consult **finding tools**, such as digests and citators. See Illustration 2-2. These finding tools are neither primary nor secondary authority. They should never be noted or cited in memoranda or court documents. Among the finding tools are **digests**, which are books containing case abstracts arranged according to publisher-assigned topics rather than in chronological order. **Annotated statutes** also include case abstracts written by the publishers. **Citators**, such as *Shepard's,*® provide you with listings of cases and some secondary authorities.

PRACTICE POINTER

Attorneys do not look favorably on paralegals who cite finding tools as authority.

---

4. Hybrid Sources of Authority

Hybrid sources of authority contain primary authorities, secondary authorities, regulations, cases, and finding tools. Hybrid sources of

authority include looseleaf services, formbooks, and proof of facts. These resources can be useful in finding multiple authorities. However, be certain that you distinguish the primary and secondary authorities and finding tools and that in most cases, you cite only the primary authorities.

5. Nonlegal Sources

You often must consult nonlegal sources, such as newspapers or corporate information statements. These sources are not authoritative. Never use nonlegal sources to determine the law that governs a case. However, they can assist you in your work. Sometimes it is necessary to cite these sources as relevant **factual authority** in a motion or a brief. These sources often provide insight into the purpose behind a court decision or the enactment of a law.

IN-CLASS EXERCISES

FACTS
You are a paralegal in the state in which you live. You have been assigned to research whether an individual can bring an action in state court against a car dealer and the car manufacturer of a car that has been trouble-ridden since the individual purchased it eight months ago.

RESEARCH RESULTS
You have found a statute that explains lemon law actions in your state; two cases in your state that interpret the statute; a federal case that explains the lemon law's application in your state; a case from another state that explains the lemon law; an encyclopedia explanation of the statute; a periodical article in a bar journal about lemon law actions in your state; and a newspaper article that explains how to bring a lemon law action and what actions are barred.

DISCUSSION QUESTIONS FOR THE CLASS
a. What type of authority is the lemon law statute in your state?
b. What type of authority are the two cases from your state?
c. What type of authority is the case from another state?
d. What type of authority is the federal case?
e. What type of authority is the encyclopedia reference to the statute?
f. What type of authority is the periodical article?
g. What type of authority is the newspaper article?
h. Which, if any, authorities might be binding or mandatory authorities?
i. Which authorities might be noted in a memorandum to a court?

Determine whether the authorities are primary mandatory, primary persuasive, or secondary authorities, and rank authorities according to which authorities the students would use first, second, third, and so on, if at all.

CHAPTER SUMMARY

In this chapter, you learned that determining governing law involves examining jurisdiction and the hierarchy of authorities. You also learned how precedent and dicta influence governing law. As a researcher, your goal is to find cases that are similar to yours in fact and legal issue and whose holdings address an issue presented in your case. In reaching this goal, you first seek primary authorities because these authorities carry more weight with the courts than secondary authorities. Primary authorities include court decisions, statutes, court rules, constitutions, and administrative rules and regulations.

Some primary authorities are binding. If an authority is binding, a court must follow that authority. Other authorities are merely persuasive. Such authorities provide guidance to the courts and often are followed by the decision-making tribunal.

As you are researching, you often will refer to secondary authorities. Secondary authorities provide you with information to understand primary authorities. Generally, secondary authorities are commentaries prepared by experts in a particular field. These authorities often include citations to primary authorities. Secondary authorities are persuasive only. Therefore, you would rely on a primary authority rather than a secondary authority. Secondary authorities include encyclopedias, treatises, and legal periodicals.

Finding tools are designed to assist you in your research, but they are not considered authorities. These tools provide you with citations to primary and secondary authorities. Finding tools include annotated statutes, digests, and citators.

KEY TERMS

annotated statutes
binding authority
circuits
citators
conflicting authorities
dicta
digests
factual authorities
finding tools
hierarchy of authorities

holding
hybrid sources of authority
jurisdiction
mandatory authority
persuasive authority
precedent
primary authority
secondary authority
stare decisis

EXERCISES

COURT SYSTEMS
Exercises

1. What is the highest court of your state? Where can you find this information on the Internet? Give a Web site.
2. Within your state's court system, what type of authority are decisions made by the highest court named in question 1?
   a. primary binding
   b. primary persuasive
   c. secondary binding
   d. secondary persuasive
3. What is the name of the trial court of your state?
4. Are the trial court's decisions binding on the highest court of the state?
5. What is the highest court of the federal system of government?
6. Within the federal system of government, what type of authority are decisions made by the highest court named in question 5?
   a. primary binding
   b. primary persuasive
   c. secondary binding
   d. secondary persuasive
7. What is the name of the trial court of the federal government?
8. Are decisions of any federal trial court binding on any federal appellate court?
9. Are all federal appellate court decisions binding on every federal trial court? Why or why not?
10. Can state courts decide issues of federal law?
11. Can federal courts decide issues of state law?
12. What is primary authority?
13. What is binding or mandatory authority?
14. When would you use primary authority?

HOMEWORK
Research Strategy

15. Can the Arizona Legislature adopt a law that contradicts the U.S. Constitution?
16. Must the U.S. Circuit Court of Appeals for the Ninth Circuit follow a decision of the U.S. Supreme Court concerning a federal issue?
17. Must an Arkansas trial court follow a decision of the U.S. Supreme Court concerning an issue of federal law?
18. You are a paralegal assigned to research the components necessary to create a valid will in your state. List in order the types of authorities you would consult and why. Next, rank the authorities according to whether they are primary mandatory, primary persuasive, or secondary.
19. You are a paralegal who has just researched what constitutes a breach of contract in a case involving the delivery of dairy products in Wisconsin.

Rank the following authorities and list whether each is a primary binding, primary persuasive, or secondary authority.

a. a Wisconsin Supreme Court case involving a breach of contract dispute

b. a Wisconsin statute that defines breach of contract

c. a Wisconsin statute that defines the term *delivery* in a contract

d. a Wisconsin trial court case involving a breach of contract dispute

e. an Illinois Supreme Court case involving a breach of contract dispute

f. a Uniform Commercial Code section concerning breach of contract. (The Wisconsin statute is derived in part from this section but does not adopt it in total.)

20. You are researching the question of whether a company that employs 50 individuals is an employer under the federal law regulating age discrimination in employment. Your case is pending in the federal district court in Toledo, Ohio. You learn that the definitions in the age discrimination statute were derived from those already in the sex discrimination statute. Rank the following authorities and list whether each is a primary binding, primary persuasive, or secondary authority.

a. the federal age discrimination in employment statute that defines the term *employer*

b. the federal sex discrimination in employment statute that defines the term *employer*

c. a U.S. Supreme Court case that interprets the definition of *employer* contained in the federal age discrimination in employment statute

d. a U.S. Supreme Court case that interprets the definition of *employer* contained in the federal sex discrimination in employment statute

e. a decision of the Northern District Court of Ohio, Western Division, concerning the definition of *employer* under the federal age discrimination in employment statute

f. a law review article in the *University of Toledo Law Review* concerning the definition of *employer* contained in the federal age discrimination in employment statute

g. a section of an employment law treatise that explains the definition of *employer* under the federal age discrimination in employment statute

h. an Ohio Supreme Court case that explains the definition of *employer* under the federal age discrimination in employment statute

21. You are asked to research the validity of a New York statute that bars high school students from wearing t-shirts bearing antigovernment slogans. Your case is pending in the state court of New York. Rank the following authorities and list whether each is a primary binding, primary persuasive, or secondary authority.

a. the New York statute in question

b. the U.S. Constitution's First Amendment regarding free speech

c. a U.S. Supreme Court case that prohibits states from banning the wearing of symbols by high school students because such a ban violates the U.S. Constitution

d. a case decided by the highest court in New York that holds that the statute is invalid

e. a California case involving an identical statute adopted in California that holds that the statute is valid

f. an encyclopedia entry that states that such bans are invalid

g. a newspaper article in *The National Law Journal* that predicts that the U.S. Supreme Court will invalidate the New York statute

COURT DECISIONS

CHAPTER OVERVIEW

In Chapters 1 and 2, you learned about our system of government and were introduced to the concept of legal authorities. This chapter focuses on one of those legal authorities—case law, which is a primary authority. The chapter describes where to find U.S. Supreme Court cases and other federal court decisions as well as the location of many state court opinions. It also explains where you can find the most recent court decisions. You are then introduced to a topical system for locating cases and are shown how to use this system.

A. REPORTERS

Court decisions are often referred to as **case law.** Case law is one of the primary sources of our law, on both the state and the federal levels.

Finding and reading past court decisions is therefore vital to any lawyer or paralegal working on a client's case.

Several publishers publish court decisions in various forms. Many publishers have devised **reporting systems** for organizing these court decisions. The major reporting system is called the **National Reporter System** and is published by West. It includes books called **reporters** that contain many federal and state decisions in chronological order. Several other companies and government agencies also publish court decisions in chronologically arranged reporters. In all cases, the decisions are selectively reported. Many decisions never appear in print or online.

1. Slip Opinions

The first *printed* version of a court's decision is called a **slip opinion**. See Illustration 3.1. Sometimes, the slip opinion is the only report of a court's action because the case is never published in a reporter or other service. This is usually the case with trial court decisions, especially state court decisions. However, many courts, including the U.S. Supreme Court and trial courts, now place slip opinions on the Internet.

▼ Where Can You Get a Slip Opinion?

Most slip opinions are obtained from the courts. All you need is the name of the case. Sometimes you can locate the slip opinion with the name of only one of the parties involved in the case. A few courts distribute slip opinions in printed form. More commonly, however, they are available through the Internet free of charge. A list of some of the sources of these opinions is included in Appendix D. In addition, WESTLAW, LEXIS, and Loislaw, computerized legal research services, include many slip opinions online.

The official slip opinion contains a syllabus. See Illustration 3-1 point A. It is written by the Reporter of Decision. It is not part of the decision.

NET NOTE

The U.S. Supreme Court slip opinions are available at <u>supremecourtus.gov/opinions/opinions.html</u>.

ILLUSTRATION 3-1.   A Portion of a Supreme Court Slip Opinion

(Slip Opinion)   OCTOBER TERM, 2007   1

Syllabus

> NOTE: Where it is feasible, a syllabus (headnote) will be released, as is being done in connection with this case, at the time the opinion is issued. The syllabus constitutes no part of the opinion of the Court but has been prepared by the Reporter of Decisions for the convenience of the reader. See *United States* v. *Detroit Timber & Lumber Co.*, 200 U. S. 321, 337.

SUPREME COURT OF THE UNITED STATES

Syllabus

Ⓑ UNITED STATES *v.* RESSAM

CERTIORARI TO THE UNITED STATES COURT OF APPEALS FOR THE NINTH CIRCUIT

Ⓒ No. 07–455.   Ⓓ Argued March 25, 2008— Ⓔ Decided May 19, 2008

After respondent gave false information on his customs form while attempting to enter the United States, a search of his car revealed explosives that he intended to detonate in this country. He was convicted of, *inter alia*, (1) feloniously making a false statement to a customs official in violation of 18 U. S. C. §1001, and (2) "carr[ying] an explosive during the commission of" that felony in violation of §844(h)(2). The Ninth Circuit set aside the latter conviction because it read "during" in §844(h)(2) to include a requirement that the explosive be carried "in relation to" the underlying felony.

Ⓐ *Held:* Since respondent was carrying explosives when he violated §1001, he was carrying them "during" the commission of that felony. The most natural reading of §844(h)(2) provides a sufficient basis for reversal. It is undisputed that the items in respondent's car were "explosives," and that he was "carr[ying]" those explosives when he knowingly made false statements to a customs official in violation of §1001. Dictionary definitions need not be consulted to arrive at the conclusion that he engaged in §844(h)(2)'s precise conduct. "[D]uring" denotes a temporal link. Bec[...] con-temporaneous with his §1001 [...] that violation. The statute's histo[...] that Congress did not intend a rel[...] pres-ently written. Pp. 2–6

> A   Syllabus
> B   Case name
> C   Docket number
> D   Date argued
> E   Date decided
> F   Summary of how the judges voted concerning the decision

474 F. 3d 597, reversed.

Ⓕ   STEVENS, J., delivered the op[...] RTS, C. J., and KENNEDY, SOUTER, G[...] d in which SCALIA and THOMAS, JJ., [...] d an opinion concurring in part and concurring in the judgment, in which SCALIA, J., joined. BREYER, J., filed a dissenting opinion.

ILLUSTRATION 3-1. *Continued*

Cite as: 553 U. S. ____ (2008)   1

Opinion of the Court

NOTICE: This opinion is subject to formal revision before publication in the preliminary print of the United States Reports. Readers are requested to notify the Reporter of Decisions, Supreme Court of the United States, Washington, D. C. 20543, of any typographical or other formal errors, in order that corrections may be made before the preliminary print goes to press.

SUPREME COURT OF THE UNITED STATES

No. 07–455

UNITED STATES, PETITIONER *v.* AHMED RESSAM

ON WRIT OF CERTIORARI TO THE UNITED STATES COURT OF APPEALS FOR THE NINTH CIRCUIT

[May 19, 2008]

Ⓖ JUSTICE STEVENS delivered the opinion of the Court.

Respondent attempted to enter the United States by car ferry at Port Angeles, Washington. Hidden in the trunk of his rental car were explosives that he intended to detonate at the Los Angeles International Airport. After the ferry docked, respondent was questioned by a customs official, who instructed him to complete a customs declaration form; respondent did so, identifying himself on the form as a Canadian citizen (he is Algerian) named Benni Noris (his name is Ahmed Ressam). Respondent was then directed to a secondary inspection station, where another official performed a search of his car. The official discovered explosives and related items in the car's spare tire well.

Respondent was subsequently convicted of a number of crimes, including the felony of making a false statement to a United States customs official in violation of 18 U. S. C. §1001 (1994 ed., Supp. V) (Count 5) and carrying an explosive "during the commission of" that felony in violation of §844(h)(2) (1994 ed.) (Count 9). The Court of Appeals for the Ninth Circuit set aside his conviction on Count 9 because it read the word "during," as used in §844(h)(2), to

G Body of the decision

PRACTICE POINTER

Newspaper reports of slip opinions of court cases also are quickly available; however, these should never be quoted in a memorandum for an attorney or in a motion to the court because such reports have no force within the law. In addition, they may be incorrect. Only quote or cite information that comes directly from a court opinion.

---

a. Supreme Court Slip Opinions

For the U.S. Supreme Court, you can retrieve decisions from the court clerk or from its Web site. The government also offers Supreme Court slip opinions through its Case Management Electronic Case Files (CM/ECF) service and the PACER Service, pacer.psc. uscourts.gov/. The CM/ECF service is scheduled to replace PACER, Public Access to Court Electronic Records. Users must register to use this service and pay minimal fees for items retrieved. For civil cases, users can search by case number, party name, and the nature of the lawsuit. For criminal cases, searches can be done using the case number, the party, or the nature of the appeal. The best feature is that it is available 24 hours a day via the Internet. If requested, e-mail updates of case activity will be sent. *United States Law Week,* a service of the Bureau of National Affairs, allows you to access opinions daily through the Internet. It also provides information about other newsworthy legal developments. This fee-based subscription service provides highlights of significant state and federal court decisions nationwide at bna.com. In addition, you can click on the hyperlinks that allow access to the full text of U.S. Supreme Court cases, summaries, and BNA headnotes of cases, a list of cases docketed, decided and denied review. A case summary will provide some information about the topic addressed in the opinion, the docket number, a brief case history, the summary of the ruling of the case on appeal, and the attorneys involved in the case. *U.S. Law Week* continues to appear in print. It contains a list of all the cases argued, docketed, or reviewed by the U.S. Supreme Court and full text of opinions, *U.S. Law Week* also provides some synopsis of arguments and analysis of significant opinions complete with headnotes and citations to electronic links. *U.S. Law Week* and other services provide e-mail alerts concerning cases for subscribers. Subscribers indicate their areas of interest and links to these cases are sent via email to them.

NET NOTE

Free Supreme Court slip opinions also are available quickly from the Legal Information Institute of Cornell University Law School at straylight.law .cornell.edu/supct/index.html.

b. Other Slip Opinions

Slip opinions for other federal courts can be secured from the court, the Internet, WESTLAW, LEXIS, and Loislaw. State court slip opinions also are easily accessible from WESTLAW, LEXIS, Loislaw, or the Internet, but the electronic coverage may not be complete. Contact the state court if you cannot find its opinion elsewhere.

▼ How Are Slip Opinions Cited?

Slip opinions are cited according to Rule 10.8.1 of *The Bluebook: A Uniform System of Citation* (18th ed. 2005) or the *ALWD Citation Manual: A Professional System of Citation* (3rd ed. 2006). For the *Bluebook* citation, you should provide the docket number, the court, and the full (but abbreviated) date of the most recent disposition of the case.

slip opinion cite:	Gillespie v. Willard City Bd. of Educ., No. C87-7043 (N.D. Ohio Sept. 28, 1987)
with page cite:	Gillespie v. Willard City Bd. of Educ., No. C87-7043, slip op. at 3 (N.D. Ohio Sept. 28, 1987)

The *ALWD* citation would be the same. See Rule 12.18.

2. Advance Sheets

After a slip opinion is released, it is published in **advance sheets.** Advance sheets, often distributed as pamphlets, contain the full text of a decision and are paginated using the same page numbers that will be used when the decision is published in the bound reporter. Many advance sheets contain publisher's notes called **headnotes** that are designed to assist readers. These notes summarize points of law in a case and have a topic and number assigned to them. These topics and numbers assist you in finding additional cases. The timing of the publication of advance sheets varies by publisher. After decisions appear in advance sheets, they are published in the bound reporters. Many print advance sheet publications are being phased out as many courts and fee-based online services now send users slip opinions via e-mail. For example, the Fifth Circuit Court of Appeals offers to send opinions twice a day, free of charge to subscribers. Visit www.ca5.uscourts.gov/opinSub.aspx. It also will send notices of case activity just after something occurs. The user provides an e-mail address and a case number. When changes are noted on the case, they are sent to the user's e-mail address. If calendar changes or due dates are requested, these will be sent as well.

3. Bound Reporters

a. U.S. Supreme Court Decisions

A U.S. Supreme Court case is first presented as a bench opinion, published as a slip opinion, then as an advance sheet, and finally as a report

in a bound volume. For U.S. Supreme Court cases, the official, government-printed reporter is *United States Reports*. See Illustration 3-2. Illustration 3-2 includes a syllabus or summary of the case. It is not part of the court's decision and should not be quoted in any documents submitted to the court. It has no force of law. This illustration also indicates the author of the opinion and whether any judges concurred or dissented. The attorneys representing the parties are noted. Then the decision begins. This reporter, however, is not published quickly, nor does it contain any research aids. Because of this delay, commercial publishers have created reporter systems that contain the same decisions as those published in ***U.S. Reports.***

Commercial publishers produce these decisions as well. One commercial publisher, West, publishes all U.S. Supreme Court decisions in its reporter called the ***Supreme Court Reporter***. See Illustration 3-3. LexisNexis (Lexis) prints the same full text of U.S. Supreme Court decisions in its reporter called *United States Supreme Court Reports, Lawyers' Edition 2nd*. Most people simply call it the ***Lawyers' Edition.***

Within both reporters, the cases are identical to the decisions that appear in the official *U.S. Reports,* except that they also contain references prepared by the publishers to assist you in your research. These references direct you to other sources that may help you understand a point of law. For example, a publisher may direct you to a treatise that contains commentary about a point of law raised in the case reported.

▼ Is U.S. Supreme Court Docket Information Available on the Internet?

Yes. For U.S. Supreme Court docket, schedules, general information, and links to decisions, see <u>supremecourtus.gov</u>.

▼ What Happens If the Language of a Decision in the Commercial Reporters Varies from the Language in *U.S. Reports*?

If the report contained in either the *Supreme Court Reporter* or the *Lawyers' Edition* varies from the official, government-printed report, the language in *U.S. Reports* governs.

▼ Why Use the Commercial Reporters Rather Than the Official Reports?

You should review U.S. Supreme Court cases in either the *Supreme Court Reporter* or in the *U.S. Supreme Court Reports, Lawyers' Edition*. First, these reporters are published sooner than the official, government-printed version. In addition, they contain a variety of publisher's headnotes or case abstracts that assist you in your research. Often they include additional references, such as encyclopedia cite. These headnotes summarize points of law found in a case. They also include a publisher's topic designation and number. These topics and numbers tie into the commercial publisher's indexes of legal issues called **digests.** These

ILLUSTRATION 3-2.   Pages from *U.S. Reports, United Paperworks Intl. Union, AFL-CIO, et al. v. Misco, Inc.*, 484 U.S. 29 (1987)

Syllabus

UNITED PAPERWORKERS INTERNATIONAL UNION, AFL–CIO, ET AL. *v.* MISCO, INC.

CERTIORARI TO THE UNITED STATES COURT OF APPEALS FOR THE FIFTH CIRCUIT

(1) No. 86–651.   Argued October 13, 1987—Decided December 1, 1987 (2)

Respondent employer's collective-bargaining agreement with petitioner union authorizes the submission to binding arbitration of any grievance that arises from the interpretation or application of the agreement's terms, and reserves to management the right to establish, amend, and enforce rules regulating employee discharge and discipline and setting forth disciplinary procedures.   One of respondent's rules listed as causes for discharge the possession or use of controlled substances on company property.   Isiah Cooper, an employee covered by the agreement who operated a hazardous machine, was apprehended by police in the backseat of someone else's car in respondent's parking lot with marijuana smoke in the air and a lighted marijuana cigarette in the frontseat ashtray.   A police search of Cooper's own car on the lot revealed marijuana (3) gleanings.   Upon learning of the cigarette incident, respondent discharged Cooper for violation of the disciplinary rule.   Cooper then filed a grievance which proceeded to arbitration on the stipulated issue whether respondent had just cause for the discharge under the rule and, if not, the appropriate remedy.   The arbitrator upheld the grievance and ordered Cooper's reinstatement, finding that the cigarette incident was insufficient proof that Cooper was using or possessed marijuana on company property.   Because, at the time of the discharge, respondent was not aware of, and thus did not rely upon, the fact that marijuana had been found in Cooper's own car, the arbitrator refused to accept this fact into evidence.   However, the District Court vacated the arbitration award and the Court of Appeals affirmed, ruling that reinstatement would violate the public policy "against the operation of dangerous machinery by persons under the influence of drugs."   The court held that the cigarette incident and the finding of marijuana in Cooper's car established a violation of the disciplinary rule that gave respondent just

1 Docket number
2 Decision date
3 Syllabus written by reporter

als exceeded the limited authority possessed by
itrator's award entered pursuant to a collective-

ILLUSTRATION 3-2. *Continued*

29   Opinion of the Court

framed under the approach set out in *W. R. Grace*, and the violation of
such policy must be clearly shown. Here, the court made no attempt to
review existing laws and legal precedents, but simply formulated a policy against the operation of dangerous machinery under the influence of
drugs based on "general considerations of supposed public interests."
Even if that formulation could be accepted, no violation of the policy
was clearly shown, since the assumed connection between the marijuana
gleanings in Cooper's car and his actual use of drugs in the workplace is
tenuous at best. It was inappropriate for the court itself to draw that
inference, since such factfinding is the task of the arbitrator chosen by
the parties, not the reviewing court. Furthermore, the award ordered
Cooper's reinstatement in his old job or an equivalent one for which he
was qualified, and it is not clear that he would pose a threat to the
asserted public policy in every such alternative job. Pp. 42–45.

763 F. 2d 739, reversed.

WHITE, J., delivered the opinion for a unanimous Court. BLACKMUN,
J., filed a concurring opinion, in which BRENNAN, J., joined, *post*, p. 46.

David Silberman argued the cause for petitioners. With
him on the briefs were *Lynn Agee, Michael Gottesman*, and
Laurence Gold.

A. Richard Gear argued the cause and filed a brief for
respondent.*

JUSTICE WHITE delivered the opinion of the Court.

The issue for decision involves several aspects of when a
federal court may refuse to enforce an arbitration award rendered under a collective-bargaining agreement.

I

Misco, Inc. (Misco, or the Company), operates a paper con-
verting plant in Monroe, Louisiana. The Company is a party
[...] ng agreement with the United Paper-
[...] Union, AFL–CIO, and its union local
[...] ment covers the production and main-

[...] liam P. Murphy filed a brief for the National
[...] micus curiae urging reversal.
[...] illiam R. Stein filed a brief for Northwest Air-
[...] uriae urging affirmance.

4 **Syllabus**
5 **Judicial author of opinion
   and concurring opinions**
6 **Attorneys representing
   the parties**
7 **The start of the Court's opinion**

ILLUSTRATION 3-3. Pages from *Supreme Court Reporter, United Paperworkers Intl. Union, AFL-CIO, et al. v. Misco, Inc.,* 108 S. Ct. 364-365, 370 (1987)

①

②364   **108 SUPREME COURT REPORTER**   484 U.S. 29

③   ④
484 U.S. 29, 98 L.Ed.2d 286

⑤ UNITED PAPERWORKERS INTERNA-
TIONAL UNION, AFL–CIO, et
al., Petitioners

v.

MISCO, INC.

⑥ No. 86–651.

Argued Oct. 13, 1987.

Decided Dec. 1, 1987.

⑦ After arbitrator determined that employee did not violate employer's rule regarding use or possession of marijuana on company property, and ordered reinstatement of employee, the United States District Court for the Western District of Louisiana, Tom Stagg, Chief Judge, vacated arbitration award. On appeal, the Court of Appeals for the Fifth Circuit, Gee, Circuit Judge, 768 F.2d 739, affirmed, and determined that reinstatement would violate public policy against operation of dangerous machinery by persons under influence of drugs. On writ of certiorari, the Supreme Court, Justice White, held that: (1) Court of Appeals was not free to refuse enforcement of arbitrator's award on basis that it found arbitrator's fact-finding improvident; (2) arbitrator was entitled to refuse to consider evidence unknown to company at time employee was fired; (3) formulation of public policy set up by Court of Appeals did not comply with requirement that such policy must be ascertained by reference to laws and legal precedence and not from general considerations of supposed public interests; and (4) even if Court of Appeals' formulation of public policy was accepted, no violation of that policy was clearly shown.

Reversed.

Justice Blackmun filed concurring opinion in which Justice Brennan joined.

⑧**1. Arbitration** ⬅73.7(3)⑨

Courts play only limited role when asked to review decision of arbitrator; courts are not authorized to reconsider merits of award even though parties may allege that award rests on errors of fact or on misinterpretation of collective bargaining contract.

2. Labor Relations ⬅416.1

Courts have jurisdiction to enforce collective bargaining contracts, but where contract provides grievance and arbitration procedures, those procedures must first be exhausted and courts must order resort to private settlement mechanism without dealing with merits of dispute. ⑩

3. Labor Relations ⬅485

To resolve disputes about application of collective bargaining agreement, arbitrator must find facts and court may not reject those findings simply because it disagrees with them.

4. Labor Relations ⬅462, 479

Arbitrator may not ignore plain lan-

that court is convinced that he committed serious error does not suffice to overturn decision.

1 *Supreme Court Reporter* volume number
2 *Supreme Court Reporter* page number
3 Citation to official reporter
4 Citation to unofficial reporter
5 Case name
6 Docket number
7 Syllabus by reporter editor
8 West topic
9 West key number
10 West headnotes
11 Number of page of official reports

ILLUSTRATION 3-3. *Continued*

7. Labor Relations ⬉479

Arbitral decisions pertaining to collective bargaining agreements which are procured by parties through fraud or through arbitrator's dishonesty need not be enforced.

8. Labor Relations ⬉479

Arbitrator's decision, which was rendered pursuant to collective bargaining agreement, that evidence was insufficient to prove that discharged employee had possessed or used marijuana on company property in contravention of company's rule could not be reversed on basis that appellate court found fact-finding by arbitrator to be improvident.

9. Labor Relations ⬉479

Appellate court could not refuse to enforce arbitrator's award which required company to reinstate employee who had been discharged for allegedly violating company rule pertaining to use of marijuana on company property because arbitrator, in deciding whether there was just cause to discharge, refused to consider evidence unknown to company at time of discharge; arbitrator's approach was consistent with collective bargaining agreement, and with practice followed by other arbitrators, and further, even if arbitrator erred in refusing to consider disputed evidence, error was not in bad faith so as to justify setting aside award. 9 U.S.C.A. § 10(c).

10. Labor Relations ⬉479

Court's refusal to enforce arbitrator's award under collective bargaining agreement because it is contrary to public policy is specific application of more general doctrine, rooted in common law, that court may refuse to enforce contracts that violate law or public policy.

11. Labor Relations ⬉264

Courts may only refuse to enforce collective bargaining agreement when specific terms contained in agreement violate public policy.

12. Labor Relations ⬉479

Formulation of public policy based only on general considerations of supposed public interest is not type of public policy that permits court to set aside arbitration award that was entered in accordance with valid collective bargaining agreement.

13. Master and Servant ⬉47

Even if public policy considerations against operation of dangerous machinery while under influence of drugs existed, no violation of that policy was shown in case where traces of marijuana had been found in terminated employee's car; assumed connection between marijuana gleanings and employee's actual use of drugs in workplace provided insufficient basis for holding that his reinstatement would actually violate public policy.

14. Labor Relations ⬉483

Appellate court's conclusion that since marijuana had been found in terminated employee's car, employee had ever been or would ever be under influence of marijuana while he was on job and operating dangerous machinery was improper exercise in fact-finding about employee's use of drugs and his amenability to discipline, which exceeded authority of court which was asked to overturn arbitration award; parties did not bargain for facts to be found by court, but rather, fact-finding was to be made by arbitrator chosen by parties who had more opportunity to observe employee and to be familiar with workplace and its problems.

Syllabus [*]

Respondent employer's collective-bargaining agreement with petitioner union authorizes the submission to binding arbitration of any grievance that arises from the interpretation or application of the agreement's terms, and reserves to management the right to establish, amend,

---

[*] The syllabus constitutes no part of the opinion of the Court but has been prepared by the Reporter of Decisions for the convenience of the reader. See *United States v. Detroit Lumber Co.*, 200 U.S. 321, 337, 26 S.Ct. 282, 287, 50 L.Ed. 499.

ILLUSTRATION 3-3.   *Continued*

peals but alternatively argues that the judgment below should be affirmed because of erroneous findings by the arbitrator. We deal first with the opposing alternative arguments.

A

[1] Collective-bargaining agreements commonly provide grievance procedures to settle disputes between union and employer with respect to the interpretation and application of the agreement and require binding arbitration for unsettled grievances. In such cases, and this is such a case, the Court made clear almost 30 years ago that the courts play only a limited role when asked to review the decision of an arbitrator. The courts are not authorized to reconsider the merits of an award even though the parties may allege that the award rests on errors of fact or on misinterpretation of the contract. "The refusal of courts to review the merits of an arbitration award is the proper approach to arbitration under collective bargaining agreements. The federal policy of settling labor disputes by arbitration would be undermined if courts had the final say on the merits of the awards." *Steelworkers v. Enterprise Wheel & Car Corp.*, 363 U.S. 593, 596, 80 S.Ct. 1358, 1360, 4 L.Ed.2d 1424 (1960). As long as the arbitrator's award "draws its essence from the collective bargaining agreement," and is not merely "his own brand of industrial justice," the award is legitimate. *Id.*, at 597, 80 S.Ct., at 1361.

"The function of the court is very limited when the parties have agreed to submit all questions of contract interpretation[37] to the arbitrator. It is confined to ascertaining whether the party seeking (11) tration is making a claim which on its face is governed by the contract. Whether the moving party is right or wrong is a question of contract interpretation for the arbitrator. In these circumstances the moving party should not be deprived of the arbitrator's judgment,

when it was his judgment and all that it connotes that was bargained for.

"The courts, therefore, have no business weighing the merits of the grievance, considering whether there is equity in a particular claim, or determining whether there is particular language in the written instrument which will support the claim." *Steelworkers v. American Mfg. Co.*, 363 U.S. 564, 567–568, 80 S.Ct. 1343, 1346, 4 L.Ed.2d 1403 (1960) (emphasis added; footnote omitted).

See also *AT & T Technologies, Inc. v. Communications Workers*, 475 U.S. 643, 649–650, 106 S.Ct. 1415, 1418–1419, 89 L.Ed.2d 648 (1986).

[2–7] The reasons for insulating arbitral decisions from judicial review are grounded in the federal statutes regulating labor-management relations. These statutes reflect a decided preference for private settlement of labor disputes without the intervention of government: The Labor Management Relations Act of 1947, 61 Stat. 154, 29 U.S.C. § 173(d), provides that "[f]inal adjustment by a method agreed upon by the parties is hereby declared to be the desirable method for settlement of grievance disputes arising over the application or interpretation of an existing collective-bargaining agreement." See also *AT & T Technologies, supra*, at 650, 106 S.Ct., at 1419. The courts have jurisdiction to enforce collective-bargaining contracts; but where the contract provides grievance and arbitration procedures, those procedures must first be exhausted and courts must order resort to the private settlement mechanisms without dealing with the merits of the dispute. Because the parties have contracted to have disputes settled by an arbitrator chosen by the (11) ther than by a judge, it is the arbitrator's view of the facts and of the meaning[38] of the contract that they have agreed to accept. Courts thus do not sit to hear claims of factual or legal error by an arbitrator as an appellate court does in reviewing decisions of lower courts. To resolve disputes about the application of a collective-bargaining agree-

digests are organized by topic and numbers. These digests will be discussed in detail in Chapter 4.

Cases published in the *Supreme Court Reporter* also contain head-notes. See Illustration 3-3. Similar to the cases published in the *Lawyers' Edition,* the *Supreme Court Reporter* cases include topics and numbers, which West calls **key numbers.** In Illustration 3-3, the first headnote includes the topic Arbitration and the key number 73.7(3). Also included in the text is the publisher's case abstract of a point of law. West has devised a system of organizing federal and state cases according to topics coupled with key numbers. See Chapter 4 for a more detailed explanation of this system. Across the top of the page in Illustration 3-3 is the citation to the *Supreme Court Reporter.* Above the name of the case is the official citation to the *U.S. Reports* and a citation to the *Lawyers' Edition* report of this case. In addition to the official syllabus of the court, West provides a summary of each case called a **syllabus.** This syllabus should not be cited because it is not authoritative.

West recently added another feature called **West Codenotes.** These indicate whether a statute cited in the case has been ruled unconstitutional, preempted, or modified in one of 25 ways. These are placed between the headnotes and the opinion's text.

Note the small numbers in front of some words in Illustration 3-3. Those numbers indicate the page number in which that text would appear in the official reports.

The *Lawyers' Edition* also includes headnotes, or the publisher's summaries of points of law presented in each case. These headnotes are arranged by publisher-designated topics and numbers in a series of volumes called *United States Supreme Court Digest, Lawyers' Edition.* Head-notes and digests are explained in detail later in Chapter 4. You should not quote from these headnotes because they are not authoritative.

▼ How Do You Locate a Reported Case?

Cases have citations that are similar to addresses. For example, "108 S.Ct. 364" is a citation. The number "108" is the volume of the reporter that contains the case. "S.Ct." is the abbreviation for the *Supreme Court Reporter* that contains the case and finally, "364" is the first page the case appears on within the reporter. See Illustration 3-3. Another example of a citation is "581 N.E.2d 885." The number "581" indicates the volume that contains the case. "N.E.2d" is the abbreviation for the reporter, the *North Eastern Reporter Second Series.* The last number, "885," is the first page of the case. This citation identifies the case, *Thompson v. Economy Super Marts.* See Illustration 3-4.

At the top of Illustration 3-4, next to the circled "1" is this same *West's North Eastern Reporter* citation. Above the name of the case, you can find the official (that is, state government-printed) citation and a citation to *West's Illinois Decisions Reporter.*

ILLUSTRATION 3-4. *West's North Eastern Reporter; Thompson v. Economy Super Marts, Inc., 581 N.E.2d 885 (Ill. App. Ct. 1991)*

THOMPSON v. ECONOMY SUPER MARTS, INC.
Cite as 581 N.E.2d 885 (Ill.App. 3 Dist. 1991) ——— ① Ill. **885**

provided for both of them on the instrument. Therefore, the defendant argues, since the intention of the Bank was to obtain a mortgage of the premises from both joint tenants and only one joint tenant signed the mortgage, the instrument should be found to be unenforceable as was the contract in *Dineff*.

Dineff is clearly distinguishable from the instant case. In *Dineff*, the plaintiff was attempting to enforce an agreement to convey the entire interest in the jointly held property without the signatures of both cotenants. The court pointed out that there was no prayer for partial performance against the cotenant who had signed the agreement. (*Dineff*, 27 Ill.2d at 482, 190 N.E.2d at 311.) It is well established that one cotenant cannot convey the interest of another cotenant without proper authority.

Here, however, the plaintiff is not attempting to foreclose on the entire interest in the property. The foreclosure complaint is against only the undivided one-half interest of the joint tenant who signed the mortgage.

[4] We disagree with the defendant's argument that the clear intention of the parties required the defendant's signature

that the names of both husband and wife appear in the body of the instrument and in the acknowledgment. The rule seems to be general that a deed naming two or more parties as grantors, executed by only a portion of them, is valid as to

those executing it." *Heckmann*, 283 Ill. at 513, 119 N.E. at 642.

It is clear that Mr. Stauffenberg intended to mortgage the real estate. There is nothing in the mortgage to indicate that it was not to be binding unless the defendant signed it also. We see no reason to deviate from the established rule that when a property owner attempts to convey a greater interest in the property than he actually has, that the conveyance is valid to the extent of his interest and void only as to the excess.

For the reasons stated above, the order of the trial court dismissing the complaint is reversed. This cause is remanded for further proceedings.

Reversed and remanded.

GORMAN and McCUSKEY, JJ., concur.

221 Ill.App.3d 263 ②
163 Ill.Dec. 731 ③

Cherryl E. THOMPSON,
Plaintiff–Appellant,

v.

ECONOMY SUPER MARTS, INC., a Division of Weems & Bruns Corp., a Corporation, and Weems & Bruns Corp., a Corporation, Defendants–Appellees. ④

No. 3–90–0662. ⑤

Appellate Court of Illinois,
Third District.

Nov. 8, 1991.

Customer allegedly injured when she slipped on lettuce leaf in produce section of grocery store brought negligence action against store owners. The Circuit Court, 12th Judicial Circuit, Will County, Michael H. Lyons, J., granted defendants' posttrial motion for judgment notwithstanding verdict after jury found customer to be 55% contributorily negligent and awarded her ⑥

1 Citation to *West's North Eastern Reporter*
2 Citation to official reporter
3 Citation to unofficial reporter
4 Case name
5 Docket number
6 Syllabus by reporter editor
7 West key numbers and headnotes
8 *Ward* case cited in Illustration 4-3

ILLUSTRATION 3-4. *Continued*

damages. the Appellate Court, Haase, J., held that: (1) where foreign substance causing slip of business invitee is on premises due to negligence of proprietor or his servants, it is not necessary to establish their actual or constructive knowledge of the substance, but if substance is on premises through acts of third persons, time element during which substance was present is material factor to establish

⑥ knowledge of, or notice to, proprietor; (2) even where there is proof that foreign substance causing slip of business invitee was related to defendant's business, where no further evidence is offered other than presence of substance and occurrence of injury, defendant is entitled to directed verdict, as such evidence is insufficient to support necessary inference of negligence; and (3) evidence of negligence of grocery store was not sufficient to permit customer to recover from store owners.

Affirmed.

⑦ 1. Negligence ⚖=32(2.8)

Defendant owes business invitee on defendant's premises duty to exercise ordinary care in maintaining premises in reasonably safe condition.

2. Negligence ⚖=44, 48

Where business invitee is injured by slipping on premises, liability may be imposed if substance causing slip was placed by negligence of proprietor or his servants; or if substance was on premises through acts of third persons or there is no showing how it got there, liability may be imposed if it appears that proprietor or his servant knew of presence of substance, or that substance was there sufficient length of time so that in exercise of ordinary care its presence should have been discovered.

3. Negligence ⚖=48

Where foreign substance causing slip of business invitee is on premises due to negligence of proprietor or his servants, it is not necessary to establish their actual or constructive knowledge of the substance, but if substance is on premises through acts of third persons, time element during which substance was present is material

factor to establish knowledge of, or notice to, proprietor.

4. Negligence ⚖=136(22)

Where there is proof that foreign substance causing slip of business invitee was product sold or related to defendant's operations and invitee offered some further evidence, direct or circumstantial, however slight, such as location of substance or business practices of defendant from which it could be inferred that it was more likely that defendant or his servants, rather than a customer, dropped the substance on the premises, trial court should allow negligence issue to go to jury.

5. Negligence ⚖=121.1(8)

Even where there is proof that foreign substance causing slip of business invitee was related to defendant's business, where no further evidence is offered other than presence of substance and occurrence of injury, defendant is entitled to directed verdict, such evidence being insufficient to support necessary inference of negligence.

6. Negligence ⚖=134(5)

Evidence of negligence of grocery store was not sufficient to permit customer allegedly injured when she slipped on lettuce leaf in produce section of store to recover from store, even though leaf was described as wilted and was found near unsupervised produce section where vegetables were packed on ice; no direct or circumstantial evidence made it more likely that store's servants, rather than customer, dropped the leaf, and customer presented no evidence that ice which packed produce was directly above water spot or any evidence regarding how ice was packed or how easy it might have been to jar ice loose and spill it to the floor.

James J. Morici, Jr., argued, Anesi, Ozmon & Rodin, Ltd., Chicago, for Cherryl E. Thompson.

Kenneth T. Garvey, Robert Spitkovsky, Jr. and Kevin P. O'Connell, argued, Bresnahan & Garvey, Chicago, for Economy Super Marts, Inc.

ILLUSTRATION 3-4.   *Continued*

THOMPSON v. ECONOMY SUPER MARTS, INC.   Ill. **887**

Cite as 581 N.E.2d 885 (Ill.App. 3 Dist. 1991)

Justice HAASE delivered the opinion of the Court.

The plaintiff, Cherryl E. Thompson, brought this negligence action against the defendants, Economy Super Marts, Inc. and Weems & Bruns Corp., to recover damages for personal injuries she sustained when she slipped on a lettuce leaf in the produce section of the defendants' grocery store. A jury awarded the plaintiff $12,974.96 in recoverable damages after finding that she was 55% contributorily negligent. Thereafter, the trial court granted the defendants' post-trial motion for a judgment notwithstanding the verdict. The plaintiff appeals from that decision.

The plaintiff testified at trial that on July 3, 1986, she picked up a watermelon in the produce section of the defendants' store and began to walk through the produce aisle. At that point, she slipped and fell on a lettuce leaf and water. She had not seen the leaf or the water before her fall and did not know how long they were there. She noted that the lettuce leaf was green and brown, had dirt on it, and appeared beat up. According to the plaintiff, her fall occurred about two or three feet to the left of the produce aisle. She also stated that the fruits and vegetables in the produce aisle were kept on ice.

Terida Thompson, the plaintiff's daughter, substantially corroborated the plaintiff's testimony. Additionally, she stated that the lettuce leaf looked old and like it had been there awhile. She further stated that she had walked through the produce aisle once before the accident occurred and did not see any water or a lettuce leaf on the floor prior to the plaintiff's fall.

Gene Pesavento, the assistant store manager, testified that it was his duty to make sure that all areas in the grocery store were clear and free of debris. He agreed that the produce department requires constant surveillance to ensure that debris is not left on the floor. He also agreed that debris poses a tripping hazard.

Pesavento further testified that no one was specifically charged with the responsibility of constantly monitoring the floor of the produce department. He explained

that the defendants' employees knew that they were supposed to keep an eye on the entire store, and not specifically one area.

Phil Woock, the store's general manager, testified that he was not working at the time of the plaintiff's accident. He stated that the store's floor was dry mopped and swept every night in July, 1986. In addition, the floors were swept during the day as needed, and spills were cleaned as needed. The floors were professionally mopped and waxed every Wednesday night, and the plaintiff's accident occurred on a Thursday. Woock further testified that a part-time employee was on duty in the produce department at the time of the accident, but he could have been working in the back room when it occurred. Woock also testified that all store workers have the responsibility of keeping the floor clean if no one is working in the produce department at a particular time.

Donald Schreiner and Rubin Amazan each testified that they were working at the store at the time of the plaintiff's accident, but did not witness the fall. They both stated that they did not observe a lettuce leaf on the floor after inspecting the floor following the accident.

Based on the foregoing evidence, the jury found that the plaintiff suffered $28,833.24 in damages, but it awarded her only $12,974.96 because it found that she was 55% contributorily negligent. Thereafter, the defendants filed a post-trial motion requesting that the trial court enter a judgment notwithstanding the verdict. The trial court subsequently granted the defendants' motion, finding that: (1) no evidence was presented that the defendants had actual or constructive notice of the lettuce leaf and water for a sufficient length of time that its presence should have been discovered; and (2) the jury's award of damages was a compromise verdict and could not be sustained.

On appeal, the plaintiff initially argues that the trial court erred in granting a judgment notwithstanding the verdict. She contends that the court mistakenly found that she did not present any evidence that

ILLUSTRATION 3-4. *Continued*

the defendants had actual or constructive notice of the lettuce leaf.

[1–3] It is well-settled that a defendant owes a business invitee on the defendant's premises a duty to exercise ordinary care in maintaining the premises in a reasonably safe condition. (*Ward v. K Mart Corp.* (1990), 136 Ill.2d 132, 143 Ill.Dec. 288, 554 N.E.2d 223; *Perminas v. Montgomery Ward & Co.* (1975), 60 Ill.2d 469, 328 N.E.2d 290.) Where a business invitee is injured by slipping on the premises, liability may be imposed if the substance was placed there by the negligence of the proprietor or his servants, or, if the substance was on the premises through acts of third persons or there is no showing how it got there, liability may be imposed if it appears that the proprietor or his servant knew of its presence, or that the substance was there a sufficient length of time so that in the exercise of ordinary care its presence should have been discovered. (*Olinger v. Great Atlantic & Pacific Tea Co.* (1961), 21 Ill.2d 469, 173 N.E.2d 443; *Wroblewski v. Hillman's, Inc.* (1963), 43 Ill.App.2d 246, 193 N.E.2d 470.) Thus, where the foreign substance is on the premises due to the negligence of the proprietor or his servants, it is not necessary to establish their knowledge, actual or constructive; whereas, if the substance is on the premises through acts of third persons, the time element to establish knowledge or notice to the proprietor is a material factor. *Blake v. Dickinson* (1975), 31 Ill.App.3d 379, 332 N.E.2d 575.

[4, 5] Where there is proof that the foreign substance was a product sold or related to the defendant's operations, and the plaintiff offers some further evidence direct or circumstantial, however slight, such as the location of the substance or the business practices of the defendant, from which it could be inferred that it was more likely that the defendant or his servants, rather than a customer, dropped the substance on the premises, the trial court should allow the negligence issue to go to the jury. (*Donoho v. O'Connell's, Inc.* (1958), 13 Ill.2d 113, 148 N.E.2d 434.) However, even where there is proof that the foreign substance was related to the defendant's business, but no further evi-

dence is offered other than the presence of the substance and the occurrence of the injury, the defendant is entitled to a directed verdict, such evidence being insufficient to support the necessary inference. *Olinger v. Great Atlantic & Pacific Tea Co.* (1961), 21 Ill.2d 469, 173 N.E.2d 443; *Wroblewski v. Hillman's, Inc.* (1963), 43 Ill. App.2d 246, 193 N.E.2d 470.

[6] The plaintiff argues that she satisfied the requirements set forth in *Donoho* of introducing "further evidence, however slight, such as the location of the substance or the business practice of the defendant, from which it could be inferred that it was more likely that the defendant or his servants, rather than a customer, dropped the substance on the premises." She contends that evidence of the wilted lettuce leaf and the fact that it was found near the unsupervised produce section where vegetables were packed on ice was sufficient to allow the case to go to the jury under *Donoho.*

We disagree. The Illinois Supreme Court in *Donoho* undertook an extensive analysis of the circumstances under which negligence could be inferred from the conduct of the defendant when it was uncertain who was responsible for the foreign substance dropped on the premises. In *Donoho,* the plaintiff slipped and fell on an onion ring at the defendant's restaurant. It was unknown who dropped the onion ring. Yet, the court found that from the circumstantial evidence, it could be reasonably inferred that it was more likely that the onion ring was on the floor through the acts of the defendant's servants rather than a customer. The court based its decision on the additional circumstantial evidence that the onion ring on which the plaintiff slipped was located by a table cleared by a bus boy, under the bus boy's practice of clearing tables food particles could drop to the floor, and testimony that after the bus boy cleared the table in question no one else ate there before the plaintiff fell.

In the present case, however, there was no direct or circumstantial evidence indicating that it was more likely that the defendants' servants dropped the item than a customer. Furthermore, the plaintiff did not present any evidence that the ice, which

ILLUSTRATION 3-4. *Continued*

PEOPLE v. SOLANO   Ill. **889**
Cite as 581 N.E.2d 889 (Ill.App. 3 Dist. 1991)

packed the produce, was directly above the water spot. Nor did she present any evidence regarding how the ice was packed or how easy it might have been to jar it loose spilling it to the floor. Moreover, there was no specific evidence that the plaintiff's business practice was unusual or created any special hazard.

The plaintiff also relies on *Perminas v. Montgomery Ward & Company* (1975), 60 Ill.2d 469, 328 N.E.2d 290, in support of her position. In *Perminas*, the plaintiff slipped on a skateboard-like object in an aisle of the defendant's store. There, one of the defendant's employees actually had knowledge that the object was creating a dangerous condition. The court imposed liability on the defendant because the defendant, after receiving notice through its employee that its product was creating a dangerous situation, failed to return its premises to a safe condition or warn its customers.

We find that the plaintiff's reliance on *Perminas* is misplaced. In the present case, unlike *Perminas*, the defendants did not have actual or constructive knowledge of the situation. Furthermore, the record in the instant case does not contain any evidence regarding the length of time the substance was on the floor from which it could be inferred that the defendants had constructive notice.

After reviewing the evidence in the aspect most favorable to the plaintiff, we conclude that the evidence so overwhelmingly favored the defendants that no contrary verdict could ever stand. Accordingly, we find that the trial court properly granted the defendants' motion for a judgment notwithstanding the verdict. Our resolution of the foregoing issue renders the parties' remaining issues moot.

The judgment of the circuit court of Will County is affirmed.

Affirmed.

McCUSKEY, J., and STOUDER, P.J., concur.

221 Ill.App.3d 272
163 Ill.Dec. 735

The PEOPLE of the State of Illinois, Plaintiff–Appellee,

v.

Juan SOLANO, Defendant–Appellant.

No. 3–91–0067.

Appellate Court of Illinois, Third District.

Nov. 8, 1991.

Sixteen-year-old defendant was convicted of reckless homicide and driving under the influence of alcohol by the 13th Judicial Circuit Court, LaSalle County, James Lanuti, J., and he appealed. The Appellate Court, McCuskey, J., held that: (1) degree of harm to passenger in defendant's car was aggravating factor that trial judge could consider in imposing sentence, and (2) trial judge could likewise consider defendant's prior underage drinking and level of alcohol in defendant's blood.

Affirmed.

1. Criminal Law ⟺1147, 1208.2
Sentencing is matter of judicial discretion and, absent abuse of discretion by trial court, sentence may not be altered on review.

2. Criminal Law ⟺986.2(1)
Defendant's history, character and rehabilitative potential, along with the seriousness of defendant's offense, need to protect society, and need for deterrence and punishment, must be equally weighed at sentencing.

3. Criminal Law ⟺986(3), 1144.17
Sentencing judge is presumed to have considered mitigating circumstances before court, and there is no requirement that judge recite and assign value to each circumstance presented.

4. Automobiles ⟺359
Trial judge sufficiently considered motorist's rehabilitative potential, young age,

Reprinted with permission of Thomson Reuters/West.

▼ How Are U.S. Supreme Court Cases Cited?

Cite U.S. Supreme Court cases according to *Bluebook* Rule 10, especially Table T.1. Once a U.S. Supreme Court case is published in an advance

sheet of the *U.S. Reports,* the *U.S. Reports* citation, and only the *U.S. Reports* citation, is the proper citation. Do not include parallel citations with the official *U.S. Reports* cite.

> **correct:**   *Erie R.R. v. Tompkins,* 304 U.S. 64 (1938)
> **incorrect:** *Erie R.R. v. Tompkins,* 304 U.S. 64, 58 S. Ct. 817, 82 L. Ed. 1188 (1938)

The citation would be the same based upon *ALWD* Rule 12.4(c).

However, if a Supreme Court opinion has been published in the *West's Supreme Court Reporter* but not yet in the *U.S. Reports,* the *Supreme Court Reporter* citation should be used. *See Bluebook* Table T.1 and *ALWD* Rule 12.4(c).

If a Supreme Court opinion has not yet been published in *U.S. Reports,* the *Supreme Court Reporter,* or *Lawyers' Edition,* then you should cite to *United States Law Week. See Bluebook* Table T.1 and *ALWD* Rule 12.4(c).

> **U.S.L.W. cite:**   *Ashcroft v. The Free Speech Coal,* 70 U.S.L.W. 4237 (Apr. 16, 2002).

Place the court designation for U.S. Supreme Court, "U.S.," in parentheses with the full date following. *See Bluebook* Rule 10.5.

Again, the same rules apply for *ALWD* citation and the citation would be as follows:

> *Ashcroft v. The Free Speech Coalition,* 70 U.S.L.W. 4237(US April 16, 2002).

b. Other Federal Case Reports

▼ Where Do You Find Decisions of Other Federal Courts?

Many published opinions of the U.S. Courts of Appeals can be found in *West's* **Federal Reporter.** In addition to printing the decisions of the U.S. Courts of Appeals, the current series contains some decisions of the Temporary Emergency Court of Appeals. See Illustration 3-5 for court coverage during specific years.

West's **Federal Supplement,** a publication started in 1932 to connect with the *Federal Reporter,* includes decisions of the U.S. District Courts, the U.S. Court of Claims from 1932 to 1960, the U.S. Court of International Trade (formerly known as the U.S. Customs Court), and the Judicial Panel on Multidistrict Litigation. See Illustration 3-5.

In 2001, West started publishing *West's Federal Appendix.* It is an offshoot of the *Federal Reporter.* It contains U.S. Court of Appeals decisions that are not designated by the court for publication. Similar to the other West reporters, both the print and online cases included in this publication contain headnotes and other West enhancements.

Not all federal appellate court or district court decisions are published. In some instances, the judges of these courts determine whether to submit their decisions to the publishers. In other cases, the publishers selectively print decisions. Unpublished opinions are available from the courts.

ILLUSTRATION 3-5. *West's Federal Reporter and Federal Supplement Coverage*

West's Federal Reporter Coverage (F., F.2d, F.3d)	
U.S. Circuit Courts	1880 to 1912
Commerce Court of the United States	1911 to 1913
U.S. District Courts	1880 to 1932
U.S. Court of Claims (1960 to 1982)	1929 to 1932
U.S. Court of Appeals (formerly United States Circuit Court of Appeals)	1891 to date
U.S. Court of Customs and Patent Appeals	1929 to 1982
U.S. Emergency Court of Appeals	1943 to 1961
Temporary Emergency Court of Appeals	1972 to date
West's Federal Supplement Coverage (F. Supp.)	
U.S. District Courts	1932 to date
U.S. Court of Claims	1932 to 1960
U.S. Court of International Trade (formerly U.S. Customs Court)	1956 to date
Judicial Panel on Multidistrict Litigation	1968 to date

PRACTICE POINTER

Some courts have special rules concerning the use of unpublished decisions. Check all applicable rules whenever you plan to use an unpublished case as an authority for a point of law.

▼ How Are *Federal Reporter* and *Federal Supplement* Decisions Cited?

Cite *Federal Reporter* and *Federal Supplement* decisions according to *Bluebook* Rules 10.1 through 10.5 and Table T.1 Note that for the *Federal Reporter,* the abbreviation is "F." If the *Federal Reporter* cited belongs to the second or third series, "2d" or "3d" should be placed next to the "F." For the *Federal Supplement,* the reporter is abbreviated "F. Supp." or "F. Supp. 2d." In parentheses you should place an abbreviation that denotes the appropriate court and then the date of the decision. Be certain to include a geographic designation for the district courts.

***Federal Reporter* case:**	*Zimmerman v. N. Am. Signal Co.,* 704 F.2d 347 (7th Cir. 1983)
***Federal Supplement* case:**	*Musser v. Mountain View Broad.,* 578 F. Supp. 229 (E.D. Tenn. 1984)

The *ALWD* citations would be similar for these cases based upon Rule 12. The only difference is "Mountain" would be abbreviated "Mt." in the second citation.

▼ Are Decisions Published in Any Other Reporters?

Several publishers of looseleaf services and specialized reporters also publish some federal decisions. Sometimes they duplicate opinions found in the West series. West also publishes some specialized reporters, such as the **Federal Rules Decisions** (F.R.D.). This reporter contains decisions in which a federal rule of civil or criminal procedure is at issue. *Federal Rules Decisions* includes not only cases but speeches, articles, and reports of judicial conferences. Another specialized reporter is *West's Education Law Reporter*. It is a compilation of selected state and federal education-related decisions from 1982 to date.

West publishes some noteworthy federal and state decisions in its *American Law Reports* (A.L.R.) series. For information about this series, see Chapter 6. Some decisions are found only in looseleaf services or specialized reporters.

4. Computerized Reporting

▼ Can You Find Decisions on the Internet and Through Fee-Based Computer Services?

Yes. Many published and unpublished federal and state decisions are online on WESTLAW, LEXIS, Loislaw, Versuslaw, and through the Internet. Many courts provide decisions on the Internet free of charge or for a nominal fee. For example, the federal CM/ECF and the Pacer service provide access to most federal court decisions. Many state courts provide these decisions as well. The Internet is much cheaper than using WESTLAW, LEXIS, Loislaw, or Versuslaw. You can rely on official cites, and it is available 24 hours a day. Often, however, material has not been proofread, and it is lacking research aids. In addition, cases may be difficult to locate.

On WESTLAW, LEXIS, Loislaw, and Versuslaw, cases are organized into databases or files and can be accessed through key word and other searches. Unlike most cases that may be found on the Internet, cases that appear within WESTLAW or LEXIS databases contain publishers' research aids.

To access cases through the Internet, go directly to a court's Web site. Review Appendix D and the Net Note below.

The United States Judiciary also provides the public with electronic access to case and docket information of the federal appellate, district, and bankruptcy case. Most court information can be obtained through the Internet and Pacer provides links to the courts through its Web site, pacer.psc.uscourts.gov.

If you know the case citation, you can easily find the case on WESTLAW, LEXIS, or Loislaw provided that it is available in the database.

On WESTLAW, begin at the search page. See Illustration 3-6. On the left side of the page, you will find a field labeled "Find by Citation." To find the case, 856 N.E2d 1048, you would enter the citation as shown. Click on the go button and the case would appear.

Now view Illustration 3-6 section B. It is the LEXIS search page. If you click on the "Get by Citation: field and enter the above citation, the same case should appear. Finally, review Illustration 3-6 section C. It is the search page for Loislaw. If you enter the same citation in the case cite field at the top of the opening page, the same case will appear. If you are within a database, you can place the citation in the case cite field on the search page displayed in section D of Illustration 3-6.

NET NOTE

U.S. Courts Generally
uscourts.gov

U.S. Supreme Court
Docket, Schedules, General Information, and Links to Decisions
supremecourtus.gov

Opinions
First Circuit Court of Appeals
www.ca1.uscourts.gov/
Second Circuit Court of Appeals
www.ca2.uscourts.gov/
Third Circuit Court of Appeals
www.ca3.uscourts.gov/
Fourth Circuit Court of Appeals
www.ca4.uscourts.gov/
Fifth Circuit Court of Appeals
www.ca5.uscourts.gov/
Sixth Circuit Court of Appeals
www.ca6.uscourts.gov/internet/index.htm
Seventh Circuit Court of Appeals
www.ca7.uscourts.gov/
Eighth Circuit Court of Appeals
www.ca8.uscourts.gov/
Ninth Circuit Court of Appeals
www.ca9.uscourts.gov/
Tenth Circuit Court of Appeals
www.ca10.uscourts.gov/
Eleventh Circuit Court of Appeals
www.ca11.uscourts.gov/
Federal Circuit Court of Appeals
www.cafc.uscourts.gov
D.C. Circuit Court of Appeals
www.cadc.uscourts.gov

ILLUSTRATION 3-6A. Finding a Case in WESTLAW

Welcome to Westlaw - Illinois

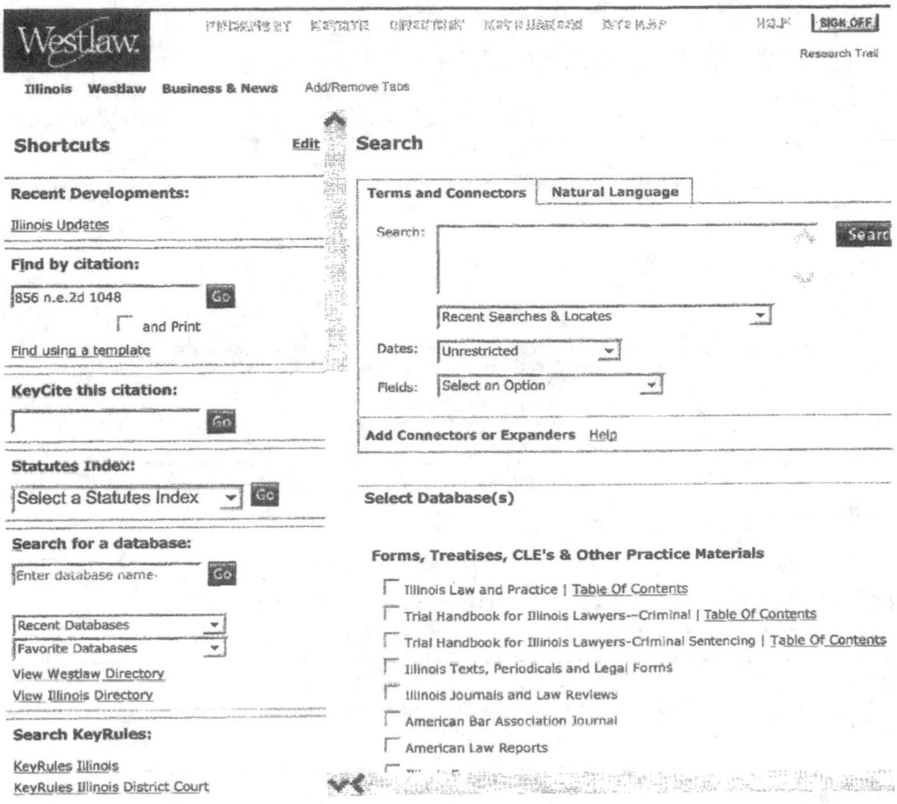

Reprinted with permission of Thomson Reuters/West.

ILLUSTRATION 3-6B.   Finding a Case in LEXIS

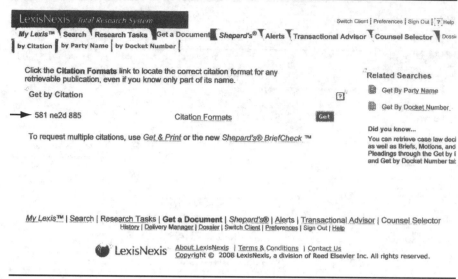

Reproduced by permission of LexisNexis. Further reproduction of any kind is strictly prohibited.

ILLUSTRATION 3-6C.   Finding a Case in Loislaw: Loislaw Welcome Page

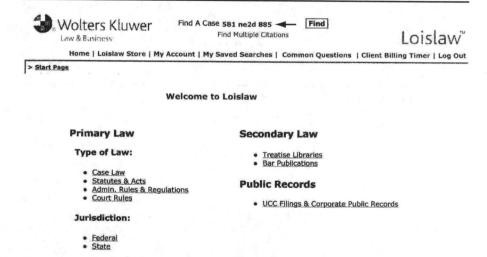

Reprinted with the permission of Loislaw, www.loislaw.com.

ILLUSTRATION 3-6D.   Loislaw Search Page

Search Illinois Appellate Court Reports

New: Thesaurus Searching - Type the thesaurus symbol (~) before search terms to include synonyms in your search results. More...

SelectCite

Search Entire Document

Date Range: All Dates

Case Cite   *for example: 29 Ill. App.2d 168   or   172 N.E.2d 803*

581 N.E.2d 885

Case Name   *for example: smith and jones   or   smith v state*

Appellate Court

Docket Number

Judge & Court Appealed

Attorneys on Appeal

Majority Opinion Justice

Majority Opinion Text

Concurring Justice

Concurring Opinion

Dissenting Justice

Dissenting Opinion

Currency

Reprinted with permission of Thomson Reuters/West.

Maps of the federal circuits with links to federal circuit courts' Web sites are provided by several universities and the government. The government site is www.uscourts.gov/links.html. It gives you access to appellate, district, bankruptcy, and other special courts. Many universities also provide federal opinions.

PRACTICE POINTER

Be careful of the source of the Internet opinion. Check court rules for citing and relying on opinions available on the Internet. Both the *Bluebook* and *ALWD* warn researchers not to cite to an Internet case if it is available in a reporter, an online database, or printed source, such as a looseleaf.

▼ How Do You Know Whether a Case Is Published or Only Available Online?

WESTLAW and LEXIS provide the print citations for all cases that are published in hard copy. If this information is absent or the publisher indicates that it is not published, it is not. Instead, WESTLAW provides its own citation for this case. LEXIS also indicates its own citation for cases it publishes only online. LEXIS also has been augmenting its database with headnotes. West recently added headnotes and other research tools to some state opinions reported only online.

Because of the high costs of computer research, it is often best to review the cases in print if they are available. However, use the computer whenever cases are not available in your library or the opinion you are seeking is an unpublished decision. Note that some courts have special rules for the use of unpublished cases.

▼ How Are Decisions Reported Only on WESTLAW or LEXIS Cited?

Bluebook Rule 18 explains how you should cite an unpublished decision found only on either WESTLAW or LEXIS. (If a decision is published in a hard-copy reporter, you should not use the WESTLAW or LEXIS citation.)

After the case name is the docket number. In the example that follows, that number is "No. 82-C-4585." Next is the year of the decision, followed by "WL" for WESTLAW. The WESTLAW number assigned to the case follows that. If a spot cite is provided, precede the screen or page number with an asterisk. Finally, in the parentheses, place the court and the full date.

WESTLAW cite: *Clark Equip. Co. v. Lift Parts Mfg. Co.*, No. 82-C-4585, 1985 WL 2917, at *1 (N.D. Ill. Oct. 1, 1985)

The *ALWD* citation based on since Rules 12, especially Rules 12.12, would be as follows the docket number and the abbreviation for company is dropped because it is the second business designation:

Clark Equip. Co. v. Lift Parts Mfg., 1985 WL 2917, at *1 (N.D. Ill. Oct. 1, 1985)

For LEXIS citations, the *Bluebook* requires that you state the name of the case, the docket number, the year of the decision, the name of the LEXIS file that contains the case, the name "LEXIS" to indicate that the case is found on LEXIS, and the document number. Last, place the court and the full date in parentheses. However, the *ALWD* citation drops the docket number.

LEXIS cite:	*Barrett Indus. Trucks v. Old Republic Ins. Co.,*
***Bluebook* citation:**	No. 87-C-9429, 1990 U.S. Dist. LEXIS 142, at *1 (N.D. Ill. Jan. 9, 1990)
***ALWD* citation:**	*Barrett Indus. Trucks v. Old Republic Ins.*, 1990 U.S. Dist. LEXIS 142, at *1 (N.D. Ill. Jan. 9, 1990)

5. State Reporters

▼ Where Can You Find State Court Decisions?

Many states continue to publish state decisions in their own reporters. In those states, the state publication is the official reporter. Some states authorize private publishers to publish the official reports. For example, West's regional reporters have been adopted as official state reporters in various states.

▼ Are There Any Unofficial Reports of State Cases?

Yes. In addition to its publication of some states' official reporters, West publishes seven **regional reporters** that contain state cases. See Illustrations 3-7 and 3-8. The regional reporters are not based on actual geographic regions. For example, Illinois is in the American Midwest region, but the regional reporter that contains Illinois decisions is the *North Eastern Reporter.*

The regional reporters contain decisions from several different states. Some states have designated the West regional reporter as the official reporter of their state decisions.

PRACTICE POINTER

In theory, the text of a case published in the state reporter should be identical to that in the regional reporter. If the two differ, then the language of the official version governs.

ILLUSTRATION 3-7.   West's Regional Reporters Coverage

Regional Reporter	States Covered
West's Atlantic Reporter (A. or A.2d)	Connecticut, Delaware, Maine, Maryland, New Hampshire, New Jersey, Pennsylvania, Rhode Island, Vermont, and the District of Columbia
West's North Eastern Reporter (N.E. or N.E.2d)	Illinois, Indiana, Massachusetts, New York, and Ohio
West's North Western Reporter (N.W. or N.W.2d)	Iowa, Michigan, Minnesota, Nebraska, North Dakota, South Dakota, and Wisconsin
West's Pacific Reporter (P. or P.2d)	Alaska, Arizona, California, Colorado, Hawaii, Idaho, Kansas, Montana, Nevada, New Mexico, Oklahoma, Oregon, Utah, Washington, and Wyoming
West's South Eastern Reporter (S.E. or S.E.2d)	Georgia, North Carolina, South Carolina, Virginia, and West Virginia
West's South Western Reporter (S.W. or S.W.2d)	Arkansas, Kentucky, Missouri, Tennessee, and Texas
West's Southern Reporter (So. or So. 2d)	Alabama, Florida, Louisiana, and Mississippi

▼ Why Would You Use the Regional Reporter Rather Than the Official State Reporter?

The regional reporter contains the publisher's headnotes designed to assist you. See Illustrations 3-4 and 3-9. These notes guide you to the publisher's topical index of cases called a digest. You also might use the regional reporter because it is published sooner than the official reporter.

▼ How Are State Cases Cited?

Cite a state case according to *Bluebook* Rule 10. Note especially *Bluebook* Rule 10.3.1 and Table T.1, which instruct on which state reporter to cite and when.

If you are citing a state case in a document submitted to a court in the same state, you should provide the citations required by local rule. That is often both the official citation, if one exists, and the regional citation. The official citation should be listed first.

When you cite a state case in a memorandum addressed to a federal court or to a court of a different state, you should include only the regional citation, according to both the *Bluebook* and the *ALWD* manuals.

ILLUSTRATION 3-8.   West National Reporter System

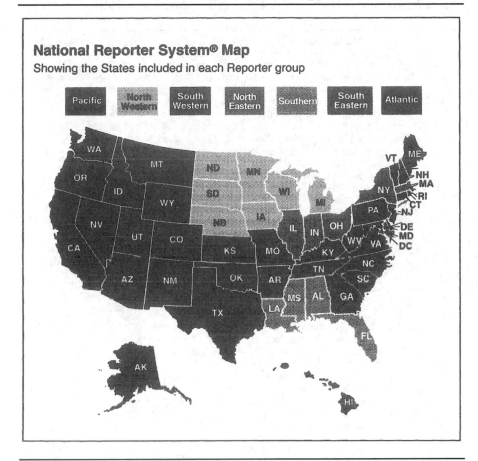

National Reporter System® Map
Showing the States included in each Reporter group

| Pacific | North Western | South Western | North Eastern | Southern | South Eastern | Atlantic |

Reprinted with permission of Thomson Reuters/West.

If you are only using the regional citation, you must remember to place the abbreviation for the deciding court in parentheses. See *Bluebook* Rule 10.4. You can remember this if you consider the reasoning behind it. Most libraries outside of the state have no need to purchase materials that are merely persuasive because of the cost involved and the space necessary to store the reports. Therefore, they are likely only to have the regional reporter—a more economic version of out-of-state cases.

The following are *Bluebook* examples of how an Illinois Appellate Court case would be cited in a brief prepared for the Illinois Supreme Court and in one prepared for the U.S. District Court for the Northern District of Illinois.

Illinois Supreme Court brief:	*Thompson v. Econ. Super Marts,* 221 Ill. App. 3d 263, 581 N.E.2d 885, 163 Ill. Dec. 731 (1991)
U.S. District Court (N.D. Ill.) brief:	*Thompson v. Econ. Super Marts,* 581 N.E.2d 885 (Ill. Ct. App. 1991)

ILLUSTRATION 3-9. West Case Report *Kellerman v. Car City Chevrolet-Nissan*, 713 N.E.2d 1285 (Ill. App. Ct. 1999)

KELLERMANN v. CAR CITY CHEVROLET–NISSAN   Ill. **1285**
Cite as 713 N.E.2d 1285 (Ill.App. 5 Dist. 1999)

the trade or commerce of selling real estate'" within the intended scope of the Act. *Zimmerman*, 156 Ill.App.3d at 168–69, 109 Ill.Dec. 541, 510 N.E.2d 409. The court concluded: "We find no support in Illinois law for the proposition that an individual selling his own home is liable to a purchaser under the Consumer Fraud Act." *Zimmerman*, 156 Ill.App.3d at 168, 109 Ill.Dec. 541, 510 N.E.2d 409. The Appellate Court, Third District, followed *Zimmerman* in *Anderson v. Stowell*, 183 Ill.App.3d 862, 863–64, 132 Ill.Dec. 289, 539 N.E.2d 852 (1989).

[5] Although the language of the Act does not express the distinction established in *Zimmerman*, the legislature has apparently accepted that interpretation of the Act's intended coverage. The legislature has amended the Act several times since *Zimmerman* was decided more than a decade ago, but it has taken no action to abrogate that case. See *Scarsdale Builders, Inc. v. Ryland Group, Inc.*, 911 F.Supp. 337, 339 (N.D.Ill.1996) (noting the continuing viability of the *Zimmerman* exception to the Act's scope). When the legislature chooses not to amend a statute to reverse a judicial construction, we must presume that it has acquiesced in the court's statement of legislative intent. *People v. Drakeford*, 139 Ill.2d 206, 215, 151 Ill.Dec. 337, 564 N.E.2d 792 (1990). By failing to so amend the Act after *Zimmerman*, the legislature has implicitly accepted the holding that an individual who casually sells his or her own single-family home is not subject to liability under the Act. See *Drakeford*, 139 Ill.2d at 215, 151 Ill.Dec. 337, 564 N.E.2d 792. Therefore, we conclude that *Zimmerman* is an accurate statement of the law.

According to plaintiffs' complaint, the Smiths are individuals whose fraudulent conduct occurred during the course of the sale of their own single-family home, which they had owned for at least 12 years. Under *Zimmerman*, the Smiths were not engaged in a "trade or commerce" under section 2 of the Act. As a result, count III of plaintiffs' amended complaint did not assert a valid claim, and the trial court properly dismissed it.

The Smiths have asked us to determine that this appeal is frivolous and to impose sanctions upon plaintiffs pursuant to Supreme Court Rule 375(b) (155 Ill.2d R. 375(b)). A frivolous appeal is one that is not reasonably well-grounded in fact and not warranted by existing law or a good-faith argument for the extension, modification, or reversal of existing law. 155 Ill.2d R. 375(b); *Gunthorp v. Golan*, 184 Ill.2d 432, 441, 235 Ill.Dec. 21, 704 N.E.2d 370 (1998).

[6, 7] Rule 375(b) sanctions are penal and should be applied only to cases that fall strictly within the terms of the rule. *Beverly v. Reinert*, 239 Ill.App.3d 91, 101, 179 Ill.Dec. 789, 606 N.E.2d 621 (1992). We find that plaintiffs made a good-faith argument based upon a reasonable interpretation of the language of the Act, and we therefore decline to find that this appeal is frivolous.

For these reasons, the order of the circuit court of Du Page County is affirmed.

Affirmed.

INGLIS and McLAREN, JJ., concur.

306 Ill.App.3d 285

239 Ill.Dec. 435

₍₂₈₅₎**Kevin E. KELLERMANN and Kathleen A. Kellermann, Plaintiffs–Appellants.**

v.

CAR CITY CHEVROLET–NISSAN, INC. Defendant–Appellee.

No. 5–98–0142.

Appellate Court of Illinois, Fifth District.

July 21, 1999.

Rehearing Denied Aug. 5, 1999.

Visitor who slipped and fell on snow at auto sales lot sued lot owner for negligence. The Circuit Court, Clinton County, John W.

ILLUSTRATION 3-9.   *Continued*

McGuire, J., dismissed claim. Appeal was taken. The Appellate Court, Welch, J., held that natural-accumulation rule precluded owner's liability for injuries.

Affirmed.

Goldenhersh, J., filed a dissenting opinion.

1. Appeal and Error ⬥893(1)

Appellate Court reviews de novo the dismissal of a complaint for failure to state a cause of action.

2. Appeal and Error ⬥895(2)

Under a de novo standard of review, Appellate Court need not give deference to the circuit court's decision.

3. Negligence ⬥210

In a negligence action, one of the essential elements is the existence of a duty to exercise reasonable care.

4. Negligence ⬥1692

Question of whether a duty is owed is a question of law.

5. Negligence ⬥1037(4), 1040(3)

As general rule, a landowner or a possessor of land has a duty to an invitee or a licensee to exercise ordinary or reasonable care in maintaining his premises in a reasonably safe condition.

6. Negligence ⬥1095

Where a business invitee is injured by slipping and falling on defendant's premises, liability may be imposed if the substance was placed there by the negligence of the proprietor or his servants or, if the substance was on the premises through acts of third persons or there is no showing how it got there, liability may be imposed if the proprietor or his servant knew of its presence or if the substance was there a sufficient length of time so that in the exercise of ordinary care its presence should have been discovered.

➤ 7. Negligence ⬥1076

"Natural-accumulation rule" provides that a landowner does not have a duty to a business invitee to remove natural accumulations of snow and ice.

> See publication Words and Phrases for other judicial constructions and definitions.

8. Negligence ⬥1134

If the snow or ice on which a business invitee slips and falls was produced or accumulated by artificial causes or if the snow or ice was produced or accumulated in an unnatural way because of landowner's own use of the area concerned, liability will be imposed on landowner.

9. Negligence ⬥1133

Pursuant to natural-accumulation rule, owner of outdoor automobile sales lot was not liable for injuries to visitor who slipped on accumulated snow and ice, regardless of allegation that slip-and-fall occurred in a display area, that owner encouraged potential customers to go there, and that owner directly benefitted from having a display area.

10. Negligence ⬥210, 213

In determining whether a duty exists, court must consider the following factors: (1) the reasonable foreseeability of the injury, (2) the likelihood of injury, (3) the magnitude of the burden of guarding against it, and (4) the consequences of placing that burden upon the defendant.

11. Negligence ⬥1133

Reason for rule protecting landowners from liability for injuries arising from naturally accumulated snow and ice is because it would be unreasonable, in a climate where those conditions are common, to force a landowner to expend the money and labor necessary to constantly keep the areas safe.

12. Constitutional Law ⬥70.1(9)

Request to overrule rule protecting landowners from liability for injuries resulting from natural accumulations of ice and snow should be addressed to the legislature, not to the Appellate Court.

‖₁₂₈₆James B. Wham, Jennifer W. Price, Wham & Wham Attorneys, Centralia, for Appellants.

ILLUSTRATION 3-9. *Continued*

KELLERMANN v. CAR CITY CHEVROLET–NISSAN   Ill. **1287**
Cite as 713 N.E.2d 1285 (Ill.App. 5 Dist. 1999)

Stephen C. Mudge, Tara English, Reed, Armstrong, Gorman, Coffey, Gilbert & Mudge, P.C., Edwardsville, for Appellee.

Justice WELCH delivered the opinion of the court:

Plaintiffs, Kevin E. Kellermann and Kathleen A. Kellermann, appeal the circuit court of Clinton County's dismissal of counts IV and V of their second amended complaint filed against defendant, Car City Chevrolet–Nissan, Inc. (Car City). Counts IV and V of the complaint allege that due to defendant's negligence, plaintiffs sustained injuries when Kevin slipped and fell on snow which had accumulated on defendant's sales lot. The circuit court applied the natural-accumulation rule, finding that defendant was not liable for injuries incurred by plaintiffs when Kevin slipped and fell on snow which had |287naturally accumulated on defendant's lot. Plaintiffs now appeal the dismissal of counts IV and V of their amended complaint, arguing that the natural-accumulation rule should not apply. For the following reasons, we affirm the decision of the circuit court.

On January 18, 1997, Kevin Kellermann and his wife, Kathleen, were walking on the auto sales lot of Car City in Centralia, Illinois. The lot is outdoors and contains numerous automobiles and trucks that are placed on display to allow an inspection by potential customers. According to the complaint, snow accumulated on the lot, making the lot "slick, icy[,] and hazardous." Plaintiffs do not allege that the accumulation of snow was unnatural or that a dangerous condition was created by defendant. The complaint does not describe the size of the auto sales lot, the size of the display area on the auto sales lot, or whether Kevin was distracted by anything on the lot.

In their complaint, plaintiffs allege that defendant was negligent for (1) failing to maintain a safe car-sales lot, (2) failing to remove the accumulation of snow and ice, (3) failing to place salt or cinders on the snow and ice, (4) failing to barricade the area containing the slick snow and ice, (5) failing to prevent customers' access to the area containing the snow and ice, (6) failing to warn the customers of the snow and ice, and (7) displaying the vehicles on the snow and ice when defendant knew that potential customers would go upon the area to examine the vehicles.

On January 17, 1998, the circuit court conducted a hearing concerning plaintiffs' second amended complaint. Although plaintiffs apparently requested that the circuit court create an exception to the natural-accumulation rule, the circuit court stated, "Perhaps such an exception should and may some day be created by the higher courts[;] however[,] at this time it appears clear to this court that under the general rule stated in *Timmons v. Turski*, 103 Ill.App.3d 36, 58 Ill.Dec. 884, 430 N.E.2d 1135 (1981), a property owner is not liable for injuries resulting from an icy condition which is a natural one." Accordingly, the circuit court dismissed plaintiffs' second amended complaint with prejudice. We shall now review this decision by the circuit court and address plaintiffs' arguments on appeal.

[1, 2] We review *de novo* the circuit court's dismissal of plaintiffs' complaint for the failure to state a cause of action. See *Kotarba v. Jamrozik*, 283 Ill.App.3d 595, 596, 218 Ill.Dec. 659, 669 N.E.2d 1185 (1996). Under a *de novo* standard of review, we need not give deference to the circuit court's decision. See *Von Meeteren v. Sell–Sold, Ltd.*, 274 Ill.App.3d 993, 996, 211 Ill.Dec. 115, 654 N.E.2d 577 (1995).

[3, 4] In the instant case, plaintiffs allege that defendant was negligent in maintaining its sales lot. In a negligence action, one of the essential elements is the existence of a duty to exercise |288reasonable care. See *Unger v. Eichleay Corp.*, 244 Ill.App.3d 445, 449, 185 Ill.Dec. 556, 614 N.E.2d 1241 (1993). The question of whether a duty is owed is a question of law. See *Roberson v. J.C. Penney Co.*, 251 Ill.App.3d 523, 526, 191 Ill.Dec. 119, 623 N.E.2d 364 (1993). If defendant does not owe a duty to plaintiffs to exercise reasonable care, then no cause of action for negligence will exist. See *Sparacino v. Andover Controls Corp.*, 227 Ill.App.3d 980, 986, 169 Ill.Dec. 944, 592 N.E.2d 431 (1992).

[5, 6] It is the general rule in Illinois that a landowner or a possessor of land has a duty to an invitee or a licensee to exercise ordi-

ILLUSTRATION 3-9. *Continued*

nary or reasonable care in maintaining his premises in a reasonably safe condition. See *Thompson v. Economy Super Marts, Inc.,* 221 Ill.App.3d 263, 265, 163 Ill.Dec. 731, 581 N.E.2d 885 (1991). Accordingly, where a business invitee is injured by slipping and falling on defendant's premises, liability may be imposed if the substance was placed there by the negligence of the proprietor or his servants or, if the substance was on the premises through acts of third persons or there is no showing how it got there, liability may be imposed if the proprietor or his servant knew of its presence or if the substance was there a sufficient length of time so that in the exercise of ordinary care its presence should have been discovered. See *Thompson,* 221 Ill.App.3d at 265, 163 Ill.Dec. 731, 581 N.E.2d 885.

[7, 8] There is also a rule in Illinois known as the natural-accumulation rule. The natural-accumulation rule provides that a landowner does not have a duty to a business invitee to remove natural accumulations of snow and ice. See *Watson v. J.C. Penney Co. Inc.,* 237 Ill.App.3d 976, 978, 178 Ill.Dec. 929, 605 N.E.2d 723 (1992). Even if the snow and ice remain on the property for an "unreasonable" length of time, it has been held that no liability will be imposed on the proprietor as long as the snow and ice is a natural accumulation. See *Foster v. George J. Cyrus & Co.,* 2 Ill.App.3d 274, 279, 276 N.E.2d 38 (1971) (where this court rejected a rule that would require property owners to remove natural accumulations of snow and ice after a reasonable length of time or be liable for injuries suffered by their tenants). However, if the snow or ice was produced or accumulated by artificial causes or if the snow or ice was produced or accumulated in an unnatural way because of defendant's own use of the area concerned, liability will be imposed. See *McCann v. Bethesda Hospital,* 80 Ill.App.3d 544, 548, 35 Ill.Dec. 879, 400 N.E.2d 16 (1979).

The natural-accumulation rule was first recognized in Illinois by our supreme court in *Graham v. City of Chicago,* 346 Ill. 638, 178 N.E. 911 (1931). In *Graham,* plaintiff sued the City of Chicago when she slipped and fell on a patch of ice that had formed on a city sidewalk. The Illinois Supreme Court adopted the natural-accumulation rule, holding that it would be "unreasonable to compel a city to expend the money and perform the labor necessary to keep its walks reasonably free from ice and snow during winter months." *Graham,* 346 Ill. at 643, 178 N.E. 911.

|₂₈₉This rule was later extended beyond cities and municipalities to allow landlords to escape liability for injuries incurred by tenants who slipped and fell on naturally accumulated snow and ice while on the landlord's premises. In *Cronin v. Brownlie,* 348 Ill. App. 448, 109 N.E.2d 352 (1952), a tenant slipped and fell on a walk that was covered with naturally accumulated snow and ice. This court applied the natural-accumulation rule and stated:

"In our northern climate where ice and snow come frequently and are accepted by all, it appears to us that the [natural-accumulation] rule adopted by the majority of the states finding no liability against the landlord is more reasonable and persuasive * * *. * * * [I]t appears to us to be unreasonable and somewhat impractical to require a landlord to remove ice and snow from sidewalks used jointly by his tenants where the ice and snow arise from natural causes." *Cronin,* 348 Ill.App. at 456, 109 N.E.2d 352.

Since *Cronin,* Illinois courts have consistently applied the natural-accumulation rule to all types of businesses. *Riccitelli v. Sternfeld,* 1 Ill.2d 133, 115 N.E.2d 288 (1953) (natural-accumulation rule applied to path through snow on sidewalk adjoining filling station); *Galivan v. Lincolnshire Inn,* 147 Ill.App.3d 228, 101 Ill.Dec. 18, 497 N.E.2d 1331 (1986) (natural-accumulation rule applied to parking lot at an Inn); *Thompson v. Tormike, Inc.,* 127 Ill.App.3d 674, 82 Ill.Dec. 919, 469 N.E.2d 453 (1984) (natural-accumulation rule applied to parking lot of restaurant); *Smalling v. LaSalle National Bank of Chicago,* 104 Ill.App.3d 894, 60 Ill.Dec. 671, 433 N.E.2d 713 (1982) (natural-accumulation rule applied to parking lot at shopping center); *Lohan v. Walgreens Co.,* 140 Ill.App.3d 171, 94 Ill.Dec. 680, 488 N.E.2d 679 (1986) (natural-accumulation rule applied to snow

ILLUSTRATION 3-9.   *Continued*

KELLERMANN v. CAR CITY CHEVROLET–NISSAN   Ill.   **1289**
Cite as 713 N.E.2d 1285 (Ill.App. 5 Dist. 1999)

and ice that naturally accumulated outside store but had been tracked inside). In addition, Illinois courts have applied the natural-accumulation rule to all areas on a defendant's property (*i.e.,* on a sidewalk, on a parking lot, inside a store, or on the step of an entranceway (see *Gehrman v. Zajac,* 34 Ill.App.3d 164, 340 N.E.2d 184 (1975) (tenant))). Plaintiffs fail to cite a single case that has created an exception to the natural-accumulation rule on the basis of where the fall occurred or on the basis of what kind of business was being conducted on the property.

[9] In the instant case, plaintiffs request that we not apply the natural-accumulation rule because Kevin slipped and fell on a display area on defendant's property. Plaintiffs contend that because defendant encourages plaintiffs to go to the display area, defendant should maintain that area as "a safe place for customers to come upon and inspect the automobiles displayed for sale." Furthermore, plaintiffs contend that because defendant directly benefits from having the display area, it should shoulder the burden of keeping that area safe or close the area in the presence of snow and ice.

[10, 11] |₂₉₀In determining whether a duty exists, the court must consider the following factors: (1) the reasonable foreseeability of the injury, (2) the likelihood of injury, (3) the magnitude of the burden of guarding against it, and (4) the consequences of placing that burden upon the defendant. See *Maschhoff v. National Super Markets, Inc.,* 230 Ill.App.3d 169, 172, 172 Ill.Dec. 304, 595 N.E.2d 665 (1992). The reason our courts have consistently found that a landowner does not have a duty to keep premises safeguarded against the potential dangers of naturally accumulated snow and ice is because it would be unreasonable in our climate to force a defendant to expend the money and labor necessary to constantly keep the areas safe. See *Graham v. City of Chicago,* 346 Ill. 638, 178 N.E. 911 (1931); *Cronin v. Brownlie,* 348 Ill.App. 448, 109 N.E.2d 352 (1952). A similar rationale is explained in American Jurisprudence Second:

"[I]n a climate where there are frequent snowstorms and sudden changes in temperature, these dangerous conditions appear with a frequency and suddenness which defy prevention, and usually, correction; consequently, the danger from ice and snow in such locations is an obvious one, and the occupier of the premises may expect that an invitee on his premises will discover and realize the danger and protect himself against it." 62A Am.Jur.2d *Premises Liability* § 699 (1990).

Based on the reasons noted above, Illinois courts have consistently determined that no duty exists for a defendant to remove, monitor, or exercise reasonable care in making reasonably safe an area which contains naturally accumulated snow and ice.

In the instant case, we shall not depart from Illinois's well-established natural-accumulation rule. We believe that defendant owes no duty to plaintiffs to exercise reasonable care toward protecting its outdoor display area from the hazards associated with the natural accumulation of snow and ice. As we have repeatedly noted, in our northern climate, snow and ice can occur frequently and unpredictably. Furthermore, snow and ice is a hazard in this part of the country, and that hazard is known to all. As our courts have consistently found it an unreasonable burden for a business to keep small areas such as parking lots, sidewalks, and entryways safe from naturally accumulated snow and ice, we believe that it would be even more burdensome to require an automobile dealership to monitor its entire display area. Is not almost every automobile that is for sale on defendant's lot on display? Although plaintiffs fail to describe the dimensions of the display area, common sense tells us that such an automotive display area is normally much larger than an average parking lot, sidewalk, or entryway. Our acceptance of plaintiffs' request would effectively require all outdoor businesses to constantly |₂₉₁monitor its entire business activity area or close its entire business activity area at the first sign of snow or ice. We believe that to place such expense and burden on a property owner is unreasonable.

[12] Therefore, we believe that the natural-accumulation rule is applicable to the in-

ILLUSTRATION 3-9. *Continued*

stant case. A result different would essentially overrule the natural-accumulation rule. As this court has previously stated, we are not the proper forum in which the natural-accumulation rule should be overruled. See *Watson v. J.C. Penney Co.*, 237 Ill.App.3d 976, 978–79, 178 Ill.Dec. 929, 605 N.E.2d 723 (1992) (this court stated that the plaintiff's request to overrule the natural-accumulation rule should be addressed "to the legislature, which formulates the public policy of this State and which could change this 'antiquated rule' if it wished."). Accordingly, the circuit court correctly applied the natural-accumulation rule and properly dismissed plaintiffs' complaint.

On another matter, on September 30, 1998, we entered an order indicating that we would take with this appeal a motion filed by defendant to strike portions of plaintiffs' reply brief. For the reasons explained in plaintiffs' response to the motion to strike, we deny said motion.

For the foregoing reasons, the dismissal by the circuit court of counts IV and V is hereby affirmed.

Affirmed.

RARICK, P.J., concurs.

Justice GOLDENHERSH, dissenting:

I respectfully dissent. The circuit court ruled, and Car City urges us to agree, that the natural-accumulation rule would apply to the instant case and that adhering to plaintiff's position would result in an abrogation of this longstanding rule. Plaintiffs, on the other hand, contend that they are not attempting to abrogate the natural-accumulation rule but, rather, that under these particular circumstances the general rule of premises liability concerning the duty of a possessor of land toward its business invitees should be the rule of law applied by the courts. I agree with plaintiffs' position.

The courts have specifically imposed a duty on the possessor of land in situations where a hazard was open and obvious but the harm to an invitee may reasonably be anticipated, such as when an invitee's attention is distracted by goods on display or for some other reason the invitee is not focused on the hazard. See *Ward v. K mart Corp.*, 136 Ill.2d 132, 143 Ill.Dec. 288, 554 N.E.2d 223 (1990). In *Ward*, our supreme court determined such duties as follows:

⌊₂₉₂"A rule more consistent with an owner's or occupier's general duty of reasonable care, however, recognizes that the 'obviousness' of a condition or the fact that the injured party may have been in some sense 'aware' of it may not always serve as adequate warning of the condition and of the consequences of encountering it. It is stated in Prosser & Keeton on Torts:

'[I]n any case where the occupier as a reasonable person should anticipate an unreasonable risk or harm to the invitee notwithstanding his knowledge, warning, or the obvious nature of the condition, something more in the way of precautions may be required. This is true, for example, where there is reason to expect that the invitee's attention will be distracted, as by goods on display, or that after a lapse of time he may forget the existence of the condition, even though he has discovered it or been warned; or where the condition is one which would not reasonably be expected, and for some reason, such as an arm full of bundles, it may be anticipated that the visitor will not be looking for it.' W. Keeton, Prosser & Keeton on Torts, § 61, at 427 (5th ed.1984).

See also 5 F. Harper, F. James & O. Gray, The Law of Torts, § 27.13, at 244–47 (2d ed.1986); J. Page, The Law of Premises Liability, § 4.6, at 80–85 (2d ed.1988).

This is the position taken by the Restatement (Second) of Torts, section 343A (1965). That section provides in pertinent part:

'(1) A possessor of land is not liable to his invitees for physical harm caused to them by any activity or condition on the land whose danger is known or obvious to them, *unless the possessor should anticipate the harm despite such knowledge or obviousness.*' (Emphasis added.)

Comment *e* of section 343A(1) states the general rule that the owner or occupier may reasonably assume that invitees will

ILLUSTRATION 3-9.   *Continued*

KELLERMANN v. CAR CITY CHEVROLET–NISSAN   Ill. **1291**
Cite as 713 N.E.2d 1285 (Ill.App. 5 Dist. 1999)

exercise reasonable care for their own safety, and that ordinarily he need not take precautions against dangers which are known to the visitor or so obvious that the visitor may be expected to discover them. Comment *f,* however, explains that reason to expect harm to visitors from known or obvious dangers may arise 'where the possessor has reason to expect that the invitee's attention may be distracted, so that he will not discover what is obvious, or will forget what he has discovered, or fail to protect himself against it. * * * In such cases the fact that the danger is known, or is obvious, is important in determining whether the invitee is to be charged with contributory negligence, or assumption of risk. It is not, however, conclusive in determining the duty of the possessor, or whether he has acted reasonably under the circumstances.' Restatement (Second) of Torts, § 343A, comment *f,* at 220 (1965).

⌐293The manifest trend of the courts in this country is away from the traditional rule absolving, *ipso facto,* owners and occupiers of land from liability for injuries resulting from known or obvious conditions, and toward the standard expressed in section 343A(1) of the Restatement (Second) of Torts (1965)." *Ward,* 136 Ill.2d at 148–50, 143 Ill.Dec. 288, 554 N.E.2d 223.

This court applied *Ward* and section 343A in *Maschhoff v. National Super Markets, Inc.,* 230 Ill.App.3d 169, 172 Ill.Dec. 304, 595 N.E.2d 665 (1992) (delivery man slipped and fell on liquid buildup in store). After citing *Ward* and quoting extensively from comment *f* of 343A, this court concluded that the injury was reasonably foreseeable, that plaintiff could have been distracted from the obvious conditions, and that, therefore, the questions of the defendant's breach of duty and the plaintiff's comparative negligence were properly submitted to the jury.

As directed by our supreme court in *Ward,* we must consider whether in the instant case the imposition of a duty meets with the following factors:

"We recognize that the Restatement speaks to the more general question of liability, and not specifically to the exis-

tence of a duty. But we think the principles expressed there are consistent with the general duty of reasonable care owed to invitees and licensees, and they are relevant to the resolution of whether an injury was reasonably foreseeable. We emphasize, however, that since the existence of a duty turns in large part on public policy considerations, the magnitude of the burden of guarding against the injury, and the consequences of placing that burden upon the defendant, as well as the likelihood of injury and the possible serious nature of such an injury[,] must also be taken into account." *Ward,* 136 Ill.2d at 151, 143 Ill.Dec. 288, 554 N.E.2d 223.

The standards of premises-liability duty, as delineated in *Ward,* appropriately apply in the instant case. We have a situation in which the possessor of land is aware of the hazards posed by ice and snow and with such knowledge seeks to bring the invitee into the business-activity part of its premises with the intent of, and taking actions toward, diverting the invitee's attention and changing the invitee's focus to the goods and services offered by the possessor of land. Under those circumstances, it is reasonably foreseeable by the possessor of land that an injury such as this might occur, and under these circumstances, it is both reasonable and appropriate that the burden should fall on the possessor of land. It is not an onerous burden on that possessor to alleviate the hazardous conditions so that the attention and focus of the invitee might safely be focused on the possessor's business activities. In comparison, the circumstances of the instant case pose a substantial likelihood of injury. I also note that the activities of diverting the invitee's attention and focus are for the benefit of the possessor294 of land, and accordingly, it is not unreasonable to place this duty on that party.

Choosing to apply the duties delineated in *Ward* and the *Restatement,* rather than the natural-accumulation rule, does not constitute an abrogation of the natural-accumulation rule. That doctrine is quite alive and well, as noted in the cases cited by the majority. In those instances involving injuries on business premises, the rule has been readily applied to those areas adjacent to and

ILLUSTRATION 3-9. *Continued*

1292 Ill. **713 NORTH EASTERN REPORTER, 2d SERIES**

utilized in the approaching of the area of commercial activity (sidewalks, parking lots), whereas the instant case involves the actual area of business activity. We may infer from these cases that the possessor of the business property has no reason to, and is not likely to, make any effort to divert the attention of a prospective customer who is approaching his commercial-activity area. In the instant case, however, the prospective customer who has entered the business-activity area is in the midst of an obvious hazard known to the property owner, and the property owner is actively diverting the customer's attention and focus to his commercial activities. We should be hard put to conclude that under these circumstances the type of injury as occurred in this case would not be reasonably foreseeable. Concurrently, we should rea-

sonably conclude that removing the hazard the invitee faces when engaging in the possessor's business activity is a minor burden on that possessor of land, given the hazard's foreseeability and the commercial benefits from successful engagement with the invitee. The difference between the approaches to business establishment and the commercial-activity area of that business are clear, qualitative, and crucial. The *Ward*/Restatement rule appropriately applies.

Reprinted with permission of Thomson Reuters/West.

The *ALWD Citation Manual* rule, however, notes that only one source should be cited when citing a case in an office memo. The case source should be cited in the following order based on availability: A West reporter (regional reporters for state cases); another print reporter in which the case appears; an online source; a looseleaf service; or any other sources in which the case appears. Parallel citations should not be used unless required by local rules or if it would be particularly helpful to the reader.

An example of *ALWD* citation for a Pennsylvania state court case is as follows:

Socha v. Workers' Compen. Appeal Bd., 725 A.2d 1276 (Pa. Cmmw. 1999). Note: The *Bluebook* abbreviation for compensation would be Comp. Because they differ, always check abbreviations before submitting citations.

However, the cite for the *Thompson* case under *ALWD* rules would be as follows:

Thompson v. Econ. Super Marts, 221 Ill. App. 3d 263, 581 N.E.2d 885 (1991).

The Illinois Appellate 3d citation must be included because local Illinois rules require parties to cite to the official reporter.

Some states now have adopted so-called public domain or neutral citations as their official cites. These cites allow readers to find their case in a computerized system that does not rely on commercial publishers. Cites to commercial reporters such as West's may be used to augment public domain citations.

Bluebook Rule 10.3.3 requires that you cite public domain citations as follows: case name, followed by the year of the decision, the deciding court, the sequential number of the decision, and the parallel cite if available. To cite to a specific portion of the decision, you may add a reference to the paragraph.

public domain citation: State v. Kienast, 1996 S.D. 111 ¶ 2, 553 N.W.2d 254

Cite neutral citations according to 12.16 of the *ALWD* manual. First, use the format specified by the court or include the case name, the year of the decision, the court abbreviation, the opinion number, and then a citation to a reporter or online source. The above case would be cited as follows:

State v. Kienast, 1996 SD 111, 553 NW2d 254.

CHAPTER SUMMARY

In this chapter, you learned about case law and about the reporters that contain supreme court, federal, and state decisions. Case law consists of court-adopted decisions. These decisions are primary authorities. These authorities generally are organized chronologically. Several publishers have established case reporters that are books, usually in series format, which contain court decisions.

Decisions are first published in slip opinions, generally a typed set of pages. Next, advance sheets are published. These decisions usually look similar to the final case reporter version of a decision.

Next, bound reporters that carry the case decision reports are published. For the Supreme Court decisions, three reporters are available. The *United States Reports* is published by the government. The *United States Supreme Court Reports, Lawyers' Edition* is published by LEXIS. The *Supreme Court Reporter* is published by West. The commercial publishers' reports include publishers' notes and annotations, such as headnotes designed to assist you in your research.

Many other federal court decisions are published in *West's Federal Supplement, West's Federal Reporter,* and *West's Federal Appendix*. State court decisions often are found in a state-published case reporter and in West's regional reporters. Some looseleaf publishers also report decisions, and West reports some opinions in specialized reporters. These commercial reporters have headnotes that assist you in your research. These headnotes contain case abstracts concerning a point of law raised in a case and a topic and number that refer you to a topical system for finding additional similar cases discussed in the next chapter.

Today, slip and other opinions often are available free of charge or for a nominal fee on the Internet from official court sites.

KEY TERMS

advance sheets

case law

digests

Federal Reporter

Federal Rules Decision

Federal Supplement

headnotes

key numbers

Lawyers' Edition

National Reporter System

regional reporter

reporters

reporting systems

slip opinion

Supreme Court Reporter

syllabus

U.S. Law Week

U.S. Reports

West Codenotes

EXERCISES

REPORTER EXERCISES

1. List the three reporters that contain the decision in Illustration 3-4.
2. What reporter or reporters would you look in to find a published Illinois Supreme Court decision?
3. What reporter or reporters would you look in to find a published U.S. Court of Appeals decision decided in 1991?
4. What reporter or reporters would you look in to find a U.S. District Court decision from 1930?
5. What is contained in the *Federal Rules Decisions*?
6. What sources would you look in to find a U.S. Supreme Court decision one to two weeks after the case was decided by the Court? (List at least four sources.)
7. What is the advantage of using the *Lawyers' Edition* to review a Supreme Court case?
8. What is the advantage of using a West's regional reporter in researching rather than the *Illinois Reports*?
9. When you are beginning a research assignment, what is the first thing that you should determine? How is this determined?
10. Are headnotes cited? Why, or why not?

TREASURE HUNT

11. Find 507 F. Supp. 1091. What is the key number and topic for the second headnote?
12. Find 825 F.2d 257. What court decided this case?

13. Find 819 F.2d 630. What is the docket number for this case? List the names of the attorneys who argued this case.
14. Find 373 N.E.2d 1371. List the presiding judge and the date the case was decided.
15. Find 432 N.E.2d 1123. List the official citation for this case, the name of the plaintiff, and the name of the defendant.
16. Find 222 N.E.2d 561. List the name of the judge who wrote the opinion.
17. Using the Internet, find the *Kellerman v. Car City Chevrolet—Nissan* case illustrated in Illustration 3-8. Where did you find it?
18. Find the Government Print Office's U.S. Supreme Court decisions on the Internet. What is the Web site address?
19. Go to the U.S. Courts Web site. What links to other courts are available? Please provide the Web sites for at least three links.
20. Go to the U.S. 5th Circuit Court of Appeals Web site. Find the court's local rules. What is the Web address for these rules?
21. Find 2002 WL1592517 (CA 7. Ill.).
    a. What does this say about publication in the Federal Reporter?
    b. Who is the trial judge?
    c. What is the date the case was argued?
    d. What is the date it was decided?

4

DIGESTS

CHAPTER OVERVIEW

This chapter focuses on the use of **digests,** topically organized indexes. You will be taught how to use the West's digests, the largest and most diverse digest system. The skills you learn will help you to use other publishers' digests. Topical searching, as well as research, using headnotes and key numbers will be explored.

A. CONTENT OF DIGESTS AND ORGANIZATION

▼ What Are Digests, and What Do They Contain?

Publishers have developed systems called digests that index the law by topics or legal issues. For example, West's digests contain more than 400 topics. To see some of those topics, review Illustration 4-1.

ILLUSTRATION 4-1. West's Digest Topics

ILLUSTRATION 4-1. *Continued*

223	Intoxicating Liquors	275	New Trial	323	Receivers	367	Subscriptions
224	Joint Adventures	276	Notaries	324	Receiving Stolen Goods	368	Suicide
225	Joint-Stock Companies and Business Trusts	277	Notice	325	Recognizances	369	Sunday
		278	Novation	326	Records	370	Supersedeas
226	Joint Tenancy	279	Nuisance	327	Reference	371	Taxation
227	Judges	280	Oath	328	Reformation of Instruments	372	Telecommunications
228	Judgment	281	Obscenity			373	Tenancy in Common
229	Judicial Sales	282	Obstructing Justice	330	Registers of Deeds	374	Tender
230	Jury	283	Officers and Public Employees	331	Release	375	Territories
231	Justices of the Peace			332	Religious Societies	376	Theaters and Shows
232	Kidnapping	284	Pardon and Parole	333	Remainders	378	Time
232a	Labor Relations	285	Parent and Child	334	Removal of Cases	379	Torts
233	Landlord and Tenant	286	Parliamentary Law	335	Replevin	380	Towage
234	Larceny	287	Parties	336	Reports	381	Towns
235	Levees and Flood Control	288	Partition	337	Rescue	382	Trade Regulation
236	Lewdness	289	Partnership	338	Reversions	384	Treason
237	Libel and Slander	290	Party Walls	339	Review	385	Treaties
238	Licenses	291	Patents	340	Rewards	386	Trespass
239	Liens	292	Payment	341	Riot	387	Trespass to Try Title
240	Life Estates	294	Paupers	342	Robbery	388	Trial
241	Limitation of Actions	295	Penalties	343	Sales	389	Trover and Conversion
242	Lis Pendens	296	Pensions	344	Salvage	390	Trusts
245	Logs and Logging	297	Perjury	345	Schools	391	Turnpikes and Toll Roads
246	Lost Instruments	298	Perpetuities	346	Scire Facias	392	Undertakings
247	Lotteries	300	Pilots	347	Seals	393	United States
248	Malicious Mischief	302	Pleading	348	Seamen	394	United States Magistrates
249	Malicious Prosecution	303	Pledges	349	Searches and Seizures	395	United States Marshals
250	Mandamus	305	Possessory Warrant	349a	Secured Transactions	396	Unlawful Assembly
251	Manufactures	306	Postal Service	349b	Securities Regulation	396a	Urban Railroads
252	Maritime Liens	307	Powers	350	Seduction	398	Usury
253	Marriage	307a	Pretrial Procedure	350h	Sentencing and Punishment	399	Vagrancy
255	Master and Servant	308	Principal and Agent			400	Vendor and Purchaser
256	Mayhem	309	Principal and Surety	351	Sequestration	401	Venue
257	Mechanics' Liens	310	Prisons	352	Set-Off and Counterclaim	402	War and National Emergency
257a	Mental Health	311	Private Roads	353	Sheriffs and Constables		
258a	Military Justice	313	Process	354	Shipping	403	Warehousemen
259	Militia	313a	Products Liability	355	Signatures	404	Waste
260	Mines and Minerals	315	Prohibition	356	Slaves	405	Waters and Water Courses
265	Monopolies	316	Property	356a	Social Security and Public Welfare		
266	Mortgages	316a	Prostitution			406	Weapons
267	Motions	317	Public Contracts	357	Sodomy	407	Weights and Measures
268	Municipal Corporations	317a	Public Lands	358	Specific Performance	408	Wharves
269	Names	318	Public Utilities	359	Spendthrifts	409	Wills
270	Navigable Waters	319	Quieting Title	360	States	410	Witnesses
271	Ne Exeat	319h	Quo Warranto	361	Statutes	411	Woods and Forests
272	Negligence		Racketeer Influenced and Corrupt Organizations	362	Steam	413	Workers' Compensation
273	Neutrality Laws	320	Railroads	363	Stipulations	414	Zoning and Planning
274	Newspapers	321	Rape	365	Submission of Controversy	450	Merit Systems Protection
		322	Real Actions	366	Subrogation		

1. Headnotes and Key Numbers

These topics are continually being revised. In the digest, you find **headnotes** or case abstracts in which the publishers assign a topic and number to a point of law. The headnotes assist you in finding other cases that are relevant to the issues presented in your case. Cases are read by editors, and each issue is put into a topic category. The specific legal issue is then assigned a number to accompany the topic. This enables you to match cases discussing the same issues of law. Digests also contain references to the publisher's other resources and law review articles.

The most comprehensive digest system is published by West. The **West key number system** is divided into digest topics, such as bankruptcy, civil rights, criminal law, negligence, double jeopardy, and damages. Illustration 4-1 shows the list of West digest topics. LexisNexis publishes a digest for U.S. Supreme Court cases and a series covering state cases. Other publishers also prepare state digests. West's state digests contain references to decisions of federal courts sitting within that state that pertain to the state's legal issues. West's regional digests do not contain federal cases. In addition to these digests, West and other publishers print topical digests, such as the *Education Law Digest*.

2. Types of Digests

The *West American Digest System* is a comprehensive set of all of West's reported federal and state cases. See Illustration 4-2. This system includes the *Century Digest,* which contains cases decided between 1658 and 1897. It does not contain key numbers. However, a West index allows you to cross-reference cases in the first and second *Decennial Digest* to convert them to the equivalent key number.

ILLUSTRATION 4-2.   Assorted Digests

American Digest System
West's General Digests
Century Digest
Decennial Digests
General Digests

Digests that Abstract All U.S. Supreme Court Cases
U.S. Supreme Court Digest (West)
U.S. Supreme Court Digest, Lawyer's Edition

Other Federal Court Digests
Federal Digest
Modern Federal Practice Digest
West's Federal Practice Digest 2d
West's Federal Practice Digest 3d
West's Federal Practice Digest 4th: contains all of the federal court cases reported by West, including U.S. Supreme Court cases

State Cases
West Regional Digests: indexes cases reported in the reporter bearing the same name
   North Western Digest
   South Eastern Digest
   Pacific Digest
   Atlantic Digest
West does not publish a digest for the *North Eastern Reporter,* the *Southern Reporter,* or the *South Western Reporter*
Individual State Digests: West publishes digests for most of the 50 states and the District of Columbia; however, it publishes a combined digest for South Dakota and North Dakota and a combined digest for West Virginia and Virginia. It does not publish separate digests for Utah, Delaware, and Nevada. Digest summaries for those cases appear in their respective regional digest products.

Specialized Digests
Federal Sentencing Guidelines Digest
West's Bankruptcy Law Digest
West's Texas Family Law Digest

ILLUSTRATION 4-2. *Continued*

West's Military Justice Digest
West's U.S. Federal Claims Digest
West's Veterans Appeals Digest
West's Education Law Digest

The *Decennial Digests* is a multiple-volume digest that includes state and federal court cases from all U.S. jurisdictions between 1997 to date. Presented in ten-year increments, it contains points of law which are summarized in headnotes and classified using the West Key Number System. Older *Decennial Digests* contain all of the abstracts from West's regional, state, and federal digests. *General Digests* also are included in this system. These also include all West cases and are presented in one-year increments.

United States Supreme Court opinions are indexed in a digest called the *United States Supreme Court Digest*, in *West's Supreme Court Digest*, and in *West's Federal Practice Digest* series.

3. Organization of Digests

▼ How Are Digest Systems Organized?

Most digest systems are organized by topic. Case abstracts of points of law are prepared by the publisher, and these points of law are then assigned topics. Within each topic, points of law are assigned numbers. In the West system, this match of a topic and a number is called a "key number." Key numbers are the cornerstones of the West system. Key numbers correspond to specific points of law presented in a case. See Illustrations 3-4 and 3-9. The case abstracts are not authoritative and should never be cited. These case abstracts contain a publisher's summary of a point of law, the case name, and a citation. See Illustration 4-3.

Illustration 4-3 is a page from the *West's Illinois Digest.* The *Thompson* case is noted in the second column by the circled "3." Note that the case abstract contained on this digest page is identical to the first headnote contained in Illustration 3-4. However, the key number is different. At the top of Illustration 4-3 is the word *Negligence*. This indicates the topic. Next to it is a key and the number 1076. This is the key number. The deciding court and the year of the decision are noted at the beginning of the abstract.

The West key number system is altered frequently. Recently, the negligence key numbers were changed substantially. Go to Illustration 3-4, the *Thompson v. Economy Super Marts* case. On page 886 of the case, the first headnote contains a notation of 32.8. That is the key number assigned to that headnote topic. When the headnote topics were revised, that number changed. To find the current headnote number that corresponds to a topic, you would review a table such as the one shown in Illustration 4-4. To determine the new key number, you need to review the "Key Number Translation Table" found in the digest.

ILLUSTRATION 4-3. Page from *West's Illinois Digest*

(1)⟷1076 NEGLIGENCE (2)   38 Ill D 2d—420

For later cases, see same Topic and Key Number in Pocket Part

to such licensee is to not wilfully or wantonly injure him.

> Wesbrock v. Colby, Inc., 43 N.E.2d 405, 315 Ill.App. 494.

Where plaintiff, after making some purchases in defendant's store, was injured when she fell down basement steps as she attempted to make use of telephone located in stairway of store which was not intended for public use, and there was no evidence that clerk who showed plaintiff where telephone was had authority to give plaintiff permission to use it, plaintiff at time she received her injuries was a "licensee", and not an "invitee", and hence could not recover for her injuries, in absence of any willful or wanton misconduct by defendant.

> Wesbrock v. Colby, Inc., 43 N.E.2d 405, 315 Ill.App. 494.

Ill.App. 2 Dist. 1942. Although one operating a business to which the public is invited is not an "insurer" of safety of patrons, he has the duty to use reasonable care to keep premises in a reasonably safe condition so that patrons will not be injured by reason of any unsafe condition of the premises, and a failure to do so is actionable negligence in case an injury results therefrom.

> Crump v. Montgomery Ward & Co., 39 N.E.2d 411, 313 Ill.App. 151.

An owner of store in propping open the doors at entrance of store owed the same duty to its invitees to use reasonable care for their safety as it did to provide safe equipment.

> Crump v. Montgomery Ward & Co., 39 N.E.2d 411, 313 Ill.App. 151.

Ill.App. 2 Dist. 1939. The law raises on the part of a proprietor of a store an implied invitation to the public to come into his building or upon his premises should they seek to do business with him, and he is under a legal obligation to exercise ordinary and reasonable care to make his premises safe for the protection of his customers.

> Todd v. S. S. Kresge Co., 24 N.E.2d 899, 303 Ill.App. 89.

A proprietor of a store is not an insurer against all accidents and injuries to customers coming to his place of business.

> Todd v. S. S. Kresge Co., 24 N.E.2d 899, 303 Ill.App. 89.

Ill.App. 3 Dist. 1993. Person is "business invitee" on land of another if that person enters land by express or implied invitation, if entry is connected with owner's business or with activity conducted by owner on land, and if owner receives benefit.

> Leonardi v. Bradley University, 192 Ill.Dec. 471, 625 N.E.2d 431, 253 Ill.App.3d 685, appeal denied 198 Ill.Dec. 544, 633 N.E.2d 6, 155 Ill.2d 565.

Ill.App. 3 Dist. 1993. Store owner did not assume duty to remove all tracked-in water from its store when it placed two mats near its outside entrance; owner's duty extended only to maintaining with reasonable care the mats it installed.

> Roberson v. J.C. Penney Co., 191 Ill.Dec. 119, 623 N.E.2d 364, 251 Ill.App.3d 523.

Ill.App. 3 Dist. 1991. Defendant owes business invitee on defendant's premises duty to exercise ordinary care in maintaining premises in reasonably safe condition.

> Thompson v. Economy Super Marts, Inc., (3) 163 Ill.Dec. 731, 581 N.E.2d 885, 221 Ill.App.3d 263.

Ill.App. 3 Dist. 1987. A "business invitee" is one who enters upon the premises of another in response to an express or implied invitation for the purpose of transacting business in which the parties are mutually interested.

> Simmons v. Aldi-Brenner Co., 113 Ill.Dec. 594, 515 N.E.2d 403, 162 Ill.App.3d 238, appeal denied 119 Ill.Dec. 398, 522 N.E.2d 1257, 119 Ill.2d 575.

The owner or occupier of land owes to persons present on the premises as business invit[...] [...]nd reas[...] [...]are reas[...] [...]es.

> [...]ec. [...]38, [...]22

| 1 Key number |
| 2 Topic |
| 3 *Thompson* case |

Liability of a storekeeper to his customers must be founded on fault.

> Simmons v. Aldi-Brenner Co., 113 Ill.Dec. 594, 515 N.E.2d 403, 162 Ill.App.3d 238, appeal denied 119 Ill.Dec. 398, 522 N.E.2d 1257, 119 Ill.2d 575.

Ill.App. 3 Dist. 1985. Storekeeper is not insurer of customer's safety.

> Nicholson v. St. Anne Lanes, Inc., 91 Ill. Dec. 9, 483 N.E.2d 291, 136 Ill.App.3d 664, appeal denied.

Ill.App. 3 Dist. 1982. Duty of owner of commercial enterprise to provide reasonably safe means of ingress and egress from place of business for use of his patrons is not abrogated by presence of accumulation of ice or snow which is natural.

> Kittle v. Liss, 64 Ill.Dec. 307, 439 N.E.2d 972, 108 Ill.App.3d 922.

Ill.App. 3 Dist. 1980. Duty owed to business invitee is to exercise ordinary care in maintaining premises in a reasonably safe condition.

> Hayes v. Bailey, 36 Ill.Dec. 124, 400 N.E.2d 544, 80 Ill.App.3d 1027.

For legislative history of cited statutes

ILLUSTRATION 4-4.   Key Number Translation Table from
West's Illinois Digest 2d

NEGLIGENCE   38 Ill D 2d—52

TABLE 1

KEY NUMBER TRANSLATION TABLE

FORMER KEY NUMBER TO PRESENT KEY NUMBER

The topic NEGLIGENCE in the American Digest System has been extensively revised to reflect current developments in the law.

This table indicates the location, in the revised topic, of cases formerly classified to the earlier Key Numbers.

In many instances there is no one-to-one relation between the Key Numbers, new and old. This table recognizes only significant correspondence. When there is more than one new Key Number to which headnotes formerly under a particular number have been reclassified, the new Key Numbers are listed in numerical order, with the most significant correspondence indicated in bold type. For the present classification of a particular case, see the Table of Cases.

The absence of a Key Number indicates that there is no useful parallel.

Former Key Number	Present Key Number	Former Key Number	Present Key Number
1	200, 202	32(2.7)	1204(1, 3, 6), 1205(7, 9)
2	210, 220	32(2.8)	1076–1078
3	230, 231	32(2.9)	1037(8)
4	232, 233	32(2.10)	1037(7), 1204(1)
5	236, 322	32(2.11)	1204(8)
6	222, 238, 259	32(2.12)	1040(2–4)
7	216, 237, 257	32(2.13)	1040(4), 1079
8	281–285	32(2.14)	1037(7)
9	200, 210, 233	32(2.15)	1037(2), 1076
10	213	32(2.16)	1037(7), 1076, 1102
11	274, 275	32(2.17)	1060, 1076
12	291–295	32(2.18)	570, 1060, 1315
13	273	32(3)	1037(1), 1052, 1076
14	481, 483	32(4)	1016, 1066, 1076
15	484	33(1)	1045(3, 4)
16	305	33(2)	1045(2)
17	236, 342; R R 277.5	33(3)	1067
18	222, 259, 341, 343	34	1071, 1151
19	303(1–3), 306	35	1071, 1152
20	253, 307	36	125–1127
21	341–344	37	191–1197
22	305–307	38	1010, 1140
22.5	Autos 181(1, 2, 4); Mun Corp 705(3)	39	1172–1178
23(1)	1172–1176	41	1130
23(2)	R R 277.5	42	1140, 1204(2), 1205(7)
24	212, 251, 253, 302	43	1119, 1125, 1151, 1204(2)
25	221, 332	44	1076, 1104(6, 8)
26	253, 351–355	45	1117
27	Prod Liab 41, 47, 49	46	1010, 1013
28	1032, 1033	47	1037(4), 1040(3)
29	1011, 1204(1)	48	1088, 1089, 1104(6)
30	1104(8)	50	1024, 1037(4), 1076, 1078, 1162
31	1025, 1204(5–7)	51	1140, 1205(7)
32(1)	1037(4), 1040(3), 1076	52	1020, 1037(4), 1040(3), 1076
32(2)	1040(2), 1050	54	1011, 1263
32(2.1)	1050	55	1205(7–9)
32(2.2)	1040(2, 3)	56(1)	370, 375
32(2.3)	1037(2, 4), 1076	56(1.1)	371, 373
32(2.4)	1037(6), 1050	56(1.2)	375, 379
32(2.5)	1076	56(1.3)	372
32(2.6)	1040(2)		

1 Old key number
2 New key number

Reprinted with permission of Thomson Reuters/West.

See Illustration 4-4. Go to Key Number 32.(2.8) in the table. It indicates that the new number is 1076-1078.

The theory of the key number system is that if you have a good case on point and you want to find similar cases on point, you look under the topic and the key number assigned to the point in your case. The case abstracts listed under that topic and key number should be similar to your case. To find cases similar to the point of law noted in the first headnote of the *Thompson* case, you would review Negligence key number 1076 in the more current digests. One of the cases that is found under that key number is *Kellermann v. Car City Chevrolet–Nissan,* 306 Ill. App.3d 285, 713 N.E.2d 1285 (1999) shown in Illustration 3-9. See headnote 7 of that case. It is Negligence 1076. Review the language of the case that corresponds to that headnote and compare it with case language that corresponds with headnote 1 of the *Thompson* case. To find the case language that corresponds to the headnote, find the bracketed numbers in the case text. The two cases address similar issues. However, note that the headnotes are not identical. They summarize what the court in each case said about this topic.

A case generally has multiple key numbers because a case abstract and a corresponding topic and key number are prepared for each point of law raised in a case. See Illustration 3-9.

PRACTICE POINTER

The same West digest system is used for all states. Therefore, you can find a good case in one state and look up the relevant key number in another state's digest. That will lead you to cases that are similarly decided in the second state.

B. STEP-BY-STEP GUIDE TO THE DIGEST SYSTEM

▼ How Do You Use a Digest System?

You might use one of several methods for finding cases within a digest: the descriptive word index method, the topic outline method, and the one good case method.

1. Descriptive Word Index Method

▼ What Is the Descriptive Word Index Method?

One method you might use is the **descriptive word index method.** This index is included in each West digest. Other digest series have similar

indexes. Before you review the digest, brainstorm for words that might be indexed. You must separate the facts into various categories. These categories will assist you in brainstorming.

To categorize the materials, first review the facts. Select only the important or relevant facts. How do you determine which facts are relevant? Facts are relevant if they might have a bearing on the outcome of a case. These are facts that the courts will look at to make their determinations of the law.

Let's suppose that you are asked to research the claims a client might have against a supermarket for a slip and fall accident in a grocery store. In this case, your client slipped on a banana peel in the produce section of the supermarket while she was speaking on a cellular telephone.

First, determine what facts are legally relevant. How do you as a researcher make this determination? You must first determine the legal issues presented. Negligence is one theory. The question posed is, Was the store owner negligent? The second question to consider is, Was the woman also negligent? Negligence is a broad area of the law.

Next, you should brainstorm to develop a list of possible words to review in the digest. Brainstorming is important because a publisher might index a subject differently than you would index it. For example, slip and fall accidents at hotels or motels are not indexed under hotel or motel in the West digest. Instead, they are found under the topic Innkeepers.

Consider the people, the places, and the things involved in your case, as well as the basis for any action and any defenses. These are manageable categories. Consider also the relationships between people. In this case, we have a grocer and a patron. Next, think about the location of the incident. Where did the accident occur? It occurred in the produce section of a grocery store. Finally, determine what happened. A woman slipped on a banana peel while talking on a cellular telephone.

Next, develop a relationship between the facts to one another. For example, does the grocer owe a duty to his patron to prevent the patron from slipping and falling inside his store? Does the patron owe a duty to herself to ensure that she does not fall?

Once you have determined these relationships, you should find synonyms for the words you plan to research. Use a thesaurus or an encyclopedia to find synonyms and other additional search words. For example, *grocer* might be indexed. But other words might be used in its place. Try *store owner, market owner,* or *shopping center owner.* For *patron,* an index might contain the words *customer, shopper,* or *invitee,* a legal term of art. Cases may have dealt with a shop owner's liability for a slip and fall accident, but banana peels may not have been involved. Research slip and fall accidents that occurred on surfaces covered with food or other slippery items such as snow or water as well as those that occurred on dry surfaces.

Now frame the legal issues: Did the owner clean the floor? If so, did he do it in a timely fashion? Did the owner ensure his patrons' safety? Was the woman negligent because she walked while talking on the telephone?

ILLUSTRATION 4-5. Results of Brainstorming Session

People or Parties	Place	Things
Customer	Grocery store	Banana peel
Patron	Shopping center	
Buyer	Supermarket	
Purchaser	Shop	
Shopper	Store	
Grocer		
Supermarket		
Grocery store		
Store		
Shop		
Shopping center		

Activity	Action	Defense
Slip	Negligence	Contributory negligence
Fall	Negligence	Comparative negligence

The results of your brainstorming session for the grocery slip and fall might be recorded as indicated in Illustration 4-5.

Once you have brainstormed, review the descriptive word index. Look under the most obvious topics first, such as negligence, slip and fall, customer, or grocery store. Once you have reviewed these words, the digest will lead you to topics and key numbers. See Illustration 4-6.

Illustration 4-6 is a sample page from *West's Illinois Digest 2d* Descriptive Word Index. Under the word *premises liability* and *stores and business proprietors,* you see a variety of subtopics such as Standard of Care and Insurer of Safety. Many of these subtopics refer you to the Negligence topic with the designation "Neglig." The number next to the topic designation is the key number. Under the subtopics Standard of Care and Insurer of Safety, the notation is "Neglig 1076." This topic and key number should have cases that are relevant. After reviewing this page, you would retrieve the volume with the Negligence topic (each volume's binding gives an alphabetical range of topics) and follow the numbers to the key numbers suggested in the descriptive word index. In this case, you would review Negligence key number 1076. Reading the case abstracts (such as those found in Illustration 4-3), you could determine the cases relevant to your own. Each digest case abstract contains a notation of the deciding court, a publisher's statement concerning the issue of law, and a citation. Under key number 1076, you would find a case abstract that refers to headnote 1 of the *Thompson v. Economy Super Marts* case.

ILLUSTRATION 4-6.   Sample Page from *West's Illinois Digest 2d* Descriptive Word Index

66A Ill D 2d–45   **PREMISES**

References are to Digest Topics and Key Numbers

PREMISES LIABILITY—Cont'd
STATUS of entrant—Cont'd

Exceeding invitation or license, **Neglig** ⚎ 1052
Invitee. See subheading INVITEE, under this heading.
Licensee. See subheading LICENSEE, under this heading.
Rejection of status distinctions, **Neglig** ⚎ 1053
Relative degrees of care, **Neglig** ⚎ 1051
Standard of care dependent on status, **Neglig** ⚎ 1036
Trespasser. See subheading TRESPASSERS, under this heading.

STATUTES, **Neglig** ⚎ 1002

STATUTORY requirements,
Duty of care, **Neglig** ⚎ 1025
Safe workplace laws. See subheading SAFE workplace laws, under this heading.
Standard of care, **Neglig** ⚎ 1079
Violation of requirements in general,
Building and structures in general, **Neglig** ⚎ 1101
Firefighters, **Neglig** ⚎ 1210
Plaintiff's conduct or fault, **Neglig** ⚎ 1295
Police, **Neglig** ⚎ 1210
Stairs and ramps, hand and guard rails, **Neglig** ⚎ 1110(3)
Swimming pools, **Neglig** ⚎ 1129

STORE and business proprietors,
Breach of duty,
Criminal acts of third persons, **Neglig** ⚎ 1162
Displays and shelves, **Neglig** ⚎ 1119
Falling merchandise, **Neglig** ⚎ 1119
Third persons, acts of, **Neglig** ⚎ 1162
Business invitee. See subheading BUSI- NESS invitee, under this heading.
Duty of care,
Generally, **Neglig** ⚎ 1022-1024
Criminal acts of third persons, **Neglig** ⚎ 1024
Discovery, **Neglig** ⚎ 1023
Foreseeability, **Neglig** ⚎ 1022
Ice and snow, **Neglig** ⚎ 1022
Inspection, **Neglig** ⚎ 1023
Third persons, acts of, **Neglig** ⚎ 1024
Warning, **Neglig** ⚎ 1022
Standard of care,
Generally, **Neglig** ⚎ 1076-1078
Criminal acts of third persons, **Neglig** ⚎ 1078
Discovery, **Neglig** ⚎ 1077
Inspection, **Neglig** ⚎ 1077

PREMISES LIABILITY—Cont'd
STORE and business proprietors—Cont'd
Standard of care—Cont'd

Insurer of safety, **Neglig** ⚎ 1076
Third persons, acts of, **Neglig** ⚎ 1078

STRICT liability,
Buildings and structures in general, **Neglig** ⚎ 1101
Floors, cleaning or waxing, **Neglig** ⚎ 1104(8)

STRUCTURAL work laws,
Safe workplace laws, **Neglig** ⚎ 1204(7)

SUBCONTRACTORS,
Construction, demolition and repairs, **Neglig** ⚎ 1205(9)
Injury or loss, **Neglig** ⚎ 1251

SUPPLIERS,
Construction, demolition and repairs, **Neglig** ⚎ 1205(10)

SWIMMING pools,
Attractive nuisance doctrine, **Neglig** ⚎ 1177
Breach of duty, **Neglig** ⚎ 1129
Complaint, **Neglig** ⚎ 1524(4)
Evidence,
Burden of proof, **Neglig** ⚎ 1565
Presumptions and inferences, **Neglig** ⚎ 1596
Weight and sufficiency, **Neglig** ⚎ 1671
Hotels and motels, **Inn** ⚎ 10
Jury instructions, **Neglig** ⚎ 1737
Jury questions and directing verdict, **Neglig** ⚎ 1709
Plaintiff's conduct or fault, **Neglig** ⚎ 1290
Proximate cause, **Neglig** ⚎ 1234
Violation of statutory requirements, **Neglig** ⚎ 1129

THEATERS. See heading **THEATERS AND SHOWS**, generally.

THIRD persons, acts of,
Breach of duty,
Generally, **Neglig** ⚎ 1161-1162
Store and business proprietors, **Neglig** ⚎ 1162
Duty of care,
Generally, **Neglig** ⚎ 1019
Store and business proprietors, **Neglig** ⚎ 1024
Plaintiff's conduct or fault, **Neglig** ⚎ 1292
Standard of care,
Generally, **Neglig** ⚎ 1070
Store and business proprietors, **Neglig** ⚎ 1078

Reprinted with permission of Thomson Reuters/West.

2. Topic Outline Method

▼ What Is the Topic Outline Method?

Another method you can use to locate cases is the **topic outline method.** If you were asked to research a slip and fall problem similar to the one noted above, you might already suspect that negligence is the designated topic. You then would find the negligence topic in the appropriate volume of the digest series. At the beginning of the topic, you would review a topic outline, which is similar to a table of contents. See Illustration 4-7. Review the outline and note the key numbers that might be relevant to your case. Note any related topics. You might want to consider them if you decide that this topic is not appropriate. Premises liability seems appropriate and was the heading in the descriptive word index. Review the topics and key numbers below those words. The words "Standard of Care" appear as they did in the index. Scan down the list of key numbers and topics below those words. Note key number 1076 is for the "general" standard of care information. Note that number 1075 pertains to "care required of store and business proprietors." Both key numbers are relevant to the issue you are researching.

3. One Good Case Method

▼ What Is the One Good Case Method?

You also can use the **one good case method** to find cases when you already have found a case on point. If you have a West report of the case, the report will contain headnotes or abstracts with topic and key number designations. See Illustrations 3-4 and 3-9. Note the topic and key number designations for the points contained in the case that are relevant to your research; next, go to the relevant digest. For example, if you were researching an issue of federal law, you would review the *Federal Practice Digest, Fourth* first. However, if you are researching a question of Arizona law, you should review the Arizona digest. Next, go to the topic and find the key number. Review the case abstracts. The case abstracts contained in the digests are identical to the headnotes. Compare Illustrations 3-4 and 4-3; note headnote 1 of the *Thompson* case and the case abstract on the digest page.

▼ Are There Any Other Ways to Find Cases in the Digests?

Yes. If you have the name of a case on point but you do not have information about the key numbers contained in the case, you can look up the case name in the table of cases. It will list the case name and any applicable key numbers.

▼ Once You Have a Relevant Topic or Key Number, What Comes Next?

Once you find a relevant topic and key number using any of these methods, then you must be certain to check that topic and key number

ILLUSTRATION 4-7. *West's Illinois Digest 2d* Topic Outline

38 Ill D 2d—32

NEGLIGENCE

SUBJECTS INCLUDED

General civil negligence law and premises liability, including duty, standards of care, breach of duty, proximate cause, injury, defenses, and comparative fault, whether based on the common law or statute, as well as procedural aspects of such actions

General civil liabilities for gross negligence, recklessness, willful or wanton conduct, strict liability and ultrahazardous instrumentalities and activities

Negligence liabilities relating to the construction, demolition and repair of buildings and other structures, whether based on the common law or statute

General criminal negligence offenses and prosecutions

①SUBJECTS EXCLUDED AND COVERED BY OTHER TOPICS

Accountants or auditors, negligence of, see ACCOUNTANTS ⊶8, 9

Aircraft, accidents involving, see AVIATION ⊸141–153

Attorneys' malpractice liability, see ATTORNEY AND CLIENT ⊸105–129.5

Banks, liabilities of, see BANKS AND BANKING ⊸100

Brokers, securities and real estate, liabilities of, see BROKERS

Car and highway accidents, see AUTOMOBILES

Common carriers, liabilities to passengers, see CA[**1 Related subjects**]

Domestic animals, injuries by or to, see ANIMALS

Dram Shop liability and other liabilities for serving alcohol, see INTOXICATING LIQUORS ⊸282–324

Drugs, liabilities relating to manufacture, sale and dispensing of, see DRUGS AND NARCOTICS ⊸17–22

Educational institutions and personnel, liabilities of, see SCHOOLS and COLLEGES AND UNIVERSITIES

Electricity-related injuries, see ELECTRICITY ⊸12–19(13)

Elevators, liabilities of owners to passengers, see CARRIERS

Employers, liabilities for injuries to their own employees, see EMPLOYERS' LIABILITY

Employers, liabilities for acts committed by their employees or for negligent hiring or retention of employees, see MASTER AND SERVANT ⊸300–313

Exculpatory clauses prospectively waiving negligence liability, see CONTRACTS ⊸114, 189

Explosion, fireworks and blasting injuries, see EXPLOSIVES ⊸6–12

Firearms, injuries inflicted with, see WEAPONS ⊸18

Food, injuries caused by, see FOOD ⊸25

Flooding others' lands or polluting others' water supply, see WATERS AND WATER COURSES

Governments, negligence liability of, see COUNTIES, DISTRICT OF COLUMBIA, MUNICIPAL CORPORATIONS, STATES, TOWNS, TERRITORIES, and UNITED STATES

ILLUSTRATION 4-7. *Continued*

---

38 Ill D 2d—33 NEGLIGENCE

Homicide by negligence, see AUTOMOBILES and HOMICIDE

Hospitals, liabilities of, see HOSPITALS ⚷7

Hotels, motels, inns and boarding houses, liabilities of, see INNKEEPERS ⚷10–11(12), 14.1

Insurers, liabilities of, see INSURANCE and WORKERS' COMPENSATION

Lease of personal property, liabilities relating to, see BAILMENT

Lease of real property, liabilities relating to, see LANDLORD AND TENANT

Manufacture, sale or distribution of products, liabilities relating to, see PRODUCTS LIABILITY and SALES

Maritime accidents and injuries, see ADMIRALTY, COLLISION, FERRIES, PILOTS, SALVAGE, SEAMEN, SHIPPING and WHARVES

Medical malpractice and liabilities of health care professionals in general, see PHYSICIANS AND SURGEONS ⚷14–18.130

Mines and quarries, injuries in excavation and operation of, see MINES AND MINERALS ⚷118

Natural gas and propane, injuries from escape or explosion of, see GAS ⚷14.50–20(6)

Negligence as measure of criminal intent generally, see CRIMINAL LAW ⚷23

Negligent misrepresentation, see FRAUD ⚷13(3)

Nursing homes, day care centers and similar group homes, injuries in, see ASYLUMS ⚷6, 7

Pesticides, herbicides and fertilizers, liabilities involving, see AGRICULTURE ⚷7, 9.13

Railroads, liabilities to non-passengers, see RAILROADS and URBAN RAILROADS

Release from liability after injury, see RELEASE

Security personnel and private investigators, see DETECTIVES ⚷4

Sports and public amusements, liabilities of proprietors, managers, and sponsors, see THEATERS AND SHOWS

Wrongful death actions, procedural aspects of, see DEATH

For detailed references to other topics, see Descriptive-Word Index

---

> **2 Key numbers**

Analysis

② **I. IN GENERAL,** ⚷200–205.

II. NECESSITY AND EXISTENCE OF DUTY, ⚷210–222.

III. STANDARD OF CARE, ⚷230–239.

XVII. PREMISES LIABILITY, ⚷1000–1320.

    (A) IN GENERAL, ⚷1000–1004.

    (B) NECESSITY AND EXISTENCE OF DUTY, ⚷1010–1025.

ILLUSTRATION 4-7. *Continued*

(C) STANDARD OF CARE, ☞1030–1079.

(D) BREACH OF DUTY, ☞1085–1162.

(E) ATTRACTIVE NUISANCE DOCTRINE, ☞1172–1178.

(F) RECREATIONAL USE DOCTRINE AND STATUTES, ☞1191–1197.

(G) LIABILITIES RELATING TO CONSTRUCTION, DEMOLITION AND REPAIR, ☞1201–1205.

(H) STATUTORY CAUSES OF ACTION FOR POLICE AND FIREFIGHTERS, ☞1210.

(I) PROXIMATE CAUSE, ☞1220–1247.

(J) NECESSITY AND EXISTENCE OF INJURY, ☞1250–1251.

(K) PERSONS LIABLE, ☞1260–1269.

(L) DEFENSES AND MITIGATING CIRCUMSTANCES, ☞1280–1320.

XVIII. **ACTIONS,** ☞1500–1750.

(A) IN GENERAL, ☞1500–1508.

(B) PLEADING, ☞1510–1542.

(C) EVIDENCE, ☞1550–1685.

    1. BURDEN OF PROOF, ☞1550–1573.
    2. PRESUMPTIONS AND INFERENCES, ☞1575–1604.
    3. RES IPSA LOQUITUR, ☞1610–1625.
    4. ADMISSIBILITY, ☞1630–1642.
    5. WEIGHT AND SUFFICIENCY, ☞1650–1685.

(D) QUESTIONS FOR JURY AND DIRECTED VERDICTS, ☞1691–1719.

(E) INSTRUCTIONS, ☞1720–1747.

(F) VERDICT AND FINDINGS, ☞1750.

XIX. **CRIMINAL NEGLIGENCE,** ☞1800–1809.

––––––––––––

I. IN GENERAL.

☞200. Nature.

201. Distinction between negligence and intentional conduct.

202. Elements in general.

203. Constitutional, statutory and regulatory provisions.

204. What law governs.

205. Preemption.

II. NECESSITY AND EXISTENCE OF DUTY.

☞210. In general.

〰〰〰〰〰〰

XVI. DEFENSES AND MITIGATING CIRCUMSTANCES.—Continued.

570. ——— Professional rescuers; "firefighter's rule".

575. Imputed contributory negligence.

▶ **XVII. PREMISES LIABILITY.**

(A) IN GENERAL.

☞1000. Nature.

1001. Elements in general.

1002. Constitutional, statutory and regulatory provisions.

1003. What law governs.

1004. Preemption.

ILLUSTRATION 4-7. *Continued*

(B) NECESSITY AND EXISTENCE OF DUTY.

☞1010. In general.

1011. Ownership, custody and control.

1012. Conditions known or obvious in general.

1013. Conditions created or known by defendant.

1014. Foreseeability.

1015. Duty as to children.

1016. —— In general.

1017. —— Trespassing children.

1018. Duty to inspect or discover.

1019. Protection against acts of third persons in general.

1020. Duty to warn.

1021. Duty of store and business proprietors.

1022. —— In general.

1023. —— Duty to inspect.

1024. —— Protection against acts of third persons.

1025. Duty based on statute or other regulation.

(C) STANDARD OF CARE.

☞1030. In general.

1031. Not insurer or guarantor.

1032. Reasonable or ordinary care in general.

1033. Reasonably safe or unreasonably dangerous conditions.

1034. Status of entrant.

1035. —— In general.

1036. —— Care dependent on status.

1037. —— Invitees.

    (1). In general.

    (2). Who are invitees.

    (3). Not insurer as to invitees.

    (4). Care required in general.

    (5). Public invitees in general.

    (6). Implied invitation.

    (7). Persons working on property.

    (8). Delivery persons and haulers.

1040. —— Licensees.

    (1). In general.

    (2). Who are licensees.

XVII. PREMISES LIABILITY.—Continued.

▶ (C) STANDARD OF CARE.—Continued.

☞1040. —— Licensees.—Continued.

    (3). Care required in general.

    (4). Social guests.

1045. —— Trespassers.

    (1). In general.

    (2). Who are trespassers.

    (3). Care required in general.

    (4). Knowledge, discovery or acquiescence.

1050. —— Distinctions between types of entrants.

ILLUSTRATION 4-7. *Continued*

1051. —— Relative degrees of care.
1052. —— Change of status; exceeding scope of invitation or license.
1053. —— Rejection of status distinctions.
1060. Police, firefighters and other public servants.
1065. Care as to children.
1066. —— In general.
1067. —— Trespassing children.
1070. Protection against acts of third persons generally.
1071. Off-premises injuries.
1075. Care required of store and business proprietors.
→ 1076. —— In general.
1077. —— Inspection and discovery.
1078. —— Protection against acts of third persons.
1079. Standard established by statute or other regulation.

(D) BREACH OF DUTY.

1085. In general.
1086. Defect or dangerous conditions generally.
1087. Knowledge or notice in general.
1088. —— In general.
1089. —— Constructive notice.
1090. Miscellaneous particular cases.
1095. Slips and falls in general.
1100. Buildings and structures.
1101. —— In general.
1102. —— Doors, entryways and exits.
1103. —— Windows.
1104. —— Floors.
    (1). In general.
    (2). Knowledge of condition or danger.
    (3). Falls in general.
    (4). Inequalities in surface.
    (5). Rugs, carpets and mats.
    (6). Water and other substances.
    (7). Objects and debris.
    (8). Cleaning and waxing.

Reprinted with permission of Thomson Reuters/West.

in the bound volume of the digest, in any pocket parts, and in any supplemental pamphlets.

▼ What Are Pocket Parts?

Pocket parts are pamphlets that are usually inserted in a slot at the back of a bound book. If the pocket part is too thick, the publishers often will

print it as a small pamphlet. These pamphlets contain the most current cases and publisher references to related sources.

▼ How Do You Use the Pocket Parts?

To find cases in the pocket parts or in the pamphlets, you should find the topic that is listed alphabetically and then locate the appropriate key number. See Illustration 4-8. These are pocket parts updating the digest page shown in Illustration 4-3. Scan the page. At the bottom of the first column, you will find key number 1076. On the third page of the illustration, it refers to *Green v. Jewel Food Stores, Inc.* A number 1 is next to the *Green* note in the pocket part. A WESTLAW print of the case is shown in Illustration 4-9. The first headnote is 1076. Review page 2. Note the bracketed numbers and find number 1. That section of the case corresponds to the first headnote. It deals with an issue that is similar to both the *Thompson* and the *Kellermann* cases. Review Illustration 3-4, headnote 1, and Illustration 3-9, headnote 7.

4. Online Digest Search

▼ Can Digests Be Searched Online?

You can search online for topics and key numbers on WESTLAW only. However, topics may be searched on LEXIS. Because WESTLAW is a West product, it has exclusive access to the key number system. Key number searches are invaluable when you do not have a digest for a particular state. Suppose you are presented with the same slip and fall issue noted above. You need to find Ohio law, but you only have the Illinois digest or an Illinois case on point. You could use a key number search on the computer to find similar cases decided in Ohio.

To do this search, you could use one of several methods. You could review the *Illinois Digest* for an appropriate key number. You could use a key number you found in a case to find other cases. A second method is to use the Key Number Search screen on WESTLAW. On that page, you would enter search terms to find an appropriate key number. See Illustration 4-10. Then you would enter the key number found. WESTLAW then would provide a Custom Digest for the jurisdiction you select. Finally, you can enter search terms to find the appropriate key number.

How would you use a key number found in a case to create a Custom Digest?

Look closely at Illustration 4-9. Under each of the headnotes is a number similar to the key number. For headnote 1, the number is 272k1076. That number is the key number needed to do a search on WESTLAW for similar cases. Using that number for a specific jurisdiction allows you to create a custom digest. For WESTLAW, 272 is the numerical designation for negligence topics. Each West digest topic is assigned a numerical counterpoint. K is for key number and 1076 corresponds to the print key number.

ILLUSTRATION 4-8.   Pocket Parts for *Illinois Digest 2d*

⚙540   NEGLIGENCE   476

the conduct of a third person, or some other causative factor, is the sole proximate cause of plaintiff's injuries.—Thomas v. Johnson Controls, Inc., 279 Ill.Dec. 798, 801 N.E.2d 90, 344 Ill. App.3d 1026, rehearing denied.

⚙570. —— **Professional rescuers; "firefighter's rule".**

Ill.App. 2 Dist. 2003. Because the grounding of fireman's rule is found in a compromise of rights between firemen and owners or occupiers, the rule cannot be expanded beyond its limited context of landowner/occupier liability.—Randich v. Pirtano Const. Co., Inc., 281 Ill.Dec. 616, 804 N.E.2d 581, opinion supplemented on denial of rehearing.

XVII. PREMISES LIABILITY.

(A) IN GENERAL.

⚙1002. **Constitutional, statutory and regulatory provisions.**

Ill.App. 2 Dist. 2003. Under due process clause, statute providing that owner or occupier of premises owes fire fighters a duty of reasonable care in maintenance of premises could not be applied retroactively to cause of action that had accrued prior to effective date of statute. U.S.C.A. Const. Amend. 14; S.H.A. 425 ILCS 25/9f.—Randich v. Pirtano Const. Co., Inc., 281 Ill.Dec. 616, 804 N.E.2d 581, opinion supplemented on denial of rehearing.

(B) NECESSITY AND EXISTENCE OF DUTY.

⚙1010. **In general.**

Ill.App. 1 Dist. 2003. In premises liability cases, including those where a guest suffered injury while on hotel premises, Illinois courts determine whether a duty of care exists by considering the common law duty factors of (1) reasonable foreseeability of the injury; (2) likelihood of the injury; (3) magnitude of the burden on the defendant of guarding against the injury; and (4) consequences of placing the burden on the defendant.—Schmid v. Fairmont Hotel Company-Chicago, 280 Ill.Dec. 936, 803 N.E.2d 166, 345 Ill.App.3d 475.

⚙1012. **Conditions known or obvious in general.**

Ill.App. 1 Dist. 2003. In premises liability cases, the open and obvious nature of a condition generally affects whether the resulting harm was foreseeable, which, in turn, is relevant in determining whether a duty and proximate cause exist; in these cases, the open and obvious nature of a dangerous condition may preclude recovery, unless one of various exceptions is present.—Blue v. Environmental Engineering, Inc., 280 Ill.Dec. 957, 803 N.E.2d 187, 345 Ill.App.3d 455.

The exceptions to the rule that the open and obvious nature of a dangerous condition precludes recovery include: (1) the distraction exception—where the possessor of the property has reason to expect that an invitee's attention may be distracted and therefore will not notice the danger; and (2) the deliberate encounter exception—where the possessor has reason to expect that the invitee will proceed to encounter the known or obvious danger because to a reasonable man in his position the advantages of doing so would outweigh the apparent risk. Restatement (Second) of Torts § 343A.—Id.

1 Key number
2 Court and year
3 Headnote

Ill.App. 1 Dist. 2003. A party who owns or controls land is not required to foresee injuries if the potentially dangerous condition is open and obvious; the term "obvious" means that both the condition and the risk are apparent to and would be recognized by a reasonable person, in the position of the visitor, exercising ordinary perception, intelligence, and judgment.—Green v. Jewel Food Stores, Inc., 278 Ill.Dec. 875, 799 N.E.2d 740, 343 Ill.App.3d 830, rehearing denied.

In applying the distraction exception to the open and obvious doctrine, a court considers whether, despite the obviousness of a hazard, defendant should have anticipated the harm to plaintiff.—Id.

⚙1013. **Conditions created or known by defendant.**

N.D.Ill. 2003. Under Illinois law of negligence, building owner has duty to correct dangerous conditions on premises of which he knows or reasonably should know.—Ohio Cas. Group v. Dietrich, 285 F.Supp.3d 1128.

⚙1014. **Foreseeability.**

Ill.App. 1 Dist. 2003. In premises liability cases, including those where a guest suffered injury while on hotel premises, Illinois courts determine whether a duty of care exists by considering the common law duty factors of (1) reasonable foreseeability of the injury; (2) likelihood of the injury; (3) magnitude of the burden on the defendant of guarding against the injury; and (4) consequences of placing the burden on the defendant.—Schmid v. Fairmont Hotel Company-Chicago, 280 Ill.Dec. 936, 803 N.E.2d 166, 345 Ill.App.3d 475.

Ill.App. 1 Dist. 2003. A party who owns or controls land is not required to foresee injuries if the potentially dangerous condition is open and obvious; the term "obvious" means that both the condition and the risk are apparent to and would be recognized by a reasonable person, in the position of the visitor, exercising ordinary perception, intelligence, and judgment.—Green v. Jewel Food Stores, Inc., 278 Ill.Dec. 875, 799 N.E.2d 740, 343 Ill.App.3d 830, rehearing denied.

(C) STANDARD OF CARE.

⚙1037(4). **Care required in general.**

Ill.App. 1 Dist. 2003. The exceptions to the rule that the open and obvious nature of a dangerous condition precludes recovery include: (1) the distraction exception—where the possessor of the property has reason to expect that an invitee's attention may be distracted and therefore he will not notice the danger; and (2) the deliberate encounter exception—where the possessor has reason to expect that the invitee will proceed to encounter the known or obvious danger because to a reasonable man in his position the advantages of doing so would outweigh the apparent risk. Restatement (Second) of Torts § 343A.—Blue v. Environmental Engineering, Inc., 280 Ill.Dec. 957, 803 N.E.2d 187, 345 Ill.App.3d 455.

⚙1076. —— **In general.**

Ill.App. 1 Dist. 2003. Duty of reasonable care of store owner, based on distraction exception to open and obvious rule, encompassed risk that customer, while exiting store, would be distracted by unattended shopping cart and trip and fall over irregular pavement.—Green v. Jewel Food Stores, Inc., 278 Ill.Dec. 875, 799 N.E.2d 740, 343 Ill. App.3d 830, rehearing denied.

A business operator generally owes his customers a duty to exercise reasonable care to maintain his premises in a reasonably safe condition.—Id.

† **This Case was not selected for publication in the National Reporter System**

ILLUSTRATION 4-8. *Continued*

itself does not impose a duty upon the occupier or controller of the premises to prepare for their safety.—Luu v. Kim, 256 Ill.Dec. 667, 752 N.E.2d 547, 323 Ill.App.3d 946, appeal denied 261 Ill. Dec. 349, 763 N.E.2d 319, 196 Ill.2d 544.

Under *Kahn* doctrine, owner or occupier of land has a duty to protect children from a dangerous condition on the premises where: (1) the owner or occupier knew or should have known that children habitually frequent the property; (2) a defective structure or dangerous condition was present on the property; (3) the defective structure or dangerous condition was likely to injure children because they are incapable, because of age and immaturity, of appreciating the risk involved; and (4) the expense and inconvenience of remedying the defective structure or dangerous condition were slight when compared to the risk to children.—Id.

Ill.App. 4 Dist. 2005. Generally, owners and occupiers of land do not have a duty to maintain their property in a way that promotes the safety of trespassers; however, an exception exists where they know, or should know, that: (1) children habitually frequent the land; (2) a dangerous condition exists on the property; (3) such condition is likely to cause injury to those children because, by reason of their immaturity, they are incapable of appreciating the risks involved; and (4) the expense or inconvenience of remedying the condition is slight compared to the risk to children.—Morris ex rel. Morris v. Williams, 296 Ill.Dec. 65, 834 N.E.2d 622, 359 Ill.App.3d 383.

If the condition on the land involves obvious risks that trespassing children generally would be expected to appreciate and avoid, no duty to remedy it ensues.—Id.

⚓**1070. Protection against acts of third persons generally.**

Ill.App. 1 Dist. 2006. Generally, Illinois law does not impose a duty to protect another from a criminal attack by a third person, unless the attack is reasonably foreseeable and the parties stand in one of four special relationships, namely, (1) common carrier and passenger, (2) innkeeper and guest, (3) business invitor and invitee, and (4) voluntary custodian and protectee.—Iseberg v. Gross, 304 Ill.Dec. 1, 852 N.E.2d 251, 366 Ill. App.3d 857, rehearing denied, appeal allowed 308 Ill.Dec. 324, 861 N.E.2d 655, 222 Ill.2d 574.

Ill.App. 1 Dist. 2002. Nonresident landowners who allowed their vacant building to fall into a complete state of disrepair were not liable for death of homeless person, who was beaten to death by an unknown assailant; landowners owed no special duty to homeless person, who was a trespasser, and there was no evidence that assault was foreseeable, even though numerous and various criminal activities occurred on property over the years, as none involved murder or even crimes of violence or violent conduct against another individual.—Salazar v. Crown Enterprises, Inc., 262 Ill.Dec. 906, 767 N.E.2d 366, 328 Ill.App.3d 735, appeal denied 266 Ill. Dec. 447, 775 N.E.2d 9, 199 Ill.2d 579.

Ill.App. 1 Dist. 2001. Breach of duty arising from a landowner's voluntary undertaking to provide for security of entrants is established where entrant shows the landowner failed to exercise reasonable care in the voluntary undertaking, and the failure increased the risk of harm to entrant.—Landeros v. Equity Property and Development, 254 Ill.Dec. 351, 747 N.E.2d 391, 321 Ill.App.3d 57, rehearing denied, appeal denied 261 Ill.Dec. 349, 763 N.E.2d 319, 196 Ill.2d 544.

Ill.App. 2 Dist. 2005. An owner or occupier of land has a duty to protect his or her business invitees against the foreseeable criminal acts of third parties; however, the existence of a special relationship and foreseeability are not the only factors to be considered in determining whether a duty exists.—Haupt v. Sharkey, 295 Ill.Dec. 47, 832 N.E.2d 198, 358 Ill.App.3d 212, appeal denied 300 Ill.Dec. 365, 844 N.E.2d 37, 217 Ill.2d 562.

Ill.App. 2 Dist. 2001. The status of business invitee is relevant to determining whether a landowner has a duty to protect another against criminal acts by third parties.—Elizondo v. Ramirez, 257 Ill.Dec. 497, 753 N.E.2d 1123, 324 Ill.App.3d 67.

Ill.App. 3 Dist. 2005. An exception to the rule that a landowner does not owe a duty to protect lawful entrants from criminal attacks by third parties arises when the landholder and the entrant stand in a special relationship with one another, such as (1) common carrier and passenger, (2) innkeeper and guest, (3) custodian and ward, and (4) business invitor and invitee.—Dearing v. Baumgardner, 294 Ill.Dec. 862, 831 N.E.2d 1187, 358 Ill.App.3d 540, appeal denied 300 Ill.Dec. 364, 844 N.E.2d 36, 217 Ill.2d 560.

Landowners did not owe a duty to protect social guest from a criminal attack by third parties; landowners and social guest did not stand in a special relationship with each other that would create a duty, and the third parties who injured social guest, who were also guests of landowner, were not "conditions on the land" that landowners were required to warn social guest about.—Id.

Landowners did not have a duty to warn social guest about third parties, who were additional social guests of landowners; the danger presented by the third parties was readily apparent as the third parties were a belligerent and intoxicated couple that were engaged in a public physical confrontation.—Id.

⚓**1071. Off-premises injuries.**

Defects in sidewalks or other public ways, see MUNICIPAL CORPORATIONS ⚓808 and HIGHWAYS ⚓199; automobile accidents see AUTOMOBILES ⚓269, 289.

Ill.App. 1 Dist. 2000. The law does not recognize a duty on the part of a property owner to fence the land of another or to post warning signs thereupon.—Calhoun ex rel. Calhoun v. Belt Ry Co. of Chicago, 246 Ill.Dec. 804, 731 N.E.2d 332, 314 Ill.App.3d 513, appeal denied 250 Ill.Dec 455, 738 N.E.2d 924, 191 Ill.2d 526.

Landowner is under no general duty to erect fencing or provide warnings on his or her land so as to deter others, particularly trespassers, from entering neighboring property on which exists a dangerous condition not caused or maintained by the landowner and over which the landowner has no control.—Id.

⚓**1076. —— In general.**

→ **C.A.7 (Ill.) 2001.** Under Illinois law, business owes its customers, as invitees, duty to take reasonable care to avoid injuring them.—Peterson v. Wal-Mart Stores, Inc., 241 F.3d 603.

Under Illinois law, store's duty to customers is not merely to prevent careless spillage by its employees but also to be on lookout for spillage by whomever caused spill and to clean it up promptly.—Id.

C.A.7 (Ill.) 1999. Under Illinois law, a business owes the public the duty of exercising reasonable care in maintaining the premises in

---

† **This Case was not selected for publication in the National Reporter System**

ILLUSTRATION 4-8. *Continued*

reasonably safe condition. S.H.A. 740 ILCS 130/2.—Lane v. Hardee's Food Systems, Inc., 184 F.3d 705.

Ill. 2006. Special relationship between a business invitor and invitee gives rise to an affirmative duty on the part of invitors to aid or protect invitees against unreasonable risk of physical harm; overruling *Stutz v. Kamm*, 204 Ill.App.3d 898, 149 Ill.Dec. 935, 562 N.E.2d 399. Restatement (Second) of Torts §§ 314A, 344.—Marshall v. Burger King Corp., 305 Ill.Dec. 897, 856 N.E.2d 1048, 222 Ill.2d 422, rehearing denied.

Fast food restaurant, an establishment open to the general public for business purposes, was in a special invitor-invitee relationship with its customers, giving rise to duty to aid or protect customers against unreasonable risk of physical harm. Restatement (Second) of Torts §§ 314A, 344.—Id.

①**Ill.App. 1 Dist. 2003.** Duty of reasonable care of store owner, based on distraction exception to open and obvious rule, encompassed risk that customer, while exiting store, would be distracted by unattended shopping cart and trip and fall over irregular pavement.—Green v. Jewel Food Stores, Inc., 278 Ill.Dec. 875, 799 N.E.2d 740, 343 Ill.App.3d 830, rehearing denied.

A business operator generally owes his customers a duty to exercise reasonable care to maintain his premises in a reasonably safe condition.—Id.

Ill.App. 1 Dist. 2003. A tavern operator is not an insurer of its patrons.—Sameer v. Butt, 277 Ill.Dec. 697, 796 N.E.2d 1063, 343 Ill.App.3d 78, rehearing denied.

Ill.App. 1 Dist. 2002. In an action based upon negligence, general rule regarding duty of a business occupier of any premises is that it must provide a reasonably safe means of ingress to and egress from premises, but ordinarily it will not be held liable for any injuries incurred on a public sidewalk under control of municipality, even though sidewalk may also be used for ingress or egress to premises.—Friedman v. City of Chicago, 267 Ill.Dec. 627, 777 N.E.2d 430, 333 Ill.App.3d 1070.

Ill.App. 1 Dist. 2002. Store, tavern, or restaurant owners owe a duty of ordinary care to their business invitees.—Salazar v. Crown Enterprises, Inc., 262 Ill.Dec. 906, 767 N.E.2d 366, 328 Ill. App.3d 735, appeal denied 266 Ill.Dec. 447, 775 N.E.2d 9, 199 Ill.2d 579.

Ill.App. 2 Dist. 2001. The relationship of business invitor and invitee did not exist between property owners and guest at party killed by another guest, although money was charged for attendance and 50 to 70 people attended, where party was not a business open to the public.—Elizondo v. Ramirez, 257 Ill.Dec. 497, 753 N.E.2d 1123, 324 Ill.App.3d 67.

The relationship of business invitor and invitee, which imposes a duty of care, may arise where the owner or occupier of land holds the land open to the public for business purposes.—Id.

The collection of a small fee, by someone who, absent the fee, would otherwise clearly not be a business invitor, is insufficient to establish the special relationship of business invitor and invitee that would allow the imposition of negligence liability for the criminal acts of third parties.—Id.

To establish the relationship of business invitor-invitee sufficient to impose a duty to guard against the criminal acts of third parties, the premises involved must be a business open to the general public.—Id.

Ill.App. 3 Dist. 2006. The operator of a business owes his invitees a duty to exercise reason-

able care to maintain his premises in a reasonably safe condition for use by the invitees.—Pageloff v. Gaumer, 302 Ill.Dec. 674, 849 N.E.2d 1086, 365 Ill.App.3d 481.

Campground and its owner did not have a duty to keep the ground clear of fallen walnuts and thus, could not be liable to camper who tripped on a walnut that fell from a tree near her campsite for breach of such a duty; camper was aware of the existence of the walnuts and of the tripping danger posed by them, burden of guarding against injury caused by fallen walnuts would be extremely onerous, and imposing such a burden on campground owner would, as a practical matter, result in an inability to have walnut trees near campgrounds.—Id.

Campground and its owner had no duty to warn camper who tripped on a walnut that fell from a tree near her campsite of the danger posed by walnuts and other items on the ground in wooded campgrounds; campground customers were already well aware of the potential for a trip or fall caused by stepping on such items.—Id.

Ill.App. 5 Dist. 2003. The general duty of reasonable care of possessor of land has toward its business invitees does not extend to all risks of harm encountered by invitees while on defendant's premises. Restatement (Second) of Torts §§ 318, 344, 390.—Cobb v. Martin IGA & Frozen Food Center, Inc., 271 Ill.Dec. 748, 785 N.E.2d 942, 337 Ill.App.3d 306, appeal denied 275 Ill. Dec. 74, 792 N.E.2d 305, 204 Ill.2d 657.

The duty owed by a possessor of land to a business invitee is not absolute. Restatement (Second) of Torts §§ 318, 344, 390.—Id.

⬚**1077. —— Inspection and discovery.**

C.A.7 (Ill.) 2001. Under Illinois law, store's duty to customers is not merely to prevent careless spillage by its employees but also to be on lookout for spillage by whomever caused spill and to clean it up promptly.—Peterson v. Wal-Mart Stores, Inc., 241 F.3d 603.

Under Illinois law, store's satisfaction of duty of inspection for spills and clean up does not require continuous patrolling of aisles, but it may require, in self-service stores where customer traffic is heavy and probability of slip and fall therefore high, frequent and careful patrolling.—Id.

⬚**1078. —— Protection against acts of third persons.**

N.D.Ill. 2001. Illinois law does not impose a duty to protect another from a criminal attack by a third person unless the attack was reasonably foreseeable and the parties were common carrier and passenger, innkeeper and guest, business invitor and invitee, or voluntary custodian and protectee.—Ryan v. U.S., 156 F.Supp.2d 900.

Ill. 2006. Duty of care that arises from the business invitor-invitee relationship encompasses protecting invitee from negligent act of a third person. Restatement (Second) of Torts §§ 314A, 344.—Marshall v. Burger King Corp., 305 Ill.Dec. 897, 856 N.E.2d 1048, 222 Ill.2d 422, rehearing denied.

Even if a business invitor's lack of knowledge of prior, similar incidents of negligent conduct should limit duty of care to protect invitees against unreasonable risk of physical harm posed by third persons, allegations raised in negligence complaint filed against fast food restaurant by estate of patron, who was killed when a vehicle crashed through wall of restaurant while patron was eating, were sufficient to support determination that restaurant owed a duty to take reason-

† This Case was not selected for publication in the National Reporter System

ILLUSTRATION 4-9.   WESTLAW Printout of Case *Green v. Jewel Food Stores*

Westlaw.

799 N.E.2d 740
343 Ill.App.3d 830, 799 N.E.2d 740, 278 Ill.Dec. 875
(Cite as: 343 Ill.App.3d 830, 799 N.E.2d 740, 278 Ill.Dec. 875)

Appellate Court of Illinois,
First District, Second Division.
Robert GREEN and Doris Green, Plaintiffs-Appellants,
v.
JEWEL FOOD STORES, INC., Defendant-Appellee.
No. 1-02-1856.

Sept. 9, 2003.
Rehearing Denied Oct. 10, 2003.

Customer brought negligence action against corporation seeking damages for injuries sustained when she fell while exiting corporation's store. The Circuit Court, Cook County, David G. Lichtenstein, J., granted corporation's motion for summary judgment. Customer appealed. The Appellate Court, Cahill, J., held that duty of reasonable care of corporation, based on distraction exception to open and obvious rule, encompassed risk that customer would be distracted by unattended shopping cart and trip and fall over irregular pavement.

Reversed and remanded.

West Headnotes

[1] Negligence ☞1076
272k1076 Most Cited Cases

[1] Negligence ☞1291(3)
272k1291(3) Most Cited Cases
Duty of reasonable care of store owner, based on distraction exception to open and obvious rule, encompassed risk that customer, while exiting store, would be distracted by unattended shopping cart and trip and fall over irregular pavement.

[2] Negligence ☞202
272k202 Most Cited Cases
Plaintiff states a cause of action for negligence by establishing: (1) that defendant owed a duty of care to plaintiff; (2) defendant breached the duty; (3) an injury occurred; and (4) the injury was proximately caused by defendant's breach.

[3] Judgment ☞181(33)

272k181(33) Most Cited Cases
Whether a duty of care exists for negligence action is a question of law which may be decided on a motion for summary judgment.

[4] Negligence ☞1076
272k1076 Most Cited Cases
A business operator generally owes his customers a duty to exercise reasonable care to maintain his premises in a reasonably safe condition.

[5] Negligence ☞210
272k210 Most Cited Cases
To decide whether a duty exists court considers: (1) foreseeability that defendant's conduct will result in injury to another; (2) likelihood of injury; (3) burden of guarding against injury; and (4) consequences of placing that burden on defendant.

[6] Negligence ☞1012
272k1012 Most Cited Cases

[6] Negligence ☞1014
272k1014 Most Cited Cases
A party who owns or controls land is not required to foresee injuries if the potentially dangerous condition is open and obvious; the term "obvious" means that both the condition and the risk are apparent to and would be recognized by a reasonable person, in the position of the visitor, exercising ordinary perception, intelligence, and judgment.

[7] Negligence ☞1012
272k1012 Most Cited Cases

[7] Negligence ☞1286(3)
272k1286(3) Most Cited Cases
In applying the distraction exception to the open and obvious doctrine, a court considers whether, despite the obviousness of a hazard, defendant should have anticipated the harm to plaintiff.
**741 *830 ***876 Roosevelt Thomas of Westrate & Holmstrom, P.C., Dowagiac, MI, for Appellant.

Paul A. Tanzillo and Andrew T. Fleishman, of McBreen, Kopko, McKay & Nora, Chicago, for Appellee.

ILLUSTRATION 4-9. *Continued*

Westlaw.

799 N.E.2d 740
343 Ill.App.3d 830, 799 N.E.2d 740, 278 Ill.Dec. 875
(Cite as: 343 Ill.App.3d 830, 799 N.E.2d 740, 278 Ill.Dec. 875)

Page 2

**831 Justice CAHILL delivered the opinion of the court:

Plaintiffs Robert and Doris Green appeal from an order of summary judgment entered in favor of defendant, Jewel Food Stores, Inc. Plaintiffs contend that the trial court erred in disposing of their negligence complaint by finding that defendant owed no duty to the plaintiffs. We believe the undisputed facts of this case fall within the distraction exception set out in *Ward v. K mart Corp.*, 136 Ill.2d 132, 143 Ill.Dec. 288, 554 N.E.2d 223 (1990), and require that the question of duty be resolved against defendant. We reverse and remand.

The Greens filed a complaint seeking damages for injuries sustained when Doris fell while exiting defendant's store in Oaklawn, Illinois. Plaintiffs alleged that defendant negligently maintained an inherently unsafe environment at the store's exit where there were unattended shopping carts and a one-inch ridge in the pavement. Doris claimed that the unsafe conditions were the proximate cause of her injury, a broken patella (kneecap). Her husband Robert sought damages for loss of consortium. The trial court granted defendant's motion for summary judgment, finding: (1) defendant did not breach a duty of care owed to plaintiffs; (2) the record was uncontested with no unanswered questions of fact; and (3) there was no unreasonably unsafe condition on defendant's property as a matter of law.

The pleadings, depositions and photographs of record show that Doris and her husband's cousin, Eleanor Hastie, entered defendant's store at about 9:30 a.m. on **742 ***877 November 16, 1997. Doris was visiting from Michigan and had not previously shopped at that store. Robert waited in the car while the women shopped. Doris exited the store, carrying her purse over her shoulder and a plastic shopping bag containing one or two items in her hand. Hastie was behind Doris. A customer exiting in front of Doris pushed an empty shopping cart toward a cart storage area. When Doris noticed the cart was rolling down a slope toward the parking lot, she grabbed it by the handle to stop it. She then fell.

In a recorded statement on November 20, 1997, Doris said as she and Hastie exited the store, a man ahead of them "just gave his cart a shove." Doris said, "I grabbed for [the cart]

so it wouldn't be out in the cars or hit a car." When asked why she thought she fell, Doris replied, "I really don't know what caused it * * * unless it was this bump that [Robert] said was there." The bump referred to a ridge between the cement sidewalk and the asphalt paving of the parking lot that Robert noticed and photographed when he returned to the scene the next day. Doris later stated in a discovery deposition on September 19, 2000, "[t]here was a ridge, but I think [it was] the cart that made me fall." She estimated the ridge to have been about one inch high.

*832 Robert also gave a deposition on September 19, 2000. He said he saw Doris exit the store and then saw her on the ground. He did not see her fall but believed she fell because "when she grabbed that cart I think she didn't notice this little ridge" where the cement was "a little higher" than the asphalt. He said he did not notice the ridge until he returned to the scene the next day.

Hastie gave a deposition on May 23, 2001. She said she was walking 10 to 12 feet behind Doris and she believed Doris fell because she lost her balance as she reached out to grab the empty cart.

Ginger Lane, defendant's employee, gave a recorded statement on December 8, 1997, in which she said she saw Doris after the fall. Lane said Doris was on the ground on an incline that was dry and clean with no cracks in the pavement.

The standard of review of a trial court's grant of a motion for summary judgment is de novo. *Morris v. Margulis*, 197 Ill.2d 28, 35, 257 Ill.Dec. 656, 754 N.E.2d 314 (2001). We construe all evidence strictly against ~~~ liberally in favor of the nonmoving p~~~ *Joliet & Eastern Ry. Co.*, 165 Ill.2d ~~~ 662, 649 N.E.2d 1323 (1995).

[1][2][3] A plaintiff states a cause of action for negligence by establishing: (1) that the defendant owed a duty of care to the plaintiff; (2) the defendant breached the duty; (3) an injury occurred; and (4) the injury was proximately caused by the defendant's breach. *Quintola v. Village of Niles*, 154 Ill.2d 201, 207, 181 Ill.Dec. 631, 608 N.E.2d 882 (1993). Whether a duty of care exists is a question of law which

ILLUSTRATION 4-9. *Continued*

Westlaw

799 N.E.2d 740   Page 3
343 Ill.App.3d 830, 799 N.E.2d 740, 278 Ill.Dec. 875
(Cite as: 343 Ill.App.3d 830, 799 N.E.2d 740, 278 Ill.Dec. 875)

may be decided on a motion for summary judgment. *Curatola,* 154 Ill.2d at 207, 181 Ill.Dec. 631, 608 N.E.2d 882.

[4][5][6] A business operator generally owes his customers a duty to exercise reasonable care to maintain his premises in a reasonably safe condition. *Ward,* 136 Ill.2d at 141, 143 Ill.Dec. 288, 554 N.E.2d 223. To decide whether a duty exists, we consider: (1) the foreseeability that the defendant's conduct will result in injury to another; (2) the likelihood of injury; (3) the burden of guarding against injury; and (4) the consequences of placing that burden on the defendant. *Curatola,* 154 Ill.2d at 214, 181 Ill.Dec. 631, 608 N.E.2d 882. A party who owns or controls land is not **743 ***878 required to foresee injuries if the potentially dangerous condition is open and obvious. *Bucheleres v. Chicago Park District,* 171 Ill.2d 435, 447-48, 216 Ill.Dec. 568, 665 N.E.2d 826 (1996). The term " obvious" means that " 'both the condition and the risk are apparent to and would be recognized by a reasonable [person], in the position of the visitor, exercising ordinary perception, intelligence, and judgment.' " *Deibert v. Bauer Brothers Construction Co.,* 141 Ill.2d 430, 435, 152 Ill.Dec. 552, 566 N.E.2d 239 (1990), quoting Restatement (Second) of Torts § 343A, Comment *b,* at 219 (1965). In *Deibert,* however, the supreme court noted that, even though a deep rut in the ground at a *833 construction site was an obvious hazard, it was foreseeable that the injured employee's attention would be distracted by the possibility of construction debris being thrown from an adjacent balcony. *Deibert,* 141 Ill.2d at 438, 152 Ill.Dec. 552, 566 N.E.2d 239.

Plaintiffs rely on the reasoning that governed our supreme court's decision in *Ward,* 136 Ill.2d at 147, 143 Ill.Dec. 288, 554 N.E.2d 223. Plaintiffs argue that open and obvious conditions do not necessarily relieve a defendant of a duty of reasonable care. In *Ward,* the supreme court held that a property owner owed a duty of care to a customer even though the customer was injured after encountering an obvious condition, if the defendant should reasonably anticipate that the plaintiff would be distracted. There, the plaintiff was injured when, while carrying a large mirror he had just purchased at defendant's store, he walked into a concrete post located just outside the store entrance. *Ward,*

136 Ill.2d at 138, 143 Ill.Dec. 288, 554 N.E.2d 223. The court concluded that the defendant owed the plaintiff a duty of care because it was reasonable to expect that the plaintiff's attention might be distracted from the pole, an obvious condition, as he carried a large item from the store. *Ward,* 136 Ill.2d at 149-50, 143 Ill.Dec. 288, 554 N.E.2d 223, adopting the reasoning in Restatement (Second) of Torts, § 343A, Comment *f,* at 220 (1965). The Restatement provides:

"Such reason to expect harm to the visitor from known or obvious dangers may arise, for example, where the possessor [of land] has reason to expect that the invitee's attention may be distracted, so that he will not discover what is obvious, or will forget what he has discovered, or fail to protect himself against it. Such reason may also arise where the possessor has reason to expect that the invitee will proceed to encounter the known or obvious danger because to a reasonable man in his position the advantages of doing so would outweigh the apparent risk. In such cases the fact that the danger is known, or is obvious, is important in determining whether the invitee is to be charged with contributory negligence, or assumption of risk. [Citation.] It is not, however, conclusive in determining the duty of the possessor, or whether he has acted reasonably under the circumstances." Restatement (Second) of Torts, § 343A, Comment *f,* at 220 (1965).

The court in *Ward* held that the proper inquiry in deciding whether the distraction exception applies to the open and obvious doctrine is "whether the defendant should reasonably anticipate injury to those entrants on his premises who are generally exercising reasonable care for their own safety, but who may reasonably be expected to be distracted, as when carrying large bundles, or forgetful of the condition after having momentarily encountered it." *Ward,* 136 Ill.2d at 152, 143 Ill.Dec. 288, 554 N.E.2d 223. Whether the hazardous condition itself operated as adequate notice of its presence or whether additional precautions were required *834 to satisfy the defendant's **744 ***879 duty of care are questions properly left to the trier of fact. *Ward,* 136 Ill.2d at 156, 143 Ill.Dec. 288, 554 N.E.2d 223.

The narrow question in this case is, should defendant have

ILLUSTRATION 4-9. *Continued*

Westlaw.

799 N.E.2d 740
343 Ill.App.3d 830, 799 N.E.2d 740, 278 Ill.Dec. 875
(Cite as: 343 Ill.App.3d 830, 799 N.E.2d 740, 278 Ill.Dec. 875)

343 Ill.App.3d 830, 799 N.E.2d 740, 278 Ill.Dec. 875

END OF DOCUMENT

Reprinted with permission of Thomson Reuters/West.

You could click on the Key Search icon. It would provide space for a key number search. See Illustration 4-10. You would enter 272k1076. It would find cases similar to *Green, Thompson,* and *Kellermann.* They would be in shown in a WESTLAW Custom Digest similar to that shown in Illustration 4-11. The first case listed is *Marshall v. Burger King Corp.,* 856 N.E.2d 1048. It is the most recent case that involves the relevant negligence topic discussed in headnote 272k1076. The headnote listed in the Custom Digest mentioned the duty owned to a business invitee. Note the number 1 in Illustration 4-11. It is where the *Green* case appears in the Custom Digest. A number 2 is next to the *Kellermann* case (shown in Illustration 3-9). *Hills v. Bridgeview Little League Ass'n,* 713 N.E2d 616 (1999) is listed in the digest next to the number 3. Again, the digest tells the researchers that this Illinois court discusses the definition of "business invitee." Note the number 4. It appears next to the *Thompson v. Economy Super Marts, Inc.,* 581 N.E.2d 885 (1991) shown in Illustration 3-4. It again discusses the question of the duty a business owes to an invitee. Now review the cases, note the similarities between the cases. They are not identical in facts or in the legal analysis. However, portions of the cases can be related to one another so that as a researcher you develop a better understanding of the relevant case law concerning the duty owed by a business to an invitee.

How would you search for the WESTLAW digest topic number if you found a topic and key number in the print digest?

If you did not have a good case, but wanted to do an online key number search with a topic and key number that you already had obtained from the print digest. You could review the broad list of WESTLAW digest topics and find the number that corresponds to the digest topic you are seeking to research.

ILLUSTRATION 4-10.   WESTLAW Key Number Search Page

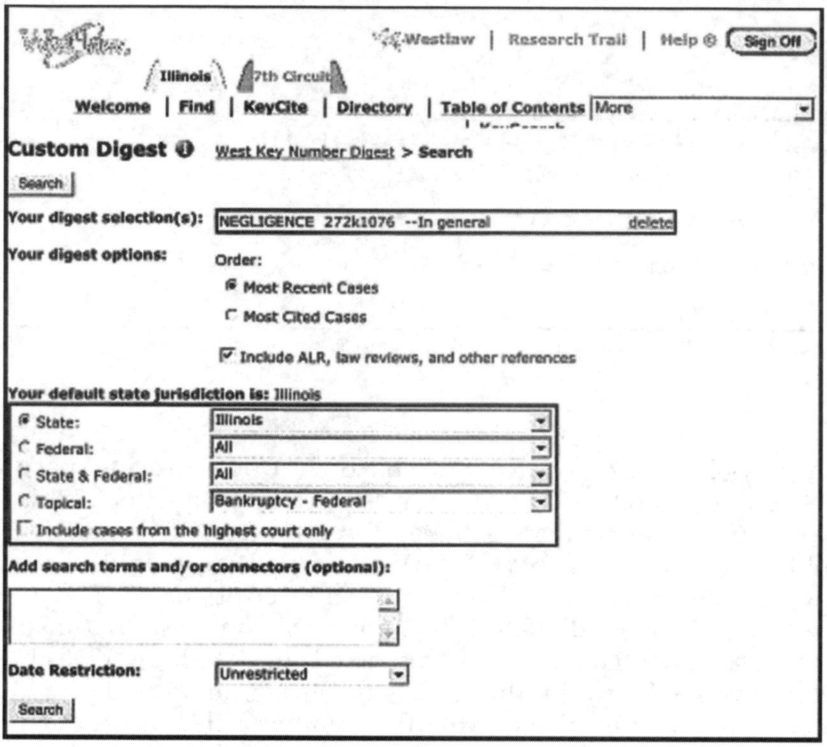

Reprinted with permission of Thomson Reuters/West.

ILLUSTRATION 4-11. Sample WESTLAW Custom Digest

Headnotes

▷
Marshall v. Burger King Corp., 856 N.E.2d 1048
  272 NEGLIGENCE
    272XVII Premises Liability
      272XVII(C) Standard of Care
        272k1075 Care Required of Store and Business Proprietors

272k1076 k. In general.
Ill.,2006
Special relationship between a business invitor and invitee gives rise to an affirmative duty on the part of invitors to aid or protect invitees against unreasonable risk of physical harm; overruling *Stutz v. Kamm*, 204 Ill.App.3d 898, 149 Ill.Dec. 935, 562 N.E.2d 399. Restatement (Second) of Torts §§ 314A, 344.

▷
Marshall v. Burger King Corp., 856 N.E.2d 1048
Ill.,2006
Fast food restaurant, an establishment open to the general public for business purposes, was in a special invitor-invitee relationship with its customers, giving rise to duty to aid or protect customers against unreasonable risk of physical harm. Restatement (Second) of Torts §§ 314A, 344.

ⓒ
Pageloff v. Gaumer, 849 N.E.2d 1086
Ill.App.3.Dist.,2006
The operator of a business owes his invitees a duty to exercise reasonable care to maintain his premises in a reasonably safe condition for use by the invitees.

ⓒ
Pageloff v. Gaumer, 849 N.E.2d 1086
Ill.App.3.Dist.,2006
Campground and its owner did not have a duty to keep the ground clear of fallen walnuts and, thus, could not be liable to camper who tripped on a walnut that fell from a tree near her campsite for breach of such a duty; camper was aware of the existence of the walnuts and of the tripping danger posed by them, burden of guarding against injury caused by fallen walnuts would be extremely onerous, and imposing such a burden on campground owner would, as a practical matter, result in an inability to have walnut trees near campgrounds.

ⓒ
Pageloff v. Gaumer, 849 N.E.2d 1086
Ill.App.3.Dist.,2006
Campground and its owner had no duty to warn camper who tripped on a walnut that fell from a tree near her campsite of the danger posed by walnuts and other items on the ground in wooded campgrounds; campground customers were already well aware of the potential for a trip or fall caused by stepping on such items.

▷
Green v. Jewel Food Stores, Inc., 799 N.E.2d 740
Ill.App.1.Dist.,2003
① Duty of reasonable care of store owner, based on distraction exception to open and obvious rule, encompassed risk that customer, while exiting store, would be distracted by unattended shopping cart and trip and fall over irregular pavement.

ILLUSTRATION 4-11.   *Continued*

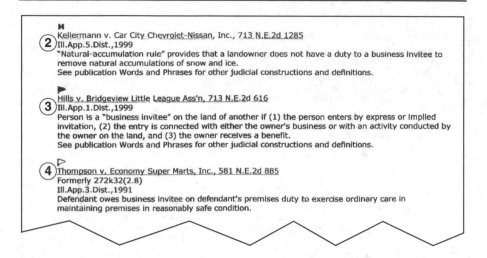

H
(2) Kellermann v. Car City Chevrolet-Nissan, Inc., 713 N.E.2d 1285
Ill.App.5.Dist.,1999
"Natural-accumulation rule" provides that a landowner does not have a duty to a business invitee to
remove natural accumulations of snow and ice.
See publication Words and Phrases for other judicial constructions and definitions.

(3) Hills v. Bridgeview Little League Ass'n, 713 N.E.2d 616
Ill.App.1.Dist.,1999
Person is a "business invitee" on the land of another if (1) the person enters by express or implied
invitation, (2) the entry is connected with either the owner's business or with an activity conducted by
the owner on the land, and (3) the owner receives a benefit.
See publication Words and Phrases for other judicial constructions and definitions.

(4) Thompson v. Economy Super Marts, Inc., 581 N.E.2d 885
Formerly 272k32(2.8)
Ill.App.3.Dist.,1991
Defendant owes business invitee on defendant's premises duty to exercise ordinary care in
maintaining premises in reasonably safe condition.

Reprinted with permission of Thomson Reuters/West.

WESTLAW provides an extensive alphabetical listing of topics. See Illustration 4-12. Next to the arrow is 272 Negligence. That is the broad topic. By clicking the mouse on the plus sign, the list is expanded and specific negligence key number ranges are shown. Next to the A is the notation "premises liability, K1000-K1320." Those key numbers deal with that topic. In a negligence case involving a slip and fall on a premises or at a store, these would be relevant. If you click the pointer on that plus sign, additional key numbers will appear. See Illustration 4-13. It shows K1076. That headnote focuses on the "care required of store and business proprietors" generally. It is the same headnote involved in the *Kellermann* and *Green* cases. It is the newer key number for the same topical headnote referenced in the *Thompson* case.

▼ Can You Find a Relevant Topic and Key Number to Search on WESTLAW by Entering Search Terms?

Yes. You can search for the appropriate key number by inserting relevant words on the WESTLAW key number search page. See Illustration 4-14. The words "store owner duty of care to invitee" are listed in the search field. The jurisdiction is Illinois. The computer yields various negligence topics and key numbers. 272K1076 is the listed first in the results. Once you have that key number, you would click on it or you enter the key number as shown in Illustration 4-12 and the Custom Digest would appear.

Each West case reported online includes two research aid links next to each headnote. One is called KeyCite Notes and the other is called Most Cited Cases.

If you are reviewing a case, you can click on the KeyCite Notes link next to the relevant headnote. It will provide you with the option to select the citing references you wish to review. For example, you can

ILLUSTRATION 4-12.   WESTLAW Online Topics

Westlaw.   FIND&PRINT   KEYCITE   DIRECTORY   KEY NUMBERS   SITE MAP   HELP   SIGN OFF

Research Trail

Illinois   Westlaw   Business & News   Add/Remove Tabs

West Key Number Digest | NY Official Digest (2nd & 3rd Series) | Canadian Abridgment

- ☐ ⊞ 🔗 1 ABANDONED AND LOST PROPERTY
- ☐ ⊞ 🔗 2 ABATEMENT AND REVIVAL
- ☐ ⊞ 🔗 4 ABORTION AND BIRTH CONTROL
- ☐ ⊞ 🔗 5 ABSENTEES
- ☐ ⊞ 🔗 6 ABSTRACTS OF TITLE
- ☐ ⊞ 🔗 7 ACCESSION
- ☐ ⊞ 🔗 8 ACCORD AND SATISFACTION
- ☐ ⊞ 🔗 9 ACCOUNT
- ☐ ⊞ 🔗 10 ACCOUNT, ACTION ON
- ☐ ⊞ 🔗 11 ACCOUNT STATED
- ☐ ⊞ 🔗 11A ACCOUNTANTS
- ☐ ⊞ 🔗 12 ACKNOWLEDGMENT
- ☐ ⊞ 🔗 13 ACTION
- ☐ ⊞ 🔗 14 ACTION ON THE CASE
- ☐ ⊞ 🔗 15 ADJOINING LANDOWNERS
- ☐ ⊞ 🔗 15A ADMINISTRATIVE LAW AND PROCEDURE
- ☐ ⊞ 🔗 16 ADMIRALTY
- ☐ ⊞ 🔗 17 ADOPTION
- ☐ ⊞ 🔗 18 ADULTERATION
- ☐ ⊞ 🔗 19 ADULTERY
- ☐ ⊞ 🔗 20 ADVERSE POSSESSION
- ☐ ⊞ 🔗 21 AFFIDAVITS
- ☐ ⊞ 🔗 23 AGRICULTURE
- ☐ ⊞ 🔗 24 ALIENS, IMMIGRATION, AND CITIZENSHIP
- ☐ ⊞ 🔗 25 ALTERATION OF INSTRUMENTS
- ☐ ⊞ 🔗 25T ALTERNATIVE DISPUTE RESOLUTION
- ☐ ⊞ 🔗 26 AMBASSADORS AND CONSULS

ILLUSTRATION 4-12.   *Continued*

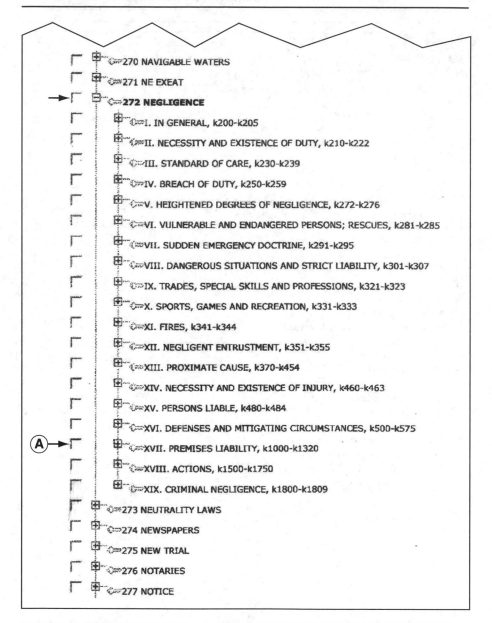

Reprinted with permission of Thomson Reuters/West.

ILLUSTRATION 4-13. Expanded List of WESTLAW Topics and Key Numbers for Premises Liability

Tree Content Page

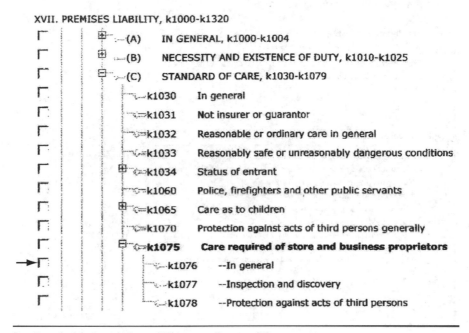

XVII. PREMISES LIABILITY, k1000-k1320

- (A) IN GENERAL, k1000-k1004
- (B) NECESSITY AND EXISTENCE OF DUTY, k1010-k1025
- (C) STANDARD OF CARE, k1030-k1079
  - k1030   In general
  - k1031   Not insurer or guarantor
  - k1032   Reasonable or ordinary care in general
  - k1033   Reasonably safe or unreasonably dangerous conditions
  - k1034   Status of entrant
  - k1060   Police, firefighters and other public servants
  - k1065   Care as to children
  - k1070   Protection against acts of third persons generally
  - **k1075**   **Care required of store and business proprietors**
    - → k1076   --In general
    - k1077   --Inspection and discovery
    - k1078   --Protection against acts of third persons

Reprinted with permission of Thomson Reuters/West.

ILLUSTRATION 4-14. WESTLAW Key Number Search Page and Sample Results

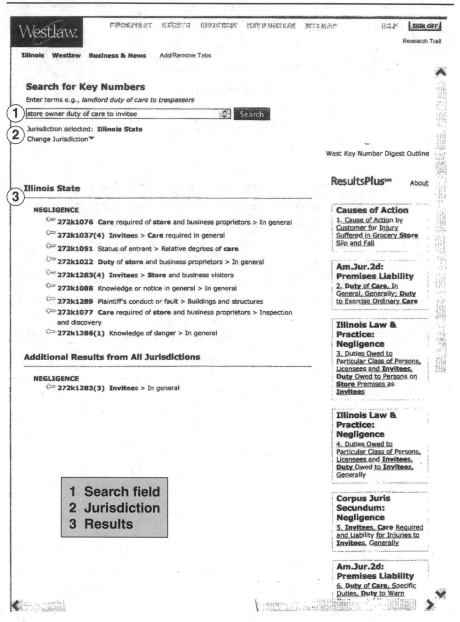

Reprinted with permission of Thomson Reuters/West.

ILLUSTRATION 4-15. List of LEXIS Legal Topics

LexisNexis *Total Research System*

Switch Client | Preferences | Sign Out | ? | Help

My Lexis™ | Search | Research Tasks | Get a Document | *Shepard's®* | Alerts | Transactional Advisor | Counsel Selector | Doss

by Source | by Topic or Headnote | by Guided Search Form | by Dot Command

Use this page to find legal data based on **areas of law and related legal topics**. Using this page can help you target your legal issue, identify appropriate sources, and formulate your search request.   Show Me...

Look for a Legal Topic   ?

Option 1: Find a Legal Topic

                                                                    Find

Type in your research issue as an individual term, phrase, list or sentence. Enclose phrases in quotation marks.

Option 2: Explore Legal Topics

Administrative Law
Agency Rulemaking, Governmental Information, Judicial Review, ...

Admiralty Law
Finds & Salvage, Shipping, Sovereign Immunity & Liability, ...

Antitrust & Trade Law
Monopolization, Price Discrimination, Sherman Act, ...

Banking Law
Bank Activities, Bank Expansion, National Banks, ...

Bankruptcy Law
Case Administration, Discharge & Dischargeability, Exemptions, ...

Business & Corporate Law
Agency Relationships, Mergers & Acquisitions, ...

Civil Procedure
Jurisdiction, Pleading & Practice, Appeals, ...

Civil Rights Law
Conspiracy, Practice & Procedure, Voting Rights, ...

Commercial Law (UCC)
Sales (Article 2), Leases (Article 2A), Bulk Sales (Article 6), ...

Communications Law
Broadcasting, Cable Systems, Telephone Services, ...

Computer & Internet Law
Censorship, Civil Actions, Privacy & Security, ...

Constitutional Law
The Presidency, The Judiciary, Bill of Rights, ...

Contracts Law
Consideration, Formation, Types of Contracts, ...

Copyright Law
Civil Infringement Actions, Publication, Subject Matter, ...

Criminal Law & Procedure
Criminal Offenses, Arrests, Search & Seizure, ...

Education Law
Athletics, Departments of Education, Students, ...

Energy & Utilities Law
Federal Oil & Gas Leases, Mining Industry, Utility Companies, ...

Environmental Law
Environmental Justice, Solid Wastes, Zoning & Land Use, ...

Estate, Gift & Trust Law
Annuities, Estate Administration, Trusts, ...

Evidence
Documentary Evidence, Relevance, Testimony, ...

Family Law
Adoption, Child Support, Marital Duties & Rights, ...

Governments
Courts, Legislation, Local Governments, ...

Healthcare Law
Actions Against Facilities, Insurance, Treatment, ...

Immigration Law
Admission, Immigrants, Nonimmigrants, ...

Insurance Law
Life Insurance, Motor Vehicle Insurance, Reinsurance, ...

International Law
Dispute Resolution, Immunity, Treaty Formation, ...

International Trade Law
Dispute Resolution, Imports & Exports, Trade Agreements, ...

Labor & Employment Law
Employee Privacy, Employer Liability, Wrongful Termination, ...

Legal Ethics
Client Relations, Practice Qualifications, Sanctions, ...

Military & Veterans Law
Military Justice, Defense Powers, Veterans, ...

Patent Law
Infringement Actions, Subject Matter, Utility Requirement, ...

Pensions & Benefits Law
Employee Benefit Plans, Multiemployer Plans, ...

Public Contracts Law
Bids & Formation, Dispute Resolution, Terminations, ...

Public Health & Welfare Law
Food & Nutrition, Healthcare, Social Services, ...

Real Property Law
Brokers, Deeds, Zoning & Land Use, ...

Securities Law
Blue Sky Laws, Investment Advisers, Liability, ...

Tax Law
Excise Taxes, International Taxes, State & Local Taxes, ...

Torts
Intentional Torts, Negligence, Products Liability, ...

Trade Secrets Law
Civil Actions, Misappropriation Actions, Protection of Secrecy, ...

Trademark Law
Infringement Actions, Likelihood of Confusion, Subject Matter, ...

Transportation Law
Air Transportation, Interstate Commerce, ...

Workers' Compensation & SSDI
Benefit Determinations, Compensability, Coverage, ...

Key:
    Click to see information about this topic.

LexisNexis   About LexisNexis | Terms & Conditions | Contact Us
Copyright © 2008 LexisNexis, a division of Reed Elsevier Inc. All rights reserved.

Reproduction by permission of LexisNexis. Further reproduction of any kind is strictly prohibited.

ILLUSTRATION 4-16.   Expanded List of LEXIS Legal Topics for Torts and Premises Liability

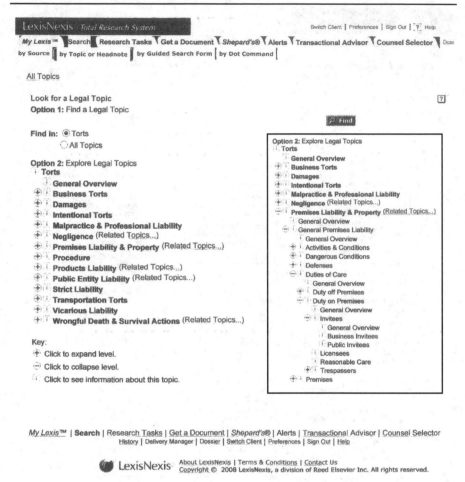

Reproduced by permission of LexisNexis. Further reproduction of any kind is strictly prohibited.

ILLUSTRATION 4-17.   LEXIS Search Page

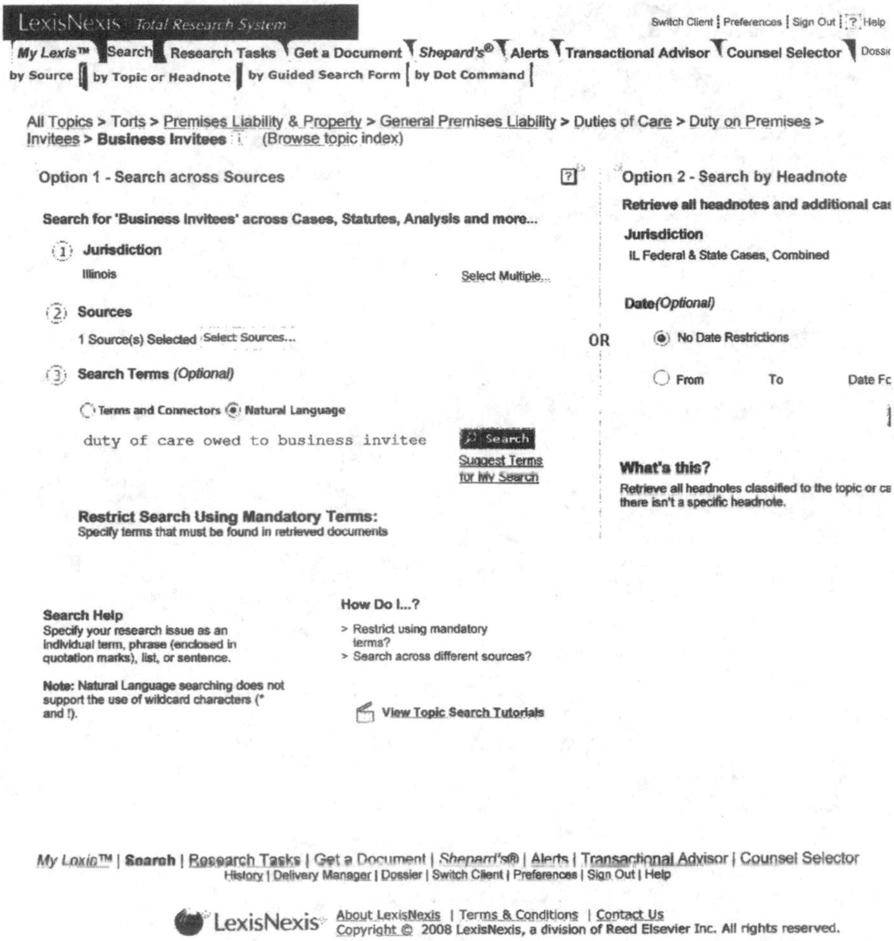

Reproduced by permission of LexisNexis. Further reproduction of any kind is strictly prohibited.

ILLUSTRATION 4-18.   List of Suggested LEXIS Search Terms

LexisNexis *Total Research System*   Switch Client | Preferences | Sign Out | ? Help

My Lexis™ Search Research Tasks Get a Document *Shepard's®* Alerts Transactional Advisor Counsel Selector Dossie

by Source | by Topic or Headnote | by Guided Search Form | by Dot Command |

All Topics > Torts > Premises Liability & Property > General Premises Liability > Duties of Care > Duty on Premises >
Invitees > **Business Invitees** i   (Browse topic index)

Option 1 - Search across Sources   ?   **Option 2 - Search by Headnote**

Search for 'Business Invitees' across Cases, Statutes, Analysis and more...   **Retrieve all headnotes and additional ca:**

1. **Jurisdiction**   **Jurisdiction**
   Illinois   Select Multiple...   IL Federal & State Cases, Combined

2. **Sources**   **Date***(Optional)*
   1 Source(s) Selected Select Sources...   OR   ● No Date Restrictions

3. **Search Terms** *(Optional)*   ○ From   To   Date Fc
   ● Terms and Connectors ○ Natural Language

                          🔍 Search
                          Suggest Terms
                          for My Search   **What's this?**
                                                 Retrieve all headnotes classified to the topic or ca
                                                 there isn't a specific headnote.

1 **Suggest Words and Concepts for Entered Terms:**

store	injury	possession	premise
arrest	negligence	check	customer
damage	slip opinion	summary judgment	deposit slip
sold	credit	police officer	credit card
reasonable doubt	robbery	search	admissible
automobile	card	deposit	identified

Suggested Terms for Topic: There are no suggested terms.

Search Connectors   **How Do I...?**
and   and   > Restrict by date on the Search by Topic form?
or   or   > Search across different sources?
w/N   within N words
pre /N   precedes by N words
w/p   in same paragraph
>More Connectors & Commands...   📄 View Topic Search Tutorials

My Lexis™ | Search | Research Tasks | Get a Document | *Shepard's®* | Alerts | Transactional Advisor | Counsel Selector
History | Delivery Manager | Dossier | Switch Client | Preferences | Sign Out | Help

LexisNexis   About LexisNexis | Terms & Conditions | Contact Us
Copyright © 2008 LexisNexis, a division of Reed Elsevier Inc. All rights reserved.

Reproduced by permission of LexisNexis. Further reproduction of any kind is strictly prohibited.

select state cases and law review journals and articles. Then the service will provide you with a list of these sources that cite the case and legal issue that you are researching.

The other new tool is called Most Cited Cases. This aid allows you to find the most cited cases for a particular point of law. You click on this icon next to a headnote or point of law and it will provide the most cited cases and tell you how many cases cite that proposition.

LEXIS also offers the ability to search by topics. See Illustrations 4-15 and 4-16 for a list of LEXIS legal topics. In the LEXIS search page, similar to the one shown in Illustration 4-17, you would fill in the

jurisdiction field (number 1), select the sources (number 2), and enter search terms (number 3). Two options are provided for the entering search terms. LEXIS will suggest terms when a research selects one of the topics shown in Illustration 4-18. The other method is Natural Language. Using that method, a researcher can enter terms without using LEXIS search connectors. LEXIS search techniques will be explained in detail in Chapter 10. In Illustration 4-17, the terms "duty of care owed to business invitee" are entered with the Natural Language option selected. Entering these terms will yield cases similar to those found on WESTLAW using the key number 272k1070.

CHAPTER SUMMARY

In this chapter, you learned about digests that can assist you in locating similar cases on point. The digests are tied to the commercial reporters' headnotes that contact case abstracts concerning a point of law raised in a case. Each headnote contains a topic and a number that refer you to a topical system for finding additional similar cases. West's National Reporter System™ is linked to its digest system both in print and online. This system enables researchers to find applicable topics in one state and review the same topics in a different state digest to find similar cases. The online databases also allow researchers to research multiple states.

When you research a legal issue in a digest, you can review its index to find a relevant topic and number that directs you to cases on point. In the West system, the numbers are called key numbers. Another method for using the digest is to review the outline presented before each topic. You also might find a good case on point and locate other similar cases by using the digest topic and numbers listed in the publisher's headnotes that appear at the beginning of a case reporter.

In the next chapter, you will learn how to ensure that the cases you found are good law.

KEY TERMS

descriptive word index method	pocket parts
digests	topic outline method
headnotes	West American Digest system
one good case method	West key number system

EXERCISES

DIGEST RESEARCH

1. Research the following issue in the appropriate digest.

Your firm's client was fired from her job because she was 69 years old. She had worked for 40 years in this position. When she was fired, she was

replaced with a 25-year-old woman. Your firm's client has a master's degree; the 25-year-old has a bachelor's degree.

You only need to consider what federal law claims she might have against her former employer. Her case would be brought in the U.S. District Court for the Northern District of Ohio.

Brainstorm: What words would you review? What topics and key numbers did you find? List them. List two relevant cases.

2. You must determine whether a former employee can assert the attorney-client privilege in your state when a third party, not the former employee, brings an action against the former employer.

Brainstorm: What words would you review? What topics and key numbers did you find? List them. List two relevant cases.

3. Using the Pocket Parts in Illustration 4-8, do the following treasure hunt.
   Find the Illinois Seventh Circuit opinion that relates to key number 1076 decided in 2001.
   a. What is the name?
   b. Are there any other CA7th cases?
   c. What is that name and citation?
   d. Where in the federal digest would you find these cases?
4. Go to the federal digest mentioned in question 3d.
   a. Find a 1990 Ninth Circuit case under key number 1076?
   b. Now find a 2006 District of Columbia case.
5. Now look at the key number translation table in the same digest. Review key number 1078. What were the old key numbers for that number?

COMPUTER RESEARCH
Portfolio Assignment for Digest Research
6. Read the following fact situation. Answer the questions following the situation.

FACTS

Nate Late, a business owner, has two partners in the operation of Loose Cannon Manufacturing in Gurnee, Illinois. He owns $33\frac{1}{3}$ percent of a $3 million company. Late is ill, but not dying. He is grooming a 26-year-old, Ivan T. All, to run the business. He tells his family he likes All and wants to teach him the business. Nate Late dies.

The most current will leaves Late's estate to his wife of 24 years, Shirley Late, and his only son, Lou Sier. Mr. All tells Mrs. Late that her husband told All he intended to give the 26-year-old his one-third interest in Loose Cannon. This conversation took place in front of a bank president. No written record exists concerning Late's intention to give his stock to All. However, family members knew that Late intended for All to run the business and for All to get something if the business was sold. None of the family believed that Late intended to give the business to newcomer Ivan T. All. Late's shares of stock

were never given to All. The shares were in the safety deposit box shared by Late and his wife.

Mrs. Late said that Mr. Late planned to give her the shares. He told her this when he opened the joint safety deposit box and gave her the key.

You work for a firm that has been retained by Mrs. Late. She would like to know if All can prove that Mr. Late gave All Mr. Late's interest in the company.

DIGEST QUESTIONS

a. What digest is appropriate for this problem?
b. How would you find the appropriate digest topics? Note in detail two methods for finding the appropriate digest topics. Next, review two topics.
c. What topics did you review?
d. Did you find additional topics that should be reviewed? If so, review those now.
e. What topics and key numbers are relevant to this problem?
f. Review the case abstracts listed under one of the topics and key numbers. Which cases are relevant? Note two below. Copy the case abstract or photocopy the case abstracts. Review two cases.

COMPUTER EXERCISES FOR DIGEST TOPICS

7. Search for Negligence key number 1086, cases in all 50 states. Print the search and the first page of the citation list of the cases.
8. Using the computer, prepare and list a headnote search of topic Bankruptcy 3079 in Minnesota. Print your search and the first page of the list of cases you find.
9. Find 713 N. E2d 1285. What is the topic number and key number for headnote 2?
10. Find 984 F.2d 218 online on WESTLAW.
    a. What is the name of the case?
    b. Who are the plaintiffs?
    c. Who are the defendants?
    d. What is the topic number and key number for headnote number 4?
    e. What is the former key number for that headnote?
    f. Is the appellant's brief for this case available on WESTLAW? If so, how would you find it?

5

VALIDATING

CHAPTER OVERVIEW

This chapter teaches you how to ensure that a case that you find is good law and how to find additional cases using citators. To ensure that a case is current or is still good law, you must validate or update your research findings. A case is good law if its ruling has not been reversed or overruled by another court's decision. Validating or Shepardizing, as it is commonly called, is one of the most important tasks you must do as a researcher. It is also referred to as citechecking. To do this, you must review citators.

A. *SHEPARD'S*

▼ What Is a Citator?

Citators are services that note when a court has mentioned or relied on a case. The citator may be found on the computer or in print. The *Shepard's* **citator system** is the most pervasive in print. It is found in printed form and

on the Internet at lexis.com and law.lexisnexis.com/shepards. Citators are used to validate a case. In addition, you can use them to locate relevant primary authorities, including cases and statutes, and secondary authorities, such as law review articles and *American Law Reports,* that may assist you in finding additional primary authorities or in understanding the legal issues presented in your research. You also can review citators to determine the direct history of a case. This history describes the progress of a specific case and all of the decisions made by different courts pertaining to it.

▼ What Do You Learn from Reviewing *Shepard's* Citations?

Shepard's provides a list of parallel citations and the history of the case you are reviewing. The **case history** explains whether the case has been appealed and the results of that appeal. If it is a trial court case, *Shepard's* indicates whether it was appealed and lists the appellate citation. For state cases such as the *Thompson* case (discussed in Chapter 4), *Shepard's* contains parallel citations in parentheses. See Illustration 5-1. The parallel citations are reported the first time *Shepard's* reports a case in print; they are not reported in subsequent *Shepard's* reports. In Illustration 5-1, the parallel citation is next to number 3. However, *Shepard's* online report of a case contains the parallel citations each time you review the case. See Illustration 5-2. First the official citation, 221 Ill. App. 3d 263 is listed. It is followed by numerous parallel citations.

Shepard's lists all cases that mention or cite the case you are **Shepardizing.** For example, the *Thompson* decision mentions or cites *Ward v. K-Mart Corp.,* 136 Ill. 2d 132, 554 N.E.2d 223 (1990) on page 888 of the case. See Illustration 3-4. The *Shepard's* listing for the *Ward* case includes a notation that it is cited in the *Thompson* case, 581 N.E.2d 885, on page 888. See Illustrations 3-4 and 5-3.

Review Illustration 5-3. The citation for the *Ward v. K-Mart* case is 554 N.E.2d 223. This page is from the *Shepard's* volume that includes citations to the *Northeastern Reporter.* In that *Shepard's* collection, you would search for citations for Volume 554 of the *Northeastern Reporter.* Next to the number 1, you will find the volume number. In this case, it is 554. The volume number will appear at the top of the page on either the right or left corner. The reporter name will appear at the top of the page in the middle. See number 4 in Illustration 5-3. To find the *Ward* case, you would look for the number of the first page of the *Ward* case— 223. That appears in the third column of this *Shepard's* listing. A number 3 is next to the first page number of the *Ward* case. The first two citations in parentheses are the parallel citations for the *Ward* case. Following the parallel citations is the list of cases that mention or cite the *Ward* case. The *Thompson* case cites the *Ward* case. It appears next to the number 5. It tells the researcher that the citation appears on page 888 of the *Thompson* case.

Shepard's also references West's headnote system. In Illustration 5-4, the small raised 7 between the N.E.2d symbol and 888 in the *Thompson* notation of the *Ward Shepard's* report indicates that the citing case,

ILLUSTRATION 5-1. *Shepard's Northeastern Reporter Citations, 2007 Volume 12 Thompson v. Economy Super Marts, Inc., 581 N.E.2d 885*

NORTHEASTERN REPORTER, 2d SERIES   Vol. 581

684NE⁹828
802NE⁸1259
Miss
645So2d894
~ 645So2d902
—822—
Shea v
Edwards
1991
(221IIA219)
(163IID668)
708NE¹488
Cir. 7
250F3d509
1998USDist
[LX17734
—824—
Downers Grove
v Illinois State
Labor Relations
Bd.
1991
(221IIA47)
(163IID670)
Cert den
587NE1013
613NE319
f 613NE321
638NE²1146
654NE³611
654NE⁴611
662NE136
668NE¹1121
668NE²1121
668NE³1121
704NE⁴888
723NE³391
j 783NE104
—831—
Brown v Char-
lestowne Group,
Ltd.
1991
(221IIA44)
(163IID677)
Cir. 8
105FS2d1037
131FS2d²1085
—833—
Aetna Casualty
& Surety Co. v
Crowther, Inc.
1991
(221IIA275)
(163IID679)
606NE⁴639
Cir. 7
2000USDist
[LX7729
2000USDist
[LX17139
2001USDist
[LX9205

2001USDist
[LX14593
2002USDist
[LX1418
2004USDist
[LX4692
2006USDist
[LX13777
2006USDist
[LX50888
791FS741
Cir. 10
12FS2d1178
Ore
f 17P3d1081
—837—
People v Pack-
ard
1991
(221IIA295)
(163IID683)
s 632NE335
618NE1164
724NE²995
f 724NE997
—839—
People v
Denny
1991
(221IIA298)
(163IID685)
590NE974
600NE⁷460
f 600NE²461
f 600NE³461
612NE⁶1333
622NE²886
j 658NE1261
666NE877
669NE²1239
719NE¹309
781NE1133
817NE182
826NE1289
Cir. 7
f 1998USApp
[LX28186
1998USDist
[LX19259
1999USDist
[LX17238
—842—
In re Estate of
Stanford
1991
(221IIA154)
(163IID688)
Cert den
587NE1015
591NE947
630NE809
645NE355

—849—
In re D.D.H.
1991
(221IIA150)
(163IID695)
—852—
People v Sau-
cier
1991
(221IIA287)
(163IID698)
f 615NE³751
625NE126
656NE442
702NE580
731NE¹⁰436
820NE585
—857—
Trettenero v
Civil Service
Com.
1991
(221IIA326)
(163IID703)
d 762NE500
—860—
Lindholm v
Holtz
1991
(221IIA330)
(163IID706)
662NE⁹601
f 698NE⁴168
f 704NE⁴895
744NE⁹937
Cir. 7
2000USDist
[LX2684
2004USDist
[LX27954
2006USDist
[LX62152
2007USDist
[LX7958
249FS2d1047
2000Bankr LX
[1432
2003Bankr LX
[414
215BRW168
215BRW⁵374
271BRW⁵301
295BRW287
320BRW372
f 355BRW732
Wash
873P2d532
—864—
People v Haun
1991
(221IIA164)
(163IID710)
Cert den
602NE463

c 585NE¹⁹140
c 592NE1114
604NE428
f 604NE¹⁴496
f 604NE¹⁶496
604NE¹⁸499
f 606NE¹⁹665
613NE743
625NE1140
625NE¹⁸1144
626NE⁹756
j 665NE1344
689NE¹²676
689NE¹⁴676
f 827NE25
—873—
In re Marriage
of Salata
1991
(221IIA336)
(163IID719)
598NE⁸1012
604NE443
—877—
Holmstrom v
Kimis
1991
(221IIA317)
(163IID723)
596NE⁴711
596NE720
605NE⁵1083
606NE⁴275
616NE⁴1012
616NE⁵1012
622NE⁴101
628NE²207
631NE⁵265
636NE⁵1149
658NE⁶505
678NE⁵379
686NE⁵1253
703NE⁴413
716NE⁴1267
716NE⁵1267
721NE⁴749
722NE⁵1163
735NE²685
805NE1248
Va
415SE239
—882—
Cadle Co. II,
Inc. v Stauf-
fenberg
1991
(221IIA267)
(163IID728)
684NE1038
687NE¹1198
687NE²1198
687NE³1198
Fla
737So2d1250

—885—
(1) Thompson v
Economy Super
(2) Marts
1991
(3) (221IIA263)
(163IID731)
648NE³100
j 648NE101
650NE¹262   (6)
713NE¹1288
713NE²1288
(5) 721NE¹624
721NE³624
d 721NE625
721NE⁴625
Cir. 7
184F3d⁴707
40Fed Appx
[1001
f 114CaR2d480
f 36P3d19
—889—
People v
Solano
1991
(221IIA272)
(163IID735)
—892—
People v Ocon
1991
(221IIA311)
(163IID738)
614NE873
828NE²363
~ 830N
851N
859N
f 859N
Io
544N
—8
People
Timb
19
(221I
(163I
d 614N
614N
668NE¹1022
f 693NE¹398
—898—
Selph v North
Wayne Commu-
nity Unit School
Dist. No. 200
1991
(221IIA177)
(163IID744)
66AL15n

—901—
Mirly v Basola
1991
(221IIA182)
(163IID747)
642NE¹1266
645NE³240
—904—
People v Gold
1991
(221IIA187)
(163IID750)
Cert den
591NE26
597NE³935
602NE1373
—907—
People v Rol-
land
1991
(221IIA195)
(163IID753)
Ga
j 542SE98
—911—
In re Applica-
tion of Multime-
dia KSDK, Inc.
1991
(221IIA199)
(163IID757)
691NE²128
808NE²1112
Cir. 7
805FS32
883FS1142
12AL171n
—914—
Standard Inv.
Co.
1991
s 536NE311
s 586NE843
j 626NE834
f 756NE¹558
—922—
Beno v State
1991
s 570NE1371
Continued

1	**Case name**
2	**Decision date**
3	**Parallel citation**
4	**Citing cases**
5	**Distinguished case**
6	**Dissenting opinion cites *Thompson***

1135

ILLUSTRATION 5-2. Online *Shepard's* Report for *Thompson v. Economy Super Marts*, 581 N.E.2d 885

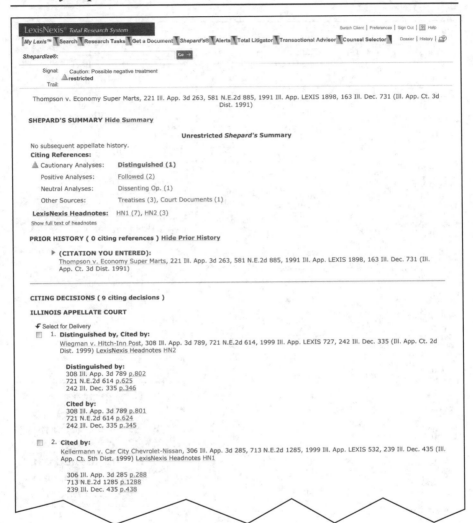

ILLUSTRATION 5-2.   *Continued*

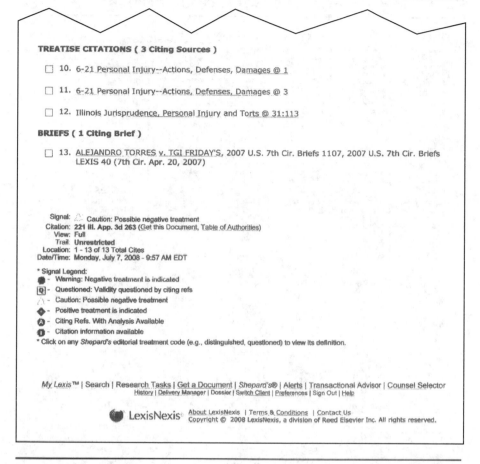

TREATISE CITATIONS (3 Citing Sources)

☐ 10. 6-21 Personal Injury--Actions, Defenses, Damages @ 1

☐ 11. 6-21 Personal Injury--Actions, Defenses, Damages @ 3

☐ 12. Illinois Jurisprudence, Personal Injury and Torts @ 31:113

BRIEFS (1 Citing Brief)

☐ 13. ALEJANDRO TORRES v. TGI FRIDAY'S, 2007 U.S. 7th Cir. Briefs 1107, 2007 U.S. 7th Cir. Briefs LEXIS 40 (7th Cir. Apr. 20, 2007)

Signal: △ Caution: Possible negative treatment
Citation: **221 Ill. App. 3d 263** (Get this Document, Table of Authorities)
View: **Full**
Trail: **Unrestricted**
Location: 1 - 13 of 13 Total Cites
Date/Time: Monday, July 7, 2008 - 9:57 AM EDT

* Signal Legend:
● - Warning: Negative treatment is indicated
Q - Questioned: Validity questioned by citing refs
△ - Caution: Possible negative treatment
◆ - Positive treatment is indicated
A - Citing Refs. With Analysis Available
I - Citation information available
* Click on any *Shepard's* editorial treatment code (e.g., distinguished, questioned) to view its definition.

My Lexis™ | Search | Research Tasks | Get a Document | *Shepard's*® | Alerts | Transactional Advisor | Counsel Selector
History | Delivery Manager | Dossier | Switch Client | Preferences | Sign Out | Help

LexisNexis   About LexisNexis | Terms & Conditions | Contact Us
Copyright © 2008 LexisNexis, a division of Reed Elsevier Inc. All rights reserved.

Thompson, refers to the text found within the portion of the *Ward* case the publisher designated as headnote 7. See the numbers 5 and 6 in Illustration 5-3 and numbers 1 and 2 in Illustration 5-4.

The online version of *Shepard's* has references to LexisNexis headnotes. The print version does not.

For some citing authorities, *Shepard's* provides additional information about the court's **treatment** of the citing case. For example, the *Shepard's* citation may include the letter *a* at the front of the citations list. That would indicate that the case has been affirmed on appeal. See Illustration 5-5. *Shepard's* may indicate with other abbreviations whether a case has been dismissed, modified, reversed, criticized, explained, followed, limited, questioned, or overruled. See Illustration 5-6. In this way you can find the **negative history** of a case, which tells you how other courts have viewed it and if any cast doubt on its validity. Not all of these court cases, however, have a direct relationship to the cited case.

ILLUSTRATION 5-3. *Shepard's Northeastern Reporter Citations, Ward v. K-Mart Corp.*, 554 N.E.2d 223 (Ill. 1990)

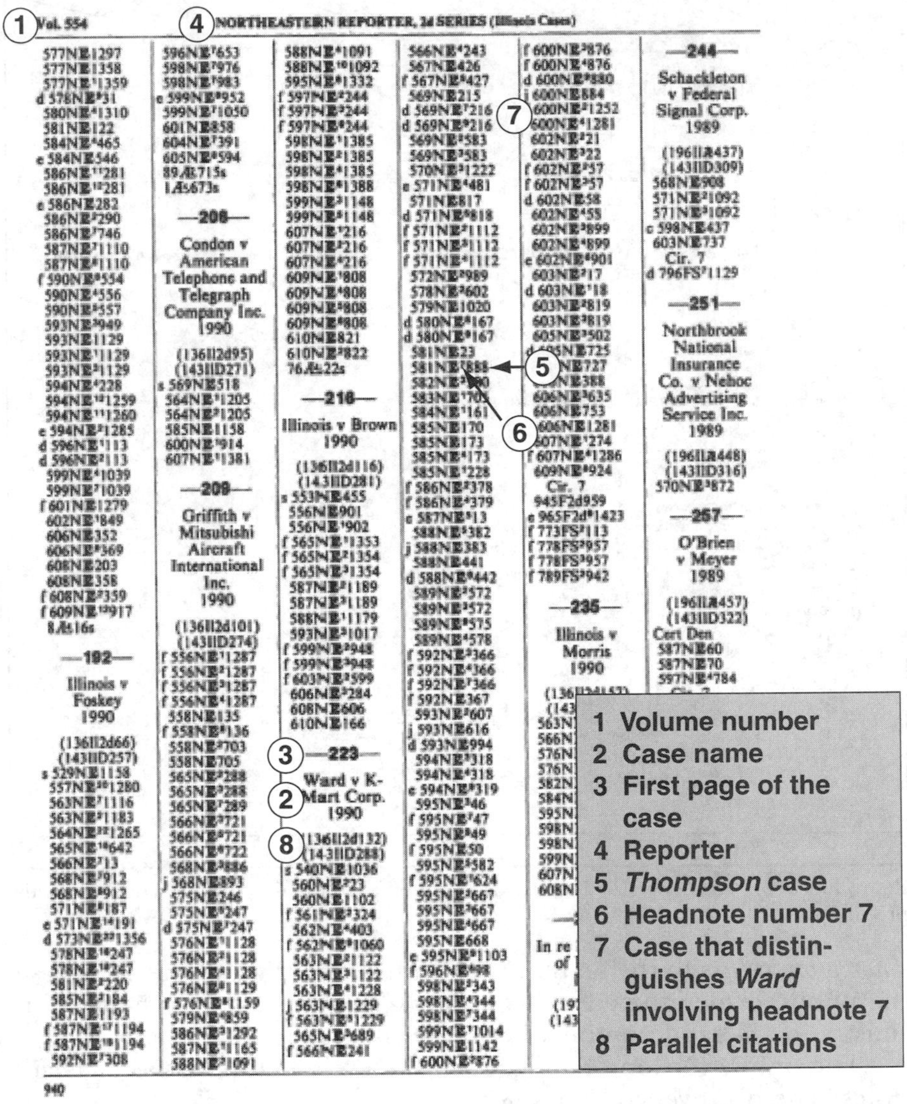

Vol. 554 — NORTHEASTERN REPORTER, 2d SERIES (Illinois Cases)

The reproduced Shepard's page includes the following case-unit headings among the citation columns:

—206—
Condon v American Telephone and Telegraph Company Inc.
1990
(136Il2d95)
(143IlD271)

—209—
Griffith v Mitsubishi Aircraft International Inc.
1990
(136Il2d101)
(143IlD274)

—192—
Illinois v Foskey
1990
(136Il2d66)
(143IlD257)

—216—
Illinois v Brown
1990
(136Il2d116)
(143IlD281)

—223—
Ward v K-Mart Corp.
1990
(136Il2d132)
(143IlD288)

—235—
Illinois v Morris
1990

—244—
Schackleton v Federal Signal Corp.
1989
(196Il2437)
(143IlD309)

—251—
Northbrook National Insurance Co. v Nehoc Advertising Service Inc.
1989
(196Il2448)
(143IlD316)

—257—
O'Brien v Meyer
1989
(196Il2457)
(143IlD322)
Cert Den

Legend (callouts):

1 Volume number
2 Case name
3 First page of the case
4 Reporter
5 *Thompson* case
6 Headnote number 7
7 Case that distinguishes *Ward* involving headnote 7
8 Parallel citations

940

ILLUSTRATION 5-4. *Shepard's Northeastern Reporter Citations,*
Ward V. K-Mart Corp., 554 N.E.2d 223 (Ill. 1990)

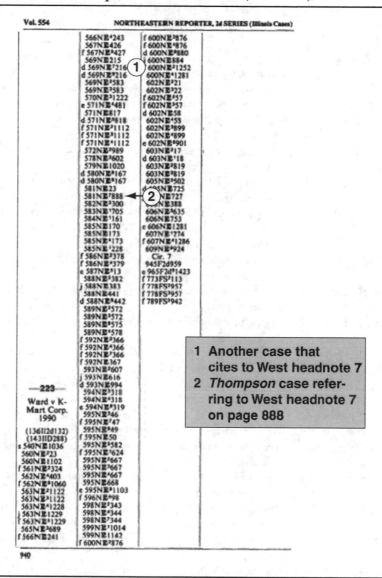

1 Another case that
  cites to West headnote 7
2 *Thompson* case refer-
  ring to West headnote 7
  on page 888

Reproduced by permission of LexisNexis. Further reproduction of any kind is strictly
prohibited.

ILLUSTRATION 5-5. *Shepard's* Case Analysis Abbreviations

CASE ANALYSIS–ABBREVIATIONS

HISTORY OF CASES

a	(Affirmed)	On appeal, reconsideration or rehearing, the citing case affirms or adheres to the case you are *Shepardizing*.
cc	(Connected case)	The citing case is related to the case you are *Shepardizing*, arising out of the same subject matter or involving the same parties.
D	(Dismissed)	The citing case dismisses an appeal from the case you are *Shepardizing*.
De/ Cert den	(Denied)	The citing case has denied further appeal in the case you are *Shepardizing*.
Gr	(Granted)	The citing case has granted further appeal in the case you are *Shepardizing*.
m	(Modified)	On appeal, reconsideration or rehearing, the citing case modifies or changes in some way, including affirmance in part and reversal in part, the case you are *Shepardizing*.
r	(Reversed)	On appeal, reconsideration or rehearing, the citing case reverses the case you are *Shepardizing*.
Reh den	(Reh./recon. denied)	The citing order denies rehearing or reconsideration in the case you are *Shepardizing*.
Reh gran	(Reh./recon. granted)	The citing order grants rehearing or reconsideration in the case you are *Shepardizing*.
s	(Same case)	The citing case involves the same litigation as the case you are *Shepardizing*, but at a different stage of the proceedings.
S	(Superseded)	On appeal, reconsideration or rehearing, the citing case supersedes or is substituted for the case you are *Shepardizing*.
TD	(Transfer den)	Transfer Denied by the Indiana Supreme Court.
TG	(Transfer gran)	Transfer Granted by the Indiana Supreme Court.
US cert den		The citing order by the U. S. Supreme Court denies certiorari in the cases you are *Shepardizing*.
US cert dis		The citing order by the U. S. Supreme Court dismisses certiorari in the case you are *Shepardizing*.
US cert gran		The citing order by the U. S. Supreme Court grants certiorari in the case you are *Shepardizing*.
US reh den		The citing order by the U. S. Supreme Court denies rehearing in the case you are *Shepardizing*.
US reh dis		The citing order by the U. S. Supreme Court dismisses rehearing in the case you are *Shepardizing*.
v	(Vacated)	The citing case vacates or withdraws the case you are *Shepardizing*.
W	(Withdrawn)	The citing decision or opinion withdraws the decision or order you are *Shepardizing*.

ILLUSTRATION 5-6.   *Shepard's* Treatment of Cases Abbreviations

CASE ANALYSIS–ABBREVIATIONS

TREATMENT OF CASES

c	(Criticized)	The citing opinion disagrees with the reasoning/result of the case you are *Shepardizing*, although the citing court may not have the authority to materially affect its precedential value.
ca	(Conflicting Authorities)	The citing opinion notes conflicting lines of authority on an issue, without taking a position on which line of authority should be applied.
d	(Distinguished)	The citing case differs from the case you are *Shepardizing*, either involving dissimilar facts or requiring a different application of the law.
e	(Explained)	The citing opinion interprets or clarifies the case you are *Shepardizing* in a significant way.
f	(Followed)	The citing opinion relies on the case you are *Shepardizing* as controlling or persuasive authority.
h	(Harmonized)	The citing case differs from the case you are *Shepardizing*, but the citing court reconciles the difference or inconsistency in reaching its decision.
j	(Dissenting Opinion)	A dissenting opinion cites the case you are *Shepardizing*.
~	(Concurring Opinion)	A concurring opinion cites the case you are *Shepardizing*.
L	(Limited)	The citing opinion restricts the application of the *Shepardized* case, finding that its reasoning applies only in specific limited circumstances.
o	(Overruled)	The citing case expressly overrules or disapproves all or part of the case you are *Shepardizing*.
op	(Overruled in part)	The citing opinion expressly overrules in part the cited case.
q	(Questioned)	The citing opinion questions the continuing validity or precedential value of the case you are *Shepardizing* because of intervening circumstances, including judicial or legislative overruling.
qo	(Overruled as stated in)	The citing opinion notes that the continuing validity of an earlier opinion you are *Shepardizing* is in question because it has been overruled in an earlier decision.
qop	(Overruled in part as stated in)	The citing opinion notes that the continuing validity of an earlier opinion you are *Shepardizing* is in question because it has been overruled in part in an earlier decision.
qab	(Abrogated as stated in)	The citing opinion states that the decision that you are Shepardizing has been reversed, vacated, abrogated or invalidated by an earlier decision.
qabp	(Abrogated in part as stated in)	The citing opinion states that the decision that you are Shepardizing has been reversed, vacated, abrogated or invalidated in part by an earlier decision.
su	(Superseded)	The citing reference, typically a session law or other record of legislative action, or a record of administrative action, supercedes the statute, regulation or order you are *Shepardizing*.

OTHER

\# The citing case is of questionable precedential value because review or rehearing has been granted by the California Supreme Court and/or the citing case has been ordered depublished pursuant to Rule 976 of the California Rules of Court. (Publication status should be verified before use of the citing case in California.)

Shepard's can be used to research almost every federal and state case reported in print in the past 200 years. It now includes some cases considered unreported because they only appear online. However, these citations are only to unreported LEXIS cases. See Illustration 5-7. Find the circled "2" located by volume 554 and page 223. The first case listed is 2005 IllAppLX[49. That is a case available only on LEXIS. The last case listed in that entry is located above the number 240. It is 2004 USDist[LX20740. It also is a case found only on LEXIS. *Shepard's* is part of LexisNexis. *Shepard's* publishes a variety of citation books for federal and state authorities. See Illustration 5-8. Among the authorities that can be Shepardized are cases, statutes, constitutions, codes, jury instructions, administrative decisions, copyrights, trademarks, patents, and regulations as well as secondary authorities including Restatements and *American Law Reports.* Most print *Shepard's* publications are supplemented regularly. A daily update can be obtained online at lexis.com or via e-mail alert.

The list of citing references to each will vary because different *Shepard's* divisions and citators include different citing sources. For example, if you reviewed the *Thompson* case under the Illinois division of the *Shepard's Illinois Citations,* you might find a listing for an attorney general opinion or a law review article. Illustration 5-9 shows a listing of the *Ward v. K-Mart Corp.,* case. Note the number of courts that have cited this case. Compare this with Illustration 5-3. Illustration 5-9 is the more current *Shepard's* listing. That is why it includes far more cases than Illustration 5-3.

However, the attorney general opinion and the law review citations would not be listed under the *Thompson* case in the *Northeastern Reporter* division of that citator. Also, under the regional citation for the *Thompson* case in the Illinois *Shepard's,* you would find the *Northeastern Reporter* citations for the Illinois cases that cite the *Thompson* case. Each citator contains a list at the front of a volume of the sources that have been consulted to determine whether a case has been referred to within that source. See Illustration 5-10.

▼ How Do You Use *Shepard's* in Print?

First, you must determine which *Shepard's* series is the appropriate one to consult. *Shepard's* has multiple citators that might contain a particular case. For example, a state citator and a regional citator would contain the *Shepard's* for a state case. For the *Thompson* case, you would look in the Illinois citator if you knew it was an Illinois case. Next, you must review the front cover of the most current pamphlet that accompanies the *Shepard's* citations. See Illustration 5-11. In Illustration 5-11, you can see the heading "What Your Library Should Contain." This lists all of the *Shepard's* volumes and supplements you must consider to complete your review of the *Shepard's* citations for a particular case. After you view the supplement cover, gather each of the volumes and supplements mentioned on the cover. The case citations are organized by reporter, volume, and page number. Find the appropriate reporter section. For the *Thompson* case,

ILLUSTRATION 5-7. Example of *Shepard's* Illinois Citations Cumulative Supplement

(1) Vol. 551

NORTHEASTERN REPORTER, 2d SERIES (Illinois Cases)

Vol. 551

—673—
Cir. 7
2004USDist
[LX18647
—680—
790NE⁵902
—685—
2004IllAppLX
[1514
—731—
j 791NE674
d 815NE453
—737—
2004Ill LX
[1676
2005IllAppLX
[39
2005IllAppLX
[42
814NE159
820NE386
—749—
Cir. 7
2004USDist
[LX24698
—763—
807NE1231
—782—
818NE885
—1324—
820NE72

(1) **Vol. 552**

—290—
805NE653
—353—
813NE1157
—398—
f 805NE665
—421—
j 786NE1112
—429—
f 813NE118
—436—
812NE367
—726—
j 2005IllAppLX
[3
f 813NE165
j 813NE167
818NE912
—743—
2004IllAppLX
[1451
788NE233
806NE739
820NE1074

—973—
Cir. 7
2004USDist
[LX12793
2004USDist
[LX22511
2004USDist
[LX23606
—1027—
807NE1048
—1043—
814NE601
—1100—
f 818NE⁴771
—1133—
h 813NE1131
Cir. 7
378F3d⁶651
2004USDist
[LX25707
351FS2d821
—1171—
j 2004IllAppLX
[1563
—1200—
815NE87
—1382—
813NE192
817NE⁷1094

Vol. 553

—21—
2004IllAppLX
[1517
820NE1167
—39—
Cir. 7
392F3d943
2003USDist
[LX25532
—64—
Cir. 7
2004Bankr LX
[2007
—85—
808NE²28
—281—
d 2004Ill LX
[2035
810NE603
e 810NE604
810NE⁵604
810NE¹⁹604
d 810NE605
811NE656
—291—
820NE57
—301—
2005IllAppLX
[23

(3) —316—
2004IllAppLX
[1486
812NE722
—362—
818NE393
—368—
808NE1071
—424—
810NE226
811NE1284
—753—
Cir. 7
2004USDist
[LX23318
—801—
Cir. 7
f 2004USDist
[LX20949
—817—
811NE236
—1112—
Cir. 7
2004USDist
[LX25302
—1174—
Cir. 7
392F3d948
—1181—
f 2005IllAppLX
[38
d 811NE727

Vol. 554

—1—
j 2005IllAppLX
[24
—155—
f 2004IllAppLX
[1473
790NE966
813NE1120
f 820NE1107
—174—
2004Ill LX673
2004Ill LX
[1015
2004IllAppLX
[1449
788NE228
806NE756
821NE649
Cir. 7
2004USDist
[LX10233
—192—
2005IllAppLX
[29
820NE389
f 807NE¹⁷390
807NE¹⁸390
809NE749

810NE589
f 812NE⁴478
f 812NE¹⁷478
813NE⁷101
813NE⁴101
815NE¹⁷767
815NE¹⁸767
—209—
f 2004IllAppLX
[1513
2004IllAppLX
[1590
2005IllAppLX
[77
791NE169
809NE⁴207
d 809NE209
f 810NE³177
810NE⁶177
810NE⁴177
810NE⁵177
817NE938
820NE5
—216—
Cir. 7
360F3d²796
—223—
2005IllAppLX
[49
808NE1135
d 808NE1136
f 808NE1139
809NE²1257
f 809NE⁴1257
f 811NE233
d 811NE¹⁹370
812NE²447
f 816NE1407
817NE1212
f 817NE1216
Cir. 7
d 2004USDist
[LX20704
—240—
806NE711
—244—
f 812NE619
—331—
Cir. 7
2001USDist
[LX25789
—345—
810NE559
—397—
d 2005
[IllAppLX92
—409—
f 811NE290
Cir. 7
2004USDist
[LX24698
—468—
793NE875

—494—
788NE²322
—511—
815NE916
Cir. 7
2004USDist
[LX5187
—534—
2004IllAppLX
[1481
—624—
816NE410
—704—
Cir. 7
2004USDist
[LX12803
—810—
2004IllAppLX
[287
817NE540
—819—
2004IllAppLX
[1525
—961—
d 789NE911
—1071—
809NE134
—1078—
d 2004
[IllAppLX1187
818NE891
—1104—
Cir. 7
393F3d729
—1115—
809NE732
809NE⁷733
815NE1217
815NE1219
—1381—
Vol. 555

—1—
807NE986
—346—
Cir. 1
ca 298FS2d137

—719—
811NE361
816NE717
f 816NE718

Cir. 7
2004USApp
[LX24641
f 2004USDist
[LX7003
—731—
805NE⁴706
—735—
2004Ill LX
[1670
820NE411
—820—
814NE205
Cir. 7
2004USDist
[LX21346
—825—
811NE239
d 811NE240
—993—
Cir. 7
2004USApp
[LX27402
—1047—
Cir. 7
341F3d654
—1126—
817NE1109
—1218—
Cir. 4
ca 325FS2d649

Vol. 556

—236—
790NE46
807NE1115
817NE468
817NE493
—253—
811NE660
—268—
d 817NE945
j 819NE761
—300—
Cir. 7
f 326FS2d915
—539—
808NE1061
—573—
Cir. 7

—671—
e 2004Ill LX
[2030
e 821NE269

(2)

1 Volume numbers
2 Page number
3 LEXIS-only case

Reproduced by permission of LexisNexis. Further reproduction of any kind is strictly prohibited.

ILLUSTRATION 5-8. *Shepard's Case Citations*

United States Citations*
Reports citations to decisions of the U.S. Supreme Court, the U.S.C., the U.S. Constitution, Court Rules, Federal Sentencing Guidelines, and other Federal Regulatory Law
Shepard's Federal Citations
Reports citations to decisions of the U.S. Courts of Appeal, the U.S. District Court, and the U.S. Court of Claims
State, Puerto Rico, and District of Columbia cases
Each state has a Shepard's citator, as does Puerto Rico and the District of Columbia
Assorter Topical and Specialized Citators
Such as *Shepard's Bankruptcy Citations, Shepard's Criminal Justice Citations, Shepard's Environmental Law Citations, Shepard's United States Administrative Citations, Shepard's Employment Law Citations*
Shepard's Regional Citators
Cases of all 50 states divided into nine regions that correspond to West's regional reporter system

---

*Three versions are published: *United States Reports* (the Official Reporter), *Supreme Court Reporter* (West), and *Lawyers' Edition* (LEXIS).

---

the *Northeastern Reporter Second Series* is the correct division. Locate the bound volume number. See Illustrations 5-3, 5-7, and 5-9. In bold at the top corner of the page you will find a volume number. Other volumes may be contained on the same page. If the volume you wish to review is not listed in the corner, scan the page for your volume. Find the page number for the case. See Illustrations 5-3, 5-7, and 5-9. You then must repeat this procedure in each of the *Shepard's* volumes and pamphlets.

Review Illustration 5-12. This is a page from a pamphlet that must be reviewed to completely Shepardize the *Thompson* citation. In Illustration 5-12, the volume number appears on the top of the page in the corner. The page numbers are found in bold in the middle of the page. In Illustration 5-12, the volume number 582 appears boxed in the middle of the page. You then must review the citations listed before it because they refer to volume 581—the volume of the *Thompson* case. Now look for "885," the number referencing the first page of the *Thompson* case. Cases that cite to *Thompson* are listed below that number as they are in Illustration 5-12. Note that the parallel citation for the *Thompson* case is listed in parentheses. Now review Illustration 5-13. This is a supplement to the bound volume and contains newer citing references, if any. No new cases cite to the *Thompson* case in this illustration because "885" does not appear below the volume 581.

Note that the *Shepard's* citations are not Bluebook abbreviations for the reporters and that the number for each series is placed on top of the reporter abbreviations.

ILLUSTRATION 5-9. Printed *Shepard's* Reporter. *Ward v. K-Mart Corp.*, 554 N.E.2d 223 (1990)

NORTHEASTERN REPORTER, 2d SERIES **Vol. 554**

—216—
People v
Brown
1990
(136Il2d116)
(143IlD281)
s 553NE455
556NE901
556NE[1]902
f 565NE[1]1353
f 565NE[2]1354
f 565NE[3]1354
587NE[2]1189
587NE[3]1189
588NE[1]1179
593NE[3]1017
f 599NE[2]948
f 599NE[3]948
f 603NE[2]599
606NE[3]284
608NE606
610NE166
611NE19
612NE[3]901
613NE[2]1279
613NE[3]1279
f 614NE[2]1338
615NE822
619NE[2]222
620NE631
626NE418
626NE[2]423
629NE[2]564
631NE[2]475
631NE[3]475
q 638NE[2]394
d 639NE1366
647NE917
647NE1106
665NE1280
667NE[1]163
f 667NE[2]164
f 667NE[3]164
f 667NE[4]164
693NE[2]873
f 703NE[2]955
709NE[1]713
f 742NE[2]1250
762NE[2]600
762NE[3]600
768NE81
777NE[2]537
Cir. 7
360F3d[2]796
f 2002USDist
[LX11021

(4) **—223—**
Ward v K Mart
Corp.
1990
(136Il2d132)
(143IlD288)
s 540NE1036
2007Ill LX433
f 1999IllApp LX
[705
2001IllApp LX
[931
2006IllApp LX
[1236
560NE[2]23
560NE1102
f 561NE[2]324
562NE[4]403
f 562NE[9]1060
563NE[2]1122
563NE[3]1122
563NE[4]1228
j 563NE1229
f 563NE[5]1229
565NE[3]689
f 566NE241
566NE[4]243
567NE426
f 567NE[9]427
569NE215
d 569NE[7]216
d 569NE[9]216
569NE[2]583
569NE[3]583
570NE[3]1222
e 571NE[4]481
571NE817
d 571NE[6]818
f 571NE[2]1112
f 571NE[3]1112
f 571NE[4]1112
572NE[2]989
578NE[2]602
579NE1020
d 580NE[8]167
d 580NE[9]167
581NE23
581NE[7]888
582NE[3]300
583NE[1]705
584NE[1]161
585NE170
585NE173
585NE[4]173
585NE[1]228
f 586NE[2]378
f 586NE[4]379
e 587NE[5]13
588NE[5]382
j 588NE383
588NE441
d 588NE[9]442
589NE[2]572
589NE[3]572
589NE[9]575
589NE[4]578
f 592NE[3]366
f 592NE[4]366
f 592NE[7]366
f 592NE367
593NE[2]607
j 593NE616
d 593NE994
594NE[3]318
594NE[4]318
e 594NE[9]319
595NE[3]46
f 595NE[7]47
595NE[9]49
f 595NE50
595NE[5]582
f 595NE[1]624
595NE[2]667
595NE[3]667
595NE[4]667
595NE668
e 595NE[9]1103
f 596NE[5]98
598NE[2]343
598NE[4]344
598NE[7]344
599NE[1]1014
599NE1142
f 600NE[2]876
f 600NE[3]876
f 600NE[4]876
d 600NE[9]880
j 600NE884
f 600NE[7]1252
600NE[4]1281
602NE[2]21
602NE[3]22
f 602NE[2]57
f 602NE[3]57
d 602NE58
602NE[4]58
602NE[3]899
602NE[4]899
e 602NE[6]901
603NE[2]17
d 603NE[1]18
603NE[2]819
603NE[3]819
605NE[3]502
d 605NE725
j 605NE727
606NE388
606NE[3]635
606NE753
e 606NE1281
607NE[1]274
f 607NE[4]1286
609NE[8]924
612NE[3]532
612NE[7]889
614NE105
614NE[2]400
614NE1244
614NE[4]1378
614NE1379
f 614NE1380
614NE1382
j 614NE1382
d 615NE867
615NE[8]867
616NE[1]1304
617NE[2]535
e 617NE[5]539
f 617NE[2]1352
d 618NE688
618NE908
620NE[4]665
620NE1086
620NE[4]1087
621NE[6]56
622NE[3]55
d 622NE57
622NE[8]57
623NE[3]954
625NE[6]776
628NE[4]804
628NE[2]876
628NE[3]876
628NE[4]876
d 628NE[9]877
d 629NE537
629NE[1]537
629NE[3]537
629NE[9]538
630NE1020
631NE[1]269
634NE[2]391
634NE1112
634NE[2]1139
635NE1001
f 636NE[4]69
636NE[9]69
636NE962
f 636NE[9]964
f 637NE[2]515
637NE[3]515
637NE[4]515
638NE[2]691
638NE[3]692
638NE[4]692
638NE[5]694
640NE688
f 641NE1231
642NE[4]758
f 642NE830
j 642NE832
643NE[2]861
643NE[3]1360
643NE[5]1365
644NE471
645NE[2]222
646NE[4]646
646NE[3]1308
f 646NE1328
j 646NE1329
646NE1334
j 646NE1335
648NE100
j 648NE101
649NE[2]1326
649NE[3]1326
d 650NE[5]263
650NE[7]263
e 650NE646
650NE[4]647
e 654NE[8]515
654NE[9]515
654NE[2]648
654NE[4]1106
j 654NE1385
657NE19
657NE[2]670
e 660NE[4]148
660NE[9]148
f 660NE[9]224
660NE870
661NE416
662NE[6]566
e 664NE[3]695
665NE831
f 665NE832
665NE[4]836
667NE[1]679
667NE[4]1092
669NE[2]1191
672NE315
672NE[2]372
677NE[4]485
677NE[2]1316
677NE[3]1316
e 677NE1317
677NE[4]1317
679NE1295
d 679NE1296
679NE[9]1296
j 679NE1298
f 680NE[2]412
680NE[2]434
682NE[2]415
f 688NE316
688NE[4]317
689NE[3]157
f 689NE[2]370
692NE[0]1361
f 692NE[5]1362
d 692NE1363
693NE[4]504
694NE1040
694NE[5]1041
694NE[9]1041
f 694NE1042
q 694NE1043
695NE57
f 695NE[4]58
j 695NE59
f 700NE[4]1022
f 701NE[2]193
701NE[4]193
702NE[3]309
702NE1006
706NE[3]446
f 706NE[4]446
706NE[5]447
f 706NE[4]463
f 706NE[2]1040
708NE[2]1221
f 708NE[4]1221
f 710NE[2]124
~ 710NE[2]124
~ 710NE[3]124
f 710NE815
711NE778
f 711NE779
713NE624
j 713NE1290
715NE[3]715
718NE[3]348
f 718NE[2]376
f 719NE[2]180
f 719NE[4]181
721NE624
723NE[2]818
723NE[2]1205
724NE[4]202
f 725NE769
726NE[3]732
726NE[4]732
730NE1134
f 730NE[9]1215
730NE[2]1224
730NE[3]1224
f 730NE[9]1225
732NE599
j 737NE298
737NE676
f 740NE450
740NE[3]450
740NE[7]450
747NE[5]382
751NE[3]147
753NE1010
753NE1127
758NE[3]486
758NE[4]486
759NE33
760NE995
763NE[3]796
763NE[9]796
766NE[3]1123
f 766NE[4]1124
768NE[3]51
768NE[4]51
772NE223
d 772NE[9]224
774NE[3]854
778NE[8]289
778NE[9]289
d 778NE290
781NE[3]635
f 781NE[4]635
782NE[3]714
782NE[5]716
782NE[6]716
785NE[2]946
785NE[3]946
f 796NE1046
796NE[3]1047
796NE[2]1068
798NE[3]734
f 799NE741
799NE[4]742
805NE[5]705
808NE1135
d 808NE1136
f 808NE1139
809NE[2]1257
f 809NE[4]1257
f 811NE233
d 811NE[19]370
812NE[2]447
f 816NE[2]407
817NE[2]1212
817NE[3]1213
f 817NE1216
817NE[9]1216
823NE1019
824NE664
830NE729
d 831NE1190
d 832NE282

Continued

447

ILLUSTRATION 5-9. *Continued*

(3) **Vol. 554**   NORTHEASTERN REPORTER, 2d SERIES

832NE²361	f 2006USDist	584NE²1043	(143IID309)	—263—
f 832NE935	[LX10766	595NE²547	2003IIIApp LX	People v Smith
e 832NE935	2006USDist	598NE¹1375	[88	1989
849NE1088	[LX11971	598NE²1375	568NE908	(1971IA226)
851NE115	f 773FS²113	599NE²554	571NE²1092	(143IID328)
j 851NE289	f 778FS²957	607NE¹152	571NE³1092	d 577NE1299
851NE783	f 778FS³957	608NE141	c 598NE437	d 577NE²1300
852NE556	f 789FS²942	621NE63	603NE737	—266—
856NE1057	816FS²1321	627NE1238	624NE⁸440	Mondelli v
857NE944	832FS²236	627NE¹1239	626NE331	Checker Taxi
f 857NE946	840FS537	627NE²1241	f 637NE674	Co.
860NE484	964FS²1252	627NE³1241	678NE⁶62	1990
Cir. 1	994FS986	j 627NE1245	703NE985	(1971IA258)
937FS1009	8FS2d762	628NE²871	727NE⁶198	(143IID331)
Cir. 2	151FS2d³961	628NE³871	c 795NE685	567NE1365
225F3d119	369FS2d1006	632NE¹272	796NE685	576NE²¹1077
2007USDist	f 369FS2d1007	d 636NE1037	807NE673	578NE¹1219
[LX149	384FS2d1235	638NE¹212	f 812NE619	584NE¹972
410FS2d346	f 422FS2d931	650NE1014	Cir. 7	587NE⁴591
Cir. 5	h 422FS2d932	656NE1067	74F3d131	594NE1324
2002USDist	442FS2d550	660NE1300	d 796FS⁷1129	594NE³1327
[LX16713	d 442FS2d553	676NE¹1340	—251—	602NE¹⁴885
Cir. 7	Cir. 8	677NE834	Northbrook	604NE¹1149
f 1999USApp	f 202FS2d956	d 684NE³177	Nat'l Ins. Co. v	605NE¹³508
[LX434	e 202FS2d958	687NE28	Nehoc Adver-	d 605NE¹1074
945F2d959	202FS2d⁸959	f 703NE94	tising Service,	633NE²³884
e 965F2d⁹1423	202FS2d⁹959	714NE507	Inc.	634NE⁴1326
57F3d584	d 202FS2d960	714NE²509	1989	652NE¹⁴1303
153F3d481	Mass	714NE³509	(1961IA448)	658NE⁶1183
157F3d²1110	726NE956	d 714NE510	(143IID316)	660NE¹⁴144
178F3d⁶485	Ohio	~ 714NE511	570NE³872	660NE¹⁵144
186F3d²979	j 597NE509	753NE520	611NE³114	736NE178
211F3d⁴1015	c 788NE1090	753NE¹1161	612NE³105	759NE¹⁴34
211F3d⁷1015	Del	768NE²114	619NE²716	826NE1008
362F3d952	604A2d397	d 768NE115	659NE²22	—285—
474F3d957	Mich	d 772NE288		
14Fed Appx	485NW682	781NE306		
[698	491NW219	807NE7		
21Fed Appx	656NW873	f 807NE8		
[494	Miss	835NE929		
1998USDist	641So2d24	op 839NE505		
[LX14097	Mont	839NE²505		
1998USDist	f 950P2d756	f 842NE1190		
[LX15790	N M	Cir. 7		
f 1998USDist	804P2d1110	d 2006USDist		
[LX16897	N D	[LX4630		
1998USDist	676NW770	—240—		(143IID322)
[LX19261	R I	In re Marriage		s 666NE726
1999USDist	732A2d718	of Fowler		587NE60
[LX19804	Tenn	1990		587NE70
f 2001USDist	f 966SW41	(1971IA95)		597NE⁴784
[LX655	Wash	(143IID305)		d 625NE685
2001USDist	72P3d1101	624NE¹1237		625NE⁶685
[LX7478	Wyo	714NE1096		d 639NE239
2002USDist	868P2d896	719NE328		684NE412
[LX2070	868P2d897	806NE711		e 684NE413
2002USDist	—235—	Calif		684NE⁵413
[LX4658	People v	283CaR409		684NE⁶413
2002USDist	Morris	812P2d590		Cir. 7
[LX5467	1990	118A3394n		084F2d218
f 2002USDist	(136I2d157)	—244—		Cir. 8
[LX11206	(143IID300)	Schackleton v		19F3d1277
2004USDist	563NE²1244	Federal Signal		Ark
[LX11140	566NE¹989	Corp.		r 570NE331
d 2004USDist	576NE¹398	1989		s 555NE379
[LX20704	576NE399	(1961IA437)		s 581NE248
	582NE¹742			

Third column right portion (—263— continued / —298— / —305— / —313— / —294—):

—298—	—305—	—313—	—294—
Klebs v	Mercado v	In re Darnell J.	People v
Trzoski	Calumet	1990	Fabing
1990	Federal Sav. &	(1961IA510)	1990
(1961IA472)	Loan Ass'n	(143IID378)	(1961IA495)
(143IID363)	1990	Cert den	(143IID359)
558NE¹³1361	(1961IA483)	561NE688	570NE331
f 580NE⁶1193	(143IID370)	f 561NE¹1243	555NE379
617NE876	593NE⁶110	f 561NE²1243	581NE248
697NE⁵1197	594NE1312	583NE558	583NE⁵559
e 707NE76		583NE²558	669NE²1228
707NE¹577		f 583NE⁵559	f 684NE²895
j 804NE1135		669NE²1228	684NE¹896
Fla		f 684NE²895	719NE354
617So2d308		684NE¹896	
Haw		719NE354	
f 52P3d260			
j 52P3d293			
Nebr			
514NW645			
84A3681n			
84A3697n			
87A3579n			
~ 87A3604n			

> 1 **Circuit court cases are listed below circuit number**
> 2 **Reference to A.L.R.**
> 3 **Volume number**
> 4 **Page number**

Reproduced by permission of LexisNexis. Further reproduction of any kind is strictly prohibited.

ILLUSTRATION 5-10. *Shepard's* **List of Citing Sources for Illinois Citations**

SCOPE OF CITING SOURCES

The citations appearing in *Shepard's Illinois Citations* were obtained from the following publications through:

(1) STATE COURT DECISIONS

Illinois Reports	Vols. 1 Ill to 208 Il2d p. 38
Illinois Appellate Court Reports	Vols. 1 IlA to 344 Il3a p. 466
Illinois Decisions	Vols. 1 IlD to 281 IlD p. 518
Illinois Circuit Court Reports	Vols. 1 IlCC to 3 IlCC p. 524
Illinois Court of Claims	Vols. 1 IlCCL to 48 IlCCL p. 666
Opinions of the Attorney General of Illinois	1906 IlAG to 2003 IlAGN 8
Northeastern Reporter (Illinois Cases)	Vols. 1 NE to 803 NE p. 1289
Illinois Supreme Court LEXIS Documents (Ill LX)	as received
Illinois Appellate Court LEXIS Documents (IllApp LX)	as received

(2) FEDERAL COURT DECISIONS

United States Reports	Vols. 1 US to 538 US p. 1301
United States Supreme Court Reports, Lawyers' Edition	Vols. 1 LE to 158 LE p. 165
Supreme Court Reporter	Vols. 1 SC to 124 SC p. 1303
Federal Cases	Vols. 1 FC to 30 FC
Federal Reporter	Vols. 1 F to 358 F3d p. 1352
Federal Appendix	Vols. 1 Fed Appx to 87 Fed Appx p. 184
Federal Supplement	Vols. 1 FS to 299 FS2d p. 1368
Federal Rules Decisions	Vols. 1 FRD to 219 FRD p. 549
Federal Claims Reporter	Vols. 21 FedCl to 59 FedCl p. 360
Bankruptcy Reporter	Vols. 1 BRW to 303 BRW p. 866
Court of Claims	Vols. 1 CCL to 231 CCL p. 1041
Claims Court Reporter	Vols. 1 CIC to 26 CIC p. 1477
Military Justice Reporter	Vols. 1 MJ to 59 MJ p. 724
United States Supreme Court LEXIS Documents (US LX)	as received
United States Courts of Appeals LEXIS Documents (USApp LX)	as received
United States District Courts LEXIS Documents (USDist LX)	
United States Court of Federal Claims LEXIS Documents (U	
United States Bankruptcy Court LEXIS Documents (USBan	
United States Court of Appeals for the Armed Forces	
LEXIS Documents (CAAF LX)	
United States Military Courts of Criminal Appeals LEXIS D	
(CCA LX)	as received

> 1 State court decisions included
> 2 Federal court decisions included
> 3 Law reviews cited

(3) LAW REVIEWS

Chicago Kent Law Review	Vols. 1 CK to 79 CK p. 317
DePaul Law Review	Vols. 1 DeP to 53 DeP p. 159
Illinois Bar Journal	Vols. 5 IBJ to 21 ILJ p. 331
Illinois Law Bulletin	Vols. 1 ILB to 4 ILB p. 1

ILLUSTRATION 5-11.   Front Cover of a *Shepard's* Cumulative
Supplement Detailing Volumes and Pamphlets to Review

VOL. 100	MAY 2008	NO. 5

Shepard's Northeastern Reporter Citations

Annual Cumulative Supplement

Part A

WHAT YOUR LIBRARY SHOULD CONTAIN

2007 Bound Volumes (Volumes 1–16)*

*Supplemented with:
  –May 2008 Annual Cumulative Supplement Vol. 100 No. 5
    (Parts A and B)

DISCARD ALL OTHER ISSUES

LexisNexis®

ILLUSTRATION 5-12.   Page from *Shepard's Illinois Citations*

NORTHEASTERN REPORTER, 2d SERIES (Illinois Cases)   Vol. 582 ①

—786—	—837—	—892—	j 659NE447	634NE⁶391
(221IlA140)	(221IlA295)	(221IlA311)		637NE²1200
645NE²559	s 632NE335	614NE873	**Vol. 582** ①	638NE²222
	618NE1164			639NE1289
—788—		—895—		641NE914
(221IlA143)	—839—	(221IlA192)	—71—	643NE⁴1328
665NE⁵1317	(221IlA298)	d 614NE1292	(144Il2d482)	644NE²35
	612NE⁵1353	614NE²1293	614NE¹⁰12	646NE³933
—793—	622NE²886	668NE¹¹1022	622NE781	646NE³933
(221IlA25)	j 658NE1261		622NE²782	657NE⁴671
629NE⁸156	666NE877	—898—	628NE490	660NE⁴224
638NE⁸298	669NE²¹1239	(221IlA177)	631NE382	665NE⁴1267
j 669NE1278			641NE⁷318	669NE⁴652
	—842—	—901—	d 641NE319	674NE1275
—800—	(221IlA154)	(221IlA182)	641NE⁶319	Cir. 7
(220IlA1093)	630NE809	642NE¹¹1266	649NE599	f 884FS1177
	645NE355	645NE³²40	651NE149	950FS⁴1389
—804—			658NE¹⁸402	950FS⁵1389
(221IlA35)	—849—	—904—	658NE¹⁴403	
627NE²273	(221IlA150)	(221IlA187)	665NE1281	—114—
e 655NE923			665NE1304	(145Il2d1)
	—852—	—907—	670NE618	612NE1063
—809—	(221IlA287)	(221IlA195)	670NE648	
(221IlA222)	f 615NE⁷751			▓ **1 Volume number**
672NE864	625NE126	—911—	—89—	**2 Page number for**
	656NE442	(221IlA199)	(145Il2d127)	*Thompson* **case**
—817—		Cir. 7	US cert den	
(221IlA234)	—857—	883FS1142	119LE590	(145Il2d100)
617NE841	(221IlA326)	12A3171n	US cert den	f 617NE⁷858
617NE¹843			112SC2970	617NE⁷875
d 626NE1388	—860—	—914—	US cert den	617NE¹1246
e 628NE219	(221IlA330)	(221IlA205)	116SC194	625NE²716
e 628NE220	662NE²601	Cir. 7	cc 649NE364	625NE⁴717
d 636NE1106		882FS724	f 616NE329	637NE²556
655NE¹955	—864—		620NE⁷337	638NE¹665
	(221IlA164)	—1189—	620NE351	642NE⁸851
—819—	613NE743	(221IlA354)	626NE⁷156	642NE¹886
(221IlA241)	625NE1140	cc 104F3d926	631NE⁴13	j 651NE132
s 623NE841	625NE¹⁸1144	cc 888FS909	f 637NE1015	660NE²1313
612NE⁷1011	626NE⁷756	613NE387	f 643NE²⁷810	660NE⁴1313
615NE⁷1157	j 665NE1344	631NE841	645NE856	666NE²55
627NE376			f 645NE²²876	
633NE⁴854	—873—	—1202—	651NE92	—125—
664NE⁶317	(221IlA336)	(221IlA373)	658NE¹⁸410	(145Il2d43)
664NE¹317		615NE⁴1351	665NE⁶793	v 121LE5
677NE⁴442	—877—	633NE34	670NE¹⁷660	v 113SC32
	(221IlA317)	634NE1309	675NE933	615NE784
—822—	616NE⁴1012	634NE¹1312		f 621NE20
(221IlA219)	616NE⁸1012	649NE⁴1000	—108—	626NE⁴¹156
	622NE⁴101	652NE424	(144Il2d535)	628NE495
—824—	628NE⁸207	672NE²409	615NE⁴51	628NE¹²1065
(221IlA47)	631NE²265		618NE²976	629NE581
613NE319	636NE⁸1149	—1208—	619NE767	630NE⁸1274
f 613NE321	658NE⁸505	(221IlA383)	620NE⁴666	631NE⁸1324
638NE²¹146		627NE⁸58	621NE⁷54	636NE452
654NE²611	—882—	653NE⁸441	j 621NE912	g 636NE502
654NE⁸611	(221IlA267)		623NE⁴843	f 636NE¹¹661
662NE136		—1213—	623NE⁵843	f 636NE¹²661
668NE¹¹	—885— ②	(221IlA390)	623NE⁸845	f 636NE¹³661
668NE⁸	(221IlA263)	615NE⁷28	623NE⁸846	645NE269
668NE³¹121	648NE⁸100	625NE1052	630NE⁴1175	645NE¹²394
—831—	j 648NE101	f 657NE⁴1035	630NE⁸1329	661NE519
(221IlA44)	650NE⁴262	657NE⁸1035	j 632NE680	663NE⁸147
			633NE²989	665NE¹²1305
—833—	—889—	—1219—	634NE²308	665NE¹³1305
(221IlA275)	(221IlA272)	(221IlA400)	634NE⁴391	
		625NE938		

665NE⁴¹1312
665NE³⁹1316
504US724
119LE500
112SC2227
—164—
(145Il2d13)
626NE1213
32A3679n
—173—
(144Il2d525)
US cert den
121LE59
US cert den
113SC99
625NE768
628NE1023
637NE1038
640NE1342
655NE²887
US cert den
112SC1953
613NE287
617NE²249
619NE227
625NE1064
628NE⁶173
d 632NE1013
640NE944
640NE977
j 642NE1246
d 650NE982
657NE646
663NE1121
668NE580
Cir. 7
158BRW742
—183—
Case 1
657NE1093
—183—
Case 2
(221IlA586)
617NE501
—185—
(221IlA858)
613NE²830
—189—
(221IlA574)
—192—
(221IlA280)
f 638NE²331
Continued

325

Reproduced by permission of LexisNexis. Further reproduction of any kind is strictly prohibited.

You can review cases by either official or parallel citations. For example, you can find the *Thompson* citation under the listings for *Northeastern Reporter Second Series, Illinois Appellate Reports Third Series,* or *Illinois Decisions.* A U.S. Supreme Court decision can be found based on its citation in *U.S. Reports, U.S. Supreme Court Reports, Lawyers' Edition,* and *U.S. Supreme Court* reporter. For your research to be complete, you must consult multiple citation services whenever possible. This

ILLUSTRATION 5-13. Page from *Shepard's Illinois Citations*

NORTHEASTERN REPORTER, 2d SERIES (Illinois Cases)　　①Vol. 582

—137—
Case 1
s 1998
[IllAppLX194
s 693NE426

—139—
683NE¹⁸520

—191—
680NE¹⁸422
Cir. 7
d 1998USDist
[LX3988
1998USDist
[LX5095

—586—
1998IllAppLX
[²236
693NE²510

—619—
682NE435

—655—
1997IllAppLX
[539
681NE¹149
684NE⁹820

—887—
f 678NE⁴1044

—903—
c 687NE²530
j 687NE532

—1198—
Cir. 7
962FS³1053
966FS749
d 1996Bankr LX
[1202

—1220—
682NE1213
682NE³1215
57Ab15n

—1246—
687NE900

—1274—
e 682NE²⁹1119

—1342—
683NE153
683NE1010

①Vol. 581

—1—
f 1998IllAppLX
[320

—19—
Cir. 7
1998USDist
[LX2459

—44—
689NE359
689NE379
Cir. 7
f 1998USDist
[LX1048

—67—
691NE832

—73—
689NE²408

—90—
1998IllAppLX
[²138
692NE²798
Cir. 7
1998USDist
[LX2878
967FS³1048
967FS³1048

—118—
1998IllAppLX
[314
f 678NE⁴362
691NE⁴83

—138—
684NE¹801
685NE¹875
685NE²875

—145—
1998IllAppLX
[274

—154—
d 690NE159

—158—
682NE99
682NE303
f 691NE³45
691NE⁵46

—175—
1998IllAppLX
[³103
679NE³434
692NE³717

—180—
f 683NE²1259
Cir. 7
979FS⁴739

—191—
f 682NE1140

—196—
683NE²519

—236—
1998IllAppLX
[³191
1998IllAppLX
[⁴191
c 1998
[IllAppLX191
c 693NE436

—275—
691NE⁸116

—288—
Cir. 7
127F3d⁵579

—293—
cc 1998USDist
[LX4907

—329—
1998IllAppLX
[³302

—367—
1998IllAppLX
[²171
692NE²1290

—383—
1998IllAppLX
[156
692NE1226

—426—
686NE²621
f 686NE622

—637—
Cir. 1
954FS⁴436

—644—
683NE⁷932
683NE1271

—648—
1998IllAppLX
[130
685NE427
691NE98
693NE869

—651—
681NE¹547
681NE²601

—656—
1998IllAppLX
[⁴325
678NE²1105
f 688NE³84

—664—
1998IllAppLX
[⁸297
682NE⁴104
682NE³1142
682NE²1198
686NE⁸64
Cir. 3
976FS⁴296
Cir. 7
121F3d³1105
1998USDist
[LX1726
1998USDist
[LX6188
979FS⁴654

—669—
Cir. 7
956FS⁸818
211BRW280

—678—
f 1997IllAppLX
[527
f 682NE¹749
682NE²749
f 682NE750
682NE⁴750
682NE⁶752

—715—
683NE1000

—716—
683NE²457
683NE⁴457
683NE⁶457
690NE⁹1029

—728—
682NE218

—730—
f 688NE148
688NE⁸148

—739—
687NE³875

—759—
681NE¹⁸567
f 681NE568
c 681NE568

—819—
684NE⁹828

—860—
Cir. 7
1997Bankr LX
[1258
215BRW168
215BRW⁹374

—864—
689NE¹²676

689NE¹⁴676

—877—
678NE⁸379
686NE⁸1253

—882—
684NE1038
687NE¹1198
687NE¹1198
687NE³1198

—895—
f 1998IllAppLX
[¹184
f 693NE¹393

—911—
691NE²128

—1202—
691NE106
691NE¹107

①Vol. 582

②—89—
US cert den
516US872
680NE³306
j 685NE907

—108—
h 1998
[IllAppLX
1998IllA

1 Volume numbers
2 Page numbers

1998IllAppLX
[⁴216
j 1998IllAppLX
[216
1998IllAppLX
[³302
678NE³28
678NE³52
678NE⁴52
678NE⁶52
680NE⁴434
681NE³1068
f 682NE⁴1243
f 688NE⁸84
688NE²1175
690NE³622
j 693NE500
Cir. 7
1998USDist
[LX743
1998USDist
[LX2829

—120—
682NE³289
682NE⁴289

—125—
s 1998Ill LX
[361
1998Ill LX353
1998IllAppLX
[⁴⁷314

685NE906
688NE⁴⁷663
j 688NE666

—173—
e 685NE895
687NE⁴1075

—196—
682NE169

—200—
f 688NE⁴690
Cir. 7
1998USDist
[LX600

—227—
691NE³152

—265—
689NE²230

—271—
f 679NE³430

—274—
681NE⁵558
681NE¹563

679NE⁸94
680NE⁴434
681NE²92
684NE²171
687NE²546
689NE²261
690NE²1050
691NE³397

—308—
688NE³128

—317—
e 1998
[IllAppLX³177
e 692NE²831

—685—
Case 2
681NE162
691NE30

—690—
687NE1123
f 687NE1124
690NE³139

459

ensures that you will review the different sources *Shepard's* reviewed to compile a citation list.

▼ Which Citator Should You Consult for State Cases?

For state cases, you should begin with the state *Shepard's,* if available to you.

Find the official citation, if one exists, and review it. Then review the regional citation. Next, if available, review the regional *Shepard's* citator that includes that state. If you have access to a relevant topical citator, review that citator.

PRACTICE POINTER

Update any print *Shepard's* with the most current online information.

 *NET NOTE*

You can subscribe to *Shepard's* online and access daily updates within 24 to 48 hours of a decision.

B. *SHEPARD'S* ONLINE

▼ How Do You Use *Shepard's* Online?

You can access *Shepard's* online at <u>lexis.com</u> and <u>law.lexisnexis.com/ shepards</u> during any point in your research. It cannot be accessed through WESTLAW.

At the Web site, after you log on, with a click of a mouse, you can access a box to enter a citation and ask the computer to find the *Shepard's* report. See Illustration 5-14.

▼ Is *Shepard's* Online More Current Than *Shepard's* in Print?

The online *Shepard's* on LEXIS is more up to date than the print *Shepard's*. You can access daily updates.

▼ How Is *Shepard's* Different Online Than in Hard Copy?

First, the online document provides you with a *Shepard's* listing only for the case you are reviewing. See Illustration 5-2. It provides the parallel citations. Compare Illustrations 5-1 and 5-2. See also Illustration 5-15. This illustration explains the advantages of using the computerized *Shepard's* citations. The computer record of the *Shepard's* search is easier to read. Listing only one case eliminates the possibility of confusion, which often occurs with the print *Shepard's* materials. Computerized

ILLUSTRATION 5-14.   *Shepard's* Search on LexisNexis

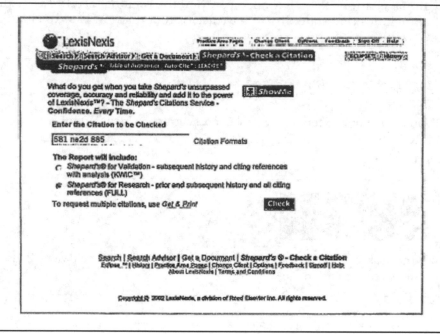

Reproduced by permission of LexisNexis. Further reproduction of any kind is strictly prohibited.

Shepard's also facilitates notetaking because the *Shepard's* can be printed, often on a single page, and does not involve the painstaking task of writing each notation. This also minimizes notetaking errors. One of the other advantages of *Shepard's* online is that the computer automatically reviews all of the *Shepard's* volumes and provides one complete list of all the *Shepard's* citations.

As you learned earlier, a print search of the same citation would require you to review multiple volumes. The computer system is much easier to use because you only need to push a few buttons or click a mouse. It also is much quicker. In addition, the computer search will find *Shepard's* citations contained in different *Shepard's* citators. For example, a search online of the *Thompson* case produces the reports of the *Shepard's Illinois Citator* and the *Shepard's Northeastern Reporter Citations* because the computer searches multiple citators at one time. The publisher's *Shepard's* treatments also are easier to understand online because the publisher includes a full word and graphic signals to tell you the value of a case. Another advantage is that you often can immediately access the citing cases online by clicking the mouse on the hyperlinked number. After you retrieve the *Shepard's* cases, you will be able to perform word searches to narrow your results. The computer system allows you to design your *Shepard's* research so that you retrieve only the cases that have a negative impact on your case. You also can retrieve cases that contain only a particular headnote or are

ILLUSTRATION 5-15. Advantages of Computerized Citation Reports

Easier to Use

—simple click of a mouse or a few buttons
—searches multiple volumes in seconds
—searches multiple citators at the same time

Easier to Read

—only one case is displayed at one time
—eliminates the confusion that often occurs with the print *Shepard's* materials

Shepard's Treatments Easier to Understand

—explained with a word; for example, the letter "E" found in the print materials is listed as "Explained" in the computerized *Shepard's* listing

Printing Function Saves Time

Allows User Immediate Access to Citing Cases Online

Shepard's Allows the User to Limit the Search of Citing References According to the User's Needs

—LEXIS: *Shepard's* searches can be limited to a particular history, treatment, or headnote number
—On LEXIS *Shepard's* includes references to LEXIS headnotes

decided by a specific court. With LEXIS, you would perform a focus search. You also may filter your search results to include a particular jurisdiction, headnote, vital points of law or fact patterns, dates, or *Shepard's* treatments such as followed by or overruled.

In addition, *Shepard's* has signal aids to help you know whether to either proceed in using an authority, to use the authority with caution, or to not use the authority. At the top of the *Shepard's* result, an orange Q may appear. That indicates that opinions exist that question the validity or precedential value of the case. A red stop sign indicates that the case is no longer good law. Other signals also appear in color. See Illustration 5-16 including a yellow triangle indicating that a researcher should use caution before relying on that case.

ILLUSTRATION 5-16. *Shepard's* Online Signal Indications

The *Shepard's* Signal™

The *Shepard's* Signal Marker indicates the standing of your case as treated by other cases (your **Cited Case**).

NOTE:

The **Cited Case** is the case you are *Shepardizing*™. The **Citing References** are citations in your *Shepard's* report that cite the case you are *Shepardizing*.

Signal

Description

Detail

Warning

Negative treatment indicated.

Includes the following analyses:

- Overruled by
- Superceded by
- Revoked
- Obsolete
- Rescinded

Questioned

Validity questioned by citing references.

Includes the following analyses:

- Questioned by

Caution

ILLUSTRATION 5-16. *Continued*

Possible negative treatment indicated.

Includes the following analyses:

- Limited
- Criticized by
- Clarified
- Modified
- Corrected

Positive

Positive treatment indicated.

Includes the following analyses:

- Followed
- Affirmed
- Approved

Citing References with Analysis

Other cases cited the case and assigned some analysis that is not considered positive or negative.

Includes the following analyses:

- Appeal denied by
- Writ of certiorari denied

Citation Information

References have not applied any analysis to the citation. For example the case was cited by case law or law reviews that do not warrant an analysis.

Includes the analysis Cited by.

NOTE:

Refer to the *Shepard's*® Citations Service Analysis Definitions for a complete list of analysis codes and definitions.

ETHICS ALERT

Some courts may sanction attorneys if they provide cases that are no longer good law to support their claims.

C. KEYCITE

WESTLAW provides a service called **KeyCite** that competes with *Shepard's*. See Illustrations 5-17 and 5-18.

KeyCite approves the direct history of a case as well as any case that impact the precedential value of a case. With it you can also retrieve all citing references that are contained within WESTLAW, including thousands of unpublished decisions as well as published cases, secondary sources, appellate briefs, trial motions, memoranda, and affidavits.

ILLUSTRATION 5-17. Screen Shot of WESTLAW KeyCite Result for *Thompson v. Economy Super Marts, Inc.*

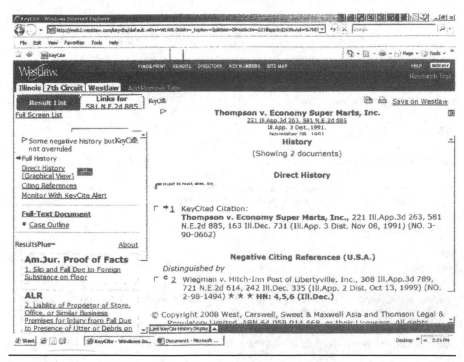

Reprinted with permission of Thomson Reuters/West.

ILLUSTRATION 5-18. WESTLAW PDF Printout of KeyCite Results for *Thompson v. Economy Super Marts, Inc.*

Westlaw.

Date of Printing: JUL 03,2008

KEYCITE

▷Thompson v. Economy Super Marts, Inc., 221 Ill.App.3d 263, 581 N.E.2d 885, 163 Ill.Dec. 731 (Ill.App. 3 Dist., Nov 08, 1991) (NO. 3-90-0662)

History

Direct History

=> 1 **Thompson v. Economy Super Marts, Inc.,** 221 Ill.App.3d 263, 581 N.E.2d 885, 163 Ill.Dec. 731 (Ill.App. 3 Dist. Nov 08, 1991) (NO. 3-90-0662)

Negative Citing References (U.S.A.)

Distinguished by

C 2 Wiegman v. Hitch-Inn Post of Libertyville, Inc., 308 Ill.App.3d 789, 721 N.E.2d 614, 242 Ill.Dec. 335 (Ill.App. 2 Dist. Oct 13, 1999) (NO. 2-98-1494) ★ ★ ★ **HN: 4,5,6 (Ill.Dec.)**

Citing References

Positive Cases (U.S.A.)

★★★ **Discussed**

H 3 Miller v. National Ass'n of Realtors, 648 N.E.2d 98, 100+, 271 Ill.App.3d 653, 657+, 207 Ill.Dec. 642, 644+ (Ill.App. 1 Dist. Nov 30, 1994) (NO. 1-92-1908) " **HN: 3,4 (Ill.Dec.)**

C 4 Jackson v. U.S. Postal Service, 2007 WL 1385368, *3+ (N.D.Ill. May 02, 2007) (NO. 06 C 2067) **HN: 5 (Ill.Dec.)**

★★ **Cited**

H 5 Kellermann v. Car City Chevrolet-Nissan, Inc., 713 N.E.2d 1285, 1288+, 306 Ill.App.3d 285, 288+, 239 Ill.Dec. 435, 438+ (Ill.App. 5 Dist. Jul 21, 1999) (NO. 5-98-0142) **HN: 1,2 (Ill.Dec.)**

▷ 6 Wind v. Hy-Vee Food Stores, Inc., 650 N.E.2d 258, 262, 272 Ill.App.3d 149, 155, 208 Ill.Dec. 801, 805 (Ill.App. 3 Dist. May 10, 1995) (NO. 3-94-0631) **HN: 1 (Ill.Dec.)**

C 7 Byrd-Tolson v. Supervalu, Inc., 500 F.Supp.2d 962, 970 (N.D.Ill. Jun 12, 2007) (NO. 06 C 3818) **HN: 1 (Ill.Dec.)**

▷ 8 Ortega v. Kmart Corp., 114 Cal.Rptr.2d 470, 480, 36 P.3d 11, 19, 26 Cal.4th 1200, 1212, 01 Cal. Daily Op. Serv. 10,516, 10516, 2001 Daily Journal D.A.R. 13,099, 13099 (Cal. Dec 20, 2001) (NO. S091888) **HN: 2 (Ill.Dec.)**

★ **Mentioned**

ILLUSTRATION 5-18. *Continued*

9 Varner v. Johnson, 40 Fed.Appx. 997, 1001 (7th Cir.(Ill.) Jul 18, 2002) (Table, text in WEST-LAW, NO. 01-3284) **HN: 4 (Ill.Dec.)**

▷ 10 Lane v. Hardee's Food Systems, Inc., 184 F.3d 705, 707 (7th Cir.(Ill.) Jul 22, 1999) (NO. 98-3935) **HN: 4 (Ill.Dec.)**

Secondary Sources (U.S.A.)

C 11 Liability of operator of grocery store to invitee slipping on spilled liquid or semiliquid substance, 24 A.L.R.4th 696 (1983)

C 12 Store or business premises slip-and-fall: Modern status of rules requiring showing of notice of proprietor of transitory interior condition allegedly causing plaintiff's fall, 85 A.L.R.3d 1000 (1978)

C 13 Liability of proprietor of store, office, or similar business premises for injury from fall due to presence of litter or debris on floor, 61 A.L.R.2d 6 (1958)

14 10 Causes of Action 605, Cause of Action by Customer for Injury Suffered in Grocery Store Slip and Fall (2008)

15 Premises Liability s 49:1, s 49:1. Spill notice requirement (2007) **HN: 4,5,6 (Ill.Dec.)**

16 Premises Liability s 49:5, s 49:5. Produce spills (2007) **HN: 6 (Ill.Dec.)**

17 28 Am. Jur. Proof of Facts 2d 167, Slip and Fall Due to Foreign Substance on Floor (2008)

18 Illinois Law and Practice Negligence s 43, s 43. Duty Owed to Invitees, Generally (2008) **HN: 2,3,4 (Ill.Dec.)**

Court Documents

Appellate Court Documents (U.S.A.)

Appellate Briefs

19 Alejandro TORRES, a/k/a Alexander Torres, Plaintiff-Appellant, v. TGI FRIDAY'S, a Foreign Corporation, Defendant-Appellee., 2007 WL 1231959, *1231959+ (Appellate Brief) (7th Cir. 2007) **Brief of Defendant-Appellee Tgi Friday's, a ...** (NO. 07-1107) ★ ★ ★ **HN: 6 (Ill.Dec.)**

20 Lenora REID, Plaintiff-Appellant, v. KOHL'S DEPARTMENT STORES, INC., Defendant-Appellee., 2007 WL 5083712, *5083712+ (Appellate Brief) (7th Cir. 2007) **Brief of Appellee, Kohl's Department Stores, Inc.** (NO. 07-3916) ★ ★ ★ **HN: 6 (Ill.Dec.)**

21 Lenora REID, Plaintiff-Appellant, v. KOHL'S DEPARTMENT STORES, INC., Defendant-Appellee., 2007 WL 5129370, *5129370+ (Appellate Brief) (7th Cir. 2007) **Reply Brief of Plaintiff-Appellant, Lenora Reid** (NO. 07-3916) ★ ★ **HN: 6 (Ill.Dec.)**

22 Dolores HOWARD, Plaintiff-Appellee, v. WAL-MART STORES, INC., et al., Defendant-Appellant., 1998 WL 34180104, *34180104+ (Appellate Brief) (7th Cir. Jul 07, 1998) **Brief of Plaintiff-Appellee Dolores Howard** (NO. 98-1781) ★ ★ **HN: 4,5 (Ill.Dec.)**

23 Dolores HOWARD, Plaintiff-Appellee, v. WAL-MART STORES, INC., Defendant-Appellant., 1998 WL 34180103, *34180103+ (Appellate Brief) (7th Cir. Jun 10, 1998) **Brief of Defendant-Appellant Wal-Mart Stores, Inc.** (NO. 98-1781) ★ ★ ★ **HN: 4,5 (Ill.Dec.)**

ILLUSTRATION 5-18. *Continued*

24 Ingrid COWAN, Appellant, v. ELLISON ENTERPRISES, INC., Appellee., 2005 WL 3627797, *3627797+ (Appellate Brief) (Ark.App. Mar 28, 2005) **Abstract and Brief for Appellee** (NO. CA-04-01281) ★ ★ **HN: 4 (Ill.Dec.)**

25 Ortega v. KMart Corp., 2001 WL 1768401, *6+ (Appellate Brief) (Cal. Jan 17, 2001) **PETITIONER KMART CORPORATION'S OPENING BRIEF ON ...** (NO. S091888) " ★ ★ ★ **HN: 1,2 (Ill.Dec.)**

26 Lettie WOODS, Plaintiff-Appellant, v. JEWEL FOOD STORES, INC., Defendant-Appellee., 2002 WL 32329052, *32329052+ (Appellate Brief) (Ill.App. 1 Dist. Feb 19, 2002) **Brief and Argument of Defendant-Appellee Jewel ...** (NO. 1-01-3269) ★ ★ ★ **HN: 2,4,5 (Ill.Dec.)**

27 Hilel H. LEWIN, Plaintiffs-Appellants, v. NATIONAL RAILROAD PASSENGER CORP., Individually and d/b/a Amtrak; Northeast Illinois Regional Commuter Railroad Corp., Individually and d/b/a Metra/Metropolitan Rail and Chicago Union Station Company, Defendants-Appellees., 2001 WL 34366054, *34366054+ (Appellate Brief) (Ill.App. 1 Dist. Dec 19, 2001) **Reply Brief for Plaintiff-Appellant Hilel H. Lewin** (NO. 1-01-2323) ★ ★ ★ **HN: 6 (Ill.Dec.)**

28 Hilel H. LEWIN, Plaintiff-Appellant, v. NATIONAL RAILROAD PASSENGER CORP., Individually and d/b/a Amtrak, Northeast Illinois Regional Commuter Railroad Corp., Individually and d/b/a Metra/Metropolitan Rail and Chicago Union Station Company, Defendant-Appellee., 2001 WL 34366057, *34366057+ (Appellate Brief) (Ill.App. 1 Dist. Dec 06, 2001) **Response Brief of Defendant-Appellee Chicago ...** (NO. 1-01-2323) ★ ★ **HN: 1 (Ill.Dec.)**

29 Hilel H. LEWIN, Plaintiffs-Appellants, v. NATIONAL RAILROAD PASSENGER CORP., Individually and d/b/a Amtrak; Northeast Illinois Regional Commuter Railroad Corp., Individually and d/b/a Metra/Metropolitan Rail and Chicago Union Station Company, Defendants-Appellees., 2001 WL 34366056, *34366056+ (Appellate Brief) (Ill.App. 1 Dist. Sep 25, 2001) **Brief and Argument for Plaintiffs-Appellants ...** (NO. 1-01-2323) ★ ★ ★ **HN: 6 (Ill.Dec.)**

30 John FARRELL and Dorothy Farrell, Plaintiffs/Appellants, v. OAK HILLS COUNTRY CLUB VILLAGE CONDOMINIUM ASSOCIATION, Floyd M. Phillips, Inc. and William Quinn & Sons, Inc., Defendants-Appellees., 2001 WL 34365930, *34365930+ (Appellate Brief) (Ill.App. 1 Dist. Sep 12, 2001) **Brief of Plaintiffs/Appellants John Farrell and ...** (NO. 1-01-2122) ★ ★ **HN: 4,5 (Ill.Dec.)**

31 Sheila HOWARD, Plaintiff-Appellant, v. CHICAGO TRANSIT AUTHORITY, a municipal corporation, Defendant-Appellee., 2001 WL 34365085, *34365085+ (Appellate Brief) (Ill.App. 1 Dist. Jul 17, 2001) **Brief of the Defendant-Appellee the Chicago ...** (NO. 1-01-0213) ★ ★ **HN: 6 (Ill.Dec.)**

32 Jill A. PAVLIK, Plaintiff-Appellant, v. WAL-MART STORES, INC., a Delaware Corporation, Defendant-Appellee., 2001 WL 34158736, *34158736+ (Appellate Brief) (Ill.App. 1 Dist. May 07, 2001) **Brief of Defendant-Appellee Wal-Mart Stores, Inc.** (NO. 1-00-3279) ★ ★ **HN: 2 (Ill.Dec.)**

33 John L. LANGSTON, Plaintiff-Appellee, v. MARTINI BROTHERS, INC., an Illinois corporation, d/b/a Martini Ranch, Defendant-Appellant., 2001 WL 34364252, *34364252+ (Appellate Brief) (Ill.App. 1 Dist. Mar 19, 2001) **Brief and Argument of Defendant-Appellant Martini ...** (NO. 1-00-4211) ★ ★ ★ ★ **HN: 4,5,6 (Ill.Dec.)**

34 Jill A. PAVLIK, Plaintiff-Appellant, v. WAL-MART STORES, INC., a Delaware Corporation, Defendant-Appellee., 2001 WL 34158735, *34158735+ (Appellate Brief) (Ill.App. 1 Dist. Feb

ILLUSTRATION 5-18.   *Continued*

Trial Court Documents (U.S.A.)

Trial Motions, Memoranda and Affidavits

104 Marilyn MILLER, Plaintiff, v. TGI FRIDAY'S, INC., a New York corporation doing business in Illinois, Defendant., 2005 WL 4857082, *4857082 (Trial Motion, Memorandum and Affidavit) (N.D.Ill. 2005) **Defendant's Reply to Plaintiff's Response to its ...** (NO. 05C006445) ★

105 Diane BROWN and Stanley Brown, Plaintiffs, v. Office DEPOT, Defendant., 2004 WL 1608613, *1608613+ (Trial Motion, Memorandum and Affidavit) (N.D.Ill. Apr 09, 2004) **Defendant's Motion for Summary Judgment** (NO. 03C2220) ★ ★

106 G. Mennen William YAGER, Plaintiff, v. ESA 0753, INC., an Illinois Corporation, d/b/a Cross-land Economy Studios, and Mitch Maneval, d/b/a Mitches Green Thumb Landscaping, Defendants., 2002 WL 32618384, *32618384 (Trial Motion, Memorandum and Affidavit) (N.D.Ill. Jan 30, 2002) **Motion for Summary Judgment and Motion to Join ...** (NO. 00C6068) ★ ★

107 Lilian E. THOMPSON, Plaintiff, v. J.C. PENNEY PROPERTIES, INC., a Delaware Corporation, Defendant., 2001 WL 34625608, *34625608 (Trial Motion, Memorandum and Affidavit) (N.D.Ill. Dec 13, 2001) **Plaintiff's Motion for Summary Judgment and ...** (NO. 00C4605) ★

108 Denise WALTON, Plaintiff, v. SUPERVALU, INC., d/b/a Shop "N Save, and Shop "N Save Warehouse Foods, Inc., d/b/a Shop "N Save, Defendants., 2008 WL 2063462, *2063462 (Trial Motion, Memorandum and Affidavit) (S.D.Ill. Apr 15, 2008) **Memorandum of Law in Support of Defendants' ...** (NO. 307CV00668) ★ ★

109 Brenda SHELTON, Plaintiff, v. SHOP 'N SAVE, Defendant., 2004 WL 3098890, *3098890 (Trial Motion, Memorandum and Affidavit) (S.D.Ill. 2004) **Memorandum of Law** (NO. 04-91WDS) ★ ★

110 Brenda SHELTON, Plaintiff, v. SHOP 'N SAVE DEFENDANTS., 2004 WL 3112191, *3112191 (Trial Motion, Memorandum and Affidavit) (S.D.Ill. 2004) **Response to Defendant's Motion for Summary ...** (NO. 04-CV-91WDS) ★

111 Elaine SUMMARIA, Plaintiff, v. AON CORPORATION, et al., Defendants., 2007 WL 4749762, *4749762+ (Trial Motion, Memorandum and Affidavit) (Ill.Cir. Sep 06, 2007) **Defendant's Reply Brief in Support of Defendant's ...** (NO. 06L9333) ★ ★

112 Vivian DAGGS, Plaintiff, v. CHICAGO TRANSIT AUTHORITY, a municipal corporation, Defendant., 2005 WL 3833480, *3833480+ (Trial Motion, Memorandum and Affidavit) (Ill.Cir. Nov 22, 2005) **Motion for Directed Verdict** (NO. 03L015715) ★ ★ ★

113 Joseph EMERSON, Plaintiff, v. FRANK'S SPORTS PAGE, INC., an Illinois corporation, d/b/a Sports Page, Brad Fosberg, Robert Stenstrom, and John Manning, Defendants., 2002 WL 32987313, *32987313+ (Trial Motion, Memorandum and Affidavit) (Ill.Cir. Feb 20, 2002) **Response to Defendants' Motion for Summary ...** (NO. 2000L13) ★ ★

114 Hilel H. LEWIN, Plaintiff, v. NATIONAL RAILROAD PASSENGER CORPORATION, a corporation, Individually and d/b/a Amtrak; Northeast Illinois Regional Corporation, individually and d/b/a Metra/Metropoloitan Rail; And Chicago Union Station Company, a corporation, Defendants., 2001 WL 35948615, *35948615+ (Trial Motion, Memorandum and Affidavit) (Ill.Cir. Apr 13, 2001) **Plaintiff's Response in Opposition to Defendant ...** (NO. 99L13842) ★ ★ ★

Reprinted with permission of Thomson Reuters/West.

In Illustration 5-16 researchers are directed to various *American Law Reports* and *Illinois Law and Practice*. In addition, you can view the case histories and be alerted via e-mail to possible court actions that may affect the validity of an authority.

KeyCite uses a system of colored flags to alert you to the history. A red case flag warns that the case is no longer good law for at least one of the points of law. A yellow flag warns that there is some negative history, but that the case has not been overruled or reversed. If the case has history that is not negative, it will have a blue H. A green C indicates that the case has citing references, but no direct or negative indirect history. Review Illustration 5-18. Note the flag. It is a yellow flag. It indicates that the case has some negative history. That history is the *Wiegman v. Hitch-Inn Post of Libertyville, Inc.* shown below the heading "Negative Citing References."

In addition, WESTLAW has developed a star system for noting the depth of the treatment a court provides to a case. Four stars means that the case was examined. Three stars mean it was discussed, and two stars indicate it was cited. One star means that the case was mentioned. Note on Illustration 5-18 the *Thompson* case was merely mentioned in *Lane v. Hardee's Food Systems, Inc.* Quotation marks indicate that the citing case directly quotes the cited case.

WESTLAW's headnotes and topics and key numbers also are incorporated into the KeyCite display. Note in Illustration 5-18 "HN: 1,2" following the *Kellermann* case. That indicates that headnotes 1 and 2 of the *Thompson* case are discussed. You can tailor your KeyCite search to focus on key numbers, topics, or jurisdictions.

Once you find a point of law within the key number system that is critical to your case, KeyCite allows you to search for the cases most often cited for that point of law. Click on the "Most Cited Cases" link next to the topic and key number listed on the KeyCite results.

▼ What Is the Difference Between *Shepard's* and KeyCite?

Researchers have noted recently that the services are very similar in nature. However, some citing references, such as some secondary authorities or treatises, may be unique to one system or the other.

▼ Why Would You Use KeyCite and *Shepard's?*

Using both services provides an additional check on the accuracy of the citation. Each also provides different references to secondary sources that might assist you in your research. For more information about secondary sources, consult Chapter 6.

▼ How Do I Access KeyCite?

From any WESTLAW screen, point your mouse at the KeyCite button and type in the citation and press Enter. If you are already viewing a case, you merely click the status flag or H or the KeyCite button on the main screen and you can instantly KeyCite your citation.

▼ Are There Any Other Online Citators?

Yes. One of the other online citators is Loislaw's **GlobalCite**.

D. GLOBALCITE

GlobalCite, a service within Loislaw, allows you to search cases, statutes, regulations, and other sources within the Loislaw database to determine whether a document has been cited. The results will list each citation of the document and a summary of the document found, and will allow you to hyperlink to the full text of those documents.

ILLUSTRATION 5-19. **GlobalCite Results for** *Thompson v. Economy Super Marts, Inc.*

GlobalCite Results List

Illinois Appellate Court Reports
THOMPSON v. ECONOMY SUPER MARTS, INC., 221 Ill. App.3d 263 (1991)

7 found (**1 - 7** shown)

Highlighted Case Treatment Terms

All Documents/Cases Reverse Chronological Order — 7
Cases Only -- Chronological Order — 7
Statutes Only — 0
Treatises Only — 0
Other Documents — 0

 # 1
Loislaw Federal District Court Opinions
BYRD-TOLSON v. SUPERVALU, INC (N.D.Ill. 6-12-2007)
Case No. 06 C 3818.
June 12, 2007
... As the owner of the supermarket, under Illinois law Moran owes business invitees the duty to maintain the premises in a reasonably safe condition to avoid injuring them. See Thompson v. Economy Super Markets, Inc., 581 N.E.2d 885, 888 (Ill.App.Ct. 1991). In this regard, Illinois law is clear, and has repeatedly emphasized, that a business owner is not an insurer of the safety of its premises, and that a triable case of negligence must be adduced or else judgment is req ...

 # 2
California Supreme Court Reports
ORTEGA v. KMART CORPORATION, 26 Cal.4th 1200 (2001)
S091888
Filed December 20, 2001
... for a period sufficient to provide the owner with constructive notice. (See, e.g., Annot. (1983) 24 A.L.R.4th 696 [collecting cases].) Additional slip-and-fall cases are in accord. (See, e.g., Thompson v. Economy Super Marts, Inc. (Ill.App.Ct. 1991) 581 N.E.2d 885, 888 [liability imposed if "substance was there a sufficient length of time so that in the exercise of ordinary care its presence should have been discovered"]; J. C. Penney Company v. Barrientez (Okla. 1965) 411 P.2d 841 [relying on Bridgman ...

 # 3
Illinois Appellate Court Reports
WIEGMAN v. HITCH-INN POST, 308 Ill. App.3d 789 (1999)
No. 2-98-1494
October 13, 1999
... The defendant relies on the rationale set forth in Thompson v. Economy Super Marts, Inc., 221 Ill. App.3d 263 (1991), Hresil v. Sears, Roebuck & Co., 82 Ill. App.3d 1000 (1980), and Hayes v. Bailey, 80 Ill. App.3d 1027 (1980). In Thompson, the plaintiff slipped and fell on a lettuce leaf and a spot of water on the floor of the produce section of the defendant's grocery store. Thompson, 221 Ill. App.3d at 263. She presented no evidence as to how long the lettuce leaf or water had been there ...

 # 4
Illinois Appellate Court Reports
KELLERMANN v. CAR CITY CHEVROLET-NISSAN INC., 306 Ill. App.3d 285 (1999)
No. 5-98-0142
Opinion filed July 21, 1999 — Rehearing denied August 5, 1999.
... the general rule in Illinois that a landowner or a possessor of land has a duty to an invitee or a licensee to exercise ordinary or reasonable care in maintaining his premises in a reasonably safe condition. See Thompson v. Economy Super Marts, Inc., 221 Ill. App.3d 263, 265 (1991). Accordingly, where a business invitee is injured by slipping and falling on defendant's premises, liability may be imposed if the substance was placed there by the negligence of the proprietor or his servants or, if ...

 # 5
United States 7th Circuit Court of Appeals Reports
LANE v. HARDEE'S FOOD SYSTEMS, INC., 184 F.3d 705 (7th Cir. 1999)
No. 98-3935
DECIDED JULY 22, 1999
... that the foreign material was related to the defendant's business, and 2) produce some evidence that makes it more likely than not that the defendant was responsible for its existence. See Donoho, 148 N.E.2d at 439; Thompson v. Economy Super Marts, Inc., 581 N.E.2d 885, 888 (Ill.App.Ct. 1991). Page 708 ...

ILLUSTRATION 5-19. *Continued*

6
Illinois Appellate Court Reports
WIND v. HY-VEE FOOD STORES, INC., 272 Ill. App.3d 149 (1995)
No. 3-94-0631
Opinion filed May 10, 1995.
... constructive notice. (Donoho, 13 Ill.2d at 122, 148 N.E.2d at 439.) In such cases, a landowner owes a business invitee a duty to exercise ordinary care in maintaining the premises in a reasonably safe condition. Thompson v. Economy Super Marts, Inc. (1991), 221 Ill. App.3d 263, 265, 581 N.E.2d 885, 888; Piper v. Moran's Enterprises (1984), 121 Ill. App.3d 644, 652, 459 N.E.2d 1382, 1388; see also Roberson v. J.C. Penney Co. (1993), 251 Ill. App.3d 523, 526, 623 N.E.2d 364, 366. ...

7
Illinois Appellate Court Reports
MILLER v. NAT'L ASSOCIATION OF REALTORS, 271 Ill. App.3d 653 (1995)
No. 1-92-1908
Opinion filed November 30, 1994. Rehearing denied March 31, 1995.
... knowledge, actual or Page 657 constructive; whereas, if the substance is on the premises through acts of third persons, the time element to establish knowledge or notice to the proprietor is a material factor." Thompson v. Economy Super Marts, Inc. (1991), 221 Ill. App.3d 263, 265, 581 N.E.2d 885.

... likely that the defendant or his servants, rather than a customer, dropped the substance on the premises, the trial court should permit the negligence issue to go the jury. Donoho v. O'Connell's, Inc. (1958), 13 Ill.2d 113, 148 N.E.2d 434; Thompson, 221 Ill. App.3d 263, 581 N.E.2d 885.

... those cases where there is no evidence to explain the origin of the substance, the plaintiff must show its presence for a sufficient amount of time so that the landowner should have discovered its existence. (Thompson v. Economy Super Marts, Inc. (1991), 221 Ill. App.3d 263, 581 N.E.2d 885, citing Olinger, 21 Ill.2d at 474.) The plaintiff who satisfies this burden imputes to the landowner constructive notice of the substance, and his failure to remove the substance may reasonably be inferred as a proximate caus ...

Case treatment terms such as affirm, agree, distinguish, dismiss, overrule, and rescind will appear in blue. Researchers must scan the cases to find these terms, however. They are not placed next to the case name in the GlobalCite search results. See Illustration 5-19.

Review the illustration. Note that all seven of the cases listed in this GlobalCite search result for *Thompson v. Economy Super Marts, Inc.* also are listed in the KeyCite and Shepard's listings. The GlobalCite, however, is not as comprehensive as the other online citators. For that reason, it is of limited assistance to you as a researcher. It is a valuable starting point, however, for researchers who use Loislaw as their primary research database.

CHAPTER SUMMARY

In this chapter, you learned that you must ensure that the law or authority you are citing is still current or valid. To determine this, you must validate or update your research findings. This process often is called *Shepardizing*. Citators not only assist you in validating the law but also provide you with citations to other authorities. You can validate an authority in both print and online.

The next chapter discusses resources called secondary authorities that help you understand legal issues and find primary authorities.

KEY TERMS

case history
citators
GlobalCite
KeyCite

negative history
Shepardize
Shepard's citator system
treatment

EXERCISES

COMPUTER EXERCISES
LEXIS

1. Shepardize the following citations:
   a. 64 N.W.2d 38
   b. 150 Ill. App. 3d 21
   c. 326 U.S. 310
2. For 326 U.S. 310, limit your treatment to negative treatment only. What are the results?

WESTLAW

3. Perform a KeyCite search for the following citations:
   a. 64 N.W.2d 38
   b. 150 Ill. App. 3d 21
   c. 326 U.S. 310

COMPUTER VALIDATING EXERCISES

4. Shepardize and KeyCite all of the following cases on the computer. Print out the first page of each result.
   a. *Consolidation Coal Co. v. Bucyrus-Erie Co.,* 89 Ill. 2d 103, 432 N.E.2d 250 (1982)
   b. *United States v. Upjohn,* 449 U.S. 383 (1981)
   c. *People v. Adam,* 51 Ill. 2d 46, 280 N.E.2d 205 (1972)
   d. *Cox v. Yellow Cab Co.,* 61 Ill. 2d 416, 337 N.E.2d 15 (1975)
   e. *Archer Daniels Midland Co. v. Koppers Co.,* 138 Ill. App. 3d 276, 485 N.E.2d 1301 (1985)
5. If available perform a GlobalCite search on the citations listed in number 4 above.
6. Perform GlobalCites for all of the cases in Number 3.

Exercises

7.
   a. Shepardize the *Kellermann* case, 713 N.E.2d 1285. Note that it is cited by 754 N.E.2d 448. Now, go to that case. What is the name of that case?
   b. What headnote of the *Kellermann* case does the case you found relate to?
   c. What is the topic and key number?

    d. Now look at key numbers 22 and 23 of the case you found. What is the topic and key number?

    e. How do these paragraphs and key numbers differ from the *Kellermann* case?

8. Perform a KeyCite search for 507 F. Supp. 1091 on Westlaw. List some of cases that have yellow flags.

9. Perform a KeyCite for 2002 WL1592517 (CA 7. Ill.). Can you perform a KeyCite for this case on WESTLAW? Can you Shepardize this case on *Shepard's* online?

10. Perform a KeyCite for 106 SCt 1415.

    a. What is the name of the case?

    b. Is there any signal indicating the validity of the case? If so, what is it?

11. Shepardize the following cases online.

    a. 816 F.2d 630

    b. 373 N.E.2d 1371

    c. 432 N.E.2d 1123

    d. 222 N.E.2d 561

12. Find 984 F.2d 218 online on WESTLAW.

    a. Is there a signal that indicates whether the case is good law?

    b. If so, what is the signal and what does it indicate?

    c. Does it apply to the entire case? If no, what part of the case does it apply to?

Hard-Copy Validation Exercises

13. Shepardize the citations listed below. Photocopy the *Shepard's* pages. List any missing volumes. Be certain to Shepardize all citations for each case or statute.

    a. 361 N.E.2d 325

    b. 80 Ill. App. 3d 315

    c. 571 F. Supp. 1012

    d. 8 U.S.C. §1449

14. Shepardize the following citations in the *Shepard's* citators and provide the official citations. Do not use the computer. Photocopy all of the relevant *Shepard's* pages. Also photocopy the list that details the *Shepard's* bound volumes and supplements you should have consulted for each citation. For each photocopy, carefully note where you found the page, for example, "1990-1991 Illinois bound volume." For each case, highlight in yellow one headnote notation. Then select one case that has a *Shepard's* notation and highlight the case in pink or blue on the photocopy and note on the page the meaning of the *Shepard's* notation. (If you prefer to hand copy each *Shepard's* page, that is acceptable too.)

    a. 129 F.R.D. 515

    b. 432 N.E.2d 250

    c. 449 U.S. 383

    d. 51 Ill. 2d 46

    e. 138 Ill. App. 3d 276

    f. 423 F.2d 487

    g. Ill. S. Ct. Rule 201

SECONDARY AUTHORITY

CHAPTER OVERVIEW

Secondary authorities are used to understand, analyze, and tie together primary authorities, or the law. Cases, statutes, and administrative regulations—all primary authorities—are frequently cited in secondary sources. Secondary authorities are useful tools for finding citations to law supporting a legal issue.

This chapter details the many sources of secondary authority, how to use the sources, and how to update them. Citation information is given for each source.

A. SECONDARY AUTHORITY: WHAT IT IS AND WHERE TO FIND IT

▼ What Is Secondary Authority?

Secondary authority describes, analyzes, and comments on primary authority. Secondary authority provides commentary on the law. Any analytical or critical discussion of the law is considered secondary authority. Generally, individuals, institutions, and publishers create secondary sources.

Secondary authority compares and contrasts judicial opinions and indicates how the law is evolving. Also, a secondary source will often tell the researcher which cases are most important and which have little merit. Secondary sources discuss statutes and administrative materials expounding on the policy motivations for enacting legislation and the accompanying regulations.

▼ Why and When Do You Use a Secondary Source?

Secondary sources are used to explain the law or a particular legal concept. Secondary sources discuss the legal rules directly without requiring the reader to unearth the issues and the holdings from the texts of judicial decisions. Secondary authority provides insight into a legal topic by discussing the most important relevant cases and statutes and by explaining how that law is applied to the facts. Because secondary sources comment on, describe, and analyze primary sources, a researcher obtains citations to primary authority. By providing access to citations, secondary sources are great finding tools. A researcher uses secondary authority to gain insight into a legal topic as well as to obtain citations to primary sources.

Paralegals use secondary sources when they are unfamiliar with a legal issue or topic and need a broad overview of the concepts written in a text format that is easily understandable. Using secondary authority provides access to primary sources because of the great number of footnotes and citations found in the secondary source.

NET NOTE

Guides to using secondary authority are at www.ll.georgetown.edu/second.

▼ What Are the Sources of Secondary Authority?

Generally, any source that comments on, analyzes, criticizes, describes, or projects the status of the law is a secondary source. Any source that states what the law should be is a secondary source. Some secondary sources are considered more prestigious and carry more persuasive authority than others. For instance, the Restatements of Law are very well respected, as are scholarly law review articles. The major sources of secondary authority are dictionaries, thesauri, encyclopedias, American Law Reports (A.L.R.), hornbooks, treatises, Restatements, legal periodicals, and newspapers. We will discuss each source separately, give examples, and illustrate which research situation would mandate their respective use.

PRACTICE POINTER

Secondary sources are great finding tools for primary authority, particularly case law. Use the secondary source to understand how case law fits together and to obtain citations. Always read the primary source, that is, the case or the statute, yourself to see if it is applicable to your research. Also, never forget to Shepardize any primary source before you rely on it as a source of authority.

B. DICTIONARIES

▼ What Is a Legal Dictionary?

The **legal dictionary** provides the legal definition of a word or term. Sometimes a case is mentioned that contains the judicial definition of that word. The two most common legal dictionaries are *Black's Law Dictionary* and *Ballentine's Law Dictionary*.

▼ When Would a Legal Dictionary Be Used?

Researchers use a legal dictionary when they do not understand the **legal meaning** of a word or term. The emphasis is on the legal meaning because the legal definition of a word often differs from its lay meaning. Sometimes you will be assigned a research project where you cannot answer or resolve the issue without first figuring out what the terms mean.

EXAMPLE

Ms. Associate asks you if Mr. Blackacre can obtain an easement by necessity to access his farm from the road by crossing his neighbor's property. You do not know what an easement is, nor do you know what

ILLUSTRATION 6-1. **Definition of** *Easement* **in** *Black's Law Dictionary*

---

earnings

a personal-injury lawsuit. And in family law, earning capacity is considered when awarding child support and spousal maintenance (or alimony) and in dividing property between spouses upon divorce. — Also termed *earning power*. See LOST EARNING CAPACITY.

earnings. Revenue gained from labor or services, from the investment of capital, or from assets. See INCOME.

  appropriated retained earnings. Retained earnings that a company's board designates for a distinct use, and that are therefore unavailable to pay dividends or for other uses. — Also termed *appropriated surplus; surplus revenue; suspense reserve.*

  future earnings. See *lost earnings.*

  gross earnings. See *gross income* under INCOME.

  lost earnings. Wages, salary, or other income that a person could have earned if he or she had not lost a job, suffered a disabling injury, or died. ● Lost earnings are typically awarded as damages in personal-injury and wrongful-termination cases. There can be past lost earnings and future lost earnings. Both are subsets of this category, though legal writers sometimes loosely use *future earnings* as a synonym for *lost earnings.* Cf. LOST EARNING CAPACITY. [Cases: Damages ☞37. C.J.S. *Damages* §§ 54–55.]

  net earnings. See *net income* under INCOME.

  ongoing earnings. See *operating earnings.*

  operating earnings. Business income calculated in violation of generally accepted accounting principles by including income items and excluding various business expenses. ● Many companies use operating earnings to favorably skew their price-earnings (P/E) ratios. Because the rationales for the underlying calculations vary from company to company, and from period to period within a company, operating earnings are almost always artificially inflated and unreliable. The term *operating earnings* is meaningless under generally accepted accounting principles. — Also termed *pro forma earnings; economic earnings; core earnings; ongoing earnings; earnings excluding special items.* See PRICE-EARNINGS RATIO.

  pretax earnings. Net earnings before income taxes.

  pro forma earnings. See *operating earnings.*

  real earnings. Earnings that are adjusted for inflation so that they reflect actual purchasing power.

  retained earnings. A corporation's accumulated income after dividends have been distributed. — Also termed *earned surplus; undistributed profit.* [Cases: Corporations ☞151. C.J.S. *Corporations* § 298.]

  surplus earnings. The excess of corporate assets over liabilities within a given period, usu. a year. [Cases: Corporations ☞152. C.J.S. *Corporations* §§ 295–299.]

earnings and profits. *Corporations.* In corporate taxation, the measure of a corporation's economic capacity to make a shareholder distribution that is not a return of capital. ● The distribution will be dividend income to the shareholders to the extent of the

corporation's current and accumulated earnings and profits. Cf. *accumulated-earnings tax* under TAX; *accumulated taxable income* under INCOME. [Cases: Internal Revenue ☞3830.1–3845. C.J.S. *Internal Revenue* §§ 381–382.]

earnings excluding special items. See *operating earnings* under EARNINGS.

earnings per share. *Corporations.* A measure of corporate value by which the corporation's net income is divided by the number of outstanding shares of common stock. ● Investors benefit from calculating a corporation's earnings per share, because it helps the investor determine the fair market value of the corporation's stock. — Abbr. EPS.

  fully diluted earnings per share. A corporation's net income — assuming that all convertible securities had been transferred to common equity and all stock options had been exercised — divided by the number of shares of the corporation's outstanding common stock.

earnings-price ratio. See *earnings yield* under YIELD.

earnings report. See INCOME STATEMENT.

earnings yield. See YIELD.

earnout agreement. An agreement for the sale of a business whereby the buyer first pays an agreed amount up front, leaving the final purchase price to be determined by the business's future profits. ● The seller usu. helps manage the business for a period after the sale. — Sometimes shortened to *earnout.*

earwitness. A witness who testifies about something that he or she heard but did not see. Cf. EYEWITNESS.

easement (eez-mənt). An interest in land owned by another person, consisting in the right to use or control the land, or an area above or below it, for a specific limited purpose (such as to cross it for access to a public road). ● The land benefiting from an easement is called the *dominant estate*; the land burdened by an easement is called the *servient estate.* Unlike a lease or license, an easement may last forever, but it does not give the holder the right to possess, take from, improve, or sell the land. The primary recognized easements are (1) a right-of-way, (2) a right of entry for any purpose relating to the dominant estate, (3) a right to the support of land and buildings, (4) a right of light and air, (5) a right to water, (6) a right to do some act that would otherwise amount to a nuisance, and (7) a right to place or keep something on the servient estate. See SERVITUDE (1). Cf. PROFIT À PRENDRE. — Also termed *private right-of-way.* [Cases: Easements ☞1. C.J.S. *Easements* §§ 2–8, 13–14, 21–22, 24, 53–55, 57–58, 89.] ←

  access easement. An easement allowing one or more persons to travel across another's land to get to a nearby location, such as a road. ● The access easement is a common type of easement by necessity. — Also termed *easement of access; easement of way; easement of passage.*

  adverse easement. See *prescriptive easement.*

  affirmative easement. An easement that forces the servient-estate owner to permit certain actions by the easement holder, such as discharging water

---

an easement by necessity is. To research the issue effectively, you would use a legal dictionary to look up easement and easement by necessity.

Examples of dictionary entries of the word *easement* are provided in Illustration 6-1. The entries in the legal dictionary are in alphabetical order. Under the word *easement* are the various types of easements.

▼ How Would You Cite to a Legal Dictionary?

The correct citation format for dictionaries is found in *Bluebook* Rule 15.7. *ALWD* format is the same.

Black's Law Dictionary 548 (8th ed. 2004)

▼ Are Legal Dictionaries Available Online?

Black's Law Dictionary is available on WESTLAW. The Directory screen, which changes constantly, indicates exactly where the dictionary is located within the WESTLAW database. The contents of *Black's* online are identical to the hard-copy version. To search for a definition online, enter the word that you want to be defined. In our example, you would enter the word *easement*. A free online legal dictionary is available at dictionary.com. Click on subject: legal. You will then be able to search the *Merriam-Webster Dictionary of Law.*

C. THESAURI

▼ What Is a Thesaurus?

A **thesaurus** provides synonyms and antonyms for words. A legal thesaurus provides synonymous terms and opposite terms for legal words. A thesaurus is the same type of source for legal and nonlegal materials.

Common legal thesauri are *Legal Thesaurus* by William C. Burton (NY: Macmillan, 2d ed. 1992) and *West's Legal Thesaurus/Dictionary* by William Statsky (St. Paul, Minn.: West Publishing 1986). Also, try thesaurus.com for an online thesaurus accessible from your desktop.

▼ Why Would You Use a Thesaurus?

A paralegal uses a thesaurus when drafting a memo about a single topic, like easement. The memo becomes very dull if the term *easement* is used over and over again. After a while you lose the reader's attention. Substituting a synonymous term makes reading the memo much more interesting. Occasionally substituting *right of way* for *easement* keeps the reader's interest.

Unfortunately, the *Bluebook* does not have an entry for citing thesauri. A writer does not cite to *Roget's Thesaurus* when using a synonym found in that work, so the same principle applies with legal thesauri.

D. ENCYCLOPEDIAS

1. Generally

▼ What Is a Legal Encyclopedia?

Just as *Encyclopedia Britannica* and *World Book* divide the realm of knowledge into subjects and discuss each subject broadly (for example, the

subjects Insects and Cities), a **legal encyclopedia** divides the law into topics and offers a broad coverage of the legal rules pertaining to each topic. The discussion is thorough but not too detailed and is oriented to the reader with legal knowledge, though not necessarily of the particular subject in question. Encyclopedias provide generalized commentary on the law.

There are legal encyclopedias such as the *Encyclopedia of the American Constitution* that cover specialized subject areas. There are encyclopedias such as **American Jurisprudence** and **Corpus Juris Secundum** that are national in scope. Finally, there are state law encyclopedias such as *Illinois Law and Practice* and *Florida Jurisprudence Second*. There are legal encyclopedias for most states.

▼ Why Would You Use an Encyclopedia?

An encyclopedia is very helpful when beginning research in an area of the law in which you have no basic knowledge of the subject or the issues. Encyclopedias divide the law into topics and subtopics and provide a generalized, clearly written discussion of the issues and the general rules. A working vocabulary and a knowledge of the general rules are obtained when using an encyclopedia. In addition, encyclopedias give credit to every tenet mentioned, so they are a marvelous source for citations.

After reading the encyclopedia entry, you must always read for yourself the cases cited in the references to determine if they are relevant to your problem.

▼ When Do You Cite an Encyclopedia as Authority?

As a general rule, encyclopedias should never be cited as authority. Encyclopedias are not scholarly sources, and authorship is institutional rather than individual. This does not detract from their helpfulness in providing a broad overview of the legal topic and in providing citations to primary source materials.

A researcher should use primary source references, even from other jurisdictions, obtained from the encyclopedia rather than cite to the encyclopedia's text. Always read the case or statute that the encyclopedia cites and rely on the primary source for authority. It is better to analogize to the law from another jurisdiction than to use an encyclopedia as authority.

The two predominant encyclopedias that are national in scope are *American Jurisprudence,* commonly referred to as Am. Jur. and Am. Jr. 2d (second series), and *Corpus Juris Secundum,* known as C.J.S.

Both encyclopedias cover the individual legal disciplines in a generalized manner. Discussion is thorough but not overly detailed. The footnotes and citations included in the sections provide citations to primary authorities. You must always read the primary source that you rely on, not only the encyclopedia's interpretation of it.

State encyclopedias also exist. In Illinois, *Illinois Law and Practice* is the encyclopedia that deals with issues of state law. *Illinois Law and Practice* is published by West and contains references to many other West publications, particularly the digests with the topics and key numbers. Check with your librarian for the encyclopedia in your state.

2. *American Jurisprudence*

▼ What Is Contained in *American Jurisprudence?*

American Jurisprudence, commonly called Am. Jur., is published by West and references other publications such as the *American Law Reports* (A.L.R.). The encyclopedia is in the second edition. The entire set is divided into topics, and the topics are arranged alphabetically.

Illustration 6-2 shows the topic outline for Easements and Licenses in Am. Jr. 2d. Notice that under the topics of Easements are various subtopics. The initial discussion of the subtopic Easements in Gross begins with a category entitled "Transfer of Easement."

The editors attempt to divide the entire body of American law into labeled topics. This gives the reader a subject approach to the law and permits the gathering of legal information, allowing the researcher to find out the general legal rules without reading the actual cases and statutes from which the rules are derived. The text explores each legal topic by providing the most important law that is relevant or the controlling legal doctrine, then discusses the exceptions to the general rules. The encyclopedia is considered to be a secondary source because it offers discussion and commentary on the law and synthesizes, or puts together, many cases. Of course, there is extensive footnoting to give proper credit or attribution to the authority discussed. This makes the encyclopedia a great finding tool, although not a substitute for reading the primary source material. The encyclopedia is a good place to begin research when you do not understand the topic and need a broad overview of the discipline. By virtue of reading about the topic, you will acquire case and statute citations to relevant materials.

Am. Jur. is organized by topic, and the volumes are updated with pocket parts. The pocket parts are called **Cumulative Supplements** and are generally published annually. Each volume of Am. Jur. is numbered, and the topics and sections contained within the volume are listed on the spine; for example, Volume 25 of Am. Jr. contains Domicil to Elections §§1-206. At the beginning of each topic is an outline listing every related subtopic. Each section within a topic refers to a subtopic; for example, under the topic of Easements and Licenses, captions indicate categories within the topics such as VI. Transfer of Easement. Under Transfer of Easement, §90 if entitled "Easement in Gross." The text of Am. Jur. 2d repeats the topic and subtopic heading. See Illustration 6-3.

ILLUSTRATION 6-2. Topic Outline for Easements and Licenses at 25 Am. Jur. 2d 495 (2004)

EASEMENTS AND LICENSES

§ 83   Right of access to make repairs or improvements; secondary easements

C. ALTERATIONS

§ 84   Generally
§ 85   Where easement is owned in common

D. INTERFERENCE WITH EASEMENT; OBSTRUCTIONS

§ 86   Generally; rights of servient owner
§ 87   Structures on or over ways; generally
§ 88   —Gates
§ 89   Right to remove obstructions

→ **VI. TRANSFER OF EASEMENT**

§ 90   Easements in gross
§ 91   Easements appurtenant, generally
§ 92   —On division of dominant tenement
§ 93   —On transfer of servient tenement; requirements as to notice

VII. DURATION, TERMINATION, AND REVIVAL

A. DURATION

§ 94   Generally
§ 95   Necessity of words of inheritance or limitation to create perpetual easement

B. TERMINATION OR EXTINGUISHMENT; REVIVAL

§ 96   Generally
§ 97   Occurrence of stated event or violation of conditions
§ 98   Abandonment
§ 99   Misuse
§ 100   Merger of dominant and servient estates
§ 101   Release; license
§ 102   Adverse possession
§ 103   Destruction or alteration of building or structure
§ 104   Foreclosure of mortgage or trust deed
§ 105   Sale for taxes; enforcement of special assessment
§ 106   Revival

VIII. ACTIONS TO ESTABLISH, ENFORCE, OR PROTECT EASEMENTS

A. IN GENERAL

§ 107   Generally

Reprinted with permission of Thomson Reuters/West.

Notice that the topic or subtopic is first discussed generally, then the subissues are explored. To update the information found in the main volume, refer to the pocket part, or supplement, under the topic and then under the section. See Illustration 6-4. In our example, the supplement has no additional material updating §90. Always check the pocket part, regardless of how recent the main volume publication date, to see if there are any new cases. For the purposes of illustration,

ILLUSTRATION 6-3. Portion of Easement Entry at 25 Am. Jur. 2d §90 (2004)

VI. TRANSFER OF EASEMENT

Research References

West's Digest References

Easements ⊜24

Annotation References

A.L.R. Digest: Easements §§ 57 to 59, 59.7

A.L.R. Index: Easements

Forms References

Am. Jur. Legal Forms 2d, Pipelines §§ 203:48, 203:49

§ 90 Easements in gross

Research References

West's Key Number Digest, Easements ⊜24

Assignment permitted—Exception of right to construct additional pipelines. Am. Ju
   Forms 2d, Pipelines § 203:48

Assignment prohibited—Exception of certain subsidiaries. Am. Jur. Legal Forms 2d, Pipelines
   § 203:49

An easement in gross, as a right personal to the one to whom it is granted, generally cannot be assigned or otherwise transmitted by him or her to another.[1] That is, because it is purely a personal right, an easement in gross is not assignable, absent evidence of the parties' intent to the contrary, and terminates upon the death of the individual for whom it was created.[2] However, there is some authority for the view that easements in gross that are taken for commercial purposes, especially those for public utility purposes such as railroads, telephone lines, and pipelines, are freely transferable,[3] and that easements in gross may be made assignable, however, by the terms of the instrument creating the right, particularly where the easement is of a commercial character, such as an easement for a pipeline, telegraph and telephone line, or railroad right-of-way.[4] When the evidence demonstrates that the parties clearly intended that an easement in gross be assignable, it is.[5]

Reprinted with permission of Thomson Reuters/West.

see the new entries in the pocket part under *Drugs and Controlled Substances.*

Narrative text generally is omitted in the pocket part, but new and updating citation references are included. This means that citations to new cases published that support the legal premises discussed in the main text are listed so that you can find the most recent authority for the legal premise. This is the same format as the pocket part in C.J.S.

Am. Jur. updates its topics with a looseleaf volume entitled *New Topic Service* in which current topics, complete with text and footnotes, are contained. The looseleaf volume is updated with great speed so that when a new topic appears, it can be included quickly rather than

ILLUSTRATION 6-4.   Cover and Sample Page Pocket Part for Volume 25 Am. Jur. 2d

AMERICAN JURISPRUDENCE

SECOND EDITION

2007 CUMULATIVE SUPPLEMENT

ISSUED IN MAY 2007

Volume 25

DOMICIL
TO
ELECTIONS (§§ 1—202)

by
The editorial staff of the Publishers

INSERT IN BACK OF BOUND VOLUME

THOMSON
* * *
WEST

For Customer Assistance Call 1-800-328-4880

IT-44

ILLUSTRATION 6-4. *Continued*

authority. United Pharmacal Co. of Missouri, Inc. v. Missouri Bd. of Pharmacy, 208 S.W.3d 907 (Mo. 2006).

§ 84 Scope and powers of state regulatory board—Validity

Cases

District of Columbia statute permitting interested party to establish prima facie case of excessive pricing of pharmaceutical product by comparing domestic wholesale price of drug with its wholesale price in one of four specified foreign countries was not facially unconstitutional under Foreign Commerce Clause, where foreign country comparison was optional approach for establishing prima facie case, and it was possible to establish prima facie case without reference to foreign drug prices. Pharmaceutical Research and Mfrs. of America v. District of Columbia, 406 F. Supp. 2d 56 (D.D.C. 2005).

§ 87 Advertising

Cases

Drug Enforcement Agency's (DEA's) finding, in deciding to approve drug manufacturing company's application for registration as importer of narcotic raw materials (NRMs) used in production of active pharmaceutical ingredients (APIs), that registration of company would promote technical advances in area was supported by substantial evidence, notwithstanding objector's assertion that company's morphine-based production technology was less efficient than its own high-thebaine poppy technology, given evidence that company had developed and patented numerous other processing technologies. Noramco of Delaware, Inc. v. Drug Enforcement Admin., 375 F.3d 1148 (D.C. Cir. 2004).

§ 89 Licensing or registration of pharmacists

Cases

To the extent plaintiffs' product liability claims with respect to a Class III medical device which had received premarket approval (PMA) from the Food and Drug Administration (FDA) sought to impose liability even though the device complied with the design as approved by the FDA or complied with the approved manufacturing process, the claims were preempted by the Medical Devices Amendment of 1976 to the Food, Drug and Cosmetics Act, and the same was true of claims based on alleged failures to warn, or inadequate warnings, arising from the warnings and labeling approved by the FDA, but to the extent that plaintiffs' claims were based on the theory that the particular device was defective in that it did not comply with the approved design or manufacturing process or that the warnings or labeling deviated from those required by the FDA, the claims were not preempted. Gilleon v. Medtronic USA, Inc., 2002 WL 31300694 (N.D. Cal. 2002).

To the extent that plaintiffs' misrepresentation claims with respect to a Class III medical device which had received premarket approval

(PMA) from the Food and Drug Administration (FDA) were premised on a theory that manufacturer was liable for withholding information from the FDA and thereby fraudulently securing approval, those claims were preempted by the Medical Devices Amendment of 1976 to the Food, Drug and Cosmetics Act, but to the extent that the fraud and misrepresentation claims were based on manufacturer's alleged misrepresentations to the general public, to plaintiffs, and to plaintiffs' physicians, such claims were not preempted. Gilleon v. Medtronic USA, Inc., 2002 WL 31300694 (N.D. Cal. 2002).

Food and Drug Administration (FDA) premarket approval (PMA) of a device for repair of abdominal aortic aneurysms resulted in preemption of state common law claims, under the Medical Devices Amendment of 1976 to the Food, Drug and Cosmetics Act, to the extent those claims sought to impose requirements that were different or in addition to those required by federal law. Gilleon v. Medtronic USA, Inc., 2002 WL 31300694 (N.D. Cal. 2002).

District court had jurisdiction under Administrative Procedure Act (APA) to resolve pharmacy's claim that Drug Enforcement Administration (DEA), in denying its request to change location pending determination of its application for modification to its registration in the context of an ongoing hearing to revoke registration, had unreasonably delayed action upon what pharmacy characterized as a routine request for change of address. Wedgewood Village Pharmacy, Inc. v. Ashcroft, 293 F. Supp. 2d 462 (D.N.J. 2003).

b. *Disciplinary Measures; Suspension or Revocation of License, Registration, or Permit*

§ 91 Particular actions as warranting disciplinary action, suspension, or revocation

Cases

Availability of administrative review under the Federal Food, Drug, and Cosmetic Act (FDCA) did not make Environmental Protection Agency's (EPA) determinations of pesticide residue tolerances on produce non-final for purposes of judicial review under the Administrative Procedure Act (APA). New York v. U.S. E.P.A., 350 F. Supp. 2d 429 (S.D. N.Y. 2004).

C. IMPORTATION AND EXPORTATION OF CONTROLLED SUBSTANCES; CONTROL OF SUBSTANCES ON VESSELS

§ 94 Generally; importation

Cases

Evidence was sufficient to support conviction for conspiring to import and to possess with intent to distribute heroin; three couriers testified in detail to several occasions when, in Colombia, they received aerosol cans filled with heroin from defendant to smuggle into United States, on their arrival in New York, couriers would give heroin to defendant's

waiting for a published volume to be printed and bound. Am. Jur. also published the *Desk Book,* which contains facts, charts, tables, statistics, and court rules of interest to attorneys. The *Desk Book* is published annually.

▼ How Do You Use Am. Jur.?

There are four basic methods of using Am. Jur. 2d.

1. **The index method.** This is the most efficient approach. At the end of the set is a multi-volume index that is printed annually. Entries are organized by descriptive word and topic and include subtopics as cross-references. An example of the index from Am. Jur. 2d is shown in Illustration 6-5.

2. **The table method.** If you have a statutory cite, use the separate Am. Jur. 2d volume entitled *Table of Statutes, Rules and Regulations Cited.* If you have a relevant *United States Code* (U.S.C.) or U.S.C.S., *Code of Federal Regulations,* or uniform law citation, the tables will indicate the precise topic and section where it is discussed.

3. **The topic outline.** This is the least efficient method. In this method you review the topics outlined at the beginning of each topic section.

4. **Access Am. Jur. on LEXIS or WESTLAW.** Although costly, you can search by word or term. This is particularly helpful when you have an unusual term. Also, all updates are integrated into the page or section retrieved so that you do not have to consult pocket part supplements.

▼ What Is the Citation Format for Am. Jur.?

Bluebook Rule 15.7 and *ALWD* Rule 26 cover legal encyclopedias. A cite for easements in §102 would be as follows:

25 Am. Jur. 2d <u>Easements and Licenses</u> §90 (2004 & Supp. 2008)

3. *Corpus Juris Secundum*

▼ What Is Contained in *Corpus Juris Secundum*?

Corpus Juris Secundum, commonly known as C.J.S., is the other predominant encyclopedia that is national in scope. C.J.S. is a West publication, and other West materials are referred to in its text. The most notable reference in C.J.S. is to the West topics and key numbers, thereby tying the encyclopedia to the West National Reporter system and the West Digests. See Illustration 6-6. This attribute makes C.J.S. a very powerful research tool.

C.J.S. is organized by titles, which are the individual legal subjects. At the beginning of each title is a section analysis that outlines the legal issues and subissues within the subject. The volumes are numbered and contain the various titles in alphabetical order. Footnotes within the text refer the reader to case citations, as in Am. Jur. 2d. Each volume of C.J.S.

ILLUSTRATION 6-5. General Index Update to Am. Jur. 2d

GENERAL INDEX

EASEMENTS—Cont'd
Actions and remedies—Cont'd
  injunctions, **Easements** § 110
  landlord and tenant, **Easements** § 109
  limitation of actions, **Easements** § 115
  parties, **Easements** § 108, 109
  pleadings, **Easements** § 114
  punitive damages, **Easements** § 112
  standing, **Easements** § 108, 109
  title and ownership, **Easements** § 109
  weight and sufficiency of evidence,
    Easements § 116
Adjoining Landowners (this index)
Adverse or hostile use. Prescription, *below*
Adverse possession
  prescription, **Easements** § 49
  termination or extinguishment, **Easements** § 102
Affirmative easements, **Easements** § 6
Agreement, creation by, **Easements** § 17
Agricultural products, **Crops** § 111
Alterations
  generally, **Easements** § 84
  access to make repairs or improvements, **Easements** § 83
  building or structure, alteration of, **Easements** § 103
  common easements, **Easements** § 85
Apparent easements
  generally, **Easements** § 7
  preexisting uses, **Easements** § 26
Appurtenant easements
  generally, **Easements** § 8
  easements in gross distinguished, **Easements** § 10
  transfer of easements
    generally, **Easements** § 91
    dominant tenement, division of, **Easements** § 92
    notice, **Easements** § 93
    servient tenement, division of, **Easements** § 93
Aviation, easements as defense to trespass or nuisances, **Aviation** § 9
Buildings or structures
  destruction of building or structure, **Easements** § 103
  interference with easements, structures on or over ways, **Easements** § 87, 88
Canals, **Canals** § 7
Change of location, **Easements** § 69
Classifications of easements, **Easements** § 5-10
Color of title, prescription, **Easements** § 57
Common easements, **Easements** § 85
Consent
  location by agreement of parties, **Easements** § 67
  permissive use. Prescription, *below*
Construction and interpretation, **Easements** § 18, 73
Contingencies, **Easements** § 97

EASEMENTS—Cont'd
Continuous use
  preexisting uses, **Easements** § 28
  prescription, continuous and uninterrupted use, **Easements** § 61-63
Contract, creation by, **Easements** § 17
Cotenancy and joint ownership, **Cotenancy** § 103
Court, location fixed by, **Easements** § 68
Covenants of Title (this index)
Covenants (this index)
Creation of easements, **Easements** § 11-63
Crops, **Crops** § 111
Damages
  generally, **Easements** § 111
  punitive damages, **Easements** § 112
Declaratory judgments, **DeclJuds** § 156
Deeds and Conveyances (this index)
Defenses, **Easements** § 115
Definition, **Easements** § 1
Destruction of building or structure, **Easements** § 103
Deviation from route, **Easements** § 70
Dominant and servient rights
  interference with easements, rights of servient owner, **Easements** § 86
  merger of dominant and servient estates, **Easements** § 100
Drains and Drainage Systems (this index)
Duration, **Easements** § 94, 95
Ejectment, **Ejectment** § 4
Eminent Domain (this index)
Estoppel, creation by, **Easements** § 13
Evidence
  presumptions and burden of proof, *below*
  weight and sufficiency of evidence, **Easements** § 116
Exception, creation by, **Easements** § 16
Exclusive use, prescription, **Easements** § 53
Existing way, **Easements** § 65
Extinguishment. Termination or extinguishment, *below*
Federal government, **Easements** § 12
Fee simple, **Easements** § 11
Forcible entry and detainer, **Forcible** § 13
Foreclosure of mortgage or trust deed, **Easements** § 104
Franchises distinguished, **Franchise** § 2
Fraud and Deceit (this index)
Gas and oil, **GasandOil** § 52
Gates, **Easements** § 88
Grant of easement, **Easements** § 14
Highways, Streets, and Bridges (this index)
Hostile use. Prescription, *below*
Implied easements
  generally, **Easements** § 19-38
  existing way, **Easements** § 65
  highways and streets, **Easements** § 20
  light, air, and view, **Adjoining** § 97, 98
  location, **Easements** § 65
  maps and plats, **Easements** § 21
  preexisting uses, *below*

EASEMENTS—Cont'd
Implied easements—Cont'd
  use of easements, **Easements** § 79
  ways of necessity, *below*
Improvements, access to make, **Easements** § 83
Indefinite easements, **Easements** § 72
In gross, easements
  generally, **Easements** § 9
  appurtenant easements distinguished, **Easements** § 10
  transfer of easements, **Easements** § 90
Inheritance, **Easements** § 95
Injunctions, **Easements** § 110
Interference with easements
  generally, **Easements** § 86-89
  gates, **Easements** § 88
  removal of obstructions, **Easements** § 89
  rights of servient owner, **Easements** § 86
  structures on or over ways, **Easements** § 87, 88
Interrupted use, prescription, **Easements** § 62
Irrigation (this index)
Judicial Sales (this index)
Knowledge. Notice or knowledge, *below*
Landlord and Tenant (this index)
Lateral support, excavations affecting, **Adjoining** § 67
Licenses in real property distinguished, **Easements** § 2, 117
Light, Air, and View (this index)
Limitation of actions, **Easements** § 115
Limitations and restrictions on use, **Easements** § 71
Lis pendens, **LisPend** § 29
Location
  generally, **Easements** § 64-70
  agreement of parties, location by, **Easements** § 67
  change of location, **Easements** § 69
  court, location fixed by, **Easements** § 68
  designation of location by parties, **Easements** § 66, 67, 69
  deviation from route, **Easements** § 70
  existing way, **Easements** § 65
  implied easements, **Easements** § 65
  prescription, **Easements** § 51
Maps and plats, implied easements, **Easements** § 21
Mechanic's liens, **Mechanics** § 39
Merger of dominant and servient estates, **Easements** § 100
Misuse, **Easements** § 99
Monopolies, restraints of trade, and unfair competition, **Monopolies** § 990
Mortgages
  foreclosure of mortgage or trust deed, **Easements** § 104
  right to easement, **Mortgages** § 816
Municipal corporations, drains and sewers, **MuncCorp** § 524

Consult Correlation Tables in text volumes for references to materials published after this index.

183

ILLUSTRATION 6-6.   Easements Entry from Pocket Part, 28A C.J.S. (1996 & Supp. 2007)

contract; and (7) by reference to boundaries or maps. Weeks v. Wolf Creek Industries, Inc., 2006 WL 1046245 (Ala. 2006).

An "easement" is a nonpossessory interest in the real property of another and arises through express grant or implication. Miller v. Kirkpatrick, 377 Md. 335, 833 A.2d 536 (2003).

The law will not permit a land-owner to create easements of every novel character and attach them to the soil. U.S. v. Blackman, 270 Va. 68, 613 S.E.2d 442 (2005).

B.   BY PRESCRIPTION

Research References

A.L.R. Library
    A.L.R. Index, Easements
    West's A.L.R. Digest, Easements ⊗1, 4 to 11

1. In General

§ 14 General considerations

Noncontiguousness does not bar the establishment of a prescriptive easement.[10.5]

[10.5]**Direct and apparent correction with dominant tenement sufficient**
Tenn.—Pevear v. Hunt, App., 924 S.W.2d 114.

§ 15 Time requisite for acquisition of easement by prescription

Cases

Rutland v. Stewart, 630 So. 2d 996 (Miss. 1994), to the extent that it hold that tacking may not be applied to establish an easement by prescription.

2. Character of Use and Enjoyment

§ 21 In general

Cases

Dominant owners' expenditure of labor and money to maintain the driveway across servient owners' land did not put servient owner on inquiry notice of claim of right for ten-year period required for prescriptive easement, given that use of the driveway was permitted by prior servient owner. Brede v. Koop, 706 N.W.2d 824 (Iowa 2005).

Landowners' failure to produce evidence to establish the boundaries of lands owned by their predecessors in title, who had become entitled to a prescriptive easement over lands owned by neighboring landowners, defeated their claim for a prescriptive easement, where landowners' property included additional land annexed to the dominant estates of their predecessor in title, the additional land created an impermissible increase in the easement's burden upon the servient estates, and the failure to establish the prior boundaries prevented the chancellor from restricting the benefit of the easement to those boundaries. Ellis v. Simmons, 270 Va. 371, 619 S.E.2d 88 (2005).

Prescriptive easement cannot be acquired without proof of adverse use, a claim of right under color of title or claim of right, use of such a kind as to put the owner of a subservient estate on notice of claim, and use that is continuous and uninterrupted adverse use for at least ten years. A.B. Cattle Co. v. Forgey Ranches, Inc., 943 P.2d 1184 (Wyo. 1997).

§ 22 Open and notorious

Cases

An easement by prescription is similar to the concept of adverse possession; it is created when a person uses another's land under a claim of right or color of title, openly, notoriously, continuously, and hostilely for ten years or more. Brede v. Koop, 706 N.W.2d 824 (Iowa 2005).

§ 23 With knowledge and acquiescence of owner

Cases

Landowners' acquiescence in mere use by neighbors of road on their property for seven years, without notice of adverse use in the form of making repairs or otherwise, did not authorize grant of prescriptive easement to neighbors; owners' acquiescence in mere use of road established, at most, a revocable license. Eileen B. White & Associates, Inc. v. Gunnells, 263 Ga. 360, 434 S.E.2d 477 (1993).

Notice to the servient owner of a claim of right to a prescriptive easement may be actual or established by known facts of such a nature as to impose a duty to make inquiry which would reveal the existence of an easement. Brede v. Koop, 706 N.W.2d 824 (Iowa 2005).

For a prescriptive easement, it must be established that the servient owner had express notice of the claim of right, not just the use of the land. Brede v. Koop, 706 N.W.2d 824 (Iowa 2005).

§ 31 Adverse or hostile

Cases

Continued use does not, by mere lapse of time, become hostile or adverse for purposes of a prescriptive easement. Brede v. Koop, 706 N.W.2d 824 (Iowa 2005).

§ 32 Adverse or hostile—Claim of right as element

Cases

Gioielli v. Mallard Cove Condominium Ass'n, Inc., 37 Conn. App. 822, 658 A.2d 134, 85 A.L.R.5th 797 (1995).

Prescriptive easement requirement of hostility refers to declarations or acts that show the declarant or actor claims a right to use the land; similarly, a claim of right requires evidence showing an easement is claimed as a right. Brede v. Koop, 706 N.W.2d 824 (Iowa 2005).

§ 36 Adverse or hostile—Use under grant, agreement, or reservation

Cases

Dominant owners' expenditure of labor and money

is updated by a pocket part that contains subsequent citations and references to support the legal premises discussed in the main volume. The pocket parts also have Library References at the beginning of various sections that indicate the correlating topic and key number in the West Digest system. C.J.S. is updated in the same manner as Am. Jur.

C.J.S. has a multivolume general index that is replaced annually. The general index is located in the last volumes of the set.

▼ How Do You Use C.J.S.?

There are three methods of using C.J.S.

1. **The general index method.** This is the most efficient method. Look up the appropriate subject in the set's general index just as you would in any encyclopedia's index to obtain references to titles and sections. If nothing is relevant, you may be given a *See also* instruction indicating that you should look up the subject using a different word.

2. **Title analysis method.** Review the title outline at the beginning of the subject or title and read the entry under the appropriate section.

3. **On WESTLAW.** WESTLAW is the only commercial database that has the full text of selected sections of CJS in the CJS database. Accessing CJS on WESTLAW permits key word searching. Updates to all entries are integrated into the document retrieved.

▼ How Is C.J.S. Cited?

Bluebook Rule 15.7 and *ALWD* Rule 26 cover legal encyclopedias. A citation to easements in §18 would be as follows:

28A C.J.S. <u>Easements</u> §18 (1996 & Supp. 2008)

4. State Law Encyclopedias

▼ Are There Any Legal Encyclopedias for State Law?

Yes, almost every jurisdiction has a legal encyclopedia. Illinois, for example, has *Illinois Law and Practice,* commonly known as I.L.P. I.L.P. is published by West and refers the reader to the other West resources such as the key numbers and the digests. West publishes many state encyclopedias such as *Florida Jurisprudence Second* and *Pennsylvania Jurisprudence Second.*

5. Online Encyclopedia Services

▼ Are Legal Encyclopedias Available on LEXIS or WESTLAW?

Legal encyclopedias are available online. Am. Jur. is on LEXIS. Selected portions of C.J.S. are on WESTLAW. Am. Jur. is on WESTLAW as well. Cornell University Legal Information Institute has a free legal encyclopedia called Wex. Wex can be accessed at <u>topics.law.cornell.edu/wex</u>.

E. *AMERICAN LAW REPORTS*

▼ What Are *American Law Reports?*

The *American Law Reports* (A.L.R.), formerly published by Lawyers Cooperative Publishing Co. and newly produced by West, contain annotations on narrow, well-defined legal topics. Each volume contains at least a half dozen annotations, or in-depth articles, about a legal issue and the pivotal case that prompted the examination of the issue. Subjects common to A.L.R. are torts, property, contracts, sales, and criminal law. Federal and state law are combined in A.L.R. until 1969. A.L.R. Federal (A.L.R. Fed.) began to be published in 1969. A.L.R. is in its 6th series. In print and updated with pocket part supplements are A.L.R., A.L.R.2d, A.L.R.3d, A.L.R.4th, A.L.R.5th, and A.L.R.6th. A.L.R. is published sequentially, just like case reporters, so that when a number of annotations are written, although they may bear no subject relationship to one another (just as with opinions), a volume of A.L.R. is published. A new volume is published about every six weeks.

Each volume of A.L.R. contains cases and annotations. The first section in each volume is a list entitled Subjects Annotated in this Volume. This provides a cross-reference for the annotations in the volume. The next section is *Table of Cases Reported,* which lists the full text decisions in the volume. Because every annotation is developed from a pivotal legal decision, A.L.R. reprints the full text of that decision before the annotation. Beginning with A.L.R.5th, the decisions are now found in the back of each volume. Researchers can also find the decisions by using the *American Law Reports Digest.* The Digest has synopses of the case opinions, and the cases themselves are cross-referenced and in A.L.R. volumes to the Digest headnotes. Following the text of each decision is the annotation, for example, the annotation entitled Locating Easement of Way Created by Necessity. The first page containing library references leads you to many other relevant practice aids. See Illustration 6-7. The next entry is a detailed outline of the annotation so that if you are interested in only a portion of the discussion, you can focus your research efforts. There is also an index so that you can see which subjects are discussed by section. See Illustration 6-8. Following the index is the Table of Jurisdictions Represented. See Illustration 6-9. The Table of Cases, Laws, and Rules makes A.L.R. a unique resource because the annotation includes every relevant statute or case from all of the appropriate jurisdictions. This is a windfall for the researcher.

▼ How Do You Use A.L.R.?

There are four basic methods of using A.L.R.

1. **The index method.** A.L.R. has a subject index for A.L.R.2d through A.L.R.5th, A.L.R. Fed., and *U.S. Supreme Court Reports, Lawyers' Edition.* See Illustration 6-10. It also contains a *Table of Statutes, Rules, and*

ILLUSTRATION 6-7. Total Client-Service Library References at 36 A.L.R.4th 769 (1985)

ANNOTATION

LOCATING EASEMENT OF WAY CREATED BY NECESSITY

by

William B. Johnson, J.D.

TOTAL CLIENT-SERVICE LIBRARY® REFERENCES

25 Am Jur 2d, Easements and Licenses §§ 64–69

Annotations: See the related matters listed in the annotation, infra.

9 Am Jur Pl & Pr Forms (Rev), Easements and Licenses, Forms 41–48

3 Am Jur Proof of Facts 2d 647, Abandonment of Easement; 5 Am Jur Proof of Facts 2d 621, Intent to Create Negative Easement; 33 Am Jur Proof of Facts 2d 669, Extent of Easement Over Servient Estate

22 Am Jur Trials 743, Condemnation of Easements

L Ed Index to Annos, Real Property; Trespass

ALR Quick Index, Access; Adjoining or Abutting Landowners; Easements; Ingress and Egress; Place or Location; Right of Way; Trespass; Way by Necessity

Federal Quick Index, Adjoining Landowners and Property; Easements and Right of Way; Ingress; Place and Location; Trespass

Auto-Cite®: Any case citation herein can be checked for form, parallel references, later history, and annotation references through the Auto-Cite computer research system.

Reprinted with permission of Thomson Reuters/West.

Regulations. A.L.R. (first series) has a separate index entitled the *Quick Index.* The index method requires that you find descriptive words for the issue or topic you are researching in one of A.L.R.'s indexes. This is a very efficient method.

2. **The digest method.** The A.L.R. Digest is organized like any other digest in topics and sections. Each section stands for a point of law. Under the digest entry is an encyclopedia reference to Am. Jur., if relevant, and to the case that stands for that premise of law. If a case is given a digest entry, then you may assume that an annotation will follow the case in the A.L.R. volume. This is a very good way to find multiple cases and multiple annotations dealing with related legal issues. This method is best when you find a good case that forms the basis for an annotation.

3. **The computerized method.** This is the best method of accessing A.L.R. annotations when available. LEXIS has the full text of A.L.R. online, as does WESTLAW. Using online access permits you to search

ILLUSTRATION 6-8. Outline of Annotation at 36 A.L.R.4th 770 (1985)

EASEMENT OF WAY BY NECESSITY—LOCATION   36 ALR4th
36 ALR4th 769

Locating easement of way created by necessity

INDEX

Reprinted with permission of Thomson Reuters/West.

for relevant annotations using the words that you think would appear in an annotation on point.

    4. *Shepard's.* This is also an excellent way to find A.L.R. annotations. *Shepard's* lists any A.L.R. citations in which the opinion you are Shepardizing is cited. See Illustration 4-3. At the end of the *Shepard's* treatment for *Illinois v. Foskey* 1990, you see 1 AL₄673s. This means that *Foskey* is cited in this A.L.R. annotation.

▼ Why Would You Use A.L.R.?

A.L.R. is best consulted when you are researching a narrow, well-defined issue, similar to how you might use a law review article. The major difference between A.L.R. and a law review article is that

ILLUSTRATION 6-9.   Table of Jurisdictions Represented at 36 A.L.R.4th 771 (1985) from WESTLAW Table of Cases, Laws, and Rules

36 A.L.R.4th 769

36 A.L.R.4th 769 (Originally published in 1985)

American Law Reports ALR4th
The ALR databases are made current by the weekly addition of relevant new cases.

Table of Cases, Laws, and Rules

First Circuit

  Bandelin v. Clark, 7 La. App. 64, 1927 WL 3637 (1st Cir. 1927) — 9[a]

  Breeden v. Lee, 2 La. App. 126, 1925 WL 3669 (1st Cir. 1925) — 2[b], 9[b]

Arkansas

  Nation v. Ayres, 340 Ark. 270, 9 S.W.3d 512 (2000) — 9[a]

  White v. Grimmett, 223 Ark. 237, 265 S.W.2d 1 (1954) — 10

California

  Kripp v. Curtis, 71 Cal. 62, 11 P. 879 (1886) — 4, 5, 7[a]

A.L.R. provides you with indexed terms, an outline, a table of law from other jurisdictions, and library references to encyclopedias, form books, and digest topics. A.L.R., however, is not considered nearly as scholarly as a law review article.

It is best not to cite A.L.R. annotations and to not rely on them as authority unless absolutely necessary. Cite to the primary source materials that A.L.R. annotations provide after reading the primary authority to determine its relevance.

▼ How Do You Cite to an A.L.R. Annotation?

Citation style for A.L.R. is found in *Bluebook* Rule 16.5.5. and *ALWD* Rule 24, as follows:

ILLUSTRATION 6-10.   A.L.R. Index Entry for Easements in A.L.R. Quick Index

ALR QUICK INDEX

EARS AND HEARING—Cont'd
Preexisting conditions
  sufficiency of proof that condition of
    skin or sensory organ resulted from
    accident or incident in suit rather than
    from preexisting condition, **2 ALR3d
    446**
  sufficiency of proof that mental or
    neurological condition complained of
    resulted from accident or incident in
    suit rather than from preexisting
    condition, **2 ALR3d 487**
Products liability, what is an unavoidably
  unsafe product, **70 ALR4th 16**
Telephone company, liability of telephone
  company for injury by noise or electric
  charge transmitted over line, **99 ALR3d
  628**
Unemployment compensation, leaving
  employment, or unavailability for particular job or duties, because of sickness or
  disability, as affecting right to unemployment compensation, **68 ALR5th 13**
Voice identification testimony, cautionary
  instructions to jury as to reliability of, or
  factors to be considered in evaluating,
  voice identification testimony, **17 ALR5th
  851**
Witnesses, deaf-mutes as, **50 ALR4th 1188**
Workers' compensation liability of successive
  employers for disease or condition allegedly attributable to successive employ-
  ments, **34 ALR4th 958**

EARTH
Soil or Earth (this index)

EARTHQUAKES
Building and construction contracts, liabilities
  or risks of loss arising out of contract for
  repairs or additions to, or installations in,
  existing building which, without fault of
  either party, is destroyed pending performance, **28 ALR3d 788**
Insurance
  business interruption insurance, **37
    ALR5th 41**
  exclusion of loss, construction and effect
    of provision excluding loss caused by
    earth movement or earthquake, **44
    ALR3d 1316**
Post-transfer damage to property, vendor's
  liability to purchaser, **18 ALR4th 1168**
Property insurance, construction and effect of
  provision excluding loss caused by earth
  movement or earthquake, **44 ALR3d 1316**
Res ipsa loquitur as applicable in actions for
  damage to property by the overflow or
  escape of water, **91 ALR3d 186**

EASEMENTS
Abandonment, loss of private easement by
  nonuse, **62 ALR5th 219**
Abstract of title, liability of one preparing
  abstract of title, for deficiencies therein, to

EASEMENTS—Cont'd
  one other than person directly contracting
    for abstract, **34 ALR3d 1122**
Access
  misuse, what constitutes, and remedies
    for, misuse of easement, **111 ALR5th
    313**
  scope of prescriptive easement for
    access (easement of way), **79 ALR4th
    604**
Access Roads (this index)
Adverse possession
  building, adverse possession based on
    encroachment of building or other
    structure, **2 ALR3d 1005**
  loss of private easement by nonuse, **62
    ALR5th 219**
  presumptions and evidence respecting
    identification of land on which prop-
    erty taxes were paid to establish
    adverse possession, **36 ALR4th 843**
Alleys (this index)
Animals, liability of person, other than owner
  of animal or owner or operator of motor
  vehicle, for damage to motor vehicle or
  injury to person riding therein resulting
  from collision with domestic animal at
  large in street or highway, **21 ALR4th 132**
Beaches and Shores (this index)
Boating, fishing, wading or recreational rights
  of public in inland streams the bed of
  which is privately owned, **6 ALR4th 1030**
Bridges (this index)
Cemeteries (this index)
Change or modification
  extent of, and permissible variations in,
    use of prescriptive easements of way,
    5 ALR3d 439
  loss of private easement by nonuse, **62
    ALR5th 219**
Consent
  grant, easement of way created by grant
    which does not specify location, **24
    ALR4th 1053**
  necessity, easement of way created by
    necessity, locating, **36 ALR4th 769**
Costs and expenses
  maintenance or repair, right of servient
    owner to maintain, improve, or repair
    easement of way at expense of
    dominant owner, **20 ALR3d 1026**
  necessity ways, way of necessity over
    another's land where a means of
    access does exit but is claimed to be
    inadequate, inconvenient, difficult, or
    costly, **10 ALR4th 447**
Covenants, taking as applied to prescriptive
  easements, **72 ALR3d 648**
Crane or derrick, liability of owner or
  occupant of premises for injury or death
  resulting from contact of crane, derrick or
  other movable machine with electric line,
  14 ALR4th 913

For assistance using this index, call 1-800-328-4880

William B. Johnson, Annotation, <u>Locating Easement of Way Cre-</u><u>ated by Necessity</u>, 36 A.L.R.4th 769 (1985 & Supp. 2008)

ALWD requires italicizing the article title.

▼ How Do You Update an A.L.R. Annotation?

A.L.R. (first series) Volumes 1 to 175 are updated in the *Blue Book of Supplemental Decisions.* This is a separate set of books that comes out every two years that updates the annotations in Volumes 1 to 175. It also indicates where annotations have been superseded or supplemented in later editions or series of the A.L.R. Entries are organized by volume and page numbers.

A.L.R.2d is updated by using the separate set entitled the *A.L.R.2d Later Case Service.* All entries are found by volume and page numbers.

The best way to update A.L.R.3d, 4th, 5th, 6th, or Fed. annotations is to consult the pocket part supplement to the volume to see if additional annotations and new statute and case law references are mentioned. Pocket parts are issued at least annually.

You can update an ALR annotation on WESTLAW or LEXIS. Retrieve the annotation on the commercial database. Weekly additions of new cases integrate the updates into the annotations.

Last, always use the Annotation History Table in the Tables volume to see if the annotation is superseded.

▼ Can A.L.R. Annotations Be Shepardized?

A.L.R. annotations can be Shepardized to see where they are cited in reported opinions and to see if a case reprinted in the A.L.R. has a parallel cite in a reporter. This information is found in *Shepard's Citations for Annotations.*

F. TREATISES AND HORNBOOKS

▼ What Are Treatises and Hornbooks?

Both hornbooks and treatises are secondary sources because they provide commentary, analysis, and criticism of the law and are written by private parties. Treatises and hornbooks help the researcher to understand the topic and, through cited references, provide citations to cases and statutes. **Treatises** are scholarly works, generally multivolume sets, that examine one legal topic, such as contracts, in great detail and with very broad coverage. **Hornbooks**, also scholarly but designed for the student of law, are generally one-volume works providing an overview of a single legal topic. The authors of hornbooks and treatises are legal scholars.

▼ How Do You Find a Thorough Treatise or Hornbook?

The best place to look for a hornbook or treatise is in the law library. The librarian will be able to refer you to the treatises that are best for the legal topic you are researching. There is a treatise for almost every legal subject. Many hornbooks are published by West Publishing Co. At the beginning of a West hornbook is a list entitled *Hornbook Series and Basic Legal Texts,* which provides all of the hornbooks categorized by legal subject.

NET NOTE

www.ll.georgetown.edu/guides/treatisefinder.cfm provides a list of treatises by topic and also indicates if the format is hard copy, online, or both.

▼ Which Treatises Are Most Noteworthy?

The following treatises are well known and respected.

> Corbin, *Contracts*
> Hazan, *Securities Regulation*
> Herzog, *Bankruptcy*
> Kratovil and Werner, *Real Estate Law*
> LaFave and Scott, *Criminal Law*
> McCormick, *Evidence*
> Nowak, Rotunda, and Young, *Constitutional Law*
> Prosser, *Torts*
> White and Summers, *Uniform Commercial Code* (this treatise is also on WESTLAW)
> Wright and Miller, *Federal Practice and Procedure*

▼ Why Do You Use a Treatise?

There are a few approaches to using a treatise. Because the treatise covers a single legal topic and is written like a text, rather than like a case opinion, it is easy to find relevant information. The amount of relevant information may present the only problem when using a treatise: so much detail is provided that you may lose sight of the focus of your research. A treatise is used to find a very detailed analysis of a point of law or a legal rule. A hornbook is used to find an overview of a point of law or a legal rule. Both sources provide the general rules of law, its exceptions, and information on how the law is evolving. Often, a treatise or hornbook offers discussion of how the legal rules are applied in specific situations or in specific factual scenarios. You should use a treatise or a hornbook to

educate yourself in a legal discipline or when an encyclopedia does not offer adequate detail in the discussion of a topic.

▼ How Do You Use a Treatise or Hornbook?

There are three methods of using a treatise or a hornbook.

1. **The table of contents method.** Treatises and hornbooks have detailed tables of contents that serve as outlines of the legal topics covered. A chapter or a subchapter often discusses the area you are researching.

2. **The table method.** Hornbooks and treatises contain tables of cases and tables of statutes. Use the relevant table when you have an excellent case or statute on point and want to understand the significance of the primary source in the context of the subject as a whole.

3. **The index method.** A subject index is found at the end of every treatise and hornbook. The index is a good place to start if you have found a word like *easement* and want to find out its relevance in property law.

▼ Are Treatises Ever Relied on as Authority?

Treatises are occasionally relied on as authority in a document when no primary authority is available on point and when it is necessary to show the progression or evolution of the law. Because scholars write treatises, they are considered to be very prestigious sources of secondary authority. Hornbooks should not be relied on for authority because they are designed for the student and are diluted versions of treatises.

▼ How Do You Cite to a Hornbook and a Treatise?

Bluebook Rules 15.1.1 and 3.4 cover citation style for treatises and hornbooks. *ALWD* Rule 22.1 uses the same format.

Wayne LaFave, *Search and Seizure: A Treatise on the Fourth Amendment* (4th ed. 2004 & Supp. 2008)

▼ Are Treatises Available Online?

More and more treatise titles are appearing online. WESTLAW, because it is part of West, makes an increasing number of treatise titles available online, and its list is growing. Often updates are available online so that you can access the newest case references. LEXIS also has an expanding number of treatises available. The benefit of using a treatise online is that you can perform full text searching whereby you construct a query and retrieve relevant information with your own selection of terms rather than relying on any of the traditional research methods. Some treatises are now available on the Internet.

▼ How Are Treatises and Hornbooks Updated?

Treatises are updated in two ways: pocket parts of supplements, which are published at least annually, and new editions. Always check to see that you are working with the most recent edition available and to see if there is a pocket part or updating supplement.

G. RESTATEMENTS OF THE LAW

▼ What Are Restatements?

Restatements of the Law, published by the American Law Institute, are the most prestigious source of secondary authority. The subjects covered are agency, conflict of laws, contracts, foreign relations, judgments, property, restitution, security, torts, and trusts. There is a Restatement on Security, but this set is only in the first edition. Each of the legal disciplines mentioned comprises a separate set of the Restatements. The authors of the Restatements write every rule of law from these legal disciplines in a form that resembles a code and not a judicial opinion. The drafters of the Restatements are "restating" the law. The purposes are to codify the common law holdings so that a researcher does not have to unearth the legal rule from the text of an opinion and to make common law principles straightforward and succinct, like statutes. The Comments and the Illustrations are most helpful in understanding the application of the rule. The Reporter's Note, following the Illustrations, contains case references in which the Restatement section has been cited. See Illustration 6-11.

▼ How Are the Restatements Updated?

Most of the Restatements are in their second series. The rules, the codified-type versions of the legal principles, are updated in the appendix. Additional case references are also included in the appendix. The appendix is organized by section in the same order as the main text. The appendix is updated annually by pocket part supplements that are organized in the same manner as the main volume, by section. Also, semiannually a pamphlet is published called the *Interim Case Citations to the Restatements of Law.*

▼ How Do You Use the Restatements?

1. **The table of contents method.** Every set of the Restatements begins with a table of contents. See Illustration 6-12. The table of contents is an outline of the entire legal discipline, by topic and then within the topic, by rule. This is not a very efficient method, but it gives the researcher insight into where the section fits into the legal discipline. For instance, §174 of the Restatement (Second) of Contracts is entitled When Duress by Physical Compulsion Prevents Formation of a

ILLUSTRATION 6-11.   Sample Pages from Restatement (Second) of Contracts

---

Ch. 10   PERFORMANCE AND NON-PERFORMANCE   § 235

on Illustration 6 to former § 267. Beach v. First Fed. Sav. & Loan Ass'n, 140 Ga. App. 882, 232 S.E.2d 158 (1977). Illustration 5 is adapted from Illustration 7 to former § 267.

Comment c. See former § 272. Illustration 6 is based on Illustration 1 to former § 268 and on Kane v. Hood, 30 Mass. (13 Pick.) 281 (1832). Illustration 7 is based on Illustration 2 to former § 268.

Comment d. This Comment replaces former § 273. See 3A Corbin, Contracts § 689 (1951); 6 Williston, Contracts § 887C (3d ed. 1962). Illustration 8 is based on Illustration 2 to former § 273 and on Beecher v. Conradt, 13 N.Y. (3 Kern.) 108 (1855); see also Kennelly v. Shapiro, 227 A.D. 488, 226 N.Y.S. 692 (1928).

Comment e. On the origin of the principle, see 6 Williston, Contracts §

830 (3d ed. 1962); Murray, Contracts § 162 (2d rev. ed. 1974). That a substantial failure to make timely progress payments is a material breach when the payments are required by a construction contract, see United States ex rel. Micro-King Co. v. Community Science Technology, Inc., 574 F.2d 1292, 1295 n.3 (5th Cir. 1978).

Comment f. Illustration 9 is based on Stewart v. Newbury, 220 N.Y. 379, 115 N.E. 984 (1917). See also Illustration 1 to former § 270. Illustration 10 is based on Clark v. Gulesian, 197 Mass. 492, 84 N.E. 94 (1908). The facts in Illustration 11 are taken from New Era Homes v. Forster, 299 N.Y. 303, 86 N.E.2d 757 (1949). Illustration 12 is based on Comment *a* to former § 270 and Illustration 1 to former § 268.

TOPIC 2.   EFFECT OF PERFORMANCE AND NON-PERFORMANCE

§ 235.   Effect of Performance as Discharge and of Non-Performance as Breach

> (1) **Full performance of a duty under a contract discharges the duty.**
>
> (2) **When performance of a duty under a contract is due any non-performance is a breach.**

Comment:

    a. Discharge by performance. Under the rule stated in Subsection (1), a duty is discharged when it is fully performed. Nothing less than full performance, however, has this effect and any defect in performance, even an insubstantial one, prevents discharge on this ground. The defect need not be wilful or even negligent. Although a court may ignore trifling departures, performance that is merely substantial does not result in discharge under Subsection (1). See Comment *d* to § 237. A duty may, of course, be discharged on some other ground. See Chapter 12. For example, a duty that has not been fully

---

Contract. This section falls under Topic 2, Duress and Undue Influence, which is part of Chapter 7, Misrepresentation, Duress, and Undue Influence.

    2. **The index method.** Use the index at the end of the set by looking up various descriptive words pertaining to your issue. Under Duress is Physical Compulsion §174. This method is moderately efficient.

    3. **The table of cases method.** When you have an excellent case on point, use the table of cases, organized in alphabetical order by

ILLUSTRATION 6-11.   *Continued*

performed may be discharged on the ground of impracticability of performance. See Chapter 11.

Illustration:

1. A contracts to build a house for B for $50,000 according to specifications furnished by B. A builds the house according to the specifications. A's duty to build the house is discharged.

b. *Effect of non-performance.* Non-performance is not a breach unless performance is due. Performance may not be due because a required period of time has not passed, or because a condition has not occurred (§ 225), or because the duty has already been discharged (Chapter 12) as, for example, by impracticability of performance (Chapter 11). In such a case non-performance is justified. When performance is due, however, anything short of full performance is a breach, even if the party who does not fully perform was not at fault and even if the defect in his performance was not substantial. Non-performance of a duty when performance is due is a breach whether the duty is imposed by a promise stated in the agreement or by a term supplied by the court (§ 204), as in the case of the duty of good faith and fair dealing (§ 205). Non-performance includes defective performance as well as an absence of performance.

Illustrations:

2. The facts being otherwise as stated in Illustration 1, A builds the house according to the specifications except for an inadvertent variation in kitchen fixtures which can easily be remedied for $100. A's non-performance is a breach.

3. A contracts with B to manufacture and deliver 100,000 plastic containers for a price of $100,000. The colors of the containers are to be selected by B from among those specified in the contract. B delays in making his selection for an unreasonable time, holding up their manufacture and causing A loss. B's delay is a breach. His duty of good faith and fair dealing (§ 205) includes a duty to make his selection within a reasonable time.

4. A contracts with B to repair B's building for $20,000, payment to be made "on the satisfaction of C, B's architect, and the issuance of his certificate." A makes the repairs but does not ask C for his certificate. B does not pay A. B's non-performance is not a breach. It is justified on the ground that performance is not due because of the non-occurrence of a condition. See Illustration 5 to § 227.

plaintiff, to find references in the Restatements. This is the most efficient method when you have a specific case on point.

4. **The online method.** The Restatements are available on LEXIS and WESTLAW. This is an efficient method to use when you know the significant vocabulary words that describe the subject. If you are unfamiliar with the terminology or the words used to describe the legal principles, then the online method is very costly and not very efficient. However, case citations for Restatement sections are kept current online and are easy to use.

▼ Can the Restatements Be Shepardized?

Yes, the Restatements can be Shepardized in the *Shepard's Restatement of Law Citations*. The *Shepard's* for the Restatements does not in any way

ILLUSTRATION 6-12.   Table of Contents from Restatement (Second) of Contracts

validate the authority because the Restatements are secondary sources. *Shepard's,* in this instance, is a citator telling the researcher which cases contain citations to the Restatements.

▼ Are the Restatements Available Online?

Yes, as mentioned earlier, the Restatements are available online on both LEXIS and WESTLAW. The advantage of searching the Restatements online is that you do not have to rely on indexing terms. However, using the Restatements online can be very expensive if you are unfamiliar with the legal terms used.

▼ How Are the Restatements Cited?

Bluebook Rule 12.8.5 indicates that Restatements are cited as follows:

Restatement (Second) of Contracts §235 (1979).

The year that the Restatement section was published is on the title page of every Restatements volume.

When citing to a Comment or Illustration that follows the Restatement section, Rule 3.5 of the *Bluebook* applies.

Restatement (Second) of Contracts §235 cmt. a, illus. 2 (1979).

See Citation Appendix for *ALWD* Rule 27 format.

H. LEGAL PERIODICALS

▼ What Are Legal Periodicals?

Legal periodicals are secondary sources ranging from very prestigious to very practical forms of authority. Scholarly law review articles are considered the most prestigious, and bar journals and commercial publications are considered the most pragmatic. The major categories of legal periodicals are:

1. academic law reviews
2. bar journals and practitioner's periodicals
3. commercial journals and newsletters
4. legal newspapers

Every conceivable subject is covered in a legal periodical. Some legal periodicals focus on a particular practice area, like estate planning. The different forms of legal periodicals have different attributes.

▼ Why Would You Use a Legal Periodical?

Legal periodicals are published quickly and keep abreast of new legal issues and laws. They are a terrific place to obtain articles discussing the impact of a Supreme Court decision or the enactment of new legislation because such information is published very quickly, far faster than any text could be printed. Also, certain legal periodicals (for example, the practitioner's journals, the journals that pertain to specific bar association sections, the commercial journals, and newsletters) cover discrete legal subject areas and enable paralegals, practitioners, and researchers to keep up with all of the new developments in their respective practice areas. The Web site for a particular legal periodical or journal is also a terrific resource.

The legal newspapers provide up-to-date information about the legal profession, the courts and significant opinions, the federal and state legislatures and significant laws, and information about law firms and the business of law. Legal newspapers also write about major and interesting cases and clients. Legal newspapers provide great insight into the realities of legal practice.

Academic law review articles are very scholarly and are excellent finding tools because of the voluminous number of cited references

in each article. Academic law review articles are often theoretical and discuss the application of a particular legal doctrine or a trend in the law. Sometimes authors of law review articles suggest how the law should hold on certain issues. Because the academic law reviews are a very prestigious source of secondary authority, sometimes these resources are relied on for persuasive purposes when no primary authority is available on point.

▼ How Do You Obtain Relevant Legal Periodical Articles?

First, the researcher must decide the type of information needed. For example, is scholarly material required, or is practical information on drafting a will needed? After deciding on the type of information required for the project, the source should be selected accordingly. If scholarly material is required, then an academic law review would be appropriate. If practical information is needed, then a practitioner's journal, bar association section newsletter, or commercial publication dealing with the legal discipline is appropriate. If the researcher needs information about a law firm, a client, or a very recent (two-week-old) Supreme Court decision, then a legal newspaper is the ideal source.

Almost all legal periodicals, regardless of format, are indexed. The major indexes are:

Current Law Index (1980 to present): the most comprehensive hard-copy index; the contents are included in the CD-ROM product entitled *Legal Resource Index.*

Index to Legal Periodicals (1908 to present): goes back farther than *Current Law Index* and contains sections on book reviews, statutes, and cases.

Kindex: includes articles related to juvenile law.

Index to Foreign Legal Periodicals (1960 to present): index to federal tax articles.

NET NOTE

Many law reviews have their own Web sites. Start with the law school Web site. Also, you can do a full-text search of journals on the Web at <u>lawreview .org</u>. The University Law School Project sponsors this site. Findlaw also has journal access at <u>stu.findlaw.com/journals</u>. Another resource is <u>ilrg.com/ indices.html</u>.

▼ Are Legal Periodicals Available Online?

Yes, legal periodicals are available online on both LEXIS and WESTLAW. LEXIS has the LAWREV library, which contains the full text articles, cover to cover, of an increasing number of law reviews. Also, the NEWS library on LEXIS contains the full text copies of legal newspapers. WESTLAW has the full text articles from an increasing number of law reviews. Most law reviews have Web addresses.

▼ How Do You Cite to a Law Review or Law Journal?

Bluebook Rule 16 and Table 14 and *ALWD* Rule 23 cover the citation form:

Mitchell N. Berman, *Justification and Excuse, Law and Morality,* 53 Duke L.J. 1 (2003).

A legal newspaper is cited according to *Bluebook* Rule 16.5.

Wayne Smith, <u>Remote Access: Striking a Balance</u>, Law Tech. News, Jan. 2005, at 11.

For abbreviations of legal periodicals not included in the *ALWD Citation Manual,* 2nd edition, go to <u>alwd.org</u>, click "ALWD Citation Manual" and select the "expanded appendices," and then click "Appendix 5."

Using all formats of secondary sources can be reinforced with the tutorial found at <u>www.ll.georgetown.edu/tutorials/second/print.html</u>.

CHAPTER SUMMARY

Secondary authorities describe, analyze, and criticize primary sources. You use secondary authorities to educate yourself about a legal topic and to find citations to primary sources.

The major sources of secondary authority are dictionaries, thesauri, encyclopedias, *American Law Reports* (A.L.R.), hornbooks, treatises, Restatements of the Law, and legal periodicals.

Dictionaries and thesauri are used to find definitions and synonyms. Encyclopedias are used to educate yourself about a legal topic. *American Law Reports* contain articles called annotations that explore a legal issue in depth. Hornbooks are written for the student of law and cover a single legal subject. Treatises cover a single legal subject but go into great detail. Restatements of the Law, produced by the American Law Institute, attempt to organize common law holdings from cases into a format resembling statutes. Legal periodicals

include academic law reviews, bar association and legal specialty publications, and legal newspapers. Law reviews are the most scholarly form of legal periodicals. Law review articles contain many citations to primary authority and are known for research accuracy.

Updating and correctly citing secondary authorities are important in your research process. Generally, it is best to rely on primary authority when writing a memo or a brief. Rely on secondary authority when there is no primary authority on point.

KEY TERMS

American Jurisprudence	legal meaning
American Law Reports	legal periodicals
Cumulative Supplements	Restatements of the Law
hornbooks	secondary authority
legal dictionary	thesaurus
legal encyclopedia	treatises

EXERCISES

COMPARING SECONDARY AUTHORITIES

1. Look up the word *easement* in a legal dictionary. Now look up the same word in a thesaurus. Compare the two sources and the information provided. What is different?

   Now look up the word *easement* in your state legal encyclopedia (if you do not have a state legal encyclopedia available, use Am. Jur. or C.J.S.). How is the term treated in an encyclopedia? How is this different from a dictionary?

ENCYCLOPEDIA RESEARCH

2. Locate the section in Am. Jur. 2d discussing *easements by necessity*. First, try to locate the section by using the index method, then by the topic outline method. Go to the encyclopedia volume for the sections that you found. Examine the treatment of *easements by necessity*. Do you see any cases from your state? Now update the section in the pocket part. Are there any new case references?

   Repeat this exercise using C.J.S. How do the encyclopedias differ? How are they similar?

3. Look up *Pawnbroker* in the index of C.J.S. or Am. Jur. 2d. Are there any encyclopedia sections discussing pawnbrokers? Now look up *Pawnbroker* in your state legal encyclopedia. Are there any relevant cases or statutes from your state?

4. Look up *gaming* in C.J.S. How is the topic organized?

Go to the index for C.J.S. and look up *casinos.* Where can you find discussion of *casinos* in C.J.S.? In the index entry *casinos,* are there references to sections outside the topic of *gaming?*

Now, go to the pocket part at the end of the volume containing the topic *gaming.* Does the pocket part contain updates to the topic of *gaming?*

List one recent case mentioned in the pocket part. Is it a state case or a federal case?

What do topic updates in the pocket part look like? How are they different, in general, than the entries in the main volume for the topic?

5. Use Am. Jur. 2d. Is there a topic called *gaming?* What similar topic covers the subject of gaming in Am. Jur. 2d?

Go to the index in Am. Jur. 2d and look up *gaming.* Where are you led to?

Compare the text in the main volume of Am. Jur. 2d that covers a topic similar to the *gaming* topic in C.J.S. How are the topics similar and how are they different?

Does Am. Jur. 2d have a pocket part to the main volume that updates the topics?

Using the index to Am. Jur. 2d, look up *casinos.* What do you find?

6. How are Am. Jur. 2d and C.J.S. similar? How are they different?

What research benefits do you obtain when consulting a legal encyclopedia?

Do either Am. Jur. 2d or C.J.S. lead you to other library resources or research tools?

7. Look up *negligence* in a law dictionary. Look up *negligence* in either C.J.S. or Am. Jur. 2d. What did you find in each source? How do the sources differ in their treatment of *negligence?*

Assignment for Encyclopedia Research

8. Read the following fact situation, which you first encountered in Chapter 4. Answer the questions following the situation.

FACTS

Nate Late, a business owner, has two partners in the operation of Loose Cannon Manufacturing in Gurnee, Illinois. He owns $33^1/_3$ percent of a $3 million company. Late is ill, but not dying. He is grooming a 26-year-old, Ivan T. All, to run the business. He tells his family he likes All and wants to teach him the business. Nate Late dies.

The most current will leaves Late's estate to his wife of 24 years, Shirley Late, and his only son, Lou Sier. Mr. All tells Mrs. Late that her husband told All he intended to give the 26-year-old his one-third interest in Loose Cannon. This conversation took place in front of a bank president. No written record exists concerning Late's intention to give his stock to All. However, family members knew that Late intended for All to run the business and for All to get something if the business was sold. None of the family believed that Late intended to give the

business to newcomer Ivan T. All. Late's shares of stock were never given to All. The shares were in the safe deposit box shared by Late and his wife.

Mrs. Late said that Mr. Late planned to give her the shares. He told her this when he opened the joint safety deposit box and gave her the key.

You work for a firm that has been retained by Mrs. Late. She would like to know if All can prove that Mr. Late gave All Mr. Late's interest in the company.

a. What topics might be relevant to this question?

b. How would you determine where to find those topics?

c. List the steps that you would take.

d. Take those steps. Note what you find.

e. Select two topics for review. Review those topics. Which topics were most relevant?

f. What additional information did you find to determine the answer to Mrs. Late's question?

g. Where did you find that information?

h. List the two most relevant cases that address this problem.

Use the Index to Legal Periodicals to find case citations and articles about this case.

9. Consult the table of cases in the Sept. '03-Aug. '04 *Index to Legal Periodicals.* Find the cite to *Amos v. Glynn County Board of Tax Assessors.* After finding the cite to the case, write it in correct citation format. Find the cite to an article discussing *Amos v. Glynn County Board of Tax Assessors.*

10. Use lawreview.org to find an article discussing "Cybercrime."

11. Consult the Subject and Author Index of the 2008 Index to Legal Periodicals. Is there an article from a country, aside from the United States, on easements? Provide the citation.

12. On WESTLAW, search Pennsylvania legal encyclopedia or *Pennsylvania Jurisprudence* for an entry on easements concerning "Private Ways and Alleys."

13. Consult *Florida Jurisprudence Second* on WESTLAW. List citations to sections concerning easements, alleys, and rights-of-way.

CONSTITUTIONS AND STATUTES

CHAPTER OVERVIEW

Constitutions and statutes occupy the highest rung in the hierarchy of authority. Constitutions are the highest form of legal authority, only to be followed by statutes. In ordinary legal dilemmas, statutes are often the controlling law. In our society statutes govern relationships like marriage and adoption, transactions like banking, and behavior like criminal acts. Learning how to find relevant statutes and constitutional provisions is very important for effective legal research.

This chapter details the research methods used to find, to cite, and to validate constitutions and statutes. The legislative process that charts the path that a statute takes from initial sponsorship through codification is outlined. This chapter gives you the skills you need to perform constitutional and statutory research.

A. CONSTITUTIONS

▼ What Is a Constitution?

A **constitution** is a document that establishes the legal structure of a state or nation and the basic legal principles that control the operation of the government and the conduct of its citizens.

▼ What Is the Relationship Between the Federal Constitution and the State Constitutions?

The U.S. Constitution is, in essence, the supreme law of the land. The state constitutions are the supreme law of each particular state. The federal constitution takes precedence over any state constitution. What does this mean? Only the U.S. Congress can repeal or redraft legislation or amend the U.S. Constitution. If a federal court determines that a state constitutional provision violates the U.S. Constitution, then the court must deem that section of the state constitution unconstitutional.

▼ Who Determines Whether a Statute Violates the U.S. Constitution?

Federal courts determine whether a statute violates the U.S. Constitution, and state courts determine if their respective state constitutions are being violated. Although courts determine if a statute violates the constitution, courts cannot rewrite or repeal statutes; only legislatures can.

▼ Can Federal and State Constitutions Be Validated?

Yes, federal and state constitutions can be validated. KeyCite and *Shepard's United States Citations* indicates if a court of law has interpreted or applied a section of the U.S. Constitution in question. KeyCite and *Shepard's* serve to validate the authority and are finding tools to obtain relevant case law decisions applying the constitutional section or amendment at issue in your research. See Illustration 7-1. Illustration 7-2 is the page from one decision cited in *Shepard's* mentioning the Fourth Amendment (see arrow in Illustration 7-1). State constitutions are validated in the particular state code *Shepard's* or on KeyCite. For a full discussion of how to validate authority, see Chapter 5.

▼ Where Are Federal and State Constitutions Found?

The full text of the current version of the U.S. Constitution as well as all the amendments are contained in the first volume of the annotated versions of the *United States Code* (U.S.C.), the *United States Code Service* (U.S.C.S.), and the *United States Code Annotated* (U.S.C.A.). Encyclopedias are also sources of unannotated versions of the U.S. Constitution.

ILLUSTRATION 7-1. Sample Page, Retrieved from LEXIS, Showing *Shepard's* Analysis of the Fourth Amendment with Citing Decisions

Copyright 2008 SHEPARD'S(R) - 101 Citing references

U.S. Const. amend. 4, U.S. Const. amend. 4

CITING DECISIONS (94 citing decisions)

U.S. SUPREME COURT

8. **Cited by:**
   Nathanson v. United States, 290 U.S. 41, 54 S. Ct. 11, 78 L. Ed. 159, 1933 U.S. LEXIS 961 (1933)
     290 U.S. 41 *p.41*
     78 L. Ed. 159 *p.159*
     54 S. Ct. 11 *p.11*

9. **Cited by:**
   Sgro v. United States, 287 U.S. 206, 53 S. Ct. 138, 77 L. Ed. 260, 1932 U.S. LEXIS 13, 85 A.L.R. 108 (1932)
     287 U.S. 206 *p.206*
     53 S. Ct. 138 *p.138*
     77 L. Ed. 260 *p.260*

10. **Cited by:**
    Grau v. United States, 287 U.S. 124, 53 S. Ct. 38, 77 L. Ed. 212, 1932 U.S. LEXIS 9 (1932)
      287 U.S. 124 *p.124*
      77 L. Ed. 212 *p.212*
      53 S. Ct. 38 *p.38*

11. **Cited by:**
    Taylor v. United States, 286 U.S. 1, 52 S. Ct. 466, 76 L. Ed. 951, 1932 U.S. LEXIS 593 (1932)
      286 U.S. 1 *p.1*
      76 L. Ed. 951 *p.951*
      52 S. Ct. 466 *p.466*

12. **Cited by:**
    United States v. Lefkowitz, 285 U.S. 452, 52 S. Ct. 420, 76 L. Ed. 877, 1932 U.S. LEXIS 446, 82 A.L.R. 775 (1932)
      285 U.S. 452 *p.452*
      52 S. Ct. 420 *p.420*
      76 L. Ed. 877 *p.877*

13. **Cited by:**
    Crowell v. Benson, 285 U.S. 22, 52 S. Ct. 285, 76 L. Ed. 598, 1932 U.S. LEXIS 773, 1932 A.M.C. 355 (1932)
      285 U.S. 22 *p.37*
      52 S. Ct. 285 *p.287*
      76 L. Ed. 598 *p.604*

14. **Cited by:**
    Blackmer v. United States, 284 U.S. 421, 52 S. Ct. 252, 76 L. Ed. 375, 1932 U.S. LEXIS 882 (1932)
      284 U.S. 421 *p.441*
      52 S. Ct. 252 *p.256*
      76 L. Ed. 375 *p.385*

ILLUSTRATION 7-1. *Continued*

15. **Cited by:**
    Husty v. United States, 282 U.S. 694, 51 S. Ct. 240, 75 L. Ed. 629, 1931 U.S. LEXIS 37, 74 A.L.R. 1407 (1931)
    282 U.S. 694 *p.694*
    51 S. Ct. 240 *p.240*

16. **Cited by:**
    Alford v. United States, 282 U.S. 687, 51 S. Ct. 218, 75 L. Ed. 624, 1931 U.S. LEXIS 36 (1931)
    75 L. Ed. 624 *p.629*

▶17. **Cited by:**
    Go-Bart Importing Co. v. United States, 282 U.S. 344, 51 S. Ct. 153, 75 L. Ed. 374, 1931 U.S. LEXIS 842 (1931)
    282 U.S. 344 *p.345*
    75 L. Ed. 374 *p.375*
    51 S. Ct. 153 *p.154*

18. **Cited by:**
    Sinclair v. United States, 279 U.S. 263, 49 S. Ct. 268, 73 L. Ed. 692, 1929 U.S. LEXIS 339 (1929)
    279 U.S. 263 *p.293*
    73 L. Ed. 692 *p.698*
    49 S. Ct. 268 *p.272*

19. **Cited by:**
    Olmstead v. United States, 277 U.S. 438, 48 S. Ct. 564, 72 L. Ed. 944, 1928 U.S. LEXIS 694, 66 A.L.R. 376 (1928)
    277 U.S. 438 *p.439*
    48 S. Ct. 564 *p.564*
    72 L. Ed. 944 *p.947*

20. **Cited by:**
    Olmstead v. United States, 276 U.S. 609, 48 S. Ct. 207, 72 L. Ed. 729, 1928 U.S. LEXIS 147 (1928)
    276 U.S. 609 *p.610*
    48 S. Ct. 207 *p.207*
    72 L. Ed. 729 *p.730*

21. **Cited by:**
    Brown v. United States, 276 U.S. 134, 48 S. Ct. 288, 72 L. Ed. 500, 1928 U.S. LEXIS 66 (1928)
    276 U.S. 134 *p.140*
    72 L. Ed. 500 *p.503*
    48 S. Ct. 288 *p.289*

ILLUSTRATION 7-2.   Page from Decision in *U.S. Reports* that Discusses the Fourth Amendment

344   OCTOBER TERM, 1930.

Syllabus.   282 U. S.

to do business within a state.   In those cases the judgment of this Court in no way restricts the further exercise of the legislative power of the state in any constitutional manner.   Here the Commission is ousted from the exercise of power which Congress has given it, and an order is sanctioned authorizing an issue of securities which it cannot be said the Commission has approved, and which this Court does not purport to say is appropriate under the statute.

MR. JUSTICE HOLMES and MR. JUSTICE BRANDEIS concur in this opinion.

GO-BART IMPORTING COMPANY ET AL. *v.* UNITED STATES.

CERTIORARI TO THE CIRCUIT COURT OF APPEALS FOR THE SECOND CIRCUIT.

No. 111.   Argued November 25, 1930.—Decided January 5, 1931.

1. A warrant issued by a United States Commissioner, addressed only to the Marshal and his deputies, and based upon, and reciting the substance of, a complaint that was verified merely on information and belief and that did not state an offense,—*held* invalid on its face, and no authority to prohibition officers to make an arrest.   P. 355.

2. Acting under color of an invalid warrant of arrest, and falsely claiming to have a search warrant, prohibition agents entered the office of a company, placed under arrest two of its officers, and made a general search of the premises.   They compelled by threats of force the opening of a desk and safe, and seized therefrom and from other parts of the office, papers and records belonging to the company and its officers.   The officers of the company were arraigned before a United States Commissioner, and by him held on bail further to answer the complaint (U. S. C., Title 18, § 591), while the seized papers were held under the control of the United States Attorney in the care and custody of the prohibition agent in charge.   The company, and its two officers individually, before

ILLUSTRATION 7-2.   *Continued*

GO-BART CO. *v.* UNITED STATES.   345

344   Syllabus.

an information or indictment had been returned against them,
applied to the District Court for an order to enjoin the use of the
seized papers as evidence and directing their return.   On a rule
against the United States to show cause, the United States Attorney
appeared and opposed the motion and an affidavit of the agent in
charge was also filed in opposition.   The applications were denied.
Held:

(1) In the proceedings before him, the Commissioner acted
merely as an officer of the District Court in a matter of which it
had authority to take control at any time.   P. 353.

(2) Notwithstanding the order to show cause was addressed to
the United States alone, the proceeding was in substance and effect
against the United States Attorney and the prohibition agent in
charge, the latter being required by the Prohibition Act to report
violations of it to the former and being authorized by the statute,
subject to the former's control, to conduct such prosecutions; and
both these officers were subject to the proper exertion of the disciplinary powers of the court.   P. 354.

(3) The District Court had jurisdiction summarily to determine
whether the evidence should be suppressed and the papers returned
to the petitioners.   P. 355.

(4) The company being a stranger to the proceedings before
the Commissioner, the order of the District Court as to it was
final and appealable.   P. 356.

(5) There being no information or indictment against the officers
of the company when the application was made, and nothing to
show that any criminal proceeding would ever be instituted in that
court against them, it follows that the order was not made in or
dependent upon any case or proceeding pending before the court,
and therefore the order as to them was appealable.   *Id.*

➡ (6) The Fourth Amendment forbids every search that is unreasonable, and is to be liberally construed.   P. 356.

(7) Assuming that the facts of which the arresting officers had
been previously informed were sufficient to justify the arrests
without a warrant, nevertheless the uncontradicted evidence requires a finding that the search of the premises was unreasonable.
Marron v. *United States,* 275 U. S. 192, distinguished.   P. 356.

(8) The District Court is directed to enjoin the United States
Attorney and the agent in charge from using the papers as evidence
and to order the same returned to petitioners.   P. 358.

40 F. (2d) 593, reversed.

Additionally, the full text of the U.S. Constitution is at <u>usconstitution</u> <u>.net/const.html</u>.

State constitutions are located in the first volume of the respective state code. Both the unannotated and the annotated state codes contain the state constitutions.

▼ How Do You Cite Federal or State Constitutions?

Bluebook Rule 11 and *ALWD* Rule 13 outline the format. The U.S. Constitution cite includes the particular article, section, and clause.

U.S. Const. art. II, §2, cl. 1

This cite is used when you are referring to the body of the Constitution. A special citation format is required when you are referring to an amendment.

U.S. Const. amend. II

State constitutions are indicated by the name of the state in the *Bluebook* abbreviated format. *Bluebook* Table 1 and *ALWD* Appendix 1 indicate the accepted state name abbreviation. The postal abbreviation is not always used. The state of Washington's postal abbreviation is WA, but the citation abbreviation is Wash. A section of the Washington state constitution would be cited as follows:

Wash. Const. art. I, §2

Years or dates are not included in citations to federal or state constitutions that are current. Parenthetical notations after the citation indicate the year only if a constitutional provision was repealed or amended. An example is the Eighteenth Amendment to the U.S. Constitution prohibiting the sale of liquor. This amendment was later repealed by the Twenty-First Amendment. *Bluebook* Rule 11 and *ALWD* Rule 13 use this example for the Prohibition amendment:

U.S. Const. amend. XVIII (repealed 1933)

▼ Are Constitutions Available on LEXIS and WESTLAW?

The full text of the U.S. Constitution, in its current format, is available on LEXIS. WESTLAW has the full text of the current U.S. Constitution as well. The individual state constitutions are available on both LEXIS and WESTLAW.

▼ Are There Any Hard-Copy Digests or Other Finding Tools That Assist with Researching Federal Constitutional Issues?

Yes, the *Supreme Court Digest* (for a detailed explanation of how to use digests, see Chapter 3) and *Shepard's United States Citations.* There are annotations discussing constitutional issues in the *American Law Reports Federal.*

Do not overlook hornbooks and treatises. Two excellent treatises on constitutional law are:

Constitutional Law by Nowak, Rotunda, and Young
American Constitutional Law by Laurence Tribe

Consult www.gpoaccess.gov for a host of legislative information beginning with the 103rd Congress and is updated daily when bills are passed.

A treatise is the best place to start researching a constitutional law issue. Treatises explain the legal issues and indicate which cases are the most important. Treatises are particularly helpful in the area of constitutional law because the issues are very complex and require a high level of analysis. For more information on secondary sources, see Chapter 6.

B. STATUTES

▼ What Are Statutes?

Statutes are the laws enacted by either a federal or a state legislature. The business of the legislature is to enact laws. Statutes, both state and federal, as well as municipal and county ordinances and charters, are primary authority.

1. The Legislative Process

▼ How Is a Statute Created Through the Federal Legislative Process?

Anyone can propose **legislation.** Very often special interest groups and law firms propose legislation. Once the legislation is proposed, a **sponsor** in the ranks of Congress must be found to introduce the legislation.

Legislation is generally introduced in the U.S. House of Representatives, but it can be introduced in the U.S. Senate. For purposes of our discussion, assume the legislation is introduced in the House. Once introduced, it is called a slip bill. The **slip bill** is given a numerical designation and is referred to the appropriate **House committee** and then often referred to a **subcommittee.** A committee print of the bill is

created. Hearings are conducted on the bill to determine its impact and effectiveness. Various experts may testify at the hearings to give input as to the possible effects of the legislation or to offer insight as to the purpose the legislation will serve. The tangible result of the hearings is the transcript of the testimony. This records the testimony of experts and lobbyists and their exhibits.

The next stage is the presentation of the committee's report. The **committee report** is a very informative resource because it generally includes the purpose of the bill and the public policies that the bill addresses. The bill is then debated on the floor of the House. The *Congressional Record,* which prints all activity occurring on the floor of both the House and the Senate, prints the transcripts of the debates. More policy information can be gathered from the debates. Flaws in the legislation can also be discerned from the text of the debates. The bill must pass by vote in the chamber of Congress in which it was initiated. In our example, the bill began in the House, so it would have to pass in the House before going to the Senate for approval.

When a bill is passed by the House and sent to the Senate, it must be referred to the appropriate committee and follow the identical route as it did in the first chamber. When the Senate passes its version of the bill, it may differ from the original House bill. Before the bill can become law, both chambers must pass the same version of the bill. If the House and the Senate pass different versions of the bill, the bill is referred to a **conference committee,** which issues a conference committee report and the conference committee version of the bill. The conference committee version is then submitted for votes in both chambers.

If both congressional chambers approve the same version, the bill is sent to the president for signing. If the president signs the bill, it becomes a slip law. If the president **vetoes** the bill, that is, refuses to approve it, the bill goes back to the Congress, and Congress may override the veto by a two-thirds majority vote in both the House and the Senate. If the president does not sign or veto the bill within ten days and the legislature is still in session, the bill automatically becomes law. Occasionally, the president uses a **pocket veto.** This occurs when there are fewer than ten days left in the legislative session and the president neither signs nor vetoes the bill, but merely waits for the session to expire. If the session expires before the president acts on the bill, the bill dies because it did not survive the legislative session. If the sponsors are still interested in passing this legislation, it must be reintroduced, in either chamber, at the beginning of the next legislative session. If both chambers pass the bill in the same exact version, then it is sent again to the president for signing. The president has the same choices: sign or veto. If the president signs the bill, it becomes a slip law.

▼ What Are Slip Laws?

Slip laws are the first written presentation of enacted laws from a legislative body. Slip laws are identified by numbers, for example, Pub. L. No. 104-145. This cite is for a federal session law, or **public**

law, for the popularly named statute called Megan's Law. The 104 indicates the congressional or legislative session, in this case the 104th Congress. The 145 indicates that it is the 145th law passed by the 104th Congress. The slip laws are published in the order that they are enacted.

Slip laws can be obtained at federal government depository libraries (many university and large city libraries are government depository libraries) thomas.loc.gov or at gpoaccess.gov, or purchased from the U.S. Government Printing Office. Slip laws can also be obtained from the law's sponsor in Congress. The annotated versions of the *United States Code* and the *United States Code Congressional and Administrative News* have advance services that publish the slip laws. Advance services are paperbound volumes that contain updated information published in advance of the bound volume or supplement.

▼ What Are Session Laws?

At the end of a congressional session, all of the laws created during the course of the session are numbered and given the designation of **session laws.** Session laws on the federal level, also known as public laws, are added to the *Statutes at Large* and receive a *Statutes at Large* citation. See Illustration 7-3 for Megan's Law in the *Statutes at Large* at 110 Stat. 1345. The text for Megan's Law in the *Statutes at Large* is identical to what is found in the earlier slip law.

▼ What Are the *Statutes at Large?*

The ***Statutes at Large*** are the compilation of the slip laws from the session of Congress that just ended. After each congressional session ends, the slip laws from that session are bound into at least one volume to form the *Statutes at Large.* The laws are published in chronological order rather than codified like the statutes because they document all legislation enacted during the congressional session. Unfortunately, the *Statutes at Large* volumes are not produced immediately after a congressional session. The *Statutes at Large* contain the public laws, or slip laws, as well as presidential proclamations and private laws. The wording of the session laws in the *Statutes at Large* is identical to the public law. The federal codes have tables indicating the *Statutes at Large* citation for a public law. See Illustration 7-3 for a reprint of the *Statutes at Large. Statutes at Large,* beginning with the 108th Congress, are available at gpoaccess.gov/statutes.

▼ What Is Codification?

Finally, the session laws are codified. **Codification** means that the session laws are grouped by subject and placed in the statutes according to their titles, which contain particular subject areas of the law. Unlike

ILLUSTRATION 7-3.   Sample Session Law Published in
Statutes at Large

Public Law 104–145
104th Congress

An Act

To amend the Violent Crime Control and Law Enforcement Act of 1994 to require the release of relevant information to protect the public from sexually violent offenders.

May 17, 1996
——————
[H.R. 2137]

Be it enacted by the Senate and House of Representatives of the United States of America in Congress assembled,

SECTION 1. SHORT TITLE.

This Act may be cited as "Megan's Law".

Megan's Law.

42 USC 13701 note.

SEC. 2. RELEASE OF INFORMATION AND CLARIFICATION OF PUBLIC NATURE OF INFORMATION.

Section 170101(d) of the Violent Crime Control and Law Enforcement Act of 1994 (42 U.S.C. 14071(d)) is amended to read as follows:

"(d) RELEASE OF INFORMATION.—

"(1) The information collected under a State registration program may be disclosed for any purpose permitted under the laws of the State.

"(2) The designated State law enforcement agency and any local law enforcement agency authorized by the State agency shall release relevant information that is necessary to protect the public concerning a specific person required to register under this section, except that the identity of a victim of an offense that requires registration under this section shall not be released.".

Approved May 17, 1996.

---

cases, which are published as the opinions are written, federal statutes are arranged by a defined group of 50 subject categories called titles. See Illustration 7-4 for the list of titles. Statutes are updated during the course of a legislative session if the legislature proposes amendments or revisions. The best finding tool for the appropriate statute on point is a good index. A new version of the *United States Code* appears approximately every six years. In the interim, the Code is updated by slip laws and session laws.

Constant updating is an essential component of statutory research. For instance, Megan's Law, found at P.L. 104-145 (1996), updated the Violent Crime Control and Law Enforcement Act of 1994 by amending the language regarding the release of information of registered sexual offenders. Since 1996, P.L. 105-119 §115(a)(3) redesignated subsection (d) as (e) and added new language concerning the release of information. This is illustrated when you compare the text of P.L. 104-145, Megan's Law, with the text found in the United States Code, at 42 U.S.C. §14071(e) in Illustration 7-5. Look carefully at Illustrations 7-5, 7-6, and 7-7 for amendments following the statute. You will see the Public Laws amending 42 U.S.C. §14071. This information helps you follow the changes in a statute's language and assists you in discerning if the statute is in its most current form. Because Congress passes new legislation

ILLUSTRATION 7-4.   Table of U.S.C. Titles

TITLES OF
UNITED STATES CODE
AND
UNITED STATES CODE ANNOTATED

1. General Provisions.
2. The Congress.
3. The President.
4. Flag and Seal, Seat of Government, and the States.
5. Government Organization and Employees.
6. Domestic Security.
7. Agriculture.
8. Aliens and Nationality.
9. Arbitration.
10. Armed Forces.
11. Bankruptcy.
12. Banks and Banking.
13. Census.
14. Coast Guard.
15. Commerce and Trade.
16. Conservation.
17. Copyrights.
18. Crimes and Criminal Procedure.
19. Customs Duties.
20. Education.
21. Food and Drugs.
22. Foreign Relations and Intercourse.
23. Highways.
24. Hospitals and Asylums.
25. Indians.
26. Internal Revenue Code.
27. Intoxicating Liquors.
28. Judiciary and Judicial Procedure.
29. Labor.
30. Mineral Lands and Mining.
31. Money and Finance.
32. National Guard.
33. Navigation and Navigable Waters.
34. Navy (*See Title 10, Armed Forces*).
35. Patents.
36. Patriotic and National Observances, Ceremonies, and Organizations.
37. Pay and Allowances of the Uniformed Services.
38. Veterans' Benefits.
39. Postal Service.
40. Public Buildings, Property, and Works.
41. Public Contracts.
42. The Public Health and Welfare.
43. Public Lands.
44. Public Printing and Documents.
45. Railroads.
46. Shipping.
47. Telegraphs, Telephones, and Radiotelegraphs.
48. Territories and Insular Possessions.
49. Transportation.
50. War and National Defense.

II

ILLUSTRATION 7-5. Sample Page Showing 42 U.S.C. §14071(e) (2006) Reprinted from access.gpo.gov

```
From the U.S. Code Online via GPO Access
[wais.access.gpo.gov]
[Laws in effect as of January 3, 2006]
[CITE: 42USC14071]


          TITLE 42--THE PUBLIC HEALTH AND WELFARE

    CHAPTER 136--VIOLENT CRIME CONTROL AND LAW ENFORCEMENT

          SUBCHAPTER VI--CRIMES AGAINST CHILDREN

Sec. 14071. Jacob Wetterling Crimes Against Children and
      Sexually Violent Offender Registration Program


(a) In general

                    (1) State guidelines

      The Attorney General shall establish guidelines for State
  programs that require--
          (A) a person who is convicted of a criminal offense against
      a victim who is a minor or who is convicted of a sexually
      violent offense to register a current address for the time
      period specified in subparagraph (A) of subsection (b)(6) of
      this section; and
          (B) a person who is a sexually violent predator to register
      a current address for the time period specified in subparagraph
      (B) of subsection (b)(6) of this section.

      (2) Determination of sexually violent predator status;
                    waiver; alternative measures

      (A) In general

      A determination of whether a person is a sexually violent
  predator for purposes of this section shall be made by a court
  after considering the recommendation of a board composed of
  experts in the behavior and treatment of sex offenders, victims'
  rights advocates, and representatives of law enforcement
  agencies.
```

```
(e) Release of information

    (1) The information collected under a State registration program may
be disclosed for any purpose permitted under the laws of the State.
    (2) The State or any agency authorized by the State shall release
relevant information that is necessary to protect the public concerning
a specific person required to register under this section, except that
the identity of a victim of an offense that requires registration under
this section shall not be released. The release of information under
this paragraph shall include the maintenance of an Internet site
containing such information that is available to the public and
instructions on the process for correcting information that a person
alleges to be erroneous.
```

ILLUSTRATION 7-6. Sample Pages Showing 42 U.S.C.A. §14071 (West 2005)

SUBCHAPTER VI—CRIMES AGAINST CHILDREN

§ 14071. Jacob Wetterling Crimes Against Children and Sexually Violent Offender Registration Program

(a) In general

(1) State guidelines

The Attorney General shall establish guidelines for State programs that require—

(A) a person who is convicted of a criminal offense against a victim who is a minor or who is convicted of a sexually violent offense to register a current address for the time period specified in subparagraph (A) of subsection (b)(6) of this section; and

(B) a person who is a sexually violent predator to register a current address unless such requirement is terminated under subparagraph (B) of subsection (b)(6) of this section.

(e) Release of information

(1) The information collected under a State registration program may be disclosed for any purpose permitted under the laws of the State.

(2) The State or any agency authorized by the State shall release relevant information that is necessary to protect the public concerning a specific person required to register under this section, except that the identity of a victim of an offense that requires registration under this section shall not be released. The release of information under this paragraph shall include the maintenance of an Internet site containing such information that is available to the public and instructions on the process for correcting information that a person alleges to be erroneous.

ILLUSTRATION 7-6. *Continued*

(Pub.L. 103–322, Title XVII, § 170101, Sept. 13, 1994, 108 Stat. 2038; Pub.L. 104–145, § 2, May 17, 1996, 110 Stat. 1345; Pub.L. 104–236, §§ 3 to 7, Oct. 3, 1996, 110 Stat. 3096, 3097; Pub.L. 105–119, Title I, § 115(a)(1) to (5), Nov. 26, 1997, 111 Stat. 2461 to 2463; Pub.L. 105–314, Title VI, § 607(a), Oct. 30, 1998, 112 Stat. 2985; Pub.L. 106–386, Div. B, Title VI, § 1601(b)(1), Oct. 28, 2000, 114 Stat. 1537; Pub.L. 108–21, Title VI, §§ 604(a), 605(a), 606, Apr. 30, 2003, 117 Stat. 688.)

① ## HISTORICAL AND STATUTORY NOTES

Revision Notes and Legislative Reports

1994 Acts. House Report Nos. 103–324, 103–489, and House Conference Report No. 103–711, see 1994 U.S. Code Cong. and Adm. News, p. 1801.

1996 Acts. House Report No. 104–555, see 1996 U.S. Code Cong. and Adm. News, p. 980.

1997 Acts. House Conference Report No. 105–405, see 1997 U.S. Code Cong. and Adm. News, p. 2942.

1998 Acts. House Report No. 105–557, see 1998 U.S. Code Cong. and Adm. News, p. 684.

2000 Acts. House Report No. 106–939, see 2000 U.S. Code Cong. and Adm. News, p. 1380.

2003 Acts. House Conference Report No. 108–10 and Statement by President, see 2003 U.S. Code Cong. and Adm. News, p. 4.

Codifications

Section 115(a)(2)(C)(ii) of Pub.L. 105–119, which directed that subsec. (b)(3)(A) be amended "by striking clauses (i) through (v)", was executed by striking clauses (i) through (iv), as the probable intent of Congress, since no clause (v) was ever enacted under subsec. (b)(3)(A) of this section.

Section 115(a)(4) and (5) of Pub.L. 105–119, which directed amendment of subsecs. (e)(2) and (f), respectively, as redesignated by "subsection (c) of this section", were executed to such subsections as redesignated by section 115(a)(3) of this Act, to reflect the probable intent of Congress.

Amendments

2003 Amendments. Heading. Pub.L. 108–21, § 605(a)(1), amended the section heading but required no change in text.

530

ILLUSTRATION 7-6. *Continued*

Ch. 136   VIOLENT CRIME CONTROL   42 § 14071
Note 2

Keeping children out of double jeopardy: An assessment of punishment and Megan's Law. 81 Minn.L.Rev. 501 (1996).

Making the case for Megan's Law: A study in legislative rhetoric. Daniel M. Filler, 76 Ind.L.Rev. 315 (2001).

Megan's Law: Branding the sex offender or benefitting the community? 5 Seton Hall Const.L.J. 1127 (1995).

Megan's Law: Can it stop sexual predators—and at what cost to constitutional rights? Joel B. Rudin, 11 Crim.Just. 3 (Fall 1996).

"Megan's Law": Community notification and the constitution. 29 Colum.J.L. & Soc.Probs. 117 (1995).

Protection and treatment: Permissible civil detention of sexual predators. John Kip Cornwell, 53 Wash. & Lee L.Rev. 1293 (1996).

Sex offender registration and community notification: Protection, not punishment. 30 New Eng.L.Rev. 183 (1995).

The quandary of Megan's Law: When the child sex offender is a child. Timothy E. Wind, 37 J.Marshall L.Rev.73 (Fall 2003)

(2)   **LIBRARY REFERENCE**

1 Citation to legislative history
2 West topics key numbers in digest
3 WESTLAW searches

American Digest System

Criminal Law ☞1222, 1226(1) to 1226(5).
Infants ☞20.
Mental Health ☞469(1) to 469(7).
Pardon and Parole ☞64, 66, 68.
Prisons ☞14.
Key Number System Topic Nos. 110, 211, 257A, 284, 310.

Research References

ALR Library

36 ALR 5th 161, State Statutes or Ordinances Requiring Persons Previously Convicted of Crime to Register With Authorities.

WESTLAW ELECTRONIC RESEARCH

(3) See Westlaw guide following the Explanation pages of this volume.

---

continually during its sessions, staying current is essential when using statutory authority. Always check the year of the code volume and the year of the supplement or pocket part when researching statutory authority. The best way to make sure that the statute is in its most current form is to use the most recent compilation of an annotated statute and to update it with the pocket part. Alternatively, if cost is not an issue, access the code section on either LEXIS or WESTLAW, and the updates will be integrated into the statute cite retrieved. See how the code section is updated and the importance of updating your research.

ILLUSTRATION 7-7. Sample Page Showing 42 U.S.C.S. §14071

*** CURRENT THROUGH P.L. 110-227, APPROVED 5/7/2008 ***

TITLE 42. THE PUBLIC HEALTH AND WELFARE
CHAPTER 136. VIOLENT CRIME CONTROL AND LAW ENFORCEMENT
CRIMES AGAINST CHILDREN

Go to the United States Code Service Archive Directory

42 USCS § 14071

§ 14071. Jacob Wetterling crimes against children and sexually violent offender registration program [Caution: See prospective amendment note below.]

(a) In general.
 (1) State guidelines. The Attorney General shall establish guidelines for State programs that require—
  (A) a person who is convicted of a criminal offense against a victim who is a minor or who is convicted of a sexually violent offense to register a current address for the time period specified in subparagraph (A) of subsection (b)(6); and
  (B) a person who is a sexually violent predator to register a current address for the time specified in subparagraph (B) of subsection (b)(6).
 (2) Determination of sexually violent predator status; waiver; alternative measures.
  (A) In general. A determination of whether a person is a sexually violent predator for purposes of this section shall be made by a court after considering the recommendation of a board composed of experts in the behavior and treatment of sex offenders, victims' rights advocates, and representatives of law enforcement agencies.

(e) Release of information.
 (1) The information collected under a State registration program may be disclosed for any purpose permitted under the laws of the State.
 (2) The State or any agency authorized by the State shall release relevant information that is necessary to protect the public concerning a specific person required to register under this section, except that the identity of a victim of an offense that requires registration under this section shall not be released. The release of information under this paragraph shall include the maintenance of an Internet site containing such information that is available to the public and instructions on the process for correcting information that a person alleges to be erroneous.

Code of Federal Regulations:
 Department of Justice--Equal treatment for faith-based organizations, 28 CFR Part 38.
 Department of Justice--Grants for correctional facilities, 28 CFR Part 91.
 Department of the Army--Law enforcement reporting, 32 CFR Part 635.
 Department of the Army--Military Police investigation, 32 CFR Part 637.

2. Reading and Understanding Statutes

▼ How Do You Read a Statute?

Each word of a statute is read for its plain meaning. Statutes are drafted using as few words as possible to state the law. The courts resolve any ambiguities that arise when applying a statute. Often litigation involves the application or interpretation or violation of a statute. When a statute has not been applied in a case previously, it is a case of first impression. Remember that the text of the statute does not discuss policy issues but policy and political climate influence how a statute will be applied. Think of the goals that the government should further and this will provide insight into relevant policy arguments concerning the application of a particular statutory provision.

The focus of statutory analysis is that legislation is adopted to apply to situations that will arise after the legislation goes into effect. An activity existing prior to passing of legislation is **grandfathered** if the legislation includes language that does not prohibit this existing activity from continuing. For instance, suppose a city passes an ordinance forbidding the operation of commercial businesses in residentially zoned neighborhoods. Under a grandfather clause, an existing business would be permitted to continue its operation; the legislation would apply only to businesses opened after the legislation took effect.

▼ What Type of Legal Authority Are Statutes?

Statutes are primary authority because codes and statutes are the laws created by the legislature. Statutes are the authority to rely on when researching. When researching, first determine the relevant jurisdiction and then check the appropriate code to see if there is a statute on point. If there is a relevant statute on point, the statute takes precedence over case law holdings that were decided prior to the statute's enactment. Statutes are enacted to control conduct like criminal acts, relationships like marriage and adoption, and transactions like banking that occur frequently in our society. Court decisions applying and interpreting statutes already enacted must be consulted to assess how a statute has been applied and analyzed.

▼ What Is the Relationship Between Statutes and Case Law?

Most cases today revolve around the application or the interpretation of a statute. Courts determine whether an individual or an institution—public, private, or government—violated a statute or whether the statute itself is unconstitutional. People, institutions, municipalities, and even state governments go to court to determine if a statute is unconstitutional.

3. How to Find Federal Statutes

▼ Where Are Federal Statutes Found?

The official, government-issued compilation of the federal statutes is the *United States Code,* or U.S.C. See Illustration 7-5, the 2006 version of 42 U.S.C. §14071(e). The most cost effective way to access the *United States Code* is at <u>access.gpo.gov</u>. Of course, you would not obtain any of the research enhancements or annotations but the ease of use is remarkable, especially if you know the code section or a key word in the provision. The U.S.C. contains most of the laws created by the U.S. Congress. The U.S. Government Printing Office publishes the U.S.C. A terrific Internet resource for federal and state codes is Cornell's Legal Information Institute at <u>law.cornell.edu</u>.

The U.S.C. is organized by title. Each title covers a specific subject area over which the U.S. Congress has authority to draft legislation. For example, Title 42 contains all statutes dealing with public health and welfare. When a new piece of legislation is enacted that pertains to public health and welfare, which includes crime prevention, it is placed in Title 42. When new statutes are enacted that replace existing statute sections, the older sections are then superseded. This differs from case law because new decisions overrule prior decisions' holdings; they do not supersede them. Sometimes only a portion of an existing statute changes when a new public law is enacted.

▼ How Often Is the U.S.C. Updated?

An official version of the U.S.C. is published every six years. Supplements updating the existing Code are published annually. During the course of the six years, new legislation is passed all of the time. It is not included in the official code until the annual supplement is published. There may be a great time lag between the law's enactment and the production of the annual supplement. New legislation retains the slip format until it becomes a session law and gets a *Statutes at Large* citation. It is important to check to see if the legislation has been repealed or superseded by a slip law or a session law in the intervening years between publications of the official code and during the time between publications of the annual supplements.

▼ Is the U.S.C. the Only Codified Version of the Federal Statutes?

No. There are two unofficial versions of the U.S.C., the *United States Code Annotated* (U.S.C.A.) published by West and the *United States Code Service* (U.S.C.S.) published by LEXIS-NEXIS. Both the U.S.C.A. and the U.S.C.S. contain the text of the laws found in the U.S.C. and also include case law annotations and excellent updating services. Unlike case law where the official and the unofficial reporters have different volume numbers and different pagination for the same case, the

citations for the unofficial codes have the same title and section designations as the U.S.C. cite. For example, the following are citations to the identical statute:

26 U.S.C. §61 (2006)

26 U.S.C.A. §61 (West 2006)

26 U.S.C.S. §61 (Lexis 2006)

▼ What Do the Unofficial Codes Contain?

NET NOTE

uscode.house.gov/search/criteria.shtml provides free access to a searchable *United States Code.* This site includes updates but always see if your code section is current by using a commercial annotated set, either the U.S.C.A. or the U.S.C.S., and then validate the cite with either *Shepard's* or KeyCite.

The unofficial codes contain references to cases that construe and apply the code section. See Illustrations 7-6 and 7-7. They are called annotated codes because they contain the case law annotations. The codes also contain references to law review articles dealing with the particular code section. The U.S.C.A. and U.S.C.S. are excellent research tools. See Illustrations 7-5, 7-6, and 7-7 for a comparison of the official and the unofficial codes.

The U.S.C.A., because it is published by West, ties the researcher into all of the other West publications. See Illustration 7-6. References are given to topic and key numbers so that the subject covered by the code section can be examined in the *West Digests* to find pertinent case law. (See Chapter 4 for a detailed discussion of digests.) References to West secondary sources and law journals are given as well. (See Chapter 6.) References to the *United States Code Congressional and Administrative News* (U.S.C.C.A.N.), published by West and containing compilations of legislative histories for major public laws since the 1950s, are contained in the U.S.C.A. (The U.S.C.C.A.N. is discussed fully in Chapter 8.)

The U.S.C.S., published by LEXIS-NEXIS, provides references to other publications that are relevant to the particular code section. See Illustration 7-7. This illustration was downloaded from lexis.com, USCS library. Note how the updating is integrated into the material retrieved.

WESTLAW has a similar feature in the U.S.C.A. database. The U.S.C.S. included related statute citations and pertinent secondary source references as well as case annotations. U.S.C.S. has consistent references to the *Code of Federal Regulations.* (See Chapter 9.)

Aside from providing excellent updates, case law annotations and law review citations, the annotated or unofficial federal codes provide the researcher with an entry into the entire research network created by the respective publisher.

▼ Is There Any Difference Between the U.S.C.S. and the U.S.C.A.?

The U.S.C.S. provides consistent references to relevant *Code of Federal Regulations* (C.F.R.) citations; the U.S.C.A. does not consistently include administrative law citations. Overall, then, the U.S.C.S. is better for researching administrative issues. The U.S.C.A. provides key numbers and topics relating to the West Digest System as well as electronic searching tips for WESTLAW query formulation.

▼ Why Would You Use an Annotated Set of the U.S.C.?

As mentioned earlier, the annotated codes offer a host of references to secondary source publications produced by the respective code's publisher as well as case law annotations. You would use an annotated, or unofficial code, because the updating through pocket parts, bound supplements, and advance session law pamphlets is very timely. Between publication of the official statutes every six years, consult an unofficial version of the U.S.C. to determine if a statute has been updated, modified, or superseded. The unofficial versions contain references to any new legislation that relates to the code section, even if it is a session law. Always check the volume's pocket part for updates. The indexes of the unofficial codes are also superior to the index of the U.S.C.

▼ How Useful Are Annotated Statutes as Finding Tools?

Annotated codes are excellent finding tools for retrieving cases that interpret the statute section in question. You do not cite to the research points and abstracts following the code section, although they are very helpful in your research. When using an annotated code section on point, you are also linked to many other resources produced by the particular code's publisher. For example, within the U.S.C.A. you would find citations to encyclopedia sections. In addition, because of the excellent updating services, the annotated codes allow you to find subsequent legislation that relates to the statute section.

▼ What Are the Research Methods Used to Find Relevant Statutes?

The research methods are the same for the U.S.C., the U.S.C.A., and the U.S.C.S. The following methods are listed in order of efficiency.

1. **Popular name table.** The popular name table is found in the last index volume. Almost every statute passed in Congress has a popular name, usually a last name of the sponsor or a description of the act's intent. If you have a popular name but not a title and section number, you can use the popular name table. See Illustration 7-8. All of the popular names for all of the code sections are listed in alphabetical order with the corresponding title and section numbers of the act, the public law numbers, and the *Statutes at Large* citations. The popular name table is an excellent research tool for finding public law numbers quickly. In Illustration 7-8, the public law number for Megan's Law is Pub. L. No. 104-145.

2. **Conversion table.** The conversion table is also at the end of the U.S.C. set, in the tables volume, and lets you find the U.S.C. citation if you have a *Statutes at Large* citation. In Illustration 7-9, our example focuses on Megan's Law using the tables in the U.S.C.A. Using the conversion table in the U.S.C.A., you are able to convert the public law number into a *Statutes at Large* citation. For example, you would obtain the citation of 110 Stat. 1345 from Pub. L. No. 104-145. The table also converts the public law number into a U.S.C.A. citation. (The public law number helps you find the legislative history of the act in the U.S.C.C.A.N. also. See Chapter 7 for more information on the U.S.C.C.A.N.)

3. **The index method.** First try to find the relevant code section by using the index. You can also find a relevant statute by checking under some of the significant terms from the act. Very often a word from the popular name of the statute is cited in the index. The index is in alphabetical order. In Illustration 7-10, our example focuses on finding Megan's Law in the U.S.C.A. Note that the index entry contains some of the terms describing the subject matter of the statute.

4. **The title outline.** If you know the particular title where the statute section is located but don't know the section number, you can look at the title outline to see if any entry in the particular title is appropriate. Illustration 7-11 shows the outline of every subchapter and section in U.S.C.A. Title 42. You must have a very clear idea of what you are looking for and knowledge about the statute's language to use the title outline method effectively. Use this method only if you cannot find a statute section by any other means.

Another excellent resource that helps you find relevant federal and state statutes is *Shepard's Acts and Cases by Popular Names—Federal and State*. As the title indicates, all of the acts and cases are organized by popular name. It is handy to use this source when you are not certain if the act is state, federal, or both and do not know which statutory compilation will have the correct statute. When using the popular name table of a code, you must know the jurisdiction and the date of enactment, but *Shepard's Acts and Cases by Popular Names* lists all acts and cases in alphabetical order regardless of jurisdiction. Look up Megan's Law in Illustration 7-12.

ILLUSTRATION 7-8.   U.S.C.A.   Popular Name Table

POPULAR NAME TABLE

MEDS Act
See Medicine Equity and Drug Safety Act of 2000

Megan's Law
See, also, AMBER Alert Act (America's Missing—Broadcast Emergency Response Alert Act)
See, also, Amber Hagerman Child Protection Act of 1996
See, also, Code Adam Act of 2003
See, also, International Parental Kidnapping Crime Act of 1993
See, also, Jacob Wetterling Crimes Against Children and Sexually Violent Offender Registration Act
See, also, National Child Search Assistance Act of 1990
See, also, Parental Kidnaping Prevention Act of 1980 (PKPA)
See, also, Prosecutorial Remedies and Other Tools to end the Exploitation of Children Today Act of 2003 (PROTECT Act)
See, also, Suzanne's Law
Short title, see 42 USCA § 13701 note
Pub.L. 104–145, May 17, 1996, 110 Stat. 1345 (42 §§ 13701 note, 14071)

Mellon Art Gallery Act
Mar. 24, 1937, ch. 50, 50 Stat. 51 (20 §§ 71 to 75)

Membrane Processes Research Act of 1992
Short title, see 42 USCA § 10341 note
Pub.L. 102–490, Oct. 24, 1992, 106 Stat. 3142 (42 § 10341, 10341 note, 10342 to 10345)

Menominee Restoration Act
Short title, see 25 USCA § 903 note
Pub.L. 93–197, Dec. 22, 1973, 87 Stat. 770 (25 §§ 903 to 903f)

Mental Health Amendments of 1967
Short title, see 42 USCA § 201 note
Pub.L. 90–31, June 24, 1967, 81 Stat. 79 (42 §§ 225a, 2681, 2684, 2687, 2688a, 2688d, 2691)

Mental Health Amendments of 1990
Short title, see 42 USCA § 201 note
Pub.L. 101–639, Nov. 28, 1990, 104 Stat. 4600 (42 §§ 201 note, 290cc–13, 299a, 300x–3, 300x–10 to 300x–12)

Mental Health Parity Act of 1996
Short title, see 42 USCA § 201 note
Pub.L. 104–204, Title VII, Sept. 26, 1996, 110 Stat. 2944 (29 § 1185a, 1185a note; 42 §§ 201 note, 300gg–5, 300gg–5 note)

Mental Health Parity Reauthorization Act of 2002
Pub.L. 107–313, Dec. 2, 2002, 116 Stat. 2457 (29 § 1185a; 42 §§ 201 note, 300gg–5)

Mental Health Parity Reauthorization Act of 2003
Short title, see 42 USCA § 201 note
Pub.L. 108–197, Dec. 19, 2003, 117 Stat. 2898 (29 § 1185a; 42 §§ 201 note, 300gg–5)

Mental Health Study Act of 1955
Short title, see 42 USCA § 201 note
July 28, 1955, ch. 417, 69 Stat. 382 (42 § 242b)

Mental Health Systems Act
Short title, see 42 USCA § 9401 note
Pub.L. 96–398, Oct. 7, 1980, 94 Stat. 1564 (42 §§ 210, 225a, 229b, 242a, 246, 289k–1, 300*l*–2, 300m–2, 1396b, 2689a to 2689c, 2689e, 2689g, 2689h, 2689q, 9401, 9411, 9412, 9421 to 9423, 9431 to 9438, 9451, 9452, 9461 to 9465, 9471 to 9473, 9481, 9491 to 9493, 9501, 9502, 9511, 9512, 9521 to 9523)
Pub.L. 97–35, Title IX, § 902(e)(1), (f)(1), (20), Aug. 13 1981, 95 Stat. 560 (42 §§ 2689, 2689a to 2689*l*, 2689n to 2689p, 2689r to 2689z, 2689aa, 9412, 9511)
Pub.L. 99–646, § 87(d)(2) to (7), Nov. 10, 1986, 100 Stat. 3624 (42 § 9511)
Pub.L. 99–654, § 3(b)(3) to (7), Nov. 14, 1986, 100 Stat. 3663, 3664 (42 § 9511)

Mental Retardation Amendments of 1967
Pub.L. 90–170, Dec. 4, 1967, 81 Stat. 527 (20 § 617; 42 §§ 2661, 2665, 2671, 2672, 2674, 2677 to 2678d, 2698 to 2698b)

ILLUSTRATION 7-9.   U.S.C.A. *Statutes at Large* **and Public Law Numbers Table**

1996   **104–146**

	§ 1(a)	110 Stat 1327	42 § 1437f
	§ 1(a)	110 Stat 1327	42 § 1437f nts
	§ 1(a)	110 Stat 1327	42 § 1437g
	§ 1(a)	110 Stat 1327	42 § 1437*l*, 1437*l* nts
	§ 1(a)	110 Stat 1327	42 § 1437p
	§ 1(a)	110 Stat 1327	42 § 1437aa nts
	§ 1(a)	110 Stat 1327	42 § 1997a, 1997b, 1997c
	§ 1(a)	110 Stat 1327	42 § 1997e, 1997f, 1997h
	§ 1(a)	110 Stat 1327	42 § 3793, 3793 nt
	§ 1(a)	110 Stat 1327	42 § 3796ii nt
	§ 1(a)	110 Stat 1327	42 § 3796ii–1 to 3796ii–8 .... Rep.
	§ 1(a)	110 Stat 1327	42 § 4852
	§ 1(a)	110 Stat 1327	42 § 5305, 5305 nt
	§ 1(a)	110 Stat 1327	42 § 5306 nt
	§ 1(a)	110 Stat 1327	42 § 7135 nt
	§ 1(a)	110 Stat 1327	42 § 13701 to 13712
	§ 1(a)	110 Stat 1327	42 § 14092
	§ 1(a)	110 Stat 1327	43 § 31i
	§ 1(a)	110 Stat 1327	43 § 50
	§ 1(a)	110 Stat 1327	43 § 1337 nt
	§ 1(a)	110 Stat 1327	43 § 1473a
	§ 1(a)	110 Stat 1327	43 § 1474b–1
	§ 1(a)	110 Stat 1327	43 § 1735 nt
	§ 1(a)	110 Stat 1327	43 § 1782 nt
	§ 1(a)	110 Stat 1327	48 § 1469b
	§ 1(a)	110 Stat 1327	48 § 1804
May 6, 1996 ....104–141...	§ 1	110 Stat 1328	20 § 1063b nt
	§ 2	110 Stat 1328	20 § 1063b
May 13, 1996 ....104–142...	§ 1	110 Stat 1329	42 § 14301 nt
	§ 2	110 Stat 1329	42 § 14301
	§ 3	110 Stat 1329	42 § 14302
	§ 4	110 Stat 1330	42 § 14303
	§ 5	110 Stat 1331	42 § 14304
	§ 6	110 Stat 1332	42 § 14305
	§ 7	110 Stat 1332	42 § 14306
	§ 8	110 Stat 1332	42 § 14307
	§ 101	110 Stat 1332	42 § 14301 nt
	§ 102	110 Stat 1332	42 § 14321
	§ 103	110 Stat 1332	42 § 14322
	§ 104	110 Stat 1335	42 § 14323
	§ 201	110 Stat 1336	42 § 14301 nt
	§ 202	110 Stat 1336	42 § 14331
	§ 203	110 Stat 1336	42 § 14332
	§ 204	110 Stat 1336	42 § 14333
	§ 205	110 Stat 1336	42 § 14334
	§ 206	110 Stat 1336	42 § 14335
	§ 207	110 Stat 1336	42 § 14336
→ May 17, 1996 ....104–145...	§ 1	110 Stat 1345	42 § 13701 nt
	§ 2	110 Stat 1345	42 § 14071
May 20, 1996 ....104–146...	§ 1	110 Stat 1346	42 § 201 nt
	§ 3(a)(1), (2)	110 Stat 1346	42 § 300ff–11
	§ 3(a)(3)	110 Stat 1347	42 § 300ff–17
	§ 3(b)(1)	110 Stat 1347	42 § 300ff–12
	§ 3(b)(2), (3)	110 Stat 1349	42 § 300ff–13
	§ 3(b)(4)	110 Stat 1351	42 § 300ff–14
	§ 3(b)(5)	110 Stat 1352	42 § 300ff–15
	§ 3(b)(6)	110 Stat 1353	42 § 300ff–16
	§ 3(c)(1)	110 Stat 1353	42 § 300ff–21
	§ 3(c)(2)	110 Stat 1354	42 § 300ff–22
	§ 3(c)(2)	110 Stat 1354	42 § 300ff–23
	§ 3(c)(3)	110 Stat 1355	42 § 300ff–26
	§ 3(c)(4)	110 Stat 1355	42 § 300ff–27
	§ 3(c)(5)	110 Stat 1355	42 § 300ff–28
	§ 3(c)(6)	110 Stat 1356	42 § 300ff–29
	§ 3(c)(7)	110 Stat 1356	42 § 399ff–31
	§ 3(d)(1)	110 Stat 1357	42 § 300ff–51
	§ 3(d)(2)	110 Stat 1357	42 § 300ff–52
	§ 3(d)(3)	110 Stat 1357	42 § 300ff–54
	§ 3(d)(4)	110 Stat 1358	42 § 300ff–55
	§ 3(d)(5)	110 Stat 1358	42 § 300ff–64
	§ 3(e)	110 Stat 1358	42 § 300ff–71
	§ 3(f)	110 Stat 1362	42 § 300ff–74
	§ 3(g)(1)	110 Stat 1362	42prec. 300ff–10
	§ 3(g)(1)	110 Stat 1362	42 § 300ff–10
	§ 3(g)(2)	110 Stat 1363	42 § 300ff–28
	§ 3(h)(1)	110 Stat 1363	42prec. 300ff–111
	§ 3(h)(1)	110 Stat 1363	42 § 300ff–111
	§ 3(h)(2)	110 Stat 1363	42 § 294N
	§ 3(h)(3), (4)	110 Stat 1364	42 § 300ff–11
	§ 4	110 Stat 1364	42 § 300ff–13

ILLUSTRATION 7-10. U.S.C.A. General Index

CHILDREN 808

CHILDREN AND MINORS—Cont'd
Restraint systems, safety seats, 23 §§ 405, 405 nt
Retirement and pensions, 38 § 1503 et seq.
  Exemptions, 38 §§ 1503, 1506
  Net worth, 38 §§ 1522, 1543
  Payment, 38 §§ 1503, 1507
  Reports, 38 § 1506
  Veterans, 38 § 1541 et seq.
Rheumatologists, 42 § 294p
Rules of Civil Procedure, this index
Runaway and Homeless Youth, generally, this index
Rural areas, stalking, 42 § 13971
Safety,
  Child Safety Pilot Program, 42 § 5119a nt
  Crimes and offenses, safe havens, 42 § 10420
  Environment, 42 § 4321 nt, EON 13045
  Grants, 42 § 9859 et seq.
  Internet, ante
  Motherhood, mortality, research, 42 § 247b–12
  Project Safe Childhood program, 42 § 16942
  Seats, safety seats, 23 §§ 405, 405 nt
  Swimming pools, 15 § 8001 et seq.
Sales, sexual exploitation, 18 § 2251A et seq.
Scholarships, development, 42 § 10901 et seq.
School Lunches, generally, this index
Schools and School Districts, generally, this index
Screening,
  Hard of hearing, 42 §§ 247b–4a, 280g–1
  Heritable disorders, 42 § 300b–8 et seq.
Sculpture, virtual child pornography, 18 § 1466A
Sealant, dentists and dentistry, 42 § 247b–14
Seals (official seals),
  Big Brothers Big Sisters of America, 36 §§ 30105, 30106
  Boys and Girls Clubs of America, 36 § 31105
Seat belts, 49 § 30127 nt
Secretary of the Treasury, this index
Security interest, Boys and Girls Clubs of America, 36 § 31105
Selling or buying, sexual exploitation, depictions, 18 § 2251A
Sentence and punishment, 18 § 3553; 18 USSG § 3B1.4
  Kidnapping, enhancement, 18 § 1201
  Sexual exploitation, post
  Victims, enhancement, 18 § 3559
  Violence, minimum terms of imprisonment, 18 § 3559
Serious emotional disturbance, mental health, community services, 42 § 290ff et seq.
Service organizations. Youth Service Organizations, generally, this index
Servicemembers group life insurance, 38 § 1967 et seq.
Services, handicapped persons, 42 § 15001 et seq.
Sex offenses,
  Crime victims, 42 § 3796aa–6

CHILDREN AND MINORS—Cont'd
Sex offenses—Cont'd
  Crime victims—Cont'd
    Court-Appointed Special Advocate Program, 42 § 13014
    Judicial officers and employees, 42 § 13024
    Televised testimony, 42 § 3793
  Definitions, Two Strikes You're Out Law, 18 § 3559
  Enhanced penalties, registered sex offenders, 18 § 2260A
  Exploitation, 18 § 2251 et seq.
  Internet, 42 § 16944
  Limitation of prosecutions, 18 §§ 2255, 3283, 3299, 3509
  Military Justice Code, 10 § 920
  Registration, offenders, 42 §§ 14071 et seq., 16901 et seq.
  Release, pretrial release, 18 § 3142
  Technology, 42 § 16944
  Training, 42 § 16944
  Transportation, 18 § 2423
  Two Strikes You're Out Law, 18 § 3559
Sex trafficking, 18 § 2251 et seq.
Sexual abuse, 18 § 2241 et seq.
  Grants, 42 § 16983
Sexual assault,
  Collaboration, 42 § 14043c–1
  Confidential or privileged information, 42 § 14043b et seq.
  Grants, 42 §§ 13925, 14043c et seq.
  Military Justice Code, 10 § 920
  Outreach services, 42 § 14045
  Prevention, 42 § 14043d et seq.
  Rural areas, 42 § 13971
  Services program, 42 § 14043g
Sexual exploitation, 18 § 2251 et seq.
  Actions and proceedings, 18 §§ 2252A, 2255
  Advertisements, 18 § 2251
  Affirmative defenses, 18 §§ 1466A, 2252A
  Attorneys, 18 § 2252A
  Books and papers, 18 §§ 2252, 2257
  Conspiracy, 18 § 2252A
  Costs, 18 § 2252A
  Custody, 18 § 2256
  Cyber tiplines, 42 §§ 5773, 13032
  Damages, 18 §§ 2252A, 2255, 2259
  Definitions, 18 § 2251 et seq.
  Digital images, 18 § 2257
  Enterprises, 18 § 2252A
  Evidence, 18 § 2252A
  Exports and imports, 18 § 2260
  Family planning services, reports, 42 § 300 nt
  Injunctions, 18 § 2252A
  Interception of wire, oral, or electronic communications, 18 § 2516
  Internet, 18 § 2251 et seq.
    Sentence and punishment, 28 § 994 nt
    Training, 42 § 16944
  Mail and mailing, 18 §§ 2252, 2252A
  Mandatory restitution, 18 § 2259
  Manufacturers and manufacturing, 18 § 2260
  Masha's Law, 18 §§ 2251 nt, 2255

ILLUSTRATION 7-11. Outline of Sections in Title 42 U.S.C.A., Public Health and Welfare, §§12901-14080

Ch. 136 VIOLENT CRIME CONTROL

Sec.

PART G—ELDER ABUSE, NEGLECT, AND EXPLOITATION, INCLUDING DOMESTIC VIOLENCE AND SEXUAL ASSAULT AGAINST OLDER OR DISABLED INDIVIDUALS

14041. Definitions.
14041a. Training programs for law enforcement officers.
14041b. Authorization of appropriations.

PART H—DOMESTIC VIOLENCE TASK FORCE

14042. Task Force.

SUBCHAPTER IV—DRUG CONTROL

14051. Increased penalties for drug-dealing in "drug-free" zones.
14052. Enhanced penalties for illegal drug use in Federal prisons and for smuggling drugs into Federal prisons.
14053. Violent crime and drug emergency areas.

SUBCHAPTER V—CRIMINAL STREET GANGS

14061. Juvenile anti-drug and anti-gang grants in Federally assisted low-income housing.
14062. Gang investigation coordination and information collection.

SUBCHAPTER VI—CRIMES AGAINST CHILDREN

14071. Jacob Wetterling Crimes Against Children and Sexually Violent Offender Registration Program.
14072. FBI database.
14073. Immunity for good faith conduct.
14074 to 14080. Reserved.

SUBCHAPTER VII—RURAL CRIME

14081. Rural Crime and Drug Enforcement Task Forces.
14082. Rural drug enforcement training.
14083. More agents for Drug Enforcement Administration.

SUBCHAPTER VIII—POLICE CORPS AND LAW ENFORCEMENT OFFICERS TRAINING AND EDUCATION

PART A—POLICE CORPS

14091. Purposes.
14092. Definitions.
14093. Establishment of Office of the Police Corps and Law Enforcement Education.
14094. Designation of lead agency and submission of State plan.
14095. Scholarship assistance.
14096. Selection of participants.
14097. Police Corps training.
14098. Service obligation.
14099. State plan requirements.
14100. Repealed.
14101. Authorization of appropriations.
14102. Reports to Congress.

355

ILLUSTRATION 7-12.   Sample Page from *Shepard's Acts and Cases by Popular Name*

**Meeting the National Education Goals:
Schools for Arkansas' Future Act**
Ark. Code 1987, 6-15-1001 et seq.

Meetings Act (Open)
Colo. Rev. Stat., 24-6-402
La. Rev. Stat. Ann., 42:4.1 et seq.

Meetings of Public Agencies Act
Ill. Rev. Stat. 1991, Ch. 102, § 41 et seq.

Megalandfill Siting Act
Mont. Laws 1991, Ch. 468

→ **Megan's Law**
May 17, 1996, P.L. 104-145, 42 U.S. Code
§ 14701, Subsec. d
Ala. Code 1975, §§ 13A-11-200 to
13A-11-203
Alaska Stat. 1962, §§ 11.56.840, 12.63.010
to 12.63.100, 18.65.087, 28.05.048,
33.30.035
Ariz. Rev. Stat. Ann., §§ 13-3821 to 13-3825
Ark. Code 1987, 12-12-901 to 12-12-909
Cal. Penal Code §§ 290 to 290.4
Colo. Rev. Stat., 18-3-412.5
Conn. Gen. Stat. 1983, §§ 54-102a to
54-102r
Del. Code of 1974, Title 11, § 4120
Fla. Stat. Ann., 775.13, 775.22
Ga. Code Ann., 42-9-44.1
Haw. Session Laws 1995, Act 160
Ida. Code 1947, 9-340, Subd. 11, Para. f;
18-8301 to 18-8311
Ill. Comp. Stat. 1992, Ch. 730, §§ 150/1 to
150/10
Ind. Code 1982, 5-2-12-1 to 5-2-12-13
Kan. Stat. Ann., 22-4901 to 22-4910
Ky. Rev. Stat. 1971, 17.500 to 17.540
La. Rev. Stat. Ann., 15:540 to 15:549
Md. Laws 1995, Ch. 142
Me. Rev. Stat. Ann. 1964, Title 34-A,
§§ 11001 to 11004
Mich. Public Acts 1994, No. 295
Minn. Stat. 1986, 243.166
Miss. Code Ann. 1972, §§ 45-33-1 to
45-33-19
Mo. Rev. Stat. 1986, 566.600 to 566.625
Mont. Code Ann., 46-23-501 to 46-23-507

N.C. Gen. Stat. 1943, §§ 14-208.5 to
14-208.10
→ N.D. Cent. Code, 12.1-32-15
Nev. Rev. Stat. Ann., 207.080, 207.151 to
207.157
N.H. Rev. Stat. 1955, 632-A:11 to 632-A:19
N.J. Stat. Ann., 2C:7-1 to 2C:7-11
N.M. Stat. Ann., 29-11A-1 to 29-11A-8
N.Y. Correction Law (Consol. Laws Ch. 43)
§§ 168 to 168V
Ohio Rev. Code 1953, 2950.01 to 2950.08
Okla. Stat. Ann., Title 57, §§ 581 to 587
Ore. Rev. Stat., 181.507 to 181.519
Pa. 1995 Pamph. Laws, No. 24
R.I. Gen. Laws 1956, 11-37-16
S.D. Codified Laws 1967, 22-22-30 to
22-22-41
Tenn. Code Ann., 40-39-101 to 40-39-108
Tex. Rev. Civ. Stat., Art. 6252-13c-1
Utah Code Ann. 1953, 53-5-212.5,
77-27-21.5
Va. Code 1950, §§ 19.2-298.1 to 19.2-390.1
Wash. Rev. Code Ann., 4.24.550, 9A.44.130,
9A.44.140, 10.01.200, 70.48.470,
72.09.330
Wis. Stat. Ann., 175.45
W. Va. Code 1966, §§ 61-8F-1 to 61-8F-8
Wyo. Stat. Ann., §§ 7-19-301 to 7-19-306

Meigs Field Airport Act
Ill. Comp. Stat. 1992, Ch. 620, § 60/1 et seq.

Melbourne Urban Renewal Act
Fla. Special Laws 1961, Ch. 61-2486

Mello-Condit-McClintock Tax Rebate Act
Cal. Revenue and Taxation Code § 17070 et
seq.

Mello-Drink Products Act
Okla. Stat. Ann., Title 63, § 1-1301.30 et seq.

**Mello-McAlister Restricted Employment
Driving Act**
Cal. Vehicle Code 1959, § 16076

Mello-Roos Community Facilities Act
Cal. Government Code § 53311 et seq.

Notice that there are both federal and state versions of Megan's Law. *Shepard's Acts and Cases by Popular Name* provides the date of codification and, for federal statutes, the *Statutes at Large* citation.

▼ How Do You Cite Federal Statutes?

Always cite to the official statutory compilation. The first entry in the citation is the title number, then the abbreviation for the statutory compilation, and then the section or paragraph number. *Bluebook* Rule 12 and *ALWD* Rule 14 detail the various rules on citing statutes and codes, state or federal. For example, Title 12, §211 of the U.S.C. would be cited as:

12 U.S.C. §211 (2006)

You always cite to the official code, the U.S.C., unless you are relying on an unofficial code for updating purposes.

The year included in the citation is the year that the code volume was published, not the year that the statute was enacted. The publication date is printed either on the title page of the bound volume or on the back of the title page. If a pocket part supplement is used, include that date as well.

42 U.S.C.A. §14071(e) (West 2005 & Supp. 2008)

In this example, the first year mentioned, 2005, is the year that the particular volume of the code was published. The second date, 2008, is the year of the pocket part supplement that updates the code volume.

If a code section is well known by a popular name, then include the name in the citation:

Strikebreaker Act, 18 U.S.C. §1231 (2006)

4. Validating and Updating Statutes

▼ How and Why Would You Validate Federal Statutes?

Remember, it is important to validate and update statutes. *Shepard's* and KeyCite provide the analytical treatment indicating how a court of law interprets or applies a statute section. *Shepard's* contains analysis that tells you whether the statute is constitutional, unconstitutional, valid, or invalid. See Illustration 7-13 for a portion of a case applying a statute and Illustration 7-14 for the corresponding *Shepard's* entry indicating the analytical treatment. Validating indicates whether a court deems the statute constitutional or unconstitutional, valid or invalid.

Shepardizing statutes does not provide information indicating whether the statute has been repealed or amended. You must update

ILLUSTRATION 7-13.   Pages from *Decision in the Federal Supplement* that Cites to 42 U.S.C. §14071

DOE v. PATAKI
Cite as 940 F.Supp. 603 (S.D.N.Y. 1996)

603

John DOE, Richard Roe and Samuel Poe, individually and on behalf of all other persons similarly situated, Plaintiffs,

v.

Hon. George E. PATAKI, in his official capacity as Governor of the State of New York, et al., Defendants.

No. 96 Civ. 1657 (DC).

United States District Court,
S.D. New York.

Sept. 24, 1996.

3. Constitutional Law ⟨⟩203

To determine whether government measure constitutes punishment, for purposes of applying constitutional prohibition against ex post facto laws, one must analyze totality of circumstances by grouping them in four areas: (1) intent, (2) design, (3) history, and (4) effects.   U.S.C.A. Const. Art. 1, § 10, cl. 1.

4. Constitutional Law ⟨⟩203

In determining whether government measure constitutes punishment, for purposes of applying constitutional prohibition against ex post facto laws, court cannot transform the factors it considers into rigid

---

(N.Y.Sup.Ct.N.Y.Co.1996) (citing statutes). The statutes resulted from growing public concern over the substantial threats presented by sex offenders and a belief that sex offenders as a group are more likely to repeat their crimes.   In enacting these laws, legislatures have articulated two goals: (i) enhancing law enforcement authorities' ability to fight sex crimes and (ii) protecting

1. In 1994, Congress enacted the Jacob Wetterling Crimes Against Children and Sexually Violent Offender Registration Program, 42 U.S.C. §§ 14071(a)–(f) (the "Federal Act").   The Federal Act initially encouraged states, through funding incentives, to enact laws requiring individuals convicted of crimes against children or sexually violent offenses to register with state law enforcement agencies.   The Federal Act also permitted law enforcement authorities to release certain information in certain limited circumstances.   *Id.* at § 14071(d).   Congress recently amended the Federal Act to provide, as an additional requirement of funding, that state and local law enforcement agencies "*shall* release relevant information that is necessary to protect the public concerning a specific person required

2.   *Registration*

Under the Act, a "sex offender" is any person convicted of a "sex offense" or a "sexually violent offense."   § 168–a(1), (2), (3).   These designations encompass 36 offenses, including attempts.   Seven of the designated offenses are misdemeanors.   (Stip. ¶ 16).[2]

→to register."   Pub.L. No. 104–145, 110 Stat. 1345 (emphasis added) (to be codified at 42 U.S.C. § 14071(d)(2)).

2. References to "Stip." are to the parties' "Stipulation of Undisputed Facts," dated August 22, 1996.

"Sex offenses" include, for example, convictions for rape in the second or third degree, sodomy in the second or third degree, or sexual abuse in the second degree, and convictions for attempt thereof.   § 168–a(2) (*citing* N.Y. Penal Law §§ 130.25, 130.30, 130.40, 130.45, 130.60 (McKinney 1987 & Supp.1996)).   "Sexually violent offenses" include, for example, convictions for rape in the first degree, sodomy in the first

---

Reprinted with permission of Thomson Reuters/West.

statutory authority by using the code's pocket part supplement and advance sheets. Most important, *Shepard's* for codes indicates the judicial treatment or interpretation of a statute, meaning how courts of law have looked at a statute's application and at whether its application was discriminatory or affected too broad or too narrow a group of people. Judges then determine if the statute has been complied with or if the

ILLUSTRATION 7-14. Sample Page from *Shepard's* on LEXIS Showing Treatment of U.S.C. References

Copyright 2008 SHEPARD'S(R) - 5 Citing references

42 U.S.C. sec. 14071 (e), 42 U.S.C. sec. 14071 (e)

(TM):
Restrictions: *Unrestricted*
FOCUS(TM) Terms: *No FOCUS terms*
Print Format: *FULL*
Citing Ref. Signal: *Hidden*

LEGISLATIVE HISTORY (1 citing reference)

1. **Renumbered to:**
   1997 Stat.
      Subsec f 111St2463

CITING DECISIONS (3 citing decisions)

MASSACHUSETTS SUPREME JUDICIAL COURT

2. **Cited by:**
   Opinion of the Justices to the Senate, 423 Mass. 1201, 668 N.E.2d 738, 1996 Mass. LEXIS 168 (1996)
      668 N.E.2d 738 *p.743*

WEST VIRGINIA SUPREME CT. OF APPEALS

3. **Cited by:**
   Haislop v. Edgell, 215 W. Va. 88, 593 S.E.2d 839, 2003 W. Va. LEXIS 167 (2003)
      215 W. Va. 88 *p.92*, (edition 2000)
      593 S.E.2d 839 *p.843*, (edition 2000)

4. **Cited by:**
   Hensler v. Cross, 210 W. Va. 530, 558 S.E.2d 330, 2001 W. Va. LEXIS 177 (2001)
      210 W. Va. 530 *p.533*
      558 S.E.2d 330 *p.333*

LAW REVIEWS AND PERIODICALS (1 Citing Reference)

5. *Article: Federal Habeas in the Information Age*, 85 Minn. L. Rev. 147 (2000)
      85 Minn. L. Rev. 147 *p.163*, (edition 2000)

statute is unconstitutional or constitutional in whole or in part. See Illustration 7-14 for Shepard's treatment of 42 U.S.C. §14071 and Illustration 7-13 where 42 U.S.C. §14071 is cited in a case listed in *Shepard's*.

▼ How Do You Update Statutes with Print Resources?

To update statutes to ensure that you have the most recent version, you must take the following steps.

1. Rely on an unofficial code, the U.S.C.A. or the U.S.C.S. After finding the appropriate code section, consult the pocket part supplement at the end of the volume or the separately published pamphlet that updates the particular volume. For example, 42 U.S.C.A. §14071(e) is viewed in the main volume. See Illustration 7-6. Then turn to the back of the volume containing the initial entry and open the pocket part supplement, to see if §14071(e) release of information is mentioned. The entries in the supplement are in numerical order just as they are in the main volume. If a section is not affected, it is just skipped over and the next affected section, in sequential order, is mentioned. See Illustration 7-15. Note that sometimes the material updating the code volume contains too many pages to be included in a pocket part so that a supplementary pamphlet, a separate paperback bound pamphlet, is published.

2. To further update a federal code section, scan the *United States Code Service Advance Service,* the U.S.C.C.A.N. advance sheets (the paperbound pamphlets that are issued monthly containing the session laws from the Congress), or the U.S.C.A. statutory supplement to find relevant slip laws from recent congressional sessions. Look for entries that are similar in name to the code section you are updating. This can also be done for state statutes by using the state session law reporter.

3. If a state statute is being updated, review the session law reporter for the legislature to see if any new session laws modify, repeal, supersede, or amend existing legislation. Also, consult the state legislative information Web site listed at the end of this chapter.

4. You can track pending legislation for the 50 states on LEXIS and on WESTLAW in the respective state bill tracking files.

5. Review the U.S.C.A. statutory supplement for federal statutes. This pamphlet indicates whether a section of the U.S.C. has been amended, repealed, or created.

5. How to Find State Statutes

▼ How Does State Statutory Research Compare with Federal Statutory Research?

State statutory research closely parallels federal statutory research. To perform state statutory research, you would use the index method, the

ILLUSTRATION 7-15.   Pocket Part Entry for 42 U.S.C.A. §14071

---

42 § 14045d   **PUBLIC HEALTH AND WELFARE**

(1) administering tribal funds and programs;

(2) enhancing the safety of Indian women from domestic violence, dating violence, sexual assault, and stalking; and

(3) strengthening the Federal response to such violent crimes.

(Pub.L. 109–162, Title IX, § 903, Jan. 5, 2006, 119 Stat. 3078.)

HISTORICAL AND STATUTORY NOTES

Revision Notes and Legislative Reports

2006 Acts. House Report No. 109–233, see 2005 U.S. Code Cong. and Adm. News, p. 1636.

References in Text

This Act, referred to in subsec. (a), is the Violence Against Women and Department of Justice Reauthorization Act of 2005, Pub.L. 109–162, Jan. 5, 2006, 119 Stat. 2960. For complete classification, see Short Title note set out under 42 U.S.C.A. § 13701 and Tables.

The Violence Against Women Act of 1994, referred to in subsec. (a), also known as VAWA, is Pub.L. 103–322, Title IV, Sept. 13, 1994, 108 Stat. 1902, as amended, which enacted 42 U.S.C.A. §§ 300w–10, 3796gg to 3796gg–5, 3796hh to 3796hh–4, 5712d, 10416, 10417, 10418, 13931, 13941 to 13943, 13951, 13961 to 13963, 13971, 13981, 13991 to 13994, 14001, 14002, 14011 to 14015, and 14031 to 14040, 16 U.S.C.A. § 1a–7a, and 18 U.S.C.A. §§ 2247, 2248, 2259, 2261 to 2266, amended 42 U.S.C.A. §§ 1988, 3782, 3783, 3793, 3796aa–1, 3796aa–2, 3796aa–3, 3796aa–5, 3796aa–6, 10402, 10407 to 10410, 10607, 13012, 13014, 13021, and 13024, 8 U.S.C.A. §§ 1151, 1154, 1186a, and 1254, 16 U.S.C.A. § 460*l*–8, 18 U.S.C.A. §§ 2245, 3156, and 3663, 28 U.S.C.A. §§ 534 and 1445, and Rule 412 of the Federal Rules of Evidence, set out in the Appendix to Title 28, repealing 42 U.S.C.A.

§§ 3796aa–4 and 3796aa–7, and enacted provisions set out as notes under 42 U.S.C.A. § 13701, 8 U.S.C.A. §§ 1151 and 1186a, and 28 U.S.C.A. §§ 534, 994, and 2074. For complete classification, see Short Title note set out under 42 U.S.C.A. §   13710 and Tables.

The Violence Against Women Act of 2000, referred to in subsec. (a), is Pub.L. 106–386, Div. B, §§ 1001 to 1603, Oct. 28, 2000, 114 Stat. 1491, as amended, which enacted 18 U.S.C.A. § 2266 and 42 U.S.C.A. §§ 280b–1c, 3789p, 3796gg–6, 3796gg–7, 3797a to 3797e, 10419, 10420, 14041 to 14041b, 14042, and 14071, amended 8 U.S.C.A. §§ 1101, 1151, 1154, 1182, 1184, 1227, 1229a, 1229b, 1255, 1367, and 1641, 18 U.S.C.A. §§ 2216A, 2261, 2262, and 2265, 20 U.S.C.A. § 1152, 28 U.S.C.A. § 1738A, and 42 U.S.C.A. §§ 3793, 3796gg, 3796gg–1 to 3796gg–3, 3796gg–5, 3796hh, 3796hh–1, 3796hh–4, 10403, 10409, 10416, 10418, 13014, 13024, 13971, 13991 to 13994, 14001, 14002, 14031, and 14032, repealed 42 U.S.C.A. § 300w–10; and enacted provisions set out as notes under 8 U.S.C.A. §§ 1101, 1229b, and 1255, 20 U.S.C.A. § 1001, 28 U.S.C.A. §§ 994 and 1738A, and 42 U.S.C.A. §§ 290bb–36, 3796gg, 3793, 3796gg–2, 13701, 13961, and 14042. For complete classification, see Short Title note set out under 42 U.S.C.A. § 13710 and Tables.

SUBCHAPTER VI—CRIMES AGAINST CHILDREN

§ 14071. Jacob Wetterling Crimes Against Children and Sexually Violent Offender Registration Program

(a) In general

(1) State guidelines

The Attorney General shall establish guidelines for State programs that require—

[See main volume for text of (A)]

(B) a person who is a sexually violent predator to register a current address for the time period specified in subparagraph (B) of subsection (b)(6) of this section.

[See main volume for text of (2) and (3); (b) to (j)]

(Pub.L. 103–322, Title XVII, § 170101, Sept. 13, 1994, 108 Stat. 2038; Pub.L. 104–145, § 2, May 17, 1996, 110 Stat. 1345; Pub.L. 104–236, §§ 3 to 7, Oct. 3, 1996, 110 Stat. 3096, 3097; Pub.L. 105–119, Title I, § 115(a)(1) to (5), Nov. 26, 1997, 111 Stat. 2461 to 2463; Pub.L. 105–314, Title VI, § 607(a), Oct. 30, 1998, 112 Stat. 2985; Pub.L. 106–386, Div. B, Title VI, § 1601(b)(1), Oct. 28, 2000, 114 Stat. 1537; Pub.L. 108–21, Title VI, §§ 604(a), 605(a), 606, Apr. 30, 2003, 117 Stat. 688; Pub.L. 109–162, Title XI, § 1153(b), Jan. 5, 2006, 119 Stat. 3113.)

Effective Date of Repeal

Pub.L. 109–248, Title I, § 129, July 27, 2006, 120 Stat. 600, provided that this section is repealed the later of 3 years after July 27, 2006 and 1 year after the date on which the software described in 42 U.S.C.A. § 16923 is available.

98

ILLUSTRATION 7-15. *Continued*

HISTORICAL AND STATUTORY NOTES

Revision Notes and Legislative Reports

  2006 Acts. House Report No. 109–233, see 2005 U.S. Code Cong. and Adm. News, p. 1636.

  Statement by President, see 2006 U.S. Code Cong. and Adm. News, p. S35.

Amendments

  2006 Amendments. Subsec. (a)(1)(B). Pub.L. 109–162, § 1153(b), struck out "unless such requirement is terminated under" and inserted "for the time period specified in".

Effective and Applicability Provisions

  2006 Acts. Pub.L. 109–248, Title I, § 129(b), July 27, 2006, 120 Stat. 601, provided that: "Notwithstanding any other provision of this Act [enacting 18 U.S.C.A. §§ 2245, 2250, 2252C, 2254, 2257A, 2260A, 3299, and 4248, and 42 U.S.C.A. §§ 3765, 3797ee, 3797ee-1, 16901, 16902, 16911 to 16929, 16941 to 16945, 16961, 16962, 16971, and 16981 to 16991, amending 18 U.S.C.A §§ 1001, 1101, 1153, 1154, 1201, 1227, 1465, 1466, 1467, 1591, 2241, 2242, 2243, 2244, 2251, 2252, 2252A, 2252B, 2253, 2255, 2257, 2258, 2260, 2422, 2423, 3142, 3509, 3559, 3563, 3583, 3592, 3621, 3771, 4042, 4209, 4241, and 4247, 21 U.S.C.A. § 841, 28 U.S.C.A. § 534, and 42 U.S.C.A. §§ 671, 5772, 5780, 13032, and 4135a, repealing 42 U.S.C.A. §§ 14071 to 14073, enact-

ing provisions set out as notes under 18 U.S.C.A. §§ 2251 and 2257, and 42 U.S.C.A. §§ 671, 5611, 13701, 14071, and 16901, and amending provisions set out as notes under 10 U.S.C.A. § 951, 28 U.S.C.A. § 994, and 42 U.S.C.A. § 13751], this section [repealing 42 U.S.C.A. §§ 14071 to 14073] shall take effect on the date of the deadline determined in accordance with section 124(a) [42 U.S.C.A. § 16924(a), which provides for implementation of this subchapter before the later of 3 years after July 27, 2006 and 1 year after the date on which the software described in 42 U.S.C.A. § 16923 is available]." See 42 U.S.C.A. § 16901 et seq.

Compliance period

  Pub.L. 109–162, Title XI, § 1153(a), Jan. 5, 2006, 119 Stat. 3113, provided that: "A State shall not be treated, for purposes of any provision of law, as having failed to comply with section 170101 (42 U.S.C. 14071) [this section] or 170102 (42 U.S.C. 14072) of the Violent Crime Control and Law Enforcement Act of 1994 until 36 months after the date of the enactment of this Act [Jan. 5, 2006], except that the Attorney General may grant an additional 24 months to a State that is making good faith efforts to comply with such sections."

LAW REVIEW AND JOURNAL COMMENTARIES

Balancing the protection of children against the protection of constitutional rights: The past, present and future of Megan's Law. Comment, 42 Duq. L. Rev. 331 (2004).

Keeping children out of double jeopardy: An assessment of punishment and Megan's Law. 81 Minn.L.Rev. 501 (1996).

Making the case for Megan's Law: A study in legislative rhetoric. Daniel M. Filler, 76 Ind. L.Rev. 315 (2001).

Megan's Law: Branding the sex offender or benefitting the community? 5 Seton Hall Const. L.J. 1127 (1995).

Megan's Law: Can it stop sexual predators—and at what cost to constitutional rights? Joel B. Rudin, 11 Crim.Just. 3 (Fall 1996).

"Megan's Law": Community notification and the constitution. 29 Colum.J.L. & Soc.Probs. 117 (1995).

Protection and treatment: Permissible civil detention of sexual predators. John Kip Cornwell, 53 Wash. & Lee L.Rev. 1293 (1996).

Sex offender registration and community notification: Protection, not punishment. 30 New Eng.L.Rev. 183 (1995).

The quandary of Megan's Law: When the child sex offender is a child. Timothy E. Wind, 37 J.Marshall L.Rev.73 (Fall 2003)

LIBRARY REFERENCES

American Digest System

  Criminal Law ⟞1222, 1226(1) to 1226(5).
  Infants ⟞20.
  Mental Health ⟞469(1) to 469(7).

Pardon and Parole ⟞64, 66, 68.
Prisons ⟞14.
Key Number System Topic Nos. 110, 211, 257A, 284, 310.

Research References

ALR Library

36 ALR 5th 161, State Statutes or Ordinances Requiring Persons Previously Convicted of Crime to Register With Authorities.

§ 14072. FBI database

Effective Date of Repeal

  Pub.L. 109–248, Title I, § 129, July 27, 2006, 120 Stat. 600, provided that this section is repealed the later of 3 years after July 27, 2006 and 1 year after the date on which the software described in 42 U.S.C.A. § 16923 is available.

title outline method, the popular name table, or the conversion table approach, just as you would with the federal materials. Even the precise, succinct language of the state statutes is similar to the federal statutes because of the canons of construction and models of statutory parallelism that are adopted by drafters of legislation. Compare North Dakota's version of Megan's Law, shown in Illustration 7-16, to the federal version, shown in Illustration 7-6. See also Illustration 7-12 for other state statutes for Megan's Law.

State statutes are enacted by the state legislatures and appear in the slip law format first, then become session laws, and finally are codified and incorporated into the state statutory codes. Current state legislation also can be found in state bar bulletins, legal newspapers, and on the Internet. Consult the end of this chapter for Internet addresses for state legislative information.

PRACTICE POINTER

Always read a statute according to its plain meaning; that is, interpret the language just as it is written. After reading a statute, summarize the language in a few sentences, in your own words. This will help when you then want to use the statute in a written document. Your language and the statutory language won't contrast so sharply. Remember to cite to all statutory authority that you rely on, even if it is written in your own language. Be sure that any statute that you rely on is updated.

▼ How Can You Tell Whether a State Code Is the Official or the Unofficial Statutory Compilation?

Bluebook Table T.1 and *ALWD* Appendix 1 answer this question. Under each state in Table T.1 is the boldface heading **Statutory compilations,** with information indicating the official format of the state code. *ALWD* indicates the official code with a star. For example, under Wisconsin you find:

Statutory compilations: Cite to Wis. Stat. if therein.

This indicates that Wis. Stat., the *Bluebook* abbreviation for the *Wisconsin Statutes,* is the official statutory compilation for Wisconsin. Under the Statutory compilations heading, the names of the state code, in the official and the unofficial format, are listed along with the *Bluebook* abbreviation.

Sometimes a state has more than one statutory compilation, or there is not official compilation. When this occurs, follow the *Bluebook* or *The ALWD Citation Manual* for guidance when citing.

ILLUSTRATION 7-16. Sample Page Showing North Dakota Century Code §12.1-32-15

LEXSTAT N.D. CENT. CODE, § 12.1-32-15

NORTH DAKOTA CENTURY CODE
Copyright (c) 2008 by Matthew Bender & Company, Inc.
a member of the LexisNexis Group.
All rights reserved.

*** THIS DOCUMENT IS CURRENT THROUGH THE 2007 LEGISLATIVE SESSION ***
*** ANNOTATIONS CURRENT THROUGH MARCH 20, 2008 ***

TITLE 12.1 Criminal Code
CHAPTER 12.1-32 Penalties and Sentencing

Go to the North Dakota Code Archive Directory

N.D. Cent. Code, § 12.1-32-15 (2008)

12.1-32-15. Offenders against children and sexual offenders -- Sexually violent predators -- Registration requirement -- Penalty.

1. As used in this section:

a. "A crime against a child" means a violation of chapter 12.1-16, section 12.1-17-01.1 if the victim is under the age of twelve, 12.1-17-02, 12.1-17-04, subdivision a of subsection 6 of section 12.1-17-07.1, section 12.1-18-01, 12.1-18-02, 12.1-18-05, chapter 12.1-29, or subdivision a of subsection 1 or subsection 2 of section 14-09-22, or an equivalent offense from another court in the United States, a tribal court, or court of another country, in which the victim is a minor or is otherwise of the age required for the act to be a crime or an attempt to commit these offenses.

b. "Department" means the department of corrections and rehabilitation.

c. "Mental abnormality" means a congenital or acquired condition of an individual that affects the emotional or volitional capacity of the individual in a manner that predisposes that individual to the commission of criminal sexual acts to a degree that makes the individual a menace to the health and safety of other individuals.

d. "Predatory" means an act directed at a stranger or at an individual with whom a relationship has been established or promoted for the primary purpose of victimization.

e. "Sexual offender" means a person who has pled guilty to or been found guilty, including juvenile delinquent adjudications, of a violation of section 12.1-20-03, 12.1-20-03.1, 12.1-20-04, 12.1-20-05, 12.1-20-05.1, 12.1-20-06, 12.1-20-07 except for subdivision a, 12.1-20-11, 12.1-20-12.1, or 12.1-20-12.2, chapter 12.1-27.2, or subsection 2 of section 12.1-22-03.1, or an equivalent offense from another court in the United States, a tribal court, or court of another country, or an attempt to commit these offenses.

f. "Sexually dangerous individual" means an individual who meets the definition specified in section 25-03.3-01.

g. "Temporarily domiciled" means staying or being physically present in this state for more than thirty days in a calendar year or at a location for longer than ten consecutive days, attending school for longer than ten days, or maintaining employment in the jurisdiction for longer than ten days, regardless of the state of the residence.

ILLUSTRATION 7-16. *Continued*

N.D. Cent. Code, § 12.1-32-15

8. An individual required to register under this section shall comply with the registration requirement for the longer of the following periods:

a. A period of fifteen years after the date of sentence or order deferring or suspending sentence upon a plea or finding of guilt or after release from incarceration, whichever is later;

b. A period of twenty-five years after the date of sentence or order deferring or suspending sentence upon a plea or finding of guilt or after release from incarceration, whichever is later, if the offender is assigned a moderate risk by the attorney general as provided in subsection 12; or

c. For the life of the individual, if that individual:

(1) On two or more occasions has pled guilty or nolo contendere to, or been found guilty of a crime against a child or as a sexual offender. If all qualifying offenses are misdemeanors, this lifetime provision does not apply unless a qualifying offense was committed after August 1, 1999;

(2) Pleads guilty or nolo contendere to, or is found guilty of, an offense committed after August 1, 1999, which is described in subdivision a of subsection 1 of section 12.1-20-03, section 12.1-20-03.1, or subdivision d of subsection 1 of section 12.1-20-03 if the person is an adult and the victim is under age twelve, or section 12.1-18-01 if that individual is an adult other than a parent of the victim, or an equivalent offense from another court in the United States, a tribal court, or court of another country; or

(3) Is assigned a high risk by the attorney general as provided in subsection 12.

---

6. Researching Statutes Online

▼ Are the Federal Statutes Available on LEXIS and WESTLAW?

Yes, the complete texts of the U.S.C. and the U.S.C.A. (published by West) are available on WESTLAW. The U.S.C.S. is available in full text on LEXIS. See Illustration 7-7 for an example. Both LEXIS and WESTLAW have added the browse enhancement to the statutes databases, enabling you to view the code sections preceding and following the code section that you retrieved. The browse feature emulates researching code sections in a hardbound format because you often look at related code sections when you find the section of the statutes with information on point. If cost is a factor, check access.gpo.gov or thomas.loc.gov.

▼ Are State Statutes Available on LEXIS and WESTLAW?

Yes, the full text of all 50 state statutory compilations are available on both WESTLAW and LEXIS. On LEXIS, you can search all 50 state codes simultaneously. Slip laws are available for all 50 states on LEXIS and WESTLAW in the respective state legislative service file.

Cornell's Legal Information Institute permits you to access and to search all 50 state statutory compilations at no charge. The site is www.law.cornell.edu/states.

▼ Can Statutes Be Validated on LEXIS and WESTLAW?

Shepard's for all statutes is now available on LEXIS. You can validate statutes on WESTLAW by using KeyCite.

▼ How Do You Update Federal Statutes Online?

Updating statutory authority online is achieved through the point-and-click method. Once you have the relevant statutory provision on the screen, there will be a caption indicating that the statute is current through a particular date or session law. Citations to any slip laws or session laws updating the statute will be given. If the updating documents are available online, WESTLAW marks the updating document with a jump marker, and LEXIS marks it with an equal sign followed by a number. Merely point and click the identifying icon and you will link to the updating document. Before you perform this on either LEXIS or WESTLAW, call customer service for guidance.

▼ Are Statutes Available on the Internet?

Yes, the U.S.C. is available on the Internet at uscode.house.gov, thomas.loc.gov, and www.law.cornell.edu. Remember to validate any statutory provision that you use to see how a court has applied it. Also, double check to see if the provision is current by consulting the last date updated on the site.

CHAPTER SUMMARY

This chapter led you through the legislative process, where you learned the steps a bill goes through to become law. Also, this chapter detailed constitutional and statutory research on the state and federal levels. You learned how to find, to cite, and to validate pertinent constitutional provisions. You learned about the different ways to perform statutory research—federal and statee—and how to update, validate, and cite statutes.

KEY TERMS

codification

committee report

conference committee

constitution

grandfathered

House committee

legislation

pocket veto

public laws

session laws

slip bill

slip law

sponsor

statutes

Statutes at Large

Statutory compilations

subcommittee

United States Code

United States Code Annotated

United States Code Service

veto

EXERCISES

RESEARCHING BY POPULAR NAME

To answer questions 1-9, look up the Americans with Disabilities Act of 1990.

1. What date was the act enacted originally? Where is the information? List at least two places.
2. List the names of the four substantive titles of the act. What are they called in the codified version?
3. Provide the public law number for the act. List at least two places where this information is found.
4. Explain what the numbers included in the public law number mean.
5. Provide the U.S.C. citation for the act. List the steps you followed to find this information.
6. Provide the *Statutes at Large* citation for the act. List at least two places where this information is found.
7. What is the definition of *employer* under the act?
8. Does the definition of *employer* under Title I of the act differ in the U.S.C.A. from the definition found in the *Statutes at Large* when the law was originally enacted? If so, how?
9. Find the *United States Code* section for the Americans with Disabilities Act on the Internet at thomas.loc.gov.

For questions 10-16, look up the Energy Conservation and Production Act in the U.S.C.'s popular name table. Note in particular the section discussing State Utility Regulatory Assistance.

10. Write the U.S.C. citation in *Bluebook* format. (Remember to look at the most recent amendments.)
11. After you find the U.S.C. cite, look up the U.S.C.A. entry for the code section. Compare the entries and the annotations. Note the research

enhancements that a West publication provides. Write down any key numbers and any U.S.C.C.A.N. references.

12. Look up the U.S.C.S. entry for the code section. Note the research aids that U.S.C.S. provides. Note that you see administrative regulation references in the U.S.C.S.

13. What C.F.R. citation is referred to in the code section? (Remember to use the supplements and the pocket parts to ensure that you are looking at the most current version of the statute.)

14. Are there any cases that discuss or interpret the statute? If so, look up two cases and see how the statute is treated in the opinions.

15. Shepardize the statute citation.

16. Find the statute on the Internet at thomas.loc.gov.

For questions 17-18, use your state statutes to find the sections that pertain to pawnbrokers and moneylenders.

17. Write the official state code cite in correct *Bluebook* format. Next, write the annotated cite if available. Compare the entries.

18. Are there any cases that discuss or interpret the statute? If so, look them up and see how the statute is treated in the opinion. Finally, Shepardize or KeyCite the statute citation.

19. Use GPOACCESS.GOV to find the United States Code section containing the provisions from Megan's Law.

20. List three ways to find Megan's Law online. Name the sites consulted.

21. Search either thomas.loc.gov or access.gpo.gov for any federal bills or resolutions in the current Congress concerning the registration of sexual offenders.

Appendix

STATE LEGISLATIVE INFORMATION

Alabama	www.legislature.state.al.us
Alaska	w3.legis.state.ak.us
Arizona	azleg.state.az.us
Arkansas	www.arkleg.state.ar.us
California	
Legislative Information	leginfo.ca.gov
Colorado	www.leg.state.co.us
Connecticut	cga.ct.gov
Delaware	legis.delaware.gov
District of Columbia	dccouncil.washington.dc.us
Florida	leg.state.fl.us
Georgia	www.legis.state.ga.us
Hawaii	capitol.hawaii.gov
Idaho	legislature.idaho.gov
Illinois	ilga.gov
Indiana	in.gov/legislative
Iowa	www.legis.state.ia.us
Kansas	kslegislature.org
Kentucky	lrc.ky.gov
Louisiana	legis.state.la.us
Maine	janus.state.me.us/legis
Maryland	mlis.state.md.us
Massachusetts	www.state.ma.us/legis/legis
Michigan	legislature.mi.gov
Minnesota	www.leg.state.mn.us
Mississippi	billstatus.ls.state.ms.us
Missouri	moga.mo.gov
Montana	leg.mt.gov
Nebraska	nebraskalegislature.gov
Nevada	leg.state.nv.us
New Hampshire	gencourt.state.nh.us
New Jersey	www.njleg.state.nj.us
New Mexico	legis.state.nm.us
New York Senate	senate.state.ny.us
Assembly	assembly.state.ny.us
North Carolina	ncga.state.nc.us
North Dakota	legis.nd.gov
Ohio	legislature.state.oh.us
Oklahoma	www.lsb.state.ok.us
Oregon	www.leg.state.or.us
Pennsylvania	www.legis.state.pa.us
Rhode Island	www.rilin.state.ri.us
South Carolina	www.scstatehouse.net

South Dakota	legis.state.sd.us
Tennessee	www.legislature.state.tn.us
Texas	www.capitol.state.tx.us
Utah	le.state.ut.us
Vermont	www.leg.state.vt.us
Virginia	legis.state.va.us
Washington	leg.wa.gov/legislature
West Virginia	www.legis.state.wv.us
Wisconsin	legis.state.wi.us
Wyoming	legisweb.state.wy.us

LEGISLATIVE HISTORY

CHAPTER OVERVIEW

Paralegals are called on to monitor the status of bills and proposed legislation currently being considered on the federal and state levels and to compile legislative histories of laws already passed and codified to ascertain the policy or intended effect of the legislation. The process of compiling all of the components of the legislative process leading to the enactment of a statute, called **legislative history,** is growing in importance as the need for the interpretation of statutes in litigation increases.

A. LEGISLATIVE INFORMATION

Researching a legislative history requires that you retrace the law making process of enacted law from the initial bill through the committee reports through the various versions of the bill to the final version and the enacted law. Legislative histories are very informative because the

information gathered from the committee reports and the speeches or legislative debates given on the floor of the legislative body provides insight into the purpose and intent of the legislation.

A fantastic source of information on legislative history, including many links, is at llrx.com/resources7.htm.

1. Finding the Text of Pending Legislation

Bills currently going through the process of being enacted into law are classified as **pending legislation.** Paralegals are called on to monitor pending legislation and to make sure that the information is as current as possible. The legislative information sites for all of the jurisdictions at the end of Chapter 7 may be of assistance.

LEXIS and WESTLAW have current federal and state bills online. LEXIS has the text of current pending federal bills as well as the full text of federal committee and conference reports dating back to January 1990. The text of most pending state bills is available also.

WESTLAW has bills, 1995 to the present, online and Billcast, which has the summaries of pending legislation from all 50 states and the U.S. Congress. Billcast also contains statistical odds of passage in each chamber. WESTLAW also has state pending legislation and the text of bills for states online.

On the state level, each state has a legislative library from which you can request the copy of the particular bill in question. If the librarian cannot provide a copy of the bill, he or she will generally direct you to the member of the state House or Senate who sponsored the bill or to the appropriate committee. Pending legislation for all 50 states can be tracked on LEXIS and WESTLAW.

www.house.gov is the site for the United States House of Representatives server. This site contains committee reports. Committee activites from the past three days are posted here. This is a good site to bookmark when you are tracking legislation for it links you to bills in full-text format. It has a directory of House members complete with addresses, both postal and e-mail, and telephone numbers. This site posts activity currently on the House floor.

2. Tracking Pending Legislation

On the federal level, the *Congressional Index* is updated weekly when Congress is in session and provides information on voting records and the status of bills during the prior week. The status of the bill means where the bill in question is in the legislative process, whether it is in committee or subcommittee hearings, or whether it is being debated on the floor. Note that *Congressional Index* does not print the text of the bills.

Another source for tracking pending federal legislation is the ***Congressional Quarterly Weekly Report.*** This source is helpful for policy information regarding bills currently being considered in Congress and for voting records.

Thomas.loc.gov has the capability to monitor pending legislation online at no cost.

On the state level, almost every state has either a state legislative Web site, a state bar association, or a state legislative library that provides information as to the status of bills that are currently being created and considered. See the list of state legislative Web sites at the end of Chapter 7.

B. LEGISLATIVE HISTORIES

▼ Where Do You Find Copies of Public Laws?

Public laws, which are the federally enacted laws, can be obtained by contacting the law's sponsor in the House or the Senate. Also, the U.S. Government Printing Office issues pamphlets for each public law passed. In addition to USCCAN, these can be obtained at a government depository library. (Many university libraries and large city libraries are government depository libraries.) The *United States Code Service* (U.S.C.S.) publishes paperback advance sheets with the public laws enacted during the prior month. The *United States Code Annotated* (U.S.C.A.) also prints paperback advance sheets each month that contain all of the public laws enacted during the prior month.

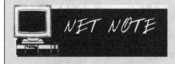

The steps for tracing federal legislation are located at www.ll.georgetown.edu/guides/legislative_history.cfm.

Public laws starting with the 93rd Congress are available online at thomas.loc.gov.

▼ How Do You Research Legislative Histories of Laws That Are Already Enacted?

Commercial publishers compile the most accessible sources of legislative histories for laws that are already enacted. The most user-friendly hard-copy source of commercially compiled federal legislative histories is the *United States Code Congressional and Administrative News* (U.S.C.C.A.N.). U.S.C.C.A.N., which began publication in the 1950s, is published by West, and references to U.S.C.C.A.N. are provided in the U.S.C.A. Often a U.S.C.A. entry to a statute enacted since U.S.C.C.A.N.'s publication will contain a reference to the U.S.C.C.A.N. citation, which outlines the legislative process that the statute underwent prior to enactment.

U.S.C.C.A.N. is organized by congressional session; the congressional session is indicated on the spine of each volume. Each session's public laws, also indicated on the spine of each volume, and the legislative history of the public laws are arranged in numerical order according to public law number. See Illustrations 8-1 and 8-2.

U.S.C.C.A.N. is a good place to find legislative history and a copy of a public law, provided it is not too recent. For copies of recent public laws (one-month old), consult the pamphlets at the end of the U.S.C.A., U.S.C.S., and U.S.C.C.A.N. sets.

Legislative histories are also available on WESTLAW in the LH database. The coverage begins in 1948.

▼ How Do You Use U.S.C.C.A.N. in Conjunction with the U.S.C.A.?

In Illustration 7-6, look at the reprint of 42 U.S.C.A. §14071(e) from the main code volume of the U.S.C.A. Notice the heading that follows the text of the statute: Historical and Statutory Notes. It is in this part of the U.S.C.A. that you obtain references to the public laws that created the statute and to the appropriate U.S.C.C.A.N. cite that contains the legislative history for the public law that was codified in the U.S.C.

Thomas.loc.gov provides free access to legislative information, including public laws, beginning in the 93rd Congress. It also contains the Congressional Record beginning with the 101st Congress and committee reports starting with the 104th Congress as well as links to federal government Web sites. This is a valuable site to find legislative information from the current Congress that may impact a particular federal statute. You can search by bill number, by popular name, or by word.

ILLUSTRATION 8-1.   Sample Pages from U.S.C.C.A.N. Showing Pub. L. No. 104-145

PUBLIC LAW 104–145 [H.R. 2137]; May 17, 1996

MEGAN'S LAW

For Legislative History of Act, see p. 980.

An Act to amend the Violent Crime Control and Law Enforcement Act of 1994 to require the release of relevant information to protect the public from sexually violent offenders.

Be it enacted by the Senate and House of Representatives of the United States of America in Congress assembled,

SECTION 1. SHORT TITLE.

This Act may be cited as "Megan's Law".

SEC. 2. RELEASE OF INFORMATION AND CLARIFICATION OF PUBLIC NATURE OF INFORMATION.

Section 170101(d) of the Violent Crime Control and Law Enforcement Act of 1994 (42 U.S.C. 14071(d)) is amended to read as follows:

"(d) RELEASE OF INFORMATION.—

"(1) The information collected under a State registration program may be disclosed for any purpose permitted under the laws of the State.

"(2) The designated State law enforcement agency and any local law enforcement agency authorized by the State agency shall release relevant information that is necessary to protect the public concerning a specific person required to register under this section, except that the identity of a victim of an offense that requires registration under this section shall not be released."

Approved May 17, 1996.

Megan's Law.

42 USC 13701 note.

LEGISLATIVE HISTORY—H.R. 2137:
HOUSE REPORTS: No. 104–555 (Comm. on the Judiciary).
CONGRESSIONAL RECORD, Vol. 142 (1996):
   May 7, considered and passed House.
   May 9, considered and passed Senate.
WEEKLY COMPILATION OF PRESIDENTIAL DOCUMENTS, Vol. 32 (1996):
   May 17, Presidential remarks.

110 STAT. 1345

Reprinted with permission of Thomson Reuters/West.

▼ What Are Other Ways to Find Relevant Legislative History in U.S.C.C.A.N.?

The popular name tables in the U.S.C., U.S.C.A., and U.S.C.S. provide references to the public law numbers for the statutes. If you have the public law number of a statute, then you can find the legislative history in U.S.C.C.A.N. because it is organized by public law number.

▼ Is Legislative History Primary Authority?

Legislative history is not primary authority but is considered to be secondary authority because it provides material to interpret the

ILLUSTRATION 8-2.   Sample Pages from U.S.C.C.A.N.
Showing the Legislative History of Pub. L. No. 104-145

MEGAN'S LAW

P.L. 104–145, see page 110 Stat. 1345

DATES OF CONSIDERATION AND PASSAGE

House: May 7, 1996

Senate: May 9, 1996

Cong. Record Vol. 142 (1996)

House Report (Judiciary Committee)
No. 104–555, May 6, 1996
[To accompany H.R. 2137]

No Senate Report was submitted with this legislation.

HOUSE REPORT NO. 104–555

[page 1]

The Committee on the Judiciary, to whom was referred the bill
(H.R. 2137) to amend the Violent Crime Control and Law Enforcement Act of 1994 to require the release of relevant information to
protect the public from sexually violent offenders, having considered the same, report favorably thereon with an amendment and
recommend that the bill as amended do pass.

    •   •   •   •   •

[page 2]

PURPOSE AND SUMMARY

This bill would amend a provision enacted as part of the Violent
Crime Control and Law Enforcement Act of 1994 (Public Law 103–
322). Title XVII of that Act, the "Jacob Wetterling Crimes Against
Children and Sexually Violent Offender Registration Act" (42
U.S.C. 14071), requires States to implement a system where all
persons who commit sexual or kidnapping crimes against children
or who commit sexually violent crimes against any person (whether
adult or child) are required to register their addresses with the
State upon their release from prison. The 1994 Act also provides
that law enforcement agencies may release "relevant information"
about an offender if they deem it necessary to protect the public.
This bill will require the release of such information when law enforcement officials deem it to be necessary to protect the public.

While the 1994 Act does not mandate that States comply with its
provisions, a State's failure to implement such a system by September 1997 will result in that State losing part of its annual federal
crime-fighting funding.

ILLUSTRATION 8-2. *Continued*

MEGAN'S LAW

P.L. 104-145

BACKGROUND AND NEED FOR THE LEGISLATION

Perhaps no type of crime has received more attention in recent years than crimes against children involving sexual acts and violence. Several recent tragic cases have focused public attention on this type of crime and resulted in public demand that government take stronger action against those who commit these crimes.

In partial response to this demand, Congress passed Title XVII of the Violent Crime Control and Law Enforcement Act of 1994 (Public Law 103-322). That title, the "Jacob Wetterling Crimes Against Children and Sexually Violent Offender Registration Act," attempted to address the concerns about these crimes by encouraging States to establish a system where every person who commits a sexual or kidnapping crime against children or who commit sexually violent crimes against any person (whether adult or child) would be required to register his or her address with the State upon their release from prison. As a further protection, the 1994 Act required States to allow law enforcement agencies to release "relevant information" about an offender if they deemed it necessary to protect the public.

The 1994 Act provision with respect to notification only required States to give law enforcement agencies the discretion to release offender registry information when they deemed it necessary to protect the public. It has been brought to the attention of the Committee, however, that notwithstanding the clear intent of Congress that relevant information about these offenders be released to the public in these situations, some law enforcement agencies are still reluctant to do so. This bill would amend the 1994 Act to mandate that States require their law enforcement agencies to release "relevant information" in all cases when they deem it "necessary to protect the public."

The bill also amends the 1994 Act to provide that information collected under a State registration program may be disclosed for any purpose permitted under the laws of that State. The 1994 Act required that information collected by the registration program be

[page 3]

kept confidential. In some instances this requirement limited public access to what had been public records before the 1994 Act became law. H.R. 2137 will correct this unintended consequence of the 1994 Act by allowing each State to determine the extent to which the public may gain access to the information kept by the State.

HEARINGS

The Committee's Subcommittee on Crime held one day of hearings on H.R. 2137 on March 7, 1996. Testimony was received from two witnesses, Representative Dick Zimmer of New Jersey, the sponsor of H.R. 2137, and Kevin Di Gregory, Deputy Assistant Attorney General, Department of Justice, with no additional material submitted.

statutes. In the legislative branch of our government, primary authority is limited to constitutions, statutes, codes, charters, and ordinances.

▼ How Do You Cite Legislative History Found in U.S.C.C.A.N.?

Legislative history materials found in U.S.C.C.A.N. follow *Bluebook* Rule 13.4 and *ALWD* Rule 15. The correct cite for a U.S. Senate Report reprinted in U.S.C.C.A.N. is:

S. Rep. No. 13, 102d Cong., 2d Sess. 111 (1991), <u>reprinted in</u> 1991 U.S.C.C.A.N. 12.

▼ How Do You Cite to a Legislative History of a Statute?

Bluebook Rule 13 and *ALWD* Rule 15 detail the format for the components of the legislative process: the bill, the committee report, the debates, and the transcripts of the hearings.

▼ What Are Some Other Sources of Legislative Information?

Congressional Information Service (CIS) has been produced since 1970. CIS is a source of detailed compiled legislative histories. CIS has an index, which is published annually, that allows you to find the reference to the relevant public law. After you find the reference to the relevant legislation, you are instructed to consult the abstracts detailing the components of the legislative history for the relevant public law. The abstracts are very informative and should be consulted because you can find out if the information you need is found in the complete document. CIS is exhaustive in its coverage of legislative history information for public laws. Unfortunately, to obtain the full text of the document, you must have access to the microfiche set and to a microfiche reader/printer. After consulting the abstracts and finding the appropriate information, ask the librarian for assistance you in obtaining the microfiche card that contains the full text document.

The CIS index is also available online on LEXIS.

The *Congressional Record* contains the text of all of the proceedings from the floor of the U.S. Congress. It is published every day that Congress is in session. The *Congressional Record* has been in print since the 1870s. It is currently available on LEXIS and WESTLAW as well as at thomas.loc.gov.

Sometimes it is necessary to consult a privately published legislative history. You should see your law librarian for this or contact the sponsor of the public law to find out more detailed information.

▼ How Do You Research State Legislative Histories?

Each state compiles legislative resources in a different manner, which complicates the task of research. Most states do not have commercially

GPO Access at www.gpoaccess.gov contains Government Printing Office documents with links to the *Congressional Record, Congressional Bills*, and congressional publications.

The United States Senate Web site at www.senate.gov offers information about every Senate committee as well as a biographical directory of Senate members. This is also available for the House of Representatives at www.house.gov.

PRACTICE POINTER

When retrieving a document from a government Web site, use your software's "Find" feature to locate relevant text within the document.

compiled legislative histories in hard-copy format. Some states have printed indexes, but the actual documents are on microfiche. Each state has a legislative library that you can call for more information. Large public libraries and university libraries, particularly law school libraries, are good places to obtain state legislative history information. Session law services are available for every state.

The Law Librarians' Society of Washington, D.C., has a legislative sourcebook online. This site, at llsdc.org/sourcebook, includes state legislative history information.

PRACTICE POINTER

Researching legislative histories can be time-consuming. Ask the attorney that you are working for about a time budget for the project before performing a legislative history. Also, contact a librarian at a large academic law library for assistance when performing legislative histories.

ILLUSTRATION 8-3. <u>Thomas.loc.gov</u> **Search Results for 110th Congress and Bills Containing "Jacob + Wetterling"**

IV

110TH CONGRESS
1ST SESSION

H. RES. 572

Encouraging employers and online dating sites to use sex offender registries for background checks.

IN THE HOUSE OF REPRESENTATIVES

JULY 25, 2007

Mr. KING of New York submitted the following resolution; which was referred to the Committee on the Judiciary

---

RESOLUTION

Encouraging employers and online dating sites to use sex offender registries for background checks.

Whereas registries tracking sex offenders are important tools in protecting against recidivism among sex offenders;

Whereas the Jacob Wetterling Crimes Against Children and Sexually Violent Offender Registration Act (the "Wetterling Act", 42 U.S.C. 14071), established guidelines for the 50 States, the District of Columbia, and territories to require sex offenders to register where they reside, work, and attend school, as applicable;

Whereas the Adam Walsh Child Protection and Safety Act (the "Walsh Act", Public Law 109–248), expanded the range of offenses that require registration in the Wetterling Act, as well as extended the requirement to register to juveniles convicted of serious sex offenses;

2

Whereas the Walsh Act requires all jurisdictions to implement at least the registration requirements described in title I of the Walsh Act by July 27, 2009; and

ILLUSTRATION 8-3. *Continued*

Whereas section 120 of the Walsh Act established the Dru
Sjodin National Sex Offender Public Website to enable
the public to obtain relevant information for each sex offender by a single query for any given zip code or geo-
graphical radius: Now, therefore, be it

1   *Resolved,* That the House of Representatives encour-

2 ages—

3   (1) employers to check the names of potential

4   employees with the Federal and State sex offender

5   registries when hiring for positions that involve

6   teaching, supervising, interacting with, or working in

7   the general vicinity of children;

8   (2) online dating sites to check the names of

9   site members and individuals seeking site member-

10   ship with the Federal and State sex offender reg-

11   istries, and take appropriate measures to prevent in-

12   appropriate use of such sites, including prohibiting

13   access to individuals that are listed on such reg-

14   istries; and

15   (3) all States and jurisdictions to expeditiously

16   implement at least the registration requirements de-

17   scribed in title I of the Walsh Act before July 27,

3

1   2009, and to the greatest extent possible implement

2   stricter requirements than those so described.

○

▼ What Additional Sources for Legislative Information Are Available?

The following sources provide additional assistance in researching legislative information.

Congressional Staff Directory
Congressional Yellow Book
State Yellow Book
The United States Government Manual

CHAPTER SUMMARY

This chapter defined pending legislation and provided the tools to monitor pending legislation. U.S.C.C.A.N. is highlighted as the best tool for compiling a legislative history of a federal statute. Thomas.loc.gov offers easy access to legislative information from the 93rd Congress to date and is very cost effective to use. You are also introduced to other resources to perform more detailed legislative histories, both federal and state.

An online legislative history tutorial is at www.ll.georgetown.edu/guides/legislative_history.cfm.

KEY TERMS

Congressional Information Service
Congressional Quarterly Weekly Report
Congressional Record
legislative history

pending legislation
public laws
United States Code Congressional and
Administrative News

EXERCISES

1. Find the legislative history of the Brady Handgun Violence Prevention Act. This is a federal act. Cite the legislative history of the act in *Bluebook* format.
2. Find the legislative history of the Depository Library Act of 1964. This is a federal act. Cite the legislative history of the act in *Bluebook* format.
3. Name two components of a typical legislative history.
4. Why would you perform a legislative history of an act?

5. What information would you gather when performing a legislative history?

6. Search thomas.loc.gov to see if there are any bills from the current Congress that update or address the Brady Handgun Act.

7. Search thomas.loc.gov to find bills for the Rural America Energy Act of 2007.

CHAPTER 9

ADMINISTRATIVE MATERIALS AND LOOSELEAF SERVICES

CHAPTER OVERVIEW

In Chapter 7 you learned about the enactment of statutes and how to research them. Some statutes create administrative agencies and provide these agencies with a variety of powers. In this chapter, you learn about the creation of administrative agencies, the powers of these agencies, and the authority that they generate. You are shown how to locate these authorities as well as how to update and validate them. By the chapter's end, you will know how to use administrative materials and will understand their importance and relationship to other primary and secondary sources.

A. INTRODUCTION

▼ What Is Administrative Law?

Administrative rules and regulations are essential to the practice of law in a variety of areas, such as taxation, environmental law, education, and health care law. Federal and state administrative agencies regulate many aspects of our lives ranging from the safety of the products we purchase to the amount of hazardous wastes that can be placed in our landfills. Although administrative law governs many facets of daily life, appointed, rather than elected, individuals create this law.

▼ How Can Administrative Agencies Create Law When This Is the Job of Congress?

Congress and other legislative bodies delegate their power to create law to **administrative agencies** by enacting **enabling statutes.** Delegating authority to the agencies relieves Congress of the daily enforcement of detailed regulations.

▼ How Do Administrative Agencies Operate?

On the federal level, administrative agencies often fall under the control of the executive branch of the government. To determine which executives control a particular agency, several sources should be consulted. The *United States Government Manual* provides information about all federal government agencies. This information includes a brief description of the agency's functions, how it was created, and how it is controlled. Although every cabinet post has an agency beneath it, some agencies are not associated with cabinet posts, such as the National Aeronautics and Space Administration (NASA). Often, agency staff members, other than those who hold cabinet posts, are hired because of their expertise and qualifications in an area of law. These experts do not leave their posts at the end of a legislative term.

NET NOTE

The *United States Government Manual* is available online at <u>www.gpoaccess</u> <u>.gov/gmanual</u>. Also an organization chart is found in Illustration 1-2.

Agencies often are called bureaus, boards, commissions, corporations, or administrations. All agencies create law in the form of **rules** or **regulations.** Agencies function in an **adjudicatory** or **quasi-judicial** manner when they hear cases involving the application of a particular regulation and then issue written opinions of their findings.

Agencies create rules or regulations regularly, conduct hearings concerning particular issues, make decisions, and enforce Congress's mandates. The agency regulations adopted, or promulgated, are similar to statutes except that they are far more detailed. The administrative regulations explain how to apply the laws briefly outlined by Congress in the enabling legislation.

For example, Congress delegates to the U.S. Food and Drug Administration (FDA) authority to deal with the daily concerns regarding food products. FDA regulates the labeling of all consumer food products based on a Congress-adopted law that created that FDA. The regulations are very specific. Among the details specified is the definition of principal display panel and the fact that it should be "large enough to accommodate all the mandatory label information required to be placed thereon." See regulation shown in Illustration 9-1.

B. REGULATIONS

▼ How Are Regulations Adopted?

The process for adoption of regulations varies. The agency or the legislature determines what procedures must be followed before a regulation is adopted. In general, the agency requests comments from the public, conducts one or more hearings, and then decides whether to adopt a regulation. The agency concerns itself with the details. Agency regulations are revised, repealed, and created daily.

▼ What Type of Authority Is an Administrative Regulation or Rule?

The regulations and other documents adopted by federal agencies and published in the *Federal Register* and the *Code of Federal Regulations* (see next section) are primary authority because they are issued by a government body acting in its official law making capacity.

C. FINDING ADMINISTRATIVE LAW

1. Generally

▼ Where Do You Find Federal Administrative Law?

Federal regulations are found in two official sources: the ***Code of Federal Regulations*** and the ***Federal Register.*** The *Code of Federal Regulations,* or the C.F.R. as it is known, contains all of the final administrative regulations. The C.F.R. is published annually, and different titles are published during different quarters of the year. The *Federal Register* is the daily newspaper for our administrative agencies and for our executive branch of the government. The *Federal Register* contains all of the

ILLUSTRATION 9-1. Sample Pages from the *Code of Federal Regulations*

Pt. 101

of a food described in this section shall be exempt from declaration of the statements which paragraphs (a) and (b) of this section require immediately following the name of the food. Such exemption shall not apply to the outer container or wrapper of a multiunit retail package.

(e) All salt, table salt, iodized salt, or iodized table salt in packages intended for retail sale shipped in interstate commerce 18 months after the date of publication of this statement of policy in the FEDERAL REGISTER, shall be labeled as prescribed by this section; and if not so labeled, the Food and Drug Administration will regard them as misbranded within the meaning of sections 403 (a) and (f) of the Federal Food, Drug, and Cosmetic Act.

[42 FR 14306, Mar. 15, 1977, as amended at 48 FR 10811, Mar. 15, 1983; 49 FR 24119, June 12, 1984]

PART 101—FOOD LABELING

Subpart A—General Provisions

②Sec.
101.1 Principal display panel of package form food.
101.2 Information panel of package form food.
101.3 Identity labeling of food in packaged form.
101.4 Food; designation of ingredients.
101.5 Food; name and place of business of manufacturer, packer, or distributor.
101.9 Nutrition labeling of food.
101.10 Nutrition labeling of restaurant foods.
101.12 Reference amounts customarily consumed per eating occasion.
101.13 Nutrient content claims—general principles.
101.14 Health claims: general requirements.
101.15 Food; prominence of required statements.
101.17 Food labeling warning, notice, and safe handling statements.
101.18 Misbranding of food.

Subpart B—Specific Food Labeling Requirements

101.22 Foods; labeling of spices, flavorings, colorings and chemical preservatives.
101.30 Percentage juice declaration for foods purporting to be beverages that contain fruit or vegetable juice.

①21 CFR Ch. I (4–1–08 Edition)

Subpart C—Specific Nutrition Labeling Requirements and Guidelines

101.36 Nutrition labeling of dietary supplements.
101.42 Nutrition labeling of raw fruit, vegetables, and fish.
101.43 Substantial compliance of food retailers with the guidelines for the voluntary nutrition labeling of raw fruit, vegetables, and fish.
101.44 Identification of the 20 most frequently consumed raw fruit, vegetables, and fish in the United States.
101.45 Guidelines for the voluntary nutrition labeling of raw fruit, vegetables, and fish.

Subpart D—Specific Requirements for Nutrient Content Claims

101.54 Nutrient content claims for "good source," "high," "more," and "high potency."
101.56 Nutrient content claims for "light" or "lite."
101.60 Nutrient content claims for the calorie content of foods.
101.61 Nutrient content claims for the sodium content of foods.
101.62 Nutrient content claims for fat, fatty acid, and cholesterol content of foods.
101.65 Implied nutrient content claims and related label statements.
101.67 Use of nutrient content claims for butter.
101.69 Petitions for nutrient content claims.

Subpart E—Specific Requirements for Health Claims

101.70 Petitions for health claims.
101.71 Health claims: claims not authorized.
101.72 Health claims: calcium and osteoporosis.
101.73 Health claims: dietary lipids and cancer.
101.74 Health claims: sodium and hyper-t
101.75
a
h
101.76
p
c
101.77
g
t
nary heart disease.
101.78 Health claims: fruits and vegetables and cancer.
101.79 Health claims: Folate and neural tube defects.
101.80 Health claims: dietary noncariogenic carbohydrate sweeteners and dental caries.

> 1 **Title**
> 2 **Sections**
> 3 **Authority**
> 4 *Federal Register* **citation**
> 5 **Text**

ILLUSTRATION 9-1. *Continued*

Food and Drug Administration, HHS

§ 101.2

101.81 Health claims: Soluble fiber from certain foods and risk of coronary heart disease (CHD).

101.82 Health claims: Soy protein and risk of coronary heart disease (CHD).

101.83 Health claims: plant sterol/stanol esters and risk of coronary heart disease (CHD).

Subpart F—Specific Requirements for Descriptive Claims That Are Neither Nutrient Content Claims nor Health Claims

101.93 Certain types of statements for dietary supplements.

101.95 "Fresh," "freshly frozen," "fresh frozen," "frozen fresh."

Subpart G—Exemptions From Food Labeling Requirements

101.100 Food, exemptions from labeling.

101.105 Declaration of net quantity of contents when exempt.

101.108 Temporary exemptions for purposes of conducting authorized food labeling experiments.

APPENDIX A TO PART 101—MONIER-WILLIAMS PROCEDURE (WITH MODIFICATIONS) FOR SULFITES IN FOOD, CENTER FOR FOOD SAFETY AND APPLIED NUTRITION, FOOD AND DRUG ADMINISTRATION (NOVEMBER 1985)

APPENDIX B TO PART 101—GRAPHIC ENHANCEMENTS USED BY THE FDA

APPENDIX C TO PART 101 NUTRITION FACTS FOR RAW FRUITS AND VEGETABLES

APPENDIX D TO PART 101—NUTRITION FACTS FOR COOKED FISH

(3) AUTHORITY: 15 U.S.C. 1453, 1454, 1455; 21 U.S.C. 321, 331, 342, 343, 348, 371; 42 U.S.C. 243, 264, 271.

(4) SOURCE: 42 FR 14308, Mar. 15, 1977, unless otherwise noted.

EDITORIAL NOTE: Nomenclature changes to part 101 appear at 63 FR 14035, Mar. 24, 1998, 66 FR 17358, Mar. 30, 2001, and 66 FR 56035, Nov. 6, 2001.

Subpart A—General Provisions

§ 101.1 Principal display panel of package form food.

(5) The term *principal display panel* as it applies to food in package form and as used in this part, means the part of a label that is most likely to be displayed, presented, shown, or examined under customary conditions of display for retail sale. The principal display panel shall be large enough to accommodate all the mandatory label information required to be placed thereon

by this part with clarity and conspicuousness and without obscuring design, vignettes, or crowding. Where packages bear alternate principal display panels, information required to be placed on the principal display panel shall be duplicated on each principal display panel. For the purpose of obtaining uniform type size in declaring the quantity of contents for all packages of substantially the same size, the term *area of the principal display panel* means the area of the side or surface that bears the principal display panel, which area shall be:

(a) In the case of a rectangular package where one entire side properly can be considered to be the principal display panel side, the product of the height times the width of that side;

(b) In the case of a cylindrical or nearly cylindrical container, 40 percent of the product of the height of the container times the circumference;

(c) In the case of any otherwise shaped container, 40 percent of the total surface of the container: *Provided, however,* That where such container presents an obvious "principal display panel" such as the top of a triangular or circular package of cheese, the area shall consist of the entire top surface. In determining the area of the principal display panel, exclude tops, bottoms, flanges at tops and bottoms of cans, and shoulders and necks of bottles or jars. In the case of cylindrical or nearly cylindrical containers, information required by this part to appear on the principal display panel shall appear within that 40 percent of the circumference which is most likely to be displayed, presented, shown, or examined under customary conditions of display for retail sale.

§ 101.2 Information panel of package form food.

(a) The term *information panel* as it applies to packaged food means that part of the label immediately contiguous and to the right of the principal display panel as observed by an individual facing the principal display panel with the following exceptions:

(1) If the part of the label immediately contiguous and to the right of the principal display panel is too small

11

proposed and final administrative regulations as well as executive orders and proclamations often issued by the president.

▼ Where Do You Find State Administrative Law?

States have agencies similar to those of the federal government. Most states have administrative materials that are organized and published in the same manner as those of the federal government. The major differences between the state systems and that of the federal government are that the state materials are not published as frequently and are not updated as often.

The amount of administrative materials states publish sometimes is quite voluminous. Some states have an administrative register but do not publish an administrative compilation. Other states have an administrative compilation but do not publish an administrative register.

One way to determine whether a state has an administrative compilation or an administrative register is to consult *The Bluebook: A Uniform System of Citation* (18th ed. 2005). The *Bluebook*'s Table T.1, United States Jurisdictions lists the administrative materials and the citation format for each state. By reviewing a particular state in the table, you also can determine whether a state has an administrative compilation. Another way is to review *The ALWD Citation Manual: A Professional System of Citation* (3rd ed. 2006), Appendix 1.

The major obstacle you face when researching state administrative law is the lack of uniformity among the 50 states' administrative materials in their format, scope, and editing. The indexes to the state publications are often difficult to use, and commercial publishers generally do not publish additional indexes. Also, some states publish their administrative materials only on an irregular basis.

Some of the state administrative codes overlap materials covered in the federal code. For example, both the federal government and the state of Illinois regulate food labeling.

The coverage of state administrative regulations on LEXIS, WESTLAW, and Loislaw is constantly changing. Therefore, check the directories. Using codes online, especially codes from other states, can be easier than trying to access print copies of the codes.

The Internet also offers access to various state regulations. Try accessing a state's home page to find its administrative regulations.

2. Specific Sources

a. Federal Register

The *Federal Register,* a pamphlet published Monday through Friday except on legal holidays, contains all of the regulations adopted by

the federal agencies, any regulations the agencies are considering adopting, and any agency notices. It often includes agency policy statements and discussions of comments received concerning agency actions. Executive orders and presidential proclamations also are found in the *Federal Register*. Documents are published in chronological order and are not codified. The *Federal Register* is available in print and on WESTLAW, LEXIS, and Loislaw, as well as on the Internet. See Illustration 9-2.

ILLUSTRATION 9-2. *Federal Register* Online

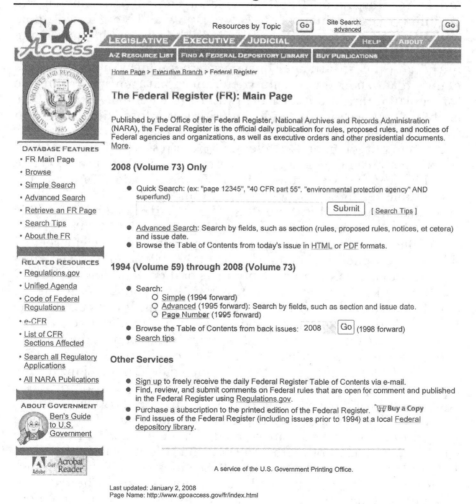

The *Federal Register* is available at www.gpoacces.gov/fr/index.html.

▼ How Do You Use the *Federal Register* in Print?

To use the *Federal Register,* you could review the table of contents or the index. See Illustration 9-3. The table of contents is found at the beginning of each volume of the *Federal Register* and is organized alphabetically by agency name. The index is published monthly and cumulated for 12 months. The table of contents or the index can be difficult to use because they are arranged by agency rather than by subject. Because of this organization, you first must determine what agency is responsible for regulating the conduct or activity you are researching. A review of the enabling statute should provide you with this information. Next, you should find the agency listing in the index and review any topics under each agency heading that are relevant to your research. For example, if you are researching regulations concerning telemarketing and Do Not Call List fees and you know that the Federal Trade Commission is responsible for these operations, you would go to table of contents and look for that agency. Note Illustration 9-3. It is a page of the table of contents from the *Federal Register* published on July 25, 2008. Next to one of the arrows, it states that there are rules concerning telemarketing sales rule fees published in this edition of the *Federal Register.* The numbers next to the words are page numbers of the *Federal Register.*

Now look at Illustration 9-4. It is the *Federal Register* pages 43354 and 43355 that are noted in the table of contents. It explains that the Federal Trade Commission is updating fees for entities accessing the Do Not Call Registry. The page also indicates the part of the Code of Federal Regulations in which this regulation will appear. It is 16 CFR part 310. It notes the agency, the Federal Trade Commission. It summarizes the regulation and details its effective dates. It also provides a contact person if you have any questions. In this case, it is Kelly A. Horne.

Return to Illustration 9-3. This table of contents also indicates that notices and proposed rules are printed in this edition for various agencies. For example, a notice from the Fish and Wildlife Service appears at *Federal Register* pages 43468 and 43469. See Illustration 9-5. This notice invites the public to comment before action is taken. The dates for submitting comments are shown as well as the format and methods for submitting comments. An e-mail address as well as a regular mail address are provided.

Finally background information and other *Federal Register* citations are included to help you understand the process. To complete your

ILLUSTRATION 9-3.   Table of Contents Page of the
Federal Register

III

Contents

①Federal Register
Vol. 73, No. 144

②Friday, July 25, 2008

Agricultural Marketing Service
PROPOSED RULES
Irish Potatoes Grown in Colorado; Reinstatement of the
    Continuing Assessment Rate, 43375–43378
Walnuts Grown in California; Increased Assessment Rate,
    43378–43381

Agriculture Department
See Agricultural Marketing Service
See Commodity Credit Corporation
See Forest Service
④*See* National Agricultural Statistics Service
NOTICES
Privacy Act; Systems of Records, 43398–43400

Army Department
See Engineers Corps
NOTICES
Privacy Act; System of Records, 43413–43418
Privacy Act; Systems of Records, 43418–43434

**Blind or Severely Disabled, Committee for Purchase From
People Who Are**
See Committee for Purchase From People Who Are Blind
    or Severely Disabled

Census Bureau
NOTICES
Agency Information Collection Activities; Proposals,
    Submissions, and Approvals, 43406–43407

Centers for Medicare & Medicaid Services
NOTICES
Agency Information Collection Activities; Proposals,
    Submissions, and Approvals, 43449–43450 ⑤
Medicare Program:
    Advisory Panel on Ambulatory Payment Classification
        Groups; Announcement of Three New Members,
        43450–43451
    Practicing Physicians Advisory Council; Request for
        Nominations and Meeting, 43451–43453

③**Coast Guard**
RULES
Special Local Regulations for Marine Events:
    Patapsco River, Inner Harbor, Baltimore, MD, 43358–

1	Volume
2	Date
3	Agencies
4	Category: rules, proposed rules, and notices
5	Page numbers

Procurement List; Additions and Deletions, 43403–43405

Commodity Credit Corporation
NOTICES
Cotton and Peanuts; 2008-Crop Marketing Assistance Loans
    and Loan Deficiency Payments, 43400

Defense Department
See Army Department
See Engineers Corps
PROPOSED RULES
Civilian Health and Medical Program of the Uniformed
    Services/TRICARE:
    Inclusion of TRICARE Retail Pharmacy Program in
        Federal Procurement of Pharmaceuticals, 43394–
        43397
NOTICES
Privacy Act; Systems of Records, 43411–43413

③**Drug Enforcement Administration**
④RULES
Control of a Chemical Precursor Used in the Illicit
    Manufacture of Fentanyl as a List I Chemical, 43355–
    43357

Education Department
NOTICES
Agency Information Collection Activities; Proposals,
    Submissions, and Approvals, 43438–43439

Engineers Corps
NOTICES
Availability of Information Bulletins:
    Replacement Lock, Sault Lock Complex, Sault Sainte
        Marie, MI, 43434
Environmental Impact Statements; Availability, etc.:
    Nebraska Department of Roads Nebraska Highway 12
        Niobrara East and West Project, 43434–43435
    Nourishment of 25,000 feet of Beach in Topsail Beach,
        Pender County, NC, 43435–43438

③**Environmental Protection Agency**
RULES
Determination of Attainment for the Ozone National
    Ambient Air Quality Standards for Nonattainment
    Areas:
    Delaware, District of Columbia, Maryland, Pennsylvania,
        and Virginia, 43360–43362
④PROPOSED RULES
Federal Requirements Under the Underground Injection
    Control (UIC) Program:
    Carbon Dioxide (CO2) Geologic Sequestration (GS) Wells,
        43492–43541
National Ambient Air Quality Standards for Lead;
    Extension Comment Period; Correction, 43489 ⑤
NOTICES
Administrative Settlement:
    Bally TCE Superfund Site, Bally, Berks County, PA,
        43439–43440
Agency Information Collection Activities; Proposals,
    Submissions, and Approvals, 43440–43441
Award of United States-Mexico Border Program Grants
    Authorized by the Consolidated Appropriations Act,
    2008, and Grant Guidance, 43441

ILLUSTRATION 9-3.   *Continued*

ILLUSTRATION 9-4.   Sample *Federal Register* Page

(9)   (10)

(8) 43354   Federal Register / Vol. 73, No. 144 / Friday, July 25, 2008 / Rules and Regulations

adequate controlled airspace to contain aircraft executing Standard Instrument Approach Procedures (SIAPs) and Obstacle Departure Procedures (ODPs). Two SIAPs are being amended for the Kivalina Airport. Additionally, one textual ODP is being developed. This action revises existing Class E airspace upward from 700 feet (ft.) and 1,200 ft. above the surface at Kivalina Airport, Kivalina, AK.

DATES: *Effective Date:* 0901 UTC, September 25, 2008. The Director of the Federal Register approves this incorporation by reference action under title 1, Code of Federal Regulations, part 51, subject to the annual revision of FAA Order 7400.9 and publication of conforming amendments.

FOR FURTHER INFORMATION CONTACT: Gary Rolf, AAL–538G, Federal Aviation Administration, 222 West 7th Avenue, Box 14, Anchorage, AK 99513–7587; telephone number (907) 271–5898; fax: (907) 271–2850; e-mail: *ary.ctr.rolf@faa.gov*. Internet address: *http://www.alaska.faa.gov/at*.

SUPPLEMENTARY INFORMATION:

History

On Thursday May 29, 2008, the FAA proposed to amend part 71 of the Federal Aviation Regulations (14 CFR part 71) to revise Class E airspace upward from 700 ft. above the surface and from 1,200 ft. above the surface at Kivalina, AK (73 FR 30827). The action was proposed in order to create Class E airspace sufficient in size to contain aircraft while executing instrument procedures for the Kivalina Airport.

will be published subsequently in the Order.

The Rule

This amendment to 14 CFR part 71 revises Class E airspace at the Kivalina Airport, Alaska. This Class E airspace is revised to accommodate aircraft executing new and amended instrument procedures, and will be depicted on aeronautical charts for pilot reference. The intended effect of this rule is to provide adequate controlled airspace for Instrument Flight Rules (IFR) operations at the Kivalina Airport, Kivalina, Alaska.

The FAA has determined that this regulation only involves an established body of technical regulations for which frequent and routine amendments are necessary to keep them operationally current. It, therefore—(1) is not a "significant regulatory action" under Executive Order 12866; (2) is not a "significant rule" under DOT Regulatory Policies and Procedures (44 FR 11034; February 26, 1979); and (3) does not warrant preparation of a regulatory evaluation as the anticipated impact is so minimal. Since this is a routine matter that will only affect air traffic procedures and air navigation, it is certified that this rule will not have a significant economic impact on a substantial number of small entities under the criteria of the Regulatory Flexibility Act.

The FAA's authority to issue rules regarding aviation safety is found in Title 49 of the United States Code. Subtitle 1, Section 106 describes the authority of the FAA Administrator. Subtitle VII, Aviation Programs, describes in more detail the scope of the agency's authority.

Federal Aviation Administration amends 14 CFR part 71 as follows:

PART 71—DESIGNATION OF CLASS A, CLASS B, CLASS C, CLASS D, AND CLASS E AIRSPACE AREAS; AIRWAYS; ROUTES; AND REPORTING POINTS

■ 1. The authority citation for 14 CFR part 71 continues to read as follows:

Authority: 49 U.S.C. 106(g), 40103, 40113, 40120; E.O. 10854, 24 FR 9565, 3 CFR, 1959–1963 Comp., p. 389.

§ 71.1   [Amended]

■ 2. The incorporation by reference in 14 CFR 71.1 of Federal Aviation Administration Order 7400.9R, *Airspace Designations and Reporting Points*, signed August 15, 2007, and effective September 15, 2007, is amended as follows:

Paragraph 6005   Class E Airspace extending upward from 700 feet or more above the surface of the earth.

*   *   *   *   *

AAL AK E5   Kivalina, AK [Revised]

Kivalina, Kivalina Airport, AK
(Lat. 67°44′10″ N., long. 164°33′49″ W.)

That airspace extending upward from 700 feet above the surface within a 6.5-mile radius of the Kivalina Airport, AK; and 3.9 miles either side of the 317° bearing from the Kivalina Airport, AK, extending from the 6.5-mile radius to 11.1 miles northwest of the Kivalina Airport, AK; and that airspace extending upward from 1,200 feet above the surface within a 73-mile radius of the Kivalina Airport, AK.

*   *   *   *   *

Issued in Anchorage, AK, on July 17, 2008.

Anthony M. Wylie,
Manager, Alaska Flight Services Information Area Group.

[FR Doc. E8–16977 Filed 7–24–08; 8:45 am]
BILLING CODE 4910–13–P

---

(1) **FEDERAL TRADE COMMISSION**

(2) **16 CFR Part 310**

RIN: 3084–AA98

Telemarketing Sales Rule Fees

(1) **AGENCY.** Federal Trade Commission.

(3) **ACTION:** Final rule.

(4) **SUMMARY:** The Federal Trade Commission (the "Commission" or "FTC") is amending its Telemarketing Sales Rule ("TSR") by updating the fees charged to entities accessing the National Do Not Call Registry ("the Registry") so that they conform to the fee structure specified in the recently enacted Do-Not-Call Registry Fee Extension Act of 2007.

---

1 Agency	10 *Federal Register* date
2 C.F.R. part	11 Authority for rule
3 Action	12 Supplemental information
4 Summary	
5 Dates	
6 Addresses	
7 Contact person and phone number	
8 Page numbers	
9 Volume	

ILLUSTRATION 9-4. *Continued*

⑨   ⑩

Federal Register / Vol. 73, No. 144 / Friday, July 25, 2008 / Rules and Regulations   43355 ⑧

⑤ **DATES:** *Effective Date:* This amendment will become effective on October 1, 2008.

⑥ **ADDRESSES:** Requests for copies of this document should be sent to: Public Reference Branch, Federal Trade Commission, Room 130, 600 Pennsylvania Avenue, NW., Washington, DC 20580. Copies of this document are also available on the Internet at the Commission's Web site: *http://www.ftc.gov.*

FOR FURTHER INFORMATION CONTACT: ⑦ Kelly A. Horne, (202) 326–3031, Division of Planning & Information, Bureau of Consumer Protection, Federal Trade Commission, 600 Pennsylvania Avenue, NW., Washington, DC 20580.

⑫ **SUPPLEMENTARY INFORMATION:** To comply with the Do-Not-Call Registry Fee Extension Act of 2007 (Pub. L. 110–188, 122 Stat. 635) ("Act"), the Commission is revising the Final Amended Fee Rule in the following manner: The revised rule decreases the annual fee for access to the Registry for each area code of data to $54 per area code, or $27 per area code of data during the second six months of an entity's annual subscription period. The maximum amount that would be charged to any single entity for accessing area codes of data is decreased to $14,850. The revised rule retains the provisions regarding free access to the first five area codes of data by all entities, as well as free access by "exempt" organizations. As required by the Act, it expands the definition of "exempt" organizations to include any person permitted to access, but not required to access, the do-not-call registry, not only under the TSR, the Federal Communication Commission's do-not-call rules found at 47 CFR 64.1200, or any other Federal law, but also under *any other Federal regulation.*

Additionally, in accordance with the Act, beginning after fiscal year 2009, the dollar amounts charged shall be increased by an amount equal to the amounts specified in the Final Amended Fee Rule, whichever fee is applicable, multiplied by the percentage (if any) by which the average of the monthly consumer price index (for all urban consumers published by the Department of Labor) ("CPI") for the most recently ended 12-month period ending on June 30 exceeds the CPI for the 12-month period ending June 30, 2008. Any increase shall be rounded to the nearest dollar. There shall be no increase in the dollar amounts if the change in the CPI is less than 1 percent. The adjustments to the applicable fees, if any, shall be published in the **Federal Register** no later than September 1 of each year.

Administrative Procedure Act; Regulatory Flexibility Act; Paperwork Reduction Act

The revisions to the Fee Rule are technical in nature and merely incorporate statutory changes to the TSR. These statutory changes have been adopted without change or interpretation at this time, making public comment unnecessary. Therefore, the Commission has determined that the notice and comment requirements of the Administrative Procedure Act do not apply. *See* 5 U.S.C. 553(b). For this reason, the requirements of the Regulatory Flexibility Act also do not apply. *See* 5 U.S.C. 603, 604.

Pursuant to the Paperwork Reduction Act, 44 U.S.C. 3501–3521, the Office of Management and Budget ("OMB") approved the information collection requirements in the Amended TSR and assigned the following existing OMB Control Number: 3084–0097. The amendments outlined in this Final Rule pertain only to the fee provision (sec. 310.8) of the Amended TSR and will not establish or alter any recordkeeping, reporting, or third-party disclosure requirements elsewhere in the Amended TSR.

■ Accordingly, the Federal Trade Commission amends part 310 of title 16 of the Code of Federal Regulations as follows:

PART 310—TELEMARKETING SALES RULE

■ 1. The authority citation for part 310 continues to read as follows:

⑪ **Authority:** 15 U.S.C. 6101–6108; 15 U.S.C. 6151–6155.

■ 2. Revise §§ 310.8(c) and (d) to read as follows:

§ 310.8   Fee for access to the National Do Not Call Registry.

*   *   *   *   *

(c) The annual fee, which must be paid by any person prior to obtaining access to the National Do Not Call Registry, is $54 for each area code of data accessed, up to a maximum of $14,850; *provided,* however, that there shall be no charge to any person for accessing the first five area codes of data, and *provided further,* that there shall be no charge to any person engaging in or causing others to engage in outbound telephone calls to consumers and who is accessing area codes of data in the National Do Not Call Registry if the person is permitted to access, but is not required to access, the National Do Not Call Registry under this Rule, 47 CFR 64.1200, or any other Federal regulation or law. Any person accessing the National Do Not Call Registry may not participate in any arrangement to share the cost of accessing the registry, including any arrangement with any telemarketer or service provider to divide the costs to access the registry among various clients of that telemarketer or service provider.

(d) Each person who pays, either directly or through another person, the annual fee set forth in § 310.8(c), each person excepted under § 310.8(c) from paying the annual fee, and each person excepted from paying an annual fee under § 310.4(b)(1)(iii)(B), will be provided a unique account number that will allow that person to access the registry data for the selected area codes at any time for the twelve month period beginning on the first day of the month in which the person paid the fee ("the annual period"). To obtain access to additional area codes of data during the first six months of the annual period, each person required to pay the fee under § 310.8(c) must first pay $54 for each additional area code of data not initially selected. To obtain access to additional area codes of data during the second six months of the annual period, each person required to pay the fee under § 310.8(c) must first pay $27 for each additional area code of data not initially selected. The payment of the additional fee will permit the person to access the additional area codes of data for the remainder of the annual period.

*   *   *   *   *

By direction of the Commission.

Donald S. Clark,
Secretary.

[FR Doc. E8–17064 Filed 7–24–08; 8:45 am]

BILLING CODE 6750–01–P

DEPARTMENT OF JUSTICE

Drug Enforcement Administration

21 CFR Part 1310

[Docket No. DEA–299F]

RIN 1117–AB12

Control of a Chemical Precursor Used in the Illicit Manufacture of Fentanyl as a List I Chemical

AGENCY: Drug Enforcement Administration (DEA), Department of Justice.

ACTION: Final rule.

SUMMARY: The Drug Enforcement Administration (DEA) is finalizing the

ILLUSTRATION 9-5.   Notice in the *Federal Register*

(8) 43468   Federal Register / Vol. 73, No. 144 / Friday, July 25, 2008 / Notices

(marks: (12) above "Register"; (9) above "Friday")

(1) DEPARTMENT OF THE INTERIOR

Fish and Wildlife Service

[FWS–R3–R–2008–N0118; 30136–1265–0000–S3]

Leopold and St. Croix Wetland Management Districts in Wisconsin

(1) AGENCY: Fish and Wildlife Service, Interior.

(2) ACTION: Notice of availability: Draft comprehensive conservation plan and environmental assessment; request for comments.

(3) SUMMARY: We, the U.S. Fish and Wildlife Service (Service), announce the availability of draft comprehensive conservation plans (CCP) and environmental assessments (EA) for the Leopold and St. Croix Wetland Management Districts (District(s), WMD(s)) for public review and comment. In the draft CCP/EAs, we describe how we propose to manage these districts for the next 15 years.

(4) DATES: To ensure consideration, we must receive your written comments by August 25, 2008. Open house style meetings will be held during the comment period to receive comments and provide information on the draft plan. Special mailings, newspaper articles, Internet postings, and other media announcements will inform people of the meetings and opportunities for written comments.

(5) ADDRESSES: Send your comments or requests for more information by any of the following methods. You may also drop off comments in person.

• *Agency Web Site:* View or download a copy of the documents and **(10)** comment at *http://www.fws.gov/midwest/planning/leopold* and *http://www.fws.gov/midwest/planning/stcroix.*

• *E-mail:* **(11)** *r3planning@fws.gov.* Include "Leopold Draft CCP/EA" or "St. Croix Draft CCP/EA", as appropriate, in the subject line of the message.

• *Fax:* 608–745–0866 for Leopold WMD and 715–246–4670 for St. Croix WMD.

• *U.S. Mail:* Comments for Leopold WMD can be mailed to: District Manager, W10040 Cascade Mountain Road, Portage, Wisconsin 53901. Comments for St. Croix WMD can be mailed to: District Manager, 1764 95th Street, New Richmond, Wisconsin 54017.

(6) FOR FURTHER INFORMATION CONTACT: Tom Kerr, St. Croix WMD, 715–246–7784 or Steve Lenz, Leopold WMD, 608–742–7100.

SUPPLEMENTARY INFORMATION:

Introduction

With this notice, we continue the CCP process for Leopold and St. Croix WMDs, which we started in 71 FR 20722 (April 21, 2006). For more about the initiation process, see that notice. Leopold and St. Croix WMDs are located in Wisconsin. Established in 1993, the Leopold WMD manages 53 waterfowl production areas (WPAs) totaling more than 12,000 acres in 17 southeastern Wisconsin counties. The District also administers 48 conservation easements within an eastern Wisconsin area of 34 counties. The St. Croix WMD, also established in 1993, manages 41 WPAs totaling 7,500 acres within an eight-county District of west-central Wisconsin. The District also administers 14 conservation easements. WPAs consist of wetland habitat surrounded by grassland and woodland communities. While WPAs are managed primarily for ducks and geese, they also provide habitat for a variety of other wildlife such as grassland birds, shorebirds, wading birds, mink, muskrat, wild turkey, and deer.

Background

The CCP Process

The National Wildlife Refuge System Administration Act of 1966, as amended by the National Wildlife Refuge System Improvement Act of 1997 (16 U.S.C. 668dd–668ee), requires us to develop a comprehensive conservation plan for each national wildlife refuge and wetland management district. The purpose in developing a CCP is to provide managers with a 15-year strategy for achieving district purposes and contributing toward the mission of the National Wildlife Refuge System, consistent with sound principles of fish and wildlife management, conservation, legal mandates, and our policies. In addition to outlining broad management direction on conserving wildlife and their habitats, plans identify wildlife-dependent recreational opportunities available to the public, including opportunities for hunting, fishing, wildlife observation, wildlife photography, and environmental education and interpretation.

CCP Alternatives and Our Preferred Alternative

Priority Issues

During the public scoping process, we, other governmental partners, and the public identified several priority issues, which were organized into five topics: Habitat management; habitat loss and fragmentation; land acquisition;

public use; and service identity. To address these issues, we developed and evaluated the following alternatives during the planning process. The themes and approaches within the alternatives are consistent between the Districts.

Under all alternatives federally listed threatened and endangered species would be protected; coordination would occur with the Wisconsin Department of Natural Resources; visitors would feel safe and the resources would be protected through law enforcement; a proposal would be developed to construct new headquarters and shop facilities; and any undertaking would be analyzed for its potential to affect historic properties.

Alternative 1, Waterfowl Emphasis— Current Management Direction

Under Alternative 1 the activities of the Districts would continue as in the past with current staffing and resources. The target for each District would be to restore 150 acres of grassland per year. The 15 year target for wetland restoration would be 50 percent of the drained wetlands for Leopold WMD and 75 percent for St. Croix WMD. Up to 20 percent of the woodlands and oak savannah would be inventoried with the objective of restoring approximately 25 percent of the identified potential savannah. Invasive species would be inventoried and treated with the recognition that only a small portion of the affected acres would be dealt with. Land acquisition would continue as funds were available with the intent of establishing larger complexes of wetlands and grasslands. An objective would be to raise the quality of the visitor services programs over time, reaching a higher level of rating within 5 years. The rating would be based on the evaluation standards of the Refuge Annual Performance Plan, which use the criteria for quality described in the Service Manual. Five (Leopold) and two (St. Croix) WPAs would be more fully developed with visitor services facilities. The volunteer and partnership programs would continue at 2008 levels. Contacts with neighbors would continue to be limited and general knowledge of the District and Service identity and missions would remain unchanged.

Alternative 2, Waterfowl Emphasis With Increased Consideration for Other "Priority" Species and Low/Moderate Consideration for Visitor Services

Under Alternative 2, the types of habitat management activities of the Districts would continue, but with more acres affected. Monitoring of habitat and wildlife would increase compared to the

1 Agency	6 Contact person	10 Web site
2 Action	7 Terms of notice	11 E-mail address
3 Summary	8 Page number	12 Volume
4 Dates	9 *Federal Register* date	
5 Addresses		

ILLUSTRATION 9-5. *Continued*

Federal Register / Vol. 73, No. 144 / Friday, July 25, 2008 / Notices 43469

current direction. Visitor services would improve about at the rate and extent of the current direction. The target for each District would be to restore 200 acres of grassland per year. The 15 year target for wetland restoration would be 75 percent of the drained wetlands for Leopold WMD and 90 percent for St. Croix WMD. Up to 90 percent of the woodlands and oak savannah would be inventoried with the objective of restoring approximately 75 percent (Leopold) and 80 percent (St. Croix) of the identified potential savannah. Invasive species would be inventoried on 100 percent of the Districts and would be treated on 25 percent (Leopold) and 50 percent (St. Croix) of District lands. Land acquisition would continue as funds were available with the intent of establishing larger complexes of wetlands and grasslands. An objective would be to raise the quality of the visitor services programs over time, reaching a higher level of rating within 5 years. Five (Leopold) and two (St. Croix) WPAs would be more fully developed with visitor services facilities. The volunteer and partnership programs would increase. Contacts with neighbors would increase slightly and general knowledge of the District and Service identity and missions would increase slightly. Full implementation of this alternative would require the addition of 1.5 full-time equivalents (Leopold) and 2.5 full-time equivalents (St. Croix) to the current staff.

Alternative 3, Waterfowl Emphasis With Low Increase in Management for Other Wildlife and Increased Consideration for Visitor Services

Under Alternative 3, the types and amounts of habitat management activities undertaken by the Districts would be similar to Alternative 1. Visitor services would expand and improve in quality compared with Alternative 1. Outreach activities would also be greater. An objective would be to raise the quality of the visitor services programs over time, reaching two high levels of rating within 5 years. Seven (Leopold) and four (St. Croix) WPAs would be more fully developed with visitor services facilities. The volunteer and partnership programs would increase. Contacts with neighbors would increase and additional information would be provided to them. The general knowledge of the District and Service identity and mission would increase among neighbors and the community. Full implementation of this alternative would require the addition of 1.5 full-time equivalents (Leopold) and 2.5 full-

time equivalents (St. Croix) to the current staff.

Alternative 4, Waterfowl Emphasis With Increased and Balanced Consideration for Other "Priority" Species, Their Habitats, Visitor Services and Neighborhood Relationships (Preferred Alternative)

Alternative 4 incorporates components of Alternatives 2 and 3. Under this alternative the types of habitat management activities of the Districts would continue, but with more acres affected. Monitoring of habitat and wildlife would increase compared to the current direction. Visitor services would expand and improve in quality compared to the current direction. Outreach activities would also be greater. The target for each District would be to restore 200 acres of grassland per year. The 15 year target for wetland restoration would be 75 percent of the drained wetlands for Leopold WMD and 90 percent for St. Croix WMD. Up to 90 percent of the woodlands and oak savannah would be inventoried with the objective of restoring approximately 75 percent (Leopold) and 80 percent (St. Croix) of the identified potential savannah. Invasive species would be inventoried on 100 percent of the Districts and would be treated on 25 percent (Leopold) and 50 percent (St. Croix) of District lands. The Districts would develop a monitoring program to determine waterfowl recruitment. Land acquisition would continue as funds were available with the intent of establishing larger complexes of wetlands and grasslands. Seven (Leopold) and four (St. Croix) WPAs would be more fully developed with visitor services facilities. The volunteer and partnership programs would increase. Contacts with neighbors and the expected effects would be the same as Alternative 3. Full implementation of this alternative would require the addition of 3.5 full-time equivalents (Leopold) and 3.5 full-time equivalents (St. Croix) to the current staff.

Public Meetings

We will give the public an opportunity to provide comments at public meetings. You may obtain the schedule from the addresses listed above (see **ADDRESSES**). You may also submit comments anytime during the comment period by writing to the above addresses.

Public Availability of Comments

Before including your address, phone number, e-mail address, or other personal identifying information, you

should know that your entire comment—including your personal identifying information—may be made publicly available. While you may ask us in your comment to withhold your personal identifying information from public review, we cannot guarantee that we will be able to do so. All comments become part of the official public record, and we handle requests for such comments in accordance with the Freedom of Information Act, NEPA, and Service and Departmental policies and procedures.

Dated: May 22, 2008.

Charles M. Wooley,

Acting Regional Director, U.S. Fish and Wildlife Service, Fort Snelling, Minnesota.

[FR Doc. E8–17106 Filed 7–24–08; 8:45 am]

BILLING CODE 4310-55-P

DEPARTMENT OF THE INTERIOR

Bureau of Land Management

[WY–030–5101–ER–K103; WYW–167155]

Notice of Intent To Announce a Proposed Environmental Impact Statement (EIS) for the Chokecherry and Sierra Madre Wind Energy Project, Announce a Proposed EIS To Amend Rawlins Resource Management Plan, and Announce a Public Comment Period and Public Meetings for Obtaining Comments

AGENCY: Bureau of Land Management.

ACTION: Notice of Intent (NOI) to (1) announce a proposed Environmental Impact Statement (EIS) for the Chokecherry and Sierra Madre Wind Energy Project; (2) announce a proposed EIS to amend Rawlins Resource Management Plan; and (3) announce a public comment period and public meetings for obtaining comments.

SUMMARY: Pursuant to Section 102(2)(C) of the National Environmental Policy Act (NEPA) of 1969, an EIS will be prepared by the Bureau of Land Management (BLM), Rawlins Field Office, Wyoming, for the Chokecherry and Sierra Madre Wind Energy Project in Carbon County, Wyoming. The EIS will analyze the impacts of issuing rights-of-way for a wind energy project and ancillary facilities (consisting of access roads, electric power gathering cables, an electric transmission line, and electric substations).

DATES: Public meetings will be held to inform the public and obtain comments. Dates, times, and locations of meetings will be announced at least 15 days in advance through local media, news releases, and posting to the BLM Web

research, you also must check multiple indexes or tables of contents even if they appear to overlap because some citations may be omitted in one of the indexes.

If you had found this information in the index of the *Federal Register,* you would need to search for the appropriate date of the pamphlet that contains the page.

The *Federal Register* begins a new volume each year. The issues are consecutively paginated from the first day that the government offices are open during the year through the last day that the government offices are open during the year. For example, a March 1 *Federal Register* might contain pages 2600-4200. The March 2 *Federal Register* would begin on page 4201. It is not uncommon for the page number in the last issue to be 60,000.

Page numbers are not listed on the outside binding of the *Federal Register.* However, dates are listed. Therefore, you must determine the date of the *Federal Register* publication that contains the page that you are seeking. To do this, use the index table entitled Federal Register Pages and Dates. This table provides you with the date of the *Federal Register* that contains the relevant information. Another alternative is to consult a commercially prepared index to the *Federal Register.* Once you find the appropriate pamphlet, go to the *Federal Register* page.

Review the sample page of the *Federal Register* shown in Illustration 9-4. It is pages 43355 and 43356 of the 2008 *Federal Register.* First, note the department at the top of the rule. It is the Federal Trade Commission. You then are provided with the C.F.R. title and parts affected by this rule: in this case, title 16 of the C.F.R., part 310. A brief summary and a more detailed summary of the agency's action are included. Next to the word "Action," you are told that this is a final rule.

On the second page of the Illustration 9-4, the effective date of the rule is provided. In addition, you are provided with a contact person for additional information as well as supplementary information. The rule change is shown on the second page. It includes a note to the section of the United States Code that provides the agency with authority to make this rule. In this case, it is 15 U.S.C. 6101-6108 and 15 U.S.C. 6151-6155.

▼ How Do You Search the *Federal Register* on the Internet?

The *Federal Register* can be found at the government-sponsored Web site www.gpoaccess.gov/fr. You can locate a specific *Federal Register* page by following the online search directions. See Illustration 9-2. The page will appear in Adobe Acrobat Portable Document Format, known as PDF. That essentially allows it to look exactly like the page of the printed *Federal Register.* You also can search the *Federal Register* by key word. Click the mouse to place a check mark in the box in front of the *Federal Register* you wish to search. Type in your search terms in the search box and submit the search. If you typed in "food labeling" and clicked on the 2008 *Federal Register* box, you would receive a variety of results. An example of these results is shown in Illustration 9-6. The

ILLUSTRATION 9-6. Internet *Federal Register* Search Result Page

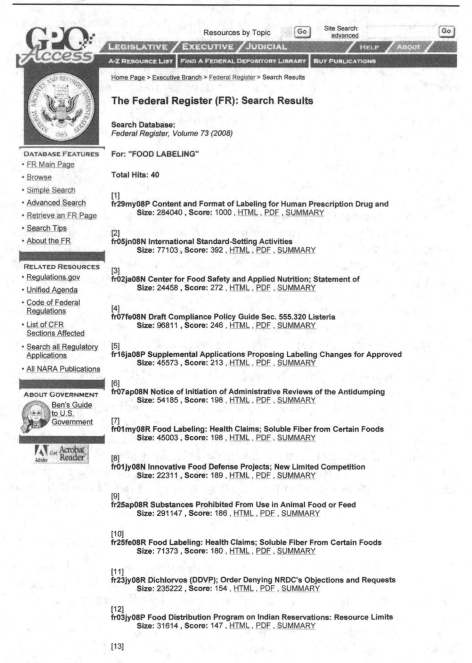

first result is for a May *Federal Register* page that details a proposed rule concerning format for labeling human drugs. You know it is from that date because it states "fr29my08P." That means *Federal Register* 29 May 2008. You can access this in HMTL or PDF format. The PDF format will look like the printed page in Illustrations 9-4 and 9-5. You must have the Adobe Acrobat Reader computer program to view the file in this manner. You also can browse the table of contents for a daily issue or past issues online at the *Federal Register* site.

▼ How Can You Use LEXIS and WESTLAW to Retrieve the *Federal Register?*

Another simple method to retrieve *Federal Register* information concerning an adopted or proposed regulation is a computer search of either LEXIS and WESTLAW. You can search these *Federal Register* databases without regard to a publisher's choice of indexing terms. You may use your own terms to determine whether any regulations concerning your research topic are contained within the *Federal Register.*

b. Code of Federal Regulations

During the course of the year, the regulations found in the *Federal Register* are incorporated into a codified version called the **Code of Federal Regulations.** The code is comprised of 50 titles similar to the titles used in the statutory codes. However, not all 50 titles mirror the titles used in the *United States Code.* Some titles, such as 26, the Internal Revenue Code, do follow the title of the U.S.C. Title 26 of the C.F.R. contains the Treasury regulations that instruct the researcher on how to apply the relevant statutory code section. The C.F.R. titles are organized by agency, not subjects. The C.F.R. is further divided into chapters, subchapters, parts, and sections. Check the back of each volume for a list of federal agencies and their C.F.R. titles and chapters.

The C.F.R. is prepared and published by the U.S. Government Printing Office. However, the C.F.R. is available online through the Government Printing Office and online services such as WESTLAW, LEXIS, and other fee-based companies.

PRACTICE POINTER

The regulations on the Internet are easy to search and accessible through most public libraries.

▼ How Often Is the C.F.R. Updated?

The C.F.R. titles are updated quarterly. Titles 1 to 16 are updated January 1 of the cover year. Titles 17 to 27 are updated April 1 of that year, and titles 28 to 41 are updated on July 1 of that year. Titles 42 to 50 are updated on October 1 of the cover year.

▼ How Do You Use the C.F.R. in Print?

To use the C.F.R in print, consult the index that contains listings of subjects, agencies, and references to the regulations codified within the C.F.R. volumes. See Illustration 9-7. The index also provides a list of C.F.R. titles, chapters, subchapters, and parts, and an alphabetical list of the agencies in the C.F.R. This index is revised once a year as of January 1.

To research a particular topic in the index, you first must locate the name of the agency. Assume that you are looking for regulations concerning the food labeling of raw fruit, vegetables, and fish. First, you need to review the enabling statute to determine the agency responsible for such regulation. Once you have made that determination, you are ready to review the index. In this case, the responsible agency is the U.S. Food and Drug Administration. You would find that agency name listed in alphabetical order in the index. Next, you would review the topical listings below the agency name. In this case, the topic of possible interest is "labeling." This index page refers you to title 21, part 101 of the C.F.R. for the labeling regulations.

The next step is to go to the C.F.R. volumes. The title and part numbers are listed on the binding. Review the appropriate part and chapter. Within the part, you will find a listing of the statutory authority that is the basis for the regulation. If you have not already consulted this statute, find the statute and review it.

Illustration 9-1 is the page of the C.F.R. referred to under the "labeling" topic in the index: title 21, part 101 of the C.F.R. concerning food labeling. You should scan the sections listed to find relevant sections. For example, suppose you are researching whether health claims may be made concerning raw fruit and the labeling required. You can scan the subpart list and see a listing for section 101.14 "Health Claims: general requirements" shown in Illustration 9-1. You would review that section and any other relevant sections. The C.F.R. part also specifies the enabling statutes. In this case, the enabling statutes are the Fair Packaging and Labeling Act and the Federal Food, Drug, and Cosmetic Act. Citations to the U.S.C. for each act are included. In addition, the citation to the *Federal Register* publication is noted. Finally, the text of the regulation begins under the heading "Subpart A—General Provisions." The government's Web site for the C.F.R. is <u>www.gpoaccess.gov/cfr/index.html</u>.

Commercial publishers also produce various print indexes to the C.F.R. The commercial indexes have many advantages. The indexing

ILLUSTRATION 9-7.   *Code of Federal Regulations* **Index Sample Page**

⑥
CFR Index

①
Food and Drug Administration

Voluntary filing of cosmetic product experiences, 21 CFR 730

Voluntary filing of cosmetic product ingredient and cosmetic raw material composition statements, 21 CFR 720

Voluntary registration of cosmetic product establishments, 21 CFR 710

Delegations of authority and organization, 21 CFR 5

Employee standards of conduct, supplement, 45 CFR 73a

Employee standards of conduct and conflicts of interest, 21 CFR 19

Enforcement of Federal Food, Drug, and Cosmetic Act and Fair Packaging and Labeling Act, 21 CFR 1

Enforcement policy, recall guidelines, 21 CFR 7

Environmental impact considerations, 21 CFR 25

1 Agency
2 Topic
3 C.F.R. citation
4 Title
5 Part
6 Index name

firmed as

as safe

FR 170

dhesives and gs, 21 CFR

djuvants, production aids, and sanitizers, 21 CFR 178

Indirect food additives, general, 21 CFR 174

Indirect food additives, paper and paperboard components, 21 CFR 176

Indirect food additives, polymers, 21 CFR 177

Indirect food substances affirmed as generally recognized as safe (GRAS), 21 CFR 186

Permitted for direct addition to food for human consumption, 21 CFR 172

Permitted in food on interim basis or in contact with food pending additional study, 21 CFR 180

Petitions, 21 CFR 171

Prior-sanctioned food ingredients, 21 CFR 181

Secondary direct, permitted in food for human consumption, 21 CFR 173

Substances generally recognized as safe (GRAS), 21 CFR 182

Substances prohibited from use, 21 CFR 189

Food for human consumption
Acidified, 21 CFR 114
Administrative rulings and decisions, 21 CFR 100
Bakery products, 21 CFR 136
Cacao products, 21 CFR 163
Cereal flours and related products, 21 CFR 137
Cheeses and related cheese products, 21 CFR 133
Common or usual name for nonstandardized, 21 CFR 102
Drinking water, processing and bottling of, 21 CFR 129
Eggs and egg products, 21 CFR 160
Emergency permit control, 21 CFR 108
Fish and shellfish, 21 CFR 161
Food dressings and flavorings, 21 CFR 169
Frozen desserts, 21 CFR 135
Fruit butters, jellies, preserves, and related products, 21 CFR 150
Fruit juices, canned, 21 CFR 146
Fruit pies, 21 CFR 152
Fruits, canned, 21 CFR 145
Good practices in manufacturing, packing, or holding human food, 21 CFR 110
Infant formula, 21 CFR 107
Infant formula quality control procedures, 21 CFR 106
Irradiation in production, processing and handling of food, 21 CFR 179

② Labeling, 21 CFR 101 ③
Macaroni and noodle products, 21 CFR 139
Margarine, 21 CFR 166
Milk and cream, 21 CFR 131   ④
② Nutritional quality guidelines, ㉑ CFR 104 ⑤
Quality standards for foods with no identity standards, 21 CFR 103
Seafood inspection program, 21 CFR 197
Special dietary use, 21 CFR 105
Standards, general, 21 CFR 130

269

terms are not limited to agency names. Information can be retrieved by subject, agency, topic, and key word. The commercial indexes generally are updated and published more frequently than the government index, and they contain better instructions concerning their use.

▼ How Do You Search the C.F.R. on the Computer?

Online computer searches may allow easier access to regulations than an index. You can search the full text of the regulations at the government's Web site or on both the WESTLAW and LEXIS systems. With these searches you do not need to rely on the terms contained within the index. Current regulations can be searched online as well as many superseded regulations. If you go to the government Web site, you can search for a regulation by entering key words, a C.F.R. citation, or by browsing the titles. See Illustration 9-8.

NET NOTE

The government's Web site for the C.F.R. is www.gpoaccess.gov/cfr/index.html.

▼ Why Would You Use Old Regulations?

Often a case will turn on a regulation that was in place at the time of the incident involved. For example, suppose you are representing a client involved in a car accident in 2007. The experts say that the accident occurred because the car manufacturer failed to use a safety device—one that was required by federal regulations. The car was manufactured in 2001. You must research the 2001 regulations to determine what safety regulations applied to that manufacturer.

▼ How Do You Update and Validate Regulations?

Updating is one of the most important tasks you must perform when you review agency regulations. This is especially important because the regulations change frequently. Because the C.F.R. is published annually with quarterly updates, you must determine the currentness of the document. The **List of CFR Sections Affected,** or L.S.A., enables you to update a C.F.R. citation. The L.S.A. identifies which sections have been changed, updated, or removed: in essence, which C.F.R. sections have been affected in any way. A monthly L.S.A. is published with the C.F.R. The L.S.A. also appears daily in the Readers Aids section of the *Federal*

ILLUSTRATION 9-8. *Code of Federal Regulations* **Online Main Page**

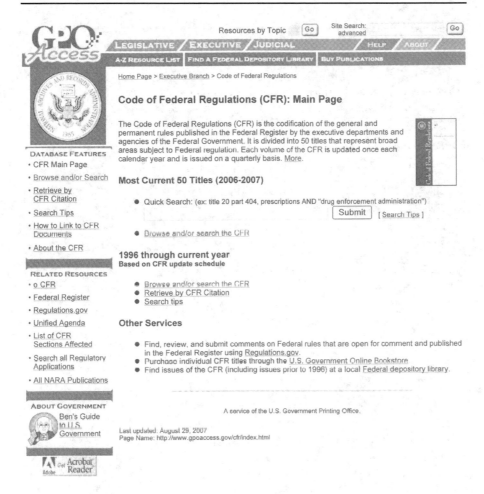

Register. It is organized by title. See Illustration 9-9. It is a page from the *Federal Register* of C.F.R. parts affected from July 1 through July 8 when this *Federal Register* was published. Changes to regulations are first published in the *Federal Register*. Therefore, you must check not only the monthly L.S.A. pamphlet, but portions of a daily *Federal Register*. Each issue of the *Federal Register* contains a section entitled "CFR Parts Affected in This Issue." See Illustration 9-10. At the end of each issue of the *Federal Register* is a section entitled "Reader Aids" that contains a column summarizing the month's changes in various regulations. See Illustration 9-9.

ILLUSTRATION 9-9. *Federal Register* Page with C.F.R. Parts Affected Shown

i

Reader Aids

Federal Register

Vol. 73, No. 131

Tuesday, July 8, 2008

CUSTOMER SERVICE AND INFORMATION

Federal Register/Code of Federal Regulations

General Information, indexes and other finding aids	202–741–6000
Laws	741–6000

Presidential Documents

Executive orders and proclamations	741–6000
The United States Government Manual	741–6000

Other Services

Electronic and on-line services (voice)	741–6020
Privacy Act Compilation	741–6064
Public Laws Update Service (numbers, dates, etc.)	741–6043
TTY for the deaf-and-hard-of-hearing	741–6086

ELECTRONIC RESEARCH

World Wide Web

Full text of the daily Federal Register, CFR and other publications is located at: http://www.gpoaccess.gov/nara/index.html

Federal Register information and research tools, including Public Inspection List, indexes, and links to GPO Access are located at: http://www.archives.gov/federal_register

E-mail

FEDREGTOC-L (Federal Register Table of Contents LISTSERV) is an open e-mail service that provides subscribers with a digital form of the Federal Register Table of Contents. The digital form of the Federal Register Table of Contents includes HTML and PDF links to the full text of each document.

To join or leave, go to http://listserv.access.gpo.gov and select *Online mailing list archives, FEDREGTOC-L, Join or leave the list (or change settings);* then follow the instructions.

PENS (Public Law Electronic Notification Service) is an e-mail service that notifies subscribers of recently enacted laws.

To subscribe, go to http://listserv.gsa.gov/archives/publaws-l.html and select *Join or leave the list (or change settings);* then follow the instructions.

FEDREGTOC-L and **PENS** are mailing lists only. We cannot respond to specific inquiries.

Reference questions. Send questions and comments about the Federal Register system to: fedreg.info@nara.gov

The Federal Register staff cannot interpret specific documents or regulations.

FEDERAL REGISTER PAGES AND DATE, JULY

CFR PARTS AFFECTED DURING JULY

At the end of each month, the Office of the Federal Register publishes separately a List of CFR Sections Affected (LSA), which lists parts and sections affected by documents published since the revision date of each title.

3 CFR

Proclamations:

8272	38297
(Proc. 7912 of 6/29/ 2005 See: Proc. 8272)	38297
(Proc. 8213 of 12/20/ 2007 See: Proc. 8272)	38297
(Proc. 8240 of 4/17/ 2008 See: Proc. 8272)	38297

Executive Orders:

13467	38103
EO 10450 of 4/27/1953 (see: EO 13467)	38103
EO 10577 of 11/23/ 1954 (see: EO 13467)	38103
EO 10865 of 2/20/1960 (see: EO 13467)	38103
EO 12171 of 11/19/ 1979 (Amended by: EO 13467)	38103
EO 12333 of 12/4/1981 (see: EO 13467)	38103
EO 12829 of 1/6/1993 (see: EO 13467)	38103
EO 12958 of 4/17/1995 (see: EO 13467)	38103
EO 12968 of 8/2/1995 (Amended by: EO 13467)	38103
EO 13381 of 6/27/2005 (Revoked by: EO 13467)	38103

Administrative Orders:

Memorandums:

Memorandum of June 26, 2008	37351

7 CFR

301	37775
989	38307

Proposed Rules:

253	38155

9 CFR

Proposed Rules:

71	38343
94	37892

10 CFR

Proposed Rules:

430	38159

14 CFR

39	37353, 37355, 37358, 37775, 37778, 37781, 37783, 37786, 37789, 37791, 37793, 37795, 38311, 38883, 38885, 38887, 38889, 38891, 38893, 38895, 38898, 38900, 38905
71	37797, 38109, 38313, 38314
97	37360

Proposed Rules:

39	37898, 37900, 37903, 38160, 38346, 38933, 38935, 38937
71	37905

15 CFR

745	38908
774	38908

17 CFR

210	38094
228	38094
229	38094
249	38094

Proposed Rules:

230	37752
240	37752, 39182

18 CFR

37	39092

19 CFR

201	38316
210	38316

21 CFR

530	38110

25 CFR

Proposed Rules:

293	37907

26 CFR

1	37362, 37797, 38113, 38910
25	37362
26	37362
31	37371
53	37362
55	37362
156	37362
157	37362
301	37362, 37804, 38915
602	37371

Proposed Rules:

1	37389, 37910, 38162, 38940
26	37910
301	37910

29 CFR

4003	38117

Proposed Rules:

4001	37390
4022	37390
4044	37390

30 CFR

938	38918

ILLUSTRATION 9-10.   C.F.R. Parts Affected in a *Daily Federal Register*

CFR PARTS AFFECTED IN THIS ISSUE

A cumulative list of the parts affected this month can be found in the Reader Aids section at the end of this issue.

7 CFR
3...29573
46.......................................29573
110.....................................29573
205.....................................29575
246.....................................29573
278.....................................29573
1150...................................29573
1160...................................29573

9 CFR
77.......................................29579

12 CFR
230.....................................29582
Proposed Rules:
Ch. 18.................................29658

15 CFR
Proposed Rules:
735.....................................29660
742.....................................29660

26 CFR
1...29596
Proposed Rules:
1 (5 documents) 29662,
   29663, 29671, 29675, 29668

28 CFR
75.......................................29607

33 CFR
117 (2 documents) 29622
165 (2 documents) 29623,
                            29624

36 CFR
17.......................................29626

40 CFR
35.......................................29627
262.....................................29910
282.....................................29628

44 CFR
65.......................................29633
67 (4 documents) 29634,
            29637, 29638, 29639
Proposed Rules:
67 (3 documents) 29683,
                29692, 29694

45 CFR
Proposed Rules:
1611...................................29695

48 CFR
Ch. 2..................................29644
207.....................................29640
208.....................................29640
215.....................................29643
216 (2 documents) 29640,
                            29643
217.....................................29643
219.....................................29644
237.....................................29640
Proposed Rules:
246.....................................29710

50 CFR
648.....................................29645
660.....................................29646
Proposed Rules:
15.......................................29711
660.....................................29713

┌───┐
│ *PRACTICE POINTER*   │
│   │
│ Current "Reader Aids" pages of the *Federal Register* now contain a notation │
│ for the relevant Web sites.   │
└───┘

▼ How Is the Updating Performed in Practice?

Assume that you have found the regulation that defines the standard for labeling of food in the *Federal Register*. It is 21 C.F.R. §101. Assume also that it is May 4, 2008, and you want to determine if this regulation has been changed since it was last published. You want to be certain that you determine whether there have been any changes to the relevant section through the date of your search.

You should now review the current L.S.A. pamphlet. For our purposes, consult Illustration 9-11. This pamphlet discloses any changes to the regulations that occurred between April 1, 2008, and May 30, 2008. Find the title you want to update: in this case, title 21. Next review Illustration 9-11. Scan the sections column and determine whether section 101 has been changed. In this case, it has not been altered. If had been altered, it would have been listed with a number on the same line. The five-digit number is the *Federal Register* page on which the changes appear.

This pamphlet only includes changes through March 31, 2008. Therefore, you need to determine whether any changes were made to the section after that up until the date of your research, May 5, 2008. First, check the last *Federal Register* for April. Turn to the "Reader Aids" section in the back and look at the column entitled "CFR Parts Affected In April." Check to see if your citation is listed there. See Illustration 9-12. Next check the May 5, 2008 *Federal Register,* Reader Aids for May. See Illustration 9-13. In this case, part 101 of title 21 was not affected. If there had been changes, you would need to review those *Federal Register* pages to determine if any of the modifications are relevant to your research.

The process is similar online. Go to the L.S.A. Web site at www.gpoaccess.gov/lsa/index.html. See Illustration 9-14. You can search for the relevant title by browsing or using search terms. In addition, you can check monthly pamphlets, the current list of C.F.R. parts affected, and the list of C.F.R. parts affected today. This is the most current search available. To find Readers Aid List of C.F.R. parts affected for a particular month, go to the *Federal Register* Web site and browse past issues. You will be able to view a *Federal Register* for the last date of a month and easily navigate to the Readers Aid section.

ILLUSTRATION 9-11.   L.S.A. Monthly Pamphlet Page

CHANGES APRIL 2, 2007 THROUGH MARCH 31, 2008

656.30 (a), (b) and (c) revised;
  (e)(3) added **27946**
656.31 Revised **27946**

Proposed Rules:

122 ....**51730**
295 12037
404 ....37496, 41649, 43202, 61218, 62607,
                        70527
.... 10715, 12923, 14409
405 ....37496, 41649, 45701, 61218, 62607
....10715
411 ....**45191**
416 ....37496, 41649, 61218, 62607, 72641
....10715, 12923
422 ....**45991**
616 ....**62145**
655 ....8538, 16243

TITLE 21—FOOD AND DRUGS

Chapter I—Food and Drug Administration, Department of Health and Human Services (Parts 1—1299)

1.231 (h)(2) revised 15883
1.234 (d)(2) revised 15883
1.235 (d)(2) revised 15883
2.125 Regulation at 71 FR 70873
  confirmed **20942**
14.100 (a)(4) added **41221**
17.2 Introductory text revised 15884
20.100 (c)(43) added **41017**
  (c)(44) added **69118**
25.20 (m) revised **69118**
25.33 (a) introductory text, (c),
  (d) introductory text and (g)
  revised **69119**
74.2053 Added **33666**
  Regulation at 72 FR 33666 confirmed **45328**
101.17 (h)(2) revised **46378**
101.80   (c)(2)(ii)(B),   (iii)(A),
  (e)(1)(iii), (iv), (2)(iii) and (iv)
  revised; interim **52789**
101.81   (c)(2)(ii)(A)(*6*)   added;
  (c)(2)(iii)(A)(*2*) revised; interim 9947
111 Added **34942**
111.27 (b)(1) revised 13124
111.75 (a)(1) revised; interim **34968**
  Regulation at 72 FR 34968 comment period extended **52790**
111.95 (b)(6) added; interim **34968**

Regulation at 72 FR 34968 comment period extended **52790**
172.735   Heading,   introductory
  text and (a) revised **46896**
172.841 (b) and (c) revised **46564**
173.375 Revised **67576**
179 Actions on petitions **17394**
  Policy statement **39557**
184.1065 (b) revised 8606
184.1140 (b) revised 8606
184.1155 (b) revised 8606
184.1165 (b) revised 8607
184.1240 (b) revised 8607
184.1261 (b) revised 8607
184.1262 (b) revised 8607
184.1265 (b) revised 8607
184.1287 (b) revised 8607
184.1297 (b) revised 8607
184.1298 (b) revised 8607
184.1307 (b) revised 8607
184.1307a (b) revised 8607
184.1307b (b) revised 8607
184.1307c (b) revised 8607
184.1321 (b) revised 8607
184.1322 (b) revised 8607
184.1323 (b) revised 8607
184.1324 (b) revised 8607
184.1355 (b) revised 8607
184.1386 (b) revised 8607
184.1445 (b) revised 8607
184.1449 (b) revised 8607
184.1521 (b) revised 8607
184.1537 (b) revised 8607
184.1540 (b) revised 8607
184.1545 (b) revised 8607
184.1553 (b) revised 8607
184.1555 (c)(3) revised 8608
184.1639 (b) revised 8608
184.1655 (b) revised 8608
184.1764 (b) revised 8608
184.1768 (b) revised 8608
184.1769a (b) revised 8608
184.1848 (b) revised 8608
184.1851 (b) revised 8608
184.1854 (b) revised 8608
184.1859 (b) revised 8608
184.1865 (b) revised 8608
184.1923 (b) revised 8608
184.1950 (b) revised 8608
184.1984 (b) revised 8608
201.26 Added; interim **73599**
201.66 (c)(5)(ii)(H) added; eff. 6–
  19–08 ....**71785**
  (c)(5)(vii) amended; interim 403
201.105 (c)(2) and (d)(1) revised **69119**
201.115 (a) and (b) revised **69119**

NOTE: Boldface page numbers indicate 2007 changes.

ILLUSTRATION 9-12.   Reader Aids C.F.R. Parts Affected During April

i

Reader Aids

Federal Register

Vol. 73, No. 84

Wednesday, April 30, 2008 ③

CUSTOMER SERVICE AND INFORMATION

Federal Register/Code of Federal Regulations
General Information, indexes and other finding aids ... 202–741–6000
Laws ... 741–6000

Presidential Documents
Executive orders and proclamations ... 741–6000
The United States Government Manual ... 741–6000

Other Services
Electronic and on-line services (voice) ... 741–6020
Privacy Act Compilation ... 741–6064
Public Laws Update Service (numbers, dates, etc.) ... 741–6043
TTY for the deaf-and-hard-of-hearing ... 741–6086

ELECTRONIC RESEARCH

World Wide Web
Full text of the daily Federal Register, CFR and other publications is located at: **http://www.gpoaccess.gov/nara/index.html**
Federal Register information and research tools, including Public Inspection List, indexes, and links to GPO Access are located at: **http://www.archives.gov/federal_register**

E-mail
FEDREGTOC-L (Federal Register Table of Contents LISTSERV) is an open e-mail service that provides subscribers with a digital form of the Federal Register Table of Contents. The digital form of the Federal Register Table of Contents includes HTML and PDF links to the full text of each document.
To join or leave, go to **http://listserv.access.gpo.gov** and select *Online mailing list archives, FEDREGTOC-L, Join or leave the list (or change settings);* then follow the instructions.
PENS (Public Law Electronic Notification Service) is an e-mail service that notifies subscribers of recently enacted laws.
To subscribe, go to **http://listserv.gsa.gov/archives/publaws-l.html** and select *Join or leave the list (or change settings);* then follow the instructions.
FEDREGTOC-L and **PENS** are mailing lists only. We cannot respond to specific inquiries.
Reference questions. Send questions and comments about the Federal Register system to: **fedreg.info@nara.gov**
The Federal Register staff cannot interpret specific documents or regulations.

FEDERAL REGISTER PAGES AND DATE, APRIL

17241–17880	1
17881–18148	2
18149–18432	
18433–18700	
18701–18942	
18943–19138	
19139–19388	
19389–19742	
19743–19958	
19959–20148	
20149–20524	
20525–20778	
20779–21016	
21017–21214	
21215–21518	
21519–21806	
21807–22048	
22049–22270	
22271–22784	
22785–23062	
23063–23320	
23321–23938	30

① **CFR PARTS AFFECTED DURING APRIL**

At the end of each month, the Office of the Federal Register publishes separately a List of CFR Sections Affected (LSA), which lists parts and sections affected by documents published since the revision date of each title.

④ **3 CFR**
Proclamations:
7746 (See 8228)	18141
7747 (See 8228)	18141
7987 (See 8228)	18141
8097 (See 8228)	18141
8097 (See 8240)	21515
8114 (See 8240)	21515
8214 (See 8228)	18141
8228	18141
8229	18425
8230	18427
8231	18429
8232	18431
8233	19387
8234	19953
8235	19955
8236	20147
8237	20521
8238	21017
8239	21213
8240	21515
8241	21805
8242	22269
8243	22779
8244	22781
8245	22783
8246	23063

Executive Orders:
11651 (See Proclamation 8228) ... 18141
12302 (See Proclamation 8240) ... 21515
13389 (Amended by 13463) ... 22047
13390 (Amended by 13463) ... 22047
13463 ... 22047

Administrative Orders:
Memorandums:
... f March ... 19957
... f April ... 20523
...s:
...March ... 17241
...March ... 17879
...March ... 18147
...April ... 22265
... ... 23012
... ... 18943
731 ... 20149
1201 ... 21019, 21415

1210	21019
1215	21019
1601	22049
7401	18944

Proposed Rules:
351	20180

④ **7 CFR** ⑥
1	18433
246	21807
301	18701, 22785
457	17243
959	21023
983	18703
985	19743, 21215
1150	19959
1463	23065

Proposed Rules:
28	20842
301	17930
319	17930
920	20002
989	21551
1980	19443

④ **8 CFR**
212	18384
214	18944
235	18384
274a	18944

Proposed Rules:
103	21260
214	21260
215	22065
217	22065
231	22065
235	22065

9 CFR
77	19139
94	17881, 20366

Proposed Rules:
201	21286

10 CFR
2	22786
26	21690
50	22786
51	22786
52	22786
100	22786

Proposed Rules:
20	19749
32	19749
50	19443
431	18858
820	19761

12 CFR
1	22216
2	22216
3	22216

④ ⑤ (circled annotation markers)

Callout key:
1 C.F.R. parts affected during the month
2 Food labeling title
3 Date of *Federal Register*
4 C.F.R. titles
5 C.F.R. parts
6 *Federal Register* page showing changes

ILLUSTRATION 9-12. *Continued*

ii   Federal Register / Vol. 73, No. 84 / Wednesday, April 30, 2008 / Reader Aids

4................................22216	71 ....18222, 19019, 19174,	210................................18440
5................................22216	19777, 20843, 20844, 21857,	211................................18440
7................................22216	21858, 23136	312................................22800
9................................22216	91................................20181	510................18441, 23066
10................................22216	93................................20846	520................................18441
11................................22216	141................................20181	522 ....17890, 21041, 21042,
12................................22216		21819
16................................22216	**15 CFR**	526................................18441
19................................22216	748................................21035	556................................21819
21................................22216	774................................21035	558 ....18441, 18958, 19432
22................................22216	**Proposed Rules:**	589................................22720
23................................22216	736................................21076	700................................20785
24................................22216	740................................21076	**Proposed Rules:**
26................................22216	742................................21076	872................................22877
27................................22216	744................................21076	1300................................22294
28................................22216	748................................21076	1308................................19175
31................................22216	752................................21076	
32................................22216	760................................21076	**22 CFR**
34................................22216	772................................21076	40................................23067
37................................22216	922................................20869	41................18384, 23067
40................................22216		53................................18384
208................................21690	**16 CFR**	304................................21528
218................................20779	**Proposed Rules:**	309................................18154
225................................21690	23................................22848	**Proposed Rules:**
268................................17885	303................................18727	121................................19778
325................................21690	305................................17263	
559................................21690		**23 CFR**
560................................21690	**17 CFR**	**Proposed Rules:**
563................................21690	200................................17810	924................................22092
507................................21690	230................................20367	
Proposed Rules:	232................................20367	**25 CFR**
701................................22836	239 ....17810, 20367, 20512	**Proposed Rules:**
705................................22836	240 ....17810, 20782, 22017	26................................19179
740................................22839	247................................20779	27................................19179
792................................22289	249 ....20782, 22017, 23328	
951................................20552	274................................23328	**26 CFR**
		1 ....18159, 18160, 18708,
14 CFR	**18 CFR**	18709, 19350, 23069
23................19746, 22271	35................................17246	54................................20794
39 ....18433, 18706, 19961,	39................................21814	301 ....18442, 19350, 21415,
19963, 19967, 19968, 19971,	158................................19389	23069, 23342
19973, 19975, 19977, 19979,	260................................19389	602................18709, 23069
19982, 19983, 19986, 19989,	**Proposed Rules:**	**Proposed Rules:**
19993, 20159, 20367, 20525,	35................................23137	1 ....18729, 19450, 19451,
21220, 21222, 21225, 21227,	38................................22849	19942, 20201, 20203, 20067,
21229, 21231, 21233, 21235,	40................21859, 22856	21860, 21861, 22300
21237, 21240, 21242, 21244,	131................................23137	20................................22300
21519, 21521, 21523, 21526,	154................................23137	26................................20870
21811, 22787, 22789, 22791,	157................................23137	31................................18729
22793, 22795	250................................23137	54................................20203
60................................23321	281................................23137	301 ....20870, 20877, 22879
61................................17243	300................................23137	
71 ....17887, 17888, 18151,	341................................23137	**27 CFR**
18436, 18437, 18438, 18439,	344................................23137	4................................22816
18956, 18957, 19143, 19995,	346................................23137	9................................22273
19997, 19998, 20161, 20162,	347................................23137	24................................22816
20163, 20526, 20527, 20780,	348................................23137	27................................22816
20781, 21813, 23321, 23322,	375................................23137	**Proposed Rules:**
23323, 23324	385................................23137	9................................22883
73................................21246		
97 ....18152, 19998, 20527,	**19 CFR**	**28 CFR**
20520, 20324	12................20782, 23334	**Proposed Rules:**
135................................20104	113................................20782	28................................21083
250................................21026	163................................20782	
Proposed Rules:	**Proposed Rules:**	**29 CFR**
25................21286, 21289	4................................22065	2550................................23349
39 ....17258, 17260, 17935,	122................................22065	4022................................20164
17937, 18220, 18461, 18719,		4044................................20164
18721, 18722, 18725, 19015,	**20 CFR**	**Proposed Rules:**
19017, 19766, 19768, 19770,	655................................19944	1926................................21292
19772, 19775, 21072, 21074,	**Proposed Rules:**	
21553, 21556, 21851, 21853,	404................20564, 22871	**30 CFR**
21855, 22088, 22090, 22840,	416................................20564	75................................21182
22845, 23132, 23134		250................20166, 20170
43................................20181	**21 CFR**	270................................20170
61................................20181	189................................20785	

281................................20170		
282................................20170		
756................................17247		
946................................21819		
Proposed Rules:		
916................................22887		
930................................21087		
938................................17268		
31 CFR		
103 ....19452, 21179, 22101		
800................................21861		
32 CFR		
501................................23350		
502................................23351		
Proposed Rules:		
199................................17271		
1900................................20882		
33 CFR		
100................................21824		
117 ....17249, 17250, 18960,		
18961, 19746, 20172, 21043,		
22277		
165 ....18961, 20173, 20797,		
21247, 21880, 21883, 23351		
169................................23310		
325................................19594		
332................................19594		
Proposed Rules:		
100................................22303		
117................................21090		
150................................10780		
165 ....18222, 18225, 19780,		
20220, 20223, 21294, 22108		
168................................20232		
334................................21296		
34 CFR		
200................................22020		
Proposed Rules:		
200................................23154		
36 CFR		
219................................21468		
242................18710, 19433		
1253................................18160		
Proposed Rules:		
2................................23388		
13................................22890		
242................20884, 20887		
1190................................21092		
1191................................21092		
1280................................18462		
37 CFR		
Proposed Rules:		
2................................22894		
202................................23390		
38 CFR		
3................................23353		
17................................20530		
75................................19747		
Proposed Rules:		
3................20566, 20571		
5................19021, 20136		
17................................20579		
20................................20571		
53................................19785		
39 CFR		
111................................20532		

(4)
(2)
(5)
(6)

ILLUSTRATION 9-13. *Federal Register* Reader Aids Sections Showing C.F.R. Parts Affected in May

i

Reader Aids

Federal Register

Vol. 73, No. 87

Monday, May 5, 2008

CUSTOMER SERVICE AND INFORMATION

Federal Register/Code of Federal Regulations

General Information, indexes and other finding aids	202–741–6000
Laws	741–6000

Presidential Documents

Executive orders and proclamations	741–6000
The United States Government Manual	741–6000

Other Services

Electronic and on-line services (voice)	741–6020
Privacy Act Compilation	741–6064
Public Laws Update Service (numbers, dates, etc.)	741–6043
TTY for the deaf-and-hard-of-hearing	741–6086

ELECTRONIC RESEARCH

World Wide Web

Full text of the daily Federal Register, CFR and other publications is located at: **http://www.gpoaccess.gov/nara/index.html**

Federal Register information and research tools, including Public Inspection List, indexes, and links to GPO Access are located at: **http://www.archives.gov/federal_register**

E-mail

FEDREGTOC-L (Federal Register Table of Contents LISTSERV) is an open e-mail service that provides subscribers with a digital form of the Federal Register Table of Contents. The digital form of the Federal Register Table of Contents includes HTML and PDF links to the full text of each document.

To join or leave, go to **http://listserv.access.gpo.gov** and select *Online mailing list archives, FEDREGTOC-L, Join or leave the list (or change settings);* then follow the instructions.

PENS (Public Law Electronic Notification Service) is an e-mail service that notifies subscribers of recently enacted laws.

To subscribe, go to **http://listserv.gsa.gov/archives/publaws-l.html** and select *Join or leave the list (or change settings);* then follow the instructions.

FEDREGTOC-L and **PENS** are mailing lists only. We cannot respond to specific inquiries.

Reference questions. Send questions and comments about the Federal Register system to: **fedreg.info@nara.gov**

The Federal Register staff cannot interpret specific documents or regulations.

FEDERAL REGISTER PAGES AND DATE, MAY

23939–24138	1
24139–24496	2
24497–24850	5

CFR PARTS AFFECTED DURING MAY

At the end of each month, the Office of the Federal Register publishes separately a List of CFR Sections Affected (LSA), which lists parts and sections affected by documents published since the revision date of each title.

2 CFR

1200	24139

3 CFR

Proclamations:

8247	24133
8248	24135
8249	24137

Executive Orders:

EO 13464	24491

12 CFR

Proposed Rules:

712	23982
741	23982

14 CFR

21	24497
39	23939, 23942, 24141, 24143, 24145, 24147, 24149, 24151, 24153, 24155, 24157, 24160, 24162, 24164, 24168
95	23944
97	24171

Proposed Rules:

39	23988, 23990, 23993, 23995

18 CFR

381	23946

21 CFR

101	23947

26 CFR

Proposed Rules:

1	24186

30 CFR

Proposed Rules:

732	24120
785	24120
870	24120
872	24120

32 CFR

204	23953
706	24173

Proposed Rules:

199	24509

33 CFR

155	24497
156	24497

Proposed Rules:

117	24510

165	24513

40 CFR

51	24174
52	23957, 23959, 24174, 24175, 24500
70	24174
71	24174

Proposed Rules:

52	23998, 24187, 24515
704	24187
720	24187
721	24187
723	24187

42 CFR

Proposed Rules:

418	24000

44 CFR

64	24178

Proposed Rules:

67	24036

47 CFR

24	24180
27	24180
76	24502

Proposed Rules:

76	24515

48 CFR

9904	23961

49 CFR

29	24139

Proposed Rules:

18	24188
19	24188
107	24519
523	24352
531	24190, 24352
533	24190, 24352
534	24352
536	24352
537	24352

50 CFR

17	23966
229	23970
660	23971
679	24184

Proposed Rules:

80	24523

ILLUSTRATION 9-14. List of C.F.R. Sections Affected Main Page on Internet

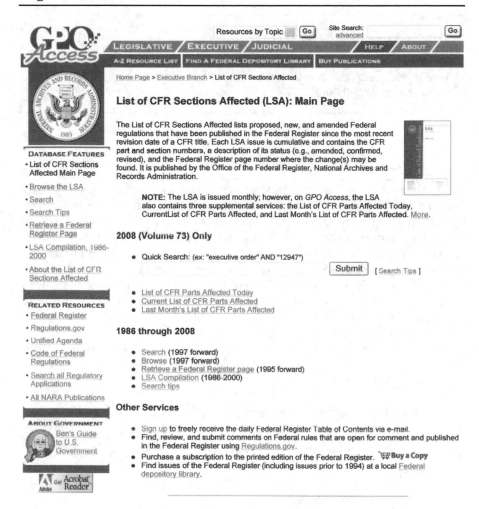

On LEXIS and WESTLAW, the changes to the regulations already are incorporated.

PRACTICE POINTER

Current "Reader Aids" pages of the *Federal Register* now contain a notation for the relevant Web sites.

▼ How Do You Validate or Shepardize a C.F.R. Citation?

Cases that construe an administrative regulation are compiled in the *Shepard's Code of Federal Regulations Citations.* The citations are organized by title and then by section. The publisher's analysis is similar to that given to statutes. (For a detailed explanation of how to Shepardize, consult Chapter 5 and Appendix A.) A court cannot repeal an administrative regulation. Shepardizing, however, indicates whether the regulation continues to be valid. However, Shepardizing an administrative regulation does not replace the need to update the regulation in the manner discussed in the prior sections. Updating the regulation provides the most current version of the citation. In contrast, Shepardizing the cite reveals the judicial interpretations of the citation. Both tasks, Shepardizing and updating, must be performed for research to be thorough and complete.

▼ How Are the C.F.R. and the *Federal Register* Cited?

Citations to the C.F.R. and the *Federal Register* should follow *Bluebook* Rule 14.2. Title 21 of the C.F.R., part 101 from 2005 is cited per the *Bluebook* as

> 21 C.F.R. pt. 101 (2008)

Title 21 of the C.F.R., §101.62 from 2008 would be written as

> 21 C.F.R. §101.62 (2008)

It will be the same based on the *ALWD* Rule 19.1.

A *Federal Register* entry from volume 70 beginning on page 35030 from June 16, 2005, would be cited based on the *Bluebook* Rule 14.2 as

> Temporary Final Rule, 70 Fed. Reg. 35030 (June 16, 2005)

However, based on *ALWD* rules, it would be cited as follows:

> 70 Fed. Reg. 35030 (June 16, 2005).

D. DECISIONS

▼ What Else Do Administrative Agencies Do?

Agencies function in a quasi-judicial capacity when they conduct **hearings.** Hearings may resemble court proceedings. However, most hearings are informal. An **administrative law judge** (ALJ) hears cases involving the application of a particular regulation. Often these cases involve the violation of a regulation. After the hearing, the ALJ, who may be an agency employee or an independent attorney, issues an opinion that serves as primary authority. However, most agency decisions do not have the same binding effect as court decisions. Some agency decisions can be appealed in the courts if the parties are not satisfied with the results. Often, however, the federal courts follow agency decisions concerning areas in which the agencies have developed expertise. To determine whether a court will follow an agency ruling, you must review court and agency decisions.

ETHICS ALERT

Some federal agencies permit paralegals to appear before them without an attorney present.

The Administrative Procedure Act requires agencies to publish their decisions and to make them available to the public. Researchers can contact a particular agency to obtain a decision. Administrative rulings are found frequently in the areas of labor, environmental, tax, securities, occupational safety and health, energy, and immigration law.

▼ What Kind of Authority Are Administrative Decisions?

Administrative decisions, like decisions of various courts, are primary authorities. Some of these decisions can be appealed to the courts after all agency remedies have been satisfied. For example, an ALJ will determine whether an individual is disabled and qualifies for Social Security. This decision is made following a hearing. The ALJ's decision then can be appealed to the U.S. District Court and subsequently to higher federal courts. The enabling statute defines the type of review each agency decision will be accorded. However, the precedential value of the agency's decision varies. Some agencies do not bind themselves to follow previous decisions. However, the courts may find that an agency's decision is very persuasive, particularly in areas in which an agency has developed an expertise.

▼ Can Administrative Agency Decisions Be
Shepardized?

Yes, administrative agency decisions can be Shepardized. The citations
are contained in *Shepard's U.S. Administrative Citations.*

▼ Other Than the Agency Itself, Where Can You Find
Administrative Agency Decisions?

Sometimes a commercially published service prints administrative
agency decisions. Many agency decisions are also available on
WESTLAW and LEXIS. Looseleaf services covering a specific legal
topic such as food and drug law or environmental law publish many
of the decisions.

E. LOOSELEAF SERVICES

▼ What Are Looseleaf Services?

Looseleaf services cover one topic thoroughly. The publishers compile
administrative decisions, rules, regulations, and editorial comments
within a single source. Looseleaf services are published in all areas
covered by administrative law: environmental, labor, energy, and government contracts law. Many researchers think of looseleaf services as
mini-libraries because they contain a variety of resources relating to a
single legal topic.

Because the looseleafs are not bound volumes but are actually
looseleaf notebooks, they are easily updated by adding and removing
pages. Most looseleaf services are updated weekly, some more frequently. Once you become familiar with a practice area, particularly
a heavily regulated area of the law, you quickly become familiar with the
looseleaf services used in that area.

PRACTICE POINTER

Do not rely on the language of a primary authority you find in a looseleaf.
Check the official version of the authority if one exists.

▼ How Are Looseleaf Services Used?

Although looseleaf services are valuable resources because they contain
everything a practitioner needs to research a heavily regulated area of
the law, they are quite cumbersome to use. The following instructions
should make using looseleaf services easier.

1. Analyze your problem to determine the topic. Is it a tax, environmental, securities, or energy law issue? Select a looseleaf service for that topic area.
2. Determine the type of material you are seeking. Do you need administrative regulations, court decisions, or agency decisions?
3. Review the instructions at the beginning of the looseleaf service that you have selected. Most services are organized by paragraph numbers and not by page numbers. Most services have a section entitled "How to Use This Service."
4. Review the various indexes to locate the specific material you are seeking. In general, you should review the general or topical index and then the current material index. If you are looking for a specific document, such as an agency decision, and you have the citation, use the finding tables or lists to obtain it.
5. Read the texts of the primary materials such as rules, regulations, and deisions and the secondary source commentary.
6. Update and validate your findings by using citators, including *Shepard's* or a service provided by the looseleaf publisher, and by looking through the "Current Materials" section.

▼ Can Looseleafs Be Retrieved Online?

More and more looseleaf services are being used online. Subscriptions to looseleaf services are expensive, require shelf space, and are labor intensive to update and to maintain. Online use eliminates the subscription cost, permits the cost of its use to be charged to the client as online time, and avoids the labor required to update the looseleaf because the computerized version always is current.

Using the looseleaf services online is advantageous for the paralegal. The multiple indexes in the hard copy are difficult to use. You must use the terms selected by the indexer. In contrast, when accessing the service online, you have the benefit of full text searching. You can enter your query and select your own words. Another advantage of using looseleaf services online is that you can validate your research instantly at the terminal by using *Shepard's* online.

▼ What Type of Authority Are Looseleaf Services?

Looseleaf services as a whole are considered secondary authority because they are not published by a government body in its official law making capacity. However, looseleaf services contain primary resources such as agency decisions, and frequently a looseleaf service is the only hard-copy resource for the decision. When citing to an agency decision obtained in a looseleaf service, that decision is primary authority.

RESEARCHING ADMINISTRATIVE LAW: SUMMARY

1. Find the enabling statute.
2. Find judicial opinions concerning the enabling statute.
3. Find agency regulations.
   a. Review the index for the appropriate title or look up title paralleling the statutory title and skim the contents.
   b. Or, look up the agency by name in the index. It will direct you to a C.F.R. part.
4. Find case adjudications. Consult looseleaf services, *Shepard's* and other citators, and the U.S.C.A. or U.S.C.S. annotations.
5. Validate and update your research.

CHAPTER SUMMARY

Administrative agencies and their power and authority are created by the federal and state legislatures when they enact enabling statutes. These agencies operate on a daily basis to enforce these legislative mandates.

As part of their enforcement duties, the agencies adopt rules and regulations and hold quasi-judicial hearings.

Rules and regulations of the federal administrative agencies can be found in the *Code of Federal Regulations*. These regulations also are available online. A daily paper called the *Federal Register* also reports any new or proposed regulations. States also have codes of regulations and generally a daily record of new and proposed administrative rules and regulations.

Updating these authorities is essential. You must use the *List of C.F.R. Sections Affected* (L.S.A.) to update a C.F.R. citation. These lists are organized by title and section and are included in the daily *Federal Register* publications. You must review both the monthly L.S.A. pamphlets and the *Federal Register* to update a C.F.R. section properly.

Decisions of administrative agencies also can be validated in a manner similar to other case decisions.

Looseleaf services focus on one area of the law. They contain both primary authorities such as statutes, administrative rules, and cases, and secondary authorities such as expert commentary. Some looseleaf services also have digests and citators and some can be found online.

The next chapter will explain how and when to use the computerized legal research systems.

KEY TERMS

adjudicatory
administrative agencies
administrative law judge (ALJ)
Code of Federal Regulations (C.F.R.)
enabling statutes
Federal Register

hearings
List of C.F.R. Section Affected (L.S.A.)
looseleaf services
quasi-judicial
regulations
rules

EXERCISES

FEDERAL REGULATIONS

1. Find a federal regulation that concerns the number of parts of lead allowable in drinking water.
   a. List each source that might contain the regulation.
   b. Map out your search strategy.
   c. List at least two sources and how you would find a regulation in each.
   d. List topics you might consult.
   e. List at least one regulation.
   f. Update the regulation using the hard-copy materials. What steps did you take?
   g. List the citation in proper *Bluebook* and *ALWD* format.
2. Find a federal tax regulation that specifies how the value of estate property will be determined.
   a. List each source that might contain the regulation.
   b. Map out your search strategy.
   c. List at least two sources and how you would find a regulation in each.
   d. List topics you might consult.
   e. List at least one regulation.
   f. Update the regulation using the hard-copy materials. What steps did you take?
   g. List the regulation in proper *Bluebook* and *ALWD* format.

STATE REGULATIONS

3. In your state, where would you look to find state regulations?
4. Find a state regulation that deals with the question of physician licensing
   a. List each source that might contain the regulation.
   b. Map out your search strategy.
   c. List at least two sources and how you would find a regulation in each.
   d. List topics you might consult.
   e. List at least one regulation.
   f. Update the regulation using the hard-copy materials. What steps did you take?
   g. List the citations in proper *Bluebook* and *ALWD* format.
5. You must find a federal regulation that concerns small toy parts and children under the age of three years.
   a. List each source that might contain the regulation.
   b. Map out your search strategy.
   c. List at least two sources and how you would find a regulation in each.
   d. List topics you might consult.
   e. List at least one regulation.
   f. Update the regulation using the hard-copy material. What steps did you take?
   g. List the citation in proper *Bluebook* and *ALWD* format.

COMPUTERIZED LEGAL RESEARCH

CHAPTER OVERVIEW

This chapter explains the basic concepts of WESTLAW and LEXIS use and the way information is organized on the systems. Three fundamental electronic research skills are explored:

1. query formulation,
2. document retrieval, and
3. validation of authority.

Although this chapter focuses exclusively on online services, using computer-assisted legal research in specific research situations is discussed throughout this book. Legal databanks are really just additional, albeit powerful and expensive, research tools. Familiarity with online searching will help you master computerized legal research.

A. INTRODUCTION

LEXIS is an online research system owned by Reed Elsevier, Inc., a British-Dutch publishing business. West, owned by Thomson Reuters, a major legal publisher, also decided to create computerized legal databases and named their system WESTLAW. Loislaw, owned by WoltersKluwer, is a legal database that offers research and updates for WoltersKluwer treatises.

A revolution in legal research occurred with the advent of computerized legal research. Researchers can now obtain documents, cases, statutes, bills, regulations, attorney general opinions, slip laws, and many other forms of information, legal and factual, from a myriad of jurisdictions and print it out in full text without leaving the office. In addition, researchers do not have to use an index when obtaining material online. Researchers can select terms or words that need to appear in the ideal document on point. The researcher can then combine the relevant terms in a query, which is used to search the appropriate databank for documents with those words or terms. Computerized research systems continually increase the amount of information and the variety of documents they contain.

Although commercial databanks are costly to use, they offer research enhancements that the scattered, free sites on the Internet often lack. Currently, though, www.gpoaccess.gov and thomas.loc.gov are excellent updated resources for federal statutory and regulatory information.

▼ What Are the Benefits of Using Computerized Legal Research?

The greatest benefit of computerized legal research is that all sources available through the online vendor, **LEXIS** or **WESTLAW,** are accessible through a single computer terminal. You do not have to travel to various libraries to obtain the information that you need. Also, the material online is never off the shelf or checked out. It is always up-to-date. Currentness is essential in legal research, and the commercial online databases keep everything as current as possible. (See Chapter 5, for example, on how to validate cases on LEXIS and WESTLAW.)

▼ What Are the Major Disadvantages of Using Computerized Research Services?

The first major disadvantage is cost. Online research is very expensive, and the charges for searching, connect time, and subscribing add up

very quickly. A half-hour search can easily cost well over $100. You can avoid some of the high fees by engaging in a special contract with LEXIS or WESTLAW. Many types of contracts can be negotiated, including contracts for single-state research. Although the vendors have made online research easier and easier by adding many user-friendly features—like menu-driven searching and point-and-click search capabilities when accessing the services via the Internet—many skills must be developed to search online effectively and efficiently.

PRACTICE POINTER

Before using commercial databases to perform any research or cite checking, ask the attorney assigning the project if it is permissible. Sometimes budgets are very low and there isn't any extra money for computerized research.

---

1. Uses for LEXIS and WESTLAW

Computerized legal research is a very powerful search tool to find cases that discuss unique fact patterns. For example, suppose you want to find cases that deal with a slip-and-fall issue on a shag carpet. An encyclopedia or digest index may have entries under "slip and fall" and possibly under "carpet," but it is very unlikely that there would be an index entry under "shag." LEXIS and WESTLAW permit you to search "shag carpet" to see where those words appear in a document.

With computerized legal research you also can find documents, cases, statutes, and articles when you only have some information from the cite but not the complete cite. Suppose you hear about a promising Florida Supreme Court case on point. You know the case was decided in April 2003 and the judge's name was Murphy, but you do not have a clue as to the case name. Knowing the court, the year, and the judge will lead you to the case on LEXIS or WESTLAW.

2. Additional Features

LEXIS and WESTLAW are used very effectively for cite checking, updating, and validating authority. (See Chapter 5 for a full discussion of citators, *Shepard's,* and KeyCite.) The online systems enable you to obtain the subsequent history of a case. Retrieving updated statutory and administrative materials on LEXIS and WESTLAW is another valuable use of the systems' capabilities because you do not have to consult a number of hard-copy sources to find the most current version of a statute or a regulation. Also, administrative and statutory materials have cumbersome and difficult-to-use indexes, and the full text search capabilities of LEXIS and WESTLAW permit you to obtain documents

by combining the words and terms relevant to your research problem. Case law and code research from other jurisdictions is also suited to online retrieval because you do not have to find out-of-state primary sources in hard-copy format. An underused feature of computerized legal research is to access looseleaf services online; subscription and filing fees are saved and the material is always current.

PRACTICE POINTER

LEXIS and WESTLAW have excellent online training. For LEXIS, go to support.lexisnexis.com, and for WESTLAW, go to westlaw.com and click "Training Options."

B. USING WESTLAW AND LEXIS

▼ How Does Computerized Research Work?

WESTLAW and LEXIS work in a similar fashion. All computerized legal research systems require careful query formulation and selection of search terms to obtain the most relevant information available. Both are **literal searching devices,** meaning that the computer system cannot answer a question but instead searches for the appearance of the words or terms that you select in the text of the document. The information that you retrieve after executing a search is a group of documents containing your search terms.

Both LEXIS and WESTLAW now rely on the Internet as the gateway to their respective databanks. The systems are ceasing to support user-installed software. With Net access, both systems are now very intuitive and menu driven. You no longer have to locate the names of libraries or databases within the systems but merely have to point and click on the type of resource you want. The mechanics of using LEXIS and WEST-LAW are now similar to using an Internet browser.

You begin by creating a list of words that would appear in the ideal document on point. (You should educate yourself on the topic before you get online so that you have a research vocabulary that includes synonymous terms.) Then you figure out the relationship between the ideal words or terms. How close together would they appear in the document? Would the words and terms appear in the same sentence? In the same paragraph? Within 100 words of one another? This involves thinking about the context of the words within the document's text and how those words should appear without losing their contextual significance.

LEXIS and WESTLAW have made the process of selecting the terms and determining the terms' contextual relationship simpler by the

introduction of **natural language searching** on WESTLAW and **Freestyle** in LEXIS. Both Freestyle and natural language let you search in plain English using sentences and phrases without selecting connectors between the terms. (More on connectors later in the chapter.) The system then selects the significant terms from your search and looks for documents containing those terms. Whether you search using a group of words separated by connectors, or use natural language or Freestyle, computerized legal research scans the databank for the appearance of those words and retrieves the documents for you.

Electronic retrieval systems do not replace traditional research sources. LEXIS and WESTLAW are literal searching tools that cannot analyze or reach conclusions, legal or factual. LEXIS and WESTLAW search for terms within the parameters that you specify, the connectors. The systems are excellent for searching terms that are not ordinarily included in traditional indexes. They are also good for searching for specific facts or legal terms. Remember that the most successful searching occurs after some preliminary research has been performed using secondary sources and digests and, if possible, primary authority. Preliminary research makes you aware of the vocabulary used in topic discussions and the wording in on-point opinions. *One warning:* The service is very costly when you are using it at a law firm or a corporation. LEXIS and WESTLAW are not suited to researching broad legal concepts like *breach of contract.* Use your judgment to determine if computerized or hard-copy research is the best route. The best and most effective research uses a combination of hard-copy and computerized sources, drawing on the strengths of both. Computerized research is yet another tool in your arsenal of sources.

1. The Basics

▼ How Is Information Organized?

Information on both LEXIS and WESTLAW is organized as follows:

1. by jurisdiction: individual states and federal cases and statutes;
2. by topic: for example, bankruptcy, tax, or contracts; or
3. by format: for example, law reviews, looseleaf services, or news articles.

2. Search Formulation

▼ What Is a Search or Query?

LEXIS and WESTLAW are literal searching systems. You must determine the words or terms that you want to appear in a document on point. Your **search** or **query** is the group of terms or words that you select, separated by connectors, that you enter into the system to retrieve on target information. Suppose you want to find cases discussing Seminole

Indians in Florida, particularly near St. Augustine, and their water, land, or property rights. The terms that you would select are:

Seminole Indian
St. Augustine
water right
land right
property right

These are the terms that would appear in the ideal opinion. Use a thesaurus to find synonymous terms to expand the number of documents you will retrieve. Next, you must determine the placement of the terms in the document's text. Do you want the terms to be close together and to all fall in the same sentence? Do you want the terms to be anywhere in the document? In the same paragraph? Will the contextual meaning or significance of the terms be lost if they are too far apart? Will you fail to retrieve many documents if you indicate that they should be close together? You indicate the proximity of the terms by using connectors.

a. Connectors

Connectors are the special words or symbols devised by WESTLAW and by LEXIS that link your search terms together to indicate your search terms' physical placement in the document's text. Connectors tell LEXIS and WESTLAW the proximity of the search terms in relation to one another. LEXIS uses the following connectors:

and—indicates that the terms are anywhere in the document but both terms must appear in the document. For example, in typing **seminole and indian,** the word *and* indicates that both terms must appear in the document.

or—indicates that one term or the other term or both terms must appear in the document. A blank space on WESTLAW indicates "or." For example, on LEXIS, typing **seminole or indian** would cause the retrieval system to look for the occurrence of either *Seminole* or *Indian* or both words in the document. To search for these synonymous terms on WESTLAW, input **seminole indian.** The *or* connector is most frequently used for synonymous terms, like *car or vehicle or automobile.* This maximizes the possibility of retrieving a greater number of on-point documents.

w/n—means within *n* number of words. You determine how close the words should appear in relation to one another. In our example, you could use **seminole w/5 indian,** which would tell LEXIS to search for the word *Seminole* to appear within 5 words of *Indian.*

Pre/n—This connector is unique to LEXIS and is identical to *w/n* except that the first word must precede the second. You are able to set the spacing. For example, **seminole pre/5 indian** would search for the word *Seminole* to precede the word *Indian* by 5 words.

w/s—indicates that the two words must appear in the same sentence in any order. You can also use */s* instead of *w/s*. **Seminole w/s indian** would search for the two terms to appear in the same sentence in any order.

w/p—instructs LEXIS to search for the terms within the same paragraph in any order. You can also use */p* instead of *w/p*. **Seminole w/p indian** would search for the appearance of those terms in the same paragraph in any order.

and not—excludes terms. Use it as your last connector. For example, **seminole and indian and not tribe** would retrieve documents with the words *Seminole* and *Indian* anywhere in the document but no documents with the word *tribe* would be retrieved.

WESTLAW's connectors are very similar to those of LEXIS, but as indicated earlier, WESTLAW does have a few unique features:

&—identical to the LEXIS **and.**

[blank space]—typing a blank space between two or more terms indicates *or*. For example, the search **auto car vehicle** translates into *auto or car or vehicle*. The **or** connector is most frequently used to indicate synonymous terms, but it is also used to link antonyms or opposites like *day or night*.

/s—WESTLAW pioneered the within-the-same-sentence connector. It is very handy because you do not have to estimate the proximity of the words to one another. If the words fall in the same sentence, you retrieve the document. Sentences can vary in length, and **/s** approximates written English.

+s—indicates that the two words must appear in the same sentence, but the first term must precede the second. For example, **seminole +s indian** would search for *Seminole* and *Indian* to appear in the same sentence, but *Seminole* must precede *Indian*.

/p—indicates that the two terms appear within the same paragraph. The search **seminole /p indian** would search for those two terms' appearance in the same paragraph in any order.

+p—searches for two terms to appear in the same paragraph, but the first term must precede the second. In our example, **seminole +p indian** would retrieve documents with *Seminole* occurring before *Indian* in the same paragraph.

/n—you can customize the proximity of terms on WESTLAW just as you can on LEXIS. For example, **seminole /5 indian** would search for the word *Seminole* to appear within 5 words of *Indian*.

+n—this connector allows you to establish the number of words between terms, but the first term must appear before the second. For example, **seminole +5 indian** searches for documents with *Seminole* falling 5 words before *Indian*.

%—excludes the term following the connector.

The following table summarizes connectors.

Description	LEXIS	WESTLAW
terms within the same document	and	&
either or both terms within the same document	or	[blank space]
terms appear within specified number of words of each other	w/n	/n
same as w/n but first term precedes second term	pre/n	+n
terms within the same sentence, any order	w/s	/s
terms within same sentence; first term precedes second term	–	+s
terms within same paragraph, any order	w/p	/p
excludes terms following the connector	and not	%

b. Quotations

Sometimes you want to search for a specific phrase or a complete name. The spaces between the words would be interpreted as *or* on WEST-LAW. Sometimes you want to search for a phrase that includes articles that are not terms located by either system. In these instances, place the phrase or name in quotations and the system will search for all the terms within the quotes as a unit. For example, you would use quotations to search for cases discussing Megan's Law or the Americans with Disabilities Act. If you do not use quotes, WESTLAW would interpret *Megan's Law* to be *Megan's* or *Law*. To obtain the exact phrase in a document enter it as follows: "Americans with Disabilities Act."

c. Plurals

LEXIS and WESTLAW automatically search for regular plurals. For example, if you enter the word *pattern*, *patterns* is automatically

searched. Irregular plurals like *children* are not automatically searched when the singular term is entered.

d. Irregular Plurals

LEXIS and WESTLAW have two symbols that assist you in searching for irregular plurals and for words that could have various endings stemming from the root word. The symbol * is like a Scrabble blank: You use it to replace a letter in a term. For example, suppose you are searching for articles about women. Documents on point could have the term *woman* or *women,* so your query would be typed as **wom*n** to increase the potential of retrieving on-point information. If you want documents about children, you could use the term **child*** and retrieve documents with *child* or *children.* The word *childhood* would not appear, however, because you only reserved three spaces after the root of *child.* If you want all possible endings of a word following its root, regardless of the amount of letters, use ! In our example, **child!** would retrieve *children, childhood, child,* and *childish.*

e. Hyphenated Words

If you place a space between two search terms on LEXIS, the system will automatically search for the hyphenated version of the word. For example, if you are searching for documents containing the term *full-text,* and you enter **full text** as your query, you will retrieve documents with *full-text* as well as *full text.* On WESTLAW, if you use **full-text** as your query, the system will search for the appearance of *full-text* and *full text.* WESTLAW interprets a blank space as an *or,* so you must put phrases in quotes so that the system searches for the existence of the phrase or term. For example, you can enter **"full text"** and WESTLAW will search for *full-text* and *full text.* The quotes are useful for phrases such as *res ipsa loquitor* so that the entire phrase will be searched for as a whole.

f. Noise Words or Articles

LEXIS and WESTLAW do not search for the occurrence of articles. Omit *the, a, an,* and *and* from your search queries. The frequent appearance of articles (or "noise words") in text would slow down the computer system if it had to search for them.

g. Capitalizing Proper Nouns and Other Terms

You do not have to worry about capitalization style. LEXIS and WESTLAW are not case sensitive, meaning that the databases do not discern between upper- and lowercase letters but search by matching words. Your query can be written as **united w/1 states** and you will retrieve relevant documents.

3. Other Ways to Restrict Your Search to Retrieve On-Point Information

a. Date and Court Restrictors

Date and court **restrictors** in your query help to narrow your search. On both LEXIS and WESTLAW, you can limit your search to look for documents from a particular time frame. On LEXIS, you can restrict your search for information on the Seminole Indians to after 2007, before August 31, 2008, or to a specific date. The searches would look as follows: **seminole w/5 indian and date aft 2007** for documents after 2007; **seminole w/5 indian and date bef 8/31/08** for documents before August 31, 2008; or **seminole w/5 indian and date = 10/1/08** for documents pertaining to the date of October 1, 2008. WESTLAW has the equivalent method of restricting the date in the search query. On WESTLAW, you would search for documents after a certain date as follows: **seminole /5 indian and da(aft 2007);** before a certain date: **seminole /5 indian and da(bef 8/31/08);** from a specific date: **seminole /5 indian and da(10/1/08).**

Court restrictors are another method of ensuring that the documents retrieved are pertinent. On WESTLAW, to retrieve cases from Florida courts enter the following: **co(florida).** You can also search by level of court. If you want only Florida Supreme Court cases, your search would include the following on WESTLAW: **seminole /5 indian & co(high).** This search would ensure that you would only receive cases from Florida's highest court.

On westlaw.com you no longer have to remember these commands, but merely fill in the blanks after clicking a date restriction box. It is important to know that searches can be constructed with specific date parameters to add precision to the information retrieved.

On LEXIS you can limit the courts to only the jurisdictionally relevant ones by using the court segment in the query. An example of this is when you are searching all federal cases and want only those actually decided in Florida. A search using the court segment would look like this: **seminole w/5 indian and court(florida).**

b. Other Restrictors

The following table summarizes the symbols and abbreviations used for search query restriction.

Description	LEXIS	WESTLAW
replaces a letter in a word or term	*	*
unlimited endings following the root of the word	!	!
date after	date aft 1/1/08	da(aft 1/1/08)
date before	date bef 1/1/08	da(bef 1/1/08)
date is	date = 1/1/08	da(1/1/08)
court	court(florida)	co(florida)
level of court		co(high)

c. Fields

Cases and other documents on LEXIS contain **segments** and on WEST-LAW contain **fields** that can be searched. Date and court restrictors are examples of segments or fields. LEXIS also has case name, judge, and counsel segments for cases, and WESTLAW has counsel, judge, case name, and topic (from the West Digest topics). Every category of information on each database has different segments or fields. Lexis.com and westlaw.com have point-and-click features. Just read the screen, point, and click. It is helpful to understand the underlying concepts to achieve more effective searching.

▼ Why Does Integrating Traditional and Computerized Resources Result in the Most Effective Computerized Legal Research?

Beginning your research with traditional sources allows you to become educated in the area of law and to learn the pertinent vocabulary used in decisions and in statutes. (See Chapter 6 for a complete discussion of secondary authorities.) A vocabulary of the words used in on-point opinions lets you construct your search queries most effectively. Online research is very costly, and you cannot afford to use the time online to educate yourself on a topic. It is, in fact, cost-effective to print out the citations and to read sources in hard copy if they are easily obtained.

EXAMPLE

You are asked to find Florida cases discussing abuse of process. Your first reaction to the assignment is that you do not even know what abuse of process is. This is the strategy that you would follow:

1. Consult secondary source materials to educate yourself and to acquire a research vocabulary for search formulation.

2. Begin the education process with a dictionary. Abuse of process is a tort and occurs when the process of the courts is used for an improper purpose. Here's an example of abuse of process: An individual enters into a contract with another to purchase rare coins. The two parties draw up an installment contract specifying monthly payments for 10 years. After possessing the coins for 2 years and after making the agreed-on monthly payments, the buyer decides that the market value of the coins has fallen and does not want to continue to make the monthly payments. The buyer sues the seller for fraud, claiming that he was deceived as to the true value of the coins. The buyer sues for fraud not because a fraud actually occurred but because he wants to get out of the contract. This is an abuse of process.

3. Decide the jurisdiction that the materials should be from. Search for the appropriate LEXIS library and file name or WESTLAW database on the site. The supervising attorney requested Florida cases, so Florida is the appropriate jurisdiction. Determining the appropriate jurisdiction enables you to select a library and a file on LEXIS or a database on

WESTLAW. In this instance, you would select the FLA library and the FLCTS file on LEXIS or the FL-CS database on WESTLAW.

4. Determine the terms that would appear in the ideal opinion. *Abuse* and *process* would be the terms in this example.

5. Decide the relationship that the terms would have to one another in the text—the proximity of the terms. It is important to ensure that contextual meaning is not lost. This is where you decide what connectors you will use. We are looking for cases defining abuse of process. *Of* is a noise word, so we ignore it for purposes of listing terms for our query, but we know that it falls between two important words. The terms must be close together to retain their contextual meaning in the document. You select *w/3*. The query would be **abuse w/3 process.**

6. You want to maximize the retrieval of on-point documents. A court can discuss the definition as abusing the process of the courts. To get this decision as well, use a root with a *!*. Your query would be **abus! w/3 process.**

7. To obtain the most recent decisions, add a date restrictor. To search for cases after 2007 on LEXIS would require you to add *and date aft 2007* in the query. On WESTLAW, *& da(aft 2007)* should be added to your query. LEXIS version: **abus! w/3 process and date aft 2007.** WESTLAW version: **abus! /3 process & da(aft 2007).**

8. If you are frustrated in your attempts to search, call WESTLAW customer service at 1-800-WESTLAW or LEXIS customer service at 1-800-543-6862.

4. Retrieving the Results of Your Research

On LEXIS, the system tells you that there are a certain number of documents containing the information in your query. WESTLAW also indicates that a certain number of documents have been found. How do you bring these documents on to the screen to view? On WEST-LAW, the system automatically defaults to **term mode** where you see the appearance of your search terms highlighted in the document's text. A few pages will be skipped, and you will once again see the appearance of your search terms. LEXIS has a parallel method of viewing the document called **KWIC,** which is an acronym for **key word in context.** You see your search terms surrounded by 25 words of the document's text. Term and KWIC are very efficient formats to view documents initially to determine if the material is on point.

On both LEXIS and WESTLAW, you can view the citations of documents found. On LEXIS, the format is **cite.** On WESTLAW, the cases are displayed in cite format, and you can select full text by merely pointing and clicking.

Viewing documents online in full text is time consuming and costly. It is best to obtain citations online and go to the hard-copy resources to read the documents.

▼ Are There Any Other Ways to Retrieve Documents?

On LEXIS and WESTLAW, you can retrieve a specific statute or a case if you know the citation. On WESTLAW, you would use the FIND command indicated by **fi.** If you want to see the text of 121 So. 2d 319 on WESTLAW, you would type **fi 121 so2d 319** and press **[enter].** To view the text of a statute on WESTLAW, you would type **fi 28 usc 1485** and press **[enter].** On LEXIS, you would click the "get a document" tab to obtain the text of an opinion or statute.

The following chart compares the retrieval options for LEXIS and WESTLAW.

Description	LEXIS	WESTLAW
search terms surrounded by a limited number of words from the document's text (generally 25 words of text)	KWIC	term
full text viewing the entire document	full	page mode (p)
citations to documents retrieved	cite	the letter l
finding a case when you know the cite	get a document	fi
finding a statute when you know the cite	get a document	fi

An important note: You do not have to be in a database on WESTLAW to use the FIND (for statutes and cases) command or in a library and file on LEXIS to click "get a document." You can request a document citation at any point in your research, and it will be retrieved by entering the requisite command or by clicking "get a document."

5. Point-and-Click Enhancements

Online search engines, provided by West and LEXIS, always ensure that the information and search capabilities are current. Additionally, both vendors have made the research services much easier to use by allowing you to use the commands of your Internet browser combined with point-and-click capability instead of learning the searching nuances of each system. The Net sites have greatly simplified searching on both systems.

LEXIS is at lexis.com. On LEXIS, the source directory has replaced the libraries. Instead of constructing a query at the top of the page, you click on the terms box. Everything is completely menu driven. At the base of the screen are the retrieval formats in little boxes: Cite List, KWIC, and Full Text. You merely click on the format. Also, just as on any other Web site, you can link to other resources. While reading a

document you may see a cite to another document in the text. If the cite is highlighted in blue, you can click on the cite and you then go to the text of the cited document. To go back to the original source, just click your Web browser back.

Lexis.com has graphics at the beginning of each case to indicate the analysis that case has received. A red stop sign indicates that the case is no longer good law and that there is strong negative analysis. A blue circle means that the available analysis is neutral.

Westlaw.com is just as simple to use as Lexis.com. WESTLAW also has point-and-click capabilities and hypertext links to cited authorities. WESTLAW developed KeyCite, a case law validating service with graphics to indicate the strength of the authority. WESTLAW relies on flags to indicate how a case has been treated by subsequent courts.

6. Accessing Other Online Services

Shepard's is available on LEXIS, and online fees are incurred based on use. The beauty of online cite checking is that you do not have to worry about all of the books being on the shelf or about updating the material. The online services do it. LEXIS permits customized *Shepard's* retrieval by court, jurisdiction, or analysis. Reed Elsevier, the parent company of LEXIS, owns *Shepard's,* so *Shepard's* data is updated nightly online. Additionally, Lexis provides the treatment that the citing case offers regarding the decision you are validating. *Shepard's* on LEXIS has color-coded symbols to alert you to the treatment that the case received. Also, you can customize your *Shepard's* retrieval by selecting only negative or positive treatment.

You do not need a document on the screen to Shepardize online with LEXIS. You can click on *Shepard's* when signing on. You can then type in the next citation and press **[enter]** while the *Shepard's* analysis is on the screen, and the information will reflect the analytical treatment of the succeeding document. You can go through entire lists of citations this way without entering a LEXIS library.

Case validation on WESTLAW is called **KeyCite.** KeyCite is as current as WESTLAW. As soon as a case is placed on WESTLAW, it receives KeyCite analysis and is included in that database. KeyCite includes thousands of unpublished opinions and references to law reviews. You can also customize your KeyCite search by focusing on a particular jurisdiction, date ranges, and court level. Cases receive stars to indicate the level of treatment in the cited case. Four stars indicate that there is more than a page of treatment in the cited case, three stars equal one page of discussion, two stars have up to a paragraph, and one star indicates that your case is included in a string cite. The stars immediately alert you to the depth of treatment in the citing case, which can be a big time saver during research.

A red flag pops up in KeyCite when a case has negative history. This visual clue indicates when a case is no longer good law for one of its points. A yellow flag means that the case has not been overruled but has

received some criticism. A blue "H" means that the case has been discussed. You can KeyCite a case by pointing and clicking the KeyCite icon or by typing in **KC.** You can KeyCite a wide range of primary and secondary sources in addition to cases and statutes. On LEXIS, you can Shepardize a document on the screen by merely clicking on the *Shepard's* tab. (For a full discussion of cite checking, see Chapter 5.)

7. Comparing LEXIS and WESTLAW

a. Differences Between LEXIS and WESTLAW

LEXIS has the **NEWS library,** which lets you access full text articles from hundreds of periodicals. It is an excellent way to perform factual research.

Shepard's, owned by LEXIS, is updated nightly and covers all cases and statutes from the 50 states and federal government as well as many regulations and other resources.

WESTLAW permits you to search the West topics and key numbers online. This is very convenient because you can customize digest searching by adding date and court restrictors and significant fact terms.

News information on WESTLAW can be searched as a whole by entering the ALLNEWS database. Dow Jones is part of this database. WESTLAW contains hundreds of newspapers, newsletters, journals, and wire services. WESTLAW has a new validation and citing service called KeyCite. KeyCite tells you the status of the case, its analytical treatment by subsequent courts, and the depth of the treatment.

b. Similarities Between LEXIS and WESTLAW

Both LEXIS and WESTLAW permit you to research myriad cases, statutes, administrative regulations, articles, factual information, and other documents online using natural language searches that eliminate the cumbersome restrictions imposed by indexes. WESTLAW's natural language searching capability is entered through a database. When it is time to construct your query, natural language will be an entry on the screen. You will have a choice of a terms and connectors search or a natural language search when entering your query. You can then construct your query as a phrase or sentence without connectors. Both LEXIS and WESTLAW have menu-driven searching systems with point-and-click capability so you can search effectively without becoming very familiar with the system. Both are kept up-to-date and permit you to find documents without having to travel from your keyboard. Both databanks are tied to the respective publisher's materials. In summary, LEXIS and WESTLAW are quite similar but competing products that are very powerful when put to use effectively.

▼ How Do You Use the Computer Most Efficiently?

As discussed earlier in the chapter, the most effective and efficient research is performed after you educate yourself on the topic using

hard-copy resources. Doing traditional research gives you a vocabulary that you can use to construct your search queries. It is most efficient and cost-effective to obtain citations to relevant documents online and to read the documents in hard-copy format if they are readily available.

▼ What Are the Other Computerized Research Services That Are Available?

Loislaw, owned by WoltersKluwer, is a commercial database containing state and federal cases, statutes, and regulations. It is a cost-effective alternative to LEXIS and WESTLAW and is a particularly attractive commercial research option for small law firms. Loislaw also offers the ability to cite check statutes and cases. Loislaw is accessed via loislaw.com. On the site, there are online tutorials that include tips for constructing searches. The site is very user friendly with on-screen icons for point and click search capability. Many firms have Loislaw subscriptions bundled with their purchases of WoltersKluwer treatises and looseleaf services. This enables users of these WoltersKluwer print products to update these resources continuously.

LEXIS has the NEWS library, which was called NEXIS until recently. It is an excellent source for full-text news and periodical articles. It is updated daily and is invaluable when performing factual research on an individual, a corporation, or an event.

Dow Jones is also available on WESTLAW. WESTLAW has a link to *West News* which consists of wire services and the *Wall Street Journal,* plus hundreds of newspapers and business periodicals.

CHAPTER SUMMARY

Computerized legal research opens up a vast realm of research possibilities for the paralegal. You are no longer limited to the resources available at your firm or school library. This chapter detailed the basic skills and concepts required to use LEXIS and WESTLAW, the two major online legal research systems. Additionally, Loislaw, a WoltersKluwer product, provides a cost effective online research alternative. LEXIS and WESTLAW were also compared to highlight each system's distinguishing features.

Search query formulation is very important for effective online searching. The skills required to construct queries are used for LEXIS and WESTLAW, as well as for Loislaw. Retrieving information in a variety of formats is possible too.

Effective research online comes with careful planning before accessing a commercial database. Learn the vocabulary for your topic. Evaluate whether the expense of online services is justified and within the budget.

Online research is not a panacea but an additional and powerful research tool.

KEY TERMS

connectors

field

Freestyle

key word in context (KWIC)

KeyCite

LexCite

LEXIS

literal searching devices

natural language searching

NEWS library

query

restrictors

search

segment

Shepard's

term mode

WESTLAW

EXERCISES

1. One fine autumn day, Jim and Jean decide to drive to the country in search of the perfect pumpkin. After driving an hour and a half, they pull into Pete's Pumpkin Patch, whose sign states "10,000 pumpkins—state's largest pumpkin patch!" Pete's Pumpkin Patch is packed with shoppers. Jim and Jean eye the perfect pumpkin. As Jim is reaching for the pumpkin, Bob reaches for the very same pumpkin. Bob is a little low on patience that day. Instead of offering to look for another pumpkin, Bob punches Jim right in the jaw. Jim wants to sue Bob for battery.

   The problem raises the issue of whether Bob has committed a battery by punching Jim. The attorney that you work for wants you to sign on to LEXIS or WESTLAW and find the statute for battery for your jurisdiction. If your jurisdiction does not have a battery statute, find a case discussing battery.
   a. How would you construct the query?
   b. What sources would you consult before going online to become aware of the terms or words that you would use in your query?
   c. What library and file would you select on LEXIS or what database would you select on WESTLAW?
   d. Print out your document in KWIC on LEXIS or term mode on WESTLAW.
2. Imagine that you are employed as a paralegal at a law firm in Detroit. A partner in the firm has just finished interviewing a client who lives in Munster, Indiana. The partner requests that you find out for him whether the courts of Indiana recognize the "Totten" trust as a valid legal instrument in that state.
   a. How would you educate yourself before going online?
   b. Formulate a search query based on the given information.
   c. What library and file would you select on LEXIS or what database would you select on WESTLAW?
   d. Print the relevant code sections in full format on LEXIS or in page mode on WESTLAW.
3. Mrs. Donahue comes to your firm because she wants to sue her dentist for malpractice. On April 27, 2008, Mrs. Donahue went to her dentist to have a

chipped bridge removed and replaced. In removing her bridge, the dentist broke her tooth. Mrs. Donahue had considerable pain due to the broken tooth. In addition, Mrs. Donahue incurred substantial expenses to repair the broken tooth and to replace the bridge with dental implants.

Now that you have done some research and have read some cases, you are familiar with the vocabulary used in relevant court decisions. You are now best equipped to perform online research economically and efficiently.

   a. Use LEXIS or WESTLAW to find two cases after 1990 that are relevant to Mrs. Donahue's problem.

   b. Print the cases in KWIC format or Best Mode.

   c. Shepardize or KeyCite the cases and print out these results.

4. Use either LEXIS or WESTLAW to find any cases from the U.S. Court of Appeals discussing Megan's Law.

   a. What is your query?

   b. Print out the list of citations.

   c. Shepardize the cites on LEXIS or KeyCite the cites on WESTLAW.

5. Use either LEXIS or WESTLAW to search *American Jurisprudence 2nd* for references to easements in gross. Try to find one reference that defines an "easement in gross."

CHAPTER **11**

PRACTICE RULES

CHAPTER OVERVIEW

This chapter provides an overview of practice rules, the sources that contain these rules, and how to find primary and secondary authorities that explain and interpret these rules. You also learn how to ensure that the rule you are relying on is valid. For our purposes, this chapter primarily focuses on the many rules that surround litigation because these rules are the most comprehensive ones you will review and research as paralegals. Most techniques useful for researching these litigation rules also are useful for investigating other rules, such as rules regarding patent and trademark proceedings, workers' compensation, and other administrative law areas as well as ethics rules.

A. OVERVIEW OF RULES OF PRACTICE

▼ What Are Rules of Practice?

Rules govern the practice of law, especially litigation. Some of these rules also govern the conduct of the lawyers, the litigants, and the judges.

▼ What Rules Govern Procedures in the Federal Courts?

The most extensive set of procedural rules for litigation is the **Federal Rules of Civil Procedure.** These rules direct an attorney on how to conduct himself or herself in a court proceeding. They cover matters such as the filing of a complaint to begin an action, service of the complaint on the defendant, the answer to the complaint and subsequent motions, and the discovery of information. Postjudgment motions and appeals also are addressed in these rules.

▼ Do the Federal Rules Control Proceedings in State Courts?

The federal rules control the course of a civil case pending in federal court only. They do not govern proceedings in any of the state courts. Within the confines of the federal courts, these rules are **primary binding authorities.** Many state courts have patterned their procedural rules after the federal rules. Therefore, the decisions interpreting the federal rules that are similar in nature to the state court rules sometimes are very **persuasive authorities** in the state courts.

▼ What Federal Courts Follow the Federal Rules of Civil Procedure?

All U.S. trial courts follow the federal rules. These rules are not applicable to the U.S. Bankruptcy courts, the appellate courts, or the U.S. Supreme Court. Nor do these rules generally apply in administrative proceedings. See Illustration 11-1.

▼ Are the Federal Trial Courts Governed by Any Other Rules?

The federal district courts also follow the **Federal Rules of Evidence** for motion practice and trial proceedings, and, in criminal cases, the courts are governed by the **Federal Rules of Criminal Procedure.** In addition, many federal courts have adopted a set of rules called **local rules of court** that dictate the small details of practice before each court. For example, the local rules of one Ohio district specify the size of the paper on which to file motions or how many interrogatory questions can be asked during discovery. You should carefully review the local rules any time you have an action pending in a federal court. In addition to a set of local rules, some courts have general orders that have the effect of local rules. Be sure to note whether the court has such rules. Local rules also can vary among judges within the same court. For example, the

ILLUSTRATION 11-1.   Courts and the Applicable Rules

U.S. District Courts
Federal Rules of Civil Procedure
Federal Rules of Criminal Procedure
Federal Rules of Evidence
Local Rules and Orders

U.S. Appellate Courts
Federal Rules of Appellate Procedure
Federal Rules of Evidence
Local Rules and Orders

U.S. Supreme Court
Rules of the Supreme Court
Federal Rules of Evidence

U.S. Bankruptcy Courts
Bankruptcy Rules
Federal Rules of Evidence
Local Rules and Orders

Federal Rules of Civil Procedure discovery rules allow local courts to determine whether the courts want to follow the federal discovery rules or adopt their own. These provisions have allowed judges within the same courts to adopt different rules of discovery than other judges who sit in the same federal district court.

Most local rules are available online. See Findlaw's list at findlaw.com/ 10fedgov/judicial/district_courts.html. You also can search for rules using search engines.

▼ What Rules of Procedure Do Federal Appellate Courts Follow?

The U.S. Courts of Appeals follow the **Federal Rules of Appellate Procedure.** These rules are similar in nature to the Federal Rules of Civil Procedure because they are primary binding authority and can be researched in the federal codes.

▼ What Rules Govern Practice Before the U.S. Supreme Court?

The **Rules of the Supreme Court** control practice before that court. Again, these rules are primary binding authority.

ETHICS ALERT

Courts may sanction attorneys for failing to follow court rules. Be certain to check not only federal or state rules for the court, but local rules as well.

PRACTICE POINTER

If you are assisting with litigation, be sure that you know what general and local rules govern your work. Read those rules carefully.

B. RESEARCHING RULES OF PRACTICE

1. Sources

▼ Where Do You Find These Rules in the Print Materials?

All federal rules of civil and criminal procedure, the evidentiary rules, the appellate procedure rules, and the Supreme Court rules, as well as the bankruptcy rules and official forms, are found in the U.S.C., the official federal code printed by the government, as well as annotated statutory codes, *United States Code Annotated* (U.S.C.A.), published by West, and *United States Code Service* (U.S.C.S.), published by LEXIS. See Illustration 11-2.

NET NOTE

The *United States Code* is available at www.gpoaccess.gov/uscode.

These annotated code versions are the best sources for the most current rules. The drafters' commentary is found in the official *United States Code* (U.S.C.). These codes are discussed in detail in Chapter 7. Several publishers produce the local federal court rules, including West, which publishes the Federal Local Court Rules 3d. These rules also can be found in a variety of other sources, including deskbooks and treatises.

ILLUSTRATION 11-2.   Where Can You Find the Rules?

U.S. District Courts

Federal Rules of Civil Procedure
28 U.S.C.
28 U.S.C.A.
28 U.S.C.S.
Various Web sites and treatises

Federal Rules of Criminal Procedure
18 U.S.C.
18 U.S.C.A.
18 U.S.C.S.
Various Web sites and treatises

Federal Rules of Evidence
U.S.C.
U.S.C.A.
U.S.C.S.
Various Web sites and treatises

Local Rules and Orders
Courts
Federal and local court rules
Books
Various Web sites and treatises

U.S. Appellate Courts

*Federal Rules of Appellate
Procedure*
28 U.S.C.
28 U.S.C.A.
28 U.S.C.S.
Various Web sites and treatises

Federal Rules of Evidence
U.S.C.
U.S.C.A.
U.S.C.S.
Various Web sites and treatises

Local Rules and Orders
Courts
Federal and local court rules
Books
Various Web sites and treatises

U.S. Supreme Court

Rules of the Supreme Court
Federal Rules of Evidence
U.S.C.
U.S.C.A.
U.S.C.S.
Various Web sites

U.S. Bankruptcy Courts

Bankruptcy Rules
Federal Rules of Evidence
Local Rules and Orders
U.S.C.
U.S.C.A.
U.S.C.S.
Various Web sites and treatises

Attorney deskbooks, as the name implies, generally are kept at each paralegal's or attorney's desk. These books usually are paperback and contain a full set of the federal rules, local rules, and sometimes the state rules for the state where the deskbook is set. These deskbooks are updated annually and are more convenient to use than a full code.

▼ Are the Federal Rules Available Online?

LEXIS, WESTLAW, and Loislaw offer the Federal Rules of Civil Procedure, the Federal Rules of Appellate Procedure, the Federal Rules of Criminal Procedure, the Federal Rules of Evidence, and the Rules of

ILLUSTRATION 11-3.   A Local Court Rule of U.S. District Court of the Northern District of Ohio

Local Civil Rules -- Northern District of Ohio

Rule 10.1 **General Format of Papers Presented for Filing**

Attorneys are required to file documents electronically, absent a showing of good cause, unless otherwise excused by the rules, procedures or Orders of the Court, pursuant to LR 5.1. The formatting requirements described below apply to documents presented on paper. Documents that are filed electronically should follow the same formatting provisions, where applicable.

All pleadings, motions, and other documents presented for filing shall be on 8½ x 11 inch white paper of good quality, flat and unfolded and shall be plainly typewritten, printed, or prepared by a clearly legible duplication process and double-spaced except for quoted material. Each page shall be numbered consecutively.

Only the original shall be filed. No duplicate of any document shall be accepted by the Clerk of Court, except upon written order of the Judicial Officer assigned to the case.

In instances wherein documents are being filed in consolidated or related cases, an additional copy shall be filed for each case number stated in the case caption. In the interest of completeness of the case files, the original document shall be placed in the lead case file and copies of the document shall be placed in each consolidated or related case file.

All documents presented for filing or lodging shall be pre-punched with two (2) normal-size holes (approximately 1/4 inch diameter), centered 2 3/4 inches apart, 1/2 to 5/8 inch from the top edge of the document.

The top margin of the first page of each document filed shall be three (3) inches for use by the Clerk to permit space for the file-stamp without stamping over case information. The title of the Court shall be centered below this 3-inch space.

Signatures on all documents submitted to the Court shall include the typewritten name, address, telephone number, facsimile number, e-mail address and the attorney's Ohio Bar Registration Number, if applicable.

This Rule does not apply to:

(a) Documents filed by pro se litigants, except that the signatures on all documents submitted by pro se litigants must include a typewritten or printed name, address, daytime telephone number, facsimile number and e-mail address, if available, or

(b) Documents filed in removed actions prior to removal from the state courts.

Last revised 6/5/06. *See* Historical Notes for full revision history.

the United States Supreme Court, as well as some state and local federal court rules. In addition, other fee-based online services such as Versus-Law, www.versuslaw.com, provide some rules. An example of a rule found online is found in Illustration 11-3.

NET NOTE

Many court and other Internet sites contain the federal civil and criminal rules of procedure, appellate procedure rules and Supreme Court rules.

LexisNexis also offers links through lexisone.com. Review court Web sites listed in Chapter 3. Many contain links to court rules.

PRACTICE POINTER

Be certain that the rules found on the Internet are from official rule sources before you rely on them.

2. Steps in Researching Rules and Court Decisions

▼ How Do You Research a Federal Rule?

First, review the rule in either the U.S.C., U.S.C.A., or U.S.C.S. See Illustration 11-2 for guidance on which source contains the rule you are seeking. Each of these publications has an index that allows users to find rules by topic. Next, you will want to locate court decisions and possibly secondary authorities that explain and interpret the rule.

▼ How Do You Find Cases or Secondary Authorities That Interpret and Explain the Federal Rules?

The annotated codes contain excerpts of cases that explain and interpret the federal rules, as well as references to secondary sources such as encyclopedias and law review articles. See Chapter 7 for a complete discussion of the use of annotated codes.

One of the easiest ways to find cases is to look on the spine of the annotated code volumes for the volume that contains the rules you are researching. Turn to the page that contains the rule. Following the rule is an index of words that lists numbers indicating certain cases. The

research strategy is similar to that involved in researching other statutory materials, explained in Chapter 7. Brainstorm for search words. Find the appropriate topic, and then review the case annotations. The annotations also are updated with pocket parts or supplementary pamphlets that should be reviewed for the most current citations to authorities.

Although some cases that deal with the federal rules are found in West's *Federal Supplement* or the *Federal Reporter,* many are published in a separate reporter called the **Federal Rules Decisions.** This reporter contains federal civil and criminal cases that focus on the federal rules.

In addition to the annotated codes, selected secondary sources such as looseleaf services and treatises focus on the federal rules. The *Federal Rules Service 3d,* published by West, contains the text of the federal civil rules, local district and appellate rules, and annotations concerning cases, law review articles, and other secondary sources that interpret and explain the rules. This service includes headnotes. The service has a topical digest system with headnotes and an index to its digest similar to the digests discussed in Chapter 4. The *Federal Rules Digest 3d,* also published by West, helps you locate cases interpreting the federal rules.

Decisions of the U.S. Supreme Court, Courts of Appeals, District Courts, Claims Court, Court of Military Appeals, Tax Court, and other federal courts can be found in the service. These cases are published more quickly than other sources, and sometimes the *Federal Rules Service* is the only source of a published opinion.

The *Federal Rules of Evidence Service* can assist you in researching the evidence rules. Also published by West, this service includes a digest that includes civil and criminal cases that interpret the Federal Rules of Evidence. Headnotes are used as well as an index system.

The *Federal Procedure Rules Service* is a series of volumes published by West. This service contains the Federal Rules of Civil Procedure, the Federal Rules of Criminal Procedure, the Federal Rules of Evidence, the Rules of the Court of International Trade, the Federal Rules of Appellate Procedure, and the Rules of the United States Supreme Court. Pamphlets that accompany the volume are divided by circuit and contain the appellate and district court local rules for the circuit. The method for using this treatise is similar to that of the digests or encyclopedias. You can use the index or the table of contents, or you can find the topic by reviewing the selected topics listed on the spines of the volumes.

▼ What Sources Are Available to Help Interpret These Rules?

Two multivolume treatises, *Federal Practice and Procedure,* known as Wright and Miller, its original authors, and published by West and *Moore's Federal Practice* published by LexisNexis Matthew Bender are widely regarded and very persuasive secondary authorities that explain

If you are dealing with the Seventh Circuit Court of Appeals, a good reference book is the *Practitioner's Handbook for Appeals to the United States Court of Appeals for the Seventh Circuit,* found online at www.ca7.uscourts.gov/rules/handbook.pdf. The Second Circuit Court of Appeals practitioners should defer to the "Handbook for Appeals to the Second Circuit," prepared by the Federal Court of the Association of the Bar of the City of New York. See the *2nd Circuit Handbook* at www.ca2 .uscourts.gov/Docs/COAManual/everything%20manual.pdf. The Committee on the Federal Courts of Cincinnati Chapter of the Federal Bar Association prepared the "Practitioner's Handbook for the Sixth Circuit." For the 8th Circuit, see the *Practitioner's Handbook for Appeals to the United States Court of Appeals for the Eighth Circuit* at www.ca8.uscourts.gov/newrules/ coa/handbook.pdf.

the federal rules and provide references to primary and secondary authorities.

Many circuits have handbooks that are prepared by local bar federal courts committees or the courts. These guides provide you with background and practical information about the courts as well as the time frame and procedure for filing appellate documents.

Another useful resource for you might be the federal rules committee comments concerning any changes in the rules or the committee's commentary regarding the purpose and origin of the rule.

The federal rules, the rulemaking process, proposed rule changes, and commentary are all available on the Web at www.uscourts.gov/rules.

Do not forget to consider resources such as encyclopedias, legal periodicals, and the A.L.R. series. For more information about these sources, see Chapter 6.

Consider a review of the federal digests under the topic Federal Civil Procedure for the federal civil rules and other related topics for other sets of federal rules. These digests provide citations to primary and secondary authorities. For a more detailed explanation of how to use the digests, consult Chapter 4.

▼ How Would You Cite the Various Federal Rules?

The federal rules should be cited in accordance with *Bluebook* Rule 12.8.3 and *ALWD* Rule 17 as follows:

> Fed. R. Civ. P. 56
> Fed. R. Crim. P. 1
> Fed. R. App. P. 26
> Fed. R. Evid. 803

The local appellate court rules are cited based on the same rule:

> 7th Cir. R. 1

The *ALWD* Citation would be as follows:

> Fed. R. Civ. P. 56
> Fed. R. Crim. P. 1
> Fed. R. App. P. 26
> Fed. R. Evid. 803

The *ALWD* Citation for local appellate court rules would be as follows:

> 7th Cir. R. 1

▼ How Would You Cite a Decision Contained in the *Federal Rules Decisions?*

The abbreviation for the *Federal Rules Decisions* is F.R.D. in both the *ALWD* and the *Bluebook* citation guides. A case would be cited according to *Bluebook* and *ALWD* as follows:

> Barrett Indus. Trucks v. Old Republic Ins. Co., 129 F.R.D. 515 (N.D. Ill. 1989).

C. STATE RULES OF PRACTICE

▼ What Rules Control the Conduct of State Proceedings?

Most states have adopted rules of civil and criminal procedure. Many of these rules are patterned after the Federal Rules of Civil or Criminal Procedure. Some states have adopted evidence codes, while others rely on the common law and have not approved any evidentiary codes. Note that some of the states that have not adopted evidence codes rely on the Federal Rules of Evidence for guidance. The rules of the state courts control conduct similar to that dealt with in the federal rules. For example, the federal rules describe the procedure and the requirements for the dismissal of a case. Similarly under state codes, the rules explain the circumstances that would allow a court to dismiss a case and the procedure to follow to obtain such an order. In addition to

state codes, many state courts have local rules or orders similar to local rules issued by the federal courts. Again, check with these courts to determine whether such rules exist for each court.

▼ Where Would You Find State Rules and Local Rules for State Courts?

The states often include the rules of criminal and civil procedure and the evidentiary rules in their statutory codes. Deskbooks may contain the statewide and local court rules. Many bar association directories also contain the rules, and several commercially published directories of lawyers contain the state and local orders of courts in the area covered by the directory. Many state court Web sites have links to the state and local rules. Go to FindLaw, lp.findlaw.com, and search under the states. Click on the hyperlink for the state and you often will find the state's rules of procedures. For example, if you click on Ohio, you will find rules at www.sconet.state.oh.us/Rules. Go to lexisONE at lexisone.com. It will link you to many court rules. In addition, these rules are available on WESTLAW, LEXIS, and Loislaw.

▼ Are Annotations for State Rules Available?

Yes, many annotated statutory codes contain references to cases and secondary authorities that explain or interpret the state procedural rules. These codes can be used in a manner similar to that of the federal annotated codes. For more information about how to use these annotated codes, see Chapter 7.

▼ Are There Any Significant State Rule Treatises or Secondary Authorities?

Each state's set of rules varies, as does the type and number of secondary authorities available to you as researchers. Check with your librarian for relevant materials. Consider reviewing the materials discussed above, such as federal treatises, and those discussed below, such as continuing legal education materials. These may be helpful because the states' rules often are patterned after the federal rules.

D. ENSURING CURRENCY

▼ How Do You Ensure That You Are Reviewing the Most Current Version of the Rule?

First, update the rule in print using the pocket parts and pamphlets that accompany the annotated codes. Next, ensure that the rule is valid and current by Shepardizing it and performing a KeyCite search online. Validating a rule also helps you to find cases and other authorities

that cite the rule. Validate both federal and state rules by following the same procedures used for the process for cases and statutes. For a more detailed explanation, consult Chapters 5 and 7.

For the federal rules, *Shepard's United States Citations* should be used because it includes citations for all federal rules. To use this in print, look for the rule number and set of rules listed at the top of the page. Then find the rule on the page. Citing sources such as cases will be listed. Note that the rules sometimes have subdivisions and that *Shepard's* lists citations below those subdivisions as well. Some libraries have *Shepard's Federal Rule Citations,* a specialized *Shepard's* devoted entirely to the federal rules and their citing authorities. The process for the use of this citator is similar to that of other *Shepard's* citators.

▼ Can Federal Rules Be Validated Online?

Yes. You can validate rules found in the U.S.C. and U.S.C.A. on WESTLAW using KeyCite and those found in the U.S.C.S. on LEXIS using *Shepard's.* Loislaw provides GlobalCite to help validate federal rules.

▼ Can State Rules Be Shepardized?

Yes. State rules are part of the specific state citator prepared by *Shepard's.* Use these in the same manner as the other *Shepard's* citators noted above.

▼ Can State Rules Be Shepardized Online?

Yes. A growing number of states' rules can be Shepardized online as part of the individual state's codified statutes.

CHAPTER SUMMARY

The rules that govern the conduct of cases brought before courts vary depending on the court in which an action is pending. Federal rules govern proceedings in the federal courts, and state rules control actions in the state courts.

These rules are primary authorities and generally can be found in statutory compilations. They also are contained in reference books called deskbooks. The statutory compilations can direct you to cases that interpret and explain these rules. Secondary authorities such as treatises and legal periodicals often explain these rules and provide you with citations to other primary authorities, including cases, that focus on the rules. Many rules are available online.

These rules are validated in a manner similar to statutes. When you validate a rule, you also find additional citing authorities.

The next chapter explains ethical rules and how to locate them, as well as how to find cases that interpret these rules. You also learn how to validate the rules.

KEY TERMS

attorney deskbooks
Federal Rules of Appellate
Federal Rules of Civil Procedure
Federal Rules of Criminal Procedure
Federal Rules Decisions
Federal Rules of Evidence

local rules of court
Procedure
persuasive authorities
primary binding authorities
Rules of the Supreme Court

EXERCISES

1. Find Federal Rule of Civil Procedure 12 in a print source.
   a. What does this rule address?
   b. Where did you find this rule?
   c. Now find the rule online from an official source. Where did you find it?
2. If the U.S.C.A. was unavailable, where would you look for a Federal Rule of Evidence? List two other sources.
3. What set or sets of rules or orders apply to cases pending in the U.S. District Court in your state or area?
4. What set or sets of rules or orders apply to motions and briefs in a case before the U.S. Circuit Court of Appeals in your state or area?
5. What set or sets of rules or orders apply to a trial in a federal court?
6. What set or sets of rules or orders apply to a trial in your state court?
7. What set or sets of rules apply to attorneys practicing in the bankruptcy courts generally?
8. What reference books would you use to find such bankruptcy rules?
9. What federal rule concerns a motion to dismiss for lack of jurisdiction?
10. What federal rule sets forth the criteria for a summary judgment motion?
11. What rules govern practice before the U.S. Supreme Court?
12. What sources contain citations to cases and other authorities that interpret or explain the federal rules?
13. Where would you find rules for the Indiana Supreme Court on the Internet?
14. Find rules on the Internet that concern juvenile procedure in Ohio.
15. Find a local rule concerning pro se parties in the family division of Florida's 11th Judicial Circuit Court.

ETHICAL RULES

CHAPTER OVERVIEW

In Chapter 11, you learned about procedural rules. In this chapter, the discussion concerns ethical rules. You learn where to find these rules in print and online and how to retrieve primary and secondary authorities that explain or interpret these rules. You also are shown how to locate ethics opinions, both in print and online. Finally, you are taught about ensuring the currency of these rules.

A. RULES OF PROFESSIONAL RESPONSIBILITY

For the practice of law, individual states determine the rules that regulate the conduct of lawyers. Some of those rules dictate an attorney's

ethical behavior, while others control an attorney's **ability to practice,** such as state licensing rules.

Each court has rules that govern the conduct of lawyers and litigants. Many state courts also have rules that regulate the activities of lawyers who never appear in court. For example, the high courts in many states have rules concerning licensing and registration of attorneys. You always should consider whether any rules exist that govern your conduct or the litigation process you are involved in. Some rules specify how attorneys must supervise paralegals.

Paralegals must be able to research ethical rules that control the conduct of attorneys and their staffs.

ETHICS ALERT

Attorneys are responsible for ensuring that paralegals follow the rules that govern attorneys. However, you must know what rules to follow so that you do not jeopardize your supervising attorney or your job.

▼ Is There a National Code of Ethics?

No. Each state has its own set of rules that control the conduct of its lawyers. Lawyers must follow these rules of conduct and must supervise you and ensure that you also follow these rules. Many of these state rules are patterned after the American Bar Association's *Model Code of Professional Responsibility* or the American Bar Association's *Model Rules of Professional Conduct.* These rules govern issues such as conflicts of interest; client confidentiality; communications; fairness; responsibilities of supervisory lawyers, law firms, and associations regarding nonlawyer assistants; unauthorized practice of law; disqualification from a case; and the reporting of professional misconduct. In most cases, the rules require that attorneys ensure that paralegals follow the same rules designed for attorneys. To date, no state has adopted separate ethical rules that control paralegal conduct or that subject the paralegal to disciplinary action rather than the attorney when the paralegal violates the rules. However, several states have advisory rules for paralegals. Paralegals cannot be sanctioned for failing to follow these rules. They merely offer paralegals some direction in how to conduct themselves. Many ask that you follow attorney codes. In addition, many ethics experts believe that the regulation of paralegals will be forthcoming. In addition to the rules of professional responsibility, cases that interpret the rules also govern the conduct of lawyers.

▼ What Type of Authority Are These Rules and Cases?

Rules adopted by a jurisdiction and the subsequent court decisions are primary binding authorities. The *ABA Model Code of Professional*

Responsibility and the *ABA Model Rules of Professional Conduct* are secondary authorities, as are any of the drafters' comments about the origin and purpose of these rules. However, these ethics rules and comments are very persuasive secondary authorities because most state ethics codes or rules are patterned after the ABA models.

▼ When Would You Review the Rules for Ethical Conduct and the Applicable Cases?

You will be asked to review the ethical rules whenever issues involving ethics are presented. Self-interest also demands that you be familiar with the rules. You must follow the rules that govern attorneys. As clients, attorneys, and paralegals become more mobile, conflicts of interest have become a frequent topic for research.

B. RESEARCHING ETHICAL QUESTIONS

1. Primary Sources and Annotated Sources

Many rules of professional responsibility are contained within the codifications of the state's statutes. In addition, deskbooks or pamphlets (single-volume references found in most paralegals' and attorneys' offices) often contain the model rules or codes. These are updated annually and are more convenient than reviewing an entire code to find an ethical rule. To find cases, you would use the annotated sources.

▼ What Is the Value of an Annotated Source for the Rules and Codes?

The annotated rule sources are valuable in a manner similar to the annotated codes. These sources provide citations to primary authorities, such as court decisions, that interpret the rules and citations to secondary authorities such as treatises, and law review articles. See Chapter 7 for additional discussion of annotated codes. Some looseleaf publishers also publish ethics cases.

▼ Where Can You Find the *ABA Model Rules of Professional Conduct* and the *ABA Model Code of Professional Responsibility*?

An excellent secondary source for your research are the ABA model rules found in the *Annotated Model Rules of Professional Conduct* published by the ABA Center for Professional Responsibility. The annotated rules book contains the full text of the rules coupled with citations to any interpretations of the rules in court decisions or informal and formal ABA opinions. This source also includes the drafters' commentary about the purpose and design of each rule. The ABA's *Annotated Model Code of Professional Responsibility* and the *Code of Judicial Conduct* focuses on the ABA model code, the predecessor of the model rules.

This publication also includes case citations and commentary concerning the model code.

The American Bar Association's Center for Professional Responsibility posts the *ABA Model Rules of Professional Conduct* at abanet.org/cpr/mrpc/mrpc_home.html. Click on Table of Contents for the rules. There is a comparison available between the Rules and the *ABA Model Code of Professional Responsibility.* Comments to the rules also are located at the ABA site. The most recent changes are noted here.

▼ What Other Secondary Sources Are Useful for Ethics Researchers?

In addition to the ABA annotated sources, many states have annotated guides for their rules of professional conduct. The ABA Web site above provides sources to help you understand the rules. The ABA site also contains a link to the ABA/BNA *Lawyers' Manual on Professional Conduct,* an updated resource that focuses on ethics issues. It also has links to many state ethics sites.

▼ How Do You Use the Annotated Sources?

The methods for using each of these sources generally involves a review of the table of contents or the index. The ABA annotated model rules, for example, lists each rule in the table of contents. This method is useful if you already know what rule you wish to review. Next to the rule is a list of the topics covered by the rule. You could read through each heading to see if the rule applies to your situation. However, it might be more efficient to review the alphabetical index at the back of the annotated rules. Within the index, you will find a variety of topics and cross-references to various subject areas, as well as citations to the rule.

2. Other Useful Authorities

The ABA and many state and local bar associations render **advisory ethics opinions** for attorneys. These opinions are secondary authorities. The ABA issues both formal and informal opinions. Although an **ABA opinion** is a secondary authority that has no force of law, in the ethics area, it is often a very persuasive authority because many ethics rules or codes that govern lawyers are based on the ABA models. The informal and formal opinions generally are issued after a party requests that the ABA provide such an opinion.

The ABA Center for Professional Responsibility provides summaries of some of the ABA ethics opinions online at <u>abanet.org/cpr/pubs/ethicopinions</u> <u>.html</u>. In some cases, the entire opinion is available. The indexes and full opinions can be obtained for nominal fees from the ABA.

PRACTICE POINTER

Advisory ethics opinions often are excellent sources of rules and cases.

▼ Do State Bar Associations Publish Ethics Opinions Similar to Those Prepared by the ABA?

Yes. Some organizations publish pamphlets or books that contain their opinions while others can be found by reviewing continuing legal education materials, which are discussed in Chapter 13. Some are accessible through the Internet, and others are available from online services.

3. Research Process

▼ How Would You Research an Ethical Question?

First, you would review the rule. Second, you should review any annotations, especially those found in the annotated codes or the annotated rule books or comments. You can review rules and comments at the ABA Web site, <u>abanet.org/cpr/mrpc/mrpc_toc.html</u>. Next, read any cases or informal and formal opinions. Shepardize the cases. Sometimes it is necessary to study a secondary authority to better understand an ethical dilemma. If necessary, perform a search of the rule on the computer to see if any additional cases can be found.

▼ Can You Find State Ethical Rules on WESTLAW and LEXIS?

You can review the ethical rules and perform searches for authorities that discuss these rules on both LEXIS and WESTLAW. You can access many state ethics rules on both services. For a detailed explanation of how to research using these fee-based services, see Chapter 10.

First, you should research the case databases. Next, you might want to search the ethics opinion databases. These databases will provide any

informal or formal ethics opinions that may have been released by a state, county, or city bar association.

Next, you might want to review the ABA databases. These databases contain secondary authority that has not been adopted in total by any jurisdiction. However, this secondary authority is very persuasive because most states have patterned their ethics rules according to the ABA model rules or model code.

NET NOTE

You also can find links to state ethics opinons and state ethics rules through the ABA Web site. The Web site is <u>abanet.org/cpr/links.html</u>.

To find ethics opinions of particular interest for paralegals, see the National Association of Legal Assistants Web site, <u>nala.org/net.htm</u> or the National Federation of Paralegal Association's Web site, <u>paralegals.org</u>.

▼ Can Ethics Rules Be Validated?

Yes. *Shepard's Professional and Judicial Conduct Citations* lists authorities that cite the ABA Model Code sections or the ABA Model Rules. Each ABA rule is listed in bold at the top of the page with a notation about whether it is a model rule or part of the model code. The ABA rules and code can be Shepardized as well as the Code of Judicial Conduct and opinions of the ABA Standing Committee on Ethics and Professional Responsibility. It draws from U.S. Supreme Court opinions, lower federal court decisions, state court decisions, ethics opinions, and articles in some law reviews. See Chapter 5 for more information concerning validating authorities.

4. Sample Research Problem

<u>*EXAMPLE*</u>

You have been asked to research a conflict of interest question. You work for an attorney who represented K. K. Industries in a matter against R. J. Enterprises in a contract dispute in 2007. R. J. Enterprises has now asked your boss to represent its company against Reynolds Wide Haulers in an unrelated contract dispute. Reynolds Wide Haulers, however, is the parent company of K. K. Industries. Your boss wants to know what rules govern such representation. Your firm is located in Ohio, which has adopted the *ABA Model Rules of Professional Conduct*.

First, brainstorm for possible search topics. Next, look in the index to the Ohio statutes. If you don't find any references concerning conflicts of interest, try the *ABA Model Rules*. One source would be the *ABA*

Annotated Model Rules of Professional Conduct. You could look in the index under conflict of interest. You might find topics such as "existing client," "interest adverse to client," or "former client." You would then be directed to rules to review.

The text of each rule is contained in the annotated resource. After each rule is a comment section that explains the rule. Following the comments is a comparison of the model code and the model rules. Finally, there is a list of authorities, including primary authorities.

Next, you should review the authorities. Finally, you should validate the rule and authorities.

▼ How Would You Cite an Ethics Rule Found in the *ABA Model Rules of Professional Conduct?*

The rules for citation of ethics codes are found in *Bluebook* Rule 12.8.5. Rule 1.10 of the *ABA Model Rules of Professional Conduct* would be cited as follows:

Model Rules of Prof'l Conduct R.1.10 (2008)

The *ALWD* citation rules for the *ABA Model Rules of Professional Conduct* are found in Rule 27.3 and it would be cited as follows:

Model R. Prof. Conduct 1.10 (ABA 2008)

▼ How Would You Cite an ABA Ethics Opinion?

The rules for citation of ethics opinions are contained in *Bluebook* Rule 12.8.6. A *Bluebook* citation of an ABA opinion would be as follows:

ABA Comm. on Prof'l Ethics and Grievances, Informal Op. 1526 (1988)

Based upon *ALWD* Rule 17.4, the *ALWD* citation for the same opinion would be as follows:

ABA Informal Ethics Op. 1526 (1988).

CHAPTER SUMMARY

Each state has ethical rules that govern the conduct of lawyers and litigants. Many of these rules are patterned after the *ABA Model Rules of Professional Conduct* or the *ABA Model Code of Professional Responsibility.*

Often these rules are found in state statutory compilations or attorney deskbooks. The statutory codes provide references to other primary authorities, such as cases and related rules, and to secondary sources. A variety of secondary

sources, such as treatises, legal periodicals, and A.L.R. annotations, explain and interpret these rules and include citations to primary authorities.

Many ethical rules are available online, as are some secondary sources that explain and interpret these rules.

In addition to state ethics opinions, the ABA and other bar associations issue advisory ethics opinions. These opinions are secondary authorities. However, they may be very persuasive authorities. These can be found in both print and online.

Both the ethics rules and opinions can be validated in print and online. The method for validating these authorities is similar to that used for cases, statutes, and rules governing court proceedings.

The next chapter will focus on practical resources that assist you in your research, such as continuing legal education materials, formbooks, and legal directories.

KEY TERMS

ABA opinion   ability to practice
Model Code of Professional Responsibility   advisory ethics opinion
Model Rules of Professional Conduct   ethical behavior

EXERCISES

You are working as a paralegal for a firm that is defending a personal injury action against a manufacturer of recreational bikes. The plaintiff, a resident of Findlay, Ohio, was injured while riding one of the bikes in an event known as the Hancock Horizontal Hundred. While working for the defendant's law firm, Cryer, Wolf and Nonnemaker, you attend depositions and strategy conferences between counsel representing the defendant and counsel representing the codefendant. You had many conferences with witnesses, transcribed statements, and prepared letters to clients after reviewing the files. Although you are working hard on this case, billable hours throughout the firm are down, and you are laid off. You are given two weeks to find a job.

A sole practitioner in Findlay, a town of 25,000, tentatively offers you a job, but you first must do some research. This attorney represents the plaintiff in the above-mentioned action. Before the practitioner will allow you to begin work, you must research whether his firm can hire you and whether the firm can continue to represent the plaintiff in this action.

1. Map out your research plan. What sources will you consult?
2. For each source, note whether you will find secondary or primary authority or both.
3. As you list each print source, note your next step and why you would go to the next source.
4. List all online sources: abanet.org/cpr/mrpc/mrpc_toc.html.

PRACTITIONER'S MATERIALS

CHAPTER OVERVIEW

In the preceding chapters, you have learned how to find primary and secondary authorities and how to use the resources that contain these authorities. This chapter focuses on some practical sources, such as formbooks and continuing legal education materials, for you to consider. In addition, you are taught about jury instruction sources and about how and when to use them.

A. FORMBOOKS

Some courts, such as bankruptcy courts, require specific forms. Also, some types of legal documents must be drafted in the statutory form

established by the state's legislature. For example, in many states that have living will statutes, living wills must be drafted using the statute's "magic language" to be valid. To assist you in drafting such documents with the appropriate language, some publishers have compiled **form-books.** Formbooks can provide you with many federal and state court forms as well as examples of forms that contain the language appropriate for a particular statute. Other forms such as wills provide suggested draft documents for users. These forms can save you time and help in your drafting. However, you must be careful when using these standardized forms for drafting documents that are not standardized, such as wills. Ideally, these forms properly incorporate the language that would make the document legally valid in your state. That, however, is not always the case. Be careful to see whether the form is up to date.

PRACTICE POINTER

You must know what language the current law requires or double-check with the court if you are using a court form. Do not substitute your independent judgment when you use these forms.

Some formbooks such as West's provide references to authorities and library sources such as key numbers and encyclopedia materials. However, these books are generally used only for forms.

▼ What Formbooks Are Available?

Many publishers offer court formbooks. For example, West publishes many formbooks including the *Federal Local Court Forms 3d* book. In the probate, real estate, and transaction areas, a variety of publishers issue forms. Some formbooks are available online and other forms can be downloaded. This saves you time. That way, you no longer need to photocopy or hand copy forms.

Some state and federal agencies and courts have their own forms that can be downloaded from a Web site. For example, the U.S. District Court for the Northern District of Ohio places court forms on its Web site. One such form is shown in Illustration 13-1. It is available at www.ohnd.uscourts.gov. Click on online forms. This form is listed as Certificate of Judgment. The court provides this in a text format that can easily be printed and filled in.

ILLUSTRATION 13-1. U.S. District Court for the Northern District of Ohio Form for Certificate of Judgment for Registration in Another District

---

* AO 451 (Rev. 12/93) Certification of Judgment

UNITED STATES DISTRICT COURT

DISTRICT OF _____

V.

**CERTIFICATION OF JUDGMENT
FOR REGISTRATION IN
ANOTHER DISTRICT**

Case Number:

I, _____ Clerk of the United States district court certify that the

attached judgment is a true and correct copy of the original judgment entered in this action _____, as it
Date

appears in the records of this court, and that

IN TESTIMONY WHEREOF, I sign my name and affix the seal of this Court.

_____
Date

_____
Clerk

_____
(By) Deputy Clerk

*Insert the appropriate language: ..."no notice of appeal from this judgment has been filed, and no motion of any kind listed in Rule 4(a) of the Federal Rules of Appellate Procedure has been filed." ..."no notice of appeal from this judgment has been filed, and any motions of the kinds listed in Rule 4(a) of the Federal Rules of Appellate Procedure (•) have been disposed of, the latest order disposing of such a motion having been entered on [date]." ..."an appeal was taken from this judgment and the judgment was affirmed by mandate of the Court of Appeals issued on [date]. ..."an appeal was taken from this judgment and the appeal was dismissed by order entered on [date]."

(• Note: The motions listed in Rule 4(a), Fed. R. App. P., are motions: for judgment notwithstanding the verdict; to amend or make additional findings of fact; to alter or amend the judgment; for a new trial; and for an extension of time for filing a notice of appeal.)

▼ How Do You Use Formbooks?

Often included in the formbook set is a page that explains how to use the guide or formbook. Consider starting with the index. Brainstorm to determine what words would be helpful and then look up the forms. You also can use the table of contents method with most formbooks.

PRACTICE POINTER

Always check if a specific form is required by statute or rule.

ETHICS ALERT

If you use a form and change it substantially, be certain that an attorney reviews it. Otherwise, this could be considered the unauthorized practice of law.

Check the FindLaw Web site for forms, findlaw.com, or the lexisONE site, lexisone.com. Other Web sites also provide forms.

B. OTHER PRACTITIONER'S MATERIALS

1. Checklists

▼ Do Any Publications Contain Lists of What Steps You Should Follow to Complete a Project?

Many commercial publishers produce **checklists.** These checklists are for a variety of topics, such as estate planning, routine corporate matters, or matrimonial matters. Some checklists provide citations to authorities. Most are updated regularly.

In addition to the commercial checklists, continuing legal education materials often contain checklists and practical information that may be as valuable for paralegals as it is for lawyers.

You can search the Internet for checklists. If you enter the term "legal checklists" into various search engines, you will find many such lists. Be careful to consider whether the source is reputable or not.

2. Continuing Legal Education Materials

Continuing legal education (CLE) materials generally explain an area of the law. They tend to be written by individual attorneys who are respected practitioners in a particular area. Within each state, a variety of continuing legal education materials are available. These are secondary authorities and have little or no persuasive value. Therefore, do not cite these materials to a court. However, they can be an invaluable tool in helping you learn about any area of the law. Unfortunately, many states do not update these quickly, and many of the materials lack adequate indexes. You generally must use the table of contents, which may not be comprehensive enough for your needs. However, for new areas of the law, these materials might be your only secondary source of information. Often bar associations present seminars with accompanying CLE materials whenever a major change in the law is made.

▼ Are CLE Materials Available Online?

Some national CLE publications can be found online on WESTLAW and LEXIS. Loislaw provides a limited number of state CLE publications.

▼ How Do You Find CLE Materials?

Check with the law librarian or the attorney who assigned the project. You also could browse through the library catalog or the library shelves. Finally, you might call the local or state bar associations for guidance about their publications.

3. Handbooks

▼ What Other Valuable Practitioner's Materials Are Available?

Several publishers produce **handbooks** that provide you with special information about a specialized type of practice such as estate planning, real estate, or trial practice. Sometimes they contain research references and case citations as well as trial aids.

4. Jury Instructions

Jury instructions are provided to juries just after they are sworn in and before they deliberate in a case. These instructions explain to the jury members their duties and the applicable law in the case they are considering. In general, attorneys representing all litigants have an opportunity to draft jury instructions and work with a judge to develop a fair and accurate statement of the law that the jurors should be told to apply. Paralegals often assist in finding the appropriate instruction or in the drafting of the instructions. Improperly drafted jury instructions can affect the outcome of a case. Some jury instructions reference

books are similar to formbooks because they provide you with sample instructions. Others, however, are pattern or approved instructions.

▼ What Are Pattern Jury Instructions, and How Do They Differ from Other Jury Instructions?

Pattern or **approved jury instructions** must be used in many states. For example, Illinois practitioners must use their state's pattern instruction if one exists concerning a specific point. If an instruction does not exist or if it inaccurately states the current law, then an attorney can submit a proposed jury instruction that varies from the pattern instruction. Be certain that the jury instructions, especially criminal instructions, are up to date. Check the regular supplementary pamphlets. In all cases, review the law and the jury instructions in tandem. Some states have "model" or sample jury instructions that they treat similar to pattern or approved instructions. Often verdict forms on which juries enter their findings are included in both the pattern and model jury instructions.

PRACTICE POINTER

Always determine whether pattern or approved instructions are required.

ETHICS ALERT

Failure to use pattern or approved jury instructions may result in sanctions for an attorney.

Jury instructions generally contain the text of the instruction and case or statutory authorities from which the instruction was derived.

▼ Do the Federal Courts Have Pattern Jury Instructions?

Some federal courts such as the Seventh Circuit Court of Appeals have pattern jury instructions. The criminal pattern jury instructions for that court are posted on the Web at www.ca7.uscourts.gov/pjury.pdf. One of these instructions is shown in Illustration 13-2. However, most federal courts generally are guided by the instructions found in *Federal Jury Practice Instructions 5th and 6th,* available from West. These samples are widely regarded. Along with the proposed jury instructions, this source includes citations to relevant authorities and some commentary

about the origin of the instruction. West also publishes pattern jury instructions for many federal circuits.

ILLUSTRATION 13-2.   A Pattern Criminal Jury Instruction of the U.S. Seventh Circuit Court of Appeals

1.05 DEFINITION OF "DIRECT" AND "CIRCUMSTANTIAL" EVIDENCE

Some of you have heard the phrases "circumstantial evidence" and "direct evidence." Direct evidence is the testimony of someone who claims to have personal knowledge of the commission of the crime which has been charged, such as an eyewitness. Circumstantial evidence is the proof of a series of facts which tend to show whether the defendant is guilty or not guilty. The law makes no distinction between the weight to be given either direct or circumstantial evidence. You should decide how much weight to give to any evidence. All the evidence in the case, including the circumstantial evidence, should be considered by you in reaching your verdict.

Committee Comment

The phrase "circumstantial evidence" is addressed here because of its use in common parlance and the likelihood that jurors may have heard the term outside the courtroom.

There may be cases where a more explicit comparison of direct and circumstantial evidence would be helpful. In such cases, the Court may give examples, e.g., direct proof that it is raining is the testimony of a witness, "I was outside a minute ago and I saw it raining"; circumstantial evidence that it is raining is the sight of someone entering the courtroom carrying a wet umbrella.

▼ Are Jury Instructions Available Online?

Yes. WESTLAW, LEXIS, and Loislaw have a selection of jury instructions online. For example, the California pattern jury instructions can be accessed on WESTLAW and LEXIS. Many federal and state court Web sites provide links to applicable jury instructions.

▼ What Type of Research Should Be Done Before You Draft Jury Instructions?

First, you should be somewhat familiar with the case and the underlying law of the case. However, if you are just asked to retrieve a jury instruction this may not be necessary. Jury instructions are read to the juries deliberating a variety of cases. Some jury instructions include references to primary authorities that often are the basis for the instruction. Sometimes these sources can be useful in finding primary binding

authority. However, you should carefully read the source to ensure that it in fact states the law as described in the jury instruction.

▼ How Do You Find Jury Instructions?

Browse through the online catalog and library shelves and ask the library staff. Once you locate the proper jury instructions, use the index or table of contents to find the appropriate jury instruction.

NET NOTE

A variety of popular press magazines and newspapers are available on the Web. Many are available free. However, some charge a nominal subscription fee.

5. Other Tools

▼ What Other Tools Might a Paralegal Use in Researching a Problem?

Use your ingenuity when researching any problem. Often you are asked to research factual questions as well as legal questions. For example, your firm may want some information about a corporation one of your clients hopes to acquire, and you have been asked to find as much information as possible. One source would be *Dun & Bradstreet Reports,* which provides information about the corporate officers, the date of incorporation, and capitalization. Additional information often can be obtained from the state's secretary of state.

Also consider reviewing popular press magazines. Many local libraries and law libraries have computerized indexes to such magazines.

Brainstorm whenever you are approached about a problem and always consider the sources at the local library.

▼ How Do You Locate Lawyers and Law Firms in Other States or Within a State?

A well-known source is the **Martindale-Hubbell Law Directory,** which lists most attorneys nationwide. This is a voluntary directory, however, so some attorneys have chosen to be excluded. In addition to the free individual listings that include the person's name, address, degrees, and the name of the institute from which the person obtained his or her law degree, some firms pay to publish larger firm directories that list the firm, its areas of expertise, if any, the names of the individual

attorneys, and a biography about each attorney. In addition, Martindale has a rating system for lawyers based on solicitations of confidential opinions of members of the bar. Martindale is available free on the Web at martindale.com. You can use the Lawyer Locator service in a variety of ways. You can search by lawyer, location and area of practice, by firm, by corporate law department, by U.S. Government Office, or by U.S. law faculty.

FindLaw has an online lawyers' directory. Again, this is a voluntary service, and not all attorneys have chosen to be listed.

Many states have statewide legal directories that provide the name of federal and state offices, addresses, and phone numbers. In addition, information about the federal, state, and local courts often are noted. An alphabetical attorney roster explains about how to contact an individual attorney.

CHAPTER SUMMARY

Paralegals find that formbooks can be invaluable tools. These commercially published books provide guidance in drafting real estate contracts, court motions, estate plans, and the like. However, these are only guides, and the paralegal should always double-check the accuracy and timeliness of the forms they contain.

Practitioner's materials such as checklists and continuing legal education books can be of great assistance to paralegal researchers. Checklists offer step-by-step guidance for handling a variety of legal matters ranging from a real estate closing to the preparation of a will. CLE materials generally concentrate on individual areas of the law and are particularly good at explaining new or developing legal topics. The type and variety of continuing legal education materials available vary by state.

Jury instructions, including pattern jury instructions, are drafted when a case is presented to a jury. Various books provide sample jury instructions concerning various legal issues. When a state has adopted pattern jury instructions, these instructions must be used.

Legal directories provide information about lawyers, their law firms, and their practices. Some directories also include information about local court phone numbers, rules, and court reporters. There are national and local legal directories.

KEY TERMS

checklists
CLE materials
formbooks
handbooks

jury instructions
Martindale-Hubbell Law Directory
pattern jury instructions

EXERCISES

FORMBOOKS

1. Find a sample power of attorney for your state. What book did you review and why?

CHECKLISTS

2. Find a real estate closing checklist for a residential real estate closing. Where did you look and why?

CLE MATERIALS

3. Find a continuing legal education book that covers estate planning in your state. Where did you look and why?

HARD-COPY JURY INSTRUCTIONS

4. Locate a civil jury instruction for nominal damages in your state.
5. Find a criminal jury instruction for reasonable doubt.
6. Find a criminal jury instruction for the definition of *recklessly* in your state.

JURY INSTRUCTIONS ONLINE

7. Access the Washington state pattern instructions and find the instruction that defines *compensatory damages*.
8. Access the Illinois pattern instructions and find the instruction that defines *punitive damages*.
9. Find the federal jury instruction that explain *retaliatory discharge*.

USING THE *MARTINDALE-HUBBELL LAW DIRECTORY*

10. For attorneys listed in the front section of the *Martindale-Hubbell Law Directory*, what does the abbreviation 851 in the law school code section indicate?
11. What is an AV rating in *Martindale-Hubbell*?

RESEARCH STRATEGY

CHAPTER OVERVIEW

Research involves planning. The more planning, the more effective the research. This chapter gives you step-by-step techniques to use when researching. You begin by educating yourself on a legal topic that pertains to the issue you are researching. You are then advised to note all of the pertinent information that you find during the research process so that you have a complete record of your findings and complete citations to those findings. Finally, you are reminded to update and to validate all of your findings.

Focusing on your issue and knowing when to stop researching are two skills that you must master. As a paralegal, you must always evaluate how much time it takes to research and to weigh cost with accuracy and thoroughness. This chapter helps you achieve the necessary balance required to effectively research a legal topic.

Topics.law.cornell.edu/wex/legal_research provides an overview of the main resource categories for legal research. Review this Web site's offerings to look at the "big picture" and to check on your thoroughness.

A. DEFINE THE ISSUES AND DETERMINE AREA OF LAW

▼ Where Do You Begin Your Research?

First, gather all facts that are relevant to your problem and define the legal issues. The **facts** and the law guide your research. Ask a lot of questions of the client and of the attorney who assigns the problem. Clarify anything that is unclear. Frame the issue or review the issue framed by the attorney assigning the project.

Discerning the area of law is the second phase in beginning your research. The issues and the facts indicate what area of law is involved in the problem. If you are unclear as to the jurisdiction or the issues, ask the attorney. For example, will the question be resolved by tort law? By constitutional law? By the law of real property?

Make a list of important terms or words that describe the facts and the legal problem. These words help later when you are using an index. You may also want to use a legal dictionary to look up any word or term that sounds unfamiliar. (See Chapter 6 for a discussion on secondary sources.)

B. REFINING RESEARCH

▼ How Do You Refine Your Research Strategy?

After defining the legal issues and determining the area of law to research, you have to devise a systematic approach to the research process.

At times your knowledge of an area of law is not complete. The best way to gain an overview of the subject is by consulting secondary sources.

Hornbooks or textbooks about a particular subject are helpful because they explain the law in everyday language and indicate the legal rules and important cases. Generally, treatises are too detailed for the time constraints that you will be under; however, sometimes they may be valuable. (See Chapter 6 for a complete discussion of secondary sources.)

A quick way to find the appropriate legal rule, particularly when the issue involves state law and you do not know whether a statute or a case governs the situation, is to consult a *West Law Finder.* For example, *West's Texas Law Finder* can be used to find the controlling law relating to dramshops. The appropriate statute citation is indicated. If a case controlled in this instance, a citation to the case would be included.

Once you have educated yourself in the area of law, turn to a legal encyclopedia to obtain case citations. If a statute is involved, use an annotated statute for the relevant jurisdiction. This is particularly helpful when you are performing research for a problem dealing with state law.

For an overview of the law, in a format that is not too scholarly or detailed, use a legal encyclopedia. State legal encyclopedias are helpful in areas of state law research and enable you to find the general legal rule and citations to important cases quickly. Reading the pertinent encyclopedia section also helps you to create a **research vocabulary** that you can use when consulting indexes or constructing search strategies on LEXIS and WESTLAW. Legal encyclopedias can also provide you with citations to primary authority.

Once you find an excellent case or cases, go to the digests and use the one good case method. (See Chapter 4 for a detailed discussion on digest use.)

Most important, once you find pertinent authority to address the issue that you are researching, you must update and validate the authority. Updating and validating authority is performed by using *Shepard's* or Key-Cite. *Shepard's* and KeyCite indicate whether the case or the statute that you are relying on is still good law by providing citations showing how subsequent courts viewed the decision. The cited cases in *Shepard's* or KeyCite are also newer cases that interpret the legal rule you are researching. Remember to update your *Shepard's* information by consulting the hard-copy supplements. If you are using LEXIS to validate the authority, Shepardize the cites. If you are using WESTLAW, use KeyCite. If time and money allow, use all of the updating and citing sources available online.

At this point, reexamine the issue that you formulated when you received the assignment. Review the vocabulary words that you listed to describe the legal issue and the factual scenario. Revise the issue to reflect your enhanced knowledge of the subject. Create an outline of the subissues raised by the problem. Remember three terms—reexamine, review, and revise—when you are performing research to find relevant information. Research involves educating yourself; as you learn more about an issue, your research becomes more focused and more precise.

Remember to stay focused on your issue or issues. While gathering relevant information, it is easy to stray into related but inapplicable

areas. Staying focused on your issues also is cost-effective because you do not waste valuable time on irrelevant information.

C. DIAGRAMMING THE RESEARCH PROCESS

▼ What Is the Purpose and Technique for Record Keeping?

Record keeping and **note taking** are essential to effective legal research because they leave a written audit trail of all the sources consulted and the information derived from those sources. Records should also include sources consulted that did not contain pertinent information so that you do not reexamine those sources if you must expand your research at a later time. Another essential component of record keeping is to write the official *Bluebook* citation for each source that contains information helpful to your research. Establishing the complete citation at the time you are researching means you do not need to retrace your research steps to obtain citation information later on, particularly when you are writing.

Write out the proper *Bluebook* or *ALWD* citation for every source, document, case, and statute that you use. Take notes as you read and indicate in parentheses the page on which you found the information from within the text of the source. For instance, if the case begins on page 1382, but the holding is on page 1389, write out the holding and then indicate parenthetically (1389) so that you know exactly where the information was found within the document.

Make a list of each source that you consult. List sources, citations, and any information obtained from the consulted source on a separate sheet. For example, you may find a useful A.L.R. annotation. Put the A.L.R. annotation at the top of the page in the correct *Bluebook* format. List all pertinent information relating to your research issue and the pages on which you found that information. Add any pertinent cites to cases and to statutes listed in the source to the sheet. The objective is to create a sheet of information that includes all of the relevant data obtained from the source consulted so that you do not have to go back and review the source again. Also include information indicating whether you Shepardized the document and the date Shepardized or KeyCited so that you may redo it if too much time lapses. Note any significant information obtained from *Shepard's* or KeyCite about the document, for instance, if the case was criticized.

EXAMPLE OF RECORD KEEPING

Below is an example of a case brief that supplies the primary authority for a legal memo addressing the topic of the effective rejection of a defective product. Some of the material in the brief has been created

for the purpose of the example. Pinpoint citations are noted for all parallel cites.

CITATION

Olson Rug Co. v. Smarto, 55 Ill. App. 2d 348, 204 N.E.2d 838 (App. Ct. 1965)

FACTS

On March 16, 1962, Marty and Rose Smarto signed a contract with Olson Rug Company for the purchase of $450.62 worth of carpeting. They paid $120.00 as a down payment and agreed to pay the balance in monthly installments. The contract clearly stated that if the Smartos defaulted on payments, not only did the outstanding balance become immediately due, at Ill. App. 2d 349, 204 N.E.2d 839, but Olson Rug had irrevocable authority to have an attorney represent them and seek to have a judgment confessed against them. At N.E.2d 841. Prior to signing the agreement, Olson Rug assured the Smartos that the color and nap of the carpet would withstand their intended use for it. At Ill. App. 2d 350. Two weeks after installation of the carpet, the color faded and the nap lost its original shape. After two more weeks, the Smartos notified Olson Rug's agent and asked him to take the carpet back. At N.E.2d 842. He refused the request. The Smartos did not return the carpet, continued to use it, and apparently stopped paying installments. At Ill. App. 2d 351. Approximately one year later Olson Rug sought a judgment by confession against the Smartos for the outstanding balance and court costs. At Ill. App. 2d 351 and N.E.2d 842.

ISSUE

Whether buyer's continued use of the carpet for more than one year after discovering that the seller delivered a defective product demonstrates effective rejection. At Ill. App. 2d 351 and N.E.2d 841.

HOLDING

No, buyer's continued use of the carpet for more than one year after having discovered the defects does not indicate a timely rejection of the carpet or defective goods. At Ill. App. 2d 351 and N.E.2d 841.

RATIONALE

A buyer, upon discovering goods to be defective shortly after delivery, should soon thereafter return or offer to return the goods to the seller. The Smartos neither returned the carpeting nor offered to return it. For that reason, the court held that the Smartos, through their more than one-year-long delay, waived their right to rescind the carpet purchase contract. At Ill. App. 2d 350 and N.E.2d 840.

DISPOSITION

The appellate court affirmed the circuit court's decision to deny the defendants' motion to open or vacate the judgment confessed against them. At Ill. App. 2d 351 and N.E.2d 841.

All of the page numbers, indicating where the information is found within the text of the case, are included. This helps you when you are writing your memo and must include citation references to the case. You will not have to go back to the reporter and review the case again when your brief contains all of the page references and the complete *Bluebook* citation.

Lib.law.washington.edu/ref/guides.html provides terrific guides for using the specific resources as well as research guides for many legal disciplines.

D. EXAMPLE OF RESEARCH STRATEGY

PROBLEM

Mrs. Jones bought a fur coat from John J. Furriers. The coat was labeled 100 percent raccoon. One day Mrs. Jones was smoking a cigarette and a hot ash accidentally fell on the coat while she was wearing it. The ash melted a hole in the coat. Mrs. Jones knew that fur burns, but acrylic melts.

1. How to Phrase the Issue If You Are Researching the Fur Labeling Problem

ISSUE

Whether a furrier is liable to a consumer for mislabeling a product.

2. First Steps

First, perform **background research** using secondary sources to educate yourself about the area of law. This helps you become familiar with the types of legal materials controlling the issue. The background research provides information indicating whether the topic (in our problem, fur labeling) is controlled by statutes, cases, or regulations and whether federal or state law controls. You should develop a research vocabulary from your readings that helps you use the index volumes more effectively.

Start with the descriptive word index of the relevant state statute and the descriptive word index of the *United States Code Annotated* (U.S.C.A.) or the *United States Code Service* (U.S.C.S.) to see if any federal statutes have been violated. The words to check would be **label, fur**, and **product mislabeling.** You can also start your research at www.gpoaccess .gov/uscode to see if there are any relevant U.S. Code provisions by searching: label fur product misleading. After retrieving the relevant

code section(s), check the annotated statutes to see if any relevant cases are cited discussing or analyzing the issue. Any relevant cases would be validated by using *Shepard's* or KeyCite. Validation also leads you to any newer cases discussing the issue.

After determining that the relevant cases and statutes are valid, a thorough reading of the decisions is necessary. You should make a list of all of the cites checked at this point and place a check next to the cites that are valid. Add a check next to the cite after you have read the full text of the opinion or statute. This will save you time later if you expand your research. You can merely review your list of cites to see if it is valid and to see if you read the full text of the authority.

3. What Sources to Consult and Why

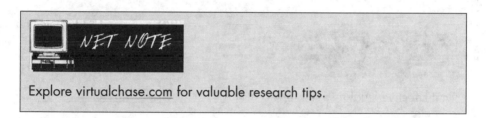

Explore virtualchase.com for valuable research tips.

1. Consult the U.S.C.A. or the *United States Code Service* (U.S.C.S.) because fur labeling is regulated by the Federal Trade Commission. You can search the U.S. Code online via LEXIS, WESTLAW, or www.gpoaccess.gov, or use one of the hard-copy annotated sets. An annotated code provides recent case references as well as references to administrative material (particularly the U.S.C.S., which provides references to administrative materials; see Chapter 7 for a discussion of statutes). Also, consumer fraud issues could be researched. Use the index to the U.S.C.A. and look up the applicable research terms that you derived from the secondary sources.

2. Consult the *Code of Federal Regulations* (C.F.R.) to see the particular agency rules pertaining to fur labeling and intentional mis-labeling. Use the index to the C.F.R. to find the appropriate titles that discuss furs, fur labeling, labeling, and labeling requirements. The research vocabulary that you generate are the words you look up in the index. (See Chapter 9 for C.F.R. use.)

3. Consult the *American Law Reports* (A.L.R.) because this is a narrow, well-defined issue and the A.L.R. may have explored this issue thoroughly. A.L.R. is easy to search on LEXIS or WESTLAW. The Federal Trade Commission might regulate fur labeling. (See Chapter 6 for a discussion on using the A.L.R.)

4. What to Do After Completing Hard-Copy Research

Create a body of information on which to base your memo. Detailed note taking and careful citation to references on sheets of paper for each source are performed here. Also, keep a complete list of all

sources consulted, whether a statute, case, regulation, periodical article, or other source. Your list of sources consulted helps later on when you may have to expand your research. You can then check the list to see if you already reviewed a source and to see if it was pertinent.

Remember to Shepardize or KeyCite any primary authority that you use in your memo, for this ensures that the authority, whether it is a case, statute, or regulation, is still good or valid law.

Outline the issues that you discuss in your memo or letter. Insert the applicable legal authority under the outline entry.

Review your outline and evaluate whether you have sufficient legal authority to support and to resolve the issues raised by the problem. If you have sufficient authority, begin to write. If you do not have sufficient authority, expand your research. Check your notes and the list of materials found to help you avoid duplicating your efforts and wasting time.

Cost-effective legal research tips are at www.ll.georgetown.edu/guides/cost.cfm.

5. Combining Computerized Research Methods with Hard-Copy Method

The principal difference between the hard-copy method and the combination computerized and hard-copy method is that instead of using indexes to the statutes, C.F.R., and the A.L.R., you construct a search query and search the materials online. You also search legal periodicals online with search queries. The validation, Shepardizing, is performed online as well.

Performing background research using secondary sources is very important for educating yourself in the area of law and for generating a research vocabulary to use later when constructing the research queries for LEXIS or WESTLAW. Secondary source research is still most efficiently and cost-effectively done with hard-copy sources.

Computerized legal research requires you to select precise words to retrieve documents that contain those words and that are on point. Using LEXIS and WESTLAW is most productive after you are versed in the subject and are aware of the words that judges, legislatures, and agencies use when writing about a legal topic.

6. Using Online Services in the Fur Labeling Problem

1. Using LEXIS, first search the U.S.C.S. for the appearance of any statutes addressing fur labeling. The query constructed and entered

is **fur w/s label!**. *Fur* is an essential factual term. The connector *w/s* (the group of letters indicating to LEXIS the relationship between fur and label!) indicates that *fur* must be within the same sentence as *label*. This connector parallels written English and ensures that the terms keep their significance in the context of the document. For instance, using the connector *and* instead of *w/s* would require LEXIS to search for the appearance of the words fur and label anywhere in the document regardless of their proximity to one another. The exclamation point (!) after *label* indicates to LEXIS to search for all possible endings for the word *label*, so that *labeling* would be picked up as well as *labeled* and *labels*. You are using LEXIS instead of the index to the U.S.C.S.

2. Use the same search again to see if any federal administrative regulations are relevant. Search the C.F.R online with the query **fur w/s label!**. Review the sections of the C.F.R. retrieved to see if any are on point. You are using LEXIS instead of the C.F.R. index. Remember that you can update C.F.R. citations on LEXIS. (See Chapter 9 for a discussion on updating C.F.R. provisions.)

3. Use the same search a third time to find A.L.R. annotations, using the query **fur w/s label!**. Once again, your query is a substitute, for using the index to the A.L.R. You will find annotations discussing fur labeling and references to primary authority.

4. Use Google to see if any other resources are relevant. Be sure to just look at the first page of hits. Search: regulations fur labeling. Any statutory or regulatory information obtained by searching Google must be updated and validated.

5. Read the text of any material that you found on LEXIS. It is most cost-effective to use the citations to the materials found on LEXIS and read the full text source in hard-copy format, if the hard copy is available. Take detailed notes. List all of the sources that you consult. Write the correct citation for each source. Update and Shepardize or Key-Cite any primary authority on which you will rely. Use either LEXIS or WESTLAW to obtain the C.F.R. section and to make sure that the C.F.R. provision is current. (See Chapter 10 for information on computer-assisted legal research.)

6. At this point, you must create an outline of the issues and sub-issues to be addressed. Insert the appropriate legal authority under each outline category. Expand your research if you do not have sufficient authority.

SUMMARY CHECKLIST

I. When you receive the problem:
   a. Clarify legal issues being researched
   b. Determine relevant jurisdiction
   c. Determine area of the law
   d. Gather all of the facts

    e. Draft a statement of the issue or question that you are researching

II. Introductory research

    a. Educate yourself in the area of law

    b. Scan a hornbook or textbook on the subject

    c. Learn the relevant vocabulary

    d. Note the major cases

    e. Make an outline of the issues and subissues of your problem

III. Targeted research

    a. Use a legal encyclopedia or an annotated statute (use descriptive word index), particularly helpful for matters involving state law, to find discussion of legal issue and relevant case and statute citations.

    b. Go to the digest for the relevant jurisdiction, and use the one good case method to find other cases.

    c. Shepardize or KeyCite to find other cites and to validate your citations before relying on them as authority.

    d. Brief cases and relate them to one another (see Chapter 23 on Synthesis).

    e. Review the outline of the issues and subissues that you drafted. Revise the outline to reflect your increased knowledge of the subject.

IV. Computerized research

    a. Particularly helpful when the facts are unique and the legal issue is narrow (for instance, whether malpractice occurred during the insertion of a chin implant), not broad (for instance, whether a breach of contract occurred)

    b. Best to be thorough and combine computerized and hard-copy methods

    c. Google the search terms to see if any other information comes up in the first page of hits and update any citations to primary authority.

V. Create an audit trail of your research

    a. Take notes of sources and location, including page number, in *Bluebook* format.

    b. Note whether Shepardizing or KeyCiting has been completed and date completed.

VI. Organizing your research findings

    a. Review the outline of the issues and the subissues that you created and revise it to reflect any new knowledge.

    b. Insert the applicable authority discussing the relevant subissue under the appropriate outline heading.

    c. Review the filled-in outline to make sure that you have found adequate authority to address each subissue listed.

    d. If you have sufficient legal authority, begin to write. If you do not have sufficient legal authority, expand your research.

Always check your list of sources consulted when you are expanding your research to make sure that you do not waste precious time with sources that you have already consulted.

PRACTICE POINTER

Take advantage of any training offered at your firm or through legal publishers. Publishers and online database vendors offer training, very often for free, that will enhance your research skills and help you become familiar with new products. Sometimes existing products are very complex, and training will help you use the resources efficiently.

CHAPTER SUMMARY

This chapter led you through the entire research process from initially receiving the project to completing research. Refining the issue at the beginning and focusing on your important sources are as essential as knowing when to stop researching. This chapter and your own experience will guide you through this process. Keep records of all sources consulted and make sure that your citations are accurate; these help when you are ready to write. Also, do not forget to validate all necessary documents and to update all resources. Now you are equipped to write.

KEY TERMS

background research	record keeping
facts	research vocabulary
note taking	*West Law Finder*

EXERCISES

RESEARCHING IN GENERAL
1. Before you begin a research project, what general questions should you resolve with the assigning attorney?
2. What is the benefit of record keeping when researching?

HARD-COPY RESEARCH
3. You have just received a research project. Outline your research plan using hard-copy resources.
4. Read the following fact pattern and answer the questions.

Facts

John Clark comes to your firm with a question regarding the tax status of his residence. John Clark was just ordained as a Methodist minister. He will be receiving a housing allowance from First Methodist Church, where he will be an assistant pastor. He wants to know if this housing allowance can be excluded from income on his tax return even though the residence is his own.

a. How would you phrase this issue if you were researching this problem using hard-copy resources?
b. What would be your research strategy using hard-copy resources?
c. List three sources that you would consult. Why would you consult them?

HARD-COPY AND ONLINE RESEARCH COMBINED

5. Draw a flow chart of your research strategy using a combination of hard-copy and computerized resources.
6. Read the following fact pattern and answer the questions.

Facts

On November 29, 2007, Michael Jones purchased a used truck from Grimy's Auto and Truck Service. At the time of purchase, Grimy's stated that the engine was completely overhauled and consisted of rebuilt and reconditioned parts, all parts were guaranteed, and invoices for all new parts would be provided. On November 13, 2008, after using the truck for almost one year, Jones discovered that several engine parts were not rebuilt or reconditioned and other engine parts were defective, which caused the truck to break down. This resulted in lost wages and lost profits for Jones. Jones made repairs to the truck on November 13, 2008, December 13, 2008, and December 16, 2008. Jones did not attempt to return the truck and did not notify Grimy's that the truck was defective. The truck is currently disabled in Columbus, Ohio. Jones came to your firm because he wants to sue Grimy's for damages for breach of contract.

Issue

Is Jones entitled to receive damages for breach of contract because the truck does not conform to the terms of the agreement? Remember that Grimy's will assert that Jones continued to use the truck for more than a reasonable time and failed to return the truck or to notify Grimy's of its defects in a timely manner.

a. What would be your research strategy if you were using a combination of hard-copy and computerized resources?
b. How would you educate yourself on the relevant topic so that you could find primary sources?
c. List one secondary source and two primary sources that you would consult. Why would you consult these sources?
d. Use either LEXIS or WESTLAW and formulate a search query that you could use to find primary authority.

LEGAL WRITING

GETTING READY TO WRITE

CHAPTER OVERVIEW

Writing involves planning—the more planning, the more effective the written document. Legal writing has three components: prewriting (which includes researching and planning your written document), drafting, and revising. This chapter explains how to draft documents and how to revise your work so that it is written clearly and concisely. This chapter provides step-by-step techniques to use when preparing to write. You must systematically prepare to write by determining the purpose, audience, and organization of the document and carefully revise your work product to tailor it precisely to the assignment, the client, and the facts. The focus of this chapter is the fundamentals of good writing. Specific tips are provided to improve your drafts.

A. WRITING GOALS AND HOW TO ACHIEVE THEM

The keys to writing well are clarity and organization. Your readers must understand what you are trying to convey to them. Whether you are writing a letter or a memorandum, your communication must be clear so that it can be understood. Often several proper formats, used at different times, will make your writing easier to read and understand.

▼ How Do You Plan Your Communication and Revise It?

You must think about what you want to say. Outline the communication. Next, write it using correct grammar and spelling, and most important, rewrite it several times. As you rewrite your letters and memos, you will always find that you can eliminate unnecessary words and legalese. Use simple words even though you know more elaborate ones. Doing so makes your writing inviting rather than pompous.

B. THE WRITING PROCESS

Follow a method or format when preparing to write to make the actual drafting process easier. Focus on the mechanics and components of the writing process rather than the finished product. The method that follows is a checklist to ensure thoroughness and to give you confidence in your newly acquired skills. The fundamental components of process writing are assessing the document's purpose and intended audience, drafting a detailed outline before writing, revising your findings into the categories of purpose and audience, and outlining and revising your work.

1. Preparing to Write: Purpose and Audience

▼ How Do You Complete the Research Process and Make the Transition to Writing?

Remember that what we plan as we prepare to write is as important as the final product. The more time you can put into the process, the better the product. Spend at least 50 percent of the time budgeted for writing in the **prewriting stage.** However, time management is crucial with any assignment because time is money and knowing when to stop researching and when to begin writing is important. Therefore, when the project is assigned ask how much time you should spend on the project. What is the budget? A good clue as to when you have completed your research is when you do not retrieve any new information; the same sources keep appearing. Ask your law librarian or another paralegal to briefly review your research strategy and ask if there are any other avenues that he or she would have taken.

Take detailed notes and make careful citations to references for each source. Also, keep a complete list of all sources consulted, whether

a statute, case, regulation, periodical article, or other source. Your list of sources consulted helps later on, when you may have to expand your research. You can then check the list to see if you already reviewed a source and to see if it was pertinent.

Shepardize any primary authority that you use in your memo. *Shepard's* ensures that the authority, whether it is a case, statute, or regulation, is still good or valid law. Never start to write using a source of authority without Shepardizing it first.

llrx.com/columns/grammar10.htm has tips on word selection in legal writing.

a. Purpose

▼ What Is the Purpose of the Document?

When you sit down to write, begin by asking yourself: What is the **purpose** of the document that I am preparing? Because a legal document has a variety of goals (to inform, persuade, or advise), you must determine the document's intent before writing. The purpose determines the posture and the format of your work product. If the document is to inform the attorney as to all available law on a particular issue, it is neutral in tone and takes the form of an objective memo. If your goal is to convince another party that your position is correct, then the document may be in the form of a memo for the assigning attorney, a memo for the court, a trial or an appellate brief, and the tone will be persuasive. Sometimes a persuasive document takes the form of a letter that requests an individual or entity to act in a certain way. Examples of persuasive letters are demand letters requesting payment owed, or eviction letters demanding that a tenant vacate the premises. Sometimes you must advise a client as to an action that he or she must take. The document may then be in the form of a letter giving counsel but one that is written as simply as possible; a client usually does not have a legal education. The purpose of the document determines its format and the rhetorical stance: objective, persuasive, or instructive.

http://law.cornell.edu/topics/legal_writing.html provides a brief overview of the types of legal documents.

b. Audience

▼ To Whom Are You Speaking?

As you prepare to write, determine carefully who the **audience,** or reader, is. Is the reader the assigning attorney? This is often the case when the project is the preparation of an office memo. The memo should be easy for the intended reader to understand; you should insert headings, if necessary, to guide the reader. If the document is intended for a court, then the reader will be a judge and opposing counsel, and your tone will be formal yet persuasive. The assertions or points that you want to prove should be clear and straightforward. The document should always be prepared using language that the reader can comprehend; this is also required when drafting client letters and demand letters.

PRACTICE POINTER

Ask the assigning attorney questions after you have reviewed the assignment, but before you begin to write, make sure that the purpose and audience are agreed upon.

---

2. Drafting a Detailed Outline

▼ How Do You Organize Your Ideas?

The next stage is to prepare an **outline** of whatever document you are writing. If it is an office memo, outline the issues and subissues of points that you want to articulate. Make sure that the outline flows logically. See if there are any gaps by reviewing your outline carefully. Organization is crucial to effective legal writing to ensure completeness. Having a complete outline also helps when you have to put your project down for a considerable period of time, or when you must work on more than one matter at a time and want to easily pick up where you left off.

Organize your research findings according to where they are pertinent in your outline. It is best to let your issues or assertions determine where the research should be placed rather than letting the sources determine the placement in the document. Never use your sources as your outline; rely on the issues.

3. Revision: The Final Part of the Process

PRACTICE POINTER

When revising, consult a dictionary to ensure that all of the words are properly spelled and used. Check a thesaurus to vary your terms.

Rewriting is a continuous part of the writing process and a vital final step. Reread the material after you have reviewed your word choices and eliminated unnecessary words. Rewriting may seem like a tedious waste of time, but it is one of the most important steps in preparing a well-written document.

Review all the steps you have taken in the prewriting stage. Ask yourself: Is the purpose of the document being prepared according to the assignment, and is it meeting the client's needs? Does the document clearly fulfill its goal of either informing, persuading, or advising? Do the language and format reflect the purpose?

Examine your intended audience. What language is appropriate for the intended reader? What level of sophistication is required? Ask yourself about voice (how it will sound), diction (word choice), and rhetoric (the way you use speech).

Review your outline. Check to see if the outline is well organized, logical, and flows smoothly. At this point, reexamine the issues or assertions that you want to include and make sure that the points are clearly discernible. Insert the appropriate research findings in the relevant place in the outline, as well as the necessary facts and the conclusions that you want to draw. Now you are ready to write. After you write the first draft, revise and pay attention to the following details.

PRACTICE POINTER

Review documents in files to see the firm's writing style.

---

4. Example of Process Writing Techniques

Ms. Partner calls you into her office and asks you to prepare a client letter to Mrs. Jones advising her as to a course of action that she can take to rectify the problem of her mislabeled fur coat. The facts of the problem are as follows: Mrs. Jones bought a fur coat from John J. Furriers. The coat was labeled 100-percent raccoon. One day Mrs. Jones was smoking a cigarette and a hot ash fell on the coat while she was wearing it. The ash melted a hole in the coat. Mrs. Jones knew that fur burns, but acrylic melts.

First, what is the purpose of the document? The document's goal is to advise Mrs. Jones as to a course of action against the seller, John J. Furriers. The partner specified the document's form, a letter.

Next, you must examine your audience. Who is your reader? Is Mrs. Jones an attorney? Probably not. You can ask the attorney making the assignment for some background information about the client. This will help you tailor a document to the reader's precise needs. Mrs. Jones is a stock analyst. She is a sophisticated individual but she does not

possess a legal education. The language used in the letter must be understandable to Mrs. Jones. The voice—how the letter sounds—should be instructive and advisory without being condescending. The diction, or word choice, should be simple; avoid legalese.

Now outline the points that you want to address in the letter. Begin by restating the facts as you know them. List the points.

1. The fur coat was mislabeled.
2. The seller misrepresented his product.
3. If the misrepresentation was intentional, there is the possibility of fraud.
4. Mrs. Jones would like to obtain a full refund for the coat that she purchased.
5. If a refund is not given in seven days, court action will proceed.

Insert your research findings, in general language, in the appropriate spot in the outline. In a client letter of this nature there is no need to cite to authority. Use the facts and advise Mrs. Jones as to how she should proceed with the matter. Always remember that an attorney must always review and sign any letter that you prepare that gives legal advice. Only an attorney may sign such a letter.

Revise all your prewriting steps by checking your purpose, audience, and outline once again. Now you are ready to write.

PRACTICE POINTER

Prewriting preparation is time well spent. Thoroughness and accuracy are so important, and attorneys have little patience for anything besides perfection. Careful note taking, outlining, and citing will provide not only an excellent start to a writing project but ample material if you are called on to discuss a project prior to its completion.

CHECKLIST

  I. When you receive the problem
    a. Clarify the legal issues being researched.
    b. Determine the relevant jurisdiction.
    c. Determine the area of the law.
    d. Gather all the facts.
    e. Draft a statement of the issue or question that you are researching.
 II. Introductory research
    a. Educate yourself in the area of the law.
    b. Consult a legal encyclopedia for a general overview to find major cases on point.

    c. Learn the relevant vocabulary.

    d. Note the major cases.

    e. Make an outline of the issues and subissues of your problem.

III. Process writing

    a. Purpose: Determine the purpose of the document. The document's goal is either to inform, to persuade, or to advise. Select the appropriate rhetorical stance and determine the format (office memo, court memo, brief, or letter).

    b. Audience: Find out who the reader or readers will be. Determine the language that is most comprehensible to the particular reader. Select an appropriate voice for the purpose, format, and reader. Note your diction.

    c. Outline: Outline the issues, assertions, or points that you want to include. Organize research findings according to the outline. Place facts in the appropriate spot and state conclusion.

    d. Revise: Review the purpose and the audience of the intended document and check your outline for appropriateness. Revise your outline to reflect any new knowledge, legal or factual. Reread the outline to ensure that it is complete and flows logically.

A list of resources for legal writers is at <u>ualr.edu/cmbarger/resources.htm</u>.

CHAPTER SUMMARY

This chapter led you through the writing process. This will ensure thoroughness. Before writing, determine the purpose of your assignment. This will guide your writing. Also, determine the audience for your work. This will determine the style of your writing. Carefully outline the document before writing and then revise the document by preparing an outline of the material that you prepared, an after-the-fact outline. Review the after-the-fact outline to make sure that it is logically organized and includes all points that the issues require to be addressed.

    The time that you spend in the prewriting stage ensures a better work product that is produced more efficiently than one created by lunging into the writing process. Think about what you want to say, outline it, and write it using good grammar and correct spelling. Then rewrite and edit your work. Prewriting takes planning, but with the methodology outlined in this chapter you will be equipped to write.

KEY TERMS

audience   prewriting stage
clarity   purpose
organization   rewriting
outline

EXERCISES

PREPARING TO WRITE

1. Why would you use a process method for legal writing?
2. Why would you outline before you write as well as create an outline of your finished document?
3. Why is it important to determine the audience and purpose before writing?

PROCESS WRITING EXERCISE

4. Read the following fact pattern and answer the questions.

Facts

John Clark comes to your firm with a question regarding the tax status of his residence. He has just been ordained as a United Methodist minister and will be receiving a housing allowance from First United Methodist Church, where he will be an assistant pastor. He wants to know if this housing allowance can be excluded from income on his tax return even though the residence is his own.

   a. How would you phrase this issue if you were researching this problem?
   b. What would be your research strategy?
   c. Construct an outline of this problem.

5. The assignment partner requests that you draft a letter of your findings to Rev. Clark. List, in detail, the purpose, audience, and resulting outline of the letter.
6. How would the purpose, audience, and outline change if the assignment partner requests a memo concerning your research findings? Once again, how would the purpose, audience, and outline change if you are requested to prepare a court brief?

IN-CLASS

1. For this exercise, use a paper that you have already written.
   a. Examine the paper. What is the purpose and the audience?
   b. Extract an outline from the paper. Outline the ideas explained in the paper.
   c. Revise your outline to clarify your ideas.
2. Write a letter to a neighbor discussing the highlights of the past season.
   a. What is the audience and, consequently, the tone?

b. Rewrite the letter to a government official. In the rewritten letter, express dissatisfaction with a service that is supposed to be provided by the local government and was not provided adequately during the past season. For example, in the letter to your neighbor, you write about the great snowfall during the winter. In the rewritten letter to a government official, you also write about the great snowfall, but also include how the locality failed to plow sufficiently. What is the purpose and audience of the letter to the government official?

CLEAR WRITING AND EDITING

CHAPTER OVERVIEW

The key to effective writing is clarity. Preparing a first draft of a document can be quite an undertaking, but that is only a start. You have not completed your project until you have carefully edited your work and prepare one or two more drafts. This chapter provides you with guidance in editing and revising your documents and preparing them for clients, courts, and attorneys.

A. PURPOSE OF EDITING

Editing and revising are essential if you want to have well-drafted and organized documents. A well-drafted document is one in which your readers understand what you are trying to convey. Be clear and make it easy to read. Few documents are written well after one draft. Good writing entails rewriting. Each time you review your document and revise it, you improve its content and make it more understandable. **Editing** allows you to review your word choices, your grammar, your spelling, your outline and organization of each sentence and paragraph, as well as the outline and organization of the entire document. It enables you to determine whether the document you wrote is clear and will be understood by your audience. Editing also provides you with the opportunity to enhance your work with additional thoughts and clarify your document by eliminating unnecessary words, ideas, and legalese.

B. PROCESS OF EDITING

The process of editing starts with a first draft and often ends after many more drafts. After you complete your first draft, you must proofread and edit your work. Consider each word you select. Review your outline and organization for each sentence and paragraph.

When you review your draft, you should read it as if you were reading it for the first time. Pretend that you are a stranger to the project and that you don't know anything about it. Ensure that it is understandable. If you have time, put the first draft aside for a day or two and then review it again. It will give you a fresh perspective.

Next, consider whether each part follows the next. The work should flow in a logical order. Consider whether the organization of the document or of any paragraphs or sentences should be revised. Question the structure and organization of each sentence and paragraph. Change passive voice sentences to active voice. For more discussion of passive and action voice, review this chapter Section C-2 Voice.

Read your writing aloud. Do you notice anything is missing? Sometimes when you read your work aloud, you find that it is missing something needed to get you from point A to point B in the discussion. Add any such missing elements.

Note whether your writing contains transitions and easily flows from one section to the next. If it doesn't, revise it. Add transitional words, phrases, or sentences where necessary. **Transitions** help move readers from one sentence to the next and from one paragraph to the next.

Next, think about whether you can eliminate unnecessary words, a process called tightening or editing. Focus on your words. Change elaborate or unfamiliar words to simpler words—often those you used in grade school. Doing so makes your writing inviting rather than pompous. Make certain that your words provide the reader with a visual image of what you mean. Ensure that your words accurately

convey your ideas. For additional information about word choice, see this chapter Section C-1 Diction.

Review your grammar. Ensure that your punctuation is correct and that the elements of each sentence and paragraph are correct. Check your citation for errors as well.

C. SPECIFIC ITEMS TO REVIEW WHILE EDITING

1. Diction

▼ What Is Diction?

Diction means choice of words when writing. Selecting the appropriate words to express your idea precisely is a skill that is developed over time. When you are revising a document, read it over to make sure that the words you selected convey your ideas precisely. Sometimes you must use a dictionary or thesaurus to assist you in selecting the best word.

Select concrete words that allow the readers to visualize what you are saying. Read the following example:

He harmed one of his body parts in the device at issue in the case.

It is better to say:

His arm was severed when the threshing machine stalled and he fell forward in front of the machine.

The second example is clearer because the reader knows what happened and to which body part it happened: The arm was severed. The second sentence also conveys that the device was a threshing machine and that it stalled, throwing the man forward.

▼ What Are Concrete Verbs?

Use **concrete verbs** that exactly describe the action taken. Read the following examples:

The parties entered into an agreement on September 1, 2008.

There was an agreement entered into on September 1, 2008.

The parties agreed to the terms on September 1, 2008.

The last example is the best because it is the simplest and uses the word *agreed* as a verb rather than as a noun. It is the easiest sentence of the three to understand and to visualize.

The first two examples turn the verb *agree* into a noun, a process called **nominalization.** The following illustrates a second example:

The parties entered into an agreement on October 15, 1994, to make a change in the purchase price of the original contract from $1,500 to $2,000.

It is better to say:

The parties agreed to increase the purchase price of the original contract from $1,500 to $2,000.

In the second sentence, *entered into an agreement* becomes *agreed* and *to make a change* becomes *increase.* These changes eliminate the use of verbs as nouns.

Another example is as follows:

The plaintiff made a statement to police that the defendant ran a red light before the crash.

It is better to say:

The plaintiff told police that the defendant ran the red light before the crash.

or

The plaintiff stated to police that the defendant ran the red light before the crash.

Select simpler words and make sentences short. Review the following example.

Prior to 9/11, airport security was incomplete.

It is better to say:

Before 9/11, airport security was lax.

Before is a simpler word than *prior to* and *lax* is more descriptive than *incomplete.*

Review these statements and determine which is clearer.

The state driver's license bureau now requires a social security card as **verification** of a person's identity.

or

The state driver's license bureau now requires a social security card as **proof** of a person's identity.

The second sentence is clearer. The use of the simple word *proof* rather than the pompous word *verification* makes the sentence easier to understand.

▼ How Do You Avoid Legalese or Legal Speak?

Avoid **legalese** or **legal speak.** What does this mean? Use plain English that your nonattorney clients would use. Consider your audience. Clear writing avoids using unnecessary legal words. For example, do not use the word *scienter* for *intent*. At the end of an affidavit, you often see the phrase *Further affiant sayeth not,* which means that the person signing the affidavit has nothing further to say. Because that should be clear without the legalistic phrase, skip it (and others like it) that add nothing to your writing.

2. Voice

Voice is the tone of your document. In professional writing, the document's tone is formal. Selecting language that is not colloquial and avoiding slang are ways to ensure that the tone of the document is correct for the law firm or corporate legal department environment. Avoid anything that personalizes the contents. Never use the first person. Conjunctions like *can't* are more casual than *cannot*. When revising, be sensitive to the tone of your document; it should have the requisite formal voice.

▼ What Is the Difference Between Active Voice and Passive Voice?

Active voice is when the subject of the sentence is doing the action of the verb. Active voice emphasizes the actor. Active voice is the preferred voice because it is clearer, more concise, and more lively.

Active voice: Harold hit a home run.
           Diane danced the tango.

Passive voice is when the subject of the sentence is being acted on. Although passive voice has its uses, it is generally wordier and not as strong as active voice.

Passive voice: The home run was hit by Harold.
           The tango was danced by Diane.

Often the word *by* is used in a passive voice sentence. When you see the word *by*, consider rewriting the sentence.

Passive example: Their initial quote for heat stamping equipment was rejected by Bailey.

Rewritten example: Bailey rejected their initial quote for heat stamping equipment.

The second example is clearer and more concise.

Passive voice, however, is sometimes acceptable. In some cases, the person or thing performing the action is unknown. For example:

Taxes were not deducted from her paychecks.

Walker received health and life insurance benefits.

In other cases, the actor does not need to be mentioned because he or she is less important than the action. If you believe it advantageous to change the emphasis of the sentence from the person doing the action to the action, use passive voice. For example, if your client is the defendant in a proceeding and you do not want to emphasize her action, you would write a sentence in passive voice, as follows:

The action stems from a contract dispute in which goods were rejected by the defendant.

This sentence in active voice would emphasize the defendant, as follows:

The defendant rejected the goods, resulting in a contract dispute.

3. Paragraphs

A **paragraph** is a collection of statements that focus on the same general subject. Effective paragraphs have a unified purpose, a thesis or topic sentence, and transitions between sentences.

The **topic sentence** is generally the first sentence of a paragraph; it tells the reader the subject of the paragraph. This sentence also indicates that a new topic will be discussed. In legal writing, this sentence often introduces the issue or subissues that will be discussed within the paragraph.

You should use transitions to guide your reader from one paragraph to the next. Transitions tell the reader that the ideas follow from each other and are related. A transitional sentence ties two paragraphs together. Think of this sentence as a bridge. Whenever you start your new paragraph, think about how you will relate it to the previous paragraph.

4. Sentences

A **sentence** is a statement that conveys a single idea. It generally should be written in active voice and must include a subject and predicate. To

avoid confusing your reader, do not place the subject too far from the verb. The focus of your sentence should be the idea you wish to convey. Do not make your readers work too hard to understand your sentence. Be direct and to the point. Keep your sentences short, generally not more than 25 words. As with any rule, you may break this rule about sentence length, but be careful not to make your sentences too complex.

One common mistake in writing sentences is to use a sentence fragment or incomplete sentence.

Incomplete sentence: The extent of the employer's control and supervision over the worker.

Complete sentence: The court will consider the extent of the employer's control and supervision over the worker.

The first example is a sentence fragment. It is incomplete and is missing a verb. The second sentence is a complete thought. It contains both a subject and a verb.

5. Other Key Rules

Do not start your paragraph or sentence with a citation. Instead, start with the rule summarizing the cited authority.

Use quotations sparingly. Most often, you can paraphrase what a court decision or other authority states. Your words convey the concept more clearly to the reader. Direct quotations that are used to convey an idea often are cluttered with unnecessary words or do not effectively explain a concept in the context of your use of the quotation. An added bonus for you when you paraphrase a court decision or other authority is that you are forced to analyze carefully the language of the authority. This ensures that you understand the concepts presented.

Review the following paragraph. Note that unnecessary words are located in parentheses.

The plaintiff (made a statement) that in his (own) opinion, during (the course of) (a period of) a year, the defendant (completely) destroyed the furniture the plaintiff hired the defendant to restore. The defendant failed to warn the plaintiff (in advance) that he couldn't restore the piece (properly) and that the price of the work originally estimated (roughly) at $600 would now cost her $2200.

None of the words in parentheses add anything to the reader's understanding of the sentences or paragraph. The phrase *made a statement* should be shortened to *stated*. When you read your paragraphs, review each word and determine whether it adds to the sentence. If not, delete it.

REVISION CHECKLIST

1. Does the material make sense?
2. Do the words accurately convey what happened?
3. Can the reader visualize what occurred?
4. Is it logical?
5. Should the organization of the sentence be changed?
6. Does one sentence follow from the next?
7. Are there any gaps in the sentence?
8. Are there any gaps in the paragraph?
9. Does one paragraph flow into the other?
10. Should the paragraphs be rearranged?
11. Are there any punctuation errors?
12. Are any words misspelled?
13. Are there any typographical errors?
14. Are there any citation errors?

CHAPTER SUMMARY

This chapter led you through the editing process generally and then more specifically. It outlined essential items to check during your editing process.

Choose your words carefully. Select concrete verbs and avoid legalese. Most often, use active voice in which the subject of the sentence is doing the action of the verb.

Make sure your paragraphs focus on a single subject or aspect of a subject and use topic and transition sentences. Use full sentences that are direct and convey the idea you intend.

Use quotations sparingly to effectively convey your messages.

KEY TERMS

active voice   paragraph
concrete verbs   passive voice
diction   sentence
editing   topic sentence
legal speak   transitions
legalese   voice
nominalization

EXERCISES

1. Eliminate the unnecessary words from the following statements:

   At the time when the parties entered into the agreement of purchase and sale it is important to note that neither of them had knowledge of contents of the dresser drawer. Because of the fact that previous to the contract the seller did not own the dresser and the seller's mother had not had many

valuable pieces of jewelry despite having a large income, the seller had made the assumption that the dresser did not contain anything. Due to the fact that the seller had made a statement to the buyer of the fact that his mother did not own any jewelry in the buyer's thinking, he had no purpose to make any further investigation or inspection of the drawers as he might otherwise have considered making. For these reasons, there was no provision in the contract for an upward modification in the payment to be made by the buyer to the seller in the event that the dresser drawer later proved to be filled with jewels.

2. The police report said that Mr. Harris had a blood alcohol level of 1.7 based on an on-site blood alcohol test and states further that there were swerve marks on the street. The report also stated that there were no brake marks and that the driver was cited by the officer for drunk driving.
3. The personnel manager did all of the hiring and firing of the restaurant and golf course and the part-time accountant manages all bookkeeping and tax work for the restaurant and golf course.
4. Candy Graham who did not have an employment contract was, despite her freedom to set her own hours and work from her own home, also an employee.
5. Which is the best sentence? Why?
   a. A modification to the contract occurred on July 8, 1998.
   b. There was a modification of the contract July 8, 1998.
   c. Harry and Morgan modified their contract on July 8, 1998.

TIGHTENING
6. At approximately 7:30 P.M. on May 4, 1992, the plaintiff, Lidia Gregory, was weeding the front garden at her home at 2099 Vista Drive in Phoenix. She was about five feet from the street. The children also were playing in the front yard which was near the street.
7. Based on a blood alcohol test done at the scene of the accident, it was determined that Ronnie Walden was intoxicated.
8. The day the accident occurred it was very clear and had not rained to make the road slick.
9. The issue is whether or not it is a nuisance.

SCREENING FOR LEGALESE—SAY IT IN ENGLISH, PLEASE
10. In the aforementioned case, the funeral home was not found to be a nuisance because the court held that the funeral home in question was "reasonably located on the outskirts of the city."
11. Now comes the plaintiff, by and through her attorney, causes this complaint to be filed with the court.
12. Further affiant sayest not.
13. The party of the first part claims that the party of the second part said that he wanted to cause her to go out of business.

ACTIVE AND PASSIVE EXERCISES

14. Two businesses are owned by Ned and Wally Maine and they are being sued in federal court by two former workers for sex discrimination.
15. Cammy Ashton's office supplies and office were provided by Whole In One.
16. The funeral home was controlled by William Halsey and owned jointly by Halsey and Ivy Courier.

WRITING BASICS

CHAPTER OVERVIEW

This chapter reinforces grammar concepts and focuses on problem areas. It provides concrete examples of grammatically correct and incorrect sentences and explains the difference. Because it cannot address all points of grammar that students need to know, it suggests other grammar resources for your consideration.

A. PUNCTUATION

The punctuation of a sentence, especially the placement of a comma, can change the meaning of that sentence. Therefore, you must carefully place each punctuation mark. The following provides you with some basic rules for checking your punctuation placement.

1. Commas

Commas tell a reader to pause. Use commas to separate a series of items. For example:

Wally ran to the school, the store, the baseball field, and then home.

Be careful not to use commas to divide run-on sentences. These are sentences that contain two separate sentences.

Incorrect:	Tildy's role is merely advisory, although she might be called on to supply facts about the spill, her opinion probably would not form the basis of any final decision.
Correct:	Tildy's role is merely advisory. Although she might be called on to supply facts about the spill, her opinion probably would not form the basis of any final decision.

In the second example, the two sentences are correctly separated with a period. You also could use a semicolon. For some run-on sentences, you could divide the sentences with a comma and a conjunction. In the above example, that solution would not cure the problem completely because the second sentence is too long.

Commas also are used to set apart parenthetical phrases. In such a situation, commas should be used in pairs.

The defendant, Larry Dwyer, filed an answer to the complaint.

The name *Larry Dwyer* is parenthetical because the meaning of the sentence would not be changed if the name was omitted. In contrast, read the following examples:

Judges who take bribes should be indicted.

Judges, who take bribes, should be indicted.

In these examples, the phrase *who take bribes* is not parenthetical. If it was omitted, the sentence would say, "judges should be indicted." The phrase

who take bribes must be part of the sentence to convey the correct meaning. Therefore, it is not parenthetical, and the commas should be omitted.

Place commas around unnecessary words or phrases. For example, a client has one child, William, and wants to name him as the executor of her estate. In a document to name him as executor, you could use either of the following sentences and the meaning would not be altered.

> I name my son, William, as the executor of my estate.

> I name my son as the executor of my estate.

Do not place commas around words or phrases that are necessary in order to understand a sentence.

In the next example, your client has two sons, William and Randall. She wants William to be the executor of the estate. The document should read as follows:

> I name my son William as the executor of my cstatc.

The following sentence would be incorrect:

> I name my son, William, as the executor of my estate.

2. Special Comma Rules

Commas separate a year from the date.

> The plaintiff and the defendant agreed to the settlement on November 15, 1998.

Commas also set off the date from a specific reference to a day of the week.

> The judge decided the summary judgment motion on Monday, November 7, 1998.

Commas separate a proper name from a title that follows it.

> The plaintiff sued RAM Enterprises and Samuel Harris, company president.

Commas and periods should always appear inside quotation marks. This rule is often mistakenly broken.

> "But I wasn't in Toledo on the night of the murder," the defendant protested. "I was in Boca Raton with my elderly mother."

3. Semicolons

Semicolons are similar to commas because they tell a reader to pause and they break apart thoughts. Semicolons are used to separate two independent sentences.

Two sentences:	The paralegal's responsibilities are broad. They include summarization of depositions.
One sentence:	The paralegal's responsibilities are broad; they include summarization of depositions.

Semicolons separate clauses of a compound sentence when an adverbial conjunction joins the two.

> The defendants presented a good case; however, they lost.

Semicolons are used to separate phrases in a list.

> The committee members were Robert Harris, vice president of Harris Enterprises; Edna Williams, owner of Walworth Products; Barbara Halley, an attorney; and Benjamin Marcus, an accountant.

4. Colons

Colons are marks of introduction: what follow are explanations, conclusions, amplifications, lists or series, or quotations. A colon is always preceded by a main clause, one that can stand alone as a sentence. A main clause may or may not follow a colon.

> Help was on the way: Someone had called the police.

> Sandra had two assignments: a five-page paper and a book report.

> The mayor stepped to the podium: "I regretfully must submit my resignation."

Colons should appear only at the end of a main clause. They should never directly follow a verb or a preposition.

Incorrect:	The hours of the museum are: 10:00 A.M. to 6:00 P.M.
Correct:	The hours of the museum are 10:00 A.M. to 6:00 P.M.
Incorrect:	Marc loved many sports, such as: soccer, tennis, and softball.
Correct:	Marc loved many sports, such as soccer, tennis, and softball.

As with any punctuation mark, use colons only when they best serve your writing purpose. Do not overuse them.

5. Parentheses

Parentheses tell the reader that the idea is an afterthought or is outside the main idea of a sentence.

> The tort involved a banana peel (the classic culprit) and a crowded grocery store.

Use parentheses infrequently because they tend to break the flow of the sentence.

6. Double Quotation Marks

These marks enclose direct quotations.

> The judge said, "The trial date will not be continued."

Note that the first word of the quotation should be capitalized if it is a complete sentence.

7. Single Quotation Marks

These marks are used to define a quotation within a quotation.

> The client told the lawyer, "My boss said, 'You cannot be a good accountant and be a good mother,' and then he fired me."

If you end a quotation with quoted words, you place a single quotation mark and follow it with a double quotation mark.

> The witness testified, "The robber said, 'Give me all your money.' "

B. MODIFIERS

Modifiers provide a description about a subject, a verb, or an object in your sentence. If you misplace a modifier, you might confuse your reader or convey an incorrect message. A modifier should be placed in proximity to the subject, verb, or object it modifies.

Incorrect: Deadlocked for more than two days, the judge asked the jury to continue to deliberate.

Correct: The jury had been deadlocked for two days. Nonetheless, the judge asked the jury to continue to deliberate.

In the first example, the phrase *deadlocked for more than two days* incorrectly modifies the judge rather than the jury. This is a dangling modifier.

C. PARALLEL CONSTRUCTION

Parallel construction is when you make each of the phrases within your sentence follow the same grammatical pattern or number. A plural subject must have a plural verb. A singular subject must have a singular verb. You also must use parallel tenses when you are listing a series of activities. A parallel grammatical pattern makes your writing balanced.

Incorrect:	The paralegal association set the following goals: recruitment of new members, educating the community, and improvement of paralegal work conditions.
Correct:	The paralegal association set the following goals: recruitment of new members, education of the community, and improvement of paralegal work conditions.

In the correct example, the words *recruitment, education,* and *improvement* are parallel.

D. SUBJECT AND VERB AGREEMENT

Subject and verb agreement, so essential to proper sentence construction, causes great confusion for many writers. The following are sample situations in which errors are most often made. You must use plural pronouns and verbs when the subjects are plural.

Incorrect:	Software Developments Inc. sent Cheryl Faith, a company sales representative, and Mark Gaines, their plant manager, to Bailey's plant.
Correct:	Software Developments Inc. sent Cheryl Faith, a company sales representative, and Mark Gaines, its plant manager, to Bailey's plant.

The second example is correct because *Software Developments Inc.* is a singular subject; therefore, the pronoun before *plant manager* should be the singular possessive *its* rather than *their.*

Incorrect:	To assert the attorney-client privilege, the claimant must show that the statements were made in confidence and was made to an attorney for the purpose of obtaining legal advice.
Correct:	To assert the attorney-client privilege, the claimant must show that the statements were made in confidence and were made to an attorney for the purpose of obtaining legal advice.

The second example is correct because the verbs must be plural when they have a plural noun. In this example, the word *statements* should have a plural verb.

If you have a singular subject, then each of the pronouns in the sentence that describes that subject should be singular.

Incorrect: To receive this protection in the corporate setting, an individual must show that they were a decision-making employee.
Correct: To receive this protection in the corporate setting, an individual must show that he or she was a decision-making employee.

Collective nouns such as *jury, court, committee,* and *group* often pose a problem for writers. They take a singular verb because they are considered one unit. For example, *jury* is considered one unit; it refers to the group, not to individual jurors.

Incorrect: The jury were to eat lunch at noon.
Correct: The jury was to eat lunch at noon.

Compound subjects also cause confusion. Subjects joined by the word *and* usually use a plural verb, regardless of whether any or all of the individual subject are singular.

Incorrect: The attorney and the paralegal was available for the client.
Correct: The attorney and the paralegal were available for the client.

When a compound subject is preceded by *each* or *every*, the verb is usually singular.

Incorrect: Each attorney and paralegal in the room have access to the library.
Correct: Each attorney and paralegal in the room has access to the library.

When a compound subject is joined by *or* or *nor*, it takes a singular verb if each subject is singular. It takes a plural verb if each subject is plural. If one subject is singular and the other is plural, the verb follows the closest subject.

Subjects singular: An apple or an orange is my favorite snack.
Subjects plural: Apples or oranges are my favorite snacks.
Subjects singular and plural: Neither the mother nor the children were happy.

To avoid awkwardness, place the plural noun closest to the verb so that the verb is plural.

Awkward: Neither the dogs nor the cat was anywhere in sight.
  Revised: Neither the cat nor the dogs were anywhere in sight.

Indefinite pronouns may also throw up roadblocks for writers. Indefinite pronouns are those that do not refer to a specific person or thing. Some common indefinite pronouns are

all	nobody
any	none
anyone	nothing
each	one
either	some
everyone	something

Most indefinite pronouns refer to singular subjects and therefore take a singular verb.

Incorrect: Everyone are free to go. Each of the stores were open on Sunday.
  Correct: Everyone is free to go. Each of the stores was open on Sunday.

Some indefinite pronouns (all, any, none, some) may take either a singular or plural verb depending on the meaning of the word they refer to.

Singular: All of the library was quiet. (The library was quiet.)
  Plural: All of the paralegals were researching the case. (The paralegals were researching the case.)

PRACTICE POINTER

Consult these books for additional guidance:

The Elements of Style by William Strunk, Jr., and E.B. White
The Careful Writer: A Modern Guide to English Usage by Theodore Bernstein

CHAPTER SUMMARY

This chapter reviewed basic grammar rules concerning punctuation, modifiers, parallel construction, and subject-verb agreement. It emphasized the importance correct grammar plays in legal writing by demonstrating how errors like incorrect punctuation, misplaced modifiers, and faulty subject-verb agreement can affect meaning.

KEY TERMS

collective nouns
colons
commas
compound subjects
indefinite pronouns

modifiers
parallel construction
parentheses
semicolons

EXERCISES

Edit the following sentences. Name the grammar mistake in each sentence (e.g., misplaced modifier, faulty parallelism, and so forth). Then correct the error by rewriting the sentence.

1. At a time when many law firms and corporations are eliminating jobs for the purpose of elimination from the budget excess expenditures, paralegals may become more of an asset.

2. Because of the fact that paralegals' time is charged at lower rates, paralegals may be employed by law firms and corporations to perform tasks previously performed by lawyers.

3. With specificity, paralegals may be asked to perform legal research of case and statutory materials in the event that a client requests an answer to a problem of a legal nature and is concerned about saving money.

4. In the situation where a paralegal is well trained, that paralegal can be asked by an attorney to perform legal research for the purpose of determining a response to the client's question.

5. With regard to ethical considerations, paralegals can perform legal research under the supervision of an attorney.

6. Subsequent to the research, however, the attorney must be the person who renders the legal opinions that need to be made, the reason being that a paralegal cannot provide legal advice.

7. It is important to note that some states are considering allowing paralegals to practice independently.

8. Try this schedule; shower, eat breakfast, drive to the train, go to work, and come home.

9. There are only one hour and thirty-five minutes left to voir dire, the judge stated.

10. Among the defendants was Craig Fisher, David Michaels, and Mitchell White.

11. The prosecutor will attempt to within the course of the trial persuade you that the defendant committed the crime.

12. The foreman, as well as half of the jury, were late for the afternoon court session.
13. Every one of the councilmen we have named to the commission want to serve.
14. The heart of a trial are the witnesses.
15. None of the players were willing to sign contracts.
16. The substance of Walter Mondale's speeches is more similar to Jimmy Carter.
17. The house was vacated by the tenants.
18. The judge said to the jurors ", please refrain from discussing the case."
19. Four of the five jurors were men (These were Steer, Halsey, Grodsky, and Eirinberg.).
20. In her testimony, the witness said she remembered that the defendant asked her "Do you have an aspirin"?
21. These modems are shared with the other subscribers, so the more people on the connection the slower.
22. Working at a law firm from 8:30 A.M. to 5 P.M. handling high-level paralegal work may seem ideal, especially if you rarely work weekends.
23. The National Association of Paralegals said 12 percent of the law firms responded to their survey.
24. Mrs. Gephart, at first thought her son, Patrick, was dead because of the amount of blood and broken bones that surrounded the car.
25. The extent of the employer's control and supervision over the worker, including directions on scheduling and performance of work.

CASE BRIEFING AND ANALYSIS

CHAPTER OVERVIEW

This chapter teaches you a skill called case briefing. It introduces you to each of the components of a case brief: the issue, the holding, the facts, the rationale or reasoning, and the disposition. It also introduces you to the concept of dicta. You will learn what to include in each section of the brief and how to skillfully draft the brief.

Case briefing is a skill that you must master to effectively record your research results and analyze a case. Often attorneys will ask you to summarize a case in the form of a case brief. The key to a good brief

is that it must be usable. You must be able to return to the brief months after you have prepared it and still be able to quickly understand the facts, the issues, the holdings, and the reasoning of the court.

A good case brief can be done in a variety of ways. Always ask an attorney if he or she has a preference. If not, you should consider the method discussed in this chapter.

A. PURPOSE OF A CASE BRIEF

The goal in writing a case brief is to summarize a court decision. A well-drafted brief saves you time because you do not have to reread the original decision to understand its significance. You are able to review the brief to obtain any necessary information. The next goal in briefing a case is to put the components of a decision in a uniform format. This is why we have specified eight set categories for a brief: citation, procedural facts, issues, holding, facts, rationale, dicta, and disposition. However, many attorneys use their own uniform format, and sometimes that format will depend on why you are briefing a case.

Sometimes you must brief cases in response to a particular legal issue that you are researching. Sometimes you must brief cases just to summarize decisions.

Remember that a brief is a case summary in a uniform format with established categories of information. The set categories make it easier to compare and contrast decisions. Also, this enables you to see how a case supports a client's problem.

B. DIAGRAM OF A DECISION

Before you begin to write your brief, read the case thoroughly several times. See Illustration 18-1. Consider the questions the court was asked to decide. Determine the parties in the action and what each party is seeking. Sometimes this is complicated, and it helps to draw a diagram of the parties. For example, when the parties are involved in a three-way dispute such as a cross-claim, it might take some time to determine what each party is seeking. Make a column for each party in which you list an issue raised and a remedy sought. After you have read the case, you are ready to write the case brief.

Write the brief in your own words and paraphrase rather than quote a court's statements unless the statements are well phrased, concise, and understandable. Paraphrasing helps you analyze a case and allows you to understand the brief quickly when you return to it later. Also, paraphrasing cases helps when you are writing about an opinion in a memo. The memo will read more smoothly if you import the information from case brief that is written in your own voice.

ILLUSTRATION 18-1.   Sample Case, *Seymour v. Armstrong*

Westlaw.

64 P. 612
62 Kan. 720
(Cite as: 64 P. 612)   (1)

Supreme Court of Kansas.

SEYMOUR   (2)
v.
ARMSTRONG et al.

April 6, 1901.   (3)

Syllabus by the Court.

(4) 1. A contract may originate in an advertisement or offer addressed to the public generally, and, if the offer be accepted by any one in good faith, without qualifications or conditions, it will be sufficient to convert the offer into a binding obligation.

2. If the acceptor affixes conditions to his acceptance not comprehended in the proposal, there can be no agreement without the assent of the proposer to such conditions.

3. If persons carrying on a trade or business give to words and phrases a technical or peculiar meaning, they will be presumed to have contracted with reference to such meaning or usage, unless the contrary appears.

4. Where a term employed in a written contract has a meaning different from the ordinary meaning when used in connection with a trade or business, evidence is admissible to show such meaning, and the sense in which it was used by the parties.

Error from court of appeals, Northern department, Eastern division.

Action by T. F. Seymour against Armstrong & Kassebaum. Judgment for defendants was affirmed by the court of appeals (61 Pac. 675), and plaintiff brings error. Affirmed.

West Headnotes

(5) Contracts ⊂⊃18
95k18 Most Cited Cases

A contract may originate in an advertisement or offer addressed to the public generally, and, if the offer be accepted by any one in good faith, without qualifications or conditions, it will be sufficient to convert the offer into a binding obligation.

Contracts ⊂⊃23
95k23 Most Cited Cases

Where the acceptor affixes conditions to his acceptance not

comprehended in the proposal, there can be no agreement without the assent of the proposer to such conditions.

Contracts ⊂⊃175(1)
95k175(1) Most Cited Cases

Where persons carrying on a trade or business give to words and phrases a technical or peculiar meaning, they will be presumed to have contracted with reference to such meaning or usage, unless the contrary appears.

Evidence ⊂⊃456
157k456 Most Cited Cases

Where a term employed in a written contract has a meaning different from the ordinary meaning when used in connection with a trade or business, evidence is admissible to show such meaning, and the sense in which it was used by the parties.
*612 J. A. Rosen and David Martin, for plaintiff in error.

Isenhart & Alexander, for defendants in error.

JOHNSTON, J.   (6)

(7) This was an action to recover damages for the breach of an alleged contract. On February 15, 1896, Armstrong & Kassebaum, commission merchants of Topeka, inserted an advertisement in a weekly newspaper, which, among other things, contained the following proposition: "We will pay 10 1/2 c., net Topeka, for all fresh eggs shipped us to arrive here by February 22. Acceptance of our bid with number of cases stated to be sent by February 20th." On February 20, (8) 1896, T. F. Seymour, a rival commission merchant of Topeka, sent the following note to Armstrong & Kassebaum

1 Citation
2 Case name
3 Date of decision
4 Syllabus by court
5 West key numbers and headnotes (written by west editors and not part of the opinion)
6 Judge's name authoring the opinion
7 Opinion
8 Facts

ILLUSTRATION 18-1. *Continued*

Westlaw.

64 P. 612
62 Kan. 720
(Cite as: 64 P. 612)

refused to receive the eggs, and Seymour shipped them to Philadelphia, where they were sold for $391.83 less than they would have brought at the price named in Seymour's note of acceptance. For this amount the present action was brought, and the plaintiff is entitled to recover if the defendants' offer on eggs was unconditionally accepted. At (9) the trial a verdict was returned in favor of the defendants, and the result of the general finding is that the pretended acceptance of Seymour was not unconditional, and that no contract was, in fact, made between him and the defendants.

(11A) Did the negotiations between the parties result in a contract? A contract may originate in an advertisement addressed to the public generally, and, if the proposal be accepted by any one in good faith, without qualifications or conditions, the contract is complete. The fact that there was no limit as to (10) number or quantity of eggs in the offer did not prevent an acceptance. The number or quantity was left to the determination of the acceptor, and an unconditional acceptance naming any reasonable number or quantity is (12A) sufficient to convert the offer into a binding obligation. It is essential, however, that the minds of the contracting parties should come to the point of agreement,-- that the offer and acceptance should coincide; and, if they do not correspond in every material respect, there is no acceptance or completed contract. In our view, the so-called "acceptance" of the plaintiff is not absolute and unconditional. It affixed conditions not comprehended in the proposal, and there could be no agreement without the assent of the proposer to (10) such conditions. It is true, the plaintiff agreed to furnish eggs at 10 1/2 cents per dozen, but his acceptance required the defendant to pay 15 cents each for the cases in which the eggs were packed, or to return the cases, or new ones in place of them. It appears from the record that according to the usages of the business the cases go with the eggs, as was done in this case.

One of the grounds of complaint is that the court erred in admitting testimony as to the sense in which the word "net" (11B) was used in the negotiations between the parties, and in submitting to the jury the question of whether the offer of the defendants was accepted. The plaintiff is hardly in a position to question the propriety of receiving evidence as to the meaning of the word "net," used in the offer and acceptance. *613 He was the first to open an inquiry, and to bring out testimony as to what was meant by the term when used in connection with a sale of eggs. Aside from that consideration, the term appears to have a meaning in connection with the business different from the ordinary meaning, and in such case evidence of the meaning given by usage of the trade or business is admissible. If persons (12B) carrying on a particular trade or business give to words or phrases a technical or peculiar meaning, they will be

presumed to contract with reference to the usage, unless the contrary appears. There was abundant evidence to show that the use of the word "net," according to the usage of the business, includes the cases of eggs like the one in question. The witnesses stated that it means a price clear to the purchaser without commissions, cartage, or any charge for the cases. The finding of the jury, in effect, is that it was understood and agreed that the cases went with and were included in the price quoted for the eggs, and the acceptance, therefore, did not correspond with the offer, nor complete the contract. We think that under the circumstances parol testimony of the sense in which the terms were used, and as to what the parties intended by them, was properly received, and that the court properly charged the jury as to the elements entering into a contract. Cooper v. Nesbit, 45 Kan. 457, 25 Pac. 866. Others of the instructions are criticised, but we find nothing substantial in any of the objections made nor in any of the grounds assigned for reversal. The judgment of the court of appeals and the district court will be affirmed.

All the justices concurring (13)

(12A+B)

64 P. 612, 62 Kan. 720

END OF DOCUMENT

9 Procedure **10 Rationale or reasoning** **11A Issue 1** **11B Issue 2** **12A Holding 1** **12B Holding 2** **13 Disposition**

Reprinted with permission of Thomson Reuters/West.

C. ANATOMY OF A CASE BRIEF

Since a brief is a summary of a decision in a uniform format, there are set categories. You should label the remaining sections of the brief: citation, procedural history or procedure, issue, holding, rationale or reasoning, dicta (if it exists in the case), and disposition.

1. Citation

The case brief starts with a case citation, which allows you to find the case at a later date. First, note the name of the case, which is generally found at the top of the page. Then add the case citation or docket number of the case. See Illustration 18-3. Be sure to include the date of the decision and the name of the deciding court. Next, you might want to make a note concerning whether the decision is primary binding or primary persuasive authority. (For more information about binding and persuasive authority, see Chapter 2.) Follow either *Bluebook* or *ALWD* rules for case citation format.

Important tips for briefing cases are at cjed.com/brief.htm.

PRACTICE POINTER

Obtain all of the citation information when you are using the reporter or have accessed the case online. Once you record all of the citation information in the brief, you will not have to revisit the decision later to get the cite information.

ILLUSTRATION 18-2. **Sample Case,** *King v. Miller*

KING v. MILLER
1000 E.R. 108 (Karen Ct. App. 1998)

Evelyn King, an insurance agent who worked for the defendant, Miller Company, filed a lawsuit claiming that the defendant discriminated against her on the basis of her sex in violation of Title VII, 42 U.S.C. §2000e et seq. Upon a motion for summary judgment, the district court granted the motion in favor of Miller. The district court found that King was not an employee of the defendant. She did not work in a manner

ILLUSTRATION 18-2. *Continued*

consistent with an employee. The court said that King was an independent contractor. As an independent contractor, her discrimination claim was outside the protection of the federal law. King appealed the trial court's decision.

In 1992, King was hired by Miller to work as an "employee agent." As such, she was paid a salary. Income taxes and Social Security were withheld by Miller. She was promoted to "independent contract agent." King could not remain an employee agent for more than one year. When she was promoted she had to sign an agreement that stated that she was an independent contractor.

As an independent contract agent, King earned a commission on her sales and some bonuses. She did not receive any paid holidays, sick days, or vacation days. She paid for her own health, life, and disability insurance.

Miller, however, provided office space, furniture, file cabinets, rate books, forms, shared secretarial services, stamps, computers, and Miller's stationery. King purchased her own personalized stationery, pens, and business cards. Miller paid her tuition for required special insurance seminars, provided lunch at such programs, and rented the space for the sessions.

King had wanted to work for Miller because Miller had a good reputation. Before coming to Miller's office, King worked for three other insurance companies. King was a single, 30-year-old mother of two children. Before her experience in the insurance industry, she worked as a sales clerk at a local boutique.

While working as an independent contract agent for Miller, King could not sell insurance for any other company. She also could only sell insurance in the county designated by the company manager. She had to work at the Miller office three and one-half days a week and every third Saturday, attend two hour-long meetings each week, and retrieve mail every day.

King was responsible for finding her own customers and deciding which products to offer. She could set the hours she worked and she worked without direct supervision. Miller did not regularly review her work. King was fired in 1993, and a man was hired to take her place.

The district court found that based upon these facts, King was an independent contractor, not an employee, The court focused on the economic realities test. One of the factors it considered as part of its test for determining whether King was an employee or an independent contractor was Miller's right to control King. *Spirides v. Reinhardt,* 613 F.2d 826, 831 (D.C. Cir. 1979), is the leading case regarding the question of whether an individual is an employee under the federal discrimination laws or an independent contractor. The *Spirides* court adopted an 11-part test. These factors are:

> 1) the kind of occupation, whether the work is usually done under the direction of a supervisor or without a supervisor; 2) the skill required; 3) whether

ILLUSTRATION 18-2. *Continued*

the "employer" provides the equipment used and the workplace; 4) how long the individual has worked; 5) how the individual is paid, whether by assignment, piece, or time; 6) how the work relationship is to be terminated, i.e., was notice required; 7) whether vacation is provided; 8) whether retirement benefits are provided; 9) whether the employer deducts social security and income tax payments; 10) whether the work is an integral part of the employer's business; and 11) the intention of the parties.

Id.

The Karen district court focused on five of those factors: 1) the extent of Miller's control and supervision of King concerning scheduling and performance of work; 2) the kind of occupation and the nature of the skill required; 3) the division of the costs of the operation, equipment, supplies, and fees; 4) the method and form of payment and benefits; 5) length of job commitment. Central to its decision was the lack of control Miller exercised over King. The court found that King had a great deal of freedom to select her hours, her clients, and the insurance products she sold.

King must prove that an employment relationship existed between Miller and her in order to maintain a Title VII action against Miller. Independent contractors are not protected by Title VII. *Spirides,* 613 F.2d at 831. Title VII defines employee "as an individual employed by an employer." 42 U.S.C §2000E(f). "In determining whether the relationship is one of employee-employer, courts look to the 'economic realities' of the relationship and the degree of control the employer exercises over the alleged employee." See *Unger v. Consolidated Foods Corp.,* 657 F.2d 909, 915-916 n.8 (7th Cir. 1981).

On appeal, King contends that the district court placed too much weight on the "control factor" and the fact the Miller did not supervise King's work and did not dictate King's hours, products or customers. Based upon this emphasis, King argues that the district court's decision was erroneous.

However, this court finds that the district court correctly considered other facts such as that King was paid on commission, did not receive benefits, and provided many of her own supplies, including stationery and business cards.

Although this court was not asked to determine whether the district court should have considered all of the facts that were relevant to each of the 11 factors stated in the *Spirides'* economic realities test, this court finds that the district court should have done so.

Although we think that the district court should have focused its analysis on all 11 factors, we do not think that its decision is clearly erroneous; therefore, we affirm the decision of the district court in granting summary judgment for the defendant, Miller.

2. Procedural History

This section of the case brief should be labeled **procedural history** or simply procedure. These facts explain the status of the case. You will summarize how this case traveled through the court system to reach this point. See Illustration 18-3. In this section, you note the action of the prior courts. For example, if the decision concerns an appeal to a federal appellate court, note that. Also, state whether the court reversed or affirmed the lower court's decision and whether the case was remanded.

PRACTICE POINTER

Always validate any case that you brief by using *Shepard's* or KeyCite. Note the date validated at the top of the brief so that you know to update if necessary.

ILLUSTRATION 18-3. Sample Case Brief, *King v. Miller*

KING v. MILLER
1000 E.R. 108 (Karen Ct. App. 1998)

PROCEDURAL HISTORY
   The case was on appeal from the District Court's grant of summary judgment for the defendant Miller.

ISSUE
   Is King, a worker subject to only minimal company control and who was paid commissions rather than a salary and benefits, an employee protected by Title VII or an independent contractor who is outside the protection of the federal law?

HOLDING
   King, a worker subject to only minimal company control and who was paid commissions rather than a salary and benefits, was an independent contractor rather than an employee protected by Title VII.

FACTS
   King first worked for Miller as an employee agent. During that time, she received a salary and the company withheld income tax and social security payments. King later was promoted to independent contract agent.
   As an independent contract agent, King earned a commission and bonuses but did not receive a salary. She signed an agreement that stated that she was an independent contractor. As a contract agent, she did not receive paid holidays, sick days, or vacation days, and she

ILLUSTRATION 18-3.   *Continued*

paid for her own health, life, and disability insurance. King supplied her own personalized stationery, business cards, and pens. She found her own customers, decided which products to sell, and set her own hours.

For its contract agents, Miller supplied office space, furniture, file cabinets, forms, shared secretarial services, stamps, computers, and stationery. Miller also paid for required insurance seminars. Miller required that contract agents, such as King, attend weekly meetings, work in the office three and one-half days per week and every third Saturday, check their mail and retrieve messages daily, and sell only Miller insurance. Miller also restricted King's sales area. Miller did not regularly review King's work.

REASONING

In order to determine whether an individual is an employee or an independent contractor, the employment relationship between the parties needs to be evaluated based upon the economic realities and circumstances of the relationship. The court considered the control exercised by the "employer" over the worker; the method of payment; who paid for the individual's benefits, such as life and health insurance; and who paid for the operation. In this case, the court found that King was an independent contractor because she was paid on commission, she paid for her own benefits, she supplied her own supplies, and she controlled her work. The court found that she set her own hours, selected the product she sold, and generated her own clients. Based upon these facts, the appellate court found that King should be considered an independent contractor rather than an employee.

DICTA

The 11-part test set by the *Spirides* court should be applied to determine whether an individual is an employee or an independent contractor.

DISPOSITION

The Court of Appeals affirmed the district court's judgment in granting summary judgment for the defendant.

PRACTICE POINTER

After the facts and any other information you note in your brief, you should indicate in parentheses the pages from the case that contain the information noted. This step assists you when you summarize your research results in memorandum.

3. Issues

Next, list the issue or issues presented in the case. See Illustration 18-3. Although determining the issues in a case is a difficult process at first, it does get easier with practice.

The issues are the questions the parties asked the court to decide. In most cases, multiple issues are presented. To determine the issues, you must understand the legal rules that govern a particular case. If you are briefing a case and you have not been assigned an issue to research, list all the issues presented in the case. If you have been given a research assignment, you need only brief the issues that are relevant to your research, listing each one separately.

▼ How Do You Determine the Legal Issue or Issues Presented When Examining a Client's Problem?

To understand this process, assume you have been asked to research whether your firm's client, Whole In One, will be subject to the federal antidiscrimination laws. Whole In One is a seasonal restaurant and golf course in Glenview, Illinois. Two women, Victoria Radiant and Karen Walker, brought suit against Whole In One for sex discrimination. Their claims are based on a federal antidiscrimination statute commonly known as Title VII. You have been asked to research whether Whole In One is an employer and whether the women are employees under the definitions included in the federal law. During your research, you find the case of *King v. Miller*. Review Illustration 18-2.

To determine the issue, read the case. Ask yourself, "What did the parties ask the court to determine?" Sometimes the court will note the issue directly in its opinion. Other times, you must search through the opinion to determine the issue. After you have read the *King* case, you should note that it involves a question of sex discrimination. However, your research is limited to the issues that concern the definitions of *employer* and *employee*. Therefore, the case brief should focus on issues that relate to your research problem.

Once you have read the *King* case, you will find that it addresses the question of whether an individual is an employee protected by Title VII. Now you are ready to draft the issue.

▼ How Do You Draft a Statement of the Issue or Issues?

For the *King* case, you might start with this brief issue:

> Is King an employee protected by Title VII or an independent contractor who is outside the protection of the federal law?

Now that the issue is presented in question format, you could leave the issue section here. However, the issue would be more meaningful for your research if you included more information about the legal

issue the court focused on in making its determination. In its discussion, the *King* court focused on the amount of control that an employer must exercise before an individual is viewed as an employee rather than an independent contractor. You could incorporate the court's focus on control into the issue as follows:

> Is King, a worker subject to only minimal company control, an employee protected by Title VII, or an independent contractor who is outside the protection of the federal law?

You also should include relevant facts in your issue statement. Again, this will make the issue more meaningful for your research. In this case, for example, you might add some facts about the company's method of payment and its lack of provisions for benefits:

> Is King, a worker subject to only minimal company control who was paid commissions rather than salary and benefits, an employee protected by Title VII or an independent contractor who is outside the protection of the federal law?

The final issue statement is the best because it incorporates the relevant facts that affect a court's decision concerning this issue and the rule of law that will be applied.

You might wonder why the issue did not focus on the appellate court's consideration of the district court's action in granting the motion for summary judgment in favor of the defendant. Students often phrase such an issue as follows:

> Did the district court err in granting summary judgment in favor of the defendant?

However, this issue focuses too heavily on the procedural question posed in the *King* case and does not include the applicable law or any of the legally significant facts. Your issue should concern the legal, not the procedural, questions a court was asked to decide. As you learned above, the *King* case involved a motion for summary judgment.

To find the substantive legal issue, determine the legal question the parties asked the court to answer in the motion for summary judgment. In the *King* case, the parties asked the court to determine whether, as a matter of law, King was an independent contractor rather than an employee. This is the central legal issue. By focusing on this substantive issue rather than the procedural issue, your brief will be more useful to you in your research of the *Whole In One* case.

Some of you might wonder why you do not focus on the question of discrimination in your issue section. Remember the issue you were asked to answer with your research. You were asked to deal with the issues of the definitions of *employee* and *employer*. You should tailor your brief to address only these issues.

4. Holding

The next section should be your holding. A holding often is called the rule of law. Essentially a holding is the court's answer to the issue or question presented. However, it is not a yes, no, or maybe answer to the issue. The holding should be a full sentence that responds directly to the issue posed and that incorporates both the legal standards and the significant legal facts on which the answer is based. Ideally, the holding should be a nugget you can use later in a summary of your research. (This summary is called a *memorandum,* which we discuss in greater detail in Chapter 19.)

▼ How Do You Draft a Holding?

The process for drafting the holding is similar to the process for writing your issue statement. First, your holding should be a statement that answers the issue. Assume you selected the first issue statement considered in this discussion:

> Is King an employee protected by Title VII or an independent contractor who is outside the protection of the federal law?

You might consider answering it as follows:

> King is an independent contractor rather than an employee and therefore is outside the protection of Title VII.

While this statement is simple and direct, similar to the first issue statement, it does not contain any relevant facts or incorporate any legal standards. This holding should be rewritten, incorporating the elements or legal standards that would be considered. Such a change would make the holding more meaningful in the context of this research.

The rewritten issue, for which we will draft a holding, could read:

> Is King, a worker subject to only minimal company control, an independent contractor or an employee protected by Title VII?

Again, you might want to include additional facts the court considered in determining that King was an independent contractor. For the holding, rewrite the final issue statement drafted above in the form of a statement.

> King, a worker subject to only minimal company control who was paid commissions rather than salary and benefits, was an independent contractor rather than an employee protected by Title VII.

The key to drafting a good issue statement, a holding, or any other type of writing is rewriting and editing. You must make your holding broad enough so that it could be useful for various research projects

involving different fact patterns. However, you need to incorporate facts from the case at hand that make it unique and that limit the holding so that you can understand the facts that form the basis for the court's decision. Refine your statements and assess whether they are helpful in your research summary.

Also, be careful to incorporate the facts and the underlying law into your holding statement, as you did in your issue statement. A holding such as

> The district court did not err in granting summary judgment in favor of the defendant.

is not valuable for your research. It does not explain why the court found that the district court's decision was correct.

5. Facts

The next section of the brief should be the facts. Be certain to include the names of the parties, a notation concerning whether the party is a plaintiff, a defendant, an appellant, or appellee, and some details about the party, such as whether it is a corporation or an individual. State the relevant rather than procedural facts in this section. Also, explain why a party sought legal assistance.

▼ What Are the Relevant Facts?

Relevant facts are those facts that may have an effect on the legal issues decided in a particular action. To write this section, you must clearly understand the issues decided by the court. Decide which facts the court relied on to make its decision. Those are the facts that you should include in this section. The facts should be presented in a paragraph rather than in a list. Also, mention any facts that will assist you in understanding the relationship between the parties and the dispute.

In the *King* case, the court relied on facts that explained the relationship between King and the Miller Co. For example, the court considered that King earned commissions and bonuses rather than a salary. That fact should be listed. Before you write your facts statement in paragraph format, make a rough outline of all the facts that the court considered in making its decision. For the *King* case, your outline might look like this:

> King first worked as an "employee" agent
> > As an employee agent, King was paid salary, company withheld taxes
>
> King later was designated an "independent contract" agent, earned commission and bonuses but no salary

> King signed an agreement that she was an independent contractor
>
> Did not receive paid holidays, sick days, or vacation
>
> Paid for her own health, life, and disability insurance
>
> Miller supplied office space, furniture, file cabinets, forms, shared secretarial services, stamps, computers, and Miller stationery
>
> Miller paid for insurance seminars and lunches at the seminars
>
> Miller required that King attend weekly meetings, work in the office three and one-half days per week and every third Saturday, check her mail and retrieve messages daily, and sell only Miller insurance
>
> Miller restricted King's sales area
>
> Miller did not regularly review King's work
>
> King supplied her own personalized stationery, business cards, pens
>
> King found her own customers, decided which products to sell, and set her own hours

The court listed additional facts, such as:

> King had wanted to work for Miller because Miller had a good reputation
>
> Before coming to Miller's office, King worked for three other insurance companies
>
> King was a single, 30-year-old mother of two children
>
> Before her experience in the insurance industry, she worked as a sales clerk at a local boutique

Note that for its decision the court did not consider any of the facts contained in the outline under additional facts. Therefore, they are not relevant facts and should not be included in your brief. After you have made your outline and determined which facts are relevant, you should draft your facts statement in a paragraph format. A list is not as helpful as a paragraph when you want to review the brief at a later date.

▼ How Do You Organize Your Facts Statements?

Your facts statement could be written in chronological order, in topical order, or using a combination of the two methods. Chronological order often works best when the case involves facts that need to be placed in order according to when they occurred. For example, in a personal injury action that results from a car accident, a chronological set of facts is best. Start with the first fact that occurred and work forward.

A chronological organization for the facts in the *King* case would read as follows:

> In 1992, King started to work for Miller. King first worked for Miller as an employee agent. During that time, she received a salary and the company

withheld income tax and social security payments. King later was promoted to contract agent. King was fired in 1993, and a man was hired to take her place.

A topical organization is the best choice for facts that have no temporal relationship. Instead, these facts are grouped by topic or legal claim. In this case, the topic is the legal question of whether King was an independent contractor. Therefore, you would group together all the facts that relate to this question.

As an independent contract agent, King earned a commission and bonuses but did not receive a salary. She signed an agreement that stated that she was an independent contractor. As a contract agent, she did not receive paid holidays, sick days, or vacation days, and she paid for her own health, life, and disability insurance. King supplied her own personalized stationery, business cards, and pens. She found her own customers, decided which products to sell, and set her own hours.

For its independent contract agents, Miller supplied office space, furniture, file cabinets, forms, shared secretarial services, stamps, computers, and Miller stationery. Miller also paid for required insurance seminars. Miller required that contract agents, such as King, attend weekly meetings, work in the office three and one-half days per week and every third Saturday, check their mail and retrieve messages daily, and sell only Miller insurance. Miller also restricted King's sales area. Miller did not regularly review King's work.

In the *King* case, a combination of a chronological and topical organization works best. The *King* brief facts statement might read as follows:

King first worked for Miller as an employee agent. During that time she received a salary and the company withheld income tax and social security payments. King later was promoted to independent contract agent.

As an independent contract agent, King earned a commission and bonuses but did not receive a salary. She signed an agreement that stated that she was an independent contractor. As a contract agent, she did not receive paid holidays, sick days, or vacation days, and she paid for her own health, life, and disability insurance. King supplied her own personalized stationery, business cards, and pens. She found her own customers, decided which products to sell, and set her own hours.

For its contract agents, Miller supplied office space, furniture, file cabinets, forms, shared secretarial services, stamps, computers, and Miller stationery. Miller also paid for required insurance seminars. Miller required that contract agents, such as King, attend weekly meetings, work in the office three and one-half days per week and every third Saturday, check their mail and retrieve messages daily, and sell only Miller insurance. Miller also restricted King's sales area. Miller did not regularly review King's work.

The above facts statement begins with a chronological organization. It explains the beginning of the relationship between King and Miller. Next, it states all the facts that pertain to King's benefits and her control of her work. The next paragraph explains what Miller provided for the independent contract agents and what Miller required of them. Following this facts section, you should include a reasoning or rationale section in a brief.

6. Rationale

In the rationale or reasoning section, you should explain the court's thought process and relevant cases or statutes, then apply the law to the facts of the case you are briefing. Essentially, you will explain the law the court relied on in making a decision. For example, the *King* court reviewed the definition of *employee* contained in Title VII and past case precedent, such as *Spirides v. Reinhardt,* 613 F.2d 826, 831 (D.C. Cir. 1979), and *Unger v. Consolidated Foods Corp.,* 657 F.2d 909, 915-916 n.8 (7th Cir. 1981), to determine that independent contractors are not protected by Title VII. Both of these cases are from different jurisdictions. The *Spirides* case is primary binding authority only in the District of Columbia Circuit and *Unger* is primary binding authority only within the Seventh Circuit. However, both are persuasive authorities in other circuits. Explain in this section whether the court relied on binding or persuasive authority.

You also must review a decision for any tests a court considered in making its decision. In *King,* the court considered the economic realities test. Finally, note how the court applied the law to the facts of the particular case.

For the *King* case, you might include the following reasoning section in your brief:

> In order to determine whether an individual is an employee or an independent contractor, the employment relationship between the parties needs to be evaluated based on the economic realities and circumstances of the relationship. The court reviewed several of the factors set forth by the District of Columbia Circuit Court in *Spirides v. Reinhardt,* 613 F.2d 826, 831 (D.C. Cir. 1979), a persuasive authority, and the economic realities of the situation as defined by the Seventh Circuit court in *Unger v. Consolidated Foods Corp.,* 657 F.2d 909, 915-916 n.8 (7th Cir. 1981), another persuasive decision. Based upon these factors, the King court considered the control exercised by the "employer" over the worker; the method of payment; who paid for the individual's benefits, such as life and health insurance; and who paid for the operation. In this case, the court found that King was an independent contractor because she was paid on commission, she paid for her own benefits, she provided her own supplies, and she controlled her work. The court found that she set her own hours,

selected the products she sold, and generated her own clients. Based on these facts, the appellate court found that King should be considered an independent contractor rather than an employee.

Or you could prepare the reasoning section without any reference to the underlying, or embedded, case law.

In order to determine whether an individual is an employee or an independent contractor, the employment relationship between the parties needs to be evaluated based on the economic realities and circumstances of the relationship. The *King* court considered the control exercised by the "employer" over the worker; the method of payment; who paid for the individual's benefits, such as life and health insurance; and who paid for the operation. In this case, the court found that King was an independent contractor because she was paid on commission, she paid for her own benefits, she provided her own supplies, and she controlled her work. The court found that she set her own hours, selected the products she sold, and generated her own clients. Based on these facts, the appellate court found that King should be considered an independent contractor rather than an employee.

In the reasoning section, you should include an application of the law to the facts of the case and a mini-conclusion that summarizes the court's decision. In the above example, the following section is the application of the court's reasoning to the facts of the case.

In this case, the court found that King was an independent contractor because she was paid on commission, she paid for her own benefits, she provided her own supplies, and she controlled her work. The court found that she set her own hours, selected the products she sold, and generated her own clients.

In the above example, the following statement is the mini-conclusion:

Based on these facts, the appellate court found that King should be considered an independent contractor rather than an employee.

In some cases, you will find that a court bases its decision on reasons other than statutes or past cases. For example, a court might consider whether its decision would be fair under the circumstances. This type of analysis is called the court's consideration of policy, which sometimes is a question of what would benefit society, such as equal rights in an educational setting. Incorporate this policy into your reasoning section whenever it is useful for your research. After the reasoning or rationale, discuss any dicta contained in the court's decision.

7. Dicta

If a court makes a statement concerning a question that it was not asked to answer, this statement is called dicta. Although dicta does not have any binding effect, it is often useful to predict how a court might decide a particular issue in the future. Therefore, you want to include any dicta that might affect your case.

In the *King* case, the court stated that it was not asked to decide whether the district court should have considered all 11 factors before it rendered its decision. However, the court stated that the district court should have based its decision on all 11 factors. This statement by the court was dicta. It is helpful for your research problem because it states the factors that this circuit court might consider in determining whether an individual is an independent contractor rather than an employee.

The dicta section for the *King* case might read as follows:

> The 11-part test set by the *Spirides* court should be applied to determine whether an individual is an employee or an independent contractor.

8. Disposition

The final section of your brief is the disposition. The disposition of a case is essentially the procedural result of the court's decision. For example, in the *King* case, the court found that the district court's decision to grant summary judgment for the defendant was correct. Therefore, the disposition section would state:

> The court of appeals affirmed the district court's judgment in granting summary judgment for the defendant.

Finally, remember to rewrite your brief, but do not spend too much time rewriting it. Use your own words rather than many quotes from the court opinions. Paraphrasing in your own words helps you analyze the case and better understand it when you review your brief in the future. Also, paraphrasing allows you to import the information from the brief into a document that you draft later.

PRACTICE POINTER

Reread your brief as if you were unfamiliar with the case. If you cannot understand what happened, rewrite your brief.

ILLUSTRATION 18-4.   Case Briefing Process

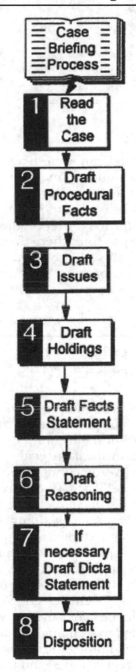

A basic overview of how to brief a case is found at www.lib.jjay.cuny.edu/research/brief.html.

IN-CLASS EXERCISE

Sometimes learning to brief can seem like an abstract exercise. The following exercise is designed to hone your brief drafting skills. It is best for students to read the illustrations for this exercise before class. Read the abridged *Molitor* case found in Illustration 18-5. Then read the case brief in Illustration 18-6. After reading the case and the brief, go back to the case and try to find where the issue, facts, holding, and rationale were obtained. This will give you insight into the information that must be gleaned from a case to write a brief.

ILLUSTRATION 18-5.   *Molitor v. Chicago Title & Trust Co.*

MOLITOR v. CHICAGO TITLE & TRUST CO.
325 Ill. App. 124, 59 N.E.2d 695 (1945)

SCANLAN, Justice.

Robert H. Molitor, plaintiff, sued Chicago Title & Trust Company, a corporation, for breach of an employment contract, and also sued Justin M. Dall for damages resulting from the breach of the said contract because of his want of authority, if the evidence should show a want of authority. A jury returned a verdict finding the issues in favor of plaintiff and against Chicago Title & Trust Company and assessing plaintiff's damages at $15,480, and also a verdict finding the issues in favor of defendant Dall. The trial court reserved rulings on motions of defendants for directed verdicts and after verdicts sustained a motion of Chicago Title & Trust Company for judgment in its favor notwithstanding the verdict against it. Plaintiff appeals from that judgment. Judgment was entered upon the verdict in favor of defendant Dall after plaintiff's motion for a new trial had been denied. Plaintiff has not appealed from that judgment. Some days after the entry of the judgment against Chicago Title & Trust Company it entered a motion for a new trial and the trial court entered an order granting the motion, but providing that "this ruling shall not become effective unless and until the order granting the motion for judgment notwithstanding the verdict shall hereafter be reversed, vacated or set aside in the manner provided by law." Plaintiff also appeals from that judgment. . . .

. . . The complaint alleges that Chicago Title & Trust Company, on or about March 20, 1936, "desiring to continue the service of plaintiff

ILLUSTRATION 18-5. *Continued*

permanently, promised and agreed that in consideration of the plaintiff giving up his residence in the State of New York, and giving up and forgoing all his other engagements and professional connections as aforesaid by moving his family to Cook County, State of Illinois, and thereafter devoting all his time exclusively to the service of the Company, that it would give plaintiff steady, continuous and permanent employment as an examiner of titles; that is to say, for and during the period of his natural life, or so long as said Company required the services of an examiner of titles and plaintiff was willing and able to do such work." Said defendant, in its answer, denies the aforesaid allegations. We may assume from the briefs filed by both parties that the trial court based his ruling upon the assumption that there was no evidence offered by plaintiff that tended to prove an enforceable agreement that plaintiff was to have permanent employment. . . .

. . . Observing these rules we find the following evidence: The Chicago Title & Trust Company is engaged, inter alia, in the business of insuring titles to and interests in real estate in Cook County and elsewhere. It employs a large number of men known as title examiners, who are especially trained and experienced in the law of real property and the validity of real estate titles. It depends upon the ability and integrity of these title examiners to discover defects, it there be any, in real estate titles. In the selection of title examiners it exercises great caution, and applicants for such position go through a long probationary period before they are given "continuous employment." In 1920 plaintiff applied for a position as title examiner and was employed on probation. He had theretofore been engaged in the practice of law in South Dakota. After a number of years of service as a probationer, he was made a regular examiner at a salary of $85 per week. In August, 1927, he quit the services of the defendant company and moved, with his family, to New York to take employment in the office of a former client, the new position paying him twice the salary he was getting as a title examiner. Because of the economic depression, he lost the New York position on February 1, 1933, and he then started to practice his profession in New York—having been admitted to the bar in New York—and by June, 1934, he was commencing to build up a paying practice. About that time one of the departments of defendant company, that was managed by Mr. Dall, was swamped with thousands of HOLC orders for title insurance, and speedy service was demanded. Mr. Dall, in letters and telegrams to plaintiff, asked him to reenter the employ of defendant company. Dall stated that the company was very busy with rush orders from the HOLC but that there was no profit in the business and that the work would probably last about six months. Plaintiff told Mr. Dall that since 1933 conditions had changed for the better for him and his family and that they now had an income; that from time to time he was getting law business which paid substantial fees; that his

ILLUSTRATION 18-5. *Continued*

wife had a music class in New York from which she derived a substantial income every month and that he might have trouble inducing her to give up her work unless plaintiff would have better prospects in Chicago than in New York. Further correspondence followed, and plaintiff finally accepted the offer of employment with the understanding that when the HOLC work gave out that Mr. Dall might be free to dispense with his services. In view of the temporary character of the agreement plaintiff decided not to move his family to Chicago. He came to Chicago on July 23, 1934, and told Mr. Dall, in a conference, that he desired to preserve his business connections in New York and to have his wife retain her music classes there, and that it would be necessary for him to be absent from his work with the defendant company when matters came up in New York that required his presence there. Mr. Dall agreed to this arrangement. Immediately following this conference plaintiff went to work for defendant company and for three or four months thereafter the title examiners were obliged to work four hours overtime every day, all day Saturdays, and some Sundays. Plaintiff spent five days in New York in the following September to attend to a legal matter in which he had been appointed referee. He was also absent from his work during the month of June, 1935, when he was conducting legal business for clients in New York and Philadelphia, and was absent again, upon like work, between December 14, 1935, and February 17, 1936. All of the absences were with the knowledge and consent of Mr. Dall. The HOLC work was tapering off in 1935, and it ended on June 12, 1936. About this time Mr. Dall was preparing for an anticipated improvement in the regular business of defendant company and he became dissatisfied with the arrangement that allowed plaintiff to be absent from his work on trips to New York, and in a conference with plaintiff it was agreed that the trips to New York caused undesirable breaks in plaintiff's work and a new arrangement as to plaintiff's employment was made. The following is plaintiff's evidence as to the agreement: Dall stated to him that the HOLC work would soon be played out but that they were looking for a big boom in regular real estate business, and he asked plaintiff to abandon his New York connections and move his family to Chicago so that he could give the company his continuous service from then on. Plaintiff replied that he would not give up his New York connections so long as there was any uncertainty about his employment in Chicago being continuous. Mr. Dall stated that two of the examiners had died, that there was now a place for plaintiff and that he could depend on the position being permanent. Plaintiff asked him what he meant by that, to which Dall replied, "You can consider yourself employed from now on—the custom here is to retain examiners as long as we can. We have men that have been here all their lives, and there is no reason why you couldn't have a job here the rest of your life." Plaintiff replied that if he could

ILLUSTRATION 18-5. *Continued*

rely on that promise he would buy a house in Chicago and move his family here, that his wife had a big music class in New York and that she would refuse to move unless he had a permanent position in Chicago, to which Mr. Dall replied, "You can rely on it being permanent." Plaintiff then accepted the position and told Mr. Dall that he would abandon his New York connections, buy a house here, and move his family to Chicago. His salary was fixed at $70 per week. Plaintiff thereupon continued in his work with defendant company and began preparations for carrying out his part of the agreement. He abandoned all his business in New York and his wife abandoned her music classes. He bought a home at 7219 Vernon Avenue and the family moved to Chicago. The defendant company loaned plaintiff $200 to enable him to move. Plaintiff thereafter continued in the employ of defendant company under the arrangements made with Mr. Dall until March 15, 1938, when he was discharged by defendant company upon the ground that business had fallen off to such an extent that the company could not afford to hold plaintiff any longer. There was evidence tending to show that defendant company about two years prior to plaintiff's discharge employed thirteen new title examiners whose salaries averaged less than $40 per week, and that only one of the thirteen was discharged at the time of plaintiff's discharge.

In passing upon plaintiff's instant contention we must assume that defendant company promised plaintiff "permanent employment" and that plaintiff accepted employment because of that promise, and the question is, What did the parties intend by "permanent employment"? Upon the oral argument counsel for the defendant contended that even under plaintiff's testimony as to the alleged agreement defendant had the right to discharge him at will. This contention is without merit and the cases cited in support of it, *Orr v. Ward*, 73 Ill. 318; *Gunther v. Chicago B. & Q Ry. Co.*, 165 Ill. App. 55, and *Fuchs v. Weibert*, 233 Ill. App. 536, have no application to the facts that must be taken as true in determining the instant contention of plaintiff. . . .

. . . In *Riefkin v. E.I. Du Pont De Nemours & Co.*, 53 App. D.C. 311, 290 F. 286, the plaintiff was induced to resign from a position with the United States government on a promise of permanent employment. After about two and one-half years of service he was discharged without cause although he had rendered satisfactory service to the defendant. In its opinion the Court of Appeals of the District of Columbia stated (290 F. at page 289):

"The circumstances surrounding the making of this contract largely control the interpretation to be given the words 'permanent employment' as used therein, for it must be assumed that the parties, knowing those circumstances, contracted with reference to them. The plaintiff held a position with the United States government, and the defendant agreed that, if he would resign from that position and take charge of the purchase of coal for the defendant, he would be given

ILLUSTRATION 18-5.   *Continued*

'permanent employment in that capacity so long as he rendered satis-factory ser-vices and was loyal to its interests.' Relying upon this agree-ment, plaintiff did resign and perform his part of the contract. May it be said that it was within the contemplation of either party that 'permanent employment,' as used in the contract, meant that the plain-tiff, the day following his resignation from his position with the govern-ment and the assumption of his new duties, could have been summarily discharged without any liability on the part of the defendant? Such a result could not have been contemplated by either party. The more reasonable view is that the parties contemplated that, so long as the defendant continued in a business requiring the purchase of coal and the plaintiff performed loyal and satisfactory service, he would continue to be employed in the capacity specified in the contract." . . .

. . . "The rule is that a contract for lifetime employment will be given effect, according to its terms, if the intention of the parties to make such an agreement is clear, even though the only consideration for it, so far as the employer is concerned, is the promise of the employee to render the service called for the contract."

But the defendant contends (a): "There was no evidence that Dall had authority to enter into the alleged contract to employ plaintiff for life or that defendant company ratified the alleged contract;" and (b) "There was no evidence that defendant company acted in bad faith in discharging plaintiff." All of these contentions involve disputed questions of fact and therefore they cannot be considered in determining the instant contention of plaintiff. After a careful consideration of the question before us we have reached the conclusion that the trial court erred in entering judgment for the defendant company not withstanding the verdict for plaintiff.

Plaintiff also contends that the trial court erred in entering the order granting the defendant a new trial. The following ground, inter alia, was urged in the motion for a new trial: "The verdict of the jury as to defendant Chicago Title & Trust Company is contrary to the manifest weight of the evidence." As this case may be tried again we refrain from analyzing and commenting upon the evidence that bears upon the instant contention. Suffice it to say that the defendants introduced evidence in support of their claim that Mr. Dall did not promise plaintiff permanent employment. The Appellate Courts of this State, upon an appeal from an order of the trial court granting a new trial, have consistently held that they would not interfere with an order of the trial court granting a new trial unless the record showed a clear abuse of discretion by the trial court in granting the motion. After a careful consideration of all of the evidence, we are satisfied that we would not be justified in holding that the trial court was guilty of a clear abuse of discretion. We have considered the further contention of plaintiff that the trial court should not have entertained the motion for a new trial and find the contention without substantial merit.

ILLUSTRATION 18-5. *Continued*

The judgment order of the Superior Court of Cook County entered May 13, 1943, entering judgment in favor of the defendant Chicago Title & Trust Company non obstante veredicto is reversed. The judgment order of the Superior Court of Cook County entered June 3, 1943, setting aside the verdict of the jury and granting the defendant Chicago Title & Trust Company a new trial is affirmed. The cause is remanded for a new trial.

SULLIVAN, P.J., and FRIEND, J., concur.

ILLUSTRATION 18-6. **Case Brief for** *Molitor v. Chicago Title & Trust Co.*

MOLITOR v. CHICAGO TITLE & TRUST CO.
325 Ill. App. 124, 59 N.E.2d 695 (1945)

PROCEDURE

Plaintiff, Molitor, appeals judgment in favor of the defendant, Chicago Title, notwithstanding the verdict and judgment granting a new trial.

ISSUE

Was there a breach of an oral contract for permanent employment when the plaintiff moved to Chicago in consideration of the defendant's promise to employ him, and when the defendant promised to employ the plaintiff for as long as he was willing and able to do the work?

HOLDING

A contract for lifetime employment is in effect if the intention of the parties is clear even if the only consideration for the contract is the promise of the employee to render the service called for by the contract.

FACTS

The plaintiff, Robert Molitor, was employed by Chicago Title & Trust as a probationary examiner for seven years before leaving and moving his family to New York to work for a former client. After losing that job, he began to practice law in New York. In June 1934, Mr. Dall of CT&T contacted the plaintiff and asked him to reenter CT&T's company temporarily. The plaintiff and Mr. Dall arranged for the plaintiff to work for a period for CT&T while retaining his law practice. He was absent from his work for CT&T to attend to his practice on several occasions with the knowledge of Mr. Dall. In June 1936, Mr. Dall offered the plaintiff a new agreement, asking him to leave his law practice and

ILLUSTRATION 18-6. *Continued*

move his family to Chicago for permanent employment with CT&T. The plaintiff replied that if he could rely on that promise of permanent employment, he would buy a house in Chicago and move his family there. Mr. Dall replied that the position was permanent. Then the plaintiff severed his New York connections and moved his family. On March 15, 1938, Mr. Dall discharged him.

RATIONALE

To decide what was meant by "permanent employment," the situation, and the relationship of the parties, and the common understanding of the meaning of the words used must be considered. The surrounding circumstances in the making of a contract must also be considered to ascertain what the parties intended by "permanent employment."

DISPOSITION

Reversed in part and remanded.

After reading *Molitor* and its briefs, read the *Heuvelman* decision found in Illustration 18-7. Although it is also decided by the Illinois Appellate Court and deals with the issue of permanent employment, it was decided 14 years after *Molitor*. Read the brief following the decision found in Illustration 18-8. You will notice that *Heuvelman* cites *Molitor*; this is an example of how legal precedent is used and why we perform case law research. Now compare the briefs for the two cases. Since both sets of briefs are drafted with the same categories (citation, procedure, issue, facts, holding, rationale, and disposition), you can compare and contrast cases easily and quickly. Compare the issues and you will see that they are very similar. Now compare the facts and the holdings and you will notice that they differ.

ILLUSTRATION 18-7. *Heuvelman v. Triplett Elec. Instrument Co.*

HEUVELMAN v. TRIPLETT ELEC. INSTRUMENT CO.
23 Ill. App. 2d 231, 161 N.E.2d 875 (1959)

SCHWARTZ, Justice.

The trial court sustained both defendant's motion for a summary judgment and its motion to strike the amended complaint, and thereupon dismissed the suit with prejudice. From these orders plaintiff has appealed. The principal issue involved turns on an alleged oral agreement for permanent employment.

The amended complaint consists of three counts. Count 1 seeks a declaratory judgment finding that plaintiff and defendant entered into

ILLUSTRATION 18-7. *Continued*

a contract for the permanent employment of plaintiff as a sales representative for the sale of electrical and radio equipment; that the contract was breached; and that plaintiff suffered damages in the sum of $250,000. . . .

. . . The pertinent facts extracted from these documents follow. From 1925 to January 1933 plaintiff was employed by an agency which served as defendant's sales representative in the Midwest. In January 1933 defendant hired plaintiff as its sole sales representative for the territory previously covered by the agency. The agreement specified no definite time of employment. In April 1933 defendant desired to secure the services of another sales representative, Jerome T. Keeney, employed by competitor of defendant, and defendant brought plaintiff and Keeney together for the purpose of having them become associated as joint representatives for the sale of defendant's products. At that meeting, as plaintiff alleges, defendant agreed that plaintiff's employment would continue as long as defendant manufactured and sold electrical equipment and as long as plaintiff acted as sales representative in that field. Plaintiff charges that it was on the basis of that agreement that he consented to enter into a partnership with Keeney. Instead of a partnership, however, a corporation was formed, the Instrument Sales Corporation, in which plaintiff and Keeney owned stock.

The business association between plaintiff and Keeney continued until 1940, when Keeney left plaintiff to join the Simpson Electric Company, a competitor of defendant. At that time Simpson also made plaintiff an offer. Plaintiff orally discussed with defendant the matter of his leaving and, as stated by plaintiff but denied by defendant, Triplett, president of defendant company, told plaintiff as they walked down State Street in Chicago, that their arrangement was a permanent one. It continued until October 1955, when defendant notified plaintiff that it terminated the relationship effective November 30, 1955.

We will first consider the motion for summary judgment as it applies to Count I. Oral contracts for "permanent employment" (meaning that as long as defendant was engaged in the prescribed work and as long as plaintiff was able to do his work satisfactorily, defendant would employ him) have been sustained, provided such contracts are supported by a consideration other than the obligation of services to be performed on the one hand and wages to be paid on the other. *Molitor v. Chicago Title & Trust Co.*, 1845, 325 Ill. App. 124, 132-133, 59 N.E.2d 695-698; *Carnig v. Carr*, 1897, 167 Mass. 544, 46 N.E 117, 35 L.R.A. 512; *Riefkin v. E. I. Du Pont, etc., & Co.*, 1923, 53 App. D.C. 311, 290 F. 286; *Eggers v. Armour & Co.*, 8 Cir., 1942, 129 F.2d 729; *Roxana Petroleum Co. of Oklahoma v. Rice.*, 1924, 109 Okl. 161, 235 P. 502. In the *Molitor* case the consideration was the giving up by the employee of a profitable law

practice in New York in order to move to Chicago in reliance on a promise of permanent employment. The *Molitor* case was supported and approved, but distinguished, in *Goodman v. Motor Products Corp.,* 1950, 9 Ill. App. 2d 57,77 132 N.E.2d 356, 366. In *Carnig v. Carr,* supra, the plaintiff gave up a going and competitive venture to go with his employer. In *Riefkin v. E. I. Du Pont, etc., & Co.,* supra, the employee gave up his position in government, a position of security and prestige. The case of *Roxana Petroleum Co. v. Rice,* supra, concerned a firm's giving up its whole law practice in order to represent a single client. Where there is no particular detriment to the employee, the act of terminating other employment is not a sufficient consideration to make the new contract binding. *Edwards v. Kentucky Utilities Co.,* 1941, 286 Ky. 341, 150 S.W.2d 916, 135 A.L.R. 642.

In the instant case the time of the first alleged conversation on which permanent employment is based is April 1933. At that time plaintiff was already employed by defendant and the formation of a partnership with Keeney, terminable at will, so far as appears from anything in the record, cannot be considered a detriment but an advantage, Keeney being a man of considerable experience and competence, as was plaintiff in this business. The alleged renewal of the offer in 1940, when plaintiff was being solicited to join Simpson, is presented in such a vague, indefinite way that it is impossible to consider it as an obligation. Plaintiff says Simpson offered him a 25% interest in a new business venture. It does not appear whether this was a gift or a capital contribution. It is not sufficient consideration for a contract of permanent employment to forgo another employment opportunity. *Lewis v. Minnesota Mutual Life Insurance Co.,* 1949, 240 Iowa 1249, 37 N.W.2d 316; *Skagerberg v. Blandin Paper Co.,* 1936, 197 Minn. 291, 266 N.W. 872.

It is our further conclusion that . . . , no contract for permanent employment was made, nor was any adequate consideration to support one shown. Such contracts extending for a long duration and resting entirely on parole should have for their basis definite and certain mutual promises. The words and the manner of their utterance should not be of that informal character which expresses only long continuing good will and hopes for eternal association. . . .

. . . The order insofar as it sustains the motion to strike Count I and enters summary judgment thereon is affirmed. The order insofar as it sustains the motion to strike Counts II and III and enters summary judgment thereon is reversed and the cause is remanded with directions to vacate the summary judgment and overrule the motion to strike Counts II and III, and for such further proceedings as are not inconsistent with the views herein expressed.

Affirmed in part and reversed in part, and cause remanded for further proceedings.

DEMPSEY, P.J., and McCORMICK, J., concur.

ILLUSTRATION 18-8. Case Brief for *Heuvelman v. Triplett Elec. Instrument Co.*

HEUVELMAN v. TRIPLETT ELEC. INSTRUMENT CO.
23 Ill. App. 2d 231, 161 N.E.2d 875 (1959)

PROCEDURE

The plaintiff appeals summary judgment for the defendant, dismissing his suit for breach of oral contract for permanent employment.

ISSUE

Whether there an oral contract for permanent employment between plaintiff and defendant?

HOLDING

No oral contract for permanent employment was made, nor was adequate consideration to support one shown by the employee forsaking another offer. . . . Instead the employer verbally extended a gesture of goodwill.

FACTS

The plaintiff was hired by the defendant as a sales representative in January 1933. The agreement specified no definite time of employment. The defendant hired another sales representative in April 1933 to work with the plaintiff. Plaintiff consented to enter into a sales partnership with the new representative on the basis of defendant's promise of permanent employment. A competitor offered plaintiff a job in 1940, which he refused after discussing it with defendant. After the other sales representative resigned, plaintiff received an offer from another employer and mentioned it to Triplett, his current employer. Plaintiff claims the defendant told him, orally, that the employment arrangement was permanent as they walked together down State Street. The defendant denies the claim. In October 1955, the defendant terminated plaintiff's employment as of November 30, 1955.

RATIONALE

The act of terminating other employment is not sufficient consideration to make a new contract binding if there is no detriment to the employee. Oral contracts for permanent employment are valid as long as they are supported by a consideration other than the obligation of services to be performed on the one hand and wages to be paid on the other. Where there is no particular detriment to the employee, the act of terminating other employment is not a sufficient consideration to make the new contract binding. When plaintiff was being solicited to join the competitor, the renewal with Triplett Electrical was presented in a vague and indefinite way and cannot be considered as an obligation. Contracts extending for long duration resting entirely on oral statements, parole, should have basis on definite and mutual promises.

ILLUSTRATION 18-8. *Continued*

Words should not be of informal character expressing goodwill and hope for eternal association.

DISPOSITION

Affirmed Count I granting defendant summary judgment on claim of breach of contract, reversed in part, and remanded.

D. CASE ANALYSIS

Comparing and contrasting decisions to assess the outcome of an issue posed by a factual scenario is called case analysis. Case analysis is particularly important when you want to see if a case applies to the client's situation. We look to prior cases to anticipate how a court will rule on the issue we are researching. You must determine if the question before the court, the issue, is the same as or different than the question the client's problem raises. You must examine the facts of the case and the facts of the client's problem to ascertain the similarities and differences. Sometimes only one component of the decision addresses one part of a client's problem. Then you must use several cases to fully address the client's situation.

Compare the briefs in Illustrations 18-6 and 18-8. The holding for *Molitor* is:

> A contract for lifetime employment is in effect if the intention of the parties is clear even if the only consideration for the contract is the promise of the employee to render the service called for by the contract.

The holding for *Heuvelman* is:

> No oral contract for permanent employment was made, nor was adequate consideration to support one shown by the employee forsaking another offer, instead the employer verbally extended a gesture of goodwill.

Note the differences in the holdings. *Molitor* states that the only consideration required to support the permanent employment contract is for the employee to perform the services required by the contract. *Heuvelman* states that a contract for permanent employment requires additional consideration beyond forgoing another employment opportunity. *Molitor* is from 1945 and *Heuvelman* is from 1959.

Now let's examine the following fact pattern:

> Howard Smith contacted Mary Dole, the senior partner of Dole, Dole & Dole regarding the situation described below.

Howard Smith is a well-regarded college administrator. For the past ten years he has been vice president for development at State University, located in Springtown, Illinois. He gained a national reputation for successful fundraising. He also held the faculty rank of full professor with tenure.

In the spring of 2004, Prestige University of Urban, Illinois, a private university 200 miles north of Springtown, was looking for a new vice president for development. Smith was encouraged by a friend at Prestige to apply for the position. Smith submitted an application to Mark Clark, Prestige's president.

Clark knew of Smith's fine reputation, and immediately scheduled interviews with Prestige's search committee. The interviews went extremely well, and at the end of the day Clark offered the job to Smith.

Smith responded, "Well, I'm very flattered. But frankly, it would have to be a major deal. I'd be giving up a happy situation and a very secure position with tenure and all."

Clark replied, "I think we can make you even happier. We will offer you $200,000 a year to start, plus a new car. And I look forward to having you at Prestige University for the rest of your life."

Smith responded, "The money is great, but I am concerned about the job security and moving 200 miles."

Clark replied, "Like I said, I look forward to your presence at Prestige for the rest of your life."

Smith immediately accepted the position at Prestige. No written document was signed. The men did shake hands immediately after Clark stated his acceptance.

Smith soon resigned his position at State, moved to Urban, purchased a home for $500,000, and started his new position as Vice President for Development at Prestige University. However, within five months, Smith and Clark had several disagreements over fundraising strategies. When the disagreements continued, Clark fired Smith, less than ten months after the agreement was reached.

Smith wants to file suit against Prestige University for the breach of an oral contract for permanent employment. Please assess whether a valid oral contract for permanent employment existed between Smith and Prestige University or whether the contract was terminable at will.

Examine the *Molitor* brief and the *Heuvelman* brief, particularly the holdings, as applied to the Smith problem set out above. *Molitor* holds that the only consideration required to support an oral contract for permanent employment is for the employee to perform the services

required by the contract. In our problem, it seemed that Smith and Clark had disagreements over how Smith was performing his job. The facts did not contain a specific job description for the Vice President for Development at Prestige. However, because of the battles between Smith and Clark over fundraising strategies, it seems that Smith was not performing his job as expected by Clark. Therefore, since Smith did not perform the services implied by their agreement, Smith did not render adequate consideration to support the permanent employment contract.

However, *Heuvelman* holds that a contract for permanent employment requires additional consideration beyond forgoing another employment opportunity. Aside from relinquishing his position at State, Smith purchased a home for $500,000 and moved 200 miles. Additional consideration, aside from forgoing another employment opportunity, exists to support a contract for permanent employment between Smith and Prestige University.

Notice how the facts are examined in our client's situation and applied to the holdings from the cases. This is the essential part of legal analysis. Also, compare and contrast the decisions. Briefing cases on a single page, in uniform categories, helps us compare and contrast decisions easily. Look carefully at the facts that the judge uses to apply the law to the issue raised in the case—this provides crucial insight into legally significant facts.

PRACTICE POINTER

When evaluating which case or cases to use, remember that cases from the appropriate jurisdiction are essential for precedent. Also, newer cases are stronger than older cases. Cases from higher courts are stronger than those from lower courts.

CHAPTER SUMMARY

A case brief has several components, including a citation, the procedural history, an issue, a holding, the relevant facts, the reasoning, and the case disposition. These briefs are designed to assist you and sometimes an attorney in understanding a case.

The brief's procedural facts statement should explain briefly how a case came before a court.

The issue statement presents the questions posed by the parties. The holding is the rule of law established by the court. The facts statement should include any relevant facts that affected the court's decision in the case. The reasoning explains how the court developed the rule of law and how it relates to the facts of the case. The disposition is the procedural result of the case.

Dicta often is included in a court decision. It is a statement made by a court concerning an issue other than one the court was asked to decide.

This chapter also provides you with your first exposure to legal analysis You learned the step-by-step process of drafting a case brief as well as how to compare cases with one another and a legal problem.

KEY TERMS

analysis	issue
case brief	legally significant fact
case citation	procedural facts
dicta	rationale
disposition	reasoning
facts	relevant facts
holding	rule of law

EXERCISES

IN-CLASS
Issues

1. Review the following issues prepared for a case brief of the *King* case. List any problems you find. Which issue of the following five is best, and why?

    Issue 1. Was the district court's decision that King was an independent contractor rather than an employee of the Miller Co. erroneous?

    Issue 2. Whether King was an employee of Miller or an independent contractor for these reasons:

    a. The control factor, in which agents are restricted in the selling of insurance as to whom or where. Agents also have mandatory requirements for working at designated times and dates. In addition, they are expected to attend weekly meetings and engage in daily office tasks.

    b. The economic factor, in which agents are not allowed to sell products for anyone but Miller and that agents are "integral" to Miller's business.

    c. As with employees, services, supplies, and education expenses are provided. Compensation is made in the form of commissions.

    d. Work hours are based on flexibility for prime selling.

    e. Performance evaluations and documents of rules of conduct are customary requirements of an employer-employee relationship.

    Issue 3. Whether, in finding the plaintiff was not an employee under the Title VII definition, the trial court erred by:

    a. failing to properly evaluate the nature of insurance sales;

    b. failing to evaluate and weigh the integral economic relationship between the defendant and the plaintiff; and

    c. failing to discuss other evidence regarding the "control" criterion used to judge eligibility.

    Issue 4. Whether the district court was clearly erroneous in determining that an insurance agent is an independent contractor rather than an

employee when the individual is paid commissions and bonuses rather than a salary and her work is not supervised by the company.

Issue 5. Does an employer have to exercise control over a worker before that individual is considered an employee under Title VII?

Holdings

2. Review the holdings below that were drafted for a brief in the *King* case, list any problems you see with each, and note which is the best.

Holding 1. The court of appeals affirmed the lower court's decision that King is an independent contractor rather than an employee of the Miller Co.

Holding 2. Because the trial court did understand the law and its factual findings are not clearly erroneous, its decision is affirmed.

Holding 3. The district court's underlying factual findings are not clearly erroneous; therefore, the decision of the district court was affirmed.

Holding 4. Yes. An employer must exercise control over a worker before that individual is considered an employee under Title VII.

HOMEWORK
Briefing

3. Brief *Kalal v. Goldblatt Bros.*, 368 N.E.2d 671 (Ill. App. Ct. 1977).
4. Brief the following case:

KREIGER v. KREIGER

No. 371

SUPREME COURT OF THE UNITED STATES

334 U.S. 555; 68 S. Ct. 1221; 92 L. Ed. 1572; 1948 U.S. LEXIS 2085

February 2-3, 1948, Argued

June 7, 1948, Decided

COUNSEL: James G. Purdy argued the cause for petitioner. With him on the brief was Abraham J. Nydick.

Charles Rothenberg argued the cause and filed a brief for respondent.

JUDGES: Vinson, Black, Reed, Frankfurter, Douglas, Murphy, Jackson, Rutledge, Burton

OPINION BY: DOUGLAS

OPINION: Opinion of the Court by MR. JUSTICE DOUGLAS, announced by MR. JUSTICE REED.

This is a companion case to *Estin v. Estin,* ante, p. 541, also here on certiorari to the Court of Appeals of New York.

The parties were married in New York in 1933 and lived there together until their separation in 1935. In 1940 respondent obtained a decree of separation in New York on grounds of abandonment. Petitioner appeared in the action; and respondent was awarded $60 a week alimony for the support of herself and their only child, whose custody she was given.

Petitioner thereafter went to Nevada where he continues to reside. He instituted divorce proceedings in that state in the fall of 1944. Constructive service was made on respondent who made no appearance in the Nevada proceedings. While they were pending, respondent obtained an order in New York purporting to enjoin petitioner from seeking a divorce and from remarrying. Petitioner was neither served with process in New York nor entered an appearance in the latter proceeding. The Nevada court, with knowledge of the injunction and the New York judgment for alimony, awarded petitioner an absolute divorce on grounds of three consecutive years of separation without cohabitation. The judgment made no provision for alimony. It did provide that petitioner was to support, maintain and educate the child, whose custody it purported to grant him, and as to which jurisdiction was reserved. Petitioner thereafter tendered $50 a month for the support of the child but ceased making payments under the New York decree.

Respondent thereupon brought suit on the New York judgment in a federal district court in Nevada. Without waiting the outcome of that litigation she obtained a judgment in New York for the amount of the arrears, petitioner appearing and unsuccessfully pleading his Nevada divorce as a defense. The judgment was affirmed by the Appellate Division, two judges dissenting. 271 N.Y. App. Div. 872, 66 N.Y.S.2d 798. The Court of Appeals affirmed without opinion, 297 N.Y. 530, 74 N.E.2d 468, but stated in its remittitur that its action was based upon *Estin v. Estin,* 296 N.Y. 308, 73 N.E.2d 113. Respondent does not attack the bona fides of petitioner's Nevada domicile.

For the reasons stated in *Estin v. Estin,* ante, p. 541, we hold that Nevada had no power to adjudicate respondent's rights in the New York judgment and thus New York was not required to bow to that provision of the Nevada decree. It is therefore unnecessary to pass upon New York's attempt to enjoin petitioner from securing a divorce or to reach the question whether the New York judgment was entitled to full faith and credit in the Nevada proceedings. No issue as to the custody of the child was raised either in the court below or in this Court. The judgment is

Affirmed.

MR. JUSTICE FRANKFURTER dissents for the reasons stated in his dissenting opinion in *Estin v. Estin,* ante, p. 549.

MR. JUSTICE JACKSON dissents for the reasons set forth in his opinion in *Estin v. Estin,* ante, p. 553.

5. Brief *Talford v. Columbia Med. Ctr. at Lancaster Sub., L.P.,* 198 S.W.3d 462 (Tex. App. 2006).
6. Brief *DeMercado v. McClung,* 55 Cal. Rptr. 3d 889 (Ct. App. 2007).

Analysis Exercises

7. Review *Seymour v. Armstrong* in Illustration 18-1. An attorney asks you to apply the holdings of *Seymour* to the following fact patterns.

Mrs. Johnson, the owner of Frocks, Etc., ordered 50 dresses at the price of $35 per dress to be delivered in one week. Mrs. Johnson ordered the dresses from ABC Dress Company and sent a contract stating that she requests 50 dresses at $35 per dress, totaling $1750 payable upon receipt of the dresses. Mrs. Johnson assumes that when ABC ships the dresses this indicates that they are assenting to the contract by their action. However, ABC sends an invoice with the dresses for $1750 plus shipping of $106. The attorney wants to know, in light of the holding in *Seymour,* if ABC is imposing a new condition in the contract, with no agreement existing between ABC and Frocks, Etc.?

8. Reread *Seymour v. Armstrong* in Illustration 18-1. Now find and read *Steele v. Harrison,* 522 P.2d 957 (Kan. 1976).

   a. Was there a meeting of the minds in the contract in *Steele?*

   b. Was there a meeting of the minds in the contract in *Seymour?*

   c. How is *Steele* similar to *Seymour?*

   d. How does *Steele* differ factually from *Seymour?*

   e. Does *Steele* apply the holding from *Seymour?*

9. Read *Farone v. Bag'n'Baggage, Ltd.,* 165 S.W.3d 795 (Tex. App. 2005). How is *Farone* factually similar to the Smith/Prestige University fact pattern in section D of this chapter? Which facts differ?

THE LEGAL MEMORANDUM

CHAPTER OVERVIEW

This chapter introduces you to the legal memorandum. You learn about your audience and how to write objectively. You are introduced to the components of the memorandum, such as the issues, conclusion or brief answer, facts, and discussion sections. The chapter concludes with a brief overview of the process of writing a memorandum.

A. THE LEGAL MEMORANDUM

▼ What Is an Objective Legal Memorandum and Why Is It Written?

An **office memorandum,** often called a memo, explains in an objective rather than a persuasive or argumentative manner the current state of the law regarding an issue. It clarifies how that law applies to a client's transaction or legal dilemma. A memo should explain the current law—both favorable and unfavorable—and any legal theories pertaining to the issues.

The balanced approach of a legal memo helps an attorney see the strengths and weaknesses of a transaction or dispute. Only when an attorney can see all sides of an issue can the attorney determine how best to represent a client. Sometimes your research will determine whether the client has a case or not. If in writing a memo you advocate a single position or attempt to persuade an attorney, the attorney cannot make an informed decision about a dispute or transaction. This can be a very costly error in terms of money, time, client loyalty, and court favor.

A memo also assists an attorney in predicting how a court might decide a particular issue. A memo could be drafted to address an issue raised as a case progresses in court. As a paralegal, you might research whether the law provides for the dismissal of an action; your research and memorandum might form the basis for such a motion to dismiss or for subsequent court documents. You might also write a memo to assist an attorney in drafting an appellate brief, a document used to appeal a trial court's decision.

B. AUDIENCE

▼ Who Reads a Memorandum?

You will usually research a legal question to determine whether a client has a claim or should proceed with a case. Following your research, you generally prepare your memo for an attorney. Your memo also might be sent to the client. Your primary audience, then, is the attorney, and the secondary audience is the client.

Often memoranda are saved in **memo banks** accessible to all firm or corporation attorneys and paralegals, so other attorneys and paralegals might review your memo.

C. COMPONENTS OF A MEMORANDUM

▼ What Is Included in a Memorandum?

A memorandum can have a variety of components arranged in different orders. The components and their order often vary from attorney to

attorney. Ask the assigning attorney if your firm or corporation has a particular style. Request a sample memo so that you can review the style he or she prefers, or go to the memo bank to review a sample. The format discussed in this chapter is one commonly accepted style. See the sample memo in Illustration 19-1. Additional sample memos may be found in Appendix C.

ILLUSTRATION 19-1. Sample Memorandum

MEMORANDUM

To: Benjamin Joyce
From: William Randall
Date: January 28, 2008
Re: *Harris v. Sack and Shop*

QUESTION PRESENTED

Is Sack and Shop, a grocery store, liable for injuries sustained by Harris, a store patron who slipped on a banana peel that had been on the grocery store floor for two days?

BRIEF ANSWER

Probably yes. Sack and Shop, a grocery store, probably will be liable based on negligence for injuries sustained by Harris, a store patron who slipped on a banana peel that had been on the grocery store floor for two days.

FACTS

Our client, Sack and Shop Grocery Store, is being sued for negligence by Rebecca Harris.

Harris went to the store to purchase groceries on July 8, 2007. While she was in the produce section, she slipped on a banana that a grocery store employee left on the floor. The employee had dropped it on the floor two days earlier and had failed to clean it up after a patron asked him to do so.

Harris sustained a broken arm and head injuries as a result of the slip and fall.

DISCUSSION

The issue presented in this case is whether Sack and Shop Grocery Store was negligent when Rebecca Harris slipped in the store's produce section. A grocer will be found negligent if a store employee breached the store's duty of reasonable care to its patrons and, as a result of that breach, the patron was injured. *Ward v. K Mart Corp.*, 554 N.E.2d. 223 (Ill. 1990). In *Ward*, the grocery store employee failed to clean up a banana peel for two days and that peel caused a patron to be injured. Similarly in our case Sack and Shop failed to remove the banana peel for two days. Therefore, Sack and Shop is likely to be found liable for the injuries Harris sustained.

ILLUSTRATION 19-1.   *Continued*

The first element to consider is whether Sack and Shop owed a duty of reasonable care to Harris. A grocery store owes a duty of care to any patron. *Ward,* 554 N.E.2d at 226. Harris was a customer in the store. Therefore, Sack and Shop owed her a duty of care.

The next question to consider is whether Sack and Shop breached its duty of reasonable care to Harris. A store will be found to have breached its duty of reasonable care to a patron if a store employee fails to properly and regularly clean the floor of the store. *Olinger v. Great Atl.& Pac. Tea Co.,* 173 N.E.2d 443 (Ill. 1961). In *Olinger,* the store was found liable because a store employee failed to clean the floor for one day and a patron slipped on a substance on the floor. 173 N.E.2d at 447. No one had told any store employee about the slippery substance. *Id.* at 447. Nonetheless, the Illinois Supreme Court found the store liable, saying that the store employees had sufficient time to notice the substance if they had used ordinary care. *Id.* In our case, Sack and Shop's employee had two days to clean the floor before Harris fell. In addition, a customer had placed the store employee on notice of the banana. Therefore, Sack and Shop breached its duty of care to Harris.

The plaintiff, however, still must establish proximate cause, that is, that the injury resulted as a natural consequence of Sack and Shop's breach of its duty. A store owner's failure to clear debris from a store floor, resulting in injury to a patron who slipped on the floor, was found to be the proximate cause of the patron's injuries. *Id.* at 449. In this case, Sack and Shop's failure to clean the peel from the floor was a breach of its duty of care to Harris. This breach resulted in injury to Harris. Sack and Shop's breach will be found to be the proximate cause of Harris's injuries.

The final element that must be established is that the plaintiff, Harris, suffered injuries. Harris sustained a broken arm and head injuries as a result of the slip and fall. Therefore, she will be able to show that she was injured.

CONCLUSION

Sack and Shop owed Harris a duty of reasonable care. The store is likely to be found to have breached that duty of reasonable care because an employee failed to remove a banana peel from the grocery store floor during the preceding two days. The injuries Harris sustained were directly caused by a slip on a banana peel. Therefore, Sack and Shop is likely to be found liable to Harris.

1. Heading

In Illustrations 19-1 and 19-2 the first part of the memo is the heading. A sample heading also is shown in Illustration 19-3. The first notation in

the heading of either illustration is the word "MEMORANDUM," placed in all capital letters at the top of the page. The next notations in both Illustrations 19-1, 19-2, and 19-3 tell the reader who the memorandum is written to and from, the date, and the subject. The regarding line, indicated by the "Re:," varies depending on the firm's style. For example, some insurance clients ask that you include claim numbers in the regarding line. Some attorneys prefer court case numbers, and still others prefer clients' billing numbers and file numbers.

ILLUSTRATION 19-2.   Sample Memorandum: Sex Discrimination Case

---

MEMORANDUM

To: Wallace Maine
From: Thomas Wall
Date: November 15, 2008
Re: Sex Discrimination Case against Whole In One No. C93 CIV 190 G12399990

QUESTIONS PRESENTED
1. Under Title VII, was Whole In One Golf Resort an employer when 14 people, including 3 full-time and 11 part-time workers, worked on any one day for 24 weeks and when 10 full-time employees were on the Whole In One payroll?

2. Under Title VII, was Walker an independent contractor rather than an employee when she worked exclusively for Whole In One, paid taxes quarterly rather than through deductions, and worked with limited company supervision?

3. Under Title VII, was Radiant an independent contractor rather than an employee when she worked with limited company supervision using company supplies and equipment and had taxes and medical deductions taken from her salary?

CONCLUSIONS
1. Whole In One was an employer. Under Title VII, an employer has at least 15 employees working for 20 or more weeks during the relevant year. Salaried employees are included in this number for each week they are on the payroll, while hourly workers are only counted on the days they actually work. In 2004, the year of the alleged discrimination, 14 workers, 3 full-time and 11 part-time people, worked for Whole In One on any day during the 24-week restaurant and golf season. However, 10 full-time workers were on the payroll. Because these part-time workers are only counted on the days that they work, the number of part-time individuals included in the count of employees is 11 for each day of the 24-week season. Because full-time workers, however, are counted for each day of a week that they are on the payroll, all 10 of the Whole In One full-time workers would be included in the count of employees. In total, Whole In One had 11 part-time workers

ILLUSTRATION 19-2.   *Continued*

and 10 full-time workers "working" for 20 or more weeks during the relevant year, bringing the total count of employees to 21. Therefore, Whole In One was an employer under Title VII.

2. Walker was an employee. The Seventh Circuit will weigh five factors to determine whether she was an independent contractor or an employee for this Title VII lawsuit. The primary focus will be on the company's control of Walker. Although Walker worked from home, set her own hours and had an impact on her commission pay, the company controlled her work by reviewing and revising it, restricting Walker's employment opportunities, and providing supplies for her. Therefore, the company exerted control over Walker and she would be considered an employee.

3. Radiant was probably an employee. To determine whether she was an employee or independent contractor for this Title VII lawsuit, the court will focus on five factors, primarily the amount of control the company exerted over Radiant's work. Whole In One provided Radiant with an office, supplies, a two-year contract, and additional training. Whole In One paid her regularly and deducted taxes from her salary. Although Whole In One did not actively supervise Radiant's work on a daily basis, she still worked in the company offices and was under the control of Whole In One. Therefore, the court probably will find that Radiant was an employee.

FACTS

Victoria Radiant and Karen Walker, two former Whole In One Enterprises workers, brought a federal sex discrimination lawsuit based upon Title VII against our client, Whole In One Enterprises, owned by Nancy and Craig Black. The lawsuit, filed in the U.S. District Court for the Northern District of Illinois, stems from the dismissal of the two women by the Blacks during 2004.

The Blacks own Whole In One Enterprises, which operates a miniature golf course and restaurant in Glenview, Illinois. During the 24-week 2004 restaurant season, 10 people worked full-time and 14 people worked part-time for Whole In One. However, no more than 14 people worked on any one day. Of those 14 people, only 3 were full-time employees. The other full-time employees regularly took days off during the summer restaurant and golf season.

Among the full-time workers was Karen Walker, who worked as a public relations director for Whole In One. Walker responded to an ad that said that "an employer" sought an individual to perform public relations work. Whole In One hired Walker without a contract and prohibited her from working for other firms. However, Walker worked from home and set her own hours. Whole In One required Walker to attend weekly staff meetings at the company offices where Whole In One would review and revise Walker's work. The company supplied Walker with paper, pencils, stamps, telephone service, and paid for

ILLUSTRATION 19-2. *Continued*

her life and health insurance. Whole In One did not withhold taxes from Walker's commissions.

Victoria Radiant, who had a two-year employment contract with the company, provided marketing services to Whole In One from October of 2002 until she was fired in 2004. Although Radiant worked in the company office, Whole In One management rarely supervised her work. The company paid for her continued education, provided her with bonuses, and deducted taxes from her weekly salary.

Applicable Statute:

The term "employer" means a person engaged in an industry affecting commerce who has 15 or more employees for each working day in each of 20 or more calendar weeks in the current or preceding calendar year. 42 U.S.C. §2000e(b) (2004).

DISCUSSION

This memo first will address whether Walker and Radiant can successfully establish that Whole In One was an employer within the meaning of 42 U.S.C. §2000e(b) (2004), commonly called Title VII.

Next, the discussion will focus on whether Radiant can establish that she was an employee protected by Title VII. Finally, the memo will explore whether Walker was an employee protected by Title VII. If Whole In One was not an employer, then the Title VII claim will be dismissed. If the court finds that neither individual is an employee, the individual's claim will be barred.

I. Was Whole In One an Employer under Title VII?

Before a federal court can consider Walker's and Radiant's claims, the plaintiffs must establish that Whole In One was an employer under the definition established in Title VII. An employer is "a person engaged in a business affecting commerce who has 15 or more employees for each working day in each of 20 or more calendar weeks in the current or preceding calendar year." 42 U.S.C. §2000e(b). The focus of this discussion will be how to calculate whether 15 employees worked for Whole In One on each working day in each of 20 or more calendar weeks and how to determine which year's employment records are relevant. The Seventh Circuit has held that full-time employees are "working" each day of a week during a week for which they are on the payroll, but part-time workers are counted only on the days that they actually work. *Zimmerman v. North American Signal Co.,* 704 F.2d 347 (7th Cir. 1983). In 2004, the year of the alleged discrimination, 14 workers, 3 full-time and 11 part-time people, worked for Whole In One on any day during the 24-week restaurant and golf season. In addition, 10 full-time workers were on the payroll. Based upon the counting method established in *Zimmerman,* these figures indicate that Whole In One had at least 15 employees working for each working

ILLUSTRATION 19-2.   *Continued*

day in each of 20 or more calendar weeks. Therefore, Whole In One was an employer under Title VII.

The central focus of this discussion will be how to calculate the number of employees. First, the relevant year must be determined. The statute states that the time to be considered is "twenty or more calendar weeks in the current or preceding year." 42 U.S.C. §2000e(b) (2004). The current year of the discrimination was 2004. Since the statute specifies "or" the preceding year, 2003 also is relevant. However, in a persuasive decision a Tennessee district court held that the "current calendar year" is the year in which the alleged discrimination occurred. *Musser v. Mountain View Broadcasting, Inc.*, 578 F. Supp. 229 (E.D. Tenn. 1984). If the court follows *Musser,* the employment records from 2004 would be relevant because Whole In One fired Walker and Radiant in 2004.

The phrase "each working day" must be clarified. "Each working day" should be taken literally and must be a day on which an employer conducts normal, full operations on that day. *Zimmerman,* 704 F.2d at 353; *Wright v. Kosciusko Medical Clinic, Inc.,* 791 F. Supp. 1327, 1333 (N.D. Ind. 1992). Whole In One operated the golf course and restaurant seven days a week. Therefore, Whole In One must have 15 employees working on all seven days of a week to be considered an employer under Title VII.

The final issue is which individuals should be counted on each of the working days. The Seventh Circuit has determined that a salaried or full-time employee is counted as working for every day of the week that they are on the payroll, whether or not they were actually at work on a particular day. *Zimmerman v. North American Signal Co.,* 704 F.2d 347 (7th Cir. 1983). However, part-time workers are counted only on the days that they actually work. *Id.; Wright,* 791 F. Supp. at 1327; *Norman v. Levy,* 767 F. Supp. 144 (N.D. Ill. 1991). In 2004, the year of the alleged discrimination, 14 workers, 3 full-time and 11 part-time people, worked for Whole In One on any day during the 24-week restaurant and golf season. As these part-time workers are only counted on the days that they work, the number of part-time individuals included in the count of employees was 11 for each day of the 24-week season. Since full-time workers, however, are counted for each day of a week that they are on the payroll, all 10 of the Whole In One full-time workers should be included in the count of employees. In total, Whole In One had 11 part-time workers and 10 full-time workers "working" for 20 or more weeks during the relevant year, bringing the total count of employees to 21. Therefore, Whole In One was an employer under Title VII.

II. Are Walker and Radiant Employees or Independent Contractors?

If the plaintiffs can show that Whole In One was an employer, the court still must determine whether Walker and Radiant were employees

ILLUSTRATION 19-2. *Continued*

entitled to Title VII protection or independent contractors. To determine whether an individual is an independent contractor or an employee, the "economic realities" of the relationship between an employer and his or her worker must be weighed. *Knight v. United Farm Bureau Mut. Ins. Co.*, 950 F.2d 377 (7th Cir. 1991); *Norman v. Levy*, 767 F. Supp. 144 (N.D. Ill. 1991); *Mitchell v. Tenney*, 650 F. Supp. 703 (N.D. Ill. 1986). The Seventh Circuit will weigh five factors to determine the economic reality of the relationship: 1) the amount of control and supervision the employer exerts over the worker; 2) the responsibility for the costs of the operation; 3) the worker's occupation and the skills required; 4) the method and form of compensation and benefits; and 5) the length of the job commitment. *Knight*, 950 F.2d at 378. Control is the most important factor. *Id.* Moreover, when an employer controls a worker in such a manner as to make that worker economically dependent upon the employer, the court is likely to find that an employment relationship exists. *Vakharia v. Swedish Covenant Hosp.*, 765 F. Supp. 461 (N.D. Ill. 1991).

The *Knight* case involved an insurance agent who was not allowed to sell insurance for any other company and who was required to attend weekly staff meetings in the office and work a specified number of hours in the office. *Knight*, 950 F.2d at 378. The insurance company provided Knight with supplies and paid for business expenses. *Id.* The insurance company trained these agents. Also, the agents were crucial to the company's continued operation. *Id.* Knight was paid on commission and did not have taxes deducted. *Id.* Knight also was free to leave the company and work elsewhere. *Id.* Based upon these facts, the *Knight* court failed to find that the agent was an employee.

Although Walker's work situation was factually similar in many ways to that of the plaintiff in *Knight*, the *Knight* case can be distinguished based upon the nature of the occupations. Knight worked in the insurance sales field. Most often, individuals who work in such positions are independent contractors rather than employees of a company. In addition, the Seventh Circuit indicated in the dicta of the *Knight* case that it might have found that Knight was an employee. *Id.* at 381.

In contrast to *Knight*, the U.S. District Court for the Northern District of Illinois found that control of an individual's livelihood could establish an employment relationship. *Vakharia v. Swedish Covenant Hosp.*, 765 F. Supp. 461 (N.D. Ill. 1991). The plaintiff in *Vakharia* was a physician who was dependent upon the hospital for business. *Id.* at 463. The district court found that this individual depended upon the hospital for patients and that when the hospital reduced the number of patients it assigned to the plaintiff, the plaintiff's livelihood was affected. *Id.* The court held that when an employer has this type of control over an individual's livelihood an employment relationship may be established.

The facts in our case are similar to the facts in the *Vakharia* case. In our case, Whole In One barred Walker from working for other

ILLUSTRATION 19-2. *Continued*

companies and required that she attend weekly staff meetings at the company offices where Whole In One would review and revise Walker's work. Since Whole in One barred Walker from working for other individuals and required that she attend meetings where Whole In One would revise her work, it seems that Walker could establish the central element of control necessary to prove an employment relationship. In addition, these facts show that Walker, similar to the plaintiff in *Vakharia,* was economically dependent upon her employer, Whole In One. Therefore, an employment relationship should be established.

However, the plaintiffs will be able to show more than control. They will be able to establish that Whole In One bore the cost of the operation of the business. Whole In One supplied Walker with paper, pencils, stamps, telephone service, and paid for her life and health insurance. These facts indicate that Whole In One was responsible for the cost of Walker's services to the company—a fact that would help to establish that Walker was an employee.

The factors that would mitigate the establishment of an employment relationship, however, are that Walker worked from home and set her own hours and Whole In One did not withhold taxes from Walker's commissions. Despite these factors, the court is likely to focus on the control Whole In One had over Walker and is likely to find that she was an employee rather than an independent contractor.

III. Was Radiant an Employee or an Independent Contractor?

Whether Radiant was an employee again turns on the amount of control Whole In One exerted over Radiant's work. The court will focus on the same factors established in *Knight* to determine whether an employment relationship exists. *Knight,* 950 F.2d at 378. Control will be the key factor the court will consider. *Id.* Radiant had a two-year employment contract with the company to provide marketing services. Whole In One also provided her with an office, supplies, and additional training. The company paid her regularly and deducted taxes from her salary. Based upon these facts, the company exerted control over Radiant. Therefore, the court is likely to find that Radiant was an employee of Whole In One.

ILLUSTRATION 19-3. Sample Memorandum Heading

MEMORANDUM

To: Sarah E. Lillian
From: Kelsey Barrington
Date: July 8, 2008
Re: Negligence Action between Sack and Shop Grocery Store and Rebecca Harris

2. Questions Presented or Issues

The next portion of the memo seen in Illustrations 19-1 and 19-2 is the questions presented section, sometimes called the issues section.

The terms **issues** or **questions presented** are synonymous. For our purposes, we will use the terms *question presented* or *questions presented*. The questions presented are the specific legal questions an attorney has asked you to research. The question presented is phrased in the form of a question concerning the legal issue posed, and it includes a reference to the applicable law and some legally significant facts. See Illustration 19-4. The legal issue in Illustration 19-4 is whether the grocery store owner was negligent and whether he owed a duty to the patron. The legally significant facts are that the patron slipped on a banana peel that had been on the grocery store floor for two days. (A detailed explanation of how to draft the questions presented is provided in Chapter 21.) Note the facts included in the questions presented section of Illustration 19-2. These facts are the legally significant facts. They are interwoven with the standard of law applicable to this case.

ILLUSTRATION 19-4.   Question Presented

Is a grocery store owner liable for injuries sustained by a store patron who slipped on a banana peel that had been on the grocery store floor for two days?

3. Conclusion or Brief Answer

You should follow the questions presented section with a brief answer or a conclusion. Brief answers and conclusions differ in format, although their purposes are similar. A brief answer is a short statement that directly answers the question or questions presented. See Illustration 19-5. A conclusion is similar, but it is usually longer. In Illustration 19-2, you will find two examples of conclusions. They are in the same order as the issues that they answer.

ILLUSTRATION 19-5.   Brief Answer

Probably yes. A grocery store owner probably will be liable based upon negligence for injuries sustained by a store patron who slipped on a banana peel that had been on the grocery store floor for two days.

▼ What Is the Difference Between a Conclusion and a Brief Answer?

Some attorneys prefer a brief answer immediately following the question or questions presented and a formal conclusion at the end

of the memo. The brief answer should be presented in the same order as the questions they answer.

For other attorneys, a conclusion without a brief answer is sufficient. A conclusion is an in-depth answer to the question presented. There is no set length for a conclusion; it should be a succinct statement that summarizes the substance of the memo. See Illustration 19-6. As you can see in Illustration 19-6, the conclusion is more in-depth than the brief answer. However, note that both the conclusion and the brief answer include references to the legally significant facts: the failure to remove the banana peel from the grocery store floor. In the conclusion, you provide your opinion concerning the case. However, a paralegal should refrain from telling an attorney how to proceed. For example, do not say "I think that we will lose this case, so we should settle it." Instead, say "This case is not likely to be won." Allow the attorney to determine whether the case should be settled. (Drafting conclusions and brief answers is explained in detail in Chapter 20.)

ILLUSTRATION 19-6.   Conclusion

A grocery store owner owes a patron a duty of reasonable care. The store owner is likely to be found to have breached that duty of reasonable care because he failed to remove a banana peel from the grocery store floor during the preceding two days. The injuries the patron sustained were directly caused by a slip on a banana peel. Therefore, the grocery store owner is likely to be found liable to the patron.

ETHICS ALERT

Refrain from providing a legal opinion. Your memorandum may be given to a client and may be construed as providing legal advice.

---

4. Facts

Following the conclusion or brief answer, you should include a facts statement that explains the status of the case and all the facts that might have a bearing on the outcome of a client's case. These facts are called legally significant facts. You should include facts that cast your client's dispute or transaction in a good light and those that shade it in a negative light. See Illustration 19-7. The presentation of facts should be balanced rather than slanted.

ILLUSTRATION 19-7.   Facts Statement

Our client, Sack and Shop Grocery Store, is being sued for negligence by Rebecca Harris.

Harris went to the store to purchase groceries on July 8, 2004. While she was in the produce section, she slipped on a banana peel that had been left on the floor by a grocery store employee. The employee had dropped it on the floor two days earlier and had failed to clean it up after a patron asked him to do so. Harris sustained a broken arm and head injuries as a result of the slip and fall.

5. Discussion

Following the facts, you will include your discussion in which you will explain the current state of the applicable law, analyze the law, and apply the law to the legally significant facts noted in the facts statement. Any problems posed in the client's case and counterarguments should be presented here. This should not be an exhaustive review of the history of the law but should be focused analysis of the current state of the law. The law should be applied to each of the legally significant facts. Note if the law is primary binding or merely persuasive authority. Use only highly persuasive secondary authorities if primary authorities are not available.

Finally, following the discussion, you should include a conclusion if a brief answer rather than a conclusion has been used earlier. Review the discussion sections in Illustrations 19-1 and 19-2. Note that Illustration 19-2 contains multiple issues and they are discussed separately within the memo.

PRACTICE POINTER

Review memos prepared previously for the attorney who assigned the memorandum. Follow that format or ask the assigning attorney what format he or she prefers.

D. STEPS IN DRAFTING A MEMORANDUM

▼ What Steps Should You Take in Drafting a Memo?

1. An attorney will assign a research problem to you. Discuss the problem thoroughly with the attorney. Be certain to ask the attorney questions to clarify the legal issues and the facts of a dispute or

transaction. Ask for guidance concerning possible topics to research and resources to consult.

2. Immediately following your meeting, draft a preliminary statement of the legal issues and the relevant facts.

3. Begin your research. To develop an understanding of the issues and the general legal rules applicable to your problem, and to provide you with some search terms, read secondary authorities such as encyclopedias and *American Law Reports.* During your research, you often will discover other issues that may be relevant, and you will find additional facts that are important. If you are uncertain whether to pursue these additional issues, ask the attorney who assigned the case whether the issues are relevant.

4. If you have additional questions about the facts of a case, ask the attorney or the client for additional facts to assist you in determining what authorities are relevant to your research.

5. Find primary binding authorities. If you are unable to find those, locate persuasive primary or secondary authorities.

6. After you find relevant authorities, validate the authorities and review the citators for more current, valuable authorities. If necessary, review these additional authorities.

7. Prepare case briefs of the relevant cases. (See Chapter 18 for a detailed discussion of case briefing.)

8. After you have completed your research, rewrite the questions presented.

9. Rewrite the facts and then draft the brief answers or conclusions (or both).

10. Next, outline the discussion section. (See Chapter 24 for a discussion of outlining and organizing the memorandum.) While you are preparing your outline, you should synthesize the legal authorities. (This process is explained in Chapter 23.) You should formulate your discussion and paragraphs in a special format called IRAC, which is an abbreviation for the formula Issue, Rule, Application, and Conclusion. (This format is discussed thoroughly in Chapter 22.) You can now begin to write your memorandum.

CHECKLIST FOR DRAFTING A MEMORANDUM

1. Discuss the case with the attorney
   a. Discuss the legal issues presented
   b. Discuss the known facts
   c. Determine whether additional facts should be investigated
   d. Determine what law governs
   e. Check the memo bank to determine firm's style and to learn whether the issue has been researched previously
2. Draft a preliminary statement of the facts
3. Draft a preliminary statement of the legal issues or questions presented

4. Research the legal issue or issues
   a. If you find additional relevant issues, discuss them with the attorney
   b. Determine whether additional facts should be considered in light of the new issues; ask the attorney or client about additional facts
   c. Research the new issues, if necessary
5. Rewrite the issues or questions presented after your research has allowed you to focus them better
6. Draft a brief answer or a conclusion (or both)
7. Rewrite the facts statement of the memo
8. Draft an outline of the discussion section of the memo; organize the discussion
9. Draft the discussion section
10. Reevaluate the facts and rewrite the facts statement to include only legally significant facts
11. Rewrite the conclusion

1. Memo Drafting Tips

You should be careful to guide your reader through each section of your memo and from issue to issue. To do this, introduce the legal issues in the facts section and again in the discussion section. Also, use headings and transitions to guide your reader into the new sections. Your memo should be clearly written, accurate, concise, and thorough. Use everyday language rather than legalese. Write the memo as if the reader is unfamiliar with the law, but do not be condescending.

Your memo should not trace the legal history of the law. Instead, it should be a statement of the current state of the law.

When you approach a legal rule, start with the rule rather than the citation for the authority. Doing so makes your discussion stronger.

Be certain that your discussion supports your conclusions. Incorporate the relevant facts into your discussion.

CHAPTER SUMMARY

The legal memorandum is composed of issues, conclusions and brief answers, facts, and a discussion section. These are written for attorneys and clients. Memoranda are designed to assist them in determining the current state of the law regarding a legal issue and how that law applies to the facts presented in a particular case.

In the next few chapters, you will learn about each one of the components of a memorandum, the questions presented, the facts, the conclusions, the brief answers, and the discussion.

KEY TERMS

brief answer
conclusion
discussion
facts statement
heading

issues
legally significant facts
memo banks
office memorandum
questions presented

EXERCISES

TRUE OR FALSE

1. A memorandum should be persuasive in its style.
2. A memorandum should present only facts that are favorable to your client's position.
3. A memorandum should inform the attorney and the client about the favorable authorities and known facts as well as the authorities and facts that pose problems for a client's case.
4. Your memorandum will never be read by a client.
5. You should include descriptive words in the facts section that slant the facts in favor of your client's position.
6. What are the components of a memorandum?

CHAPTER 20

QUESTIONS PRESENTED AND CONCLUSIONS OR BRIEF ANSWERS

CHAPTER OVERVIEW

Chapter 19 introduced you to the legal memorandum and its components. This chapter explains the reasons for drafting questions presented, issues, brief answers, and conclusions and teaches you how to draft these items.

A. QUESTIONS PRESENTED OR ISSUES

The questions presented or issues are the problems you must research to answer the attorney's or client's questions. These questions provide a preview to the reader about the applicable legal standards and the relevant facts. They are always posed in the form of a question.

▼ Who Reads the Questions Presented Statement?

The questions presented statement often is the first portion of a memorandum an attorney reviews. Many attorneys focus on these questions and the conclusions or brief answers. Some attorneys read these questions and answers without reading the entire memorandum. Therefore, your questions presented statement must be easy to understand and allow the reader to quickly grasp the legal questions that the memo will address.

1. First Draft

The first draft of the questions presented should be done following the receipt of the initial research assignment from the attorney. Draft a simple statement that explains the questions you were asked to research. For example, suppose an attorney provides you with the following facts:

> While driving a car Ronnie Randall struck Janice Kahn's son at 5:00 P.M. on August 29, 2008. It was bright and clear. No skid marks appeared on the dry street following the accident.
>
> Janice Kahn was working in her garden about five feet from the accident scene at the time of the accident. Her son was playing a game in the street before Randall's car struck him. Kahn saw the car strike her son. When she first looked up from her garden, she thought her 11-year-old son was dead. He was covered with blood and had several broken bones. However, Kahn's son was conscious after the accident.
>
> Immediately after the accident, Randall, who had a blood alcohol level of .11, was cited for drunk driving and driving with a suspended driver's license. Police had charged him with drunk driving and had suspended his license two weeks earlier after the car he was driving struck another child at the same spot. Randall has a drinking history.
>
> Following the accident, several witnesses said Randall was upset and wobbled as he walked. One witness said that Randall intentionally turned the steering wheel to hit Kahn's son. Kahn stated that Randall often swerved down her street to get her attention.
>
> Rhonda Albert, Kahn's neighbor, said she heard Randall say he would get even with Kahn after Kahn broke off a ten-year relationship with him. During Kahn and Randall's ten-year relationship, Randall was close to Kahn's son. He took him to ball games, including one in April, and attended the son's baseball games. Randall knew that Kahn's son was the most important person in her life.

Since the accident, Janice Kahn vomits daily and suffers from anxiety and headaches. Dr. Susan Faigen, Kahn's internist, states that the vomiting, anxiety, and headaches are the result of the accident.

The attorney wants you to research whether Janice Kahn has a claim against Ronnie Randall for intentional infliction of emotional distress. Your first draft of the question presented might be:

> Does Janice Kahn have a valid claim for intentional infliction of emotional distress against Ronnie Randall?

This statement is devoid of legally significant facts.

▼ What Are Legally Significant Facts?

These are facts that will have an impact on a jury's or judge's decisions concerning Kahn's claim. This question presented is too vague. To make your question more understandable in the context of Kahn's case, you must incorporate legally significant facts.

Legally Significant Facts

Kahn saw Randall strike her 11-year-old son
Randall struck the boy with his car
Kahn now suffers from anxiety, headaches, and vomiting

You might rewrite the question presented with the fact that Kahn saw Randall strike her 11-year-old son with his car. That fact is legally significant. The rewrite might read as follows:

> Does Janice Kahn have a valid claim for intentional infliction of emotional distress against Ronnie Randall when Kahn **saw** Randall strike her 11-year-old child with his car?

By incorporating some legally significant facts, you have drafted a question presented that places the issue in perspective for the reader and that clearly identifies the parties in the action. This question presented allows the reader to understand the legal issue in the context of the factual circumstances surrounding the claim.

2. Research the Issue and Revise It

Now you are ready to research the issue. After you complete your research, you determine what law applies to a claim for intentional infliction of emotional distress. Once you determine the legal standard, you rewrite the question presented to incorporate that standard and only the legally significant facts. Your rewrite should frame the questions presented around the applicable legal standard and should present the applicable legal standard in the context of the facts that will affect the determination of a claim.

In the case of Janice Kahn, you learn from a decision of the highest court in your state that intentional infliction of emotional distress is "an act done by a person which is extreme and outrageous, done with intent to cause another to suffer severe emotional distress, and which results in distress and emotional injury to another. The emotional injury must manifest itself with a physical problem." If you rewrite the question presented above to incorporate the legal standard and legally significant facts, it might read as follows:

> Does Janice Kahn have a valid claim for intentional infliction of emotional distress against Ronnie Randall after Kahn saw Randall turn his car to strike Kahn's 11-year-old child in front of her, causing her to suffer from anxiety, headaches, and vomiting?

This question presented incorporates legally significant facts and provides these facts in the context of the legal standard. Randall's intention is one of the legal factors or elements in determining whether Kahn has a claim for intentional infliction of emotional distress. The question presented notes the legally significant fact that Randall turned his car to strike the child. The fact that Kahn now suffers from anxiety, headaches, and vomiting also is legally significant and relates to the legal standard because it may show that Kahn suffers from severe emotional distress. Although you should mention legally significant facts and the legal standard, keep the issue short enough for the reader to understand.

When you have multiple questions presented, the conclusion section should answer the questions in the same order as they were presented.

IN-CLASS EXERCISE

Review the question presented in Illustration 20-1. Determine what legal issue is presented. Then find the legally significant facts that are included in the question presented.

ILLUSTRATION 20-1.   Question Presented

Is the grocery store owner liable for injuries sustained by a store patron who slipped on a banana peel that had been on the grocery store floor for two days?

3. Specificity and Precision

The facts should be specific and your characterization of the parties and the issues should be precise. For example, one of the issues posed in the

sample memo in Appendix C Illustration 2 involves the question of whether an individual is an independent contractor or an employee.

You could pose the question presented as follows:

> Under Title VII, was Walker an employee when she worked exclusively for Whole In One, paid her own taxes quarterly rather than through deductions, and worked with limited company supervision?

The facts in this case are specific: Walker paid her taxes quarterly rather than through payroll deductions. However, the question presented is not precise because it does not characterize the legal issue presented completely. The legal issue is whether Walker is an independent contractor rather than an employee. Therefore, the question presented could be refined as follows:

> Under Title VII, was Walker an independent contractor rather than an employee when she worked exclusively for Whole In One, paid her own taxes quarterly rather than through deductions, and worked with limited company supervision?

You must only ask a question in the questions presented statement, not provide an answer. You will answer the question presented in the brief answer or conclusion section.

If you have more than one issue or question presented, place them in a logical order and make that order consistent throughout the memo. The first question presented, then, should be answered first in the conclusion or brief answer statement and should be the first issue addressed in the discussion. See Illustration 19-1 in Chapter 19.

B. BRIEF ANSWERS AND CONCLUSIONS

1. Brief Answers

Brief answers are the quick answers to the question or questions presented. A brief answer is a short statement. Some attorneys prefer a brief answer that is later accompanied by a formal conclusion at the end of the memorandum. The brief answer allows an attorney to read a memo in a hurry and determine the legal issues. See Illustration 20-2.

ILLUSTRATION 20-2.   Question Presented and Brief Answer

Question Presented: Does Janice Kahn have a valid claim for intentional infliction of emotional distress against Ronnie Randall after Kahn saw Randall turn his car to strike Kahn's 11-year-old child in front of her, causing her to suffer from anxiety, headaches, and vomiting?

Brief Answer: Yes. Kahn can bring a successful action for intentional infliction of emotional distress against Ronnie Randall because she saw Randall turn his car to strike her 11-year-old son, causing her to suffer severe anxiety, headaches, and vomiting.

The brief answer should include a brief statement of the applicable law and some relevant facts. A brief answer for the question presented above in Illustration 20-1 could be presented as follows in Illustration 20-3.

ILLUSTRATION 20-3. Brief Answer

Probably yes. A grocery store owner probably will be liable based upon negligence for injuries sustained by a store patron who slipped on a banana peel that had been on the grocery store floor for two days.

In the memorandum, it would appear as in Illustration 19-1. This brief answer addresses the question presented in Illustration 19-1. The legal standard applicable to this case, negligence, is mentioned along with legally significant facts.

2. Conclusions

A conclusion also is an answer to the question presented and a summary of the discussion section. For some attorneys, a conclusion without a brief answer is sufficient. However, other attorneys prefer both a brief answer and a conclusion.

▼ How Is a Conclusion Different from a Brief Answer?

A conclusion does not have a set length, but it is generally longer than a brief answer. It is not a detailed or in-depth discussion of the legal issue presented in the case. It is a succinct summary of the substance of the memo. The conclusion should include legally significant facts and the applicable legal standard. In the conclusion, you must answer the question presented and provide your best prediction concerning the outcome of the case. It is acceptable to use terms such as *likely* or *probably* when you think that the outcome of an action is uncertain.

3. Drafting Conclusions

Before you draft your conclusion, review the questions presented and your preliminary facts statement. (A detailed explanation of the facts statement is presented in Chapter 21.)

Next, write the conclusion as an answer to the question presented and incorporate some of the relevant facts contained in the facts

section of the memo. Refine the conclusion so that the reader understands the legal standard and the applicable facts. Conclusions often work well when drafted in an IRAC formula: Issue, Rule, Application, and Conclusion. (For a thorough discussion of the IRAC formula, see Chapter 22.)

For the facts and the question presented in the *Kahn* case, the following conclusion might be prepared:

> The central question is whether Janice Kahn has a valid claim for intentional infliction of emotional distress against Ronnie Randall. To successfully prove a claim for intentional infliction of emotional distress, Khan must show that the act that caused the distress was extreme and outrageous and done with intent. In the case, Kahn saw Randall turn his car to strike her 11-year-old child. Seeing this accident caused Kahn to suffer from anxiety, headaches, and vomiting daily. Several witnesses can testify that Randall said that he intended to harm Kahn, and Kahn states that Randall turned the car to strike her son. Two factors, however, might show that Randall lacked intent: the statement that he made to the police that he did not intend to hit the child and the fact that his blood alcohol level was .11, possibly preventing him from formulating the needed intent. Kahn probably has a claim for intentional emotional distress.

This conclusion provides a summary of the writer's prediction of the outcome of the case after the legal standards are applied to the legally significant facts:

> Janice Kahn probably has a valid claim for intentional infliction of emotional distress against Ronnie Randall.

Facts such as that Kahn saw Randall turn the car to strike her son and that witnesses can testify concerning what Randall said he intended to do are relevant to the question of whether the act was extreme and outrageous. The legal standard provides that the act must be extreme and outrageous before an individual can be liable for intentional infliction of emotional distress. In addition, the extreme and outrageous act must be done with intent. Randall's intent also is discussed in the conclusion.

Many students include an authority, such as a statute or case, in the conclusion. Most often, however, your analysis of a claim requires that you synthesize a number of authorities to determine the applicable law. It would be misleading, therefore, to include only one authority in your conclusion. You might include an authority if it is the sole authority governing a claim.

When two or more questions presented are noted in the memorandum, a conclusion or a brief answer and then a conclusion for each question should be noted in the same order as the question presented. See Illustration 20-4.

ILLUSTRATION 20-4. Questions Presented Conclusion

QUESTIONS PRESENTED

1. Under Title VII, was Whole In One Golf Resort an employer when 14 people, including 3 full-time and 11 part-time workers, worked on any one day for 24 weeks and when 10 full-time employees were on the Whole In One payroll?

2. Under Title VII, was Walker an independent contractor rather than an employee when she worked exclusively for Whole In One, paid taxes quarterly rather than through deductions, and worked with limited company supervision?

3. Under Title VII, was Radiant an independent contractor rather than an employee when she worked with limited company supervision using company supplies and equipment and had taxes and medical deductions taken from her salary?

CONCLUSIONS

1. Whole In One was an employer. Under Title VII, an employer has at least 15 employees working for 20 or more weeks during the relevant year. Salaried employees are included in this number for each week they are on the payroll, while hourly workers are only counted on the days they actually work. In 2007, the year of the alleged discrimination, 14 workers, 3 full-time and 11 part-time people, worked for Whole In One on any day during the 24-week restaurant and golf season. However, 10 full-time workers were on the payroll. Because these part-time workers are only counted on the days that they work, the number of part-time individuals included in the count of employees is 11 for each day of the 24-week season. Because full-time workers, however, are counted for each day of a week that they are on the payroll, all 10 of the Whole In One full-time workers would be included in the count of employees. In total, Whole In One had 11 part-time workers and 10 full-time workers "working" for 20 or more weeks during the relevant year, bringing the total count of employees to 21. Therefore, Whole In One was an employer under Title VII.

2. Walker was an employee. The Seventh Circuit will weigh five factors to determine whether she was an independent contractor or an employee for this Title VII lawsuit. The primary focus will be on the company's control of Walker. Although Walker worked from home, set her own hours, and had an impact on her commission pay, the company controlled her work by reviewing and revising it, restricting Walker's employment opportunities, and providing supplies for her. Therefore, the company exerted control over Walker and she would be considered an employee.

3. Radiant was probably an employee. To determine whether she was an employee or independent contractor for this Title VII lawsuit, the court will focus on five factors, primarily the amount of control the company exerted over Radiant's work. Whole In One provided Radiant

with an office, supplies, a two-year contract, and additional training. Whole In One paid her regularly and deducted taxes from her salary. Although Whole In One did not actively supervise Radiant's work on a daily basis, she still worked in the company offices and was under the control of Whole In One. Therefore, the court probably will find that Radiant was an employee.

PRACTICE POINTER

When you have multiple questions presented, the conclusion section should answer the questions in the same order as they were presented.

IN-CLASS EXERCISE

Read the questions presented in Illustration 20-4.

1. Discuss the issues and conclusions.
2. After reviewing the questions presented, what legal standards do you think will determine the applicable law?
3. Does the conclusion answer the questions presented? Are the legal standards discussed? What, if any, standards are noted?

EXPLANATION FOR IN-CLASS EXERCISE

For the question presented in Illustration 20-4, the issue is whether Whole In One is an employer under Title VII. The legal standards that determine whether Whole In One is an employer center on the definition of *employer* under Title VII and case law.

Now read the conclusion. It answers the question presented. In the second and third sentences, the conclusion provides the legal standard for determining this issue. These sentences refer to the definition of *employer* contained in the Title VII statute, which states that an employer "is a person engaged in a business affecting commerce who has fifteen or more employees for each working day in each of 20 or more calendar weeks in the current or preceding calendar year." 42 U.S.C. §2000e(b). The next sentence concerning salaried employees and part-time employees is based on a synthesis of the applicable cases. Next, the relevant facts of this case are discussed and applied to the legal standards. Finally, the writer presents a single sentence summarizing how the issue is likely to be resolved based on the application of the legal standards to the facts presented.

CHAPTER SUMMARY

In this chapter, you learned how to draft questions presented, issues, brief answers, and conclusions. Questions presented or issues should incorporate legally significant facts and the rule of law. Legally significant facts are facts that will affect a decision concerning an issue of law.

Legally significant facts and the current rule of law also should be included in the conclusions in the conclusions or brief answers that answer the questions presented or issues.

Some attorneys prefer both a brief answer and a conclusion, while others require only a conclusion.

The process of writing the questions presented, issues, brief answers, and conclusions requires that you rewrite these components of a memorandum several times. The questions presented or issues should be drafted before you perform your research. The conclusions or brief answers also should be rewritten in light of the facts presented in a case.

In the next chapter, you learn how to draft facts statements for your memoranda.

KEY TERMS

brief answers	precise
conclusion	questions presented
issues	specific
legally significant facts	

EXERCISES

SHORT ANSWER

1. What is a brief answer?
2. How does a brief answer differ from a conclusion?
3. Is an issue or question presented written as a statement or a question?
4. If you have four questions presented, how many conclusions or brief answers should you have?
5. What is the purpose of a question presented?
6. What is the purpose of a conclusion?

QUESTIONS PRESENTED

Draft questions presented for memos in the following cases.

7. You work as a paralegal for the country prosecutor's office in Houcktown County. One of the assistant prosecutors asks you to research whether Bonnie Bill has committed aggravated burglary under the Houcktown Rev. Code §2911. The attorney has provided you with the following facts:

Merriweather Halsey and Bonnie Bill were at the Masonic Temple for a fundraiser to fight AIDS. During the fundraiser Bill told a drunken Halsey that she intended to steal the $8,000 fundraiser proceeds from the Masonic Temple after the fundraiser and that she intended to steal a pearl necklace from Alice McKinley.

Bill, who had helped organize the fundraiser, watched as the chairperson of the fundraiser opened the safe and placed the money in it. She memorized the combination and decided that she would use it later to steal the money.

After the fundraiser, Bill walked home to get a credit card and a crowbar to open the door if she needed it. Bill went to the Masonic Temple after the fundraiser, wearing a disguise, showed the guard her invitation, and told him that she lost her mother's diamond brooch inside. Although the guard did not remember her, he allowed her to go into the temple. She wandered around the building for about an hour with the brooch inside her purse.

When the guard decided to eat his supper and call home, Bill went to the safe. She opened it and pulled out all the money, except for $1,000.

Bill told the guard she found the brooch and then left. She went to Alice McKinley's home, entered the house through an open ground-floor window, took the pearl necklace she had seen Alice wearing earlier, and then left.

The relevant statute is as follows:

§2911 Aggravated Burglary

(A) A person is guilty of aggravated burglary when the person, by force or deception, trespasses in any house, building, outbuilding, watercraft, aircraft, railroad car, truck, trailer, tent vehicle or shelter with the purpose of committing a theft; and

(1) inflicts or attempts or threatens to inflict physical harm to another; or
(2) the person has a deadly weapon, which is any instrument, device, or thing capable of inflicting death or designed or specially adapted for use as a weapon; or
(3) the person has a dangerous ordnance such as any automatic or sawed off firearm, zip gun or ballistic knife, explosive or incendiary device; or
(4) the structure is the permanent or temporary dwelling of a person.

8. An assistant county prosecutor wants you to research whether Merriweather Halsey committed aggravated burglary based on the following facts:

Merriweather Halsey considered borrowing money from a friend who worked at the local bulb factory. She wandered into the factory around 4:00 A.M., after an AIDS fundraiser. The guard had stepped away from the door for a break. She headed toward her friend's workstation, but she stumbled into an open office where the petty cash was kept. She fell

over a secretary's desk. Her leg caught the desk and pulled open a drawer that contained $500. She thought about taking the money, but she passed out before she took it. She woke up at about 6:00 A.M., when a secretary found her and summoned the security guard.

Halsey then fell onto the security guard, causing him to crash his head into a planter. The guard cut his head and later required six stitches. Halsey thought the security guard was a robber, so she grabbed a letter opener from a nearby desk and told the security guard to back off. The security guard took the letter opener. Halsey's mind was still fuzzy from the alcohol, but she decided to pull a squirt gun out of her pocket to scare the robber.

Draft a question presented for this problem based on the aggravated burglary statute noted in question 7 above.

CONCLUSIONS

9. Draft a conclusion for the problem discussed in exercise 7.
10. Draft a conclusion for the problem discussed in exercise 8.
11. Review the following facts. Make a list of the legally significant facts. Then prepare an issue statement and a conclusion for this problem.

Your client, Hospitality Resorts International, Inc., which does business in your state, is defending an action against James Panhandle, a 70-year-old doctor from Akron, Ohio, who slipped and fell at a London hotel bearing the name Hospitality Resorts of London on January 28, 2008. Panhandle, a semi-retired general practice physician, smashed his head on some wet marble flooring next to the pool. A sign saying "slippery when wet" was set up next to the pool, but Panhandle didn't see the sign. He sustained severe and permanent injuries and was unable to practice medicine for two years.

Panhandle often stayed at the Hospitality Resorts. The resorts were known for cleanliness and hospitality. The staff was friendly and always helpful. The advertising for the resorts claimed that it was the "cleanest in the world. We stay on top of our hotels." Most advertisements stated that the hotels were independently owned and operated. Some ads, such as the one that appeared in the Doctor's Weekly, which Panhandle read, did not state that independent owners owned the London hotel. That ad boasted about the resort, "We care about you. We take care of you. We take care of your home—our resort."

Hospitality Resorts was a trade name. The company that licensed the name Hospitality Resorts to other hotels was called Hospitality Resorts International, Inc. (HRII), your client. Hospitality Resorts licensed its trade name to Fred and Ethel Carrigan of London, England, for use in a hotel there. The Carrigans called the hotel Hospitality Resorts of London. As part of the license agreement, Hospitality Resorts provided training to the staff. The Carrigans hired and fired the staff. HRII had no authority to hire and fire staff.

Panhandle did not know anything about the training or the connection between the London hotel and HRII.

HRII provided operations manuals and suggested procedures and menus. Personnel from HRII regularly traveled to London to advise the hotel employees about their jobs. HRII had no ownership interest in the

London hotel. HRII was not authorized to act on behalf of the hotel nor was the hotel authorized to act on behalf of HRII.

The license agreement between HRII and Hospitality Resort of London only provided for HRII to provide its name Hospitality Resort to the London hotel as well as some manuals and technical assistance. It did not authorize the London hotel to act as its agent and HRII was not an agent of the London hotel. HRII did include the Hospitality Resort of London in its list of Hospitality Resorts. That list appeared in many ads as well as in a brochure.

Plaintiff filed suit against the Hospitality Resort in London and Hospitality Resorts, and Hospitality Resorts International, Inc., alleging that HRII is in an agency relationship or apparent or ostensible agency relationship with the London Hospitality Resort. Thus, plaintiff claims that HRII and the London hotel are both responsible for his injuries. This suit was filed in the United States District Court for your area. All the rules of that court and the Federal Rules of Civil Procedures apply.

Does our client have a good defense to the plaintiff's claim that it was in an agency relationship with the London hotel?

Assume that the highest court in your state has held that a hotel owner can be liable based upon the theory of apparent agency. Under that theory, if a business allows another to hold itself out as its representative or the individual or entity holds itself as acting on behalf of the business, the business may be liable for the acts of the individual or entity. Also assume that a decision of the federal appellate court in your area follows your high court's decision.

12. Review this question presented and this conclusion. What legally significant facts are included in the question presented? What legally significant facts are included in the conclusion?

Question Presented

Did an actionable battery occur when Mann intentionally struck McMillan with a bucket, without McMillian's consent, causing McMillian to suffer physical and monetary injuries?

Conclusion

Mann's intentional striking of McMillan with a bucket and sand was an actionable battery.

FACTS

CHAPTER OVERVIEW

This chapter explains the purpose of a facts statement and how to draft one. To do this, you need to learn how to determine which facts are legally significant. The chapter discusses the difference between a fact

and a legal conclusion and demonstrates the different organizational structures for the facts section.

A. FACTS STATEMENT

The facts statement is a summary of the information that is relevant to the determination of whether a legal claim exists or whether a defense to such a claim can be made. It is also a summary of the status of a pending case.

A fact statement is an integral part of the office memorandum. Often, an attorney reads this statement to refresh his or her memory about the facts of the case before meeting with a client or a judge. The facts detailed in a memorandum also provide a reference point for your research and the framework for the application of the law.

1. Defining *Fact*

A fact may be a thing that is known with certainty. It can be an event. It can be an observation. The answer is not clear-cut. Some facts are pure facts, which means there is no dispute about them. For example, an individual's birth is a pure fact. Facts in the court document, such as a complaint or an answer, are asserted facts, which means the individual is claiming they occurred. Some information can be objectively tested. That is a fact. For the purpose of the facts statement, note all of this information as facts.

2. Legally Significant Facts

▼ What Facts Should Be Included in the Facts Statement?

All facts that might have an impact on the issues presented in a particular case must be included in the memo. These facts are called **legally significant facts.** A good rule is that if you plan to include a fact in your discussion of the law, it should be mentioned in the facts statement.

Legally significant facts are those facts that may affect how a court would decide a particular legal issue. To determine which facts are legally significant, you must understand the legal issue or issues presented in your case. A **legal claim** is comprised of components called **elements** that must be proven before a claim is successful. Legally significant facts are those facts that might prove or disprove any of those elements.

For example, you are asked to research the factors a court will consider when it decides whether Sack and Shop Grocery Store was liable to Rebecca Harris, a patron, for a slip-and-fall accident that occurred in the store. Ms. Harris was injured when she slipped on a banana peel that had been left on the store floor for two days.

Ms. Harris's shopping list included bananas, cherries, and strawberries. You determine that the action or legal claim is based on negligence. You learn that negligence is the breach of a duty of reasonable care that results in an injury to another person. The legal elements of negligence are as follows:

- Existence of a duty
- Breach of that duty
- Injury caused by the breach of the duty

Legally significant facts are those facts that might prove or disprove any of those elements. In this case, the legally significant facts and the legal element that they might prove or disprove would include:

- The slip and fall occurred in the store. (injury, breach)
- Rebecca Harris slipped on a banana peel that had been left on the store floor for two days. (injury, breach)
- Rebecca Harris suffered injuries as a result of the fall. (injury)
- Rebecca Harris shopped daily at the store. (duty)
- Rebecca Harris went to the store to make a purchase. (duty)

A fact that is not necessarily legally significant is:

- Rebecca Harris's shopping list included bananas, cherries, and strawberries.

This fact does not prove or disprove any of the elements.

Do not omit any legally significant facts even if you think that an attorney should remember them from client meetings. Attorneys are responsible for multiple cases, and these statements often are used to refresh their recollection. If a fact is not legally significant, you generally would exclude it. However, if the fact explains how a dispute or transaction arose or explains the relationship between the parties, then that fact should be noted. Such a **procedural fact** would assist the reader in understanding the status of a case.

Facts statements provide facts that are advantageous for your clients and those facts that are unfavorable to them. Remember that this is an objective memo. The facts should be presented in a neutral manner, devoid of emotion. Compare the following two examples.

EXAMPLE

Our client, Janice Kahn, seeks to sue Ronnie Randall for intentional infliction of emotional distress following a car accident in which Randall brutally struck Kahn's only child while the precious child was playing T-ball in the street with his friends. This brutal act was done in the presence of Ms. Kahn, a caring mother, who was gardening while watching

her child play. As a result of the incident, Kahn was devastated and emotionally distraught.

EXAMPLE

Our client, Janice Kahn, seeks to sue Ronnie Randall for intentional infliction of emotional distress following a car accident in which Randall struck Kahn's child while the child was playing T-ball in the street with his friends. After Randall struck the child, he backed up and struck the boy again, running over his head with the rear tire. Ms. Kahn was gardening nearby while watching her child play.

The first example contains several adjectives that slant the statement in favor of Kahn. The statement "Randall brutally struck Kahn's only child" characterizes the action as brutal. This is not a statement of fact. The adjective *brutal* should not be included in a facts statement. The second example is devoid of these **emotional adjectives.** Instead of using the word *brutal,* the second example details the underlying acts that constitute a brutal strike:

> After Randall struck the child, he backed up and struck the boy again, running over his head with the rear tire.

The second example allows readers to draw their own conclusions. The facts statement should not be slanted. Facts such as that Kahn was "a caring mother" or that the child was "precious" should not be incorporated into a facts statement. You should mention only facts, not legal conclusions or definitions of the law.

3. Fact Versus a Legal Conclusion

A fact is a piece of information that might explain to the reader what occurred in a particular case. In contrast, a legal conclusion is an opinion about the legal significance of a fact. Read the following facts statement:

> Our client, Janice Kahn, seeks to sue Ronnie Randall for intentional infliction of emotional distress following a car accident in which Randall maliciously struck Kahn's only child while the child was playing T-ball in the street with his friends. This malicious and intentional act was done in the presence of Ms. Kahn, a caring mother, who was gardening while watching her child play.

The statements that the act was *malicious* and *intentional* are legal conclusions because the writer makes assumptions about the state of mind of the actor. The term *malicious* is a legal element of many claims; it describes a wicked state of mind. *Intentional* also describes a legal element. You should exclude such characterizations from your facts statements. Instead, describe the acts a person committed that could

be considered malicious, or statements that could indicate that an act was intentional. For example:

> Randall struck Kahn's only child after he told a neighbor that he intended to hit the child with his car while the child was playing T-ball. Randall struck the child with his car while the car was traveling at 25 miles an hour.

The information about Randall's comments to the neighbor, coupled with the speed at which he struck the child, could indicate that Randall struck the child maliciously and intentionally. The proper place to discuss whether an act is either malicious or intentional is in the discussion section of the memo. A definition of the law also is not a statement of fact and should be noted only in the memo discussion.

4. Source of Information for a Facts Statement

Most often, information from a client interview is the basis for your facts statement. See the example in Illustration 21-7 later in this chapter. During a court dispute, information for the facts statement also can be found in witness statements, complaints, answers, or discovery materials, such as depositions and interrogatories. For these facts, note the source of the information. For transactions, information might be contained in various business records or contracts.

B. ORGANIZING THE FACTS STATEMENT

A facts statement can be organized in several ways: chronologically, by claim or defense, by party, or according to a combination of these three methods.

▼ What Are the Different Methods of Organizing a Facts Statement?

1. Chronological Organization

A chronological organization is based on the order of events. You start with the event that occurred first and end with the event that occurred last. You also can write the statement in reverse chronological order, beginning with the last event and ending with the first. For some claims, such as those stemming from an accident, a contract dispute, or a criminal case, chronological organization works well because these concerns often are ordered by time. See Illustration 21-1.

The statement in Illustration 21-1 first introduces the claim. In the succeeding paragraphs, the events are detailed in chronological order from start to finish. Illustration 21-2 starts with the last event and ends with the information about the beginning of the day.

ILLUSTRATION 21-1. Chronological Organization

Dr. James Panhandle is suing our client, Hospitality Resorts International, Inc., for negligence stemming from injuries he sustained when he slipped and fell on January 28, 2008, at the Hospitality Resort of London. The doctor seeks $8 million in damages.

On the day of the accident, children were playing in the pool at 8:00 A.M. The children splashed water out of the pool and onto the marble floor near the pool. The floor had not been mopped at any time during the day.

At 8:00 P.M., Dr. Panhandle was walking slowly out of the hotel coffee shop that was adjacent to the pool. He slipped on the wet marble floor next to the pool.

The doctor hit his head on the marble floor, causing him to crack his skull and to bleed.

ILLUSTRATION 21-2. Reverse Chronological Order

Dr. James Panhandle is suing our client, Hospitality Resorts International, Inc., for negligence stemming from injuries he sustained when he slipped and fell on January 28, 2008, at the Hospitality Resort of London. The doctor seeks $8 million in damages.

The doctor hit his head on the marble floor, causing him to crack his skull and to bleed.

At 8:00 P.M., Dr. Panhandle was walking slowly out of the hotel coffee shop that was adjacent to the pool. He slipped on the wet marble floor next to the pool.

On the day of the accident, children were playing in the pool at 8:00 A.M. The children splashed water out of the pool and onto the marble floor near the pool. The floor had not been mopped at any time during the day.

2. Organization by Claim or Defense

Facts statements also can be organized by claim or defense. In statements of this kind, legally significant facts that relate to a claim or a defense are grouped together. See Illustration 21-3. This method is useful when the issue does not concern events that can be organized by time sequence and the information involves individuals who are not parties to the action.

ILLUSTRATION 21-3. Organization by Claim or Defense

Our clients, the Black Hawks, want to know whether the attorney-client privilege can be asserted by a former company president, Debbie Irl, and a current employee, Meredith Tildy, head of the cleaning staff. These questions arose while the plaintiff's attorney was deposing

ILLUSTRATION 21-3. *Continued*

these individuals on July 8, 2008, as part of the discovery in a personal injury lawsuit stemming from a slip and fall at the stadium.

Irl, president of the Hawks at the time of the accident, left the organization in June 2008. During her tenure with the organization, she was a decision maker and she drafted the cleaning policy for the stadium. Irl had spoken with the Hawks' attorney, Ace Rudd, about the accident on July 10, 2007. Irl is not named as a party in the lawsuit and is merely a witness. During the deposition, the plaintiff's attorney asked Irl about her conversation with Rudd. Irl asserted the attorney-client privilege.

Meredith Tildy, the current head of the Hawks' cleaning staff, knew about the accident. Beer had been spilled the night before the accident. A patron told the staff to mop up the beer when it happened. Tildy knew that the cleaning staff had failed to clean up the beer. In her position, Tildy schedules the staff and decides whether the stadium should be cleaned completely each night. On July 10, 2007, Tildy spoke with Rudd, the company attorney, about the accident. The plaintiff's attorney asked Tildy about her conversation with Rudd. Based upon Rudd's advice, Tildy asserted the attorney-client privilege.

In Illustration 21-3's sample facts statement, the details are organized by claim. The first paragraph introduces the claims—the assertion of attorney-client privilege by Irl and Tildy. The next paragraph includes the facts that are legally significant to Irl's claim of attorney-client privilege. The final paragraph focuses on the facts that are legally significant to Tildy and Tildy's assertion of the attorney-client privilege. Because neither Irl nor Tildy is a party, this organization works well.

3. Organization by Party

Another way to organize the facts is to organize by party, grouping the facts according to the party the facts describe. This method is useful when multiple parties are involved in a dispute. See Illustration 21-4, which involves a dispute between three parties: a company and two individuals. The memo focuses on whether Whole In One is an employer under Title VII and whether two individuals are employees or independent contractors.

The first paragraph in Illustration 21-4 introduces the claim. The next paragraph describes one of the parties, Whole In One. The next paragraph describes another party, Walker. The final paragraph tells the reader about Radiant, the third party in the action.

ILLUSTRATION 21-4. **Organization by Party**

Victoria Radiant and Karen Walker, two former Whole In One Enterprises workers, brought a federal sex discrimination lawsuit, based upon Title VII, against our client, Whole In One Enterprises, owned

ILLUSTRATION 21-4. *Continued*

by Nancy and Craig Black. The lawsuit, filed in the U.S. District Court for the Northern District of Illinois, stems from the dismissal of the two women by the Blacks during 2007.

The Blacks own Whole In One Enterprises, which operates a miniature golf course and restaurant in Glenview, Illinois. During the 24-week 2007 restaurant season, 10 people worked full-time and 14 people worked part-time for Whole In One. However, no more than 14 people worked on any one day. Of those 14 people, only 3 were full-time employees. The other full-time employees regularly took days off during the summer restaurant and golf season.

Among the full-time workers was Karen Walker, who worked as a public relations director for Whole In One. Walker responded to an ad that said that "an employer" sought an individual to perform public relations work. Whole In One hired Walker without a contract and told her she was prohibited from working for other firms. However, Walker worked from home and set her own hours. Whole In One required Walker to attend weekly staff meetings at the company offices, where Whole In One would review and revise Walker's work. The company supplied Walker with paper, pencils, stamps, and telephone service and paid for her life and health insurance. Whole In One did not withhold taxes from Walker's commissions.

Victoria Radiant, who had a two-year employment contract with the company, provided marketing services to Whole In One from October of 2005 until she was fired in 2007. Although Radiant worked in the company office, Whole In One management rarely supervised her work. The company paid for her continued education, provided her with bonuses, and deducted taxes from her weekly salary.

4. Combination of Chronological and Claim or Party Organization

Some facts statements do not lend themselves to one type of organization. Some facts should be arranged by the order of the events, and others do not fit neatly into this arrangement. Therefore, you might group facts in chronological order and by party or claim. See Illustration 21-5.

The facts statement in Illustration 21-5 concerns the question of whether Janice Kahn can successfully pursue a claim against Ronnie Randall for intentional infliction of emotional distress after Randall struck Kahn's 11-year-old son with Randall's car. The accident itself is best described in a chronological manner because the events can be explained in a sequential order. However, the witness statements and other "facts" that relate to whether Randall intentionally struck the child and whether Randall intended to cause emotional distress when he struck the child should be organized by issue or claim.

ILLUSTRATION 21-5.   Chronological and Claim Organization

While driving a car, Ronnie Randall struck Janice Kahn's son at 5:00 P.M. on August 29, 2008. It was bright and clear. No skid marks appeared on the dry street following the accident. Janice Kahn was working in her garden about five feet from the accident scene at the time of the accident. Her son was playing a game in the street before Randall's car struck him. Kahn did not see the car strike her 11-year-old son. When she first looked up from her garden, she thought her son was dead. He was covered with blood and had several broken bones. However, Kahn's son was conscious after the accident.

Immediately after the accident, Randall, who had a blood alcohol level of .11, was cited for drunk driving and driving with a suspended driver's license. Police had charged him with drunk driving and suspended his license two weeks earlier after the car he was driving struck another child at the same spot. Randall has a history of alcohol abuse.

Following the accident, several witnesses said Randall was upset and wobbled as he walked. One witness said that Randall intentionally turned the steering wheel to hit Kahn's son. Kahn stated that Randall often swerved down her street to get her attention.

Rhonda Albert, Kahn's neighbor, said she heard Randall say he would get even with Kahn after Kahn broke off a ten-year relationship with him.

During Kahn and Randall's ten-year relationship, Randall was close to Kahn's son. He took him to ball games, including one in April, and attended the son's baseball games. Randall knew that Kahn's son was the most important person in her life.

Since the accident, Kahn vomits daily and suffers from anxiety and headaches. Dr. Susan Faigen, Kahn's internist, states that the vomiting, anxiety, and headaches are the result of the accident.

In some instances, your organization should be structured by the sequence of the events and by the parties. See Illustration 21-6.

In Illustration 21-6, the first paragraph introduces both parties, Bonnie Bill and Merriweather Halsey. The facts statement details most of the night's events in chronological order. However, the parties, Bill and Halsey, leave the fundraiser separately. At this point, the organization changes from chronological to one focusing on each party. First, facts that are legally significant to Bill's escapades are explained. These are noted in chronological order from start to finish. After the facts concerning Bill's adventure, the facts related to Halsey's acts at the bulb factory are detailed. These facts also are explained in chronological order. The final paragraph tells the reader the issues that will be considered in the memo.

ILLUSTRATION 21-6.   Chronological and Party Organization

Merriweather Halsey and Bonnie Bill were at the Masonic Temple for a fundraiser to fight AIDS. During the fundraiser Bill told a drunken

ILLUSTRATION 21-6.   *Continued*

Halsey that she intended to steal the $8,000 proceeds from the Masonic Temple after the fundraiser and a pearl necklace from Alice McKinley. Bill, who had helped organize the fundraiser, watched as the chairperson of the fundraiser opened the safe and placed the money in it. She memorized the combination and decided that she would use it later to steal the money.

After the fundraiser, Bill walked home to get a credit card and a crowbar to open the door if she needed it. Bill went to the Masonic Temple after the fundraiser, wearing a disguise, showed the guard her invitation, and told him that she had lost her mother's diamond brooch inside. Although the guard did not remember her, he allowed her to go into the temple. She wandered around the building for about an hour with the brooch inside her purse.

When the guard decided to eat his supper, Bill went to the safe. She opened it and pulled out all the money, except for $1,000.

Bill told the guard she had found the brooch and then left. She went to Alice McKinley's home, entered the house through an open ground-floor window, and took the pearl necklace she had seen Alice wearing earlier, and then left.

Merriweather Halsey considered borrowing money from a friend who worked at a local bulb factory. She wandered into the factory around 4:00 A.M., after the fundraiser. The guard had stepped away from the door for a break. She headed toward her friend's workstation, but she stumbled into an open office where the petty cash was kept. She fell over a secretary's desk. Her leg caught the desk and pulled open a drawer that contained $500. She thought about taking the money, but she passed out before she took it. She woke up about 6:00 A.M., when a secretary found her and summoned the security guard.

Halsey then fell into the security guard, causing him to crash his head into a planter. The guard cut his head and later required six stitches. Halsey thought the security guard was a robber, so she grabbed a letter opener from a nearby desk and told the security guard to back off. The security guard took the letter opener. Halsey's mind was still fuzzy from the alcohol, but she decided to pull a squirt gun out of her pocket to scare the robber.

The question is whether Bill or Halsey can be convicted of aggravated burglary under Houcktown County law.

C. WRITING THE FACTS STATEMENT

1. Prepare a List of Facts and Preliminary Statement

After you meet with an attorney to discuss your research assignment, make a list of the facts and draft a preliminary facts statement.

Illustration 21-7 shows an excerpt from a client interview. Following the interview is a list of the facts and a preliminary facts statement, Illustration 21-8, that includes all the facts provided in the interview.

ILLUSTRATION 21-7. Excerpt from a Client Interview

Attorney: What can I do for you today, Mr. Grocer of Sack and Shop?

Grocer: Rebecca Harris, one of my regular customers, is suing me for $1 million.

Attorney: What happened?

Grocer: Ms. Harris came to the store to purchase cherries, strawberries, and bananas. When she was turning the corner in the produce section, she slipped on a banana peel.

Attorney: How long had the banana peel been on the floor?

Grocer: Two days.

Attorney: Did you or any of your employees know about the banana peel on the floor?

Grocer: Yes. One of the patrons told the head of the produce department to clean up the banana peel two days before Ms. Harris fell.

Attorney: Why wasn't it picked up?

Grocer: The produce department head was in a hurry to leave and forgot to do it. The next day, he was very busy and he kicked the banana peel into a corner. Apparently it was knocked out of the corner and to the middle of the floor where Ms. Harris slipped on it.

Attorney: Were there any witnesses?

Grocer: I saw her slip.

Attorney: What was Ms. Harris doing when she slipped?

Grocer: She was walking to the green peppers.

Attorney: What day did the incident occur?

Grocer: July 8, 2008. The same day another accident occurred in the produce section that involved a piece of cut cantaloupe.

Attorney: Was Ms. Harris injured?

Grocer: She claims in the court papers that she hurt her head and broke her arm.

Attorney: Was anyone injured in the second accident?

Grocer: Yes. A man slipped on the cantaloupe and broke his finger.

ILLUSTRATION 21-8. Sample Preliminary Facts Statement Based on the Client Interview

BRIEF LIST OF FACTS:
Client: Sack and Shop Grocery Store
Plaintiff: Rebecca Harris

Slip and fall at grocery store on July 8, 2008.

Plaintiff slipped on a banana peel, which had been left on the store floor for two days.

ILLUSTRATION 21-8.   *Continued*

Harris was walking to the green peppers.

Another accident happened in the same section when a man slipped on a cantaloupe and broke his finger.

A patron told the store employee to clean up the banana peel two days earlier.

The employee kicked it into a corner.

Somehow the peel got to the middle of the floor again.

Harris came to the store to purchase cherries, strawberries, and bananas.

Our client, Sack and Shop Grocery Store, is being sued for negligence by Rebecca Harris.

Harris went to the store to purchase cherries, strawberries, and bananas on July 8, 2008.

While Harris was in the produce section, she slipped on a banana peel that had been left on the floor by a grocery store employee. The employee dropped it on the floor two days earlier and had failed to clean it up after a patron asked him to do so. The employee had kicked the peel into the corner two days before the accident. Somehow the peel found its way to the middle of the floor on the date of the accident.

Harris sustained a broken arm and head injuries as a result of the slip and fall. Another man was injured in the produce department that same day when he slipped and fell on some cantaloupe.

2. Research the Issue

After you prepare your list and preliminary facts statement, the next step is to research the legal issue or issues and to determine the applicable law.

3. Revise to Include Only Legally Significant Facts

Revise your list so that it includes only the legally significant facts, the facts that will have a bearing on the applicable law. See Illustration 21-9. To draft this list, you must determine the legal elements necessary to establish a claim. In the case of negligence, you would learn that negligence is the breach of a duty of reasonable care that results in injuries to another person. The elements then would be:

- duty of reasonable care
- breach of the duty
- a link between the breach of the duty and the resulting injuries
- injuries

You should review the facts and determine which facts may affect whether the plaintiff can establish one of these elements or whether the defendant would be able to disprove one of the elements—in other words, the legally significant facts. In this case, you should include all of the facts listed in Illustration 21-9. In that illustration, the element of the legal theory is noted in parentheses next to the legally significant fact. The fact that Harris was purchasing cherries, strawberries, and bananas is not legally significant. Similarly, the fact that another patron was injured in the produce section that day did not affect whether Harris was injured and therefore is not legally significant.

ILLUSTRATION 21-9. List of Legally Significant Facts

- The slip and fall occurred in the store on July 8, 2008. (breach and duty)
- Rebecca Harris slipped on a banana peel that had been left on the store floor for two days. (breach and duty)
- The store employee dropped the banana peel on the floor two days earlier. (breach and duty)
- A store employee knew about the banana peel on the floor two days before the accident. (breach and duty)
- The employee kicked the peel into the corner after a patron told him to clean it up. (breach and duty)
- Rebecca Harris suffered injuries as a result of the fall. (link and injuries)

4. Organize the Facts

After you have made your list of facts, decide how to organize them. After you select your organizational method, group the legally significant facts together in the organizational style you have selected.

PRACTICE POINTER

Sometimes you will use multiple organization methods.

---

5. Rewrite the Facts Statement

The facts contained in Illustration 21-9 lend themselves to a chronological organization because they can be ordered by time. Illustration 21-10 is a rewritten facts statement that includes only the legally significant facts. Finally, remember to introduce the legal issue or issues presented in the facts statement, as shown in the first paragraph of Illustration 21-10.

ILLUSTRATION 21-10. Sample Facts Statement for Slip-and-Fall Case

Rebecca Harris, a store patron, is suing our client, Sack and Shop Grocery Store, for negligence.

While Harris was in the produce department, on July 8, 2008, she slipped on a banana peel that had been left on the floor by a grocery store employee. The employee dropped it on the floor two days earlier and had failed to clean it up after a patron asked him to do so. When he was told to pick up the peel, the employee kicked the peel into the corner.

Harris sustained a broken arm and head injuries as a result of the slip and fall

CHAPTER SUMMARY

A facts statement is designed to refresh an attorney's memory about a case or to educate a new attorney about the case. It is a statement of all facts that are legally significant (facts that might affect the outcome of a legal issue). Facts that are not legally significant should be omitted from a facts statement.

Facts statements can be organized in chronological or reverse chronological order, by claim or defense, by party, or any combination of these three.

To draft your statement, make a list of the facts, plan your organization, then write the statement. Next, research the legal issue, then rewrite your facts statement because the legally significant facts may have changed based on your research.

In the next chapter, you will learn how to organize using the IRAC methodology.

KEY TERMS

asserted facts
chronological organization
elements
emotional adjectives
fact
facts statement
legal claim

legal conclusion
organization by claim or defense
organization by party
procedural fact
pure fact
reverse chronological order

EXERCISES

SHORT ANSWER

1. What is a facts statement?
2. What are legally significant facts?
3. What are pure facts?
4. What are asserted facts?
5. What are procedural facts?
6. What facts should be included in the facts statement?

7. What is the difference between a fact and a legal conclusion?
8. Where do you find the information to include in the facts statement?
9. List several methods for organizing a facts statement.
10. Explain two methods of organization.

DRAFTING A LIST OF RELEVANT FACTS

11. Review the following Uniform Commercial Code section and read the list of facts that follows. Make a list of the legally significant facts based on the statute. Next to each fact, list the relevant portion of the statute.

§2-315 Implied Warranty of Fitness for a Particular Purpose

Where the seller at the time of contracting has reason to know any particular purpose for which the goods are required and that buyer is relying on the seller's skill or judgment to select or furnish suitable goods, there is unless excluded or modified under the next section an implied warranty that the goods be fit for such purpose.

Facts

Your client is Sue A. Buyer. She lives at 3225 Wilmette Avenue, Glenview, Illinois. The defendants are Lee R. Merchant, owner of Mowers R Us, in Glenview, Illinois, and Manny U. Facture, the owner of a manufacturing concern that is not incorporated called Mowers, of Rosemont, Illinois. Ms. Buyer went to the defendant's store, Mowers R Us, to purchase a lawn mower for her new home. She was a first-time homeowner and was unfamiliar with lawn mowers. She had never operated a lawn mower because her brothers had always mowed the lawn when she was a child.

When she went to Mowers R Us, she asked to speak with the owner. She told Mr. Merchant: "I don't know anything about these mowers, and I need to talk with an expert." Mr. Merchant said, "I'm the owner, and you couldn't find a better expert anywhere in the Chicagoland area. I have been in the business of selling mowers for more than 40 years. I only sell mowers and the equipment to clean and repair them. Are you familiar with the type of lawn mower you would like?"

"No, I don't know anything about lawn mowers. I just know that I have to have a lawn mower that will mulch my grass clippings, because I cannot bag the clippings. The village of Glenview does not permit me to bag the clippings, so the clippings must remain on my lawn."

"You're absolutely correct. You must have a mulching mower," Mr. Merchant said. "That type of mower will grind the grass clippings, and you will not notice them on your grass. I have the perfect mower for you. It is a used model that will fit into your price range, only $200. It's a good brand, a Roro, and will mulch the grass as well as any of the new mowers. This one is true blue. You can purchase a separate mulching blade, which will easily attach to it for an additional $50," he added.

"Do you think that I need the mulching blade?" Ms. Buyer asked, "I've never used a lawn mower, so I don't know what to expect, and you appear to be the expert."

"I think that you could do without the mulching blade unless you want the grass ground up very fine."

"I think that I would like it ground up fine. I'll defer to your judgment. If you think a mulching blade is necessary, then I'll buy that with the mower. Do you think that this is the best mower for mulching, or should I go with a new one?"

"Absolutely the used one is best; I told you: it's a true value. It will mulch with the best of them."

"If you think it can do the job, I'll trust your judgment," said Ms. Buyer, "I'll take the mower and the mulching blade. Can you install the mulching blade? I don't know anything about the installation.

"Sure, we can install any blade for another $30."

Ms. Buyer purchased the mower and the blade. She used the mower after Mr. Merchant installed the new mulching blade. It barely cut the grass and certainly didn't mulch the clippings into fine pieces as Mr. Merchant had claimed.

She brought the mower back to Mr. Merchant. He said that he had made no warranties about the mower. He showed her the language on the receipt that said that he did not expressly warrant anything.

Ms. Buyer brought the mower to a Roro dealer. The owners of the Roro dealership, Abe Saul and Lou T. Wright, said that the mower Ms. Buyer had purchased from Mowers R Us was not a mulching mower. It was a mower built before mulching was popular. Therefore, it would not perform the mulching task. It was designed merely to cut the grass. "Any merchant who has been in business even for one year should have known that mowers built before 1970 were not designed for mulching," Mr. Wright said. He showed Ms. Buyer where the manufacturing date appeared on the mower. "Manufactured in August 1969," it said on the plate with the serial number. "Also, mulching blades cannot be placed on these old mowers. Any mower dealer should know that too," Mr. Wright added. "However, this mower isn't bad. It can cut the grass without mulching it."

Ms. Buyer brought an action against Mr. Merchant and Mr. Facture in the Cook County Circuit Court, Skokie, IL.

OBJECTIVE WRITING

12. Write three different discussions about your high school career. One discussion should present the experience in a negative manner. The second should attempt to persuade the reader that the experience was positive. Finally, write about your experience in a neutral manner, without any emotion. Compare the three discussions.

DRAFTING A FACTS STATEMENT

13. Draft a facts statement for our client, Ronnie Randall. Janice Kahn, the plaintiff, brought an action against Randall for intentional infliction of emotional distress. You should prepare your facts statement based on this excerpt from a deposition transcript, witness statements, and a police report. The facts statement will be included in a memo that discusses the issue of intentional infliction of emotional distress. For the purpose of this memo, intentional infliction of emotional distress is defined as follows:

An act by a person that is extreme and outrageous conduct, done with intent to cause another to suffer severe emotional distress, and which

results in distress and emotional injury to another. The emotional injury must manifest itself with a physical problem.

Below is a portion of Janice Kahn's deposition transcript.

Q. What were you doing when the accident occurred?
A. Working in my garden. I planted tomatoes, green peppers, carrots, and broccoli.
Q. Where is your garden located on your property?
A. In the front, near the street. It is next to a brick wall. I can't see the garden from my house.
Q. What direction were you facing in your garden?
A. North.
Q. Does that direction face the street?
A. No.
Q. What do you usually do in your garden when you work?
A. Weed it.
Q. What were you doing in your garden when the accident occurred?
A. Weeding it.
Q. Where is the street in relation to your garden?
A. About five feet.
Q. Where do the children generally play?
A. In the backyard.
Q. Where were the children playing on the day of the accident?
A. They were playing t-ball in the front yard.
Q. Were you watching the children at the time of the accident?
A. Yes I could see them.
Q. Did you see the accident occur?
A. Sort of.
Q. Did you or did you not see the accident?
A. I saw my son, who is 11 years old, on the ground covered with blood, and blood all over the front of the Cadillac.
Q. Did you actually see the driver strike your son?
A. No. But I know Ronnie hit him. I saw my son next to Ronnie's car. I heard him swerve.
Q. Did you know the driver?
A. Yes.
Q. How did you know him?
A. We met at a state fair. We dated for ten years. I broke up with him two weeks before the accident.
Q. Did he know your son?
A. He knew my son was the most important person to me, and he tried to kill him to pay me back for dumping him.
Q. Are you accusing the driver of intentionally striking your son?
A. Yes. He wanted to get back at me, so he hit my boy.
Q. What happened to your son on the day of the accident?
A. He sustained head injuries and several broken bones. He can't play t-ball for the rest of the season, and we had to cancel our vacation to the Dells because he's been hurting so much.

Q.   Was he conscious when you first saw him after the accident?

A.   He was awake, but I thought he was dead at first. He had blood everywhere. I knew the driver, Ronnie, was drunk when he hit him. He wasn't even looking where he was going. He always swerves down our street to get my attention.

Q.   Did your son speak to you right after the accident?

A.   Barely. I told him that Ronnie was speeding and trying to run him down on purpose. I was horrified to see the blood and the broken bones. I couldn't move and I was so angry at Ronnie because I knew he did this on purpose.

Q.   Did you go to the doctor after this accident?

A.   I went by ambulance with my son to the doctor. His doctor looked me over and said I was suffering from shock. Since then, I suffered from anxiety and headaches. I throw up every day.

Q.   Have you seen a doctor for your complaints?

A.   Yes. She said that they are related to the accident. I just keep thinking back to that day when the neighbor told me that Ronnie intentionally turned the wheel to hit my boy.

Q.   Was your son able to move after the accident?

A.   Slightly. He looked just like our neighbor's son did after Ronnie hit him with his car two weeks before at the same curve.

Police Report, State of Illinois

Ronnie Randall, the driver of a 2003 Cadillac, was cited for driving while under the influence of alcohol and/or drugs, reckless driving, and driving with a suspended license. I will ask the prosecutor to consider either reckless assault charges or vehicular homicide, depending upon the condition of the boy. I tested Randall for alcohol intoxication. His blood alcohol level was .11. Randall struck another boy, Tommy Albert, at the same site two weeks earlier. He was cited for reckless driving for that accident and drunk driving. As I arrested Randall, he said that he was daydreaming during the accident and that he did not mean to hit the child. There were no skid marks. The street was dry.

The boy's mother, Janice Kahn, was working in her garden about five feet from the accident scene at the time of the accident. Her son, Billy Kahn, was playing a game in the street.

Witness Statement

Two days before the accident, Rhonda Albert, a neighbor of Janice Kahn, heard Randall say that he planned to get even with Kahn after Kahn broke off her ten-year relationship with Randall. Albert saw the car strike Kahn's son. According to Albert, after the car struck the boy, Randall got out of his car and said, "Oh, my God. I didn't mean to hit him. Is he okay?" Albert could smell alcohol on Randall's breath.

Witness Statement

Rebecca Mark saw the driver, Ronnie Randall, turn the car toward Kahn's son.

REVIEW OF FACTS STATEMENTS

14. Now that you have reviewed the facts for the *Janice Kahn* case and have drafted a statement of your own, read the following statements of facts. Determine which facts statement is best. List any errors you find in any of the statements.

A. The plaintiff, a single mother, and the defendant, her ex-boy-friend, are involved in a lawsuit. The plaintiff alleges in her deposition that the defendant was driving recklessly and intentionally struck her son with his car. The defendant's motive was to pay her back for ending their relationship. He tried to kill her son for this reason. As a result of the accident, the plaintiff went into shock and suffers from anxiety, head-aches, and vomiting.

B. The plaintiff was working in her tomato garden located in the front of the property about five feet from the street. She could see the children playing in the front yard. She did not see the driver, Ronnie Randall, hit her son with his Cadillac but did see blood on the front of the Cadillac and on her son, who was on the ground.

The plaintiff dated Randall for ten years and had just ended their relationship. She states that Ronnie hit her son to pay her back for ending their relationship. Two weeks before, Ronnie had hit a neighbor's son at the same curve.

The plaintiff states that her son was covered with blood, able to move slightly. He suffered head trauma and broken bones.

The plaintiff is suffering from shock after seeing her son. She remembers a neighbor telling her that Ronnie intentionally turned the wheel to hit her son.

The plaintiff suffers from anxiety and headaches and vomits daily.

C. Janice Kahn is bringing an action against Ronnie Randall for the intentional infliction of emotional distress. Her son was recently hit by Ronnie Randall's car on the street in front of the Kahn home. At the time of the injury, Kahn was working in the front yard near her son. Her son went into the street and Randall hit him. At the time of the accident, Randall was legally drunk and driving with a suspended license.

Randall had previously told Kahn's neighbor, a Ms. Albert, that he was going to get even with Ms. Kahn over the breakup of their ten-year relationship. He also told Ms. Albert that he knew that Ms. Kahn's son was very important to her.

Since the accident, Kahn vomits daily and suffers from anxiety and headaches. She has stated that Mr. Randall often drives by her home in an erratic fashion and on another occasion hit a neighbor's child. Kahn feels that Randall hit her son intentionally. Kahn did not see the injury take place but was at her son's side immediately after the injury. Kahn also says that Randall never slowed down until after he hit her son.

D. On August 12, 2008, Janice Kahn filed a lawsuit against Ronnie Randall for intentional infliction of emotional distress stemming from an accident involving Kahn's 11-year-old son.

On July 8, 2008, Janice Kahn was weeding her tomato garden while her children played T-ball a few feet away from her in the street. As she worked, Kahn heard a car swerve. She looked up to see her son, covered in blood, lying on the ground in front of a Cadillac, driven by Ronnie Randall.

Two neighbors witnessed the accident. Rebecca Mark saw the driver, Ronnie Randall, turn the car toward Kahn's son. Rhonda Albert also saw the car strike Kahn's son. According to Albert, after the car struck the boy, Randall got out of his car and said, "Oh, my God. I didn't mean to hit him. Is he okay?"

Albert could smell alcohol on Randall's breath. Police tested his blood alcohol level and found that it was .11. Police cited Randall for drunk driving, speeding, and reckless driving.

After police arrived, an ambulance took Kahn and her son to the hospital, where he was treated for head injuries and broken bones. The doctor who treated Kahn's son told Kahn that she should be treated for shock. Since the accident, Kahn has suffered from anxiety and headaches and vomits daily. Her doctor said that the anxiety, headaches, and vomiting are the result of the accident.

The driver of the car involved in the accident was Kahn's former boyfriend. They had dated for ten years; however, Kahn broke off the relationship about two weeks before the accident. Kahn stated in her deposition that she believes Randall intentionally struck her son to pay her back for ending the relationship.

Also, two days before the accident Albert heard Randall say that he planned to get even with Kahn after Kahn broke off their ten-year relationship. However, the police report stated that Randall said that he was daydreaming during the accident and that he did not mean to hit the child. Since the breakup, Kahn has seen Randall often swerve down the street in front of her home. Two weeks before the accident, Randall hit Rhonda Albert's son with his Cadillac at the same curve.

THE IRAC
METHOD

CHAPTER OVERVIEW

The IRAC chapter focuses on the writing style used for the discussion portion of the memo. IRAC is an acronym for Issue, Rule, Application, Conclusion. These are the building blocks of a memo's discussion. You will learn to identify issues and applicable legal authority. You will also learn how to extract the legally significant facts and apply them to the relevant law to draw substantiated conclusions. You will learn to identify effective IRAC use by dissecting discussions and labeling the IRAC components, and you will learn to draft IRAC sequences as well.

A. PURPOSES OF IRAC

▼ What Is IRAC?

IRAC stands for Issue, Rule, Application, Conclusion. IRAC is the architectural blueprint for the discussion portion of a legal memo. It gives legal writing continuity and clarity and organizes the contents of the discussion. IRAC provides legal support and analysis for the issues posed by the problem and guides the writer toward a well-supported conclusion.

IRAC benefits both the writer and the reader because the components are essentially a checklist designed to ensure that the discussion is analytically well thought-out and that it contains the necessary legal authority. IRAC is very important because it lets the reader see the particular legal point being addressed, the relevant legal rule, the application of the law to the facts, and the conclusion. It is formula writing in the same way that formula movie romances, westerns, and thrillers are. The predictability of the IRAC format enables the reader to obtain the information quickly.

The CUNY Law School Writing Center Web site has handouts on using the IRAC format at www.law.cuny.edu/wc. Click "For Students." Then click the "Resources" link and then the "IRAC" link.

B. IRAC COMPONENTS

Each IRAC sequence is composed of an issue, which is really a legal element or component; the legal rule or holding from a case or statutory authority; the application, which is a demonstration of how the legal authority applies to the problem that you are writing about; and the conclusion, the final assessment of how the rule applies to the facts of your problem.

▼ What Does an IRAC Paragraph Look Like?

This fact pattern forms the basis of the IRAC paragraph example.

On August 7, 2008, Ms. Howard went to Rough & Tough Pawn Shop in Chicago to obtain a loan using a diamond ring as collateral. Rough & Tough loaned Ms. Howard $800, and she agreed to pay $75 per month

for a total of 13-1/2 months. Ms. Howard knew that she would have to pay off the balance of $1,025 in 12 months because at that time Rough & Tough would have the right to sell the ring. On September 11, 2008, Ms. Howard received a postcard from Rough & Tough stating that it was selling the shop and all of its assets to Able Pawn. Mr. Sam Able would assume the business of Rough & Tough, including all pawned items and outstanding loans. On the bottom of the postcard was a notice stating; "If you want your item, please pick it up by September 29, 2008, and pay off your note by September 29, 2008. Because Ms. Howard did not have the money to pay off the note, she decided to pay Able Pawn the $75 per month once the loan was transferred in the sale. In October 2008, Able Pawn was robbed and all the jewelry, including Ms. Howard's ring, was stolen. Able Pawn had a security alarm system and a guard dog to protect the property, but the robbers were able to circumvent these obstacles.

We will work through the following sample IRAC paragraph, based on the Howard fact pattern, and its components to illustrate how to draft an IRAC paragraph.

(**I**) Whether a bailment for the mutual benefit of Rough & Tough and Howard existed. (**R**) A pawn is a form of bailment, made for the mutual benefit of bailee and bailor, arising when goods are delivered to another as a pawn for security to him on money borrowed by the bailor. *Jacobs v. Grossman,* 141 N.E. 714, 715 (Ill. App. Ct. 1923). In *Jacobs,* the court found that a bailment for mutual benefit did arise because the plaintiff pawned a ring as collateral for a $70 loan given to him by the defendant. *Id.* (**A**) In our problem, Howard pawned her ring as collateral to secure an $800 loan given to her by Rough & Tough. (**C**) Therefore, Howard and Rough & Tough probably created a bailment for mutual benefit.

Note that the first sentence of the IRAC paragraph is a statement of the issue that will be examined in the paragraph. The issue is narrowly defined and focused on one of the analytical elements of the problem. The rule of law, the next component of the paragraph, provides the legal basis for the analysis of the issue. Then, it is appropriate to discuss some of the facts of the cited case if these facts help explain how the legal rule can be applied to your facts. Notice that everything that comes from an opinion is given citation credit.

The most important component of the IRAC paragraph is the application portion. The application is where you use the facts of your problem to demonstrate, but not to conclude, why the legal rule should apply to the issue posed. This is the legal analysis. (See Chapter 23 for more discussion.) After you let the facts speak for themselves by demonstrating how the legal rule applies to the scenario at hand, you draw a conclusion. The conclusion answers the issue posed. The issue is the question being examined in the discussion, and the conclusion is the answer.

This example illustrates how the conclusion responds directly to the issue:

Issue:	Whether a bailment for the mutual benefit of Rough & Tough and Howard existed.
Conclusion:	Therefore, Howard and Rough & Tough probably created a bailment, for it was for their mutual benefit because a loan was given upon the receipt of valuable collateral.

1. Issues

The question presented is the overall legal issue that will be resolved in the memo. A subissue in the IRAC paragraph is a point or query that must be addressed to substantiate one legal element of the problem. When analyzing and writing about a legal problem objectively, it is often important to address subissues in the order that they must be resolved to support legal analysis. For example, the general rule for arson in Illinois is the malicious burning of the dwelling house of another. The question presented for a memo on arson would be:

Whether Mr. Smith committed arson by intentionally burning down his brother's factory.

The subissues addressed in the IRAC paragraphs would be:

Whether there was a malicious burning.

Whether the factory is a dwelling house.

Whether the factory of Mr. Smith's brother constitutes the property of another person.

The subissues form the **topic sentences** of the IRAC paragraphs. They provide the analytical steps that you must take in your thought process and your legal reasoning to resolve the overall issue posed by the problem, the question presented. The topic sentences in the IRAC paragraph introduce the legal element in question that needs to be resolved to complete the steps necessary to thoroughly examine the problem and to determine a response to the question presented.

▼ What Is the Difference Between the Question Presented and the Issues in IRAC Paragraphs?

The question presented is the overall problem that must be resolved in the objective memo. The question presented for the Howard fact pattern is:

Whether Ms. Howard has a claim against Rough & Tough or against Able Pawn Shop for the value of her ring.

The subissues are determined by the legal elements or tests involved in the problem. The elements are discussed individually along with the relevant legal rule. There is a certain logical order when presenting the elements. Let the legal rules guide you in establishing the order of the subissues. Notice that each issue centers on a single step of the legal analysis necessary to fully examine the question presented.

The subissues that form the topic sentences of the IRAC paragraphs in a memo addressing Ms. Howard's problem would be as follows:

> The first issue is what type of relationship does a pawner and a pawnee have?
>
> What property rights do Ms. Howard and Rough & Tough Pawn have when they enter into a mutual bailment?
>
> Can Rough & Tough Pawn transfer its interest in Ms. Howard's property to Able Pawn?
>
> Did Rough & Tough Pawn receive the proper consent for the transfer of the ring from Ms. Howard?
>
> Is Rough & Tough liable for the loss of Ms. Howard's property after transferring its interest to Able Pawn?
>
> Is Able Pawn liable for the theft of Ms. Howard's property while it was in its possession?

All of these queries are really elements that must be addressed, step by step, to resolve the question presented.

Each of the subissues will be a topic sentence of the IRAC paragraph highlighting the analytical focus of the legal discussion in that paragraph. Each issue is a step in the thought process required to thoroughly prove all of the underlying elements necessary to address the question presented.

Notice how one issue statement logically leads into the next. A good test to see if your discussion is well organized is to write down all your issue statements from your IRAC paragraphs. If the issue statements flow logically, one to the next, then the organization of your discussion will be logical.

To analyze the problem thoroughly, a number of issues must be examined in the discussion. To make the analysis logical, the issues must be examined in a certain order.

2. Rules of Law

The legal holding or rule, or synthesized compilation of the pertinent legal rules, follows the issue at the beginning of the IRAC paragraph. (For an in-depth discussion of the process of synthesizing authority, see Chapter 23.)

A rule of law is the court's holding or a synthesis of various courts' holdings on the same point. A rule also can be a statute and the legal elements laid out by the statute. A synthesis of a statute and a case applying or interpreting the statute also constitutes a rule.

In our IRAC example, note that the first sentence is the issue, and the second sentence is the legal rule.

Issue:	Whether a bailment for the mutual benefit of Rough & Tough and Howard existed.
Rule, followed by pinpoint citation:	A pawn is a form of bailment, made for the mutual benefit of the bailee and the bailor, arising when goods are delivered to another as a pawn for security to him on money borrowed by the bailor. *Jacobs v. Grossman,* 141 N.E. 714, 715 (Ill. App. Ct. 1923).

When organizing the discussion, first discern what issues are to be addressed, then find the pertinent mandatory authority that addresses the issues raised. Do not write the discussion around the authority, but make the authority address the issues. To demonstrate clearly how the authority supports or addresses the issues raised, discuss the pertinent facts of the cited case after you state the case's holding or legal rule. This is particularly helpful when the holding is very broad. You must demonstrate that the cited case truly supports the premise discussed in the IRAC paragraph.

▼ Why Is Citation Important?

Citation is an essential component of the rule portion of the IRAC paragraph. (See Appendix B.) You must always give proper credit in *Bluebook* or *ALWD* format to any statement made that is not wholly your own. Any legal principle or authority must be attributed to its source. Proper attribution of authority tells the reader where you obtained the legal principle that supports the discussion. Most important, the cite tells the reader whether the authority is primary mandatory authority, primary persuasive, or secondary authority. A cite also provides information without including the information in the discussion's text. For example, you could write a holding as follows:

> The state of Kimberly Supreme Court held in 1983 that individuals have a right to privacy. *Jones v. City of Moose,* 121 Kim. 12, 13 (1983).

A much more effective version of the same holding to include in the rule portion of the IRAC paragraph is:

> Individuals have a right to privacy. *Jones v. City of Moose,* 121 Kim. 12, 13 (1983).

The citation itself provides the information about the court, its jurisdiction and level, and the year. The text need not repeat this information. Citations are valuable sources of information about the legal authority presented in the rule component of the IRAC paragraph.

3. Application of the Law to the Problem's Facts

▼ How Do You Use the Legally Significant Facts?

Think of the legal rule as a test or a series of elements requiring certain facts to be used to support the outcome of the test. The facts used are **legally significant facts** because they bear legal significance as to the outcome of an issue. Our arson example mentioned at the beginning of the chapter illustrates this point.

THE ARSON HYPOTHETICAL

John Smith lived in Arkville. John Smith's brother, Richard Smith, lived in Barkville Estates. Richard Smith owned a factory in downtown Barkville. John Smith was consumed by a jealous rage over his brother Richard's success and intentionally and maliciously burned down the factory in Barkville. The question to be examined is whether John Smith committed arson by intentionally and maliciously burning down his brother's factory.

The general rule for arson is the malicious burning of a dwelling house of another. This general rule would be the legal authority used in the rule portion of the IRAC paragraph.

An IRAC paragraph on this topic would be as follows:

Issue: Whether John Smith committed arson by burning down his brother's factory.

Rule: Arson is the malicious burning of a dwelling house of another. 9 Stat. §§21, 23 (1976).

Application: John Smith burned down the factory of his brother, Richard Smith. John Smith's actions were intentional and malicious. Richard resides in Barkville Estates.

Conclusion: John Smith did not commit arson because he burned down his brother's factory, not his brother's residence or dwelling house.

The **application** lays a factual foundation on which the conclusion can be based. The facts are selected because each fact illustrates a legal point related to your rule of law: the malicious act, the intentional burning down of a building, the use of the building—whether it serves as a residence or dwelling house or whether it serves another purpose. The rule indicates which facts you should examine. Once you lay the factual foundation by using the problem's facts illustrating how the law should apply, you draw a conclusion.

4. Conclusion

The conclusion resolves the issue posed at the beginning of the IRAC sequence. The conclusion should reflect directly the issue posed. If you

remove the rule and the application portions of the IRAC paragraph, the issue and the conclusion should read as if they are a question and an answer. The conclusion generally restates the issue and includes the basis for the answer. The arson example with John Smith illustrates the role of the conclusion.

Issues: Whether John Smith committed arson by burning down his brother's factory.

Conclusion: John Smith did not commit arson because he burned down his brother's factory, not his residence or dwelling house.

Notice how the conclusion responds directly to the issue posed. The conclusion focuses directly on the question raised at the beginning of the IRAC sequence. Each element of the discussion is resolved before addressing the next element or issue.

PRACTICE POINTER

Always test to see if your conclusion is focused on the issue raised by reading the issue at the beginning of the IRAC sequence, then reading the conclusion. If the issue and the conclusion read like a question and a reasoned answer that responds directly to the question raised, then you have adequately resolved the issue.

CHAPTER SUMMARY

IRAC—standing for Issue, Rule, Application, Conclusion—provides the structure for the legal discussion. The IRAC structure provides a checklist for you to make sure that you have included all the necessary components in the discussion and supported every premise with legal authority. Because it follows a predictable pattern, IRAC permits the reader to obtain information quickly. Mastering the IRAC format requires practice, which involves rereading and revising your work. Once you feel comfortable with the IRAC format, you should be confident that the discussion portions of your memos are logically ordered and analytically complete.

KEY TERMS

application	legal holding
citation	legal rule
conclusion	legally significant facts
IRAC	subissue
issue	topic sentence

EXERCISES

SHORT ANSWER

1. What does "IRAC" stand for? Define each component.
2. Why do we use the IRAC format?
3. What is a legally significant fact?

DIAGRAMMING IRAC COMPONENTS

4. Diagram the IRAC components of each paragraph in the discussion section. Note where the writing digresses from the IRAC format.

Discussion

To be successful in a claim against Rough & Tough or Able Pawn, Ms. Howard would have to prove that Rough & Tough was liable for the loss of her ring. First, for an action against Rough & Tough, she would have to show that the company had no right to transfer her pawned property without her written consent. Illinois Pawnbrokers Act, 205 Ill. Comp. Stat. 510/7 (2006). If pledged property was transferred without written consent of the property owner, the pawnbroker can be held responsible for loss or theft of pawned property because the property was in his safekeeping and was transferred illegally. *Jacobs v. Grossman,* 141 N.E. 714, 716 (Ill. App. Ct. 1923). Rough & Tough did not get a written consent for the transfer of Ms. Howard's property. In its defense the company could claim that written correspondence without the written consent would be enough to inform the pawner of the transfer of her property. Second, for an action against Able Pawn, Ms. Howard would have to show negligence in its care of her pawned ring. Illinois courts have ruled that in bailment for mutual benefit, the ordinary care or diligence that one would give to one's own property would be adequate to avoid negligence. *Id.* at 715; *Bielunski v. Tousignant,* 149 N.E.2d 801, 803 (Ill. App. Ct. 1958). Mrs. Howard would have to prove that a security system and a guard dog would not be ordinary care and diligence. In his defense Mr. Able could argue that these were sufficient to be considered ordinary care and diligence. For a claim against Village Jewelers to be successful, Ms. Howard would have to establish that she held good title to her property because a thief cannot convey good title to stolen property. *Hobson's Truck Sales v. Carroll Trucking,* 276 N.E. 89, 92 (Ill. App. Ct. 1971). Village Jewelers, which purchased the ring from the robbers, could not have good title to Ms. Howard's ring. Ms. Howard probably could have a successful claim against Rough & Tough and Village Jewelers. She probably would not be able to prove Able Pawn negligent in the care of her ring.

Does a pawnbroker have the right to transfer pawned property or interest in that property without written consent of the pawner? Pawned property cannot be transferred within a year from the pawner's default without written consent of the pawner. Illinois Pawnbrokers Act, 205 Ill. Comp. Stat. 510/7. One Illinois court ruled that a pawnbroker had no right to transfer the plaintiff's pledged diamond ring to another pawnbroker within a year of

the plaintiff's default of her loan, without written consent of the pawner. *Jacobs,* 141 N.E. at 716. In our situation, Rough & Tough sold its shop and assets to Sam Able within two months of Ms. Howard's pawning her grandmother's engagement ring. Because the sale occurred within a year of Ms. Howard's transaction with Rough & Tough, the company had a legal obligation under the Illinois statute to require a written consent for the transfer of her property. Also, the statute states that the time period for requirement of written consent for transfer of pledged property is established from the time of the pawner's default. 205 Ill. Comp. Stat. 510/7. Our client has not defaulted, and she deserves at least all the rights offered by the statute to a pawner who is in default. Rough & Tough did send Ms. Howard a postcard notifying her that it had sold all the pawned items and outstanding loans, including her ring, but it did not get her written consent for the sale of her property. Rough & Tough did not have the right to transfer Ms. Howard's ring without her written consent, and the sale of her property was probably not a legal sale.

Is a postcard sent to a pawner by a pawnbroker sufficient notice for the transfer of pawned property? Personal pawned property cannot be sold by a pawnee within one year from the time the pawner has defaulted in the interest payment unless the pawner has given written consent. Illinois Pawnbrokers Act, 205 Ill. Comp. Stat. 510/7. The statute uses a definite and clear term: "written consent." Ms. Howard did not default, and she would have at least all the rights of a pawner that did default. Therefore, the pawnbroker was required to receive her written consent before transferring her property. A postcard with written notice of a sale of pawned property is not a written consent by the pawner and would probably not be sufficient notice to constitute a legal sale.

5. Diagram the IRAC components of each paragraph in the discussion section. Note where the writing digresses from the IRAC format.

Facts

The Blacks came to us with the following problem and want to know what type of damages they are entitled to.

Mr. and Mrs. Black wanted to have a chair and a loveseat made to match the living room in their new home. The Blacks searched for weeks at various local furniture retailers for a furniture style and fabric that they liked but were unsuccessful. Finally, the Blacks went to a fabric sale at Fabric Retailers and found the upholstery fabric of their dreams. The Blacks purchased 50 yards of the fabric to make sure that they would have enough for any project. Mr. Black called all the furniture retailers in the area to inquire whether customers can have furniture covered in their own material. Finally, Comfy Furniture said that they permit customers to bring in their own material to cover upholstered furniture ordered from Comfy. The Blacks hurried over to Comfy with the 50 yards of fabric and placed an order for a chair and a loveseat using their own fabric. The price agreed on was the base price of $500 for the chair and $800 for the loveseat. Mr. Blaine, of Comfy Furniture, was their salesperson. Mr. Blaine said that the fabric was ideal for the styles selected because it required no matching. He added that there was plenty of yardage because

30 yards is adequate for jobs of this nature. The fabric was a small paisley print, with the right side having a lovely sheen and vibrant coloration. The Blacks placed the order on July 7, 2008, because they were planning a family reunion for Thanksgiving and felt that that date would give them plenty of time to completely decorate their living room. The new pieces would provide plenty of seating for the family reunion. The Blacks indicated to Mr. Blaine that they needed the furniture for the reunion. Mr. Blaine asserted that the furniture would be ready by September 15. The Blacks gave Comfy Furniture a deposit of $1,000. The loveseat and the chair were delivered to the Black home on September 10, but the furniture was upholstered with the fabric's reverse side showing. The Blacks were devastated.

Issues

Whether the Blacks are entitled to damages from Comfy Furniture for incorrectly upholstering their furniture.

Whether the Blacks are entitled to damages from Comfy Furniture for the expense of decorating their living room to match the furniture they did not receive in the agreed-on condition.

Discussion

Are the Blacks entitled to special damages from Comfy Furniture for the cost of the redecoration of their living room? An Illinois Appellate Court decided that the nonbreaching party should be put back in the position that it was in when the contract was formed. *Kalal v. Goldblatt Bros.*, 368 N.E.2d 671, 673 (Ill. App. Ct. 1977). The Blacks stated their intention at the beginning concerning the fabric, the redecoration of the living room, and the family reunion. This fact was a part of their original position. The living room was redecorated. The furniture was delivered; however, the fabric was incorrect. Therefore, the Blacks have a right to recover consequential damages for the cost of the redecoration of their living room because the end result was not achieved: correctly upholstered furniture, newly redecorated living room to match, and sufficient seating for the reunion. The conditions of the original contract were not met, and there was a breach of contract as embodied by the incorrectly upholstered furniture.

Under contract law, what damages are the Blacks entitled to pursue? Damages for breach of contract should place the plaintiff in a position he would have been in had the contract been performed. *Kalal*, 368 N.E.2d at 671. The plaintiffs in *Kalal* received a sofa that had been reupholstered in the wrong fabric after numerous delays, during which they had chosen three different fabrics in succession. *Id.* The court held that the defect could be remedied by the cost of reupholstering the sofa in the proper fabric. *Id.* at 674. The Blacks' sofa and loveseat were improperly upholstered. Comfy Furniture upholstered their furniture with the reverse side of the fabric showing. Therefore, they were entitled to damages equal to the cost of upholstering their furniture correctly. However, the Blacks' situation is distinguished from *Kalal* in that their furniture was delivered before the date set in the contract, and it can be argued by Comfy that there was time to remedy the defect before their target date of Thanksgiving.

Are the Blacks entitled to compensation for the loss of use of their furniture? The question of compensation for loss of use of the furniture was considered by both parties in *Kalal* to be appropriate since the plaintiffs in the case were without their furniture for several months while waiting for it to be reupholstered. *Id.* The Blacks have been similarly inconvenienced in that they, too, have been without the use of their new furniture. Thus, they are entitled to compensation for the loss of use of the furniture. However, it can be argued by Comfy Furniture that the furniture in the *Kalal* case was used and had been removed from the home for the purpose of reupholstering it. *Id.* In the present case, the furniture was new and had never been in the Blacks' home, and Comfy may argue that the Blacks did not actually suffer loss of use of the new furniture.

Are the Blacks entitled to damages for the expense of decorating their living room to match the furniture they did not receive in the agreed-on condition? The redecorating of the living room in *Kalal* was not in the contemplation of either party at the time the contract was executed. *Kalal,* 368 N.E.2d at 671. Subsequently, the court held that the only damages that were recoverable for breach of contract are limited to those that were reasonably foreseeable and were within the contemplation of the parties at the time the contract was executed. *Id.* at 674. By the express terms of the Uniform Commercial Code, the court cannot follow tort theories to award damages. The legislative history of the U.C.C. indicates that contractual disputes should apply to the findings of the court. *Moorman Mfg. Co. v. National Tank Co.,* 435 N.E.2d 443, 453 (Ill. 1982). The Blacks only told Mr. Blaine that they needed the furniture to be completed in time for a family reunion. Comfy knew that the Blacks were under a time constraint for the delivery, but apparently there was no communication regarding the redecorating of the living room. With regard to Comfy Furniture, the redecorating of the Blacks' living room was an unforeseeable event, and consequently they would not be held responsible for the expense. Because the fact that the redecorating of the living room was unforeseeable, it was not included within the terms of the contract. Therefore, Comfy only breached the express terms of the contract. The Blacks probably will not be awarded compensatory damages.

APPLICATION EXERCISES

6. Write an IRAC paragraph using the following information. You need not include all the information. The issue is whether the plaintiff can show that his attorney's failure to attend hearings was excusable neglect. A number of the text blocks below contain statements of rules. Other text blocks include legally significant facts. In some paragraphs, conclusions have been drawn for you. Combine the rules where necessary and form an IRAC paragraph for the issue.

   Fed. R. Civ. P. 60(b) provides for relief from judgment if plaintiffs can show that a mistake was made or that there was excusable neglect on the part of their attorney.

Rule 60(b) is an extraordinary remedy, granted in only exceptional cases. *Harold Washington Party v. Cook City. Illinois Democratic Party,* 984 F.2d 875 (7th Cir. 1993).

In this case, the plaintiff's attorney, Mark Adly, missed four court-set status hearings. He failed to appear. He failed to answer motions. Court status hearings are routinely held every three months.

Adly claims he did not have any notice of the hearings. Adly knew status proceedings normally were held. He attended depositions in this matter. Court records show that he was sent notices of the hearings to the address Adly says is correct.

"Excusable neglect may warrant relief under Rule 60(b)." *Zuelzke Tool & Eng'g v. Anderson Die Casting,* 925 F.2d 226 (7th Cir. 1991). In this case, the defendant relied on a third party who told them to refrain from further action because efforts were being made to have the defendant removed as defendant. *Id.* at 228. Anderson did not answer any complaints or file any pleadings. *Id.* The lack of response led the court to enter a default judgment against the company. *Id.* at 229. The district court refused the motion to vacate, saying that the defendant had voluntarily chosen not to control its fate in the litigation. *Id.*

7. Review the following paragraph. Note the issue, the rule, the application of law to facts, and the conclusion.

> An important factor in determining whether a funeral home is a nuisance is the suitability of its location. "Funeral homes are generally located on the edge of purely residential but not predominantly residential areas." *Bauman v. Piser Undertakers Co.,* 34 Ill. App. 2d 145, 148, 180 N.E.2d 705, 708 (App. Ct. 1962). A carefully run funeral home may be located on a property zoned for business at the edge of a residential neighborhood. *Id.* The funeral home in this case is located in a predominantly rural area. It is outside the boundary lines of the Up and Coming Acres subdivision. It is a lawful business located on a parcel zoned for business. The funeral home is in a suitable location.

8. Read the following facts carefully.

> Mr. and Mrs. Mortimer reserved the party room at Harvey's Restaurant and gave Harvey's a $500 deposit. Their party was scheduled for November 3, 2004. Mrs. Mortimer sent the invitations out on October 1, 2004. The Mortimers agreed to the quoted price of $62.50 per person. The purpose of the event was for Mr. Mortimer to establish relationships with current and prospective legal clients.

> On October 20, 2004, Mrs. Mortimer called Harvey's to confirm party details. She was informed that the party room was under demolition and could not be used for the party. Mrs. Harvey offered to lower the price to $57.50 per person and reserve a portion of the dining room. Although she believed these arrangements were not suitable, Mrs. Mortimer agreed to use the dining room since the invitations were sent and many people accepted.

Mrs. Mortimer ordered lump crab meat as an appetizer for the party. A waitress told Mrs. Mortimer that imitation crab meat was used when Mrs. Mortimer inquired about the crab's unusual crunchiness.

The Mortimers want to sue Harvey's for breach of contract and believe that they relied to their detriment on this contract. They assert that Harvey's failed to notify them of the changes in a timely manner, consequently preventing them from making other arrangements. Additionally, the Mortimers want to know if they have a cause of action for the substitution of imitation crab meat for genuine.

The following is a portion of a memo relating to one of the issues raised by the Mortimers. Read the paragraphs carefully and revise in IRAC format. Remember that each IRAC sequence can span more than one paragraph (for example, paragraph 1—issue and rule; paragraph 2—application and conclusion).

Did the Mortimers suffer a loss of business because of Harvey's Restaurant's promise of the entire party room? The Mortimers can argue that a false representation surrenders the restaurant's interest. "When parties enter into a contract for the performance of the same act in the future they impliedly promise that in the meantime neither will do anything to harm or prejudice the other inconsistent with the contractual relationship they have assumed. . . . If one party to the contract renounces it, the other may treat the renunciation as a breach and sue for damages at once." The restaurant can argue that the contract did not cover the entire performance but was modified; therefore, no harm was done to the contractual relationship. *Pappas v. Crist,* 233 N.C. 265, 25 S.E.2d 850 (1943).

The Mortimers can argue that "damages are not speculative merely because they cannot be computed with mathematical exactness, if, under evidence they are capable of reasonable approximation." *Hawkinson v. Johnston,* 122 F.2d 724 (8th Cir. 1941). The "rainmaking" potential was minimized because of the restaurant's failure to supply the room contracted for.

The restaurant would argue that the "period for which the damages can be reasonably forecast or soundly predicted in such a situation must depend on the circumstances and evidence of the particular case." *Id.* at 727. Therefore, the Mortimers can only quantify the number of RSVPs, not the number of rejects due to the smaller room.

9. This exercise will highlight organizational problems in the discussion and help you to write more logically.

Review the discussion section of a previously drafted memo. Label, in the margin, the issues, the rules, the application portions, and the conclusions. Examine each component to see where you digress from the IRAC format in the discussion. Revise the discussion to conform more closely with the IRAC format.

SYNTHESIZING CASES AND AUTHORITIES

CHAPTER OVERVIEW

You will learn about the methods of synthesis used in a memo. Synthesizing authority requires finding a common theme from two or more sources that ties together the legal rule. Cases are synthesized because it is hard to find a single decision that articulates the precise rule of law required for a memo. Often one case holding will expand another, so the two holdings can be combined, or synthesized, to reflect an accurate statement of the law.

You will also become adept at synthesizing statutory authority as well as combining case law and statutes. Statutes should be given the highest regard in the hierarchy of authority. If you find case law that applies or interprets a statute, synthesize the statute and the case holding.

A. SYNTHESIS

Synthesis is the bringing together of various legal authorities into a unified cohesive statement of the law. The process of synthesizing authority requires finding a common theme or thread that relates to the various legal rules and tying the holdings to that unified theme. Discussing related decisions and statutes separately in a memo makes your points sound more like a list than an integrated, well-thought-out whole. Synthesis adds analytical insight to your legal documents and makes reading them easier.

▼ What Is the Process of Synthesizing Legal Rules?

Enacted law that emanates from more than one statute section must be synthesized under a common legal principle to promote cohesiveness and to add your analytical viewpoint to the memo. We synthesize cases and enacted law because memos and opinion letters are organized by legal issue and not by cited references. Frequently, more than one source of primary authority addresses a particular legal issue. The synthesis of related legal principles enables you to compare and to contrast the legal rules easily as well as to demonstrate how factual applications differ and to show how legal rules expand or contract. Often enacted law and case law are synthesized because the case law applies the statute or interprets the extent to which the statute can be applied.

▼ Why Do We Synthesize Legal Authority?

The legal issues form the framework for the memo discussion. The synthesized authority groups the legal holdings together to address the issues raised.

The following example demonstrates how one case defines an easement in gross and then another case explains how an easement in gross is retained. Both cases discuss easements in gross, yet one expands on the other. The facts on which the example is based are as follows:

> Robert and Jan Murray live in Evanston and are building an addition to their house on Ashland. There is eight feet between their house and their neighbor's, Mrs. Brown's, house. The properties are adjoining. A driveway does not separate the houses, and they cannot be accessed by an alley. The Murrays' contractors and construction workers must enter Mrs. Brown's property to work on the addition. Mrs. Brown is not very pleased that workers are entering her property. The Murrays came to our office wondering whether they should purchase an easement from Mrs. Brown, their neighbor.

EXAMPLE

Should the Murrays purchase an easement in gross from Mrs. Brown? An easement in gross, sometimes called a personal

easement, is a right in the land of another, without being appurtenant to or exercised with the occupancy of the land. *Willoughby v. Lawrence,* 4 N.E. 356 (Ill. 1886). It belongs to the easement holder independent of his ownership or possession of any tract of land and does not benefit the possessor of any tract of land in his use of it. *Schnabel v. County of DuPage,* 428 N.E.2d 671 (Ill. App. Ct. 1981). The Murrays are building an addition to their house. They want to have a right to use the adjoining land to perform the construction of their addition. They do not need an easement, which would be appurtenant to the estate. The interest that the Murrays have in Mrs. Brown's land is personal and would not benefit either tract of land. Therefore, the Murrays can purchase an easement in gross from Mrs. Brown that would permit the workers to enter the Brown property.

B. TYPES OF SYNTHESIS

▼ What Are the Four Methods of Synthesizing Authority?

As we discussed previously, synthesizing primary authority requires finding a common theme that is used to unify all the sources related to the issue. The common legal theme can be developed by classifying the applicable precedent into categories. There are four basic ways to combine and to analyze legal rules to render a coherent distillation of the law:

1. **Primary authority** can be grouped by rule of law found in the text of the decision or in the statute or constitution.
2. Synthesis can be focused around the **reasoning** that a judge uses as the basis of the synthesis.
3. The various **facts** from different cases can form the foundation of the synthesis.
4. The **causes of action** are the last category of case synthesis.

In your writing you will synthesize primary authority by grouping related legal rules. All the examples focus on this method of synthesis. Detailed instruction as to how to synthesize various sources of case law, case law combined with statutory authority, as well as two sources of statutory authority follow.

C. STEP-BY-STEP PROCESS TO SYNTHESIZING LEGAL RULES

The most effective synthesis of legal rules follows conscientious case briefing and careful reading of enacted law. Case briefing requires conforming a decision into set categories: citation, procedure, issue, facts, holding, rationale, disposition. (See Chapter 19.) The following steps take you through the synthesizing process.

1. *Brief decisions.* Once you have carefully and meticulously briefed all the decisions that you plan to use in your memo, you can establish categories of legal precedent to make comparing and contrasting decisions easier. It is far simpler to compare and to contrast seven holdings from briefed decisions than to flip through photocopies of authority.

2. *Outline the problem.* The next step is to formulate the analytical outline of your letter or memo and to pinpoint the issues and subissues that must be addressed to fully explore the memo topic.

3. *Relate research to legal issues raised.* Organize the primary authority by relating the research findings to the issues raised by the problem. Remember: Legal writing is never organized around your sources of authority but around the issues raised by the problem. After pinpointing the legal issues that will be explored, decide on the general rule relating to that point of law.

4. *Under each issue, organize your primary sources by hierarchy of authority.* Enacted law comes before common law, constitutions come before statutes, newer case decisions interpreting statutes come before common law cases, higher court holdings come before lower court holdings, and newer case holdings are more relevant than older holdings on the same point of law from the same court.

5. *Compare and contrast holdings and statutes.* Using the case briefs that you prepared and the notes you made from the plain reading of the enacted law, compare and contrast the holdings and statutory texts.

6. *Formulate a statement of the law.* Your statement should incorporate all the primary sources that will be used under the subissue heading. Ask yourself: What are the similarities and differences between the various cases and statutes? How do the facts differ? What do the documents have in common?

7. *Correct citation.* Remember that you must attribute the authority for any legal statement, even if it is a clause, using the proper *Bluebook* or *ALWD* citation.

D. EXAMPLES OF CASE SYNTHESIS

This example demonstrates synthesizing the holdings from two legal decisions. A problem and two fictitious legal decisions are provided below on which case synthesis is performed.

PROBLEM

Mr. and Mrs. Black wanted to have a chair and a loveseat made to match the living room in their new home. The Blacks searched for weeks at various local furniture retailers for a furniture style and fabric that they liked but were unsuccessful. Finally, the Blacks went to a fabric sale at Fabric Retailers and found the upholstery fabric of their dreams. The Blacks purchased 50 yards of the fabric of their dreams to make

sure that they would have enough for any project. Mr. Black called all the furniture retailers in the area to inquire whether customers can have furniture covered in their own material. Finally, Comfy Furniture said that they permit customers to bring in their own material to cover upholstered furniture ordered from Comfy. The Blacks hurried over to Comfy with the 50 yards of fabric and placed an order for a chair and a loveseat using their own fabric. The price agreed on was the base price of $500 for the chair and $800 for the loveseat. Mr. Blaine, of Comfy Furniture, was their salesperson.

Mr. Blaine said that the fabric was ideal for the styles selected because it required no matching. He also offered that there was plenty of material, that 30 yards was adequate for a job of this nature. The fabric was a small paisley print, with the right side having a lovely sheen and vibrant coloration. The Blacks placed the order on July 7, 2008. They were planning a family reunion for Thanksgiving and felt that ordering in July would give them plenty of time to completely decorate their living room. The new pieces would provide plenty of seating for the family reunion. The Blacks indicated to Mr. Blaine that they needed the furniture for the reunion. Mr. Blaine asserted that the furniture would be ready by September 15. The Blacks gave Comfy Furniture a deposit of $1,000. The loveseat and the chair were delivered to the Black home on September 10, but the furniture was upholstered with the fabric's reverse side showing. The Blacks were devastated.

The legal issue is whether the Blacks are entitled to damages for the breach of the contract to upholster the furniture.

The legal principle surrounding this problem is the expectation interest in a contract. The expectation interest is the expectation of gain from the performance of the contract. The damages are assessed to give the nonbreaching party the measure of gain that he or she would have received if the contract was performed as agreed. Sometimes special or consequential damages are awarded in addition to the expectancy interest.

CASE A

The Cahill family ordered a sofa from the Acme Furniture Company in red tapestry, on June 1, 2008, due to be delivered in six weeks, on July 15, 2008. The Cahills paid $600 for the sofa at the time of the order. After 10 weeks, Acme delivered a gold sofa to the Cahill home. The Cahills called Acme to complain, and Acme picked up the sofa with the promise that it would be reupholstered in red. The sofa was delivered in green six weeks later. In the meanwhile, the Cahills decorated their living room to match the red sofa. After the sofa was delivered in green, 16 weeks after the initial order, the Cahills sued Acme for breach of contract and for damages resulting from the breach, which included the cost of redecorating their living room to match the red sofa. The legal rule is that the nonbreaching party can only collect damages to recoup the expected gain from the contract if performed as agreed. The nonbreaching party cannot receive damages

for expenses incurred that were not in contemplation at the time the contract was formed. The Cahills are entitled to damages for the upholstering of the sofa in the incorrect color and are entitled to compensation for the loss of the use of their sofa for 16 weeks as well as the cost of a new red sofa.

CASE B

Jane Smith ordered a new car from Lunar Motors on June 1, 2008. The Lunar coupe in black was ordered, but the salesperson suggested that the gray floor model, which was used only for demo drives, would represent a $300 savings off the sticker price of the Lunar coupe. Ms. Smith agreed to purchase the floor model for $12,700 rather than pay $13,000 for the special-order car. The salesperson once again asserted that the floor model was new, was used only for demo drives, and had only 5 miles on the odometer. Ms. Smith returned to Lunar Motors on June 3, 2008, paid the $12,700 for the gray floor model Lunar coupe, and drove home. While driving home, Ms. Smith noticed that the car veered dramatically to the left. Ms. Smith took the car to her mechanic, who reported that the car was in an accident previously and had been repaired, but the frame was bent in such a manner as to distort the alignment. Ms. Smith contracted to and expected to receive a new, undamaged car with mileage and wear and tear due to demo drives. Ms. Smith did not contract to receive a damaged car. The salesperson asserted the car was like new. The holding of the court is that the nonbreaching party is entitled to the gain expected from the performance of the contract as agreed, and if the contract is not performed as agreed, the nonbreaching party is entitled to receive the benefit that she would have received if the contract had been performed as agreed. Ms. Smith is entitled to a complete refund of the $12,700 she paid for the car plus the daily cost of the loss of the use of the automobile to be tabulated by the fair market rental value per day of a Lunar coupe.

To synthesize the holdings from the fictitious cases, you would find a common theme that ties together the rules of law from both decisions. Basically, both cases hold that the nonbreaching party in a contract is entitled to receive the benefit of the deal that would have been received if the contract had been performed as agreed. First, craft a general statement of the law. Then, mention the legal rules from Case A and Case B as they pertain to the general statement of the law.

EXAMPLE

Are the Blacks entitled to damages compensating them for the breach of the contract to reupholster the loveseat and the chair? Damages are assessed in a breach of contract action (to give the non-breaching party the measure of gain that he would have received if

the contract had been performed as agreed) in a very specific manner. The nonbreaching party can collect damages to recoup the gain expected from the contract if the contract had been performed as agreed. Case A; Case B. If the contract is not performed as agreed, the nonbreaching party is entitled to the benefit he would have received if the contract had been performed as agreed. Case B. The nonbreaching party cannot be compensated for expenses incurred that were not in contemplation at the time the contract was formed. Case A. In the alternative, the nonbreaching party can be compensated for expenses incurred that were in contemplation at the time the contract was formed. Case A. In our problem, the Blacks contracted to have the chair and loveseat upholstered in paisley fabric with the correct side showing. The furniture was upholstered with the wrong side of the fabric showing. When ordering the furniture, the Blacks stipulated that they needed the pieces for a family reunion and that the pieces would provide the necessary seating. The Blacks were without their furniture because of Comfy Furniture's error. The Blacks communicated the need for the seating at the time of the contract formation. The Blacks should receive the gain they expected from the performance of the contract as agreed as well as compensation for the expense of providing alternative seating for the family reunion based on the rental cost of chairs.

An ineffective case synthesis based on our hypothetical problem would be as follows.

> Are the Blacks entitled to damages from Comfy Furniture for breach of contract? In *Case B,* the court held that "the non-breaching party is entitled to the gain expected from the performance of the contract as agreed and if the contract is not performed as agreed, the nonbreaching party is entitled to receive the benefit that she would have received if the contract had been performed as agreed." *Case B.* The Blacks were the nonbreaching party and anticipated a loveseat and a chair to be upholstered in paisley with the correct side showing. Therefore, the Blacks are entitled to be compensated by a damage award to put them in a position as if the contract had been performed as agreed. Are the Blacks entitled to be compensated for not having adequate seating for the family reunion? *Case A* holds that the nonbreaching party cannot receive damages for expenses incurred that were not in contemplation at the time the contract was formed. *Case A.* The Blacks alerted Mr. Blaine, the salesperson, that the couches were needed for a family reunion at Thanksgiving. The Blacks indicated that the additional seating provided by the chair and the loveseat would be necessary at the reunion when ordering the furniture. Since the need for the seating, to be provided by the furniture, was in contemplation at the time the order was placed, the Blacks should be compensated for not having adequate seating at the time of the reunion; the damages should be measured by the cost of providing alternative seating.

This example, although clear and coherent, does not synthesize the decisions and unify the concepts articulated in the cases. Each holding

is addressed separately, although one holding relates to the other and the authority is presented more as a list than as a cohesive unit.

When you have found a relevant statute for a problem, give it the highest regard, because statutes on point govern before case law. (See Chapters 1 and 2.) Generally, synthesize statutes separately from case law holdings. However, if you find cases that interpret and apply the relevant statutes, synthesize the statute text with the application found in case law. Always apply the plain meaning rule to statutes. The plain meaning of the statute text is derived from a reading of each word at its face value.

The problem below illustrates the synthesis of a statute and a case.

PROBLEM

FACT PATTERN

On August 7, 2008, our client, Jane Howard, obtained an $800 loan from Rough & Tough Pawn Shop, using her grandmother's engagement ring as collateral. Howard agreed to make monthly payments on the loan for a minimum of 13½ months. After 12 months, Rough & Tough had the right to sell the ring and to refund Howard the difference between her outstanding debt and the price received for the ring.

On September 11, 2008, Howard received a postcard from Rough & Tough stating that its shop and its assets will be sold to Able Pawn. The postcard also stated that Able would assume the business of Rough & Tough, including the items pawned and the loans outstanding. The postcard alerted Howard to pick up the ring and to pay off her note by September 29, 2008, if Howard wanted to reclaim her property. Howard decided to continue to make her monthly payments to Able Pawn, where her loan would be transferred.

On October 1, 2008, Able Pawn was robbed and all the jewelry was stolen, including Howard's ring. The premises were protected by a security alarm system and a guard dog. The jewelry was sold to Village Jewelers in Lincoln Park.

ISSUE

The issue to be examined is whether Rough & Tough had authority to sell its interest in Howard's ring.

STATUTORY AUTHORITY

The applicable statute is from the Pawnbrokers Regulation Act, 205 Ill. Comp. Stat. 510/10 (2006).

Sale of Property. No personal property received on deposit or pledge, or purchased by any such pawnbroker, shall be sold or permitted to be redeemed or removed from the place of business of such pawnbroker

for the space of twenty-four hours after the delivery of the copy and statement required by Section 7 of this act required to be delivered to the officer or officers named therein; and no personal property pawned or pledged shall be sold or disposed of by any such pawnbroker within one year from the time when the pawner or pledger shall make default in the payment of interest on the money so advanced by such pawnbroker, unless by the written consent of such pawner or pledger.

RELEVANT CASE LAW

This decision interprets and applies the relevant statute, so the statute and the decision should be synthesized.

JACOBS v. GROSSMAN

310 Ill. 247, 141 N.E.2d 714 (1923)

DUNCAN, J.

This case is brought to this court on a certificate of importance and appeal from a judgment of the Appellate Court for the First District, affirming a judgment of the municipal court of Chicago in favor of the appellee and against appellant in the sum of $330. Appellee, Minnie Jacobs, on April 8, 1921, began an action of replevin in the municipal court of Chicago against appellant, Harry Grossman, a licensed pawnbroker, to recover possession of a diamond ring delivered by herself to appellant to secure the payment of $70 borrowed from him. A replevin bond was given for $800, and a writ of replevin issued. It was returned April 12, 1921, served but no property found. Appellee then filed a count in trover, alleging possession of the ring of the value of $400 and the conversion of it by appellant. The case was heard before the court without a jury.

On June 3, 1919, appellee placed in pawn with appellant, a licensed pawnbroker doing business at 426 South Halsted Street, Chicago, the ring, and received thereon the sum of $70. Interest on the loan was paid to June 7, 1920. The pawn ticket issued to appellee contained this statement, "This office protected by the Chicago Electric Protective Company," and described the location and name of the pawnbroker as "Metropolitan Loan Bank, 426 South Halsted St." The ticket further described the goods pawned, the amount loaned, and the time of redemption. Between October 7 and 10, 1920, appellant sold all his interest in whatever pledges he had to Jacob Klein, another duly licensed pawnbroker at 502 South Halsted Street, for the sum of $16,000 or $17,000, which represented the principal sums loaned on said pledges with interest thereon. The pledges were sold by appellant to Klein upon the express understanding that the pledgors might redeem from Klein in the same manner as they could from appellant, had he not sold his interest in the pawns. It was admitted that Klein is a reputable business man, and it was also conceded by appellant that no notice was given by him, either expressly or impliedly, to the appellee of the transfer of her property. On January 8, 1921, the pawnshop of Klein

was entered by four armed robbers. The robbers ordered the clerks employed there to hold up their hands, and they forcibly took from a safe a large number of articles, including the diamond ring in question of appellee, which has never been recovered.

There is an unimportant dispute in the record evidence as to whether appellee or her sister, after the sale of appellant's business to Klein, had called on Klein and secured an additional loan upon a diamond ring other than the one in question. The Appellate Court found that the evidence on this point showed that appellee's sister, and not appellee, was involved in that transaction. Appellant admits in his reply brief that he does not rely in any way on this testimony to show actual notice to appellee of the change in the possession of the pledge in question. As to the other material facts above set out, there is no dispute between the parties.

Counsel for appellant relies for a reversal of the judgment on two propositions: First, that a pawnbroker is bound only to use ordinary care for the safety of the pawner's property, and, if the property is lost or destroyed without the negligence of the pawnee, then he is not liable; second, that a pawnbroker has the right to assign or sell to another his interest in an article pledged to him.

A pawn is a species of bailment which arises when goods or chattels are delivered to another as a pawn for security to him on money borrowed of him by the bailor. It is the pignari acceptum of the civil law, according to which the possession of the pledge passes to the creditor, therein differing from a hypotheca. It is a class of bailment which is made for the mutual benefit of the bailor and bailee. All that is required by the common law on the part of a pawnee in the protection of the property thus entrusted to him is ordinary care and diligence. Consequently, unless a failure to exercise such care and diligence is shown, a pawnee is not answerable for the loss of the article pledged. 30 Cyc. 1169; *Standard Brewery v. Malting Co.*, 171 Ill. 602, 49 N.E. 507. This is an elementary principle, and there can be no question as to the accuracy and correctness of appellant's first proposition.

But the question arises as to whether or not appellant was guilty of negligence in transferring the interest of the pawner without giving her any notice of such transfer. Appellant's duty to her was to safely keep and protect the property pledged. It was a legal obligation on his part to appellee, from which he could not relieve himself by transferring the pledge to another without her consent. Appellee relied upon him to keep and protect her property where it would be reasonably safe, and he had in substance assured her by the language on the ticket that her property was insured or safeguarded. He violated this duty or obligation to her by transferring the possession of her property to another, to be kept at another place, which the evidence does not show to be protected by a protective company, and without giving her notice of such custody and transfer.

Whatever may be the right of the parties in a bailment for the mutual benefit of the bailor and the bailee, it is unquestionably the

law that the parties may increase or diminish these rights by stipulations contained in the contract of bailment. 30 Cyc. 1167; *St. Losky v. Davidson,* 6 Cal. 643. The sum and substance of appellant's contract was that he would keep appellee's property at his office or shop described as aforesaid, and which was protected as aforesaid. The pawning of the ring by appellee under the circumstances imposed a personal trust upon appellant to personally keep the property at his shop and under the assurance of protection as aforesaid, and he could not at his will, without the consent of appellee, transfer the possession and custody thereof to another without such consent. The rule is stated in 3 R.C.L. 112, that any attempt on the part of the bailee in an ordinary simple bailment of a pawn to sell, lease, pledge, or otherwise part with the title or possession of the bailment, constitutes a conversion in every case where the bailment can be properly regarded as a personal trust in the bailee.

There is another controlling reason for holding that appellant is liable for the loss of the ring, and for holding that he could not transfer the possession of the article pawned to him to another and escape liability for a conversion. Section 10 of the Pawnbroker's Act (Smith-Hurd Rev. St. 1923, c. 107 1/2) provides, in part, as follows:

> No personal property pawned or pledged shall be sold or disposed by any such pawnbroker within one year from the time when the pawner or pledger shall make default in the payment of interest on the money so advanced by such pawnbroker, unless by the written consent of such pawner or pledger.

Appellant claims that the proper interpretation of this statute is that it prohibits the sale of an article, including the interest of the pledger or pawner as well as his own, and does not refer to a sale of only the interest of the pawnbroker or pledgee. The statute is not subject to such construction. It should be construed to mean what it says: That the property must not be sold or disposed of by the pawnbroker without the written consent of the pledgor. The statute does not confine itself to a sale, but also forbids any disposition of the same without consent as aforesaid. It cannot be seriously disputed that appellant did dispose of the property without the consent of appellee, within the meaning of the foregoing section of the statute.

The judgment of the Appellate Court is affirmed.

Judgment affirmed.

SAMPLE SYNTHESIS

Does Rough & Tough have the authority to sell its interest in Howard's ring? Unless the pawner gives written consent, no pawned property shall be sold or disposed of by any pawnbroker within one year from the time the pawner defaults in the payment of interest on the money advanced by the pawnbroker. 205 Ill. Comp. Stat. 510/10 (2006). Where a pawnbroker neglected to give notice of the intent to sell his interest in a pawner's diamond ring and neglected to receive

written consent for such sale, the pawnbroker lacked authority to transfer his interest in the ring to another. *Jacobs v. Grossman,* 141 N.E. 714, 715 (Ill. App. Ct. 1923). Although Rough & Tough gave Howard notice of its intent to sell the shop and its assets, R&T failed to obtain Howard's written consent to sell her ring. Therefore, a court will probably find that Rough & Tough lacked the authority to sell its interest in Howard's ring to another pawnbroker.

The above example synthesizes the statute and the *Jacobs* case around the issue of a pawnbroker's authority to sell its interest in a pawned item without the consent of the pawner. Notice how the statute is mentioned first because its authority ranks higher than the case. The *Jacobs* case follows the statute because the holding is more detailed on the issue of a pawnbroker's duty to give notice before selling his interest in the pawner's ring and the facts are similar to Jane Howard's situation. Two sources of primary authority, a statute and a case, are used together in this sample synthesis because both sources relate to a single legal issue.

▼ How Do You Synthesize Two Sources of Statutory Authority?

Often you must use two or more sections of a statute in conjunction to explain the legal rule completely. Sometimes definitional provisions are located in one section and the applicable code section is located in another.

> **Facts:** Mr. Thomas was arrested on charges of domestic battery. He punched his wife in the face three times and broke her nose. Mr. and Mrs. Thomas live in Illinois, but they are living apart.
>
> **Issue:** Whether the Illinois domestic battery statute applies to an estranged husband and whether punching is considered battery.

This problem requires you to use two statutory provisions. One section defines the relevant terms, and the other section details actions that constitute domestic battery. The statutory definition of family and household members as pertaining to domestic battery follows.

725 Ill. Comp. Stat. 5/112A-3(3) (2006):

"Family or household members" include spouses, former spouses, parents, children, stepchildren and other persons related by blood or marriage, persons who share or formerly shared a common dwelling and persons who have or allegedly have a child in common.

The domestic battery statute at 720 Ill. Comp. Stat. 5/12-3.2 (2006):

(a) A person commits domestic battery if he intentionally or knowingly without legal justification by any means:

(1) Causes bodily harm to any family or household member as defined in Subsection (3) of Section 112A-3 of the Code of Criminal Procedure of 1963, as amended;

(2) Makes physical contact of an insulting or provoking nature with any family or household member as defined in subsection (3) of Section 112A-3 of the Code of Criminal Procedure of 1963, as amended.

Sample synthesis using two statutory provisions:

We must determine whether the domestic battery statute, 720 Ill. Comp. Stat. 5/12-3.2 (2006), applies to married couples living apart and if so, whether Mr. Thomas, an estranged husband, committed domestic battery by punching his wife. The domestic battery statute applies to family members. "Family members" is defined to include "spouses formerly sharing a common dwelling." 725 Ill. Comp. Stat. 5/112A-3(3) (2006). "A person commits domestic battery if he intentionally or knowingly without legal justification by any means:

(1) Causes bodily harm to any family or household member. . . ." 720 Ill. Comp. Stat. 5/12-3.2 (2006). Since Mr. Thomas is a spouse who formerly shared a common residence with his wife, he is a family or household member, and the domestic battery statute is applicable. Mr. Thomas punched his wife in the face three times, which caused her nose to break. The facts do not state that his mental capacity was altered by inebriation or severe mental illness, so his actions can be deduced to be intentional. The facts also do not indicate if Mr. Thomas was provoked to commit battery by extreme jealousy. It appears that there was no legal justification for the bodily harm inflicted on Mrs. Thomas by Mr. Thomas. Although Mr. Thomas is a spouse formerly sharing a common dwelling with Mrs. Thomas, he is a family member and is governed by the domestic battery statute. By punching his wife, breaking her nose, and causing her bodily harm, Mr. Thomas committed domestic battery.

CHECKLIST: SEVEN STEPS FOR EFFECTIVE SYNTHESIS

1. Brief your authority.
2. Outline the problem.
3. Organize the primary authority.
4. Under each issue, organize your primary sources by hierarchy of authority.
5. Compare and contrast the case holding and statutory text.
6. Formulate a statement of the law that incorporates all the primary sources that will be used under the subissue heading.
7. Attribute the authority for any legal statement by using the proper *Bluebook* or *ALWD* citation.

PRACTICE POINTER

When synthesizing authorities, always cite to every source that you use. Often the information gathered from the authority is not from the first page of the decision. You must use pinpoint cites to indicate from exactly where within the decision the information is obtained. Also, often you will use authorities more than once. This calls for subsequent citation format. Use *Bluebook* Rule 10.9 or *ALWD* Rule 12.21 for guidance on short citation when citing cases subsequently.

CHAPTER SUMMARY

Learning to synthesize authority is a mechanical process at first. Brief the cases and summarize the statutory authority. Insert the applicable authority in your outline by grouping together related statements of the law. Draft cohesive statements of the legal authority that you grouped together. Cite all authority accurately even if string citations are needed or if two separate clauses in a single sentence are each supported by a different authority.

As you become more adept at synthesis, you will see that your writing is smoother and less redundant. Synthesizing authority lets you write in one voice rather than awkwardly switching back and forth between your words and the words of the court.

KEY TERMS

causes of action	reasoning
facts	synthesis
primary authority	

EXERCISES

SHORT ANSWER

1. Why do we synthesize authority?
2. What are the four basic types of synthesis?
3. What are the steps required to synthesize legal rules?

APPLICATION

4. Read the following fact pattern and cases carefully. Draft a paragraph in which you synthesize the holdings of the cases. The issue that you will address is provided as well. Remember that proper synthesis requires you to relate the authority to a common legal theme. The problem's issue will guide you in synthesizing the authority.

Facts

On November 29, 2007, Michael Jones purchased a used truck from Grimy's Auto and Truck Service. At the time of the purchase, Grimy's stated that the engine was completely overhauled and consisted of rebuilt and reconditioned parts, that all parts were guaranteed, and that invoices for all new parts would be provided. On December 13, 2008, after using the truck for over one year, Jones discovered that several engine parts were not rebuilt or reconditioned and that other engine parts were defective. These defects caused the truck to break down, resulting in lost wages and lost profits for Jones. Jones made repairs to the truck on December 13, 2008, December 16, 2008, and December 31, 2008. Jones did not attempt to return the truck and did not notify Grimy's that the truck was defective. The truck is currently disabled in Columbus, Ohio. Jones wants to sue Grimy's for damages for breach of contract.

Issue

Whether Jones continued to use the truck for more than a reasonable time after noticing the defects and failed to properly reject the truck and to notify Grimy's as to the defects.

Case A

A buyer of goods must alert the seller as soon as he discovers that the goods are not as agreed on. A buyer must rescind a sales contract as soon as he discovers the breach or after he has had a reasonable time for examination. The buyer waives the right to rescind a contract for the sale of goods by continuing to use allegedly defective goods for more than a reasonable time.

Case B

To meet the requirements of an effective rejection, the buyer must reject the goods within a reasonable time and reasonably notify the seller.

5. Read the following fact pattern and cases carefully. Draft a paragraph in which you synthesize the holdings of the cases. The issue that you will address is provided as well.

Facts

Robert and Jane Moore live in Evingston and have to repair the gutters on their house. There is eight feet between their house and their neighbor's. The properties are adjoining; the neighboring Kandler house is north of the Moore house. The Moore's contractors and carpenters must enter the Kandler property to work on the gutters on the north side of the house. Mrs. Kandler is not very pleased that workers are entering her property. The Moores came to our office to find out what they should do. The Moores specifically asked if they should obtain an easement to grant them a right of way on Mrs. Kandler's property to make the repairs.

Issue

What legal access would allow the contractors and carpenters, repairing the gutters on the Moore house, to enter the adjoining property belonging to Mrs. Kandler?

Statutory Authority

Ch. 12 §99: If the repair and maintenance of an existing single-family residence cannot reasonably be accomplished without entering onto the adjoining land, and if the owner of the adjoining land refuses to permit entry onto that adjoining land for the purpose of repair and maintenance of the single-family residence, then the owner of the single-family residence may bring an action in court to compel the owner of the adjoining land to permit entry for the purpose of repair and maintenance where entry will be granted solely for the purposes of repair and maintenance.

Case Y

The need to enter the land of an adjoining property for the purpose of making repairs to one's own property should not mandate that an easement be acquired. An easement grants a right of way, but only the landowner can create an easement. The adjoining landowner may view the repairs as a nuisance and would not grant the easement. Sometimes repairs must be performed on a single-family residence that require entering the adjoining land. Statute Ch. 12 §99 was created to avoid the need to obtain an easement to enter adjoining land when the sole reason for the right of way is to make repairs on a single-family residence.

REINFORCEMENT EXERCISE

6. Review a memo that you have recently completed. Examine the body of the discussion carefully. Highlight a paragraph that states the rule, its application and conclusion. Examine a subsequent paragraph that expands on the initial rule by citing a separate opinion. Reformulate the rules statement to incorporate the initial rule and the subsequent rule to create a comprehensive statement of the law on that particular point.

OUTLINING AND ORGANIZING A MEMORANDUM

CHAPTER OVERVIEW

In Chapters 19-23, you learned about the components of a legal memorandum as well as some drafting pointers. This chapter teaches you how to organize the discussion section of your memorandum. You are shown some outlining techniques. These are suggested techniques only. You may have a technique of your own that works well. Feel free to use it. In this chapter, you also learn how to draft thesis paragraphs for your discussion.

A. PURPOSE OF OUTLINING

The key to a well-organized memo is a well-drafted outline. Outlining allows you to organize your discussion easily so that it is smooth and cogent. An outline ensures that you cover all the legal rules and apply all the legally significant facts to those rules. An outline also simplifies your discussion drafting.

B. STEPS TO OUTLINING

The outline should be done in two stages, each of which consists of a number of steps. In the first stage, you compile a list of legal authorities, which includes the names of and the citations to authorities, a note about the legally significant facts presented in any case, and a statement that summarizes each authority's significance to the issues presented in your research problem. See Illustration 24-1. In the second stage, you arrange the discussion sections concerning each issue and, in some cases, arrange each paragraph. See Illustration 24-2.

1. Steps in Compiling a List of Legal Authorities

1. Draft the statement of the facts, the questions presented, and the conclusions.
2. Research your issues.
3. Read the cases.
4. Brief the authorities as discussed in Chapter 18. Once you have briefed the authorities, you will write a holding for each case. These holdings should be used in your list of authorities. These holdings will summarize the significance of the authorities. If the holdings are well written, they will incorporate important facts derived from the authorities.
5. Write a summary statement for each statute or other noncase authority you plan to cite.
6. Prepare a list of each of the relevant authorities. Note that not all authorities will be relevant. Include only those that help you to determine the law involved in your case. For your list, include the name of the authority. If the authority is a case, list the holding or summary statement of the significance of the authority. Note the complete citation. It is also helpful to list whether the authority is a primary binding, primary persuasive, or secondary authority.

Now review Illustrations 24-1 and 24-4. Illustration 24-1 is a list of the significant authorities for the memo in Illustration 24-3. Illustration 24-4 is a list of authorities for the memo in Illustration 24-5, which follows the pattern of the outline in Illustration 24-2.

ILLUSTRATION 24-1.   List of Authorities

1. *Anderson v. St. Francis-St. George Hosp., Inc.,* 77 Ohio St. 3d 82, 671 N.E.2d 225 (1996): A civil battery occurs when one individual touches another individual without his or her consent and a physical injury occurs. (primary binding)

2. *Leichtman v. WLW Jacoc Communications, Inc.,* 92 Ohio App. 3d 232, 634 N.E.2d 697 (1994): A contact between a nonconsenting individual and a substance or an object such as cigar smoke is sufficient to be a touching within the context of the tort of civil battery because the substance or object would be an extension of the offender's body. (primary binding)

3. *Smith v. John Deere Co.,* 83 Ohio App. 3d 398, 614 N.E.2d 1148 (1993): A person intends his or her conduct when he or she undertakes an action with a knowing mind. (primary persuasive)

4. *Love v. Port Clinton,* 37 Ohio St. 3d 98, 524 N.E.2d 166 (1988): If a person consents to the touching, a battery has not occurred. (primary binding)

ILLUSTRATION 24-2.   Outline of Discussion

Element or Subissue 1
Issue: Did a touching occur?
Rule: Objects are extensions of body parts. Contact with a substance or an object can be touching (*Leichtman*)
Application of law to facts: Bucket contacted McMillan
Conclusion: A touching occurred
Element or Subissue 2
Issue: Did Mann intend to hit McMillan?
Rule: A person intends an act when it is done purposefully (*Smith*)
Application of law to facts: Mann purposefully threw the bucket at McMillan and said she intended to strike her
Conclusion: Mann had intent
Element or Subissue 3
Issue: Did McMillan consent to touching?
Rules: If a party consented to the touching, no battery occurred. (*Love*)
Application of law to facts: McMillan did not consent
Conclusion: A touching without consent as in this case can be a battery
Element or Subissue 4
Issue: Did McMillan suffer the requisite physical injuries as a result of the contact?
Rule: Physical injuries must result from contact for battery (*Anderson*)
Application of law to facts: McMillan sustained cuts and eye irritation from bucket and sand contact
Conclusion: McMillan had requisite physical injuries

ILLUSTRATION 24-3.   Memorandum: McMillan Battery Action

MEMORANDUM

To: William Mark
From: Ivy Courier
Date: November 7, 2008
Re: McMillan Battery Action

QUESTION PRESENTED

Did an actionable battery occur when Mann intentionally struck McMillan with a bucket, without McMillan's consent, causing McMillan to suffer physical and monetary injuries?

CONCLUSION

Mann's intentional striking of McMillan with a bucket and sand was an actionable battery.

FACTS

Our client, Mary McMillan, a 36-year-old bank teller, wants to bring an action for battery against Carol Mann, a 36-year-old mother, who threw a metal bucket filled with sand at McMillan at a local park. While McMillan sat on a park bench, she teased Mann's seven-year-old son. Mann did not like this teasing and threw a bucket filled with sand at Mary. Sand landed in McMillan's eyes while she was wearing soft contact lenses. As a result, McMillan's contacts had to be replaced. The bucket also cut McMillan's eye and cheek. She had stitches in both places. McMillan asked Mann to pay for her doctor bills and for the new contacts. Mann refused and added, "I'm not sorry. I meant to hurt you."

DISCUSSION

The issue presented is whether Mann's intentional touching of McMillan with a bucket rather than her person is an actionable battery. A battery is the intentional touching of another without consent, which causes injury. *Anderson v. St. Francis-St. George Hosp., Inc.,* 77 Ohio St. 3d 82, 671 N.E.2d 225 (1996). A touching can occur when an object rather than an individual's body contacts the other party. *Leichtman v. WLW Jacoc Communications, Inc.,* 92 Ohio App. 3d 232, 634 N.E.2d 697 (1994); *Smith v. John Deere Co.,* 83 Ohio App. 3d 398, 614 N.E.2d 1148 (1993). In this case, Mann intentionally struck McMillan with a bucket without McMillan's consent and that touching resulted in injuries. Therefore, a battery occurred.

The threshold issue is whether a touching occurred when the bucket struck McMillan. A contact between a nonconsenting party and object rather than the actor's body can be a battery. *Leichtman v. WLW Jacoc Communications, Inc.,* 92 Ohio App. 3d 232, 634 N.E.2d 697 (1994); *Smith v. John Deere Co.,* 83 Ohio App. 3d at 398, 614 N.E.2d at 1148. In *Leichtman,* one person blew cigar smoke at another person,

ILLUSTRATION 24-3. *Continued*

resulting in injuries. The court found that the cigar smoke was an extension of the person and that a contact between the smoke and the nonconsenting person met the requirement of a touching for civil battery. In this case, Mann threw the bucket at McMillan, and the bucket contacted her face. Following the reasoning in the *Leichtman* case, the bucket would be an extension of Mann's body, and the contact between McMillan and the bucket would be considered a touching under the theory of civil battery.

Next, the question to consider is whether under the statute Mann intended to touch McMillan when she struck her with the bucket. A person intends his or her conduct when he or she undertakes an action with a knowing mind. *Smith v. John Deere Co.,* 83 Ohio App. 3d 398, 614 N.E.2d 1148 (1993). In *Smith,* a police officer handcuffed the plaintiff. The court found that the officer must have intended his actions because you could not accidentally handcuff a person. *Smith,* 83 Ohio App. 3d at 399, 614 N.E.2d at 1149. In McMillan's case, Mann aimed the bucket at McMillan purposefully trying to strike her, Mann later told McMillan that she deliberately threw the bucket at her. McMillan probably will be able to establish that Mann had the statutory intent.

The next factor to consider is whether McMillan consented to the contact. If a person consents to the touching, a battery has not occurred. *Love v. Port Clinton,* 37 Ohio St. 3d 98, 524 N.E.2d 166 (1988). In our case, McMillan did not consent to Mann's throwing of the bucket at her face. Therefore, McMillan did not consent to any contact. Finally, the question is whether McMillan suffered physical injuries. A battery occurs only if a plaintiff sustains physical injuries as a result of the touching. *Anderson v. St. Francis St. George Hosp., Inc.,* 77 Ohio St. 3d 82, 671 N.E.2d 225 (1996). McMillan sustained cuts on her face and the sand flying out of the bucket into her eyes. McMillan will be able to show that she sustained physical injuries as a result of the contact with the bucket.

ILLUSTRATION 24-4. Outline of Authorities

1. *42 U.S.C. §2000e* **(1998):** The term "employer" means a person engaged in an industry affecting commerce who has fifteen or more employees for each working day in each of twenty or more calendar weeks in the current or preceding calendar year.

2. *Zimmerman v. North American Signal Co.,* **704 F.2d 347 (7th Cir. 1983):** Salaried workers or full-time workers counted as employees for every day of the week on the payroll whether they were present at work or not. Hourly paid workers are counted as employees only on the days when they are actually at work or days on paid leave. (primary binding)

ILLUSTRATION 24-4. *Continued*

3. *Musser v. Mountain View Broadcasting,* **578 F. Supp. 229 (E.D. Tenn. 1984):** "Current calendar year" is the year of discrimination. (primary persuasive)

4. *Wright v. Kosciusko Medical Clinic,* **791 F. Supp. 1327, 1333 (N.D. Ind. 1992):** "Each working day" is literal and must be a day on which an employer conducts normal, full operations. (primary persuasive)

5. *Norman v. Levy,* **767 F. Supp. 144 (N.D. Ill. 1991):** Part-time workers counted only on the days that they actually work. (primary persusive)

6. *Knight v. United Farm Bureau Mut. Ins. Co.,* **950 F.2d 377 (7th Cir 1991):** The "economic realities" of the relationship between an employer and his or her worker must be weighted by applying five factors: (1) the amount of employer control and supervision over employee, (2) the responsibility for the operational costs, (3) the worker's occupation and the skills required, (4) the form of compensation and benefits, and (5) the length of the job commitment. *Knight,* 950 F.2d at 378. Control is the most important factor. *Id.* Knight is an insurance agent, is not permitted to sell insurance for any other companies, is required to attend weekly staff meetings in the office, and works a specified number of hours in the office (primary binding). *Knight,* 950 F.2d at 378. Company provided supplies and paid for business expenses. *Id.* Essential to company operation. *Id.* Paid commissions with no deductions. *Id.* Knight not an employee.

7. *Mitchell v. Tenney,* **650 F. Supp. 703 (N.D. Ill. 1986):** The "economic realities" of the relationship between an employer and his or her worker must be weighed.

8. *Vakharia v. Swedish Covenant Hosp.,* **765 F. Supp. 461 (N.D. Ill. 1991):** When an employee is economically dependent on an employer, the court is likely to find employment relationship. Plaintiff in *Vakharia* was a physician dependent on the hospital for business *Id.* at 463. (primary persuasive)

ILLUSTRATION 24-5.   Memorandum: Sex Discrimination Case

MEMORANDUM

To: Wallace Maine
From: Thomas Wall
Date: November 15, 2007
Re: Sex Discrimination Case against Whole In One No. C07 CIV 190, G12399990

ILLUSTRATION 24-5. *Continued*

QUESTIONS PRESENTED

1. Under Title VII, was Whole In One an employer when 14 people, including 3 full-time and 11 part-time workers, worked on any one day for 24 weeks and when 10 full-time employees were on the Whole In One payroll?

2. Under Title VII, was Walker an independent contractor rather than an employee when she worked exclusively for Whole In One, paid taxes quarterly rather than through deductions, and worked with limited company supervision?

3. Under Title VII, was Radiant an independent contractor rather than an employee when she worked with limited company supervision using company supplies and equipment and had taxes and medical deductions taken from her salary?

CONCLUSIONS

1. Whole In One was an employer. Under Title VII, an employer has at least 15 employees working for 20 or more weeks during the relevant year: Salaried employees are included in this number for each week they are on the payroll, while hourly workers are only counted on the days they actually work. In 2004, the year of the alleged discrimination, 14 workers, 3 full-time and 11 part-time people, worked for Whole In One on any day during the 24-week restaurant and golf season. However, 10 full-time workers were on the payroll. As these part-time workers are only counted on the days that they work, the number of part-time individuals included in the count of employees is 11 for each day of the 24-week season. Because full-time workers, however, are counted for each day of a week that they are on the payroll, all 10 of Whole In One's full-time workers would be included in the count of employees. In total, Whole In One had 11 part-time workers and 10 full-time workers "working" for 20 or more weeks during the relevant year, bringing the total count of employees to 21. Therefore, Whole In One was an employer under Title VII.

2. Walker was an employee. The Seventh Circuit will weigh five factors to determine whether she was an independent contractor or an employee for this Title VII lawsuit. The primary focus will be on the company's control of Walker. Although Walker worked from home, set her own hours, and had an impact in her commission pay, the company controlled her work by reviewing and revising it, restricting Walker's employment opportunities, and providing supplies for her. Therefore, the company exerted control over Walker and she would be considered an employee.

3. Radiant was probably an employee. To determine whether she was an employee or independent contractor for this Title VII lawsuit, the court will focus on five factors, primarily the amount of control the company exerted over Radiant's work. Whole In One provided Radiant with an office, supplies, a two-year contract, and additional training. Whole In One paid her regularly and deducted taxes from her salary.

ILLUSTRATION 24-5. *Continued*

Although Whole In One did not actively supervise Radiant's work on a daily basis, she still worked in the company offices and was under the control of Whole In One. Therefore, the court probably will find that Radiant was an employee.

FACTS

Victoria Radiant and KarenWalker, two former Whole In One Enterprises workers, brought a federal sex discrimination lawsuit based on Title VII against our client, Whole In One Enterprises, owned by Nancy and Craig Black. The lawsuit, filed in the U.S. District Court for the Northern District of Illinois, stems from the dismissal of the two women by the Blacks during 2004.

The Blacks own Whole In One Enterprises, which operates a miniature golf course and restaurant in Glenview, Illinois. During the 24-week 2004 restaurant season, 10 people worked full-time and 14 people worked part-time for Whole In One. However, no more than 14 people worked on any one day. Of those 14 people, only 3 were full-time employees. The other full-time employees regularly took days off during the summer restaurant and golf season.

Among the full-time workers was Karen Walker, who worked as a public relations director for Whole In One. Walker responded to an ad that said that "an employer" sought an individual to perform public relations work. Whole In One hired Walker without a contract and prohibited her from working for other firms. However, Walker worked from home and set her own hours. Whole In One required Walker to attend weekly staff meetings at the company offices, where Whole In One would review and revise Walker's work. The company supplied Walker with paper, pencils, stamps, and telephone service and paid for her life and health insurance. Whole In One did not withhold taxes from Walker's commissions.

Victoria Radiant, who had a two-year employment contract with the company, provided marketing services to Whole In One from October of 2002 until she was fired in 2004. Although Radiant worked in the company office, Whole In One management rarely supervised her work. The company paid for her continued education, provided her with bonuses, and deducted taxes from her weekly salary.

APPLICABLE STATUTE

The term "employer" means a person engaged in an industry affecting commerce who has fifteen or more employees for each working day in each of 20 or more calendar weeks in the current or preceding calendar year. 42 U.S.C. §2000e(b) (2004).

DISCUSSION

This memo first will address whether Walker and Radiant can successfully establish that Whole In One was an employer within the

ILLUSTRATION 24-5. *Continued*

meaning of 42 U.S.C. §2000e(b) (2004), commonly called Title VII. Next, the discussion will focus on whether Walker can establish that she was an employee protected by Title VII. Finally, the memo will explore whether Radiant was an employee protected by Title VII. If Whole In One was not an employer, then the Title VII claim will be dismissed. If the court finds that neither individual is an employee, the individual's claim will be barred.

I. Was Whole In One an Employer under Title VII?

Before a federal court can consider Walker's and Radiant's claims, the plaintiffs must establish that Whole In One was an employer under the definition established in Title VII. An employer is "a person engaged in an industry affecting commerce who has fifteen or more employees for each working day in each of 20 or more calendar weeks in the current or preceding calendar year." 42 U.S.C. §2000e(b) (2004). The focus of this discussion will be how to calculate whether 15 employees worked for Whole In One on each working day in each of 20 or more calendar weeks and how to determine which year's employment records are relevant. The Seventh Circuit has held that full-time employees are "working" each day of a week during a week for which they are on the payroll, but part-time workers are counted only on the days that they actually work. *Zimmerman v. North American Signal Co.*, 704 F.2d 347 (7th Cir. 1983). In 2004, the year of the alleged discrimination, 14 workers, 3 full-time and 11 part-time people, worked for Whole In One on any day during the 24-week restaurant and golf season. In addition, 10 full-time workers were on the payroll. Based on the counting method established in *Zimmerman*, these figures indicate that Whole In One had at least 15 employees working for each working day in each of 20 or more calendar weeks. Therefore, Whole In One was an employer under Title VII.

The central focus of this discussion will be how to calculate the number of employees. First, the relevant year must be determined. The statute states that the time to be considered is "20 or more calendar weeks in the current or preceding calendar year." 42 U.S.C. §2000e(b) (2004). The current year of the discrimination was 2004. Because the statute specifies "or," the preceding year, 1997, also is relevant. However, in a persuasive decision a Tennessee district court held that the "current calendar year" is the year in which the alleged discrimination occurred. *Musser v. Mountain View Broadcasting*, 578 F. Supp. 229 (E.D. Tenn. 1984). If the court follows *Musser*, the employment records from 2004 would be relevant because Whole In One fired Walker and Radiant in 2004.

The phrase "each working day" must be clarified. "Each working day" should be taken literally and must be a day on which an employer conducts normal, full operations. *Zimmerman*, 704 F.2d at 353; *Wright v. Kosciusko Medical Clinic*, 791 F. Supp. 1327, 1333 (N.D. Ind. 1992).

ILLUSTRATION 24-5. *Continued*

Whole In One operated the golf course and restaurant seven days a week. Therefore, Whole In One must have 15 employees working on all seven days of a week to be considered an employer under Title VII.

The final issue is who should be counted on each of the working days. The Seventh Circuit has determined that a salaried or full-time employee is counted as working for every day of the week that he or she is on the payroll, whether or not he or she was actually at work on a particular day. *Zimmerman,* 704 F.2d at 347. However, part-time workers are counted only on the days that they actually work. *Id.; Wright,* 791 F. Supp. at 1327; *Norman v. Levy,* 767 F. Supp. 144 (N.D. Ill. 1991). In 2004, the year of the alleged discrimination, 14 workers, 3 full-time and 11 part-time people, worked for Whole In One on any day during the 24-week restaurant and golf season. As these part-time workers are only counted on the days that they work, the number of part-time individuals included in the count of employees was 11 for each day of the 24-week season. Because full-time workers, however, are counted for each day of a week that they are on the payroll, all 10 of Whole In One's full-time workers should be included in the count of employees. In total, Whole In One had 11 part-time workers and 10 full-time workers "working" for 20 or more weeks during the relevant year, bringing the total count of employees to 21. Therefore, Whole In One was an employer under Title VII.

II. Are Walker and Radiant Employees or Independent Contractors?

If the plaintiffs can show that Whole In One was an employer, the court still must determine whether Walker and Radiant were employees entitled to Title VII protection or independent contractors. To determine whether an individual is an independent contractor or an employee, the "economic realities" of the relationship between an employer and his or her worker must be weighed. *Knight v. United Farm Bureau Mul. Ins. Co.,* 950 F.2d 377 (7th Cir. 1991); *Norman,* 767 F. Supp. at 144; *Mitchell v. Tenney,* 650 F. Supp. 703 (N.D. Ill. 1986). The Seventh Circuit will weigh five factors to determine the economic reality of the relationship: (1) the amount of control and supervision the employer exerts over the worker, (2) the responsibility for the costs of the operation, (3) the worker's occupation and the skills required, (4) the method and form of compensation and benefits, and (5) the length of the job commitment. *Knight,* 950 F.2d at 378. Control is the most important factor. *Id.* When an employer controls a worker in such a manner as to make that worker economically dependent on the employer, the court is likely to find that an employment relationship exists. *Vakharia v. Swedish Covenant Hosp.,* 765 F. Supp. 461 (N.D. Ill. 1991).

The *Knight* case involved an insurance agent who was not allowed to sell insurance for any other company and who was required to attend weekly staff meetings in the office and work a specified number of

ILLUSTRATION 24-5. *Continued*

hours in the office. *Knight,* 950 F.2d at 378. The insurance company provided Knight with supplies and paid for business expenses. *Id.* These agents were trained by the insurance company and were crucial to the company's continued operation. *Id.* Knight was paid on commission and did not have taxes deducted. *Id.* Knight also was free to leave the company and work elsewhere. *Id.* Based on these facts, the *Knight* court failed to find that the agent was an employee.

Although Walker's work situation was factually similar in many ways to that of the plaintiff in *Knight,* the *Knight* case can be distinguished based on the nature of the occupations. Knight worked in the insurance sales field. Most often, individuals who work in such positions are independent contractors rather than employees of a company. In addition, the Seventh Circuit indicated in the dicta of the *Knight* case that it might have found that Knight was an employee. *Id.* at 381.

In contrast to *Knight,* the U.S. District Court for the Northern District of Illinois found that control of an individual's livelihood could establish an employment relationship. *Vakharia,* 765 F. Supp. at 461. The plaintiff in *Vakharia* was a physician who was dependent on the hospital for business. *Id.* at 463. The district court found that this individual depended on the hospital for patients and that when the hospital reduced the number of patients it assigned to the plaintiff, the plaintiff's livelihood was affected. *Id.* The court held that when an employer has this type of control over an individual's livelihood an employment relationship may be established.

The facts in our case are similar to the facts in the *Vakharia case.* In our case, Whole In One barred Walker from working for other companies and required that she attend weekly staff meetings at the company offices, where Whole In One would review and revise Walker's work. Because Walker was barred from working for other individuals and was required to attend these meetings where Whole In One would revise her work, it seems that Walker could establish the central element of control necessary to prove an employment relationship. In addition, these facts show that Walker, like the plaintiff in *Vakharia,* was economically dependent on her employer, Whole In One. Therefore, an employment relationship should be established.

However, the plaintiffs will be able to show more than control. They will be able to establish that Whole In One bore the cost of the operation of the business. Whole In One supplied Walker with paper, pencils, stamps, and telephone service and paid for her life and health insurance. These facts indicate that Whole In One was responsible for the cost Walker's services to the company. Therefore, it would help to establish that Walker was an employee.

The factors that would mitigate the establishment of an employment relationship, however, are that Walker worked from home

ILLUSTRATION 24-5. *Continued*

and set her own hours and Whole In One did not withhold taxes from Walker's commissions. Despite these factors, the court is likely to focus on the control Whole In One had over Walker and is likely to find that she was an employee rather than an independent contractor.

III. Was Radiant an Employee or an Independent Contractor?

Whether Radiant was an employee again turns on the amount of control Whole In One exerted over Radiant's work. The court will focus on the same factors established in *Knight* to determine whether an employment relationship exists. *Knight*, 950 F.2d at 378. Control will be the key factor the court will consider. *Id.* Radiant had a two-year employment contract with the company to provide marketing services. Whole In One also provided her with an office, supplies, and additional training. The company paid her regularly and deducted taxes from her salary. Based on these facts, the company exerted control over Radiant. Therefore, the court is likely to find that Radiant was an employee of Whole In One.

IN-CLASS EXERCISE

Review the list of authorities in Illustration 24-1. Each authority is followed by a summary statement, usually the holding if it is a case.

Next, review the outline of the discussion in Illustration 24-2.

Review the outline for the memo in Illustration 24-5, see Illustration 24-7: Each of the statements listed in each outline of authorities was derived from a holding found in a case brief prepared for the memos. See Illustration 24-4. A summary statement for the statute also was included in the list.

2. Organize Issues

After you have prepared a detailed list of authorities, you are ready to organize your issues and to determine each of the legal elements that your memo should address. Each legal theory is defined as several factors called elements. You can think of the elements as pieces of a puzzle. You must consider each element before you complete your discussion. You can think of your discussion of these elements as a discussion of the subissues of the questions presented. Your discussion of some of these subissues will be cursory; some elements can be discussed in a single sentence. Most subissues, however, will be discussed in one or more paragraphs, generally organized in the IRAC (Issues, Rules, Application, Conclusion) format discussed in Chapter 22.

▼ What Steps Should You Follow in Preparing Your Outline of Each of the Issues?

The first step in organizing your outline is to write a **thesis paragraph.** This is the first paragraph of your discussion. It usually is a summary of the legal issue you plan to discuss. In the thesis paragraph you introduce the issue, define the applicable rule of law, introduce each legal element, apply the legally significant facts to the rule of law, and provide a short conclusion, usually one sentence long. When you have multiple issues, such as those in the memo shown in Illustration 24-5, the thesis paragraph will introduce all the issues presented and give readers a roadmap of what will be discussed. Then, each issue will begin with a separate thesis paragraph.

3. Draft a Thesis Paragraph

The best and most typical format for the thesis paragraph is the IRAC format. (For a full discussion of this format, see Chapter 22.) The first sentence of a thesis paragraph introduces the overall issue presented in the memo. The second sentence explains the rule of law. The next sentence applies the rule of law to the facts of your case, and the final sentence states a conclusion. A general outline for a thesis paragraph, then, is:

1. Introduce the legal issue or question presented.
2. Summarize the legal rule for the question presented and each legal element to be discussed.
3. Apply the legally significant facts to the legal rule.
4. Conclude.

Review the thesis paragraph in Illustration 24-6, which is the first paragraph of the discussion section of the memo in Illustration 24-3. The first sentence introduces the issue: whether a battery occurred when Mann struck McMillan with the bucket. This sentence mirrors the question presented. See Illustration 24-3. The second sentence is the rule of law. In this sentence you introduce each of the legal elements or factors that will be discussed. In the *McMillan* case, the elements are touching, intent, lack of consent, and resulting physical injury. Each of these elements is discussed separately in the succeeding memo paragraphs. A thesis paragraph should introduce the reader to as many legal elements as possible in the thesis paragraph. The third sentence of this thesis paragraph is the application of the law to the facts. In this sentence, you explain to the reader the relationship between the relevant law and the facts of your case. In Illustration 24-6, the fact the Mann struck McMillan with the bucket without McMillan's consent was applied to the rule of law stated in the second sentence. The final sentence is a conclusion. This sentence explains to your readers your view of how the law and facts relate to each other. In the *McMillan* case, the writer concluded that a battery occurred.

ILLUSTRATION 24-6.   Thesis Paragraph

The issue presented is whether Mann's intentional touching of McMillan with a bucket rather than her person is an actionable battery. A battery is the intentional touching of another without consent which causes injury. *Anderson v. St. Francis-St. George Hosp., Inc.,* 77 Ohio St. 3d 82, 671 N.E.2d 225 (1996). A touching can occur when an object rather than an individual's body contacts the other party. *Leichtman v. WLW Jacoc Communications, Inc.,* 92 Ohio App. 3d 232, 634 N.E.2d 697 (1994); *Smith v. John Deere Co.,* 83 Ohio App. 3d 398, 614 N.E.2d 1148 (1993). In this case, Mann intentionally struck McMillan with a bucket without McMillan's consent and that touching resulted in injuries. Therefore, a battery occurred.

OUTLINE OF THESIS PARAGRAPH FOR McMILLAN CASE

1. Introduce the battery issue or question presented.
2. Summarize the legal rule: battery is the intentional touching of another without consent that results in physical injury; touching can be with an object.
3. Apply the legally significant facts to the legal rule: touching occurred when bucket struck McMillan.
4. Conclusion: battery occurred.

Next, read the sample thesis paragraph below for one of the issues presented in Illustration 24-5.

Before a federal court can consider Walker's and Radiant's claims, the plaintiffs must establish that Whole In One was an employer under the definition established in Title VII. An employer is "a person engaged in an industry affecting commerce who has fifteen or more employees for each working day in each of 20 or more calendar weeks in the current or preceding calendar year." 42 U.S.C. §2000e(b) (2004). The focus of this discussion will be how to calculate whether 15 employees worked for Whole In One on each working day in each of 20 or more calendar weeks and how to determine which year's employment records are relevant. The Seventh Circuit has held that full-time employees are "working" each day of a week during a week for which they are on the payroll, but part-time workers are counted only on the days that they actually work. *Zimmerman v. North American Signal Co.,* 704 F.2d 347 (7th Cir. 1983). In 2004, the year of the alleged discrimination, 14 workers, 3 full-time and 11 part-time people, worked for Whole In One on any day during the 24-week restaurant and golf season. In addition, 10 full-time workers were on the payroll. Based on the counting method established in *Zimmerman,* these figures indicate that Whole In One had at least 15 employees working for each working day in each of 20 or more calendar weeks. Therefore, Whole In One was an employer under Title VII.

An outline for the thesis paragraph above might look like the following example.

THESIS PARAGRAPH

ISSUE
Is Whole In One an employer?

RULE
Under Title VII, an employer has at least 15 employees working for 20 or more weeks during the relevant year. 42 U.S.C. §2000e(b) (2004). (first element) Salaried employees are included in this number for each week they are on the payroll (second element), while hourly workers are only counted on the days they actually work. (third element) *Zimmerman* (primary binding).

APPLICATION OF LAW TO FACTS
In 2004, Whole in One had 14 workers, 3 full-time and 11 part-time people, on any day during the 24-week season. Ten full-time workers were on the payroll. Part-time workers are only counted on the days that they work; they number 11 for each day of the 24-week season. All 10 full-time workers are counted each day of a week. In total, Whole In One had 11 part-time workers and 10 full-time workers "working" for 20 or more weeks during the relevant year, bringing the total count of employees to 21.

CONCLUSION
Therefore, Whole In One was an employer under Title VII.

The outline and thesis paragraph in the above example introduce multiple subissues or legal elements. Each of these elements is discussed fully in the sample memo contained in Illustration 24-5. The thesis paragraph, however, introduces the reader to the elements and provides a preview of the elements that will be discussed.

4. Determine Which Element to Discuss First

The next step is to determine which element to discuss first. If a legal claim has a threshold issue or element, it should be discussed first. A threshold issue is an issue that, if decided one way, would eliminate any further consideration of the legal claim. For example, in a breach of contract case, you must decide first whether a contract was formed before determining whether a breach occurred. Because courts sometimes change current law or approach legal claims differently than expected or than the law provides, you should fully discuss all subissues or elements, even if your threshold issue would dispose of the legal claim. For the memo in Illustration 24-3, the touching is the threshold issue. If Mann did not touch McMillan, then McMillan could not bring an action for battery. Therefore, this issue must be considered first.

5. List Elements or Subissues

Next, make a list of the elements or subissues to discuss. In the *McMillan* case, the elements list might be as follows:

> touching
> intent
> lack of consent
> physical injury

6. Add Authority

Now add the authority or authorities that relate to each element:

> touching (*Leichtman, Smith*)
> intent (*Smith*)
> lack of consent (*Anderson*)
> physical injury (*Anderson*)

7. Refine Issues

You might refine the issues so that they include facts from your case or incorporate further questions that are raised by the issues. For example, the issue of touching involves a secondary question of whether contact with an object rather than a person is a touching sufficient to constitute a battery. Your new list might be as follows:

> touching (*Leichtman, Smith*)
> object rather than person (*Leichtman*)
> intent (*Smith*)
> lack of consent (*Anderson, Love*)
> physical injury (*Anderson*)

8. Arrange the Order of Elements

Now arrange the order of the elements. Touching is the threshold element or subissue, so you should discuss it first. The order of the other issues is a value judgment. If one or more elements can be easily discussed in a single sentence, often it is best to consider them after the threshold issue. If none of the elements is a threshold issue, then consider those elements that can be discussed easily first.

9. Organize into IRAC Paragraph

After you have determined the order of the elements, organize each element or subissue into an IRAC paragraph. Introduce the issue,

present the rule, apply the law to the facts of your case, and conclude. For the *McMillan* memo, the discussion outline for each element might be as shown in Illustration 24-2. Review Illustration 24-2 and compare it to the text of the memo in Illustration 24-3. The discussion is derived entirely from the outline and follows it closely in IRAC format.

C. EXAMPLE OF OUTLINING

You should follow this same process for more complicated issues. The memo shown in Illustration 24-5 discusses several complicated issues and subissues. Review the discussion of the question of whether Whole In One is an employer, section I.

1. After you review the thesis paragraph, make a list of the elements. Your list of elements might be as follows:

Person

Engaged in industry affecting commerce

15 or more employees for each working day in each of 20 or more calendar weeks in current or preceding calendar year

2. Refine this list. Next to the element to which the authority relates, note the relevant authority from your list of authorities. Some authorities will relate to multiple elements. In such a case, note that authority next to each of the elements to which it relates. Now your list might read as follows:

Person (42 U.S.C. §2000e(b))

Engaged in industry affecting commerce (42 U.S.C. §2000e(b))

15 or more employees for each working day in each of 20 or more calendar weeks in current or preceding calendar year (42 U.S.C. §2000e(b)); *Zimmerman v. North American Signal Co.,* 704 F.2d 347 (7th Cir. 1983); *Musser v. Mountain View Broadcasting,* 578 F. Supp. 229 (E.D. Tenn. 1984); *Wright v. Kasciusko Medical Clinic,* 791 F. Supp. 1327, 1333 (N.D. Ind. 1992); *Norman v. Levy,* 767 F. Supp. 144 (N.D. Ill. 1991)

It is better to list the full name of the authority next to the element rather than the number of the authority because the numbers might be confusing later.

3. Your list of elements, however, should be revised again. Often, as in this case, the authorities will guide you as to how to further delineate the elements. Several authorities noted in the above memo focus on the word *employees* and indicate that different types of employees are counted differently for the purpose of the statute. For example, full-time or salaried workers are counted for each day that they are on the

payroll, while part-time workers only are counted on the days that they are actually at work. Add this distinction to your list of elements. Now rewrite your list as follows:

Person (42 U.S.C. §2000e(b))

Engaged in industry affecting commerce (42 U.S.C. §2000e(b)) 15 or more employees

— part-time: *Zimmerman v. North American Signal Co.,* 704 F.2d 347 (7th Cir. 1983); *Wright v. Kosciusko Medical Clinic,* 791 F. Supp. 1327, 1333 (N.D. Ind. 1992); *Norman v. Levy,* 767 F. Supp. 144 (N.D. Ill. 1991)

— full-time: *Zimmerman v. North American Signal Co.,* 704 F.2d 347 (7th Cir. 1983); *Wright v. Kosciusko Medical Clinic,* 791 F. Supp. 1327, 1333 (N.D. Ind. 1992); *Norman v. Levy,* 767 F. Supp. 144 (N.D. Ill. 1991).

Each working day in each of 20 or more calendar weeks current or preceding calendar year (42 U.S.C. §2000e(b)); *Zimmerman v. North American Signal Co.,* 704 F.2d 347 (7th Cir. 1983); *Musser v. Mountain View Broadcasting,* 578 F. Supp. 299 (E.D. Tenn. 1984); *Wright v. Kosciusko Medical Clinic,* 791 F. Supp. 1327, 1333 (N.D. Ind. 1992); *Norman v. Levy,* 767 F. Supp. 144 (N.D. Ill. 1991).

4. Note that one case defines the relevant year while another explains the phrase "each working day." Review the outline of elements below.

Person (42 U.S.C. §2000e(b))

Engaged in industry affecting commerce (42 U.S.C. §2000e(b))

15 or more employees (determining the number of employees)

— part-time: *Zimmerman v. North American Signal Co.,* 704 F.2d 347 (7th Cir. 1983); *Wright v. Kosciusko Medical Clinic,* 791 F. Supp. 1327, 1333 (N.D. Ind. 1992); *Norman v. Levy,* 767 F. Supp. 144 (N.D. Ill. 1991)

— full-time: *Zimmerman v. North American Signal Co.,* 704 F.2d 347 (7th Cir. 1983); *Wright v. Kosciusko Medical Clinic,* 791 F. Supp. 1327, 1333 (N.D. Ind. 1992); *Norman v. Levy,* 767 F. Supp. 144 (N.D. Ill. 1991)

Each working day in each of 20 or more calendar weeks (*Wright v. Kosciusko Medical Clinic,* 791 F. Supp. 1327, 1333 (N.D. Ind. 1992))

Current or preceding calendar year (42 U.S.C. §2000e(b)); *Musser v. Mountain View Broadcasting,* 578 F. Supp. 229 (E.D. Tenn. 1984)

5. Now you are ready to arrange the order of each of the elements. Determine if any of the elements should be discussed first. For the above memo, the threshold issue is how to determine whether Whole In One had 15 or more employees.

6. After you have determined the order of the elements, organize each element or subissue in an IRAC paragraph. For the above discussion, the outline of each element might be arranged as follows:

Element or Subissue 1
> Issue: For which year is the number of employees relevant?
> Rules: The current calendar year or preceding year (42 U.S.C. §2000e (2004)); the "current calendar year" is the year of the discrimination (*Musser*)
> Application of law to facts: Discrimination occurred in 2004
> Conclusion: 2004 is the relevant year

Element or Subissue 2
> Issue: What does the phrase "each working day" mean?
> Rule: "Each working day" is literal: a day of normal operations (*Zimmerman; Wright*)
> Application of law to facts: Whole In One operated the golf course and restaurant seven days a week
> Conclusion: Therefore, Whole In One must have 15 employees working on all seven days of a week to be considered an employer under Title VII

Element or Subissue 3
> Issue: Who should be counted as employees each day?
> Rule: Salaried or full-time employees counted for every day of the week that they are on the payroll (*Zimmerman*); part-time workers counted only on the days that they actually work (*Zimmerman; Wright; Norman*)
> Application of law facts: In 2004, 14 workers, 3 full-time and 11 part-time people, worked for Whole In One on any day during the 24-week season. Eleven part-time workers counted on the days that they work. Ten full-time workers counted for each day of a week. In total, Whole In One had 11 part-time workers and 10 full-time workers "working" for 20 or more weeks during the relevant year, bringing the total count of employees to 21.
> Conclusion: Therefore, Whole In One was an employer under Title VII.

Review this outline and compare it to the text of the memo in Illustration 24-5. The outline closely parallels the discussion concerning Whole In One.

PRACTICE POINTER

If your outline is well drafted, your writing of the discussion will flow from it easily.

D. MULTI-ISSUE MEMORANDUM

If you have a multi-issue memorandum, you will use many of the same techniques discussed above.

▼ How Do You Organize a Multi-Issue Memorandum?

1. Determine how many issues you will discuss. Often an attorney will help you make this determination. Decide which issue should be discussed first. Again, consider whether there is a threshold issue. In the memo above, the first issue is whether Whole In One is an employer. If Whole In One is not an employer, then Title VII will not apply and the later issues do not need to be addressed. Therefore, this issue is the threshold issue and should be placed first. However, you should still discuss the later issues even if you determine that the first issue would be decided in a manner that would dispose of a case. Courts are unpredictable and might decide the issue differently than you did.

2. Determine the legal elements you will discuss and a logical order for this discussion.

3. Prepare a detailed outline of the discussion. For each issue, not each legal element you will address, the authority related to that element, and the legally significant facts applicable to that element.

4. Write a thesis paragraph. For a multi-issue memo, such as on Whole In One, introduce the issues and explain the rules of law in the thesis paragraphs that introduce each issue. Your organization for a multi-issue memo might be as follows:

Thesis Paragraph
    Introduce all legal issues or questions presented
    Conclusions

Thesis Paragraph for Issue or Question Presented #1
    Introduce the legal issue or question presented
    Summarize the legal rule for the question presented #1 and each
       legal element to be discussed
    Apply the legally significant facts to the legal rule
    Conclusion

First Legal Element or Subissue
    Introduce the legal element
    Summarize the legal rule
    Apply the legally significant facts to the legal rule
    Conclusion

Second Legal Element or Subissue
 Introduce the legal element
 Summarize the legal rule
 Apply the legally significant facts to the legal rule
 Conclusion

Thesis Paragraph for Issue or Question Presented #2
 Introduce the legal issue or question presented
 Summarize the legal rule for the question presented #2 and each
  legal element to be discussed
 Apply the legally significant facts to the legal rule
 Conclusion

First Legal Element or Subissue
 Introduce the legal element
 Summarize the legal rule
 Apply the legally significant facts to the legal rule
 Conclusion

Second Legal Element or Subissue
 Introduce the legal element
 Summarize the legal rule
 Apply the legally significant facts to the legal rule
 Conclusion

5. Use headings to introduce new issues. Use transitions to guide the reader from one issue to another and one paragraph to another.

Illustration 24-7 is an outline of the Whole In One memo shown in Illustration 24-5.

Once you complete your outline, you are ready to begin writing your discussion. Follow your outline and use the applicable law and the facts from cases when they are useful. Illustration 24-8 reprints the last paragraph in Illustration 24-5 and the original outline for that paragraph. Once you have completed your draft, compare the draft to the outline to ensure that you have incorporated all the components in your outline and that your text matches your outline organization.

IN-CLASS EXERCISE

Review the following memo. Prepare an outline of authorities and an outline based on this memo. (This is the reverse of the process you would normally use.) Then discuss your outline. Make a list of legally significant facts and note the legal standard.

ILLUSTRATION 24-7.   Multi-Issue Outline

Thesis Paragraph
>   Introduce issues
>>   Whether Whole In One is an employer under Title VII
>>   Whether Walker is an employee under Title VII
>>   Whether Radiant is an employee under Title VII

Heading: Issue 1 or Question Presented 1
>   Introduce issue: Was Whole In One an employer under Title VII?
>   Rules: (**A**) Under Title VII, an employer has at least 15 employees working for 20 or more weeks during the relevant year. (42 U.S.C. §2000e(b) (2004)) (**first element or subissue**)
>   (**B**) Salaried employees are included in this number for each week they are on the payroll. (**second element or subissue**)
>   (**C**) Hourly workers are only counted on the days they actually work. (**third element or subissue**) (*Zimmerman*) (primary binding)
>   Application of law to facts: In 2004, Whole In One had 14 workers, 3 full-time and 11 part-time people, on any day during the 24-week season. Ten full-time workers were on the payroll. Part-time workers are only counted on the days that they work; their numbers is 11 for each day of the 24-week season. All 10 full-time workers are counted each day of a week. In total, Whole In One had 11 part-time workers and 10 full-time workers "working" for 20 or more weeks during the relevant year, bringing the total count of employees to 21.
>   Conclusion: Therefore, Whole In One was an employer under Title VII.

First Legal Element or Subissues:
>   Introduce subissue: Which is the appropriate year for counting workers?
>   Rules:
>   (A) Under Title VII, an employer has at least 15 employees working for 20 or more weeks during the current calendar year or preceding year. (42 U.S.C. §2000e(b) (2004))
>   (B) The "current calendar year" is the year of the discrimination. (*Musser*)
>   Application of law to facts: Discrimination occurred in 2004.
>   Conclusion: 2004 is the relevant year.

Second Legal Element or Subissue
>   Introduce subissue: Is "each working day" literally interpreted?
>   Rule: "Each working day" is literal: a day normal operations. (*Zimmerman; Wright*)
>   Application of law to facts: Whole In One operated the golf course and restaurant seven days a week.
>   Conclusion: Therefore, Whole In One must have 15 employees working on all seven days of the week to be considered an employer under Title VII.

ILLUSTRATION 24-7. *Continued*

Third Legal Element or Subissue

  Introduce subissue: Who should be counted?

  Rules:

  (A) Salaried or full-time employee counted for every day of the week that he or she is on the payroll (*Zimmerman*)

  (B) Part-time workers counted only on the days that they actually work (*Zimmerman; Wright; Norman*)

  Application of law to facts: In 2004, 14 workers, 3 full-time and 11 part-time people, worked for Whole In One on any day during the 24-week season. Eleven part-time workers counted on the days that they work. Ten full-time workers counted for each day of a week. In total, Whole In One had 11 part-time workers and 10 full-time workers "working" for 20 or more weeks during the relevant year, bringing the total count of employees to 21.

  Conclusion: Therefore, Whole In One was an employer under Title VII.

Thesis Paragraph to Introduce Issues 2 and 3

  Issues 2 and 3

    Introduce issues and elements: Are Walker and Radiant employees or independent contractors?

    Rules:

    (**A**) "Economic realities" of the relationship between an employer and his or her worker must be weighed (*Knight; Norman; Mitchell*) Five factors to determine the economic reality of the relationship: (1) the amount of control and supervision the employer exerts over the worker, (2) the responsibility for the costs of the operation, (3) the worker's occupation and the skills required, (4) the method and form of compensation and benefits, and (5) the length of the job commitment. (*Knight*) (first element)

    (**B**) When an employee is economically dependent on the employer, an employment relationship exists. (*Vakharia*) (second element)

    Application of law to facts: Walker worked from home, set her own hours, received pay on commission. Company controlled her work by reviewing and revising it, restricting Walker's employment opportunities, and providing supplies for her.

    Conclusion: Therefore, the company exerted control over Walker, and she would be considered an employee.

    Application of law to facts: Whole In One provided Radiant with an office, supplies, a two-year contract, and additional training, paid her regularly, and deducted taxes from her salary. She worked in company offices under the control of Whole In One.

    Conclusion: Therefore, the court probably will find that Radiant was an employee.

ILLUSTRATION 24-7. *Continued*

Reintroduction of Issue 2: Was Walker an employee or an independent contractor?

    First Legal Element or Subissue

        Introduce subissue: What factors will the court weigh to determine economic realities?

        Rule: "Economic realities" of the relationship between an employer and his or her worker must be weighed. (*Knight; Norman; Mitchell*) Five factors to determine the economic reality of the relationship: (1) the amount of control and supervision the employer exerts over the worker, (2) the responsibility for the costs of the operation, (3) the worker's occupation and the skills required, (4) the method and form of compensation and benefits, and (5) the length of the job commitment. (*Knight.* Facts: Knight worked in the insurance sales field, traditionally an independent contractor setting.)

        Application of law to facts: Walker worked from home, set her own hours. Received her pay on commission. Company controlled her work by reviewing and revising it.

        Conclusion: Walker was an employee.

    Second Legal Element or Subissue

        Introduce subissue: Was Walker economically dependent on Whole in One?

        Rule: When an employee is economically dependent on the employer, an employment relationship exists. (*Vakharia*). Facts: A physician dependent on the hospital for business establishing employment relationship.)

        Application of law to facts: Similar facts for Walker. Whole In One barred Walker from working for other companies.

        Conclusion: Because Walker was barred from working for other companies, employment relationship existed.

        Reintroduction of Issue 3: Was Radiant an employee or an independent contractor?

        Rule: Five factors weighed, primarily control of her by the company. (*Knight*) See also the Rules discussed below the thesis paragraph introducing Issues 2 and 3. There is no need to discus the Rule in as much detail in Issue 3 as in Issue 2.

        Application of law to facts: Whole In One provided Radiant with an office, supplies, a two-year contract, and additional training, paid her regularly, and deducted taxes from her salary. She worked in company offices under the control of Whole In One.

        Conclusion: Therefore, the court probably will find that Radiant was an employee.

ILLUSTRATION 24-8. Writing from an Outline

Outline

Issue 3: Was Radiant an employee or an independent contractor?

Rule: Five factors weighed, primarily control of her by the company. (*Knight*) See also the Rules below the thesis paragraph introducing Issues 2 and 3. There is no need to discuss the Rule in as much detail in Issue 3 as in Issue 2.

Application of law to facts: Whole In One provided Radiant with an office, supplies, a two-year contract, and additional training, paid her regularly, and deducted taxes from her salary. She worked in company offices under the control of Whole In One.

Conclusion: Therefore, the court probably will find that Radiant was an employee.

Paragraph Drafted from Outline

III. Was Radiant an Employee or an Independent Contractor?

Whether Radiant was an employee again turns on the amount of control Whole In One exerted over Radiant's work. The court will focus on the same factors established in *Knight* to determine whether an employment relationship exists. *Knight*, 950 F.2d at 378. Control will be the key factor the court will consider. *Id*. Radiant had a two-year employment contract with the company to provide marketing services. Whole In One also provided her with an office, supplies, and additional training. The company paid her regularly and deducted taxes from her salary. Based upon these facts, the company exerted control over Radiant. Therefore, the court is likely to find that Radiant was an employee of Whole In One.

MEMORANDUM

To: Margaret Sterner
From: Marie Main
Date: January 28, 2008
Re: *Harris v. Sack and Shop*

QUESTION PRESENTED

Is Sack and Shop, a grocery store, liable for injuries sustained by Harris, a store patron who slipped on a banana peel that had been on the grocery store floor for two days?

BRIEF ANSWER

Probably yes. Sack and Shop, a grocery store, probably will be liable based on negligence for injuries sustained by Harris, a store patron who

slipped on a banana peel that had been on the grocery store floor for two days.

FACTS

Our client, Sack and Shop Grocery Store, is being sued for negligence by Rebecca Harris.

Harris went to the store to purchase groceries on July 8, 2004. While she was in the produce section, she slipped on a banana peel that a grocery store employee had left on the floor. The employee had dropped it on the floor two days earlier and had failed to clean it up after a patron asked him to do so.

Harris sustained a broken arm and head injures as a result of the slip and fall.

DISCUSSION

The issue presented in this case is whether Sack and Shop Grocery Store was negligent when Rebecca Harris slipped in the store's produce section. A grocer will be found negligent if a store employee breached the store's duty of reasonable care to its patrons and, as a result of that breach, the patron was injured. *Ward v. K Mart Corp.,* 554 N.E.2d 223 (Ill. 1990). In *Ward,* the grocery store employee failed to clean up a banana peel for two days and that peel caused a patron to be injured. Similarly, in our case Sack and Shop failed to remove the banana peel. Therefore, Sack and Shop is likely to be found liable for the injuries Harries sustained.

The first element to consider is whether Sack and Shop owed a duty of reasonable care to Harris. A grocery store owes a duty of care of any patron. *Ward,* 554 N.E.2d at 226. Harris was a customer in the store. Therefore, Sack and Shop owed her a duty of care.

The next question to consider is whether Sack and Shop breached its duty of reasonable care to Harris. A store will be found to have breached its duty of reasonable care to a patron if a store employee fails to properly and regularly clean the floor of the store. *Olinger v. Great Atl. & Pac. Tea Co.,* 173 N.E.2d 443 (Ill. 1961). In *Olinger,* the store was found liable because a store employee failed to clean the floor for one day and a patron slipped on a substance on the floor. 173 N.E.2d at 447. No one had told any store employee about the slippery substance. *Id.* at 447. Nonetheless, the Illinois Supreme Court found the store liable, saying that the store employee had sufficient time to notice the substance if they had used ordinary care. *Id.* In our case, Sack and Shop's employee had two days to clean the floor before Harris fell. In addition, a customer had placed the store employee on notice of the banana peel. Therefore, Sack and Shop beached its duty of care to Harris.

The plaintiff, however, still must establish proximate cause, that is, that the injury resulted as a natural consequence of Sack and Shop's breach of its duty. A store owner's failure to clear debris from a store floor, resulting in injury to a patron who slipped on the floor, was found

to be the proximate cause of the patron's injuries. *Id.* at 449. In this case, Sack and Shop's failure to clean the peel from the floor was a breach of its duty of care to Harris. This breach resulted in injury to Harris. Sack and Shop's breach will be found to be the proximate cause of Harris's injuries.

The final element that must be established is that the plaintiff, Harris, suffered injuries. Harris sustained a broken arm and head injuries as a result of the slip and fall. Therefore, she will be able to show that she was injured.

CONCLUSION

Sack and Shop owed Harris a duty of reasonable care. The store is likely to be found to have breached that duty of reasonable care because an employee failed to remove a banana peel from the grocery store floor during the preceding two days. The injuries Harris sustained were directly caused by a slip on a banana peel. Therefore, Sack and Shop is likely to be found liable to Harris.

CHAPTER SUMMARY

Outlining is an important component of legal writing. It helps you organize the discussion section of your legal memorandum. To outline a legal memorandum, first draft a list of legal authorities. Second, arrange the discussion sections concerning each issue and, if necessary, arrange each paragraph of the memorandum.

The list of legal authorities should include the names and citations to the authorities, a note about the legally significant facts contained in the authority, if any, and a statement that summarizes the significance of the authority.

The legal issues of the discussion should be organized in the IRAC format discussed in Chapter 22. Each element of a legal issued should be addressed in this format.

Before you can begin writing your memorandum, you must organize your thesis paragraph. The thesis paragraph is the first paragraph of your discussion. It summarizes the legal issues you will discuss in the memorandum. This paragraph also should be organized in IRAC format, if possible.

You have been shown how to draft questions presented, issues, conclusions, brief answers, facts statements, and discussion sections. In addition, you have been taught how to synthesize authorities and how to use a legal writing convention called IRAC.

KEY TERMS

elements
list of legal authorities
outlining

thesis paragraph
threshold issue

EXERCISES

SHORT ANSWER

1. How do you organize a thesis paragraph?
2. How do you compile a list of legal authorities?
3. How do you determine which element to discuss first?
4. What format should each paragraph take?
5. Write the discussion section only for the memo below.

MEMORANDUM

To: Ruth Abbey
From: Gail Michael
Date: January 20, 2008
Re: *Kahn v. Randall,* Civ. 95 No. 988, File No. 8988977

QUESTION PRESENTED

Does Janice Kahn have a valid claim for intentional infliction of emotional distress against Ronnie Randall after Kahn saw Randall turn his car to strike Kahn's 11-year-old child in front of her, causing her to suffer from anxiety, headaches, and vomiting?

CONCLUSION

Janice Kahn probably has a valid claim for intentional infliction of emotional distress against Ronnie Randall. Kahn saw Randall turn his car to strike her 11-year-old child. Seeing this accident caused Kahn to suffer from anxiety, headaches, and vomiting daily. This act could be considered extreme and outrageous conduct if it was done with intent. Several witness can testify that Randall said that he intended to harm Kahn and Kahn states that Randall turned the car to strike her son. Two factors, however, might show that Randall lacked intent: the statement that he made to the police that he did not intend to hit the child and the fact that his blood alcohol level was .11, possibly preventing him from formulating the needed intent.

FACTS

While driving a car Ronnie Randall struck Janice Kahn's son at 5 P.M. on August 29, 2007. It was bright and clear. No skid marks appeared on the dry street following the accident.

Janice Kahn was working in her garden about five feet from the accident scene at the time of the accident. Her son was playing a game in the street before Randall's car struck him. Kahn did not see the car strike her 11-year-old son. When she first looked up from her garden, she thought her son was dead. He was covered with blood and had several broken bones. However, Kahn's son was conscious after the accident.

Immediately after the accident, Randall, who had a blood alcohol level of .11, was cited for drunk driving and driving with a suspended

driver's license. Police charged him with drunk driving and suspended his license two weeks earlier after the car he was driving struck another child at the same spot. Randall has a drinking history.

Following the accident, several witnesses said Randall was upset and wobbled as he walked. One witness said that Randall intentionally turned the steering wheel to hit Kahn's son. Kahn stated that Randall often swerved down her street to get her attention.

Rhonda Albert, Kahn's neighbor, said she heard Randall say he would get even with Kahn after Kahn broke off a ten-year relationship with him.

During Kahn and Randall's ten-year relationship, Randall was close to Kahn's son. He took him to ball games, including one in April, and attended the son's baseball games. Randall knew that Kahn's son was the most important person in her life.

Since the accident, Kahn vomits daily and suffers from anxiety and headaches. Dr. Susan Faigen, Kahn's internist, states that the anxiety, headaches, and vomiting are the result of the accident. The prevailing case is *George v. Jordan Marsh Co.*, 359 Mass. 244, 268 N.E.2d 915 (1971). In that case, the court held that one who without a privilege to do so by extreme and outrageous conduct intentionally causes severe emotional distress to another, with bodily harm resulting from such distress, is subject to liability for such emotional distress and bodily harm.

6. Write a thesis paragraph for this discussion section.

FACTS

Drake Industries has been leasing warehouse space at 2700 North Bosworth Avenue, in Chicago, Illinois, from the owner of the building, Michael Martin. Drake began leasing space from Martin beginning January 1, 2007 at $700 per month until the lease expired on December 31, 2007.

Martin offered a new lease to Drake on November 25, 2007, to be signed and returned by December 31, 2007. The new lease began January 1, 2008, and expired on June 30, 2008, and the rent increased to $850 per month, payable on the first of each month. Drake never signed or returned the new lease, but did pay the increased rent amount during the term of the unsigned lease ending June 30, 2008. Since then, Drake has continued paying $850 on the first day of each month. On August 15, 2008, Martin requested that Drake surrender the premises. Drake came to your firm to find out what type of tenancy he has and whether Martin gave Drake the proper notice to quit the premises.

DISCUSSION

Is Drake Industries a holdover tenant? A holdover tenancy is created when a landlord elects to treat a tenant, after the expiration of his or her lease, as a tenant for another term upon the same provisions contained in the original lease. *Bismarck Hotel Co. v. Sutherland*, 92 Ill.,

App. 3d 167, 415 N.E.2d 517 (1980). In *Bismarck,* defendant Sutherland's written lease expired. Bismarck presented her with a new lease that included a rent increase. She began to pay the increase but did not sign the new lease. Sutherland could not be a holdover tenant since the terms of the old lease were not extended to the terms of the new, unsigned lease. Drake Industries was offered a new lease in 2007 that included a rent increase. Since the terms were different from the original lease. Drake could not be considered a holdover tenant.

It is the intention of the landlord, not the tenant, that determines whether the tenant is to be treated as a holdover. *Sheraton-Chicago Corp. v. Lewis,* 8 Ill. App. 3d 309, 290 N.E.2d 685 (1972). When a landlord creates a new lease and presents it to the tenant, it is clear that it was his intention that a new tenancy was created. *Holt v. Chicago Hair Goods Co.,* 328 Ill. App. 671, 66 N.E.2d 727 (1946). Martin presented Drake with a new lease to sign in November 2007, with new terms beginning January 1, 2008. It was never his intention to hold over the same lease from 2007. Therefore, Drake was not a holdover tenant and has never been one. 735 Ill. Comp. Stat. 5/9-202 (West 1993) could not apply to Drake. Martin could not demand double rental fees from Drake when it remained in possession of 2700 North Bosworth after the written lease expired on December 31, 2007.

Is Drake Industries a year-to-year tenant? When the payment of rent is annual, there arises a tenancy from year to year, even if the agreement provides for a payment of one-twelfth of the annual rental each month. *Seaver Amusement Co. v. Saxe et al.,* 210 Ill. App. 289 (1918). The terms of the 2007 written lease would have to have said "$8,400 a year rent, payable in monthly installments of $750" for it to have been considered a year-to-year lease. Since the terms of the 2007 lease only provided for monthly payments and not a yearly rental rate, Drake was not a year-to-year tenant. 735 Ill. Comp. Stat. 5/9-205 (West 1993) does not apply at all to Drake. Martin would not be required to tender 60 days' notice in writing to terminate the tenancy.

Is Drake Industries a month-to-month tenant? A month-to-month tenancy is created when a tenant remains in possession of the premises after a lease expires under different terms of tenancy. *Bismarck Hotel,* 92 Ill. App. 3d at 168, 415 N.E.2d at 517. By paying Bismarck's increased rental amount, different terms of the tenancy were established, so Sutherland's tenancy was considered month to month by the court. Drake remained at 2700 North Bosworth after its lease expired in 2007 but began paying the increased rent to Martin under the new terms of the unsigned lease. This established different terms of tenancy, so Drake has been a month-to-month tenant since 2008.

What type of notice is necessary to vacate the premises? Under 735 Ill. Comp. Stat 5/9/-207 (West 2008), notice to terminate a month-to-month tenancy must be given in writing 30 days before termination before any action for forcible entry and detainer can be maintained. Drake said that on August 15, 2008, Martin "requested" that Drake surrender the premises. An oral request may not be sufficient and

Drake may maintain that proper notice has not been made and it need not surrender the premises by September 15, 2008. A forcible entry and detainer action could not be entered and maintained and Drake need not surrender the premises until proper notice has been given.

7. Review the discussion section above and draft a list of authorities. Then draft an outline of the discussion section.
8. Review the discussion section below and draft a list of authorities. Then draft an outline of the discussion section.

Are the Blacks entitled to special damages from Comfy Furniture for the cost of redecorating their living room? An Illinois appellate court decided that the nonbreaching party should be put back in the position that it was in when the contract was formed. *Kalal v. Goldblatt Bros.*, 368 N.E.2d 671, 673 (Ill. Ct. App. 1977). The Blacks stated their intention at the beginning concerning the fabric, the redecoration of the living room, and the family reunion. This fact was a part of their original position. The living room was redecorated. The furniture was delivered; however, the fabric was incorrect. Therefore, the Blacks have a right to recover consequential damages for the cost of the redecoration of their living room because the end result was not achieved; correctly upholstered furniture, newly redecorated living room to match, and a new living room look for the reunion. The conditions of the original contract were not met, and there was a breach of contract as embodied by the incorrectly upholstered furniture.

Under contract law, what damages are the Blacks entitled to pursue? Damages for breach of contract should place the plaintiff in a position he would have been in had the contract been performed. *Kalal,* 368 N.E.2d at 671. The plaintiffs in *Kalal* received a sofa that had been reupholstered in the wrong fabric after numerous delays, during which they had chosen three different fabrics in succession. *Id.* The court held that the defect could be remedied by the cost of reupholstering the sofa in the proper fabric. *Id.* at 674. The Blacks' chair and loveseat were improperly upholstered. Comfy Furniture upholstered their furniture with the reverse side of the fabric showing. Therefore, they were entitled to damages equal to the cost of upholstering their furniture correctly. However, the Blacks' situation is distinguished from *Kalal* in that their furniture was delivered before the date set in the contract, and it can be argued by Comfy that there was time to remedy the defect before their target date of Thanksgiving.

Are the Blacks entitled to compensation for the loss of use of their furniture? The question of compensation for the loss of use of the furniture was considered by both parties in *Kalal* to be appropriate since the plaintiffs in the case were without their furniture for several months while waiting for it to be reupholstered. *Id.* The Blacks have been similarly inconvenienced in that they, too, have been without the use of their new furniture. Thus, they are entitled to compensation for the loss of use of the furniture. However, it can be argued by Comfy Furniture that the furniture in the *Kalal* case was used and had been removed from the home for the purpose of reupholstering it. *Id.* In the present case, the furniture was new and had never been in the Blacks' home, and Comfy may argue that the Blacks did not actually suffer loss of use of the new furniture.

Are the Blacks entitled to damages for the expense of decorating their living room to match the furniture they did not receive in the agreed-on condition? The redecorating of the living room in *Kalal* was not in the contemplation of either party at the time the contract was executed. *Kalal,* 368 N.E.2d at 671. Subsequently, the court held that the only damages that were recoverable for breach of contract are limited to those that were reasonably foreseeable and were within the contemplation of the parties at the time the contract was executed. *Id.* at 674. By the express terms of the Uniform Commercial Code, the court cannot follow tort theories to award damages. The legislative history of the U.C.C. indicates that contractual disputes should apply to the findings of the court. *Moorman Mfg. Co. v. National Tank Co.,* 435 N.E.2d 443, 453 (Ill. 1982). The Blacks only told Mr. Blaine that they needed the furniture to be completed in time for a family reunion. Comfy knew that the Blacks were under a time constraint for the delivery, but apparently there was no communication regarding the redecorating of the living room. With regard to Comfy Furniture, the redecorating of the Blacks' living room was an unforeseeable event and consequently they would not be held responsible for the expense. Because the fact that the redecorating of the living room was unforeseeable, it was not included within the terms of the contract. Therefore, Comfy only breached the express terms of the contract. The Blacks probably will not be awarded compensatory damages.

LETTER WRITING

CHAPTER OVERVIEW

This chapter explains letter writing basics, such as format and types of letters. It provides example of a variety of letters you might use in practice.

Letter writing is one of the basic tasks you will perform as paralegals. Most letter writing conventions apply to legal correspondence in much the same way as they do to other business communications. Paralegals should be aware of the components of basic letters as well as some special rules for legal communications.

A. BASICS OF LETTER WRITING

Letter writing is done in much the same way as any other legal writing. You plan it, draft it, and revise it. In planning your communication, you must determine your audience and outline what you plan to say to your reader. When revising the letter, use proper grammar and consider any revisions that would make the letter clearer. Proofread your letter.

▼ What Formats Are Used?

Letters may be drafted using a variety of formats. Firm style or personal taste generally determines the format of your letters. The formats are **full block, block, modified block,** and **personal style.**

In a full block letter, you do not indent the paragraphs. The paragraphs, the complimentary close, and the dateline are flush left. See Illustration 25-1. For block format, all paragraphs and notations are flush left, except for the date, the reference line, the complimentary close, and the signature lines, which are just right of the center of the page. See Illustration 25-3. In a modified block style letter, the first line of each paragraph is indented about five characters. See Illustration 25-6. In a personal style letter, often written to friends, the inside address is placed below the signature at the left margin.

B. COMPONENTS OF A LETTER

1. Letterhead and Headers

A letter is divided into several sections: the date, the name and the address of the addressee called the inside address, a reference line, a greeting to the addressee, the body of the letter, and the complimentary closing.

You should draft the first page of a letter on firm letterhead. The **letterhead** is the portion of the firm's stationery that identifies the firm, generally the attorneys, and sometimes the firm's paralegals. It usually includes the firm's address and its telephone and facsimile numbers. Additional pages should not carry the firm letterhead but should be placed on matching paper with a **header** on each page. The header identifies the letter and is generally placed on the top right side of the

page. A header includes the name of the addressee, the date, and the number of the page:

Cheryl Victor
November 15, 2008
Page Two

ILLUSTRATION 25-1.   Full Block Letter

---

[1]Fuzzwell, Cubbon and Landefelt
888 Toledo Road
Ottawa Hills, Ohio 43606
(419) 535-7738

[2]November 7, 2008

[3]Via Federal Express
Mr. Stuart Shulman
Navarre Industries
708 Anthony Wayne Trail
Maumee, Ohio 45860

[4]Re: Settlement of Kramer v. Shulman

[5]Dear Mr. Shulman:

[6]I have enclosed a copy of the settlement agreement that we drafted and that has been signed by Mr. Kramer. Please sign the agreement and forward it to me at the above address by November 30, 2008.

If you have any questions, please feel free to call me at 535-7738.

[7]Sincerely,

Mara Cubbon
Legal Assistant

[8]cc: Randall Fuzzwell
[9]Enc.
[10]MAC/wlk

1. Letterhead
2. Date
3. Recipient's address and method of service
4. Reference line
5. Greeting
6. Body of the letter
7. Closing
8. Carbon copy notation
9. Enclosure of notation
10. Initials of drafter/typist

ETHICS ALERT

Check your state law as to whether your name may appear on the letterhead.

2. Date

The date should be placed at the top of the letter just below the firm's letterhead. The date is one of the key components of a letter concerning any legal matters. Date the letter with the same date as the date of mailing. This date can be crucial in determining a time line in a legal proceeding. Timing in sending documents and correspondence is often important in legal transactions and litigation matters. Therefore, be careful to include the date of mailing rather than the date of writing the letter. For example, if you prepare a letter on July 4 after the last mail pickup, you should date the letter July 5 because that is the date it would actually be mailed. This may seem like a purely technical distinction if you put the letter in the mail on July 4. However, some court cases and negotiations turn on the date of mailing.

3. Method of Transmission

If the letter is being sent by a method other than U.S. mail, it should be indicated on the top of the address and then underlined as follows:

> <u>Via Facsimile and U.S. Mail</u>
> Cheryl Victor
> Vice President
> Arizona Money Makers
> 1000 Tempe Road
> Phoenix, Arizona 85038

This notation should start at least two lines below the date. See Illustration 25-1.

4. Inside Address

The next part of the letter, the inside address, should contain the name of the person to whom the letter is addressed, the individual's title if he or she has one, the name of the business if the letter is for a business, and the address.

5. Reference Line

The reference line is a brief statement regarding the topic of the letter. For example, if the letter concerns a contract for the sale of a particular property, your reference line would say:

Re: Sale of 2714 Barrington Road, Toledo, Ohio

Some firms and corporations ask that the reference line contain a client number, claim number, or case number, so investigate your firm's style.

PRACTICE POINTER

If possible, review letters in a file written by the assigning attorney. Note the attorney's style for the reference line and follow it.

---

6. Greeting

In general, your greeting depends on how familiar you are with an individual. An individual whom you do not know should be addressed as "Dear Ms. White." If you know an individual well, you may address, formally, such that person by first name. If you are uncertain whether to address the individual by first name, use a title and the individual's last name. If you are addressing a letter to a particular person, such as the custodian of records, but you do not know the person's name, try to determine the person's name. If necessary, call a company or agency to determine the appropriate recipient for the letter. Your letter is more likely to be answered quickly if it is addressed to the appropriate person rather than "To whom it may concern." In addition, it may provide you with an opportunity to establish a rapport with the individual to whom the letter is addressed.

7. Body of Letter

The body of the letter follows the greeting and should begin with an opening sentence and paragraph that summarizes the purpose of the letter. Draft the body of the letter carefully. Outline the letter before writing it to be sure that you address all the necessary points. List each point you want to cover. For Illustration 25-1, your outline might read as follows:

1. enclose settlement agreement
2. ask for signature and return date
3. ask addressee to call if he has questions

Consider your audience. If you are writing to a layperson who is unfamiliar with the law, explain any legal terms you use often using

definitions provided in a dictionary, or use simple language. However, do not provide any legal opinions. If you are addressing your letter to an individual who is familiar with the law, such as a judge, a paralegal, an in-house counsel, or an attorney, you do not need to explain such terms. To do so might be considered condescending.

ETHICS ALERT

Do not offer any legal advice or opinions in the letter.

---

8. Closing

End your letter with a closing in which you invite a response, such as "Please do not hesitate to call if you have any questions," or thank the addressee for assistance, such as "Thank you in advance for your cooperation." Finally, end the letter with a complimentary closing such as "Sincerely," "Very truly yours," or "Best regards" placed two lines below the final line of the body of the letter. Place your name four lines below the closing to allow for a signature. Include your title, that is, paralegal or legal assistant.

ETHICS ALERT

Be sure that your reader knows that you are a paralegal rather than an attorney. The easiest way to do this is to add your title after your name in the closing.

Do not provide legal advice in your letter or represent yourself as an attorney. Ethical codes and state laws prohibit paralegals who are not licensed to practice law from providing legal opinions or from representing themselves as attorneys. To avoid any confusion or possible misrepresentation, include your title after your name when you write a letter.

9. Copies to Others and Enclosures

If you are copying a third party on the letter and want the original addressee to know this, note it with a "cc" at the bottom left margin of the letter following the closing. The cc indicates carbon copy sent to the person listed. (Although photocopies have replaced carbon copies, cc is still used.) Indicate to whom a copy of the letter was sent as "cc: Mike Sterner." See Illustration 25-2. If you do not want the original addressee to know that you copied a letter to another person, note on

the draft or file copy "bcc," which means blind carbon copy. That notation should only appear on the draft or file copy of the letter and not on the recipient's letter.

ILLUSTRATION 25-2.   Letter Confirming Deposition

Law Offices of Sam Harris
2714 Barrington Road
Findlay, Ohio 45840
(419) 267-0000

January 28, 2009

Ms. Karen Dolgin
2903 W. Main Cross Street
Findlay, Ohio 45840

Re: Deposition of Robert Harrold
     Harrold v. Sofer

Dear Ms. Dolgin:

This letter is to confirm our conversation today in which you stated that you will present the plaintiff, Robert Harrold, for a deposition at the law office of Sam Harris, 2714 Barrington Road, in Findlay, on March 18, 2009, at 2 p.m. This deposition is being rescheduled at your request because the plaintiff had a family commitment set for February 15, 2009, the date originally set for the deposition.

If you have any questions or additional problems, please feel free to call me at (419) 267-0000, extension 608.

Best regards,

Craig Black
Paralegal

cc: Sam Harris
     Wally Sofer
CMB/klm

The next notation is for **enclosures,** such as court orders, contracts, or releases. Place the abbreviation **Enc.** or **Encs.** at the bottom left margin of the letter. See Illustration 25-1.

Finally, the letter should note your initials in all capital letters as the author of the letter and then the initials in lowercase letters of the person who typed the letter. If your initials are RAS and the typist's are HVS, then the notation under the enclosure or cc notation would read RAS/hvs.

C. TYPES OF LETTERS

Paralegals write letters to clients to confirm deposition dates, meeting dates, hearing dates, or agreements. These letters are called confirming letters. Other letters provide a status report of a case or summarize a transaction. Some letters accompany documents, such as those for document productions, contracts, or settlement releases. These are called transmittal letters. Still others are requests for information. Some letters explain the litigation process to clients. See Illustration 25-3.

1. Confirming Letters

Confirming letters reaffirm information already agreed to by you and the recipient. It is a good practice to follow up any conversation with a client or an opposing attorney or paralegal with a confirming letter that summarizes the conversation, any agreements made, or any future acts to be accomplished. See Illustration 25-2. For example, after you discuss a document production with a client and set a meeting date to review the records, send a letter summarizing the conversation. Such confirming letters provide you with a reminder of the conversation and allow anyone who reviews the file later to know what you and the client discussed should you be unavailable.

If opposing counsel has agreed to produce documents or provide a witness for a deposition at a particular time, write a confirming letter to the opposing counsel summarizing these facts and asking to be contacted if there are discrepancies. Whenever a deposition is rescheduled or continued, it is imperative that a confirming letter be sent to avoid future discovery disputes. Whenever your client is deposed, send him or her a copy of the deposition for review. A sample of such a letter is found in Illustration 25-4.

2. Status Letters and Transaction Summary Letters

Often you will be asked to provide a status report of a case, especially to insurance companies and other clients. See Illustration 25-5. These letters provide clients with an overview of the current activities in a court case, transaction, or other legal matter.

Transaction summary letters often follow a business transaction such as a real estate closing. In these letters, you summarize a transaction.

ILLUSTRATION 25-3.   Letter Concerning Deposition Schedule

Law Offices of Sam Harris
2714 Barrington Road
Findlay, Ohio 45840
(419) 267-0000

January 28, 2009

Wally Sofer
Chief Executive Officer
1000 Hollywood Way
Houcktown, Ohio 44060

Re: Deposition of Wally Sofer
Harrold v. Sofer

Dear Mr. Sofer:

This letter is to advise you that you are required to submit to a deposition by the plaintiff's attorney at 10 a.m. on March 1, 2009, at the law office of Karen Dolgin, 2903 W. Main Cross Street in downtown Findlay. During this deposition, the plaintiff's attorney will ask you questions related to the above-referenced court case, and you will provide answers while under oath and in the presence of a court reporter. Mr. Harris also will be present to represent you during the deposition.

Mr. Harris and I would like to meet with you at least once before the deposition to discuss your case and this important part of your case.

I will call you Wednesday to schedule an appointment next week to prepare for your deposition.

Please bring any accident reports, citations, or other documents that relate to the accident if you have not already provided them to our office.

I look forward to speaking with you this week.

Sincerely,

Craig Black
Paralegal

cc: Sam Harris
CMB/klm

ILLUSTRATION 25-4. Letter Enclosing Deposition Transcript

Law Offices of Sam Harris
2714 Barrington Road
Findlay, Ohio 45840
(419) 267-0000

July 11, 2008

Mr. William Gary
709 Franklin Street
Findlay, Ohio 45840

Re: Deposition on July 8, 2008

Dear Mr. Gary:

Enclosed is a copy of the transcript of your July 8, 2008, deposition. Please review the transcript carefully and note any statements that were incorrectly transcribed. You may not rewrite your testimony, but you should note any inaccurate transcriptions. You may correct the spelling of names and places. If you find any serious mistakes, please call me to discuss these problems.

When you review the deposition, please do not mark the original transcript. Instead, note any discrepancies on a separate sheet of paper. Please note the page and line of any discrepancies. I will have my secretary type a list of the discrepancies, and we will discuss these changes before we send them to the court reporter. These changes must be received by the court reporter within 30 days; therefore, I would appreciate your prompt review of the transcript and would like to review your changes by July 30, 2008. If we fail to provide the changes to the court reporter within 30 days, we will forfeit your right to correct the transcript and any inaccuracies will be part of the record.

If you have any questions, please do not hesitate to call me.

Thank you for your cooperation in advance.

Best regards,

Benjamin Harris
Paralegal

Enc.
BSH/jas

ILLUSTRATION 25-5.   Status Report Letter

Cosher, Cosher and Snorer
960 Wyus Boulevard
Madison, Wisconsin 53606

June 12, 2008

Mr. Cal L. Medeep
Pockets Insurance Company
10 Wausau Way
Wausau, Wisconsin 54401

Re: <u>Kelsey v. Cocoa</u>
Your claim number: C100090888

Dear Mr. Medeep:

This letter is to provide you with a status report concerning the progress of the above-referenced matter. To date, we have requested that the plaintiff answer interrogatories and requests for admissions. I sent a copy of these requests to you about a week ago. The plaintiff is required to answer these requests within 30 days. We will send you a copy of the plaintiff's answers as soon as we receive them. We are scheduled to depose the plaintiff on September 1, 2008.

The plaintiff's attorney is scheduled to depose a representative of Oreo Company on October 13, 2008.

At this time, the court has not scheduled a settlement conference, but is likely to do so before the end of the year.

Please feel free to call if you have any questions.

Sincerely,

Alicia R. Samuel
Legal Assistant

ARS/yml

In other letters, you will request information, often from the custodian of records. See Illustration 25-6.

Often you will be responsible for coordinating document productions. Illustration 25-7 shows a sample **transmittal letter** to a client concerning a request to produce documents.

Many letters will be written to accompany documents, releases, and checks. See Illustrations 25-8 and 25-9.

ILLUSTRATION 25-6.   Request for Information

Cosher, Cosher and Snorer
960 Wyus Boulevard
Madison, Wisconsin 53606

August 12, 2008

Sarah Rachel
Custodian of Records
Federal Deposit Insurance Corp.
9100 Bryn Mawr Road
Rosemont, Illinois 60018

Re: Freedom of Information Act Request

Dear Ms. Rachel:

Based on the Freedom of Information Act, 5 U.S.C. §552 et seq., I am requesting that your agency provide copies of the following:

Each and every document that relates to or refers to the sale of the property located at 2714 Barrington Road, Glenview, Illinois, 60025.

The documents should be located in your Rosemont, Illinois office.

Under the act, these documents should be available to us within ten days. If any portion of this request is denied, please provide a detailed statement of the reasons for the denial and an index or similar statement concerning the nature of the documents withheld. As required by the act, I agree to pay reasonable charges for copying of the documents upon the presentation of a bill and the finished copies.

Thank you in advance for your cooperation in this matter.

Sincerely,

Lillian Eve Harris
Paralegal

LEH/dag

3. Demand Letter

A demand letter is a letter that states your client's demands to another party. A common letter paralegals write is a demand letter that seeks to collect debts. Such a letter may need to comply with the requirements of your state's fair-debt collection laws. See Illustration 25-10.

In a demand letter, you should include the fact that your firm represents the creditor or other client, as well as the client's desire

for full payment of the claim. Specify the amount demanded or state the action sought, and ask the debtor either to make payment or to contact your office within a certain number of days. Then state the action that the firm will take if the demand is not met within the specified time period.

ILLUSTRATION 25-7.   Request to Produce Documents

Carthage, Katz and Kramer
1001 B Line Highway
Darlington, Wisconsin 53840

February 28, 2009

Ms. Karen Taylor
Carrots and Critters Corp.
1864 Merrimac Road
Sylvania, Ohio 43560

Re: Carrots and Critters v. Rabbits and Rodents

Dear Ms. Taylor:

Enclosed please find a request from the defendants asking you to produce documents. The date scheduled for the production of these documents is April 1, 2009. Some documents may be protected from disclosure because they may contain confidential trade secret information, and others may be protected because they are communications between you and your attorney or the result of your attorney's work. We must respond in writing by March 25, 2009, in order to raise any of these claims.

As we must review the documents to determine whether any documents are protected, we should compile the documents no later than March 15, 2009. This will allow us time to review, to index, and to number each document.

I will be available to assist you in gathering documents to respond to this request. I will call you this week to schedule an appointment.

If you have any questions, please feel free to call.

Sincerely,

Eileen Waters
Paralegal

Encs.
EDW/jnn

4. Opinion Letters

Opinion and advice letters advise clients about the legal rules that apply to their situation. Most law firms will not have paralegals draft even a preliminary opinion letter. If your firm asks you to draft a preliminary letter, be sure not to sign the letter with your name or that of your attorney, and to have the attorney carefully review it before it is sent to a client or another attorney.

ILLUSTRATION 25-8.   Letter Accompanying Document

Janis, Max, & Jordan
1600 Bradley Street
Wilmette, Illinois 60091

March 4, 2009

Eve Lillian
Lake County Recorder of Deeds
18 N. County Street
Waukegan, Illinois 60085

Re: 1785 Central Street

    Deerfield, Illinois 60015

Dear Mrs. Lillian:

Enclosed please find two original quit claim deeds, one dated December 30, 2003, and one dated January 2, 2009, relating to the above-referenced property. Both deeds have been marked "exempt" from state and county transfer tax. A check for $50.00 to cover the recording fees ($25 each) is enclosed. Please record these deeds at once and return the originals to Jacki Harris at the 1785 Central Street address.

Thank you for your assistance.

Sincerely,

Jennifer Lauren
Legal Assistant

Encs.
cc: Jacki Harris
JML/jch

ETHICS ALERT

If you sign an opinion letter, this could be construed as the unauthorized practice of law. If you sign the attorney's name, without his or her consent, that is tantamount to practicing law.

ILLUSTRATION 25-9. **Letter Accompanying Check**

Hellman & Harris
Central and Carriage Way
Evanston, Illinois 60202

April 22, 2008

William German
Chicago Bar Association
124 Plymouth Court
Chicago, Illinois 60611

Re: Commercial Real Estate Contract Prepared by the Real Property Law Committee

Dear Mr. German:

Enclosed please find a check for $30.00 to cover the mailing fees and the cost of a copy of the Real Estate Contract referenced above. Please send me a copy of the contract at your earliest convenience.

Thank you for your cooperation.

Sincerely,

M. Seth Jordan
Paralegal

Enc.
cc: Rachel Jacob
MSJ/ear

If you must draft a preliminary version of an opinion letter, the process is similar to writing an IRAC paragraph. Start with a statement of the legal issue. Your next sentence, however, should answer the issue. In the paragraph following the answer to the issue, state the law and apply the legally significant facts to the law. Provide information about any legal issues that present problems and incorporate the legally significant facts into that discussion.

The final paragraph should state your conclusion or answer to the issue presented and provide your prediction of the outcome for the legal situation.

ILLUSTRATION 25-10.   Demand Letter

Law Office of Randall William
145 Franklin Street
Madison, Wisconsin 53606

April 1, 2008

Michelle Hirsh
889 Barrington Road
Middleton, Wisconsin 53608

Re: Furniture Crafters Account 4155

Dear Ms. Hirsh:

Our office represents Furniture Crafters in the collection of the $468.00 debt due on the above-referenced account. Furniture Crafters requests that you pay the full amount of the debt, $468.00, immediately.

You must pay this amount in full or contact our firm at the above telephone number or address within seven days. If we do not hear from you within seven days, we will proceed to court in this matter.

Sincerely,

Randall William
Paralegal

RAW/bgh

NET NOTE

Do not use all capital letters in an e-mail. That is considered screaming.

PRACTICE POINTER

Check with your firm concerning whether to draft any e-mails that include client secrets. E-mails can be intercepted and may not be secure. Some firms, however, have security measures in place to facilitate such communications.

> ## PRACTICE POINTER
>
> Some e-mail programs allow you to request a return receipt that lets you know that the reader opened the e-mail. For critical e-mail it is a good idea to request such a receipt. If something is time critical and you must ensure that the party received the document, e-mail is not the best method of communication. Too often e-mails are lost.

Discuss this letter with the attorney who will be signing it and be sure that it is his or her opinion rather than your own that is conveyed to the client. Be sure that the attorney reviews the letter before signing it. If the attorney does not initiate a discussion with you about the letter, you should do so to ensure that the attorney reviewed it. Although you may draft the letter for the attorney to review, be sure that the letter is signed by the attorney when sent to the recipient. Even under direction by an attorney, a paralegal can never give legal advice, suggest a change in a legal condition, or reach a legal conclusion. Opinion letters provide legal advice, suggest that a client change his legal position, and also reach a legal conclusion, this is why it is imperative that the letter is signed by the attorney supervising the matter.

5. E-mail

E-mail notes have become very common. Many of the same rules apply in the same way to an e-mail note as they would to any other letters. Consider your audience and outline what you plan to say. Use proper grammar. Proofread your e-mail. If you would address a letter using a title such as Mr. or Mrs., do so in the e-mail. Include your mailing address and your telephone number so that the party can contact you using methods other than e-mail. If you are sending an attachment such as a document to be reviewed, be sure you notify the party in advance so that the person doesn't mistakenly delete the attachment, believing it may contain a virus.

When sending emails, remember that emails can be forwarded to other recipients. Be sure to include confidentiality information if necessary stating that the email should only be viewed by the intended recipient.

CHECKLIST: RULES FOR LETTER WRITING

1. "Never give legal advice" is the first rule of letter writing for paralegals.
2. Be informative.

3. Consider your audience. If you are addressing a client, do so courteously and write at a level that the client will understand. If you were asked to answer a client's questions, be sure that you do. You should always be respectful to the addressee.
4. Choose your words carefully. You want to make certain that your words express what you intend.
5. Write succinctly and directly. Your reader is busy so you want to communicate clearly and in as few words as possible. Avoid unnecessary details.

CHAPTER SUMMARY

Letter writing is an essential part of your daily routine as a paralegal. Most letter writing conventions that apply to business communication apply to legal correspondence. However, paralegals should be careful about dating letters concerning legal matters. Letters should be dated with the date of mailing, which may or may not be the date of drafting.

A letter should contain a date, the name and address of the addressee, a reference line, a greeting to the addressee, the body of the letter, and the complimentary closing.

Confirming letters reaffirm information already agreed to between you and the recipient. Status letters provide an up-to-date review of the process of a pending matter. Transaction summary letters explain particular transactions. Letters also are written to accompany documents, such as releases and checks, or to state your client's demands to a third party, such as for payment.

As with any written document, letters should be outlined, written, and then rewritten if necessary.

It is important to avoid the unauthorized practice of law when writing letters. Do not give any legal advice in a letter that you sign. A letter must be signed by an attorney when it contains legal advice, suggests that a client change her legal position, or states a legal conclusion.

KEY TERMS

attachment	greeting
blind carbon copy (bcc)	header
block letter	inside address
body	letterhead
carbon copy (cc)	modified block letter
closing	personal style letter
confirming letter	reference line
date	request information
demand letter	status report
e-mail	transaction summary letter
enclosure line	transmittal letter
full block letter	

EXERCISES

SHORT ANSWER

1. What are the basic components of a letter?
2. What is a reference line?
3. How do you indicate that you are sending a copy of a letter to another person?
4. How do you indicate that you want someone to receive a copy, but you don't want the addressee to know that the other person received a copy of the letter?
5. What are confirming letters?
6. What is a status report letter?
7. What are transmittal letters?
8. What are demand letters?
9. Should you provide a legal opinion in a letter?

LETTER WRITING

Prepare the following letters as if you were a paralegal with the law firm of Snorer, Hackett and Blank, 1000 Madison Way, Madison, Wisconsin 53606. Addressee names are identified for you, but you may supply each one's address yourself.

10. Write a letter to Madison Insurance Corporation explaining that your law firm will be representing Carol White for a lawsuit against its insured, Harold Watson, stemming from an automobile accident that occurred on September 1, 2008. The Madison claims adjuster is Howie Mark. Harold Watson's insurance policy number is 1280. You once had a difficult time dealing with Mr. Mark and Madison Insurance in the past, so you send your letter by certified mail. Enclose a copy of the police report. Send a blind copy to your client. You write it at 5 P.M. on December 24. You realize that December 25 is a holiday and that mail will not go out until the next day.

11. Your firm represents a client, Karen Taylor, who sustained a neck injury during an automobile accident between Carter McLaughlin and Robert Carroll. Write a letter to Dr. Nancy Martin asking for a detailed report concerning the present and future medical problems of that client. Dr. Martin is an orthopedic surgeon. Indicate that you have a signed release from the client to enclose.

12. Your firm represents Margaret Weston in a divorce case. Write a short letter to her informing her of the final hearing date in her divorce case. The date is June 16, 2008, in Lucas County Domestic Relations Court, 900 W. Adams Street, Toledo, Ohio 43602.

13. Your client needs to give testimony at a deposition on November 15, 2008, at 10 A.M. at your offices. Please draft a letter asking William Hesse to be at

the deposition. Explain to him that you will meet with him in advance to discuss his testimony.

14. Your firm has just settled a case involving Karen Douglas and your client, the Wentworth Industries, in Morristown, New Jersey. The case was settled for $88,000. The Wentworth corporation paid Douglas for injuries she sustained when she fell at a Mexican hotel. You do not want to admit any liability in your letter or admit any ownership interest in the Mexican hotel, the CanCan. You merely want to tender the check to Douglas in full satisfaction of any claims she or her husband have against Wentworth. You also have the signed settlement agreement to send her and the court dismissal of the action.

15. You are assigned the preparation of a letter that explains the status of a pending insurance defense litigation matter. The matter is set for trial on November 15 of this year. Two depositions have been taken—the plaintiff's and the defendant's. Interrogatories have been answered by both sides and a settlement conference is scheduled with the judge in the case on October 31. The judge is Eve G. Halsey of Ohio Common Pleas Court in Columbus, Ohio. You expect that a representative of the restaurant where the incident took place will attend the settlement conference and that an insurance company representative also will attend as required by the local court rules. Your firm will be calling several witnesses from the restaurant to testify at the trial and you and the partner on the case, Wally Taylor, will be preparing these witnesses to testify beginning in October. Send this letter to your client, Schroeder Insurance Enterprise, 250 W. Wilson Street, Wilmette, IL 60091. The person you deal with at the insurance company is Thomas Kennedy, a claims manager. You are sending this letter via Express Mail. The letter is being typed by Taylor's secretary Jan Marie Maggio. She will send a blind copy of the letter to an associate on the case, Janis Harris. She also will send a carbon copy of the letter to Mr. Taylor.

16. The following letter was written and signed by a paralegal. Please list three problems that could arise from this letter.

January 1, 2009

Sent by Mail and Fax to:

Re: Contract to purchase real estate dated December 15, 2008

Dear Mr. Smith: Per your request the Seller hereby agrees to extend the attorney approval contingency until 5:00 P.M., January 15, 2009.

I specifically note to you that I am in receipt of your first amendment and its Exhibits A, B, and C.

As to paragraph 3 of your first amendment, I note to you that I am posting in the mail to you a proposed limited warranty and a Waiver and Disclaimer of Implied Warranty of Habitability. I request that you review the same after I have advised you that my client has reviewed

the same. I am also posting it in the mail to them. It is specifically noted that what will be provided will be a limited warranty and that we will expect the parties to sign a waiver and disclaimer and I further note that I want to end this thing and accordingly, I provide for a date of January 15, 2009.

I expressed to you that I was unhappy with the contingencies in paragraph 5 of the contract. In fairness, I request that if it does not appear that your client will be able to meet the contingencies, namely, either sell her home or secure financing, that she will notify us at the earliest date and to then voluntarily agree to a termination of the contract.

Looking forward to a closing with you soon.

Very truly yours,

Mary Walton
Paralegal

A

SHEPARDIZING AND CITE CHECKING

▼ What Is Cite Checking, or Shepardizing, and When Is It Done?

The meaning of the term *cite checking* varies. Often, the meaning depends on the particular attorney asking you to complete the project. For some attorneys, cite checking includes three components:

1. ensuring that the cited authority in fact states what the brief or memorandum tells the reader the authority states and that the correct authority is cited;
2. making certain that the citation is placed in proper *Bluebook*, *ALWD*, or court format or style; and
3. checking that the authority is still current and valid law.

When some attorneys ask you to cite check your research results, they only want you to complete the final component of the cite checking process. Others may want you to complete all three tasks or just two of the three procedures.

For the first stage, you might consider using the following process:

1. Review the brief and the citation.
2. Read the cited authority.
3. Ask yourself a series of questions:
   Does the cited authority say what the brief or memorandum states that it says?
   Should quotes be placed around the text in the brief or memorandum?

Is the correct page number for the citation listed?
What is the correct case name?
What court decided this case?
What is the date of the decision?
What is the parallel citation?
4. Make certain that you note the correct court.

For stage two, consult Appendix B. For stage three, refer to the cite checking checklist that follows.

Cite Checking Checklist

1. Make a list of the cases, statutes, rules, or other authorities you need to cite check.
2. To be thorough, search cases in all of the following sources or services: *Shepard's* (hard copy with a daily update check or online), KeyCite, and GlobalCite.

Shepardizing Cases in Hard-Copy Materials Checklist

1. Determine which *Shepard's* series is the appropriate one to consult. Is the case in the federal or state citators? Should you consult the regional rather than state citator?
2. Review the front cover of the most current pamphlet that accompanies the *Shepard's* citations to determine what volumes should be reviewed for your cite check.
3. Gather each of the volumes and supplements mentioned on the cover.
4. Find the appropriate reporter section in each volume.
5. Locate the volume number listed in bold. Check the top corner of the page until you find pages encompassing your volume number.
6. Find the page number.

Shepard's Online Checklist for Cases

1. Click on the *Shepard's* citation button and type in the citation.
2. Check for red, orange, or yellow signals and review citing references.

KeyCite Checklist

1. Access WESTLAW.
2. Click on the KeyCite button. Then type in the citation.
3. Check for red or yellow signals and review citing references.

CITATION

The *Bluebook* is the guide to citation form for all legal documents, whether office memos or Supreme Court briefs. The *Bluebook*, formally known as the *Uniform System of Citation,* 18th Edition, governs because of convention and tradition rather than by the mandate of the state legislature. The *ALWD Citation Manual,* 3rd Edition by Darby Dickerson offers easily comprehended citations. Also, the *ALWD* guide contains "Fast Formats" for every category of citation. These provide terrific examples of formats for all legal resources. New forms of citation are emerging due to the advent of nonproprietary cases in which the case is not attributed to a publisher. Generally, the *Bluebook* is the bible for citation format for all legal personnel. If ever in doubt as to citation format, rely on the *Bluebook*.

▼ What Is a Citation?

A citation is really an address indicating where the cited material can be found so that anyone reading your document can find the material if he or she wants to. The abbreviations must be consistent so that everyone knows what they mean. We rely on a similar convention with street addresses and postal

abbreviations. The abbreviation for avenue is Ave.; the postal abbreviation for New York is NY.

▼ What Documents Are Cited?

Any source of authority that you discuss in any legal document is cited. Any concept or idea that is not your own must be cited; this is called attributing authority to your ideas. Citing credits the source from which the idea or legal rule came. It also tells the reader where he or she can find the original source. Citations are used for all authority, whether it is primary authority such as a case or a statute, or secondary authority such as a treatise or a law review article. Also cited are looseleaf services, practitioners' materials, and newspaper articles.

The *Bluebook* has two citation formats, one for briefs and memos and the other for law review articles. *ALWD* has one FORMAT. Paralegals rely on the brief and memo format for citation.

▼ What Are the Components of a Citation?

Generally, the components of a cite are the name of the particular document, the volume or title where the document is located, the name of the publication that contains the document, and the specific page, section, or paragraph where the document is found. Also included is the year that a case was decided or the publication date of a book or volume of statutes. For example:

Jacobs v. Grossman, 310 Ill. 247, 141 N.E. 714 (1923)

The name of the document is the case name, *Jacobs v. Grossman*. Parallel citations are given in the example so that you can find the case in both reporters, the official reporter is always mentioned first and the unofficial reporter, mentioned second. Each state has its own rules regarding the necessity of including parallel citation information for documents submitted to its court. Some states do not have state reporters and rely on the regional reporters so parallel citation is not an issue. Always check the local court rules. The first number preceding the reporter abbreviation is the volume number of the reporter. Next is the reporter abbreviation and then the page number where the case begins in the reporter. The year that the case was decided is included in parentheses. *Bluebook* **Table T.1** lists reporter abbreviations as does *ALWD* **Rule 12.1** and Appendix 1.

Using the *Bluebook* takes practice. The *Bluebook* is organized by rules. Each rule details the citation format for each type of document. The index is very helpful in finding specific references to the citation format for an individual document such as a statute, an administrative regulation, or a law review article. For additional examples, use the Fast Formats in the *ALWD Citation Manual*. The Fast Formats are easily located in the index of the *ALWD Citation Manual*.

The following portion of the appendix provides examples of the materials mentioned in the book and sample cite formats. These examples will help you navigate your way. If the illustration here does not provide adequate information, you can turn to the *Bluebook* or *ALWD* rule mentioned to obtain more detailed treatment.

Check the ALWD Web site for the latest updates and citation details at www.alwd.org/publications/second_edition_resources.html.

▼ How Are Slip Opinions Cited?

You should provide the docket number, the court, and the full date of the most recent disposition of the case, as well as the full case name.

slip opinion cite: Gillespie v. Willard City Bd. of Educ., No. C87-7043 (N.D. Ohio Sept. 28, 1987)—*Bluebook* format, Rule 10.8.1; *ALWD* format, Rule 12.18

with page cite: Gillespie v. Willard City Bd. of Educ., No. C87-7043, slip op. at 3 (N.D. Ohio Sept. 28, 1987)

According to the *ALWD Citation Manual,* always check the local court rules to see if unpublished cases can be cited. See *ALWD* Sidebar 12.7.

▼ How Do You Cite a State Case?

Bluebook **Rule 10** and *ALWD* **Rule 12.4** discuss citation formats for state cases. Also check *Bluebook* Jurisdiction-Specific Citation Rules and Style Guides at BT.2 for local court citation rules. The first example below shows the citation for an Illinois case with parallel authority included. The second example shows the same case cited in a brief to an Illinois court or to the United States District Court for the Northern District of Illinois.

With parallel cites: Thompson v. Economy Super Marts, 221 Ill. App. 3d 263, 581 N.E.2d 885, 163 Ill. Dec. 731 (App. Ct. 1991)— *Bluebook* format

Thompson v. Economy Super Marts, 221 Ill. App. 3d 263, 163 Ill. Dec. 731, 581 N.E.2d 885 (1991)—*ALWD* format

In a brief: Thompson v. Economy Super Marts, 581 N.E.2d 885 (Ill. App. Ct. 1991)—*Bluebook* and *ALWD* formats

When you use a state decision in a memorandum or a brief, always include the regional citation. See *Bluebook* **Table T.1** and *ALWD* Appendix 2. If you are citing a state case to a state court in which the case was decided, provide both the official citation, if one exists, and the regional citation, as the first example above shows, if court rules or the assigning partner requires it. Always list the official citation first. When you cite a state case in a memorandum addressed to a federal court or to a court of a state different from the state that decided the

case, include only the regional citation as the second example above shows. If you are using only the regional citation, remember to place the abbreviation for the deciding court in parentheses. See *Bluebook* **Rule 10.4** and *ALWD* **Rule 12.6.** Additionally, follow the local court rules references in *Bluebook* blue pages BT.2. The *ALWD Citation Manual* stipulates that parallel citations are not required unless mandated by local court rules. *ALWD* Appendix 2 and *ALWD* **Rule 12.4** state this. However, if parallel citations are required, *ALWD* **Rule 12.4(c)(3)(d)** states that the regional reporter citation is last in the order.

Some states, like Oklahoma, use the regional reporter as their official reporter. Some states have adopted public domain citations as their official cites that should be cited in accordance with *Bluebook* **Rule 10.3.3** and *ALWD* **Rule 12.16** (also called neutral citations). These cites are designed to allow readers to find the case in a computerized system that does not rely on commercial publishers. Cites to commercial reporters such as West's may be used to augment public domain citations.

The public domain format is as follows: case name, followed by the year of the decision, the deciding court, and the sequential number of the decision. To cite to a specific portion of the decision, you may add a reference to the paragraph.

Public domain citation: State v. Kienast, 1996 S.D. 111 ¶ 2—*Bluebook* and *ALWD* formats

Use neutral, or public domain, citations when local court rules permit according to *ALWD* **Rule 12.16.**

▼ How Do You Cite Decisions Found in the *Federal Reporter* or the *Federal Supplement?*

Bluebook Rules **10.1-10.6 B5.1.3** and **Table T.1** and *ALWD Citation Manual* **Rule 12.6** and Appendices 1 and 4 provide detailed coverage of the citation format for cases from the *Federal Reporter* and the *Federal Supplement.* The case name is placed first and underlined. Next, place the volume number. The reporter abbreviation is next. For the *Federal Reporter*, the abbreviation is "F." The number of the series, second or third, should be placed next to the "F." For the Federal Supplement, the reporter is abbreviated "F. Supp." The page number follows the abbreviation for the reporter. Next, place an abbreviation denoting the appropriate court and the date of the decision. Be certain to include a geographic designation for the district courts.

Federal Reporter **case:**   Zimmerman v. North Am. Signal Co., 704 F.2d 347 (7th Cir. 1983)—*Bluebook* and *ALWD* formats

Federal Supplement **case:**   Musser v. Mountain View Broad., 578 F. Supp. 229 (E.D. Tenn. 1984)—*Bluebook* and *ALWD* formats

▼ How Do You Cite a Decision Contained in the *Federal Rules Decisions* Reporter?

The abbreviation for the *Federal Rules Decisions* is F.R.D. A case would be cited according to *Bluebook* **Table T.1** and *ALWD* Appendix 1, as follows:

Barrett Indus. Trucks v. Old Republic Ins. Co., 129 F.R.D. 515 (N.D. Ill. 1989)

PRACTICE POINTER

When embarking on a writing project, ask the attorney about his citation preferences and look at examples in the firm's memo and brief bank. Sometimes the attorney's preferences will differ from the local court rules when writing in-house memos.

▼ How Do You Cite a U.S. Supreme Court Case?

According to the *Bluebook,* once a U.S. Supreme Court case is published in an advance sheet of the *U.S. Reports,* the *U.S. Reports* citation, and only the *U.S. Reports* citation, is the proper citation. Do not include parallel citations. See **Rule 10, T.1** and *ALWD* **Rule 12** generally. The cite format is diagramed on page 79 of the *Bluebook.*

Erie R.R. v. Tompkins, 304 U.S. 64 (1938)—*Bluebook* and *ALWD* formats

Erie R.R. v. Tompkins, 304 U.S. 64, 58 S. Ct. 817, 82 L. Ed. 1188 (1938)—*ALWD* format permissible upon attorney request—*ALWD* **Rule 12.4(b).**

However, if a Supreme Court opinion has been published in the *West Supreme Court Reporter* but not yet in the *U.S. Reports,* the *Supreme Court Reporter* citation should be used. See *Bluebook* **Table T.1.**

If a Supreme Court opinion has not yet been published in *U.S. Reports, Supreme Court Reporter,* or *U.S. Reports, Lawyers' Edition,* then you should cite to *United States Law Week.* See *Bluebook* **Table T.1.** The court designation, U.S., should be placed in parentheses with the full date. See *Bluebook* **Rule 10.4(a).** The citation would read as follows:

UAW v. Johnson Controls, 59 U.S.L.W. 4209 (U.S. Mar. 20, 1991)

The *ALWD Citation Manual* in **Rule 12.4(b)** states to include only one source of U.S. Supreme Court opinions, in the illustrated order of preference. However, parallel citation of Supreme Court cases is permitted if attorneys request it.

▼ How Do You Use Short Citation Forms?

Short citation forms and subsequent cite formats are explained in *Bluebook* Rule 10.9. The part on footnotes does not apply to briefs and memos. Also see *ALWD* **Rule 12.21**.

Full citation:

<u>Seymour v. Armstrong</u>, 64 P. 612, 613 (Kan. 1901).

Subsequent citation when there is an intervening cite:

Seymour v. Armstrong, 64 P. at 613. *Bluebook* Rule 10.9.(a)(i)

Seymour, 64 P. 613. *Bluebook* and *ALWD* Rule 12.21(b) if using only the first party will not cause confusion.

A subsequent citation without an intervening cite requires the use of *Id.:*

Id. at 613. *Bluebook* Rule 10.9(b) and *ALWD* Rule 12.21

Use of *Id.* with parallel citations (note: follow local court rules to determine requirements for parallel citation):

Full cite

Thompson v. Economy Super Marts, 221 Ill. App. 3d 263, 581 N.E.2d 885, 163 Ill. Dec. 731 (App. Ct. 1991).

Short cite without intervening citations

Id. at 263, 581 N.E.2d at 887, 163 Ill. Dec. at 733—*ALWD* and *Bluebook* formats

▼ How Do You Cite a Decision Reported on WESTLAW?

Bluebook **Rule 18.1.1** and *ALWD* **Rule 12.12** explain how an unpublished decision found only on either WESTLAW or LEXIS should be cited. For WESTLAW, first provide the name of the case and underline it. The next part of the citation is the docket number. In the example that follows, that number is No. 82-C4585. The next part of the citation is the year that the decision was issued. Next, indicate "WL" for WESTLAW and finally the WESTLAW number assigned to the case. Place the date in the parentheses.

WESTLAW example: <u>Clark Equip. Co. v. Lift Parts Mfg. Co.</u>, No. 82-C4585, 1985 WL 2917, (N.D. Ill. Oct. 1, 1985)—*Bluebook* format
<u>Clark Equip. Co. v. Lift Parts Mfg. Co.</u>, 1985 WL 2917 (N.D. Ill. Oct. 1, 1985)—*ALWD* format, Rule 12.12(a)

▼ How Do You Cite a Decision Reported on LEXIS?

For LEXIS citations, first state the name of the case, the docket number, the year of the decision, the name of the LEXIS file that contains the case, and the name LEXIS to indicate that the case is found on LEXIS. Next place the date in parentheses.

LEXIS example: Barrett Indus. Trucks v. Old Republic Ins. Co., No. 87-C9429, 1990 U.S. Dist. LEXIS 142 (N.D. Ill. Jan. 9, 1990)—*Bluebook* format
Barrett Indus. Trucks v. Old Republic Ins. Co., 1990 U.S. Dist. LEXIS 142 (N.D. Ill. Jan. 9, 1990)—*ALWD* format

If a decision is published in a hard-copy reporter, you should not use the WESTLAW or LEXIS citation. This is stipulated in *Bluebook* **Rule 18.1** and *ALWD* **Rule 12.12(a).**

▼ How Do You Indicate a Page or Screen Number for the Case?

An asterisk should precede any screen or page numbers. See *Bluebook* **Rule 18.1.1** and *ALWD* **12.12(b).**

WESTLAW screen no.: Clark Equip. Co. v. Lift Parts Mfg. Co., No. 82-C4585, 1985 WL 2917, at *1 (N.D. Ill. Oct. 1, 1985)—*Bluebook* format
LEXIS screen no.: Barrett Indus. Trucks v. Old Republic Ins. Co., 1990 U.S. Dist. LEXIS 142, at *1 (N.D. Ill. Jan. 9, 1990)—*ALWD* format

▼ How Do You Cite Internet Resources?

Bluebook **Rule 18.2.1** covers Internet materials. *ALWD* **Rule 23.1(i)** covers electronic journals. Only rely on Internet resources if there is no other way to obtain the material, because the Internet format is transient in nature. However, if you can obtain the resource in a PDF file, then it is a reliable version. You can use Net cites as additional cites when the identical information can be obtained in hard copy as well as on the Internet, but the Net resource is more accessible. Information on including parallel citations to Net cites is detailed at *Bluebook* Rule **18.2.2.** *ALWD* **Rule 12.15** states that cases obtained on the Net can be cited only if they are unavailable in a bound reporter, looseleaf service, or on LEXIS or WESTLAW.

Karin Mitra, *Information v. Commercialization: The Internet and Unsolicited Electronic Mail,* 4 Rich. J.L. & Tech. 6 (Spring 1998), *available at* http://www.richmond.edu/jolt/v4i3/mitra.html—*Bluebook* Rule **18.2.2**

Karin Mitra, *Information v. Commercialization: The Internet and Unsolicited Electronic Mail,* 4 Rich. J.L. & Tech. 6 (Spring 1998) (http://www.richmond.edu/jolt/v4i3/mitra.html)—*ALWD* format

▼ How Do You Cite Documents Retrieved in PDF Files?

Documents are widely available for retrieval in Portable Document Format, "PDF." LEXIS and WESTLAW now permit most resources to be saved and printed in PDF. Documents in PDF maintain the pagination from the hard-copy source and do not permit end-user manipulation.

Bluebook Rule 18.2.1(c) and *ALWD* Rule 40.1(C)(3) address citing to PDF documents.

PRACTICE POINTER

It is both cost- and time-efficient to attach PDF versions of cases and statutes to emailed memos rather than printing or photocopying the resources.

▼ How Do You Cite Federal Statutes?

Always cite to the official statutory compilation. The first entry in the citation is the title number, then the abbreviation for the statutory compilation, and then the section or paragraph number. *Bluebook* **Rule 12** and *ALWD* **Rule 14** detail all the various rules pertaining to citing statutes and codes, state or federal. Always cite to the year of the code's compilation, not the year that the particular statute section was enacted. For example:

> 12 U.S.C. §211 (2006)—*Bluebook* and *ALWD* formats

If a code section is well known by a popular name, then include the name in the citation. For example:

> Strikebreaker Act, 18 U.S.C. §1231 (2006)—*Bluebook* format
> *Strikebreaker Act,* 18 U.S.C. §1231 (2006)—*ALWD* format

You may rely on an unofficial version for updating purposes. All the following are citations to the identical statute.

> 26 U.S.C. §61 (2006)—*Bluebook* and *ALWD* formats
> 26 U.S.C.A. §61 (West 2005 & Supp. 2008)—*Bluebook* and *ALWD* formats
> 26 U.S.C.S. §61 (LEXIS 2007 & Supp. 2008)—*Bluebook* format
> 26 U.S.C.S. §61 (LEXIS L. Publg. 2007 & Supp. 2008)—*ALWD* format

As with the U.S.C., the year included in the citation is the year that the code volume was published, not the year that the statute was enacted. In the U.S.C.A. example above, the first year mentioned, 2005, is the year that the particular volume of the code was published; the second date, 2008, is the year of the pocket part supplement that updates the code volume. The publication date is printed either on the title page of the bound volume or on the back of the title page.

▼ How Do You Cite a Section of a Constitution, Federal or State?

Bluebook **Rule 11** and *ALWD* **Rule 13** outline the citation format. The United States Constitution citation refers to the particular article, section, and clause being used. For example:

U.S. Const. art II, §2, cl. 1—*Bluebook* and *ALWD* formats

This cite is used when you are referring to the body of the Constitution. A special citation format is required when you are referring to an amendment currently in force. For example:

U.S. Const. amend. II

State constitutions are indicated by the name of the state in the *Bluebook* abbreviated format. *Bluebook* **Table T.1** and *ALWD* **Appendix 1** indicate the accepted state name abbreviation; this is not necessarily the postal abbreviation. For example, the state of Washington's postal abbreviation is WA, but the *Bluebook* abbreviation is Wash. A section of the Washington state constitution would be cited as follows:

Wash. Const. art I, §2—*Bluebook* and *ALWD* formats

Years or dates are not included in citations to constitutions, state or federal, that are current. Parenthetical notations after the citation indicate the year a constitutional provision was repealed or amended. An example is the Eighteenth Amendment to the U.S. Constitution prohibiting the sale of liquor. The Twenty-First Amendment later repealed this. *Bluebook* **Rule 11** and *ALWD* **Rule 13.3** cover this:

U.S. Const. amend. XVIII (repealed 1933)—*Bluebook* format

U.S. Const. amend. XVIII (repealed 1933 by U.S. Const. amend XXI)—*ALWD* format

▼ How Do You Cite to a Legislative History of a Statute?

Bluebook **Rule 13** and *ALWD* **Rule 15** detail the citation format for all the components of the legislative process: the bill, the committee report, the debates, and transcripts of the hearings.

▼ How Are the *Code of Federal Regulations* and the *Federal Register* Cited?

Rule 14 of the *Bluebook* and *ALWD* **Rule 19** provide the citation format for administrative and executive materials, which include the *Code of Federal Regulations* and the *Federal Register*. See also *Bluebook* T.1 for each

jurisdiction's administrative material. Title 21 of the C.F.R. part 101 from 2005 is cited as:

> 20 C.F.R. pt. 404 (2008)—*Bluebook* and *ALWD* formats

If you are citing to Title 21 of the C.F.R. §101.62 from 2008, it would be written as:

> 21 C.F.R. §101.62 (2008)—*Bluebook* and *ALWD* formats

A *Federal Register* entry from volume 73 beginning on page 26200, from May 8, 2008, would be cited as:

> 73 Fed. Reg. 26200 (May 8, 2008)—*Bluebook* and *ALWD* formats

▼ How Do You Cite to a Legal Dictionary?

The information for the correct citation format for dictionaries is found in **Rule 15.8** of the *Bluebook* and **Rule 25.1** of *ALWD*.

> Black's Law Dictionary 712 (8th ed. 2004)—*Bluebook* format
> *Black's Law Dictionary* 712 (8th ed., West 2004)—*ALWD* format

▼ How Are Legal Encyclopedias Cited?

ALWD **Rule 26** and *Bluebook* **Rule 15.8** discuss legal encyclopedias. A citation to the discussion of easements would be as follows:

> 25 Am. Jr. 2d *Easements and Licenses* §90 (2004 and Supp. 2007)—*Bluebook* and *ALWD* formats
> 28A C.J.S. *Easements* §18 (2004 & Supp. 2007)—*Bluebook* and *ALWD* formats

▼ How Do You Cite to *American Law Reports?*

This is found in **Rule 16.6.5** of the *Bluebook* and **Rule 24** of *ALWD*.

> William B. Johnson, Annotation, *Locating Easement of Way Created by Necessity*, 36 A.L.R.4th 769 (1985)—*ALWD* and *Bluebook* formats

▼ How Do You Cite to a Law Review or Law Journal?

Bluebook **Rule 16** and *ALWD* **Rule 23** indicate the citation form for a law review article, as follows:

> Mitchell N. Berman, *Justification and Excuse, Law and Morality*, 53 Duke L.J. 1 (2003)—*Bluebook* and *ALWD* formats

Abbreviations for the journal names are found in **Table 13** of the *Bluebook* and *ALWD* Appendix 5. A legal newspaper is cited according to *Bluebook* **Rule 16.5:**

> Wayne Smith, <u>Remote Access: Striking a Balance</u>, Law Tech. News, Jan. 2005, at 11—*Bluebook* and *ALWD* formats

ALWD **23.1(d)(3)** states if place of publication can't be discerned from title, include it in parentheses.

▼ How Do You Cite the Restatements?

Bluebook **Rule 12.8.5** and *ALWD* **Rule 27.1** indicate that the Restatements are cited as follows:

> Restatement (Second) of Contracts §235 (1979)—*Bluebook* and *ALWD* formats

Note that for *Bluebook* format the year is the year that the Restatement section was adopted. This information is given on the title page of every volume of the Restatements. When you are citing to a comment that follows the Restatement section, **Rule 3.5** of the *Bluebook* applies. For example:

> Restatement (Second) of Contracts §235 cmt. a (1979)—*Bluebook* format (date adopted)
>
> *Restatement (Second) of Contracts* §235 (1981)—*ALWD* format
>
> *Restatement (Second) of Contracts* §235 cmt a (1981)—*ALWD* format

Note that *ALWD* requires that the year is the date of volume publication—*ALWD* format, **Rule 27.1.**

▼ How Do You Cite an Ethics Rule Found in the *ABA Model Code of Professional Responsibility?*

The rules for citation of ethics codes are found in *Bluebook* **Rule 12.8.6** and *ALWD* **Rule 17.** Rule 1.10 of the *ABA Model Code* would be cited as follows:

> Model Code of Professional Responsibility Rule 1.10 (1992)

▼ How Do You Cite an ABA Ethics Opinion?

The rules for citation of ethics opinions are contained in *Bluebook* **Rule 12.8.6** and *ALWD* **Rule 17.4.** For example:

> ABA Comm. on Professional Ethics and Grievances, Informal Op. 88-1526 (1988)—*Bluebook* format

Model Code of Professional Responsibility Rule 1.10 (ABA 1992)—*ALWD* format

▼ How Do You Cite the Various Federal Rules?

Cite the federal rules in accordance with *Bluebook* **Rule 12.8.3** and *ALWD* **Rule 17** as follows:

Fed. R. Civ. P. 56
Fed. R. Crim. P. 1
Fed. R. App. P. 26
Fed. R. Evid. 803

Only include the year when the rule is no longer in force by providing the most recent year that it appeared and the year repealed. For example:

Fed. R. Civ. P. 9 (2006) (repealed 2008)—*Bluebook* 12.8.3
Fed. R. Civ. P. 9 (repealed 2008)—*ALWD* 17.2

Go to www.law.cornell.edu/citation for "An Introduction to Basic Legal Citation" by Peter Martin.

CITATION EXERCISES

For the following citations, assume that these cases are being used in a brief for the U.S. District Court for the Northern District of Ohio. Correct the citation, if possible. If not, specify what is wrong. If an item is missing, note it and tell where it belongs.

1. How would you cite the following slip opinion?
   Michele Greear, et. al., plaintiffs, vs. C.E. Electronics, Inc., et. al., defendants, decided in the United States District Court for the Northern District of Ohio Western Division, docket number C 87-7749, decided by Judge Richard B. McQuade, Jr. on September 12, 1989.

2. When responding to a motion for summary judgment, the plaintiff must submit proof of each and every element of his claims so that a reasonable jury would find in his favor.
   Anderson v. Liberty Lobby, Inc., 477 U.S. 242, 105 S.Ct. 989, 10 L.Ed. 2d 1111 (1986).

3. When the relationship of the parties is so clear as to be undisputed, it can be decided as a matter of law that no apparent or actual relationship existed.
   Mateyka v. Schroeder, 504 N.E.2d 1289 (1987).
4. In a diversity action, a court must apply the conflict of law principles of the forum state. Dr. Franklin Perkins School v. Freeman, 741 F.2d 1503, 1515, n.19 (1984); Pittway Corp. v. Lockheed Aircraft Corp., 641 F.2d 524, 526 (7th Cir.); Klaxon Co. v. Stentor Electric Mfg. Co., 313 US 487, 496 (1941).
5. Gizzi v. Texaco, 437 F.2d 308 (3rd).
6. Zimmerman v. North American, 704 F.2d 347 (1983)
7. E.E.O.C. v. Dowd, 736 F.2d 1177.
8. Musser v. Mountain View Broadcasting, 578 F. Supp. 229 (1984)
9. United States v. Upjohn, 449 U.S. 383.
10. Indicate what, if anything, is missing from this citation: Consolidation Coal Co. v. Buryus-Erie Co., 89 Ill. App. 2d 103 (1982).

CITATION PRACTICE

Provide the correct citation form for the following; use case name abbreviations found in either the *Bluebook* or the *ALWD Citation Manual*.

1. Trzcinski v. American Casualty Company
   901 Federal Reporter Second Series 1429
   Seventh Circuit Court of Appeals
   1990
2. Wade v. Singer Company
   130 Federal Rules Decisions 89
   Northern District Court of Illinois 1990
3. Pryor v. Cajda
   662 Federal Supplement 1114
   Northern District Court of Illinois 1987
4. Longman v. Jasick
   91 Illinois Appellate Court Reports Third Series 83
   46 Illinois Decisions 636
   414 North Eastern Second Series 520
   Third District Court of Appeals 1986
5. Gulf Oil Corporation v. Gilbert
   91 Lawyers Edition 1055
   330 United States Reports 501
   67 Supreme Court Reporter 839
   1947
6. Wyness v. Armstrong World Industries Incorporated
   131 Illinois Reports Second Series 403
   546 North Eastern Reporter Second Series 568
   Supreme Court of Illinois 1989
7. Title 28 of the United States Code, section 1404(a) from the year 2000.
8. Title 42 of the Code of Federal Regulations, section 29 from the year 2004.

SHORT CITATION

Write the following information in short citation format.

1. Smith v. Jones, 96 N.E.2d 17 (Ill. App. Ct. 1965).
   You are using text from p.18 of the N.E.2d.
   How would you cite this the first time?
   How would you short cite it to page 18 if it is cited in full in the immediately preceding citation?
2. Cranshaw v. Marge, 321 F.2d 97 (5th Cir. 1935).
   You need to short cite this case to reflect attributing authority to page 99 of the decision.

CITATION FOR RESOURCES OTHER THAN CASES

1. How would you cite to a federal statute that appeared in the 2008 pocket part of Title 42 of the United States Code Annotated at section 1201 that was in a volume published in 2004?
2. How would you cite a law review article that appeared in volume 78 of the Columbia University Law Review in 1985? The article is entitled Tax Aspects of Marital Dissolution, and begins on page 1587. The author is John Reese.
3. How would you cite Megan's Law found in Title 42 of the United States Code at section 14071(e) in the 2006 Code?
4. How would you cite volume 63 of the Federal Register at page 59,231 from October 1, 1991.
5. How would you cite the Procter & Gamble 2003 annual report accessed on June 5, 2004, at pg.com/investors. Choose the "Financial Results and Events" tab, and then click the "Annual Reports" link. Click "2003 Annual Report."

CITATIONS FOR ONLINE RESOURCES

1. How would you cite an unreported opinion available on LEXIS where you are relying on a statement from page 3 of that opinion? The opinion is from 2005 and was found in the US Dist Ct file. The LEXIS case number is 15976. The date of the decision is April 13, 2005. The case name is *Pane Bread Store v. Baguette Company.* The docket number is No. 05-1721.
2. You have found a new C.F.R. provision on WESTLAW and you know it was printed in hard copy in the 2005 C.F.R. The provision is in Title 5 at section 12.
3. You retrieved a recent final regulation in the *Federal Register,* volume 73 at page 90. It will be codified in the C.F.R. at 19 C.F.R. part 18. The material was accessed at www.gpoaccess.gov/fr. Please provide the citation according to the *Bluebook* or the *ALWD.*
4. You have found an article in the Yale Law Journal. You know that the journal is available in hard copy at the law school library across town and the identical article is available in full text on the Web. You want to

cite to both sources to improve access. What rule do you follow in the *Bluebook?*

The article is from volume 114, number 7, May 2005. The article is titled: "The Sarbanes-Oxley Act and the Making of Quack Corporate Governance" by Roberta Romana. The article begins on page 1521. The Yale Law Journal Internet site is www.yale.edu/yalelj.

SAMPLE MEMORANDA

ILLUSTRATION C-1. **Sample Memorandum**

MEMORANDUM

To: Benjamin Joyce
From: William Randall
Date: January 28, 2008
Re: *Harris v. Sack and Shop*

QUESTION PRESENTED

Is Sack and Shop, a grocery store, liable for injuries sustained by Harris, a store patron who slipped on a banana peel that had been on the grocery store floor for two days?

BRIEF ANSWER

Probably yes. Sack and Shop, a grocery store, probably will be liable based on negligence for injuries sustained by Harris, a store patron who slipped on a banana peel that had been on the grocery store floor for two days.

FACTS

Our client, Sack and Shop Grocery Store, is being sued for negligence by Rebecca Harris.

Harris went to the store to purchase groceries on July 8, 2007. While she was in the produce section, she slipped on a banana that a grocery store

ILLUSTRATION C-1. *Continued*

employee left on the floor. The employee had dropped it on the floor two days earlier and had failed to clean it up after a patron asked him to do so.

Harris sustained a broken arm and head injuries as a result of the slip and fall.

DISCUSSION

The issue presented in this case is whether Sack and Shop Grocery Store was negligent when Rebecca Harris slipped in the store's produce section. A grocer will be found negligent if a store employee breached the store's duty of reasonable care to its patrons and, as a result of that breach, the patron was injured. *Ward v. K Mart Corp.,* 554 N.E.2d 223 (Ill. 1990). In *Ward,* the grocery store employee failed to clean up a banana peel for two days and that peel caused a patron to be injured. Similarly in our case Sack and Shop failed to remove the banana peel for two days. Therefore, Sack and Shop is likely to be found liable for the injuries Harris sustained.

The first element to consider is whether Sack and Shop owed a duty of reasonable care to Harris. A grocery store owes a duty of care to any patron. *Ward,* 554 N.E.2d at 226. Harris was a customer in the store. Therefore, Sack and Shop owed her a duty of care.

The next question to consider is whether Sack and Shop breached its duty of reasonable care to Harris. A store will be found to have breached its duty of reasonable care to a patron if a store employee fails to properly and regularly clean the floor of the store. *Olinger v. Great Atl.& Pac. Tea Co.,* 173 N.E.2d 443 (Ill. 1961). In *Olinger,* the store was found liable because a store employee failed to clean the floor for one day and a patron slipped on a substance on the floor. 173 N.E.2d at 447. No one had told any store employee about the slippery substance. *Id.* at 447. Nonetheless, the Illinois Supreme Court found the store liable, saying that the store employees had sufficient time to notice the substance if they had used ordinary care. *Id.* In our case, Sack and Shop's employee had two days to clean the floor before Harris fell. In addition, a customer had placed the store employee on notice of the banana. Therefore, Sack and Shop breached its duty of care to Harris.

The plaintiff, however, still must establish proximate cause, that is, that the injury resulted as a natural consequence of Sack and Shop's breach of its duty. A store owner's failure to clear debris from a store floor, resulting in injury to a patron who slipped on the floor, was found to be the proximate cause of the patron's injuries. *Id.* at 449. In this case, Sack and Shop's failure to clean the peel from the floor was a breach of its duty of care to Harris. This breach resulted in injury to Harris. Sack and Shop's breach will be found to be the proximate cause of Harris's injuries.

The final element that must be established is that the plaintiff, Harris, suffered injuries. Harris sustained a broken arm and head injuries as a result of the slip and fall. Therefore, she will be able to show that she was injured.

ILLUSTRATION C-1. *Continued*

CONCLUSION

Sack and Shop owed Harris a duty of reasonable care. The store is likely to be found to have breached that duty of reasonable care because an employee failed to remove a banana peel from the grocery store floor during the preceding two days. The injuries Harris sustained were directly caused by a slip on a banana peel. Therefore, Sack and Shop is likely to be found liable to Harris.

ILLUSTRATION C-2. Sample Memorandum

MEMORANDUM

To: Wallace Maine
From: Thomas Wall
Date: November 15, 2008
Re: Sex Discrimination Case against Whole In One No. C93 CIV 190 G12399990

QUESTIONS PRESENTED

1. Under Title VII, was Whole In One Golf Resort an employer when 14 people, including 3 full-time and 11 part-time workers, worked on any one day for 24 weeks and when 10 full-time employees were on the Whole In One payroll?

2. Under Title VII, was Walker an independent contractor rather than an employee when she worked exclusively for Whole In One, paid taxes quarterly rather than through deductions, and worked with limited company supervision?

3. Under Title VII, was Radiant an independent contractor rather than an employee when she worked with limited company supervision using company supplies and equipment and had taxes and medical deductions taken from her salary?

CONCLUSIONS

1. Whole In One was an employer. Under Title VII, an employer has at least 15 employees working for 20 or more weeks during the relevant year. Salaried employees are included in this number for each week they are on the payroll, while hourly workers are only counted on the days they actually work. In 2004, the year of the alleged discrimination, 14 workers, 3 full-time and 11 part-time people, worked for Whole In One on any day during the 24-week restaurant and golf season. However, 10 full-time workers were on the payroll. Because these part-time workers are only counted on the days that they work, the number of part-time individuals included in the count of employees is 11 for each day of the 24-week season. Because full-time workers, however, are counted for each day of a week that they are on the payroll, all 10 of the Whole In One full-time workers would be included in the count of employees. In total, Whole In One had 11 part-time workers and 10 full-time workers

ILLUSTRATION C-2. *Continued*

"working" for 20 or more weeks during the relevant year, bringing the total count of employees to 21. Therefore, Whole In One was an employer under Title VII.

2. Walker was an employee. The Seventh Circuit will weigh five factors to determine whether she was an independent contractor or an employee for this Title VII lawsuit. The primary focus will be on the company's control of Walker. Although Walker worked from home, set her own hours and had an impact on her commission pay, the company controlled her work by reviewing and revising it, restricting Walker's employment opportunities, and providing supplies for her. Therefore, the company exerted control over Walker and she would be considered an employee.

3. Radiant was probably an employee. To determine whether she was an employee or independent contractor for this Title VII lawsuit, the court will focus on five factors, primarily the amount of control the company exerted over Radiant's work. Whole In One provided Radiant with an office, supplies, a two-year contract, and additional training. Whole In One paid her regularly and deducted taxes from her salary. Although Whole In One did not actively supervise Radiant's work on a daily basis, she still worked in the company offices and was under the control of Whole In One. Therefore, the court probably will find that Radiant was an employee.

FACTS

Victoria Radiant and Karen Walker, two former Whole In One Enterprises workers, brought a federal sex discrimination lawsuit based upon Title VII against our client, Whole In One Enterprises, owned by Nancy and Craig Black. The lawsuit, filed in the U.S. District Court for the Northern District of Illinois, stems from the dismissal of the two women by the Blacks during 2004.

The Blacks own Whole In One Enterprises, which operates a miniature golf course and restaurant in Glenview, Illinois. During the 24-week 2004 restaurant season, 10 people worked full-time and 14 people worked part-time for Whole In One. However, no more than 14 people worked on any one day. Of those 14 people, only 3 were full-time employees. The other full-time employees regularly took days off during the summer restaurant and golf season.

Among the full-time workers was Karen Walker, who worked as a public relations director for Whole In One. Walker responded to an ad that said that "an employer" sought an individual to perform public relations work. Whole In One hired Walker without a contract and prohibited her from working for other firms. However, Walker worked from home and set her own hours. Whole In One required Walker to attend weekly staff meetings at the company offices where Whole In One would review and revise Walker's work. The company supplied Walker with paper, pencils, stamps, telephone service, and paid for her life and health insurance. Whole In One did not withhold taxes from Walker's commissions.

ILLUSTRATION C-2.   *Continued*

Victoria Radiant, who had a two-year employment contract with the company, provided marketing services to Whole In One from October of 2002 until she was fired in 2004. Although Radiant worked in the company office, Whole In One management rarely supervised her work. The company paid for her continued education, provided her with bonuses, and deducted taxes from her weekly salary.

Applicable Statute:

The term "employer" means a person engaged in an industry affecting commerce who has 15 or more employees for each working day in each of 20 or more calendar weeks in the current or preceding calendar year. 42 U.S.C. §2000e(b) (2004).

DISCUSSION

This memo first will address whether Walker and Radiant can successfully establish that Whole In One was an employer within the meaning of 42 U.S.C. §2000e(b) (2004), commonly called Title VII.

Next, the discussion will focus on whether Radiant can establish that she was an employee protected by Title VII. Finally, the memo will explore whether Walker was an employee protected by Title VII. If Whole In One was not an employer, then the Title VII claim will be dismissed. If the court finds that neither individual is an employee, the individual's claim will be barred.

I. Was Whole In One an Employer under Title VII?

Before a federal court can consider Walker's and Radiant's claims, the plaintiffs must establish that Whole In One was an employer under the definition established in Title VII. An employer is "a person engaged in a business affecting commerce who has 15 or more employees for each working day in each of 20 or more calendar weeks in the current or preceding calendar year." 42 U.S.C. §2000e(b). The focus of this discussion will be how to calculate whether 15 employees worked for Whole In One on each working day in each of 20 or more calendar weeks and how to determine which year's employment records are relevant. The Seventh Circuit has held that full-time employees are "working" each day of a week during a week for which they are on the payroll, but part-time workers are counted only on the days that they actually work. *Zimmerman v. North American Signal Co.,* 704 F.2d 347 (7th Cir. 1983). In 2004, the year of the alleged discrimination, 14 workers, 3 full-time and 11 part-time people, worked for Whole In One on any day during the 24-week restaurant and golf season. In addition, 10 full-time workers were on the payroll. Based upon the counting method established in *Zimmerman,* these figures indicate that Whole In One had at least 15 employees working for each working day in each of 20 or more calendar weeks. Therefore, Whole In One was an employer under Title VII.

The central focus of this discussion will be how to calculate the number of employees. First, the relevant year must be determined. The statute states that

ILLUSTRATION C-2. *Continued*

the time to be considered is "twenty or more calendar weeks in the current or preceding year." 42 U.S.C. §2000e(b) (2004). The current year of the discrimination was 2004. Since the statute specifies "or" the preceding year, 2003 also is relevant. However, in a persuasive decision a Tennessee district court held that the "current calendar year" is the year in which the alleged discrimination occurred. *Musser v. Mountain View Broadcasting, Inc.,* 578 F. Supp. 229 (E.D. Tenn. 1984). If the court follows *Musser,* the employment records from 2004 would be relevant because Whole In One fired Walker and Radiant in 2004.

The phrase "each working day" must be clarified. "Each working day" should be taken literally and must be a day on which an employer conducts normal, full operations on that day. *Zimmerman,* 704 F.2d at 353; *Wright v. Kosciusko Medical Clinic, Inc.,* 791 F. Supp. 1327, 1333 (N.D. Ind. 1992). Whole In One operated the golf course and restaurant seven days a week. Therefore, Whole In One must have 15 employees working on all seven days of a week to be considered an employer under Title VII.

The final issue is which individuals should be counted on each of the working days. The Seventh Circuit has determined that a salaried or full-time employee is counted as working for every day of the week that they are on the payroll, whether or not they were actually at work on a particular day. *Zimmerman v. North American Signal Co.,* 704 F.2d 347 (7th Cir. 1983). However, part-time workers are counted only on the days that they actually work. *Id.; Wright,* 791 F. Supp. at 1327; *Norman v. Levy,* 767 F. Supp. 144 (N.D. Ill. 1991). In 2004, the year of the alleged discrimination, 14 workers, 3 full-time and 11 part-time people, worked for Whole In One on any day during the 24-week restaurant and golf season. As these part-time workers are only counted on the days that they work, the number of part-time individuals included in the count of employees was 11 for each day of the 24-week season. Since full-time workers, however, are counted for each day of a week that they are on the payroll, all 10 of the Whole In One full-time workers should be included in the count of employees. In total, Whole In One had 11 part-time workers and 10 full-time workers "working" for 20 or more weeks during the relevant year, bringing the total count of employees to 21. Therefore, Whole In One was an employer under Title VII.

II. Are Walker and Radiant Employees or Independent Contractors?

If the plaintiffs can show that Whole In One was an employer, the court still must determine whether Walker and Radiant were employees entitled to Title VII protection or independent contractors. To determine whether an individual is an independent contractor or an employee, the "economic realities" of the relationship between an employer and his or her worker must be weighed. *Knight v. United Farm Bureau Mut. Ins. Co.,* 950 F.2d 377 (7th Cir. 1991); *Norman v. Levy,* 767 F. Supp. 144 (N.D. Ill. 1991); *Mitchell v. Tenney,* 650 F. Supp. 703 (N.D. Ill. 1986). The Seventh Circuit will weigh five factors to determine the economic reality of the relationship: 1) the amount of control and supervision the employer exerts over the worker; 2) the responsibility for

ILLUSTRATION C-2.   *Continued*

the costs of the operation; 3) the worker's occupation and the skills required; 4) the method and form of compensation and benefits; and 5) the length of the job commitment. *Knight,* 950 F.2d at 378. Control is the most important factor. *Id.* Moreover, when an employer controls a worker in such a manner as to make that worker economically dependent upon the employer, the court is likely to find that an employment relationship exists. *Vakharia v. Swedish Covenant Hosp.,* 765 F. Supp. 461 (N.D. Ill. 1991).

The *Knight* case involved an insurance agent who was not allowed to sell insurance for any other company and who was required to attend weekly staff meetings in the office and work a specified number of hours in the office. *Knight,* 950 F.2d at 378. The insurance company provided Knight with supplies and paid for business expenses. *Id.* The insurance company trained these agents. Also, the agents were crucial to the company's continued operation. *Id.* Knight was paid on commission and did not have taxes deducted. *Id.* Knight also was free to leave the company and work elsewhere. *Id.* Based upon these facts, the *Knight* court failed to find that the agent was an employee.

Although Walker's work situation was factually similar in many ways to that of the plaintiff in *Knight,* the *Knight* case can be distinguished based upon the nature of the occupations. Knight worked in the insurance sales field. Most often, individuals who work in such positions are independent contractors rather than employees of a company. In addition, the Seventh Circuit indicated in the dicta of the *Knight* case that it might have found that Knight was an employee. *Id.* at 381.

In contrast to *Knight,* the U.S. District Court for the Northern District of Illinois found that control of an individual's livelihood could establish an employment relationship. *Vakharia v. Swedish Covenant Hosp.,* 765 F. Supp. 461 (N.D. Ill. 1991). The plaintiff in *Vakharia* was a physician who was dependent upon the hospital for business. *Id.* at 463. The district court found that this individual depended upon the hospital for patients and that when the hospital reduced the number of patients it assigned to the plaintiff, the plaintiff's livelihood was affected. *Id.* The court held that when an employer has this type of control over an individual's livelihood an employment relationship may be established.

The facts in our case are similar to the facts in the *Vakharia* case. In our case, Whole In One barred Walker from working for other companies and required that she attend weekly staff meetings at the company offices where Whole In One would review and revise Walker's work. Since Whole in One barred Walker from working for other individuals and required that she attend meetings where Whole In One would revise her work, it seems that Walker could establish the central element of control necessary to prove an employment relationship. In addition, these facts show that Walker, similar to the plaintiff in *Vakharia,* was economically dependent upon her employer, Whole In One. Therefore, an employment relationship should be established.

However, the plaintiffs will be able to show more than control. They will be able to establish that Whole In One bore the cost of the operation of the business. Whole In One supplied Walker with paper, pencils, stamps,

ILLUSTRATION C-2. *Continued*

telephone service, and paid for her life and health insurance. These facts indicate that Whole In One was responsible for the cost of Walker's services to the company—a fact that would help to establish that Walker was an employee.

The factors that would mitigate the establishment of an employment relationship, however, are that Walker worked from home and set her own hours and Whole In One did not withhold taxes from Walker's commissions. Despite these factors, the court is likely to focus on the control Whole In One had over Walker and is likely to find that she was an employee rather than an independent contractor.

III. Was Radiant an Employee or an Independent Contractor?

Whether Radiant was an employee again turns on the amount of control Whole In One exerted over Radiant's work. The court will focus on the same factors established in *Knight* to determine whether an employment relationship exists. *Knight*, 950 F.2d at 378. Control will be the key factor the court will consider. *Id.* Radiant had a two-year employment contract with the company to provide marketing services. Whole In One also provided her with an office, supplies, and additional training. The company paid her regularly and deducted taxes from her salary. Based upon these facts, the company exerted control over Radiant. Therefore, the court is likely to find that Radiant was an employee of Whole In One.

ILLUSTRATION C-3. Memorandum: McMillan Battery Action

MEMORANDUM

To: William Mark
From: Ivy Courier
Date: November 7, 2008
Re: McMillan Battery Action

QUESTION PRESENTED

Did an actionable battery occur when Mann intentionally struck McMillan with a bucket, without McMillan's consent, causing McMillan to suffer physical and monetary injuries?

CONCLUSION

Mann's intentional striking of McMillan with a bucket and sand was an actionable battery.

FACTS

Our client, Mary McMillan, a 36-year-old bank teller, wants to bring an action for battery against Carol Mann, a 36-year-old mother, who threw a metal bucket filled with sand at McMillan at a local park. While McMillan sat on a

ILLUSTRATION C-3.   *Continued*

park bench, she teased Mann's seven-year-old son. Mann did not like this teasing and threw a bucket filled with sand at Mary. Sand landed in McMillan's eyes while she was wearing soft contact lenses. As a result, McMillan's contacts had to be replaced. The bucket also cut McMillan's eye and cheek. She had stitches in both places. McMillan asked Mann to pay for her doctor bills and for the new contacts. Mann refused and added, "I'm not sorry. I meant to hurt you."

DISCUSSION

The issue presented is whether Mann's intentional touching of McMillan with a bucket rather than her person is an actionable battery. A battery is the intentional touching of another without consent, which causes injury. *Anderson v. St. Francis-St. George Hosp., Inc.,* 77 Ohio St. 3d 82, 671 N.E.2d 225 (1996). A touching can occur when an object rather than an individual's body contacts the other party. *Leichtman v. WLW Jacoc Communications, Inc.,* 92 Ohio App. 3d 232, 634 N.E.2d 697 (1994); *Smith v. John Deere Co.,* 83 Ohio App. 3d 398, 614 N.E.2d 1148 (1993). In this case, Mann intentionally struck McMillan with a bucket without McMillan's consent and that touching resulted in injuries. Therefore, a battery occurred.

The threshold issue is whether a touching occurred when the bucket struck McMillan. A contact between a nonconsenting party and object rather than the actor's body can be a battery. *Leichtman v. WLW Jacoc Communications, Inc.,* 92 Ohio App. 3d 232, 634 N.E.2d 697 (1994); *Smith v. John Deere Co.,* 83 Ohio App. 3d at 398, 614 N.E.2d at 1148. In *Leichtman,* one person blew cigar smoke at another person, resulting in injuries. The court found that the cigar smoke was an extension of the person and that a contact between the smoke and the nonconsenting person met the requirement of a touching for civil battery. In this case, Mann threw the bucket at McMillan, and the bucket contacted her face. Following the reasoning in the *Leichtman* case, the bucket would be an extension of Mann's body, and the contact between McMillan and the bucket would be considered a touching under the theory of civil battery.

Next, the question to consider is whether under the statute Mann intended to touch McMillan when she struck her with the bucket. A person intends his or her conduct when he or she undertakes an action with a knowing mind. *Smith v. John Deere Co.,* 83 Ohio App. 3d 398, 614 N.E.2d 1148 (1993). In *Smith,* a police officer handcuffed the plaintiff. The court found that the officer must have intended his actions because you could not accidentally handcuff a person. *Smith,* 83 Ohio App. 3d at 399, 614 N.E.2d at 1149. In McMillan's case, Mann aimed the bucket at McMillan purposefully trying to strike her, Mann later told McMillan that she deliberately threw the bucket at her. McMillan probably will be able to establish that Mann had the statutory intent.

The next factor to consider is whether McMillan consented to the contact. If a person consents to the touching, a battery has not occurred. *Love v. Port Clinton,* 37 Ohio St. 3d 98, 524 N.E.2d 166 (1988). In our case, McMillan did not consent to Mann's throwing of the bucket at her face. Therefore, McMillan did not consent to any contact. Finally, the question is whether McMillan

ILLUSTRATION C-3.   *Continued*

suffered physical injuries. A battery occurs only if a plaintiff sustains physical injuries as a result of the touching. *Anderson v. St. Francis-St. George Hosp., Inc.,* 77 Ohio St. 3d 82, 671 N.E.2d 225 (1996). McMillan sustained cuts on her face and the sand flying out of the bucket into her eyes. McMillan will be able to show that she sustained physical injuries as a result of the contact with the bucket.

HELPFUL WEB SITES

U.S. Courts Generally
www.uscourts.gov

U.S. Supreme Court
Docket, Schedules, General Information and Links to Decisions
www.supremecourtus.gov/

First Circuit Court of Appeals
www.ca1.uscourts.gov/

Second Circuit Court of Appeals
www.ca2.uscourts.gov/

Third Circuit Court of Appeals
www.ca3.uscourts.gov/

Fourth Circuit Court of Appeals
www.ca4.uscourts.gov/

Fifth Circuit Court of Appeals
www.ca5.uscourts.gov/

Sixth Circuit Court of Appeals
www.ca6.uscourts.gov/internet/index.html

Seventh Circuit Court of Appeals
www.ca7.uscourts.gov/

Eighth Circuit Court of Appeals
www.ca8.uscourts.gov/

Ninth Circuit Court of Appeals
www.ca9.uscourts.gov/

Tenth Circuit Court of Appeals
www.ca10.uscourts.gov/

Eleventh Circuit Court of Appeals
www.ca11.uscourts.gov/

U.S. Court of Appeals for the Federal Circuit
www.cafc.uscourts.gov

U.S. Court of Appeals for the District of Columbia Circuit
www.cadc.uscourts.gov/

Federal Legislation and Information

Generally
thomas.loc.gov

U.S. Senate
www.senate.gov

U.S. House
www.house.gov

Other U.S. Government Sites
Consumer Product Safety Commission (Recalls List)
www.cpsc.gov

Securities and Exchange Commission
www.sec.gov/

Edgar (SEC databases)
www.sec.gov/edgar/searchedgar.htm

Federal Register
www.gpoaccess.gov/fr/

Code of Federal Regulations
www.gpoaccess.gov/cfr/index.html

List of C.F.R. Section Affected
www.gpoaccess.gov/lsa/index.html

U.S. Code
uscode.house.gov/search/criteria.shtml

Justice Department
www.usdoj.gov

Department of Labor
www.dol.gov

Internal Revenue Service
www.irs.gov

Patent and Trademarks Office
uspto.gov/

Occupational Safety and Health Administration
www.osha.gov

National Library of Medicine
www.nlm.nih.gov

Library of Congress
www.loc.gov/index.html

Alabama
www.alalinc.net/

Alaska
Courts
www.state.ak.us/courts/
Legislation
w3.legis.state.ak.us/index.php

Arizona
Supreme Court and Court of Appeals
www.supreme.state.az.us/
Legislation
www.azleg.state.az.us/

Arkansas
Courts
courts.state.ar.us/

California
Courts
www.courtinfo.ca.gov/
Legislation
www.leginfo.ca.gov/
www.sen.ca.gov
www.assembly.ca.gov

Colorado
Courts
www.courts.state.co.us
Legislation
www.leg.state.co.us

Connecticut
Courts
www.jud.ct.gov
Legislation
www.cga.ct.gov/

Delaware
Courts
courts.delaware.gov

Legislation
www.legis.delaware.gov/

Florida
Courts
www.flcourts.org/
Legislation
www.leg.state.fl.us/

Georgia
Courts
www.georgiacourts.org
www.gasupreme.us
Legislation
www.legis.state.ga.us/

Hawaii
Courts
www.courts.state.hi.us/
Legislation
capitol.hawaii.gov/

Idaho
Courts
www.isc.idaho.gov
Legislation
www.legislature.idaho.gov

Illinois
Courts
www.state.il.us/court/
Legislation
www.ilga.gov/

Indiana
Courts
www.in.gov/judiary/
Legislation
www.in.gov/legislative/

Iowa
Courts
www.judical.state.ia.us/
www.iowacourts.state.ia.us/
Legislation
www.legis.state.ia.us

Kansas
Courts
www.kscourts.org/
Legislation
www.kslegislature.org/

Kentucky
    Courts
    www.courts.ky.gov/
    Legislation
    www.lrc.ky.gov

Louisiana
    Supreme Court
    www.lasc.org
    Legislative
    www.legis.state.la.us

Maine
    Courts
    www.courts.state.me.us/
    Legislation
    www.mainsenate.org

Maryland
    Courts
    www.courts.state.md.us/
    Legislature
    mlis.state.md.us/

Massachusetts
    Courts
    www.mass.gov/courts/
    Legislation
    www.mass.gov/legis

Michigan
    Courts
    courts.michigan.gov/
    Legislation
    www.legislature.mi.gov/

Minnesota
    Courts
    www.mncourts.gov/default.aspx
    Legislature
    www.leg.state.mn.us/

Mississippi
    Courts
    www.mssc.state.ms.us/
    Legislation
    billstatus.ls.state.ms.us/

Missouri
    Courts
    www.courts.mo.gov/
    Legislation
    www.moga.mo.us/

Montana
Courts
www.montanacourts.org
Legislation
leg.mt.gov/css/default.asp

Nebraska
Courts
www.supremecourt.ne.gov/supreme-court/index.shtml?sub1
Legislation
www.unicam.state.ne.us/

Nevada
www.nvsupremecourt.us/
Legislature
leg.state.nv.us/

New Hampshire
Courts
www.courts.state.nh.us/
Legislation
www.gencourt.state.nh.us/

New Jersey
Courts
www.judiciary.state.nj.us/
Legislation
www.njleg.state.nj.us/

New Mexico
Courts
www.nmcourts.gov
Legislation
legis.state.nm.us/

New York
Courts
www.courts.state.ny.us/
Legislation
assembly.state.ny.us/
www.senate.state.ny.us/

North Carolina
Courts
www.nccourts.org/
Legislature
www.ncga.state.nc.us/

North Dakota
Courts
www.courts.state.nd.us/court/courts.htm
Legislation
www.legis.nd.gov/

Ohio
> Courts
> www.sconet.state.oh.us/web_sites/courts/
> Legislation
> www.legislature.state.oh.us/

Oklahoma
> Courts
> www.oscn.net/
> Legislation
> www.lsb.state.ok.us/

Oregon
> Courts
> www.ojd.state.or.us/
> Legislation
> www.leg.state.or.us/

Pennsylvania
> Courts
> www.courts.state.pa.us/
> Legislation
> www.legis.state.pa.us/

Rhode Island
> Courts
> www.courts.ri.gov/
> Legislature
> www.rilin.state.ri.us/

South Carolina
> Courts
> www.judicial.state.sc.us/
> Legislation
> www.scstatehouse.net/

South Dakota
> Courts
> www.sdjudicial.com/
> Legislature
> legis.state.sd.us/

Tennessee
> Courts
> www.tsc.state.tn.us/
> Legislature
> www.legislature.state.tn.us

Texas
> Courts
> www.courts.state.tx.us/
> Legislation
> www.capitol.state.tx.us/

Utah

Courts

www.utcourts.gov/

Legislation

www.le.state.ut.us

Vermont

Courts

www.vermontjudiciary.org

Legislation

www.leg.state.vt.us/

Virginia

Courts

www.courts.state.va.us/

Legislation

www.legis.state.va.us

Washington

Courts

www.courts.wa.gov/

Legislation

www.leg.wa.gov/legislature

West Virginia

Courts

www.state.wv.us/wvsca/wvsystem.htm

Legislation

www.legis.state.wv.us/

Wisconsin

Courts

www.wicourts.gov

Legislation

www.legis.state.wi.us/

Wyoming

Courts

courts.state.wy.us/

Legislation

legisweb.state.wy.us/

Special Paralegal Sites

NFPA

www.paralegals.org/

NALA

www.nala.org/net.htm

ABA

www.abanet.org

Other Useful Web Sites
  www.findlaw.com
  www.lexisone.com
  www.abanet.org

INDEX